# BRITISH
# COLONIAL POLICY
# IN THE
# MID-VICTORIAN
# AGE

# BRITISH
# COLONIAL POLICY
## IN THE
## MID-VICTORIAN AGE

SOUTH AFRICA · NEW ZEALAND
THE WEST INDIES

W. P. MORRELL

OXFORD
AT THE CLARENDON PRESS
1969

*Oxford University Press, Ely House, London W. 1*

GLASGOW NEW YORK TORONTO MELBOURNE WELLINGTON
CAPE TOWN SALISBURY IBADAN NAIROBI LUSAKA ADDIS ABABA
BOMBAY CALCUTTA MADRAS KARACHI LAHORE DACCA
KUALA LUMPUR SINGAPORE HONG KONG TOKYO

© OXFORD UNIVERSITY PRESS 1969

PRINTED IN GREAT BRITAIN

25736

TO

E.M.M., W.D.M., J.A.N.

# PREFACE

THIS book is a partial sequel to *British Colonial Policy in the Age of Peel and Russell*, published in 1930. I was persuaded to undertake other commitments which diverted me from the study of Victorian colonial policy. After the Second World War I returned to New Zealand but an award of the Hugh Le May Fellowship by Rhodes University, Grahamstown, for the year 1951 gave me the opportunity of reverting to my former field of study. The twenty years after 1852 where my other book ended were a critical period in both South African and New Zealand history. New Zealand received a representative constitution in 1852 and immediately demanded and obtained responsible government. The Cape Colony received a representative constitution in 1853 but did not demand responsible government or obtain it for nearly twenty years. The contrast was all the more piquant because Sir George Grey served as Governor in both colonies in this very period. But if the differing course of self-government in colonies of mixed race was to be studied, there was much to be said for including the West India colonies in the survey. Most of them had had representative institutions for generations past and early in the period appeared to be moving towards responsible government of a sort. Then there occurred an explosion in Jamaica which frightened them into turning back—as it now appears, *pour mieux sauter*. The greater part of a year's leave in England in 1958 was spent on blue books and records relating to the West Indies in the Bodleian Library and the Public Record Office; but time did not permit the short visit, at least to Jamaica, which had been part of my original plan. Shipping lines to New Zealand, which in the past and again more recently have called at British West Indian ports, did not call in 1958-9. A New Zealand historian cannot but envy his colleagues in Great Britain, the United States and Canada as they flit to and fro across the Atlantic.

Many parts of the field of this book have been covered by other historians. President de Kiewiet's early book *British Colonial Policy and the South African Republics, 1848-1872* and scholarly works by Dr. A. E. du Toit, Dr. Waldemar Campbell, and Dr. J. A. I.

Agar-Hamilton—not to mention Professor Eric Walker's ency-
clopedic *History of Southern Africa*—have a good deal of ground in
common with mine; but the point of view is, I think, different.
I have tried to disentangle the threads of South African history
but to keep the aims and actions of the Imperial Government and
its organ the Colonial Office in the foreground. In the New
Zealand section of the book the late Dr. A. J. Harrop preceded
me. But his book *England and the Maori Wars*, though it brought
to light many important unpublished documents, hardly attempted an interpretation of the period. Interpretation is certainly
not lacking in the works of Professor Keith Sinclair and Dr. Harold
Miller and their interpretations have been sharply challenged at
many points by the recent book of Professor B. J. Dalton. My
own interpretation is nearer to his but the emphasis is, I think,
different. On both South Africa and New Zealand the late Professor Rutherford's biography of Sir George Grey had much that
was new to say and came closer than any of its predecessors to
explaining that complex, fascinating, but flawed personality.
Fewer books have been published on the West Indies, though the
late Dr. W. L. Mathieson, the late Lord Olivier, and Mr. Bernard
Semmel, from very different points of view, have studied the
Jamaica crisis of 1865 and Professors Philip Curtin and Douglas
Hall have thrown new light on this period of Jamaican history.
The other West Indian islands remain largely unworked ground,
except for Mr. Bruce Hamilton's book on Barbados. There is
ample room for new research on West Indian history. On general
policy Dr. C. A. Bodelsen's comprehensive survey of the literature in his *Studies in Mid-Victorian Imperialism* has placed all subsequent historians in his debt. No scholar indeed can claim to have
said the last word on any part of this period of British colonial
history and policy. All I can hope to do in this book is to make
British colonial policy more intelligible and to show how it was
affected by the personalities of Secretaries of State and senior
officials, by British public opinion—so far as it existed on colonial
questions—and by the policies of strongminded governors like
Sir George Grey and Sir Philip Wodehouse and the developing
self-consciousness of the colonies themselves.

Every historian incurs obligations to many people in writing his
books. My primary obligations are to my own University of
Otago for its generous treatment of me on study leaves and not

less for the Professorial Fellowship unexpectedly offered me on my retirement from the chair of History; and to Rhodes University for its hospitality to my family and myself during the enjoyable year in South Africa of which this book is the fruit. I have also to thank the New Zealand University Grants Committee and the University of Otago for their research grants for microfilms and photocopies of documents and articles and the Public Record Office, London, the Bodleian Library, the University of Nottingham Library and the Newcastle Trustees, the South African Public Library, and the Library of the University of the West Indies for their kindness in permitting microfilms and copies to be made of documents and other materials in their custody.

I should also like to record my indebtedness to the staff of the Public Record Office and the British Museum; to Mrs. O. D'Arcy Hart, Record Agent; to Mr. D. H. Simpson, Librarian of the Royal Commonwealth Society; to Mr. D. H. Varley, whose help was invaluable in the early stages of my work, when he was Librarian of the South African Public Library; to Professor Michael Roberts, then Professor of History, Professor D. Hobart Houghton and Dr. F. G. van der Riet, Librarian, of Rhodes University; to Professor Elsa Goveia and Mr. K. Ingram, Deputy Librarian, of the University of the West Indies; and to Mr. E. V. Quinn, Librarian of Balliol College, Oxford. In New Zealand I have had help and support from three successive Librarians of the University of Otago, and their staffs, especially Mrs. G. M. Strathern and Mr. Michael Hitchings, Hocken Librarians; the Librarians and staff of the Alexander Turnbull Library, Wellington; Mr. J. O. Wilson and the staff of the General Assembly Library; Mr. J. D. Pascoe, Chief Archivist, and Miss J. S. Hornabrook of the National Archives; Mr. R. C. Lamb of the Canterbury Public Library and Mr. C. W. Collins, Librarian, and Mrs. P. D. Shea, Deputy Librarian, of the University of Canterbury. I am grateful to the scholars who have allowed me to use unpublished work, especially Dr. E. L. G. Schnell in South Africa, but also the writers of the numerous unpublished theses cited in the footnotes and bibliography. I thank my wife for her help with the index. The book is dedicated to her and to our family, who lived with this book and travelled for it for many years.

W. P. M.

# CONTENTS

# MAPS

# I

## ISSUES: PERSONALITIES:
## CHANGING OPINIONS

BRITISH colonial policy had changed fundamentally in the twenty years after the great Reform Bill. The first Reformed Parliament, intervening over the heads of the colonial legislatures, had abolished slavery throughout the British Empire. A Select Committee of the House of Commons had attempted to lay down principles for the treatment of aboriginal peoples in and on the borders of British colonies. Under the inspiration of Edward Gibbon Wakefield, first by executive action and then by parliamentary legislation, an attempt had been made at systematic colonization of the Australian colonies and New Zealand by control of land sales and regulation of emigration. Parliament had repealed the corn laws and the navigation laws and was in process of equalizing the sugar duties and removing colonial preferences from the British tariff and, by amending the British Possessions Act, British preferences from colonial tariffs. The ministry of Lord John Russell had conceded responsible government, as recommended by Lord Durham in his great report of 1839, to Canada and its sister colonies of Nova Scotia, New Brunswick, and Prince Edward Island. Sir John Pakington, Secretary of State for the colonies in the short Derby–Disraeli administration of 1852, made some important new concessions. Under pressure from the Colonial Reformers who had harassed his predecessor Earl Grey, he took up and passed the measure Grey had prepared conferring a representative constitution on New Zealand and gave the new General Assembly control of waste lands.[1] Under pressure from the Australian colonies, he yielded them also control of their lands and land revenues, which had been withheld by the Australian Colonies Government Act 1850. Thus the attempt at

---

[1] Lord Grey had proposed to make the concession to the Provincial Councils. On this and on the whole paragraph see my *British Colonial Policy in the Age of Peel and Russell* (reprinted, Frank Cass, London, 1966).

systematic colonization on Wakefield principles was abandoned. Pakington also promised to abolish transportation to Van Diemen's Land. These concessions to the Australian colonies on contentious issues were important preliminary steps towards the acceptance of responsible government in principle by the Duke of Newcastle a few months later.

On the other hand, the Derby–Disraeli Ministry refused to yield to West Indian agitation and stop the equalization of the sugar duties and Gladstone, Chancellor of the Exchequer in the Whig–Peelite coalition which was formed after the defeat of Disraeli's budget, carried the free-trade policy further and abolished or reduced preferences on a number of articles. The Reciprocity Treaty of 1854 between the British North American colonies and the United States was an apparent exception to the general free-trade policy, though it provided for free trade in the more important colonial staples, but the reasons for it were essentially political.[1] The proposal of a committee of the Canadian Legislative Assembly for a reciprocity arrangement between Canada and the West India colonies met with some sympathy from the Governor of Barbados, Sir William Colebrooke, and from the legislatures of Barbados, St. Vincent, and Montserrat; but it was strongly discouraged by Sir William Molesworth, then Secretary of State, and by the end of 1855 this flutter of interest had died down.[2]

The enthusiasm for colonial reform which had led to the formation of the Society for the Reform of Colonial Government in 1850 had now worked itself out. The course of British colonial policy was firmly set in the direction of extending self-government. But two important interrelated questions remained to be settled. How far was it consistent with self-government that colonies should rely on Imperial troops for their internal security and external defence? And how far was it consistent with the humanitarian principles of the Abolition of Slavery Act and the Aborigines Committee's report to allow British colonists in the name of 'self-government' to govern Native tribes within their borders or large populations of emancipated slaves? The examination of these two contentious questions with special reference to

---

[1] Molesworth to Colebrooke (18 Sept. 1855) (No. 18), P.P., 1856, xliv (H.C. 431), 51.
[2] The correspondence is in H.C. 431 of 1856—a paper of 66 pages.

South Africa, New Zealand, and the West Indies is the main theme of this book.

The first question was raised by the Colonial Reformers and especially Sir William Molesworth in Lord Grey's time. Wakefield in March 1851 had submitted a long memorandum to Gladstone on the evil effects of these colonial garrisons; and in the very same month Lord Grey sent off a dispatch to Lord Elgin foreshadowing that these would be confined to Quebec and Kingston and that Canada must assume a larger share of responsibility for defence.[1] It was the outbreak of a new 'Kaffir War' in South Africa that had provoked Wakefield's memorandum, and the exasperation caused by this burdensome war contributed to the declining popularity and eventual fall of the Russell Ministry. British military expenditure in the colonies in 1851–2 was £3,000,000; civil expenditure accounted for another £500,000, and the Navy for £55,000.[2] When Aberdeen came into office, Gladstone pressed for a reduction of British forces in the Pacific. 'Lord Aberdeen, Granville, Molesworth and I were for it. We failed.'[3] Commissary-General Filder urged that the forces in the West Indies be concentrated at Jamaica and Barbados.[4] Then came the Crimean War. Since Waterloo, in the words of a recent writer, the British army had been 'not so much an army as a conglomeration of detachments scattered over the Empire'.[5] Routine ruled; military thought was stagnant; the pay and conditions of the rank and file were so poor that recruitment languished; though the army was doubled during the war, German and Swiss legions had to be enlisted to keep it up to strength; and the brilliant dispatches of W. H. Russell made the British public more aware of its deficiencies than ever in the past. With the unification of the department under a Secretary of State for War, winds of change began to blow through the War Office. One of these brought J. R. Godley, former leader of the Canterbury settlement, to the

[1] *British Colonial Policy in the Age of Peel and Russell*, pp. 497–8. Wakefield's memo. is in the *Canadian Historical Review*, v. 231–6.
[2] Abstract of Colonial Expenditure by Great Britain, P.P., 1852–3, lxii (H.C. 1000).
[3] Quoted by F. W. Hirst, *Gladstone as Financier and Economist* (London, 1931), p. 139.
[4] Memo. on the Defence of the West India Colonies (26 Feb. 1853): Newcastle Papers, Ne C 9633, Univ. of Nottingham Library.
[5] Jay Luvaas, *The Education of an Army: British Military Thought, 1815–1940* (London, 1965), p. 4.

post of Assistant Under-Secretary for War, in 1857. As such he was much concerned with problems of man-power and, says his biographer, 'he became obsessed with the waste of men and money in colonial garrisons'.[1] On all these matters Gladstone, who returned to the Exchequer in 1859, saw eye to eye with Godley. 'Economy', he wrote to his brother, 'is the first and great article ... in my financial creed.'[2] With his passionate belief in *laissez-faire* as the ruling principle of economic policy, he thought he could best help the working man by making food cheap and keeping taxes low. He fought hard for economy in the departments: 'energetically and incessantly, year after year, he directed a vigilant attention to every nook and corner of extravagance and found opportunity for savings, large or small.'[3] His hardest battle was with the Prime Minister on defence: we can follow its course in Guedalla's *Gladstone and Palmerston*.

Already, in March 1859, Godley had managed to secure the appointment of an interdepartmental committee consisting of himself, T. F. Elliot, Assistant Under-Secretary at the Colonial Office, and G. A. Hamilton, recently appointed Permanent Secretary to the Treasury. The committee's terms of reference were to establish some 'fixed and recognized principle for the guidance of the Secretary of State in determining the numerous questions of military expenditure which are continually arising in most of the colonies'.[4] It became a battleground between Godley, reinforced by Hamilton, on the one side and Elliot on the other. The majority report divided the colonies into two classes, military posts (Malta, Gibraltar, Corfu, Bermuda) and colonies proper. In the latter, the report, whilst admitting that the Imperial Government, having control of peace and war, was in honour bound 'to assist them in providing against the consequences' of its foreign policy, favoured a system of defence 'founded on two simple principles, colonial management and joint contribution at a uniform rate'.[5] Elliot, on the other hand, argued with much cogency that the diverse circumstances of the colonies precluded

---

[1] C. E. Carrington, *John Robert Godley of Canterbury* (Christchurch, 1950), p. 197. See also p. 173 on a conversation with Gladstone.
[2] Hirst, op. cit., p. 241.    [3] Ibid., p. 242.
[4] Hawes to Merivale (14 Mar. 1859), P.P., 1860, xli (H.C. 282), 1–2. Hawes, the Under-Secretary, wrote on behalf of his chief, Major-General Peel.
[5] Report of Hamilton and Godley (24 Jan. 1860), ibid., pp. 3–11. Godley privately laid his views before his friend J. E. Fitzgerald in October 1859.

any 'self-acting rule' and that other considerations besides Imperial control of peace and war, notably the valuable colonial trade, should influence Imperial policy.[1]

A divided committee was reporting to a Cabinet much divided on questions of defence. Suspicion of Napoleon III's designs and fear of the ironclads France was building had diminished confidence in the Navy, stimulated the volunteer movement, and created a demand for fortifications. Gladstone was all in favour of maintaining 'at the centre of the Empire, a powerful force by sea and land'; but he was strongly against any loan for fortifications and he thought it 'discreditable to the people of the colonies calling themselves free, to have their defence provided for . . . at the charge of England'.[2] Sidney Herbert, Secretary of State for War, on the other hand, pointed out that 'the Colonial mind is in no way educated to or prepared for this change; nor is this country as ready for it as the bearing of the case on their pockets would lead one, at first, to suppose'.[3] Thinking the estimates insufficient, he offered his resignation in April 1860; but it was refused. We may infer that the Duke of Newcastle as well as Palmerston sympathized with Herbert's point of view: in fact Gladstone had not much support in the Cabinet.[4] These interdepartmental differences came to the surface soon afterwards when Adderley drew the attention of the House of Commons to the report. Chichester Fortescue, Parliamentary Under-Secretary for the Colonies, said bluntly that his chief was 'not prepared to adopt the very simple but impossible scheme' of Godley, though he would do his best to reduce Imperial expenditure on colonial defence and would bring pressure to bear on the colonies to contribute more.[5]

Various speakers in this debate suggested a Select Committee of the House as the best way to settle the controversy and Godley jumped at the idea.[6] He suggested that General Peel might move

[1] Memo. of Elliot (28 Jan. 1860), ibid., pp. 11–19.
[2] Memo. on the Budget (20 Apr. 1860), Hirst, op. cit., p. 201. This was after Herbert's proffered resignation.
[3] Herbert to Gladstone (2 Nov. 1859); Lord Stanmore, *Sidney Herbert . . . a Memoir* (London, 1906), ii. 236. On the resignation, see ibid., pp. 248 ff.
[4] Newcastle's views may be inferred from the speech of Chichester Fortescue, cited below, Palmerston's from a letter to Gladstone (15 Dec. 1859) in P. Guedalla (ed.), *Gladstone and Palmerston* (London, 1928), p. 116.
[5] House of Commons, 31 May 1860, *Hansard*, 3rd Ser. clviii. 1826–41.
[6] Godley to Adderley (3 June 1860), *Extracts of Letters from J. R. Godley to C. B. Adderley* (privately printed, London, 1863), p. 288.

for a committee, but it was Arthur Mills, Conservative M.P. for
Taunton, a barrister who had written a book on colonial constitutions, who moved the motion on 5 March 1861. Chichester
Fortescue was critical. The subject, he said, was not a fit one for
inquiry by the House of Commons: 'it was not a question of facts
but of opinions and principles.' But later in the debate Palmerston,
agreeing that the determination of colonial contributions to
defence was a matter for the Government, deferred to the apparent wish of the House and withdrew his opposition to the
motion.[1]

The committee was a strong one. The Government was
represented by Sir George Grey and Chichester Fortescue; there
were two former conservative Ministers, General Peel and Lord
Stanley, and one of the ablest of the party's young men, Lord
Robert Cecil (the future Marquis of Salisbury); Roebuck and
Ellice had Canadian and Childers Australian experience. It
examined naval and military authorities (Admiral Erskine and
Sir John Fox Burgoyne), leading statesmen (Earl Grey, the Duke
of Newcastle, Gladstone, Lowe), civil servants like Godley,
Elliot, and Merivale, and a few colonists. In a sense the committee
merely carried on the debate that had begun in Parliament, the
Cabinet, and the departments. Few witnesses were as categorical
as Lowe, who saw no duty on the part of the mother country to
defend self-governing colonies except by her fleet in wartime and
thought it undignified to take payment from them. 'It is putting
our troops more in the position of mercenaries . . .', he told the
committee. 'They are virtually serving a foreign Government
which hires them from the Government which they are bound to
serve.' He looked forward to a time when some of the colonies
might wish to separate and when the presence of Imperial troops
might be 'a formidable obstacle in the way of an amicable separation'.[2] Gladstone, like Godley, emphasized the 'moral and social'
aspects of the question. In his opinion 'no community which is
not primarily charged with the ordinary business of its own
defence is really . . . in the full sense of the word a free community'.
But it would take time and effort to reach this position. No

---

[1] *Hansard*, 3rd Ser. clxi. 1400–21. On the relations of the Cabinet and the House
of Commons, see below, pp. 32–3.

[2] Report from Select Committee on Colonial Military Expenditure, Minutes
of Evidence, P.P., 1861, xiii (H.C. 423), 221 (QQ. 3332–3).

Colonial Minister could do a great deal unless 'supported by the popular feeling of this country much more strongly than any Colonial Minister has ever yet been'.[1] Lord Grey took a more conservative view than most witnesses unconnected with the Colonial Office. He thought that in New Zealand and even more at the Cape the Imperial Government had an additional liability because of its encouragement of colonization. On the Cape frontier it 'did so in a manner . . . calculated to increase the danger and to diminish the power of the settlers to defend themselves . . . by giving very large grants of land and placing single farm houses over an extensive district . . . in which, without the support of the home Government, they must have perished'. It would be bad policy, and bad economy, to reduce the force at the Cape, but the Imperial Government should 'retain complete authority in its own hands' and not grant responsible government as had been done, prematurely, in New Zealand.[2]

The committee's report did not endorse Lord Grey's views and took up a position close to Gladstone's. It recommended

that with respect to the South African Colonies, and all those similarly circumstanced dependencies which contain large European populations, their security against warlike tribes or domestic disturbances should be provided for, as far as possible, by means of local efforts and local organization; and that the main object of any system adopted by this country should be to encourage such efforts, not merely with a view to diminish Imperial expenditure, but for the still more important purpose of stimulating the spirit of self-reliance in Colonial communities.

South Africa and Ceylon should contribute more than they did; in New Zealand, it might not be right 'to withhold from the settlers . . . assistance in protecting themselves against the attacks of native tribes, so long as the Imperial Government retains a control over native policy', but 'their principal reliance ought to be on their own resources'. An amendment by Lord Robert Cecil to omit the qualifying phrase about control of Native policy, though supported by Sir George Grey and Fortescue, was defeated. The forces in the Australian colonies and in the West Indies should be reduced. In conclusion, the committee drew attention to the

[1] Minutes of Evidence, P.P., 1861, xiii (H.C. 423), QQ. 3780–2, 3829 (pp. 257–8, 265).
[2] Ibid., QQ. 2557, 2577–8 (pp. 153–4, 156–7).

tendency in modern warfare 'to strike blows at the heart of a hostile power': it was 'therefore desirable to concentrate the troops required for the defence of the United Kingdom as much as possible, and to trust mainly to naval supremacy for securing against foreign aggression the distant dependencies of the Empire'.[1] This was sound doctrine, though the attention of the Navy at this time was so much concentrated on changes in design with the coming of the ironclad warship that the strategic purposes of sea power in Imperial defence had been little considered.[2]

The report was perhaps less categorical than the prime mover in the matter, Godley, would have wished; but before his strength failed he was able to inform Adderley that Government had appointed a departmental committee 'to propose for the consideration of the Cabinet the best way of carrying out your recommendations'.[3] Early in the session of 1862 Mills pressed the matter further by associating the House with the recommendations of its Committee. He moved

> that this House, while it fully recognizes the claim of all portions of the British Empire on Imperial aid against perils arising from the consequences of Imperial policy, is of opinion that Colonies exercising the right of self-government ought to undertake the main responsibility of providing for their own internal order and security.

Charles Buxton, son of the chairman of the Aborigines Committee, whom he had wisely secured as his seconder, said:

> It was highly honourable both to the Government and the people of this country that the apprehension of injury resulting to the aborigines of their colonies from a discontinuance of their present system had been hitherto regarded as a powerful argument in favour of its continuance, notwithstanding the enormous expense thereby entailed. But although that policy was noble ... as a plain matter of fact, the merit of success could not be attributed to it ... He believed they might trust to the increasing thoughtfulness and love of justice of their countrymen to restrain them from any gross violation of its principles.

Missionaries in the colonies and public opinion at home were a safeguard against acts of cruelty by colonial authorities. W. E.

---

[1] Minutes of Evidence, P.P., 1861, xiii (H.C. 423), QQ. 2557, 2577–8 (pp. vi–vii).

[2] On this subject see D. M. Schurman, *The Education of a Navy* (London, 1965).

[3] Godley to Adderley (5 Aug. 1861), *Extracts of Letters from J. R. Godley to C. B. Adderley*, pp. 302–3. Godley died on 17 Nov. 1861.

Baxter, Joseph Hume's successor as M.P. for Montrose Burghs and a member of the committee, did not think the resolution went far enough and moved the addition of the words 'and ought to assist in their own external defence'. Chichester Fortescue did not oppose either resolution or amendment. As he said towards the end of his speech:

> While contending that it was not the policy or the duty of this country to abandon the colonies entirely to their own means of defence ... he did admit that it was quite possible to go too far in considering the wishes of the colonists, to forget the interests of the British tax-payer and even the true interest of the colonists themselves.[1]

The Government's acceptance of the resolution as amended ensured its passage *nem. con.* *The Times* published a sympathetic leading article the following day. But it added a word of caution: 'These things cannot be done roughly and suddenly. They must be brought about with the consent of the Colonists themselves, by showing them the justice of the case, and by firmly withhold-ing all interference in their intestine quarrels and all encourage-ment to unnecessary local wars.'[2]

Others were less considerate of colonial opinion. Imperial sentiment was at a low ebb in 1862. The seizure of the Confederate envoys on the *Trent* in November 1861 brought on a crisis in Anglo-American relations which, even though happily resolved, forced Englishmen to think very seriously about the responsibility of Great Britain for the defence of Canada. In particular it was the occasion of the first of a brilliant series of letters to the Liberal *Daily News* by Goldwin Smith, Regius Professor of Modern History at Oxford, outspokenly attacking the colonial connection as a source of expense to Great Britain and of weakness to the colonies themselves.[3]

> We have ... long felt that the Colonies did nothing for us. We now are very naturally beginning to grumble at being put to the expense of doing anything for them ... We are keeping the Colonies in a perpetual state of political infancy, and preventing the grists of their frames from being matured and hardened into bone.

Palmerston, no doubt, would not give an inch. But his successors

---

[1] House of Commons, 4 Mar. 1862, *Hansard*, 3rd Ser. clxv. 1032–61.
[2] *The Times*, 5 Mar. 1862.
[3] Goldwin Smith, *The Empire* (Oxford and London, 1863), p. vi. The first letter, reprinted at pp. 1–24, was dated 27 Jan. 1862.

would be 'more imbued with ideas and alive to the exigencies of our own age: and depend upon it such statesmen will be disposed to retrench our Empire, in order to add to our security and greatness'. The *Spectator* answered this in an able article, relying not on the stock argument of trade and emigration but on 'the alliances our colonies ensure' and their effect on 'the national tone'.

> The colonial system yields us in every part of the globe strong and faithful allies, united to us by a tie which, by a singular felicity, gives us at all times and under all circumstances their assistance without, in any corresponding degree, embarrassing our counsels. . . . With the loss of our colonial empire . . . our politics would be those of a vestry; our projects would cease to be worldwide; our very trade would be dwarfed by the thought that nowhere out of England could the Englishman feel secure of the protection of his flag.[1]

*The Times* was equally unsympathetic, pointing out that the colonists also had their rights: 'they are British subjects and as long as they choose to remain so the mother country has no right to deprive them of their heritage.'[2] But Goldwin Smith was unrepentant. He did not admit that 'the emancipation of the Colonies would reduce England to an insular position'. She would still be 'the heart and centre of a great confederacy of states belonging to her own race'. The colonists certainly had rights: 'they have a right above all, even if they do not know it themselves, to be released from the childish thraldom which, if it is prolonged, will be fatal to their hope of attaining the manly strength and stature of great nations.' He then went on to attack the Colonial Office— 'a pure bureaucracy based upon no constituency . . . a solecism in English institutions'.[3] Two days later he poured scorn on the forms of government in the colonies, 'a parody of our constitutional monarchy' and 'the concomitants of that peculiar institution, party government and Cabinet administration'.[4] Not satisfied with the Commons' vote that the colonies should pay a share of their military expenses, he asked in his fourth letter 'why should not these free communities pay the whole . . .?'[5]

[1] *Spectator,* 1 Feb. 1862.
[2] *The Times,* 4 Feb. 1862.
[3] 14 Feb. 1862, *The Empire,* pp. 25 ff.
[4] 16 Feb. 1862, ibid., p. 51. Goldwin Smith was doubtless aware that the 'peculiar institution' was the cant phrase in the U.S.A. for slavery.
[5] 7 Mar. 1862 (two days after the resolution), ibid., p. 73.

A fifth letter summed it all up: 'My argument is that a timely separation, while it is good for both parties, is especially good for the Colonists. . . . What is it that the Canadians hope to gain by remaining a province? What is it that they fear to lose by becoming a nation?'[1]

Two months later the defeat of the Canadian Ministry on its Militia Bill gave new point to Goldwin Smith's arguments. The Bill was based on the report of a Commission of which John A. Macdonald, the dominant figure in the Ministry, was a member. According to the best modern authority,

the explanation of the country's apparent apathy . . . was neither lukewarmness towards the British connexion . . . nor a spiritless reluctance to make sacrifices for the preservation of the province's national existence. It was first, a lack of conviction of the serious probability of war, and, secondly, a failure to appreciate the gravity of Canada's situation in the event of war occurring.[2]

But it was very disheartening to the Duke of Newcastle, who had managed to secure over Gladstone's opposition a guarantee of the proposed intercolonial railway from Halifax to Quebec, to see 'a measure of such vital importance to the safety of Canada made a mere stalking horse of Party Warfare'.[3] His forecast that the defeat of the Bill would make a very bad impression in England was justified. *The Times* immediately turned on the Canadians, who were apparently unwilling to defend themselves when 18,000 Imperial troops were stationed in Canada for their defence.[4] As Newcastle later warned Lord Monck, the Governor-General, 'your Ministers have succeeded in *producing* on this side the water a feeling which two months ago had no other existence than in their imaginations and in the clever but eccentric brain of Goldwin Smith'.[5] In the blunt words of the *Spectator*: 'It is, perhaps, our

[1] 21 Mar. 1862, ibid., pp. 96–7.
[2] C. P. Stacey, *Canada and the British Army, 1846–1871* (revised edition, Toronto, 1963), pp. 135–6.
[3] Newcastle to Monck (6 June 1862) (Private), Newcastle Papers, NeC10886. For Gladstone's opposition to the guarantee, ibid., NeC10891.
[4] *The Times*, 6 June 1862, quoted by Stacey, op. cit., pp. 137–8.
[5] Newcastle to Monck (26 July 1862) (Private), Newcastle Papers, loc. cit. The Duke was referring to a remark of Sandfield Macdonald, head of the Ministry formed after John A. Macdonald's defeat, that England wished to get rid of Canada.

duty to defend the Empire at all hazards; it is no part of it to defend men who will not defend themselves.'[1]

There was a debate in the House of Commons also, in which hard words were used by Adderley and even harder by Roebuck (who, however, carried no weight in the House) and Canada was somewhat tepidly defended by members of the Government. The most interesting contribution to the debate was a statesman-like speech from Disraeli, curiously ignored by his biographers, since it anticipates some of the ideas of his famous Crystal Palace speech of 1872:

> I cannot contemplate with the same feeling of indifference as the Secretary of State a separation taking place between this country and Canada. I think a great empire, founded on sound principles of freedom and equality, is as conducive to the spirit and power of a community as commercial prosperity or military force. . . . Canada . . . has many of those diverse elements which tend to change in due season a mere colonial into a national character. . . . Self-government was for a long time so obstinately refused by the mother country, and in the end so precipitately conceded, that I will not say the terms, but the principles on which the new relations between the mother country and the colonies hereafter should be regulated were never sufficiently examined and matured.

It would then have been possible to stipulate 'that every colony should adopt reasonable measures of self-defence: and . . . that there should be between the colony and the mother country free commercial intercourse'. But now it was not a question of sudden and hasty remedies but of trusting 'to the spirit and sense of the inhabitants and . . . the character, talents and resources of the governors whom we send out'. He protested against the discussion of Canadian politics in the House: the resolutions of the Parliament and people of Canada should be accepted.

If in olden days that empire was endangered because of a sense of oppression on the part of the colonists, it will in our day also be endangered if, on the part of the mother country, a sense of unfairness with regard to her connection with her dependencies should prevail. We ought not, however, to use the word 'dependencies' any longer. We should look upon those communities as a portion of a great empire in whose prosperity and honour we are all alike interested.

[1] *Spectator*, 26 July 1862, quoted by Stacey, op. cit., p. 138.

He did not despair that the present unsatisfactory relations with Canada would be 'modified and improved before long'.[1] No one else in the debate saw so clearly the glimmer of light at the end of this dark tunnel. Adderley reprinted, with a special preface on Canadian affairs, a *Letter to the Right Honourable B. Disraeli on the Present Relations of England with the Colonies* which he had published in 1861. In spite of his criticisms in the Canada debate, he was still seeking to place the relationship between Great Britain and her colonies on a basis of 'community and partnership'.[2] Goldwin Smith, in yet another letter, sarcastically asked Adderley 'why, when he implicitly admits that the substance of Imperial power over the Colonies is gone, he holds it such treason to discuss the utility of the shadow'. 'How', he inquired, 'does he propose to ensure the harmonious action of a set of independent legislatures representing constituencies of the most different character, and scattered literally all over the globe?' No, these 'cravings for a grand unity' were 'destined to find their fulfilment in the moral and intellectual rather than in the political sphere'.[3]

The Sandfield Macdonald Ministry rejected Newcastle's suggestion that it might reconsider the discarded militia plan of its predecessor and, to the disgust of the maritime provinces, broke off the negotiations for an Imperially guaranteed intercolonial railway. It did, however, introduce in August 1863, 'an improved code of militia legislation', and Canadian militia and volunteer forces increased in number and efficiency in 1863 and 1864. Meanwhile, a report by a capable Imperial officer, Lieutenant-Colonel W. F. D. Jervois, on the defence of Canada raised yet more questions for discussion between the governments.[4] Anxious though he was to 'shift the centre of responsibility' for Canadian defence from Whitehall to Canada, Gladstone at least saw that there were wider issues involved.

[1] House of Commons, 25 July 1862, *Hansard*, 3rd Ser. clxviii. 843–76. (Disraeli's speech, 867–72.) The Secretary of State was Sir George Lewis, Secretary of State for War. Mr. Robert Blake, Disraeli's latest biographer, seems to me to underrate, as Monypenny and Buckle overrated, his interest in the broader issues of colonial policy.

[2] C. B. Adderley, *Letter to the Right Honourable B. Disraeli on the Present Relations of England with the Colonies* (London, 1861).

[3] 12 Nov. 1862, Goldwin Smith, op. cit., pp. 198–201.

[4] On all this, see Stacey, op. cit., pp. 149 ff. Newcastle was convinced that J. S. Macdonald's colleague Sicotte 'came over here for the express purpose of preventing the success of the Intercolonial Railway': Newcastle to Monck (8 Jan. 1863), Newcastle Papers, NeC 10887.

I submit that the true aim of all our measures at this important juncture should be to bring the people of the British North American Colonies, regarded in one mass, as nearly to a national sentiment and position as their relation to the British Crown will permit. . . . Efforts should be made, without delay, to ascertain whether it is practicable to establish a Federation or Political Union of these Colonies.[1]

The great coalition between John A. Macdonald, Cartier, and George Brown to promote just such a measure had in fact been formed on 22 June. Defence discussions continued along with the negotiations about confederation, both being affected by anxiety about what might happen after the American Civil War had ended. The conferences on defence with the Canadian delegation which went to England in 1865 indeed produced no agreement. But at least it was now recognized that both Great Britain and Canada were willing to defend Canada.

Meanwhile the new military arrangements called for by the House of Commons were moving forward slowly. A circular dispatch from Newcastle in June 1863 announced a new rate of contribution (£40 per man) for troops stationed in the Australian colonies. Victoria was pressing for a warship to be given by Great Britain but maintained by the colony for its own defence.[2] Wodehouse at the Cape was proposing to replace the Cape Mounted Rifles by a locally raised irregular force.[3] In the course of a debate on a motion of Arthur Mills on 28 April 1863, Chichester Fortescue admitted on behalf of the Government an obligation to carry the colony of New Zealand 'through the present crisis';[4] but he did not know that within a week of his speech the colony would be involved in a renewed war and would adopt new policies which the Government would not like. The formation of the self-reliant Ministry towards the end of 1864 relieved the

---

[1] Memo. (for the Cabinet) on the Defence of Canada (12 July 1864), printed by P. Knaplund, *Gladstone and Britain's Imperial Policy* (London, 1927), pp. 228–42. Monck's dispatch on the formation of the coalition had reached the Colonial Office on 8 July (D. G. Creighton, *The Road to Confederation*, p. 81) but Gladstone hardly seems aware of it. Jervois's report was enclosed in Cardwell to Monck (6 Aug. 1864) (Confidential).

[2] B. A. Knox, 'Colonial Influence on Imperial Policy, 1858–1866: Victoria and the Colonial Naval Defence Act 1865', *Historical Studies: Australia and New Zealand*, xi (1963), 61–79.

[3] See below, Chap V.

[4] *Hansard*, 3rd Ser. clxxv. 876–98.

tension between the two governments; but then the quarrel between Sir George Grey and General Cameron revived it.[1] All this time the argument between the Chancellor of the Exchequer and the Prime Minister, the one insisting on the public demand for a reduction in naval and military expenditure, the other on the need to keep the country 'in an efficient Condition of Defence' and abreast of 'the Inventions of Science and the Progress of Improvement', continued in the background until Palmerston died, still in harness, on 18 October 1865.[2]

Very soon afterwards the other main issue involved in colonial self-government unexpectedly came to the front. In New Zealand Weld's acceptance of the policy of self-reliance, a corollary, at least in British eyes, of the assumption of responsibility for Native affairs, appeared to give moral justification for the new Imperial defence policy. But whereas this transfer of responsibility suggested some weakening in 'Exeter Hall' influences in England, the reaction to Governor Eyre's suppression of the Morant Bay rebellion in Jamaica this October showed that the great missionary bodies and the Anti-Slavery and Aborigines Protection Societies, especially when reinforced by liberal utilitarians and scientific humanists like John Stuart Mill and T. H. Huxley, were still a power in the land. The weakness of Exeter Hall had always been that it was readier to denounce abuses than to suggest practical remedies. Agitation against the policies of self-governing colonies like New Zealand perhaps did more harm than good, since any more enlightened policy must necessarily originate with the colonial legislature, and colonial opinion was apt to be antagonized by exaggerated or ill-informed (and sometimes by well-informed) criticism. On the other hand, in the Jamaica crisis these influences gave useful support to the reaction against oligarchical 'representative' institutions in favour of Crown Colony rule. A measure which nearly brought down a government in 1839 passed with general acceptance in 1866, it is true with the co-operation of the frightened Jamaica Assembly itself. Though the scope of the new Crown Colony Government's activities was reduced by the continued prevalence of *laissez-faire* ideas in England, it was this Government that introduced a number of

---

[1] See below, Chs. IX and X.
[2] The quotations are from a memo. of Palmerston of 19 Oct. 1864, Guedalla, op. cit., pp. 297 ff.

long-overdue reforms.[1] Crown Colony rule may have later become 'a political blind alley';[2] but it was not so at this stage of Jamaica's history. Trinidad, which had been a Crown Colony all along, had made good progress under the system; and the change in Jamaica gave an impetus to reform, in varying degrees, in other West India colonies. Indeed this rehabilitation of Crown Colony government was not without significance for the new colonial Empire Great Britain was about to built up in Africa and the Pacific.

The death of Palmerston, which inaugurated a new period of reform in England, seems an appropriate point at which to consider the men and institutions involved in the government of the British colonies. There had already been nine Secretaries of State since 1855. The fifth Duke of Newcastle, though by no means the ablest of the nine, had by far the longest tenure, though it was in his first short term of eighteen months that he had the best opportunity to develop a personal policy—the extension of responsible government.[3] His reputation, marred by his ill-advised choice of the War Secretaryship when the Aberdeen Ministry decided to separate War and the Colonies in June 1854, stands lower than he deserves. In this case his ambition to serve his country outran his abilities: in the hard words of Sir Frederic Rogers, 'he showed himself unequal either to managing affairs himself or to choose confidential advisers who could manage them for him'.[4] Yet he was to some extent the victim of circumstances, for, as one of his successors, General Peel, told the House of Commons, the chief cause of the Crimean calamities was 'your commencement of a great war with little means'.[5] Henry Taylor's characterization— 'he has sense and judgement to adopt, but . . . not vigour to originate or to urge'—disqualified Newcastle for managing a war but not necessarily for administering the colonies. His connection with the Colonial Reformers and membership of the Canterbury Association were evidence of a genuine interest in the colonies; and in consequence, as his biographer says, he gained 'a knowledge of colonial questions which few public men took the trouble to

[1] See below, Ch. XIII.

[2] H. H. Wrong, *The Government of the West Indies* (Oxford, 1923), p. 144.

[3] The only biography as yet is J. Martineau, *Life of Henry Pelham, fifth Duke of Newcastle* (London, 1908).

[4] *Letters of Frederic Lord Blachford* (ed. G. E. Marindin) (London, 1896), p. 225.

[5] Quoted by Martineau, op. cit., p. 192.

acquire'.[1] When he became Colonial Secretary in December 1852 his liberal principles found expression in action. A dispatch to Sir Charles Fitzroy, of which copies were sent to Victoria, South Australia, and Tasmania, foreshadowed the introduction of responsible government in New South Wales.

> All will agree as to the extreme difficulty of withholding political privileges from bodies of men to whom the maxims now prevailing in British domestic policy afford so strong a right to claim them, and of keeping our fellow-subjects in Australia on a different political footing from those to whom these rights have been fully conceded in America.[2]

About the same time the Duke's Under-Secretary, Frederick Peel, told delegates from Newfoundland that 'it was not the policy of the Imperial Government to refuse responsible government to any colony which was generally desirous of having it'.[3] The Duke did not send a copy of his New South Wales dispatch to New Zealand, but he was still a member of the Cabinet when the demand of the first General Assembly was conceded sixteen months later and must be presumed to have concurred. He was not afraid to contemplate a future concession of responsible government to Cape Colony;[4] and he planned with Sir Henry Barkly a campaign to persuade the Assembly of Jamaica to improve the working of representative institutions in the colony by providing for the appointment of certain members as organs of Government in the Assembly.[5] The Duke also carried through the policy of abandoning the Orange River Sovereignty, initiated by Lord John Russell's administration, by the Convention of Bloemfontein signed by his Special Commissioner, Sir George Clerk.

It was hardly the Duke's fault that the achievements of his first term of office were not repeated in his frustrating five-year term as Colonial Secretary in the second Palmerston administration. His first step was to reverse his predecessor's recall of Sir George

---

[1] Martineau, op. cit., p. 118.

[2] Newcastle to Fitzroy (4 Aug. 1853) (Confidential), K. N. Bell and W. P. Morrell, *Select Documents on British Colonial Policy, 1830–1860* (Oxford, 1928), p. 161.

[3] Report of Newfoundland Delegates (9 Aug. 1853), P.P., 1854–5, xxxvi (H.C. 273), 26.

[4] Newcastle to Cathcart (14 Nov. 1853) (Private), Newcastle Papers, NeC9554. But in 1862 the Duke, whilst maintaining his attitude, added: 'I by no means desire its introduction at present': Minute (9 September) on Wodehouse to Newcastle (17 July 1862) (No. 95): CO48/414.     [5] See below, Ch. XII.

Grey from South Africa, on the understanding that Sir George would carry out the policy of the new Government, which was opposed to the resumption of sovereignty over the Orange Free State. Grey, whom he had appointed in the first place, regained the Duke's confidence and won him over to plans of expansion eastwards[1]—plans not destined, however, to be realized in his lifetime. In New Zealand he was soon faced with a Maori war. He supported, and reinforced, Governor Gore Browne, though his attempt to strengthen the Governor's hand by instituting an advisory Native Council failed. But the Governor's desire to force the issue with the Waikato tribes caused misgivings: he seemed to be 'yielding too much to the anti-Native policy of a large number of the settlers'.[2] In his difficulty the Duke turned once again to Sir George Grey and accepted his offer to return to New Zealand. The failure of his Native Council Bill prepared him for Sir George Grey's decision to consult his responsible Ministers on Native affairs in the same way as on other matters. But he was disappointed in his hope that New Zealand would now implement the House of Commons resolution of March 1862 and accept the main responsibility for its own defence. The Waikato war broke out; reinforcements were asked for and sent; but the Duke complained that 'both the Colonial Government and the Legislature are constantly doing things and expressing opinions which indicate an intention to pull more and more on the English purse and do less and less for themselves'.[3] He was also 'a little uneasy' about the New Zealand Government's confiscation plans; but he did not withdraw his confidence from Sir George Grey as his successors gradually did. His instinct was to trust the man on the spot and not hamper him with detailed instructions. When we remember that Newcastle had to bear the brunt of the frustrating discussions with Canada about defence and did not live to see the deadlock broken by Canada's move towards a federation of the North American colonies, we cannot withhold our sympathy for the man who was all the time fighting a losing battle against disease. Sir Frederic Rogers, his Permanent Under-Secretary,

[1] See below, Ch. IV.
[2] Minute (18 Sept. 1861), CO209/163. Cf. also Newcastle to Sir G. Lewis (24 Sept. [1861]), Newcastle Papers, NeC10890.
[3] Newcastle to Sir G. Grey (n.d.—c. Oct. 1863) (Private), Grey Collection, Auckland Public Library.

portrays him as 'an honest and honourable man, a thorough gentleman in all his feelings and ways, and considerate of all about him
. . . painstaking, clear-headed and just'; but he found him stiff,
inaccessible (since he worked at home in the mornings and spent
only about an hour at the office), and too ready to seek safety
in a multitude of counsellors when his advisers differed.[1] Goldwin
Smith praises his devotion to business but says 'he wore himself
out with details which he ought to have left to subordinates'—
whom he did not always choose well. He was 'a decided Imperi-
alist' but 'too good-natured ever to quarrel with a friend who
wrote in support of the opposite point of view'.[2] He had the
qualities and the defects of the *grand seigneur*. He upheld unpopular
Governors against their critics and battled hard for the colonies
(and for pensions to Colonial Governors) against an unsympathetic
Treasury.[3] He was far from being a great man but he was not
an inconsiderable one.

The Duke of Newcastle had a valuable auxiliary in his
second term of office in his Irish Parliamentary Under-Secretary,
Chichester Fortescue. Fortescue's social position he perhaps owed
to the 'tact and accomplishment' of his wife, the famous Lady
Waldegrave;[4] but he was well worth his place in the Government.
With his chief in the Lords, he had the labouring oar when
colonial questions came up for debate in the House of Commons.
For this reason Fortescue acquired a special competence in New
Zealand questions. New Zealand politicans more than once
excepted him from their complaint that public men in England
were ill-informed about their affairs.[5] Not that Fortescue saw the
Maori question entirely through the colonists' eyes. He had hoped
'to keep up that which is left of the personal responsibility of the
Governor in dealing with the Natives and his position as mediator

[1] *Letters of Lord Blachford*, pp. 224–5. Also letter to Lady Rogers (17 June
1860), ibid., pp. 227–8.
[2] Goldwin Smith, *Reminiscences* (ed. A. Haultain) (New York, 1910), pp. 185–6.
[3] Cf. Newcastle to Grey (26 May 1862) (Private), Grey Coll. Also, *inter alia*,
Newcastle to Gladstone (5 Dec. 1861) and to Palmerston (17 Feb. 1862), Newcastle Papers, NeC10890. On pensions, see Newcastle to Gladstone (15 Feb.
1864), Martineau, op. cit., p. 329; Gladstone to Cardwell (2 Feb. 1865), B.M.
Add. MS. 44118. An Act (28 & 29 Vict. c. 113) was passed in 1865.
[4] *Dictionary of National Biography*. After his defeat in the general election of 1874
Fortescue was created Lord Carlingford.
[5] Cf. in particular J. C. Richmond's letter to the Editor, *The Times*, 26 May
1869.

between the two races';[1] but, having become convinced that Imperial control was 'more nominal than real', he readily acquiesced in the transfer of the Native Department to the responsible Ministry.[2] There was independence of mind as well as shrewdness and point in many of his minutes. When the Duke and the Cabinet contemplated sending Sikhs to New Zealand, he 'much doubt[ed] the wisdom of bringing coloured troops from India to fight Maoris'.[3] He was less convinced than Rogers by Sir William Martin's arguments against the confiscation policy: 'We must not be told . . . that the hostile Natives must not be treated as ordinary *rebels* (which is true and right) because they are not ordinary subjects—and in the same breath, that it is iniquitous to take their lands from them, except under the scrupulous application of English law, because they are subjects.'[4] He had little patience, on the other hand, with Governors, whether Sir George Grey in his controversy with his New Zealand Ministers or Darling in Jamaica, who spent their time in arguing when they ought to be deciding questions, in short, governing.[5] Fortescue deserved the parting tribute of the *Spectator* when, after serving another eighteen months under Cardwell, he was promoted Chief Secretary for Ireland, to his 'sound sympathies, strong judgement and thorough conversancy with his duties'.[6]

No fewer than seven men held the office of Secretary of State for the Colonies between the Duke of Newcastle's two terms. When the office was separated from the War Office, Earl Grey's cousin, Sir George Grey, who had at first declined to join the coalition Ministry, was persuaded to take it. He had twice been Parliamentary Under-Secretary in the thirties, first to Spring–Rice and afterwards to Lord Glenelg, and was a man of businesslike habits, sound judgement, and high character. He was responsible for the concession of responsible government to New Zealand and, with the support of Lord John Russell, for the important

---

[1] Minute (14 Dec. 1857), CO209/142. Fortescue, after the general election of 1857, had succeeded J. Ball as Under-Secretary to Labouchere.

[2] Minute (21 Feb. 1862), CO209/165.

[3] Minute (18 July 1863), CO209/173.

[4] Minute (16 Apr.) on Grey to Newcastle (6 Jan. 1864) (No. 9), CO209/178.

[5] Minute (21 Dec.) on Grey to Cardwell (7 Oct. 1864) (No. 143), CO209/183. On the Jamaican affair, see below, pp. 399–402.

[6] *Spectator*, 25 Nov. 1865. Fortescue was less successful, however, as Irish Secretary.

decision not to accept the Australian colonies' proposal to limit the power of disallowance of Bills to stated 'Imperial subjects'.[1] He ceased to hold the office when Aberdeen fell in February 1855, and Lord Palmerston's remark to Queen Victoria in the following November that 'Sir George Grey . . . has a strong disinclination for the Colonies' implies that he was not well suited to the post.[2] His predilection was for the Home Office, which he held with success under both Lord John Russell and Lord Palmerston. Sidney Herbert, who succeeded Grey on 6 February, resigned with Gladstone and Sir James Graham on the 21st and Palmerston turned to Lord John Russell. Russell's tenure of the Colonial Office from 1839 to 1841 had been important and successful and he had continued his interest in colonial affairs as Prime Minister. He was alive to the broader considerations of colonial policy and could rise above the Treasury point of view, which was so potent at this period. He drafted with his own hand the dispatch to Sir George Grey which committed the Imperial Government to support with a parliamentary vote Grey's plans for British Kaffraria. It was he who offered a guaranteed loan to New Zealand to pay off its debt to the New Zealand Company. But throughout this term of office he was distracted by the long-drawn-out and unsuccessful negotiations at Vienna in which he took part; and in the end his shufflings and tergiversation raised such strong feeling against him that he resigned on 13 July.

A few days later Sir William Molesworth accepted the office for which he had long seemed to be marked out. The most prominent of Lord Grey's critics, he had, in office as First Commissioner of Works as well as out of it, strongly supported the withdrawal from the Orange River Territory. An ardent supporter of colonial self-defence, he welcomed the abandonment of 'the system of defending the Boer against the native and the native against the Boer by means of British troops and at the expense of this country'.[3] At the same time he was sceptical of Sir George Grey's plans for the Xhosas: 'if they can cajole us out of land they will—if they can't they will wait their opportunity and attack us.' It was right to try the experiment, but he had 'no expectation

[1] On this see P. Knaplund, op. cit., pp. 74–7.

[2] Viscount Palmerstone to Queen Victoria (10 Nov. 1855), *Letters of Queen Victoria, 1837–1861* (ed. Benson and Esher) (London, 1908), iii. 149.

[3] Sir W. Molesworth, *Materials for a Speech in defence of the Policy of abandoning the Orange River Territory* (London, 1854), p. 25.

of success'.[1] Our policy in South Africa was to keep our frontier safe and protect our own colonists.[2] This was no longer so in New Zealand, however: 'New Zealand has obtained representative institutions and enjoying the sweets it also ought to bear the burden of self-government.'[3] But Molesworth had no chance to develop his policies: his health, always weak, was failing when he took office and he died on 22 October.

The office remained vacant nearly a month after Molesworth's death. Palmerston first offered it to Lord Stanley, who, after consulting his father, not surprisingly declined. He then hoped to tempt Sidney Herbert to detach himself from the 'peace party' and take the office; but he too declined. Finally he fell back upon Henry Labouchere, M.P. for Taunton since 1830, who after a brief term as Parliamentary Under-Secretary to Lord Normanby as Colonial Secretary, had been President of the Board of Trade first in the Melbourne, then in the Russell administration. He was now fifty-seven and had made a reputation as a hard-working administrator. The few references to him in contemporary works and his own dispatches, letters, and minutes, all give the impression of a high-principled, even-tempered, likeable man, anxious to make allowances for the difficulties of his Governors. 'Governor Wodehouse', he once wrote, 'is very disputatious in temper and is wrong in many points in his argument';[4] but this note of asperity is very unusual. Labouchere was not a man to introduce new ideas or initiate policies as Molesworth might have done; but he discharged his duties competently for two and a quarter years.

In the second Derby–Disraeli Ministry, formed in February 1858, Derby's heir Lord Stanley was Colonial Secretary. Not yet thirty-two, he was thought, not only by Disraeli, to be one of the coming men. He was able and independent, so independent that it was never quite certain on which side he stood in politics. Though he was 'indefatigable in his application to business', after three months he had to move, unwillingly, to the India Office before he had made any mark.[5] On 31 May Sir Edward Bulwer

[1] Minute (n.d.—c. Mar. 1855) and Minute of 6 Aug. 1855, CO48/361 and 366.

[2] Minute (7 Oct. 1855), CO48/367.

[3] Minute (29 Sept. 1855), CO209/129.

[4] Minute (25 Apr. 1856), CO111/310.

[5] Carnarvon in Sir A. Hardinge, *Life of the Fourth Earl of Carnarvon* (London, 1925), i. 113. On the unwilling move see *Queen Victoria's Letters*, iii. 292.

Lytton, the novelist, succeeded him. His fellow-novelist, Disraeli, had mentioned Bulwer Lytton's name to Derby, but it was not at first accepted. He would in fact have liked to go to the Lords, because, in spite of his success as a speaker, he dreaded the intervention of his wife on the hustings.[1] He held the office just over a year; but his erratic behaviour even before his breakdown in health towards the end of 1858 had shown him to be ill-suited to the routine of official life. 'He is (literally) half mad about his responsibilities, and fancies he is going to reform the whole colonial empire', wrote Godley after a visit to Knebworth. 'He gets up in the middle of the night to write dispatches and is furious if they don't actually go in twelve hours.'[2] Some of his initiatives—the cancellation of the Hudson's Bay Company's monopoly west of the Rocky Mountains and the constitution of the new gold colony of British Columbia—were well advised.[3] His opposition to a reduction of the force in New Zealand was justified by events. On the other hand, the commitment of Sir George Grey to federation at the Cape, which led to his recall, was partly due to an ill-judged dispatch of Lytton. In his later months at any rate, his Under-Secretary, the Earl of Carnarvon, to whom we shall return, was more active than he was himself.

Edward Cardwell, who succeeded the Duke of Newcastle when ill-health forced his resignation in April 1864, was the ablest administrator among the Colonial Secretaries of the period, though his full capacity was not realized until the first Gladstone Ministry made him famous as the reformer of the Army. Rogers praises his ability to 'deal well with masses of business and bring order out of disorder'.[4] Though lacking fire and eloquence, he was clear-headed and trenchant in both writing and speech. He ended the long and inconclusive discussions about the Transkei by a decision to withdraw. He satisfied Victoria by a Colonial Naval Defence Act which enabled a colony to create a local force in peace-time and place it at the Admiralty's disposal in time of war. He would not ask Parliament to guarantee a £3,000,000 loan to New Zealand: £1,000,000 would be considered a large

---

[1] *Queen Victoria's Letters*, loc. cit. and T. H. Sweet Escott, *Edward Bulwer, first Baron Lytton of Knebworth* (London, 1910).

[2] Godley to Adderley (21 Aug. 1858), *Extracts from Letters from J. R. Godley to C. B. Adderley*, p. 285.

[3] Margaret A. Ormsby, *British Columbia: A History* (Vancouver, 1958), ch. vi.

[4] *Letters of Lord Blachford*, p. 225.

sum. With the support of Lord de Grey at the War Office, he proposed to end the controversy between Sir George Grey and General Cameron by recalling them both. He met the Jamaica crisis by the appointment of a strong and well-balanced Royal Commission. 'Cardwell, like Peel, was dry, and, like Peel, somewhat stiff and formal,' says Goldwin Smith, who knew him well; but he was kind-hearted and magnanimous, 'a true comrade, a fast friend.'[1] The Office, however, did not regard him with unqualified approval. He relied less on his officials than most Secretaries of State, recorded few minutes, and wrote most of his important dispatches himself; and in Rogers's view, he paid too much heed to Parliament. 'He seemed always to feel on trial before the House of Commons. . . . He had a fine instinctive sense of what "would do" in that point of view.'[2] On Chichester Fortescue's promotion to the Irish Secretaryship, Cardwell found another able Parliamentary Under-Secretary in W. E. Forster, a man of weight and strong individuality. Forster had only eight months in the office, but in the Jamaica crisis particularly made a distinctive contribution to its work.

When the Russell Ministry failed to carry its Reform Bill and Lord Derby was called upon to form his third and last administration, Lord Carnarvon received a well-earned promotion to the Colonial Secretaryship. Carnarvon, who was still only thirty-five, was a man of high intellectual ability and warmly generous character. He was ambitious of distinction and 'less afraid of what the House of Commons would say or think of him' than Cardwell, but also more diffident and inferior in judgement.[3] His enthusiasm for Canadian confederation, now in process of accomplishment, was a real service to the Empire; his warmth and his hospitality at Highclere took away the impression of coolness about the colonial connection which Canadian statesmen had earlier received. On the other hand, his success in this field tempted him to repeat the experiment in South Africa some years later, with disastrous results. For the moment he was prepared to carry on and even press the policy of military withdrawal there: he felt it 'open to great objection if not indefensible that a force of more

---

[1] Goldwin Smith, *Reminiscences*, pp. 187–8.
[2] *Letters of Lord Blachford*, p. 225.
[3] Ibid., p. 263. Rogers did not make the comparison but it seems to me to be implied.

than four thousand men should be maintained in a Colony for objects on the whole more or as much Colonial as Imperial without any Colonial contribution worth mentioning';[1] but as Under-Secretary in 1858 he had thought the treaties with the Boer Republics 'far too one-sided and partial' and now he wondered whether there were sufficient grounds for declaring that the Transvaal had violated its engagement not to permit slavery.[2] The seeds of his expansionist policies of the seventies were already germinating in his mind.

Carnarvon had in his Parliamentary Under-Secretary, Adderley, a man whose knowledge of colonial affairs exceeded his own and probably that of any other man in public life. But Adderley, a wealthy Warwickshire squire who was not only interested in the colonies but had a strong and unfashionable belief in the possibility of their permanent connection with England on the basis of self-government, was independent to the verge of obstinacy, and did not always see things in their right proportions. 'I should not object to Sir Philip Wodehouse's plan to put Basutoland in a "territory" state for a time . . .', he wrote, 'But not one shilling should fall on the English taxpayer.'[3] There was a similar rigidity about his attitude to the withdrawal of the last regiment from New Zealand during the Maori war: 'it is said its removal would be taken by friendly tribes and colonists as a sign they can expect no longer support from England—the very thing most desirable and the state our early American Colonists throve best in.'[4] Nor was Adderley an effective speaker: Carnarvon complained of his 'inaccuracy and confusion of mind'.[5] His failure at the Board of Trade in the Disraeli administration of 1874 confirms Carnarvon's impression that this estimable man was ill-suited to official life.

When Carnarvon resigned with Lord Cranborne and General Peel on the Reform Bill, the third Duke of Buckingham and Chandos became Secretary of State for the Colonies. Unlike his extravagant father, the Duke was an excellent man of business. When he was Marquis of Chandos Disraeli had used him to

---

[1] Carnarvon to Wodehouse (26 Nov. 1866) (Private), Private Correspondence of Sir P. E. Wodehouse, 1861–9, Colonial Office Library.
[2] Minute (24 July 1858), CO48/389. Minute (n.d.—early 1867), CO48/433.
[3] Minute (30 June 1867), CO48/441.
[4] Minute (4 Sept. 1868), CO209/207.
[5] Carnarvon to Derby (7 Jan. 1867), Carnarvon Papers: quoted by D. G. Creighton, op. cit., p. 428.

overhaul the Irish departments as a Lord of the Treasury in 1852. He had been suggested as an alternative to Bulwer Lytton when Stanley left the Colonial Office in 1858 and in 1861 had been offered the Governor-Generalship of Canada. For some years he was chairman of the London and North Western Railway, though Rogers considered that the 'natural turn for detail' which he could indulge there 'injured his capacity as a minister'.[1] The Duke, 'a thoroughly honest and kind-hearted man, with a rough but friendly manner', possessed considerable independence of mind. He was against the withdrawal of all troops from the Cape: 'Imperial purposes require that such a force be maintained as will secure the permanent holding against foreign enemies of the anchorage and naval station' and the Colony could not fairly be asked to pay for this.[2] It was he who sanctioned Sir Philip Wodehouse's annexation of Basutoland and he continued his confidence in Wodehouse even though the manner of it deviated somewhat from his views.[3] He would not haggle with New Zealand about the expenses of the Maori war: it was better to cry quits. His good sense and decision of character appear in many of his minutes.

His successor, Earl Granville, was a very different sort of man. Sir Frederic Rogers thought him 'the pleasantest and most satisfactory chief of those under whom I served'. He trusted his subordinates and 'was ready to act with promptitude and authority in matters which none but a chief could handle, matters requiring action in the House of Lords or the Cabinet or the Treasury'.[4] The *Spectator* welcomed him as 'a conciliatory (and very able) minister to deal with our sometimes touchy colonies'.[5] He certainly had charm: 'if he could only *talk* to the Colonies instead of writing to them,' the same journal declared, 'we believe Lord Granville would be almost the most useful as well as the most popular colonial minister who ever persuaded, rather than ruled, the antipodes from Downing Street.'[6] But, as his nickname 'Puss' suggests, he also possessed claws. When he was transferred to the Foreign Office on Lord Clarendon's death, many would have

[1] *Letters of Lord Blachford*, p. 264.

[2] Minute (28 Oct. 1867) on Wodehouse to Buckingham (16 July 1867) (No. 64), CO48/437.

[3] Buckingham to Wodehouse (25 July 1868) (Private), Private Correspondence of Sir P. E. Wodehouse. On this subject see below, pp. 166-8.

[4] *Letters of Lord Blachford*, p. 264.   [5] *Spectator*, 12 Dec. 1868.

[6] Ibid., 23 Jan. 1869.

echoed the parting shot of the *Spectator*: 'It is with a sigh of relief that we see him quit his department before any Colony has declared at once its independence and its undying hostility to Great Britain.'[1] Both the matter and the manner of his policy had been at fault.

The Colonial Office, even in 1872, contained only twenty-six established clerks; and of these only the few senior officials really influenced policy. But their great ability, experience, and knowedge carried great weight and the frequent changes at the top of course increased their influence. Sir Henry Taylor, senior clerk of the West India department for forty-seven years, was the best known to the general public, thanks to his drama *Philip van Artevelde* and his brilliant satire *The Statesman*, 'the first book in our political literature to deal with the status and structure of the administrative branch of government'.[2] The West India department was his private empire: he had declined to take Stephen's place as Permanent Under-Secretary in 1848. When, in 1861, asthma constrained him to move to Bournemouth for four or five months each year, it was arranged that he should receive the papers there. Taylor's early years in the office had been mainly concerned with the emancipation of the slaves. Afterwards his aim was to sweep away the old representative system so that the Crown might have a free hand to legislate for the improvement of the education and status of the emancipated labourers. He met with a sharp setback in 1839 when his plans were first whittled down by the Cabinet and then thrown out by the House of Commons. This disappointment impaired his health and no doubt accentuated the cynical strain which had been evident in *The Statesman*. A minute of 1852 well illustrates Taylor's realistic appraisal of West Indian politics.

I am afraid that Governments in these days are not strong enough to govern the Colonies and that neither Governments nor Parliaments have time for the party contests involved in the attempt. But if the weakness of the Home Government is its chief disqualification as a governing power for British Guiana, it is a weakness which is not likely to be occasioned by anything else than what has hitherto

---

[1] Ibid., 9 July 1870.
[2] *The Statesman* with an introductory essay by Leo Silberman (Cambridge, 1957), p. xi. Another modern edition (Mentor Books, New York, 1958) has an introduction by C. Northcote Parkinson.

occasioned it—viz. preponderant power in the Planters, acting through the West India Body and their friends in Parliament, or those who become their friends for the purposes of Opposition.

But if the planters ever saw that the choice lay between lowering the franchise and maintaining the power of the Crown, they would prefer control by the Crown to control by the Negroes.[1] In the end, thanks to the fright given to the governing oligarchies by the Morant Bay rebellion, Taylor achieved his aim of Crown Colony government in no small degree before his retirement in 1872. The interventions of Secretaries of State were only occasional. Newcastle took a personal interest in Barkly's constitutional reform in Jamaica; possible reform there had interested Cardwell even before the rebellion and afterwards it of course became Cabinet business of high priority; both Buckingham and Granville concerned themselves with the plans for federation of the Leeward and Windward Islands. But on the whole it may be said, with only slight exaggeration, that Henry Taylor ruled not only his department of the Office but the British West India colonies.

T. F. Elliot, who had been moved from the chairmanship of the Colonial Land and Emigration Board to be Assistant Under-Secretary towards the end of 1847, retained this post until he retired on pension in December 1868. His responsibilities in the office varied from time to time but he was most influential in defence questions. He understood better than some of his contemporaries that 'the Naval Supremacy of this Country is the true foundation on which its Colonial Empire rests'.[2] His able memorandum as a member of the interdepartmental committee had some effect on the tendency to impose uniform policies on differently situated colonies. He was also out of sympathy with the prevailing cult of economy. When the Treasury proposed to halve the Kaffrarian vote in 1861, he observed that 'nothing can be more unfair to a Governor and more calculated to produce instead of avert financial difficulties and claims than suddenly to withdraw a long promised aid'.[3] A minute on the Basuto war again reveals Eliot's independence of fashionable views.

The war is the fruit of the wonderfully anomalous measures by

[1] Minute (10 Sept. 1852) on Barkly to Pakington (8 June 1852) (No. 106), CO111/290.    [2] Minute (19 Nov. 1859), CO209/150.
[3] Minute (7 May 1861) on Treasury letter of 4 May, CO48/410.

which these Boers were erected into an independent State. It will undoubtedly deserve mature consideration whether the Governor should not be encouraged to take advantage of any fair opening that the progress of events may afford, for once more bringing them within the control of the only responsible and civilized Government in South Africa.[1]

Elliot was a stickler for official form and a writer of caustic and outspoken minutes, but he had a dry wit. On F. D. Fenton's proposed abstract of English law for the Maoris he remarked: 'I wonder whether the laws of England will be more intelligible in Maori than they are in English.'[2]

All the Colonial Secretaries, with the possible exception of Cardwell, relied heavily upon the advice of the Permanent Under-Secretary. Rightly so, for both Herman Merivale and Sir Frederic Rogers, who succeeded him in May 1860, were very able and liberal-minded men. Merivale was 'somewhat combative and formidable' in appearance and manner, 'massive' in intellect (the word is Bulwer Lytton's) as well as broad and strong in frame, in conversation a man of long silences sometimes startlingly broken, but 'a remarkably good and quick writer'. He used to get through his work at the office by four, play whist (not well) till dinner, and write articles for the reviews (on all manner of subjects) in the evening. He cared nothing for outward show and refused a K.C.B. because he 'did not see the use of it'. Yet such was his reputation that he was persuaded to leave the Colonial Office, which he liked, for the India Office, where he remained Permanent Under-Secretary till his death.[3]

Merivale was a firm believer in responsible government and had no doubt carried weight with Pakington and Newcastle in their concessions to the Australian colonies. He came to think that Auckland and Taranaki with their large Maori populations might have been better kept under Crown rule for a time, but had considered responsible government 'very desirable' for New Zealand in 1854 and knew there could be no question of going

---

[1] Minute (17 Aug. 1865), CO48/427.
[2] Minute (28 Oct. 1858), CO209/145.
[3] This paragraph is based on C. Merivale, *Herman Merivale, C.B.* (reprinted from *Transactions of the Devonshire Association for the Advancement of Science*, 1844) and 'My Father in his Habit as he lived', a chapter from H. C. Merivale, *Bar, Stage and Platform* (2nd ed., London, 1902). I owe this reference and access to the first to Mr. E. V. Quinn, Librarian of Balliol College, Oxford.

back.[1] Indeed he was convinced that it was impracticable to retain Native affairs in the Governor's hands and could see no advantage in setting up a Council to assist him.[2] He was something of a sceptic about Britain's withdrawal from South African responsibilities. He accepted the necessity of reducing the forces there, which had varied from 4,000 to 10,000 men, but 'to expect that the colony can pay half of the expense even of the smallest of those numbers is quite idle'.[3] He admired Sir George Grey's native policies and wanted Shepstone to govern the tribes in Natal instead of removing large numbers out of the colony.[4] On the other hand he was 'entirely against any . . . federation or union with the Free Republics': federation meant 'one or the other of two things: either enormous expense to the mother country or the independence of South Africa'.[5] In the West Indies (where he seldom intervened) he shared Governor Hincks's dislike of Indian immigration: 'I agree with him as to the inconsistency of which we are guilty before foreign nations in at once setting up free against slave labour and yet importing labour which though not slave is certainly *not* free.'[6]

Sir Frederic Rogers had been one of the Land and Emigration Commissioners since 1846 and sole legal adviser since C. A. Wood's retirement in 1857. Since he was to carry his legal business with him, the Duke of Newcastle proposed to lighten his burden as Permanent Under-Secretary by appointing Taylor Second Assistant Under-Secretary with sole supervision of the West India department and perhaps a few more colonies;[7] but the Treasury would not agree. Rogers had to carry the extra load until Carnarvon secured the appointment of H. T. Holland as Legal Adviser in 1867.[8]

---

[1] Minutes (11 Nov. 1854 and 1 Oct. 1857), CO209/123 and 141: see below, p. 219.

[2] Minute (6 Feb. 1860), CO209/158.

[3] Minute (13 Feb. 1860), CO48/406.

[4] Minute (29 May 1854) on Pine to Newcastle (12 Mar. 1854) (Separate), CO179/35.

[5] Minutes (24 Aug. and 15 Oct. 1858), CO48/389 and 390.

[6] Minute (9 Oct. 1857) on Hincks to Labouchere (22 Aug. 1857) (No. 42), CO 28/187.

[7] Newcastle to Taylor (3 May 1860), Newcastle Papers, NeC10889. For Taylor's reply see his *Autobiography*, ii. 158–9.

[8] B. A. Knox, 'The Provision of Legal Advice and Colonial Office Reorganization, 1866–7', *Bulletin of the Institute of Historical Research*, xxxv. 178–97.

Rogers's published letters and innumerable minutes and dispatches of his drafting reveal him as a man not only of great intellectual range and power but also of remarkable literary gifts. Though he was shy of expressing an opinion on political issues, his force of character and intellect gave him great weight in counsel. Those who knew him well describe him as 'in private life . . . one of the most interesting and attractive of men' and some of his letters have delightful touches of humour. But he was essentially an aristocrat in his outlook on life and a High Church aristocrat at that.[1] He hardly concealed his scorn at the low tone of public life in the rising colonial democracies and the disingenuous shifts of colonial politicians. He regarded responsible government as equivalent in practice to independence. But he had the high-principled aristocrat's sense of duty towards Native peoples under British protection. A minute on Natal reveals his uneasy conscience.

I cannot help saying that if this great opening is neglected and this great experiment comes to disgrace and disaster, it will be a greater disgrace and a greater disaster than the failure of the similar but smaller experiment in New Zealand. In Natal we have not yet committed the (as I think) terrible error of giving purely representative institutions to a country in which we had to protect one race against another.[2]

Rogers drafted the Native Council Bill Newcastle introduced in the House of Lords in 1860, but when it had to be withdrawn and the colonial alternative turned out to be 'a mere feeding of the Home Government with words and despoiling it of power' he tried another tack.[3] 'It would be better for the Imperial Government to contribute to the education and government of the Natives than to furnish troops to control them.' Hence he would make Sir George Grey a liberal grant 'for a tolerably long period', keep a fair number of troops for, say, three years but then insist that all but a certain minimum 'must be paid for by the Colony —come peace come war'.[4] The course of events and the Waikato

---

[1] The quotation is from Sir Algernon West, *Contemporary Portraits* (London, 1920), p. 107. Cf. also Taylor, *Autobiography*, ii. 160.
[2] Minute (11 Nov. 1868) on Keate to Buckingham (24 Sept. 1868) (No. 101), CO179/90.
[3] The quotation is from a Minute of 13 Feb. 1861, CO209/156.
[4] Minute (20 Feb. 1862) on Grey to Newcastle (30 Nov. 1861) (No. 36), CO209/165.

war in particular interfered with Rogers's programme, but in any case he soon grew disgusted with the colonists' aim (as he saw it) of 'leaving with the Home Government such a shadow of responsibility as shall support a claim to have the war which their policy has caused carried on at the Imperial expense'.[1] 'I at once made up my mind', he wrote years afterwards, 'that there would be no quiet for ourselves or safety for the Natives until our troops were recalled and the colonists forced to rely on their own resources and to try mild and just methods rather than violent ones.'[2] This is not the place for tracing the course of this policy. Even Weld's self-reliant principles were more easily formulated than carried out and Sir George Grey was fertile in excuses for delaying the withdrawal of the troops which were the main buttress of his personal authority.[3] Rogers's tone in his ably drawn dispatches grew ever sharper and the relations of the two Governments more and more unfriendly.

Rogers had always been pessimistic about the future of the Imperial connection. In a letter referring to the Australian constitutions of 1854 and their attempt to limit the Imperial veto, he wrote: 'It is a great pity that, give as much as you will, you can't please the colonists with anything short of absolute independence, so that it is not easy to say how you are to accomplish what we are, I suppose, all looking to—the eventual parting company on good terms.'[4] Now he was making his own fears come true. Taylor, his close friend, saw eye to eye with him. Engrossed in their official work, they were not aware that the climate of opinion was changing.

Nor did the House of Commons see it until 1870. The influence of the House on colonial policy is indubitable, but hard to measure. Parties were in a fluid state from the break-up of Peel's Conservative Party in 1846 to the formation of Gladstone's Liberal Cabinet in 1868. Government had as yet found no substitute for the declining 'influence of the Crown' traced by Professor Foord in a famous article. Party organization was weak. Governments seldom had clear majorities and the fall of

[1] Minute of 4 Jan. 1863, Newcastle Papers, NeC 10908A.
[2] *Letters of Lord Blachford*, p. 298. This autobiographical fragment was apparently written about 1885.
[3] On all this, see below, Chs. X and XI.
[4] To R. W. Church (15 Sept. 1854), *Letters of Lord Blachford*, pp. 157–8.

Palmerston in 1858 showed how unstable even these might be. J. S. Mill remarks on the tendency of the House 'to interfere more and more in the details of administration'.[1] The creation, on Gladstone's motion, of the Committee of Public Accounts in 1861 no doubt encouraged detailed discussion of the estimates.[2] All these circumstances made the Cabinets of this period unusually sensitive to the temper of the House of Commons. When Secretaries of State told colonial Governors that Parliament would not carry this vote or guarantee that loan, they were not raising up bogies to frighten them: they meant what they said.

Governments also had to take note of the criticisms of the press and especially of *The Times*. *The Times* is said to have been responsible for the appointment of Sir William Molesworth to the Aberdeen Cabinet. It was *The Times*, through the dispatches of its correspondent W. H. Russell from the Crimea, which brought down the Aberdeen Cabinet and which had the principal share in the triumph of Lord Palmerston.[3] Perhaps this deference to the press was part of the ransom which the liberal aristocracy, which predominated in the Cabinets of the period, paid to the middle-class electorate.

Yet the change in the temper of the country, which made the Gladstone Ministry of 1868–74 a watershed between two conceptions of the Empire, did not originate with the press. The weight of newspaper opinion, as the *Spectator* admitted, was in favour of the policy of the Gladstone Ministry, which had after all just been returned with a majority of 112.[4] The change originated in the City of London. As Professor Habakkuk showed in a path-breaking chapter in the *Cambridge History of the British Empire*, at this period 'the growing pressure of competitors underlined the importance of the possession of colonial markets'; and investment in India and the colonies was increasing. The colonial bonds which, from the 'fifties onwards, were issued on London in increasing numbers were to all intents and purposes gilt-edged

---

[1] *Considerations on Representative Government* (1861), p. 235 (in Everyman's Library edition).

[2] Earl Grey, *Parliamentary Government considered with reference to Reform* (London, 1863), pp. 86 ff. Grey also remarks that 'perhaps the worst jobs of recent years have been perpetrated by means of jobs in Committee of Supply'.

[3] *History of 'The Times'* (London, 1939), vol. ii; B. Kingsley Martin, *The Triumph of Lord Palmerston* (London, 1924).

[4] *Spectator*, 26 Mar. 1870.

securities; they returned a steady 5 or 6 per cent, and they were issued near par.'[1] The fact that a serious interest in colonial affairs had always been confined to a minority perhaps increased the sensitivity of governments to minority pressure. The 'West India interest' is a case in point. Now an increasing number of business and professional men with colonial experience and connections were settling in London. A General Association of the Australian Colonies, formed in 1855, had functioned for some years. At a critical period of the Maori war New Zealand colonists in London had held regular meetings and made representations to the Government. A newspaper, the *Australia and New Zealand Gazette*, was published, generally at fortnightly intervals. On 26 June 1868 a group of 'colonists' in London, reinforced by men who had served in the colonies like the chairman, Viscount Bury, who had for three years been Superintendent of Indian Affairs in Canada, resolved to form a Colonial Society as a meeting place and centre of information about the colonies, if possible with a library. Chichester Fortescue (then in opposition) was present and moved that the Society be 'entirely non-political'.[2] The Duke of Buckingham and Sir Stafford Northcote, Secretary of State for India, agreed to send their respective Governors addresses in favour of the Society; by the time these were ready, they were out of office, but Lord Granville and the Duke of Argyll carried out the undertaking. Gladstone himself proposed the toast of the Society at its inaugural dinner; three of his Ministers (Granville, Cardwell, and Chichester Fortescue) became Vice-Presidents and Childers sat on the Council, along with both Merivale and Rogers. Soon, by permission, it became the Royal Colonial Institute.

On the other hand, the fear that the Gladstone Ministry aimed at loosening the painter, if not cutting it, was not entirely imaginary. The withdrawal of troops from the colonies was an essential part of Cardwell's army reforms. A Royal Commission on Recruiting in 1867 had expressed the view that Army service was unpopular because two-thirds of the service was overseas. This was not the only reason: the agricultural labourers, who had been the mainstay of the rank and file as the country gentry had been of

[1] *Cambridge History of the British Empire*, ii (Cambridge, 1940), 780, 796.
[2] *Proceedings of the Royal Colonial Institute* (1870); Avaline Folsom' *The Royal Empire Society: the Formative Years* (London, 1933).

the officers, were moving into the towns where there was no such military tradition: the rates of pay, in a period of rising wages, were shockingly low.[1] Cardwell 'did not anticipate much opposition, as the principle of colonial self-reliance was very generally assented to'.[2] The Derby–Disraeli administrations of 1866–8 had pressed on with the policy of withdrawal, just as he had done when he was Colonial Secretary; and neither Carnarvon nor Buckingham had any sympathy with 'Little England' views. But the known views of Granville about the tenuousness of the colonial connection and his refusal to make allowances for the special difficulties of New Zealand made these withdrawals appear part of a wider design. Kimberley in his *Journal of Events during the Gladstone Ministry* informs us of a 'gloomy discussion' on relations with the United States: 'nearly all the Ministers were of opinion that it would be impossible to defend Canada successfully against the Americans and that it is much to be desired that Canada should become independent.'[3] A month later Granville wrote in a confidential dispatch to the Governor-General of Canada, Sir John Young: 'You will be good enough to bring to my notice any line of policy or any measures which without implying on the part of Her Majesty's Government any wish to change abruptly our relations would gradually prepare both Countries for a friendly relaxation of them.'[4] 'The best solution', he told Lord Russell in reply to a critical letter, '. . . would probably be that in the course of time and in the most friendly spirit the Dominion should find itself strong enough to proclaim [its] independence.'[5] John Bright and Robert Lowe on more than one occasion and Clarendon just

---

[1] The pay of a private of infantry in 1865 was 1s. a day, with 1d. beer money. 'From this was deducted 8½d. for rations, groceries and vegetables. From the balance of 3½d. he had to pay for barrack-damages, washing and the renewal of his forage-cap, shell jacket, three shirts, razor, brushes, mits, soap, sponge and haversack': Sir J. W. Fortescue, *History of the British Army*, xiii (London, 1930), 531–40.

[2] Sir R. Biddulph, *Lord Cardwell at the War Office* (London, 1904), p. 26.

[3] *Journal of Events during the Gladstone Ministry, 1868–1874* (ed. E. Drus) (Camden Miscellany, xxi; London, 1958), p. 4.

[4] Granville to Young (14 June 1869) (Confidential), quoted by D. M. L. Farr, *The Colonial Office and Canada, 1867–1887* (Toronto, 1955), pp. 282–3. Farr's book contains the fullest discussion of this often-quoted dispatch. Granville added this paragraph to a draft by Rogers.

[5] Granville to Russell (28 Aug. 1869), quoted by Lord E. Fitzmaurice, *Life of the Second Earl Granville* (London, 1905), ii. 22.

before he died expressed similar opinions.[1] There were reasons for anxiety. The *Alabama* controversy was still unsettled; President Grant and Senator Sumner, Chairman of the Foreign Relations Committee, wanted Canada as the price of a settlement; and even Hamilton Fish, the moderate and level-headed Secretary of State, hoped for a time that Canadian independence might form part of a deal.[2] But there is no evidence that Gladstone saw Granville's confidential dispatch and no reason at all to believe that he would have lent himself to such a deal as the Americans had in mind. Kimberley, Chichester Fortescue, Childers certainly and probably others in the Cabinet were quite out of sympathy with any such policy.

The rumours of Gladstone's intentions, however, produced a sharp reaction from some of the group which had formed the Colonial Society. J. A. Youl, a banker who had been Secretary and Treasurer of the Australian Association, Henry Sewell of New Zealand, and H. Blaine, a former member of the Cape Parliament, summoned a meeting in its rooms for 4 August 1869, and with its support prepared a circular addressed to the governments of the Australian colonies (except Western Australia), New Zealand, Canada, the Cape, Natal, and, rather incongruously, Mauritius. The Government's policy seemed to be pointing to a severance of the connection. The Colonial Office was 'ill adapted for carrying on friendly intercourse with Colonial Governments or representing their wants or wishes'. The British Parliament was absorbed in domestic affairs. The circular suggested the summoning of a conference of authorized representatives of the various responsible colonial governments to meet in London perhaps in the following February.[3] Granville quickly scotched this proposal by a circular dispatch pointing out the practical objections—the diversity of the issues affecting the different colonies,

---

[1] For Bright see speeches in the House on 23 Mar. 1865 and 28 Feb. 1867, *Hansard*, 3rd Ser. clxxviii. 169 and clxxxv. 1184 (the former reprinted in his *Speeches on Questions of Public Policy* (ed. J. E. T. Rogers) (popular edition, p. 79)); for Lowe see a remark quoted in Sir A. Lyall, *Life of the Marquis of Dufferin and Ava* (London, 1905), i. 286; for Clarendon, his letter to Lord Lyons (1 June 1870), Lord Newton, *Life of Lord Lyons* (London, 1913), i. 292.

[2] See in particular A. Nevins, *Hamilton Fish: the Inner History of the Grant Administration* (New York, 1936).

[3] Youl, Sewell, and Blaine to Colonial Secretaries of New South Wales, etc. (13 Aug. 1869), P.P., 1870, xlix [C. 24], 1–2.

the adequacy of existing machinery, and the unsatisfactory character, as colonial representatives, of 'a body of gentlemen resident in London, acting in pursuance of their own views or of mere written instructions, under influence not always identical with those which are paramount in the Colony and without the guarantee which their recommendations may derive from having passed through the Governor's hands'.[1] The reach of the authors of the circular had far exceeded their grasp. The press gave it a mixed reception. *The Times* appeared to hint that such a conference might be used to negotiate a friendly separation.[2] The *Morning Post* and the *Standard* (Conservative papers), the independent *Pall Mall Gazette* and the *Spectator* were, in varying degrees, sympathetic.[3] But the unsympathetic attitude of the colonial governments killed the conference. Most of them either expressed concurrence in Lord Granville's views or simply declined to be represented. Even the New Zealand Government, misinterpreting the authors of the circular as believing 'that the time has arrived to prepare the way for National Independence', professed itself satisfied with Granville's dispatch and declined to instruct the Commissioners it was about to send to England to take part in the conference.[4] A series of meetings that winter in the Cannon Street Hotel, in which Edward Wilson, proprietor of the *Melbourne Argus*, took the leading part, attempted to keep up the pressure; and the Royal Colonial Society, though disavowing the circular and unconnected with the Cannon Street meetings, agreed to join in a deputation to Lord Granville to urge the calling of a conference of colonial representatives. On 15 December, in the words of the *Spectator*, the deputation was 'received graciously, and still more graciously snubbed'.[5] Youl and his colleagues had to admit that the conference could not take place.[6]

[1] Granville to Governors of New South Wales, South Australia, New Zealand, Victoria, Queensland, Canada, Newfoundland, Prince Edward Island (8 Sept. 1869), ibid., p. 3. Note omission of colonies without responsible government. For the authorship see *Letters of Lord Blachford*, pp. 278–9.

[2] C. A. Bodelsen, *Studies in Mid-Victorian Imperialism* (reprinted, London, 1960), p. 97. But the leading article (26 Aug. 1869) need not be so interpreted.

[3] Here I rely on Bodelsen, op. cit., p. 97, except for the *Spectator*, a file of which has been accessible to me in the Canterbury Public Library.

[4] Memo. of Fox (2 Dec. 1869), P.P., 1870, xlix [C. 51], 3–4. Replies from other governments are in C. 24, pp. 4–15.

[5] *Spectator*, 18 Dec. 1869.

[6] Youl, Sewell, and Blaine to Gisborne (23 Dec. 1869), Appendices to Journals, House of Representatives, N.Z., 1870, A—No. 6.

Yet *The Times* conceded that the 'small knot of persons' responsible for the Canon Street meetings had 'set politicians talking everywhere about the Colonies and their relations with England'.[1] Towards the end of the year Adderley published a discursive *Review of 'The Colonial Policy of Lord John Russell's Administration' by Earl Grey . . . and of subsequent Colonial History*, in which he took issue with those who 'do not see that between the alternatives of independence and separation lies the real secret of a lasting connexion—that of common partnership'.[2] In an article 'England and her Colonies' in the January number of *Fraser's Magazine*, Froude was chiefly concerned with the social question and the indifference of the Government to the direction of English emigration; but he also made the point, now hackneyed but then less familiar, that the day of small states was passing. In any case 'the breaking up of our empire . . . cannot be completed till the country has had an opportunity of declaring its pleasure'.[3] Forster also spoke out on this point to his constituents at Bradford. 'Neither in England nor in the colonies do we intend that the English Empire shall be broken up.' He avowed his hope that in the course of time statesmen might unite the colonies with the mother country 'in one great confederation'.[4] Merivale in the February number of the *Fortnightly Review*, whilst pointing out that colonies could not be made subservient to the purposes of emigration from Great Britain as Froude supposed, stated his belief that existing voluntary ties would endure.[5] Such was the public interest in the colonies that Lord Carnarvon expressed surprise at the 'silence on colonial subjects' in the Queen's Speech. He feared it meant the Government were taking the line recommended by Lowe—'a course at once cheese-paring in point of economy and spendthrift in point of character.'[6] On 26 April R. R. Torrens, first Premier of South Australia and now member

[1] *The Times*, 19 Jan. 1870.
[2] (London, 1869), p. 420.
[3] *Short Studies on Great Subjects* (London, 1893), ii. 214. Froude returned to the subject with 'The Colonies Once More' in August.
[4] *The Times*, 18 and 21 Jan. 1870.
[5] H. Merivale, 'The Colonial Question in 1870', *Fortnightly Review*, N.S. vii. 153 ff.
[6] House of Lords, 14 Feb. 1870: *Hansard*, 3rd Ser. cxcix. 193–212. Granville in reply admitted that 'at this moment a great majority of the people of this country and perhaps a still greater majority of the people of the Dominion [of Canada] desire that the connection should be continued': ibid. 219.

for Cambridge, moved for a Select Committee 'to enquire into the political relations and modes of communication between the self-governing colonies and this country'. He wanted limitation of the veto to acts infringing the royal prerogative and permission to the colonies to send envoys to England who would stand to the Secretary for the Colonies on the same footing as envoys of foreign countries to the Foreign Secretary. These suggestions found little support; but the tone of the debate was friendly to the colonies and it elicited an interesting declaration from Gladstone. 'I believe', he said, 'that the connection with our Colonies depends so entirely on will and affection that I do not regard it as bound up essentially in the maintenance of any administrative function whatever.'[1]

The settlement of the controversy with New Zealand in mid-May by its acceptance of a loan guarantee[2] was a good sign and so was the appointment of the Earl of Kimberley to the Colonial Office in Granville's place on 6 July. Kimberley was not much of a public figure but already had wide official experience, with the Foreign Office as Under-Secretary and Minister to Russia and in Ireland as Lord Lieutenant. Dilke describes him as 'a wise man who never did himself justice in conversation'. Morley thought him one of the ablest of the Whigs.[3] Whereas Granville, who had a streak of indolence in his character, relied on his officials in departmental business and drifted with the tide, Kimberley was a man of action. Uneasy though he was about the annexation of the diamond fields which were to perpetuate his name, it was Kimberley who prepared the way for the moves towards federation in South Africa which Carnarvon unfortunately forced on. His was the initiative in the intervention against the Ashantis and the forward policy in Malaya and he brought matters nearly to the point of annexation in Fiji. He secured a like-minded Parliamentary Under-Secretary when Knatchbull-Hugessen replaced the ineffective Monsell at the end of the year. His eloquent insistence, in a debate initiated by an enthusiastic but uninspiring

---

[1] *Hansard*, 3rd Ser. cc. 1817–1908. The previous question was moved (by Viscount Bury) and carried by 110 to 67. Cf. also Gladstone's speech on 7 Mar. 1873: ibid., ccxiv. 1534.
[2] See below, p. 371.
[3] S. Gwynn and G. M. Tuckwell, *Life of Sir Charles Dilke* (London, 1917), i. 391; Viscount Morley, *Recollections* (London, 1917), ii. 247. On Granville's laziness, cf. *Journal* of Kimberley (ed. E. Drus), p. 31.

Scottish member, R. A. Macfie, on 12 May 1871, that 'self-reliance did not mean separate existence', that the colonies must be made to feel 'that there was nothing to be gained by separation', won golden opinions.[1]

Exactly a week later Sir Frederic Rogers retired. His successor, R. G. W. Herbert, who had been appointed Assistant Under-Secretary when Elliot's successor Sir F. R. Sandford returned to the Education Office in February 1870 as Permanent Secretary, had gone out to Queensland as Colonial Secretary in 1859 and later became its first Premier. This first-hand colonial experience, together with his natural 'tact . . . geniality and courteous bearing', were excellent qualifications for his post at a time when, as Torrens implied in his speech in the House, the self-governing colonies were reaching forward to equality of status. Childers was soon writing to Gavan Duffy that 'the recent changes in personnel at the head of the permanent office are very favourable to the sound treatment of large questions'.[2] On 25 June 1872 the House of Commons had an inconclusive debate on Fiji. 'The question of annexing the Fiji Islands', The Times remarked, 'is one which a few years ago would scarcely have been discussed seriously by the House of Commons.' The article, after reviewing some recent contentious issues, concluded: 'Well might the Royal Colonial Institute congratulate itself, at its annual meeting held last Wednesday, on the change which appears to have passed over the spirit of Imperial statesmanship in the last year or two.'[3] Disraeli had noted the change. In his famous Crystal Palace speech (the night before the Fiji debate) he had tried to use it for the benefit of the Conservative Party: but he was not leading the movement of opinion. He was following it.

The causes of the change in the intellectual climate were complex. The success of Cardwell's policy of withdrawal, except in South Africa, and the consequent removal of this continual irritant, the renewed interest in emigration, the increased contact with the colonies of settlement as communications improved and successful colonists 'came home', the increasing attraction of the colonies to investors, the exciting and important new explorations

[1] Hansard, 3rd Ser. ccvi. 750–70 (Knatchbull-Hugessen's speech, 761–6).
[2] 19 Apr. 1872: E. S. C. Childers, Life and Correspondence of the Right Hon. H. C. E. Childers (London, 1901), i. 208.
[3] The Times, 1 July 1872.

in Africa, uneasiness at the rising power of Bismarckian Germany
—all these contributed something. And no doubt the great
majority of Englishmen disagreed with the Manchester School
and took pride in the British Empire, though they grumbled
occasionally about paying for it.[1]

[1] Cf. *Spectator*, 18 Sept. 1869 ('The Colonial Imbroglio').

# II

## THE SETTLEMENT OF THE
## FRONTIER AND THE
## NEW CAPE CONSTITUTION

IN the winter of 1851–2 the Ministry of Lord John Russell decided to limit British responsibilities in South Africa. The war which had broken out at Christmas 1850 in the recently annexed province of British Kaffraria and the rebellion of the Hottentots of the Kat River settlement had thrown doubt upon Earl Grey's theory that the best way to peace on the Cape frontier was to bring the tribes under British rule. A critical Parliament and press had urged that the colonists should be given self-government and left to manage their own frontier policy and defend themselves. The injudicious meddling of Major Warden, British Resident at Bloemfontein, in tribal quarrels in the Orange River Sovereignty, also annexed in 1848, had led to a military reverse which strengthened the reaction: Lord John Russell changed his views and, with Lord Grey's reluctant concurrence, insisted that withdrawal from the Sovereignty must be 'a settled point in our policy'. Two assistant Commissioners, Major W. S. Hogge and Mr. C. Mostyn Owen, were sent out to assist Sir Harry Smith, the High Commissioner, in frontier affairs and in January 1852 they signed the Sand River Convention recognizing the independence of the Transvaal. Soon afterwards Sir Harry, an enthusiastic expansionist, was superseded by Major-General George Cathcart.[1]

Cathcart, a humane, tactful, intellectual soldier, arrived on the frontier in April to find that Smith had practically broken the rebellion, at the cost of a heavy strain upon his inadequate army. After a short pause, in which he organized a new mounted police and reminded the settlers of their own obligations in defence,

---

[1] On all this see my *British Colonial Policy in the Age of Peel and Russell*, ch. xii. On Cathcart see especially *Correspondence of Lieutenant-General the Hon. Sir G. Cathcart* (London, 1856). Cathcart was made K.C.B. in 1853.

Cathcart in August invaded the territory of the Galeka chief Kreli beyond the river Kei and then, with the aid of a burgher force, cleared the mountain strongholds of the Waterkloof and the Amatolas. The two principal Gaika chiefs, the ineffective Sandile and his astute, strong-minded half-brother Macomo, were driven to take refuge across the Kei. Cathcart next turned northward, received the submission of the Tembu tribe and offered them terms of peace, under the loyal regent Nonesi, with a 'somewhat circumscribed' boundary.[1]

The frontier settlement was essentially Cathcart's own. Sir John Pakington, in a private letter, mooted the question of reversing the annexation of British Kaffraria and retiring to the Keiskamma.[2] Cathcart lost no time in pointing out the dangers.

Such a measure, if not now next to impossible, on account of our engagements to white settlers in British Kaffraria, who have been allowed to take root, as it were, in King William's Town, would be most impolitic and disastrous at this particular time. . . . Abandonment of the field would give to our enemies now driven beyond the Kei and expelled from their location, which has been declared forfeited, the advantage which they have so pertinaciously contended for, the recovery and reoccupation of their former territory, and even more than that, the recovery of their independence. This termination of the Contest could not fail to be proclaimed to all surrounding Native tribes, and revive the War of races . . . with renewed hopes of being able by perseverance ultimately to drive the white man into the Sea.[3]

This idea of Pakington's disappeared with him. Cathcart forced the Gaika tribe to abandon the forest and mountain country of the Amatolas and relocated them 'under the only responsible head they can ever be made to acknowledge [Sandile] in a country which is the most easily controlled which this district affords'— along the Kabousie river.[4] But if he gave short shrift to the

[1] Cathcart to Pakington (11 Feb. 1853) (No. 54), P.P., 1852–3, lxvi [1635], 218–28. The chief Mapassa and his followers had taken part in the war and lost their territory.

[2] The original of this letter may be presumed to be in the Cathcart Papers. The present Earl Cathcart informed me, in a courteous letter, that these are at present inaccessible.

[3] Cathcart to Pakington (24 Jan. 1853) (Private), Newcastle Papers, NeC9554. These sentences are repeated in dispatch No. 54 of 11 Feb.

[4] Cathcart to Pakington (15 Feb. 1853) (Private), ibid. See also Cathcart to Pakington (11 Feb. 1853), (No. 54) G.H. 23/22, Cape Archives: printed in P.P., 1852–3, lxvi [1635], 218 ff.

suggestion of the Secretary of State, he also disregarded the clamour of the frontier newspapers for further chastisement of Kreli.[1] When two of Kreli's councillors came to sue for peace, Cathcart granted it on condition that he recognized the Indwe–Kei boundary, surrendered two Hottentot rebel leaders, restrained and punished all attempts of his people to disturb the peace of Her Majesty's subjects, and made himself responsible for the lives and property of those British subjects whom he allowed to live in his territory.[2]

Cathcart was trying to exclude all the Xhosa tribes from the Cape Colony proper. But the refugee tribes, originally from Natal, commonly known as the Fingoes (*Amamfengu* = hungry people in search of work), were a special case. Governor D'Urban at their request had given them protection within the Colony and they had rendered loyal service in two wars since. Now a military column had brought out some thousands of them from the Trans-kei with their pastor and many thousand cattle.[3] The Fingoes were settled for the most part near the frontier in the 'ceded ter-ritory' between the Keiskamma and the Fish River but many became farm servants and herdsmen in the Colony. It was also part of Cathcart's plan to strengthen the defence of the eastern frontier by new settlements of European farmers in the district north of the Windvogelberg, which he named Queenstown and caused to be transferred from British Kaffraria to the Colony,[4] and by the military occupation of the Amatolas, with a village at Keiskammahoek in the heart of the mountains. British Kaffraria was to remain under the military government of Colonel John Maclean as Chief Commissioner, the Letters Patent for a civil government issued in December 1850 being left in abeyance in the meantime.[5] The moderate elements in colonial opinion realized

[1] *Cape Frontier Times* (Grahamstown), 15 Feb. and 8 Mar. 1863. The Port Elizabeth *Mercury* and *Telegraph* were also dissatisfied with the peace.
[2] Cathcart to Pakington (12 Feb. 1853) (No. 56), P.P., 1852-3, lxvi [1635], 229-30. Detail about the Hottentot leaders in Cathcart to Pakington (15 Feb. 1853), loc. cit.
[3] Rev. J. Ayliff and J. Whiteside, *History of the Abambo (Fingoes)* (Butterworth, 1912), pp. 50-1. Calderwood in 1855 put the number at 3,000-4,000.
[4] On this see P. J. Lombard, 'Die Stigting en Vroeë Geskiednis van Queens-town (1853-1859)', *Archives Year Book for South African History*, xv, vol. ii (Cape Town, 1952).
[5] Cathcart to Pakington (11 Feb. 1853) (No. 51), P.P., 1852-3, lxvi [1635], 217-18.

that these terms were as favourable as could be expected after an exhausting war, but doubted whether they would last. 'You cannot create a vacuum in South Africa,' wrote the *Grahamstown Journal*, '. . . No one supposes for a moment that the Governor's plan for settling the Amatolas will prove successful, and yet if not settled, the Kaffirs will as assuredly walk into them as that their summits will be lit up by to-morrow's sun.'[1]

The centre of controversy in South Africa after the war, however, was the Orange River Sovereignty. The Russell Ministry's policy of withdrawal was endorsed by its successors and approved by Sir George Cathcart, but it was more difficult of execution. Peace with the Basuto, who were being patiently built up into a nation by the great chief Moshesh from his stronghold of Thaba Bosigo, had been endangered by Warden's mistakes. Moshesh himself carried out a successful raid on Sikonyela and his Batlokwa in May 1852 and Cathcart could not ignore what he described as the 'incessant and latterly increasing depredations by the Basuto from the Burghers who are restrained by law from retaliation as well as from the Chief Moroko avowedly as a punishment for his services rendered on the side of the British Government in Major Warden's campaign'. On his assumption of the government he had written to Moshesh announcing his intention to visit the Sovereignty as soon as the war was over and his hope to 'meet him as a friend'. But these raids made a show of force inevitable, and in November Cathcart assembled a force of some 2,000 men to exact compensation from Moshesh and to adjust various boundaries and other unsettled questions in the Sovereignty.[2] 'I do not mean', he told the Secretary of State, 'to make it appear that I go to the Orange River to make war with Mosesch, but that I go with a sufficient force to administer strict justice with a strong arm to all.'[3] Moshesh's sons were informed that he must come to see the Governor at Platberg himself. On 15 December the two men had an interview. The Governor demanded 10,000 cattle and 1,000 horses (a severer penalty, for the Basuto had learned to fight on horseback) within three days. Moshesh promised to

---

[1] *Grahamstown Journal*, 22 Mar. 1853. Cf. also Cathcart to Newcastle (12 June 1853) (No. 19), P.P., 1854–5, xxxviii [1969], 11–12.
[2] Cathcart to Pakington (14 Nov. 1852, No. 34, and 29 Nov. 1852, No. 44), P.P., 1852–3, lxvi [1635], 183–6, 200–1.
[3] Cathcart to Pakington (13 Nov. 1852) (Private), Newcastle Papers, NeC9554.

comply, but added: 'Do not talk of war, for, however anxious I may be to avoid it, you know that a dog when beaten will show his teeth.'[1] On the 18th his son Nehemiah brought in 3,500 head of cattle. Late next day Moshesh's brother Mopeli came to Cathcart's camp near a ford over the Caledon (Cathcart's Drift) to ask for an extension of time, but in vain.

Early on the morning of 20 December the main force crossed the Caledon. The cavalry was to pass round the north of the Berea plateau, which lies between the river and Thaba Bosigo, another column under Eyre was to march across it, and both were to make a rendezvous with Cathcart's own column, which was to march round the plateau to the south, at a point within striking distance of Moshesh's stronghold. It seems that Cathcart and his staff still did not expect to have to fight. But the plateau was swarming with cattle and the cavalry, which was not expected to go up to the plateau, was misinformed about the geography of the country and found it had no choice. 'Both my commanders of columns', Cathcart ruefully complained in a private letter, 'ran wild after cattle, and did not act according to orders; so that I was left to fight the greater part of the Basuto army almost alone during half that day.'[2] Eyre reached the rendezvous, late; the cavalry never did, having had to withdraw from the plateau with their captured cattle. It seems that neither commander had realized that Thaba Bosigo was Cathcart's first objective; and when Eyre arrived, it was too late and the troops were too short of ammunition to attempt it. At sunset they retired about two miles to bivouac in a defensible position. The Basuto followed them and managed to entice a number of cattle to break out of their kraals but made no attempt to rush the camp and drew off during the night. Cathcart intended to resume operations in a day or two, when reinforced, and attack Thaba Bosigo. It stands about 300 feet above the valley, but the path up is not impossibly steep and there is no reason to believe that his force with its artillery could not have taken it, as his brigadiers wished him to do. But with superb political skill Moshesh forestalled him.

The Basuto chief had drawn the right moral from the Berea engagement. During the night Nehemiah, under the eyes of the

---

[1] Official Report of Proceedings enclosed in Cathcart to Pakington (13 Jan 1835) (No. 46), P.P., 1852-3, lxvi [1635], 205 ff.

[2] *Cathcart Correspondence*, p. 345.

French missionary Casalis but by no means at his dictation, wrote
Cathcart a letter in his father's name:

This day you have fought against my people, and taken much
cattle. . . . I beg you will be satisfied with what you have taken. I
entreat peace from you,—you have shown your power,—you have
chastised,—let it be enough I pray you; and let me be no longer considered an enemy to the Queen.[1]

Cathcart, however confident that he could turn the tables, must
have been sore at his reverse. But he had been sent to South
Africa to finish a war and limit Imperial commitments. The last
thing he wanted was to involve Great Britain in a new war and
break up the tribe of so intelligent and prudent a chief.[2] Over-
riding the wishes of his brigadiers and the advice of Assistant
Commissioner Owen, who made a written protest, he took
Moshesh's overture at its face value and responded in the same
spirit of moderation:

The words are those of a Great Chief, and of one who has the
interests of his people at heart. . . . I have taken the fine by force, and I
am satisfied. . . . I now desire not to consider you, Chief, as an enemy
of the Queen, but I must proclaim Martial Law in the Sovereignty, to
give to Commandants and Fieldcornets power to make commands in a
regular manner and, with the consent of the Resident, enter your
country in search of plundered horses and cattle. . . . And I expect you
to assist them.[3]

There is truth in Orpen's comment: 'Cathcart . . . perilled his
military reputation in the cause of justice.'[4] He did not withdraw
his troops because he had been defeated, but the withdrawal left
him open to this insinuation and was widely criticized in the
Colony. The Basuto boasted of their success; but Moshesh knew
in his heart how close he had come to ruin and was careful never
to fight against 'the Queen's soldiers' again. *The Times* was ill-
informed when it called the Berea a 'victory'; but the Duke of
Newcastle saw 'no reason to question the judgement you formed

---

[1] Enclosure in Cathcart to Pakington (13 Jan. 1853) (No. 46), loc. cit., p. 211.
On Casalis's position see Casalis to Green (3 Feb. 1853) and Cathcart to Green
(22 Mar. 1853)—a gracious acknowledgement that he had misjudged the missionaries: *Basutoland Records* (ed. Theal) (Cape Town, 1883), ii. 19–20, 41–2.

[2] On the danger to the tribe see letter of the Revd. H. Moore Dyke (28 Dec.
1852): *Basutoland Records*, i. 634–5.

[3] Cathcart to Moshesh (21 Dec. 1852), P.P., 1852–3, lxvi [1635], 211.

[4] J. M. Orpen, *History of the Basutos of South Africa* (Cape Town, 1857), p. 102.

of the course to be pursued towards the Basuto chief. The object of the expedition was accomplished by his submission, and there remained no motive for prosecuting further hostilities.'[1] This should be the verdict of history.[2]

With the return of peace to the frontier the time had come to introduce the new representative constitution framed at the Cape, which had been held up first by internal political differences and then by the war. Pakington had delayed ratification of the Constitution Ordinance and Civil List Ordinance which the Cape Legislative Council had passed in April 1852. The Duke of Newcastle, however, transmitted them to the Governor, with minor amendments, in a dispatch of 14 March 1853. There was to be a Parliament of two elective Houses, the Upper being elected by two large constituencies, eight from the Western Province and seven from the East. The franchise was low, but the property qualification for Legislative Councillors high. Persons holding offices of profit under the Crown were ineligible for the Assembly, but certain officers—the Colonial Secretary, Attorney-General, Treasurer, and Auditor-General—might take part in the deliberations of either House, though without voting rights. The only important amendment was a reversion from a franchise based mainly on property ownership to one admitting occupancy of buildings to the value of £25 as a qualification. As Newcastle said:

> It is exceedingly undesirable that the franchise should be so restricted as to leave those of the Coloured Classes who in point of intelligence are qualified for the exercise of political power, practically unrepresented. . . . It is the earnest desire of Her Majesty's Government that all her Subjects at the Cape, without distinction of Class or Colour, should be united by one bond of loyalty and common interest, and we believe that the exercise of political rights enjoyed by all alike will prove one of the best methods of attaining this object.[3]

Thus the Imperial Government inaugurated a liberal experiment which lasted approximately a hundred years. The Duke threw on the new Parliament the responsibility of meeting the demand of

---

[1] *The Times*, 28 Feb. 1853. Newcastle to Cathcart (14 Mar. 1853) (No. 37), P.P., 1852-3, lxvi [1635], 244.

[2] On the battle and its sequel see, in addition to Cathcart's dispatch and its enclosures, G. Tylden, *The Rise of the Basuto* (Cape Town and Johannesburg, 1950), ch. iv. A visit to the spot in 1951 has helped to form my views.

[3] Newcastle to Cathcart (14 Mar. 1853) (No. 40), P.P., 1852-3, lxvi [1636], 24-6.

the Eastern Provinces for a separate legislature or alternatively the removal of the seat of government to the East. The experiment of a Governor on the frontier with a Lieutenant-Governor in Cape Town had not, in Cathcart's opinion, worked well; he recommended that the General commanding the Forces be appointed Lieutenant-Governor for the frontier districts and have certain administrative functions and assistants, and the acceptance of this recommendation had a mollifying effect.[1] The prevailing mood, at any rate of the rural Dutch (Afrikaner) population, was one of apathy. The Cape was in fact accustomed to 'government by Executive Council;'[2] in time, Cathcart forecast, 'responsible governement will, I think we may fairly anticipate, be striven for at the instigation of ambitious leaders having the majority on their side', but this time was 'as yet remote'.[3]

The introduction of the constitution was, however, a convenient opportunity for broaching the question of a reduction in the Imperial force at the Cape and calling the attention of the colonists to the obligations of self-defence.

All the subjects of this great empire [Newcastle wrote] are bound to contribute to the common object of its safety. . . . It is only reasonable that local military expenses should be borne by the colonists as their very moderate contribution to the general protection, and I cannot doubt that when they are placed in respect of their civil liberties upon an equal footing with their fellow-subjects at home they will not demur to the justice of this share of a common burden being allotted to them.

The Duke suggested that the Imperial force should be reduced within eighteen months to 4,000 men, with their headquarters at Grahamstown; that a colonial militia of not less than 5,000, a sufficient proportion of them being cavalry, should be formed; and that the forts in British Kaffraria should be delivered up to the colonial authorities: these should also 'lay down such rules and regulations between the colony and the Kafirs as shall be agreed upon with the sanction of the Governor'.[4] Cathcart was in substantial

[1] Cathcart to Newcastle (14 July 1853) (Private), Newcastle Papers, NeC9554. Cathcart to Newcastle (15 Jan. 1854) (No. 1), GH23/24, Cape Archives.
[2] A. K. Fryer, 'The Government of the Cape of Good Hope, 1852-54', *Archives Year Book for South African History*, xxvii, vol. i. (Cape Town, 1964).
[3] Cathcart to Newcastle (15 Sept. 1853) (Private), Newcastle Papers, NeC9554.
[4] Newcastle to Cathcart (14 Mar. 1853) (No. 38), P.P., 1852-3, lxvi [1635], 244-6.

agreement as to the strength of the Imperial force; but he pointed out that the militia system was unpopular with the Dutch, who preponderated over the English by six to one everywhere except in Albany, Port Elizabeth, and Cape Town: what they wanted was a burgher law and this, with safeguards, Cathcart thought, would be more efficient and better suited to the country. As for the forts in Kaffraria, they did not really deserve the name.[1]

Cathcart's real complaint against the Imperial Government was that he was left in uncertainty about its policy, especially after Pakington had expressed doubts about retaining British Kaffraria. Newcastle, however, did not share these doubts and in his dispatch of 14 June 1853 he disclaimed any desire to question any of Cathcart's measures except the annexation of the Windvogelberg district to the Colony—though he later expressed some doubt whether the time had yet arrived for converting the provisional government of British Kaffraria into a more regular system.[2] Before the close of the year, however, both measures were approved.

Cathcart was now writing optimistically about the peace, security, and contentment existing on the frontier. 'The measures which have been adopted. . .', he told the Duke, 'have been all calculated as much to the benevolent powers of intervention between the Native and the Colonist as to the subjection of the one and security of the other.'[3] In a Government Notice he called the attention of the frontier farmers to 'the great benefit to their present and future comfort and security that may result from living on good terms, and above all things keeping faith, with their coloured neighbours'. They should employ Fingoes within the Colony rather than Xhosas living outside it as farm servants and if they wanted the latter should apply for them, specifying names, to the Gaika Commissioner or Resident Magistrate. This would help the chiefs to restrain their people and prevent their trespassing across the border.[4]

In British Kaffraria, Cathcart reported, the late rebels had 'taken to agriculture with a degree of enterprise never before known—

[1] Cathcart to Newcastle (15 May 1953, Nos. 12 and 13, and 14 Sept. 1853, No. 46), G.H. 23/22 and 24, Cape Archives.
[2] Newcastle to Cathcart (14 June 1853, No. 74, and 13 Oct. 1853, No. 138), P.P., 1854–5, xxxviii [1969], 67–8.
[3] Cathcart to Newcastle (15 Dec. 1853) (No. 64), ibid., p. 25.
[4] Government Notice (10 Dec. 1853), *Grahamstown Journal*, 31 Dec. 1853.

they purchased ploughs, sent men to be taught to work and hired people to plough for them'. Many lines of wagon-road had been opened through the Amatolas, where it had previously been difficult to pass even on horseback. But the purpose of these roads was military. The area should be kept as a Crown Reserve under military occupation, partly to overawe the Xhosa tribes but also 'as a salutary check against the reckless propensity of colonists to struggle on beyond the bounds of legitimate and recognized colonization, as detached squatters, tempted by visions of large profits on extensive farms, and regardless of all risks'. As he informed Chief Commissioner Maclean, 'military control, not colonization, is the principle of policy which has induced me to advise the retention of Kaffraria as a separate Government'.[1] With the Gaika Commissioner, Charles Brownlee, reporting that 'the universal desire among the Gaikas is for peace', with Queenstown firmly established in the north, 200 farms already surveyed there and the Abatembu settling down under Nonesi's regency, Cathcart could feel when he left for the Crimea that South Africa was 'in a state of perfect repose and security and with every prospect of a permanent peace and increasing prosperity'.[2]

The settlement of the Orange River Sovereignty, however, on Cathcart's own suggestion, had been left to a Special Commissioner. The Aberdeen Ministry confirmed the decision to withdraw and on 14 April 1853 Newcastle notified Cathcart of the appointment of Sir George Russell Clerk, formerly Governor of Bombay, as Special Commissioner. Believing that 'the difficulty of abandoning as well as of retaining the Orange Sovereignty has been underrated in this Country', Newcastle gave him a wide discretion.[3] But Clerk, an able, cynical, aloof man, made up his mind before he set foot in the territory. The Dutch, in a majority of 8 to 1, could not be expected to be loyal.

The Colonists (and I do not mean the Boers in particular) are self-interested and prejudiced. It is assuredly not here one is likely to doubt that all men are liars and the sort of Cormorants' appetite that all have for public money is remarkable. The missionaries of the 'Stations'

[1] Cathcart to Newcastle (15 Jan. 1854) (No. 6), G.H. 23/24, Cape Archives. Cathcart to Maclean (19 Jan. 1854), P.P., 1854, xxxviii [1969], 27-8.
[2] Brownlee to Maclean (4 Mar. 1854); Cathcart to Newcastle (17 May 1854) (No. 28), ibid., pp. 29-30, 32. *Cathcart Correspondence*, pp. 301-6.
[3] Newcastle to Cathcart (14 Apr. and 14 May 1853) (Private), Newcastle Papers, NeC9554.

are traders and shopkeepers; hence their other and sacred profession is regarded with not the least respect by the Natives. To be sure the Doctrines of freedom and 'liberal' ideas are attentively listened to, but the pupils are savages whose only possible understanding of freedom is to go and fight and kill and plunder.[1]

An assembly of delegates in Bloemfontein in the previous June had offered to relieve the Imperial Government of all trouble if a garrison of 500 troops with some guns was stationed in the territory; but this, Clerk declared, would mean bringing up a considerable support force to the frontier. The Sovereignty, in his view, was 'a vast territory, possessing nothing that can sanction its being permanently added to a frontier already inconveniently extended. . . . It imparts no strength to the British Government, no credit to its character, no lustre to the Crown.'[2] British authority was a farce.

It consists, in fact, in a dozen of Englishmen stuck down in this remote territory calling themselves a government, with ninety thousand Kafirs immediately around; a police [of one field commandant and seven field cornets]; an insufficient revenue; no credit; a land-jobbing character; with a detachment of . . . one hundred and fifty British infantry and fifty Hottentot cavalry in a starved country whose nearest support is four hundred miles off.[3]

On the other hand, many quarters in Cape Colony voiced strong opposition to withdrawal. A petition from the merchants of Cape Town signed by 'all the principal and several other mercantile firms, and the leading inhabitants of the town and neighbourhood of all professions and callings'[4] was followed by others from Swellendam, Burghersdorp, Uitenhage, Graaff Reinet, Port Elizabeth, and Grahamstown, this with 683 signatures, the largest number of any. True, they came from interested parties: 'the Sovereignty', wrote Cathcart in a private letter, 'was to them— the English speculators—a great gaming-table, and, moreover, out of reach of the police. Outlaws for debt in the colony are great land speculators in the Sovereignty; and the mortgagers in

---

[1] Clerk to Jocelyn (13 June 1953), ibid. Viscount Jocelyn was son and heir of the Earl of Roden.
[2] Clerk to Newcastle (25 Aug. and 8 Oct. 1853), P.P., 1854 xliii [1758], 24–30, 42.
[3] Clerk to Newcastle (3 Dec. 1853), ibid., p. 55.
[4] This phrase is from Darling (Lieutenant-Governor) to Newcastle (13 Nov. 1853) (No. 140), ibid., p. 12.

the colony, particularly at Cape Town, Graham's Town and Port Elizabeth say they have £50,000 at stake. . . . The Dutchman', he added, '. . . has not had time to open his mouth yet, but he is not of the same way of thinking.'¹ Yet the Dutchmen in the Sovereignty had had their chance in the assembly of 1852;² and the similar assembly which Clerk met in the little village church at Bloemfontein on 5 September 1853 did not go as he expected. On the second day of their meeting they presented to the Special Commissioner a unanimous address on Her Majesty's Government's announced intention of withdrawal.

We are unable to conceive the reasons that may have induced it to take this step. There certainly has been no desire expressed on our part for such a measure. We trust it has been no misconception in regard to our feeling of loyalty, for although we have at times given expression to our feelings of dissatisfaction in regard to local government, it was because we felt aggrieved at not participating in the advantages of good government and protection which we know Her Majesty's subjects elsewhere enjoy.³

This came from an assembly in which there were seventy-six Afrikaners and only nineteen English delegates. Clerk attributed its composition and proceedings to the machinations of colonial speculators and 'the untiring zeal of the Scotch Presbyterian clergyman of the Dutch church here'—the Revd. Andrew Murray; when many Dutch delegates left for their farms, Clerk said it was because they were 'disheartened by the difficulties which they feel to be thrown round them by the tricky character of the schemes of their British neighbours'.⁴ All this seems too farfetched. One finds it easier to accept de Kiewiet's judgement, 'that seventy-six intelligent Boers could have been driven into expressing views totally at variance with their real sentiments is inconceivable.' If they soon departed it was because 'they thought more about their farms than their independence'.⁵

¹ Cathcart to Trevelyan (18 Sept. 1853), *Cathcart Correspondence*, p. 376.
² C. W. de Kiewiet, *British Colonial Policy and the South African Republics, 1848–1872* (London, 1929), p. 66.
³ *Grahamstown Journal*, 20 Sept. 1853. The *Journal* and the *Friend of the Sovereignty* (Bloemfontein) were owned by the same firm.
⁴ Clerk to Newcastle (10 Sept. 1853), P.P., 1854, xliii [1758], 34–5.
⁵ De Kiewiet, op. cit., pp. 74–5. Cf. also J. F. Midgley, 'The Orange River Sovereignty, 1848–1854', *Archives Year Book for South African History*, xii, vol. ii (Cape Town, 1949), 521 ff.

But Clerk would not take 'No' for an answer. Before dispersing, the assembly resolved by 55 to 25 to appoint a committee 'for the purpose of considering a form of government for this territory and for communicating with Her Majesty's Special Commissioner'. It also resolved 'that the Committee be instructed not to entertain any proposals for the formation of an independent government until the following questions have been adjusted to their entire satisfaction'. Eleven questions followed, relating chiefly to treaties, tribal and farm boundaries, confiscated farms and compensation, though one of the number was 'the complete or conditional absolution of the inhabitants from their allegiance to the British Crown'.[1] Clerk's answer was ambiguous: 'Several of the proposals are very reasonable. On the other hand there are some which he [the Commissioner] cannot entertain.'[2] In fact he set himself to undermine the position of the committee, which, being urban and predominantly English, was too one-sided to be representative. Its choice of Dr. A. J. Fraser (chairman of the assembly) and the Revd. Mr. Murray as a deputation to England was not calculated to impress the Imperial Government.

Winburg became the headquarters of a party in contact with the Transvaal and critical of the committee's arrangements. Clerk went on tour, receiving (and no doubt encouraging) memorials complaining that the committee's proceedings were not satisfactory to the majority of the inhabitants. The Winburg group, in which an enterprising Belgian-Jewish trader, Adolphe Coqui, took the lead, chose new representatives and expressly empowered them 'to take over the government of this territory for and in the name of its inhabitants and jointly with those elected for the other districts . . . to constitute and become . . . the provisional government'. The document went on to suggest a future form of government and a series of fundamental laws.[3]

To strengthen Clerk's hand, Newcastle sent him a dispatch declaring that if the representatives refused to play their part 'the only resource left to Her Majesty's Government would be one which could not be adopted without regret, namely to withdraw the troops and pronounce the separation accomplished'.[4]

---

[1] *Grahamstown Journal*, 1 Oct. 1853 (with interesting analysis of parties in the Assembly). Cf. also P.P., 1854, xliii [1758], 43–4.
[2] Clerk to Chairman of Assembly (12 Sept. 1853): P.P., 1854, xliii [1758], 44.
[3] Clerk to Newcastle (10 Dec. 1853), Enclosure, P.P., 1854, xliii [1758], 63.
[4] Newcastle to Clerk (14 Nov. 1853) (No. 4), ibid., pp. 87–8. Cf. also private

Clerk thought there was a risk of riot and confusion in such an event,[1] and bent all his energies to avert it. Through the Field Commandant and Field Cornets he called a meeting in Bloemfontein on 15 February of all persons who were prepared, on behalf of the inhabitants, to discuss with him the terms on which the government would be transferred to them. His unyielding attitude had induced the moderate Afrikaners, who had been prepared to work with the 'loyalists' in the September assembly, to change their line and take part in the negotiations for independence. The September committee declared its sittings permanent and its seats inalienable, insinuated that the Boers were only being led into a trap, and disturbed the first two days of the new assembly. Clerk moved it nearer his quarters and threatened to put down any riot with a strong hand. Under the chairmanship of J. P. Hoffman, a shrewd, self-made man, Cape Town born, who spoke English well, the assembly then proceeded, in consultation with the Special Commissioner, to draw up the instrument known as the Convention of Bloemfontein, which was signed on 23 February 1854.[2] The government of the Orange River Territory was to be treated and considered henceforth as a free and independent government. The British Government disclaimed any alliance past or future with chiefs or tribes north of the Orange River, Adam Kok excepted, and Adam Kok's treaty was to be modified to remove restrictions on the alienation of Griqua lands. The Orange River Government was not to permit any vexatious proceedings towards British subjects and was to give them facilities for disposal and transfer of their properties should they leave within three years. The Government was not to permit slavery or the slave trade. There were provisions for apprehension of criminals, recovery of debts, inheritance of property, and purchase of ammunition supplies, and the Special Commissioner would recommend liberal treatment in regard to import duties. Friendly intercourse was to be promoted by the stationing of a British Agent within the Colony near to the frontier.[3]

---

letter of same date: Newcastle Papers, NeC9554. The whole procedure was based on Minutes of Merivale and F. Peel (27 Oct.) on Clerk to Newcastle (25 Aug. 1853), CO48/348.

[1] Clerk to Newcastle (4 Mar. 1854) (Private), Newcastle Papers, NeC9554.

[2] Ibid. See also Midgley, op. cit., pp. 550 ff. and (for the characterization of Hoffman) J. M. Orpen, *Reminiscences of Life in South Africa* (Durban, 1915), p. 341.

[3] The Convention is in P.P., 1857–8, xi [2352], 107–9. It is reprinted in K. N.

The pill of withdrawal was sweetened by the payment of compensation, especially to those settlers who had established themselves in the Sovereignty after, and in reliance on, the Imperial Government's confirmation of Sir Harry Smith's annexation. In November Newcastle had authorized Cathcart to draw upon the commissariat chest for £10,000 on that account.[1] This was not nearly enough. Cathcart allowed another £15,000 on his own authority, urging upon the Imperial authorities that this would prove 'economy, as well as the best policy, in the end'. Finally, after some correspondence and no doubt personal discussion, the Treasury informed the Colonial Office that £45,000 would be placed on the estimates for this purpose.[2] The parties most likely to be prejudiced by the withdrawal were in fact the chiefs. Moshesh, confident in his own strength, had less reason for apprehension than the others. After Owen had officially informed him of the intention to withdraw, Clerk saw Moshesh in October, and the interview passed without mention of the subject.[3] Clerk's advice did not deter Moshesh a few days later (27 October) from settling his old account with Sikonyela, who had attacked one of his dependents. Sikonyela fled to Bloemfontein and later to the Colony. Owen had told Moshesh that 'Sir George Clerk is most anxious that before he leaves the Sovereignty, the long disputed boundary line between yourself and the Boers should be settled so as to prevent future disputes';[4] but no such settlement was made. In January 1854 Clerk suggested to Newcastle that the matter be left where it was. Moshesh did not seem to want a treaty.

On the other hand the boers residing on that frontier were averse to any more exact demarcation of those extensive tracts of country from a sense of the advantages of trusting to availing themselves again of the fair, and even liberal spirit in which Moshesh was accustomed formerly to grant lands to them on the easiest terms possible . . . ; and from an apprehension that if the British authorities undertook to interfere further with their relations with Moshesh, it

Bell and W. P. Morrell, *Select Documents of British Colonial Policy, 1830–60*, pp. 533–6. In the main it followed the lines suggested in Newcastle's dispatch of 14 Nov.
   [1] Newcastle to Clerk (14 Nov. 1853) (Confidential), P.P., 1854, xliii [1758], 91.
   [2] Cathcart to Clerk (10 Jan. 1854), ibid. 19–20. Treasury to Colonial Office (17 June 1854), CO48/362.
   [3] Clerk to Newcastle (10 Nov. 1853), P.P., 1854, xliii [1758], 49.
   [4] Owen to Moshesh (23 Aug. 1853), *Basutoland Records*, ii. 59–60.

might be thought necessary also that British authorities should continue in the country to superintend them.

Clerk then proceeded to enlarge upon the futility of 'extending British dominion in South Africa . . . to prevent the extinction of the rights of the natives'.[1] The language lacks Clerk's usual outspokenness and cogency. Maybe he was putting up a smoke-screen to conceal his retreat from a problem which he found embarrassing. Clerk did, however, support Moshesh in his urgent desire for a British Agent residing with his tribe.

> He ought not to be left alone. He does not desire or deserve to be regarded with that degree of indifference or neglect. Such reserve on our part will naturally tend to direct his regards to alliances not yet subsisting between him and these Kaffir tribes, the most powerful of which now entertain a growing respect for him and a very different sentiment towards us.

But the new Secretary of State for the Colonies, Sir George Grey, disregarding the favourable opinion of his Under-Secretary, Frederick Peel, wanted time for consideration and for the opinion of his namesake the new Governor before approving the recommendation;[2] and no such appointment was in fact made.

The Griqua chief Adam Kok was by no means happy about the withdrawal. The article in the Bloemfontein Convention stated that his treaty would be modified to remove the restrictions on the sale of Griqua lands, 'the Chief Adam Kok having for himself concurred in and sanctioned the same'. Any such concurrence was prospective only. Adam Kok's real attitude was that '*if* my people and the Raad resolved to sell their farms and leave the country, I should not oppose, though my own views were strongly against any such measure'.[3] The British Resident at Bloemfontein, Green, took down to Philippolis new articles granting the Griquas freedom to sell, continuing the pension to the chief, and offering facilities, if he so desired, to remove with his people south of the Orange River;[4] but Kok refused to sign. His people, however,

---

[1] Clerk to Newcastle (14 Jan. 1854), P.P., 1854, xliii [1758], 72–3.

[2] *Basutoland Records*, ii. 116–17. Minutes of Peel (1 Nov.) and Sir G. Grey (3 Nov.) on Clerk to Newcastle (11 Aug. 1854), CO48/364.

[3] Adam Kok and Griqua Raad to Clerk (7 Mar. 1854), Cape of Good Hope, Votes and Proceedings of Parliament, 1861, Appendix I, A118–'61, pp. 1–3.

[4] 'Articles of Agreement' in Memo. to Kaptyn Adam Kok (17 Mar. 1854), ibid., pp. 3–4.

yielded to the pressure to sell and the Orange Free State Government, regarding his treaty as void, connived at the sales. In July Kok asked if he might reopen the question and Clerk, though his mission was completed, promised to submit the application to Her Majesty's Government.[1] It was too late. In any case, once the Imperial authorities had decided to cut loose from their responsibilities north of the Orange River, nothing could stop the steady erosion of Griqua lands. All the Imperial Government could do was to continue Adam Kok's allowance of £300 per annum from Imperial funds until arrangements could be made for its payment by the Orange Free State.[2] Sir George Clerk had called Adam Kok 'a young man of respectability and good disposition'. He did not deserve the shabby treatment he received.

In the eyes of the Imperial Government Sir George Clerk's mission had been a success. In thanking him for his services, the Duke of Newcastle expressed the hope that the Convention would 'lay the foundation of . . . secure and orderly civil administration . . . among a people who are now no longer under Her [Majesty's] dominion, but who must remain connected by ties of mutual interest and amity with their former fellow subjects'.[3] But one problem remained to vex the lawyers.

The difficulty [wrote Merivale] is as to those who owe *native* allegiance to the Crown, having been born out of the Sovereignty and within the Crown's other dominions: that is to say, almost all the white population. Can the Queen discharge *these* from their allegiance by proclaiming the independence of the Sovereignty? I think not. . . . The Crown having abandoned all jurisdiction over causes civil or criminal arising in the Orange River Territory itself, their position as British subjects would be no disadvantage to them—on the contrary an advantage, as enabling them to inherit etc. in British territory. But then the Act 6 & 7 Will. iv makes them all triable by the Courts of the Cape . . . for offences committed within their own countries.[4]

[1] Adam Kok to Clerk (12 July) and Clerk to Adam Kok (3 Aug. 1854), Cape of Good Hope, Votes and Proceedings of Parliament, 1861, Appendix I, A118–'61, pp. 8–9.
[2] Treasury to Colonial Office (12 Apr. 1856), CO48/378. See also Labouchere to Grey (16 Apr. 1856), Cape of Good Hope, Correspondence with Secretary of State for the Colonies, 1853–7, pp. 208–9; Midgley, op. cit., pp. 552–5, 562–7; J. S. Marais, *The Cape Coloured People 1652–1937* (London, 1939), pp. 56 ff.
[3] Newcastle to Clerk (12 June 1854), G.H. 1/49, Cape Archives.
[4] Minute of Merivale (26 Oct.) on Law Officers to Newcastle (28 Sept. 1853), CO48/350.

No doubt this Cape of Good Hope Punishment Act had become inoperative; but, for slightly different reasons, both he and the Law Officers of the Crown were inclined to think a new Act of Parliament advisable. The terms of Article 1 of the Convention, guaranteeing the inhabitants of the territory 'that their independence shall, without unnecessary delay, be confirmed and ratified by an instrument promulgated in such form and substance as Her Majesty may approve, finally freeing them from their allegiance to the British Crown' reinforced the argument. The delegates from the Orange River Sovereignty obtained from counsel, Roundell Palmer (the future Lord Chancellor Selborne) and Willes (later a famous common law judge), an opinion that the Crown could not by prerogative constitute any branch of its subjects an independent state. At the instance of the delegates Adderley in the House of Commons on 9 May moved an address praying Her Majesty 'to reconsider the Order in Council for the promulgation, on or before 1 August next, of a Proclamation abandoning and renouncing all Sovereignty over the Orange River Territory and its inhabitants'; he made the illegality of the proceedings one of his main grounds of attack. The others were that it overrode the wishes of the Cape colonists and the treaties with the chiefs: 'the more insignificant the people we volunteered to treat with, the more particular ought we to be in adhering to our treaties.' He forecast that the cost of abandonment would be far greater than the cost of retention.[1] But Adderley gained no support in Parliament. Sir John Pakington, spokesman for his party, declined to vote for the address. Only a handful of speculators, he believed, really wished to remain under British dominion. Sir Frederick Thesiger, Attorney-General in the previous administration, would have preferred an Act of Parliament to remove doubts, but did not think it essential. Under-Secretary Peel took the ground that the Orange River Territory was a country acquired by conquest and could therefore be ceded by the Crown: the inhabitants were not divested of their allegiance, but, if they wished, the Government would consider an Act for the purpose. On the general policy 'the Government considered it to be essentially an Imperial question—a question in which the Home Government was infinitely more interested than the local

[1] *Hansard*, 3rd Ser. cxxxiii. 52–63. I have not seen Roundell Palmer's and Willes's opinion, quoted by Adderley in his speech.

Government'. He wished they could quit Kaffraria also, but 'if we left it the Kafirs would consider themselves victorious'. 'Was any object of interest, honour or dignity involved in the retention of the Orange River Territory', he asked, 'worth this country's going to the enormous expense of maintaining peace between the aborigines and the Europeans?' He comforted himself with the thought that it would now be 'their interest to live at peace with one another'.[1] Adderley had little choice but to withdraw his motion, though he forecast that within a few years Great Britain would resume her sovereignty.

Peel's hopes that self-interest would ensure peace were not fulfilled, and within a few years the question of resumption of the sovereignty came under discussion, though not with the result Adderley expected and desired. Both Cathcart's successors, Grey and Wodehouse, thought the policy which led to the Bloemfontein Convention 'a most mistaken one'.[2] Though the majority of the Free Staters were no doubt willing enough to be left alone, their attitude before and after suggests that they could readily enough have been persuaded to accept a simple form of self-government under the Crown with a token military force which would have made hostilities with the Basuto less likely. Exeter Hall influences counted for less than in the past, but the Transvaal's system of child apprenticeship was already being attacked by the London Missionary Society, British and Foreign Anti-Slavery Society, and other such bodies as a breach of the Sand River Convention.[3] Great Britain could not abdicate her responsibilities so easily as the proponents of the policy of withdrawal imagined. It was hardly consistent with her position and policies in the Cape and in Natal. Cathcart's frontier settlement had been based on an intelligible principle, though no new one in South African history. Cape Colony was to be kept for the Europeans, whether of Dutch or English extraction, and for the Hottentots,

[1] Hansard, 3rd Ser. cxxxiii. 63–76. This debate, filling 36 columns of Hansard, was the longest on South African affairs in our period. Sir W. Molesworth privately printed *Materials for a Speech in Defence of the Policy of abandoning the Orange River Territory*, which he never delivered.
[2] Wodehouse to Buckingham (1 June 1868) (No. 40), P.P., 1868–9, xliii [4140], 61–3. On Grey's attitude see below, pp. 105 ff.
[3] Memorial of British and Foreign Anti-Slavery Society, Aborigines Protection Society, London Missionary Society, Wesleyan Missionary Society, and Peace Society (11 July) in Newcastle to Clerk (22 July 1853) (No. 3), P.P., 1854, xliii [1758], 81–2.

Malays, and former slaves who were gradually merging in the Cape Coloured people, with its mixture of European blood. British Kaffraria would continue as a kind of military frontier, bringing a section of the Xhosa tribes under British rule and other civilizing influences and thus lessening the risk of war with these tribes both within and beyond the frontier. The Fingoes were already an exception to this principle, and changes of policy and circumstance were soon to break it down; but it was at least an attempt to face the facts of the South African situation. The withdrawal from the Orange River Sovereignty, imposed by Imperial authority (with Sir George Clerk as a willing instrument) upon a reluctant South Africa, was an attempt to make South African facts conform to Imperial requirements. The Great Trek had already shown the impossibility of such policies. The Sand River and Bloemfontein Conventions were an attempt on Great Britain's part to wash her hands of the consequences of the Trek. But she had dipped her hands too deeply in South African affairs to be able to withdraw and wash them. She has not withdrawn them even now.

# III

## SIR GEORGE GREY AND THE
## EASTERN FRONTIER
### 1854-1858

W HEN Sir George Cathcart gave up the government of the Cape, the mood of revulsion against South African responsibilities was still strong in Great Britain. But the Duke of Newcastle saw work yet to be done there and, breaking the tradition of appointing a military man, he submitted to the Queen the name of Sir George Grey, who had just come home on leave after eight years in the government of New Zealand, as the man best qualified to undertake it. As Frederick Peel told the House of Commons, answering Adderley's criticism of the appointment: 'We had succeeded in conquering the Kafirs, but it was too expensive a game to keep them in forcible subjection. We must attach them to our rule.'[1] No one in South Africa had as yet seriously attempted to win the confidence of the chiefs except the Christian missionaries, who had now been working for two generations with a different purpose. With many of them enthusiasm had now degenerated into mere routine;[2] the concentration of the Hottentots of the Western Cape at the mission stations brought its own problems;[3] and the very success of their propaganda with the House of Commons Committee on Aborigines had made many of them 'bitter politicians'[4] and deepened the antagonism between them and the English settlers and Afrikaner burghers. Moreover the

[1] House of Commons, 26 June 1854: *Hansard*, 3rd Ser. cxxxiv. 713. Newcastle on 12 June, just before he gave up the Colonial Office, had communicated to Grey the Queen's approval of his appointment: Grey Collection, Auckland.
[2] See, e.g., J. Green, *The Kat River Settlement in 1851* (Grahamstown, 1853). But Green excepted the Revd. W. R. Thomson from his criticisms.
[3] See debate on motion for subdivision and grant of land at these institutions, *Advertiser and Mail's Parliamentary Debates*, 3 Aug. 1854.
[4] Bishop Gray to Revd. C. Gray in the latter's *Life of Robert Gray Bishop of Capetown* (London, 1876), i. 269. See also Clerk to Newcastle (10 Nov. 1853): P.P., 1854, xliii [1758], 51-2.

recent war, in which the Hottentots of the Kat River settlement, the pride of the London Missionary Society, had joined,
had been even more disheartening than its predecessors. If
the civilizing work of the missions among the Native peoples
of South Africa was to make progress, some new impetus was
needed.

Sir George Grey, immediately on his arrival at the Cape in
December 1854, set himself to win the confidence of colonists,
missionaries, and Xhosa chiefs alike. The American missionary
Daniel Lindley, who gives an interesting description of him—
'a spare, wiry man, with rather sharp features, light brown hair,
light grey eyes . . . about five feet ten inches high, a little stoop-
shouldered, and about forty-four years of age'—was as much taken
with him as Robert Gray, Anglican Bishop of Cape Town.[1] Grey
proved those men wrong who said after his New Zealand governorship that he could never work with a representative assembly.
There were moves for responsible government in the Cape Parliament in 1855 and 1856 but they were defeated by a combination
of Western conservatives with Easterners anxious about the
defence of the frontier under a responsible system.[2] But undoubtedly Sir George Grey's political ability, charm, and force
of personality—aided by the parliamentary leadership of the
liberal-minded Attorney-General, William Porter—contributed
to this result. As Molteno, the leader in the struggle for responsible government, said in 1871, 'When Sir George Grey was
Governor, fears were felt by many persons that his Government
was too popular. It had power to do almost what it wished.'[3]
Grey's efforts to win the confidence of the Xhosas were less
successful, but his achievements in that field of policy were noteworthy and of lasting importance. But a Governor who welcomed responsibility was bound to get into trouble with an
Imperial Government in a mood to shirk it.

In spite of Cathcart's optimistic dispatches, Grey had to face a
flurry of excitement on the frontier before the end of the year. The
overcrowding among the 20,000 Fingoes on their locations in the

[1] Lindley to Rufus Anderson (16 Nov. 1855): quoted by E. W. Smith, *Life
and Times of Daniel Lindley* (London, 1949), pp. 305–7. C. Gray, *Life of Robert
Gray*, i. 386.
[2] There was a Committee on Responsible Parliamentary Government in 1855
and a motion by Sir A. Stockenstrom in the Legislative Council, 3 Apr. 1856.
[3] House of Assembly, 1 June 1871: *Grahamstown Journal*, 9 June 1871.

MAP I. EASTERN FRONTIERS AND NATAL

Colony was giving rise to some anxiety;[1] and in October or
November the Chief Commissioner of British Kaffraria was
informed that Sandile was making overtures to the Fingo chief
Jokweni for the hand of one of his daughters in marriage, whilst
the Ndhlambi chief Umhala and Oba, a lesser chief, were also
said to be seeking marriage with daughters of influential Fingoes. Any *rapprochement* between the Fingoes inside the Colony
and the Xhosas in Kaffraria was worrying, and when the Civil
Commissioner of Queenstown on 13 December reported that
a party of Gaikas had ordered two farmers off their farm and the

[1] T. H. Bowker and J. C. Molteno in House of Assembly, 30 Aug. 1854: *South
African Commercial Advertiser*, 22 Feb. 1855. Report of Revd. H. Calderwood
(22 Jan.) in Governor Grey to Sir G. Grey, Bart. (29 Jan. 1855) (No. 19), P.P.,
1854–5, xxxviii [1969], 42–51.

Gaika chief Anta was reported to have entered the Amatolas, fear of a new outbreak spread panic on the frontier.[1] This last report was not true and the panic subsided; but it gave the Governor a pretext for asking for an assurance that the Imperial Government would not leave the Colony undefended until it had provided for its own safety and drawing attention to the danger of dispersing the troops in small detachments with large bodies of Fingoes—who, he said, 'feel and much overrate their strength'—interspersed among them. The present state of affairs was only an armed truce, for the confined location of the Gaikas so near to their lost lands in the Amatolas 'must be to them a cause of constant uneasiness and annoyance'. Yet no general plan was in operation to produce a better state of things, and though the Colonial Parliament by increased provision for defence could 'render us, I hope, sufficiently strong, with the present military force, to overawe and control the Kafir and other wavering tribes, without making any further demands upon Great Britain for troops', there would be practically no money left for plans of improvement. Grey then proceeded with fine imaginative sweep to outline the plan he had in mind and ask Imperial assistance for it—

to attempt to gain an influence over all the tribes included between the present north-eastern boundary of this colony and Natal, by employing them upon public works, which will tend to open up their country; by establishing institutions for the education of their children, and the relief of their sick, by introducing among them institutions of a civil character suited to their present condition; and by these and other like means to attempt gradually to win them to civilization and Christianity, and thus to change by degree our at present unconquered and apparently irreclaimable foes into friends who may have common interests with ourselves.

He estimated the cost of the plan at £45,000 per annum, 'of which £40,000 would require to be furnished by Great Britain'. But the charge should diminish in about three years and within eight or ten no further extraneous assistance should be required and Great Britain might hope to be relieved from 'all further care and expense connected with this colony'.[2]

---

[1] Answers to Queries proposed to the Chief Commissioner in 1855 in J. Maclean (ed.), *A Compendium of Kafir Laws and Customs* (Mount Coke, 1858), pp. 141–84.

[2] Governor Grey to Sir G. Grey, Bart. (22 Dec. 1854, No. 7, and for the phrase

Grey had not yet been three weeks in the Colony. He had not yet visited the frontier. The plan was necessarily based on the policies he had pursued in New Zealand. Nevertheless, behind the rhetoric, there is an energy of mind, a determination to look at South Africa as a whole, which carried conviction and impressed even the timid spirits of Downing Street. And after a visit to the Eastern Province and Kaffraria in the first months of the New Year, Grey carried the plan a stage further, suggesting that the defence of British Kaffraria be strengthened by the immediate dispatch of 1,000 enrolled military pensioners, ultimately to be increased to 5,000, 'upon the same regulations as they were sent to New Zealand, under the admirable system devised by Earl Grey'.[1] These men and their families should be settled on small holdings near the military posts of King William's Town and Alice. 'Probably', he declared, 'so great an increase of our force will altogether prevent hostilities from ever again breaking out in Kaffraria'; but if they did break out, the pensioners would garrison the posts and set the army free for active operations. He would undertake, when 2,000 pensioners and their families had arrived, immediately to dispense with 1,000 regular troops.[2]

Grey's whole policy was based on very different principles from Cathcart's. Cathcart's was a policy of 'military control, not colonization'—territorial segregation, apartheid if you will, but without its twentieth-century overtones. The tribes, with the exception of the Gaikas, would retain their lands. Grey's policy might be described as integration.

In a few years our frontier defence will consist of a strong European population of young men accustomed from childhood to the country, mixed up with a civilized coloured race won from heathenism and barbarism by our exertions, whom their fellow-countrymen beyond their border will be rather disposed to emulate and imitate than attack, but who, if themselves and their properties were attacked, would be far better able to defend their own country than any force we could furnish would do it for them.[3]

---

about the Fingoes, 29 Jan. 1855, No. 19): P.P., 1854–5, xxxviii [1969], 37–8, 41·
The request for an assurance was in Governor Grey to Sir G. Grey, Bart. (21 Dec·
1854) (Private), CO48/361.
    [1] See on these G. G. Gillespie, 'The Pensioner Settlements' (Univ. of Otago, M.A. thesis, 1954). His verdict is on the whole favourable.
    [2] Governor Grey to Sir G. Grey, Bart. (7 Mar. 1855, No. 35, and 17 Mar. 1855, Separate), P.P., 1854–5, xxxviii [1969], 54–5.
    [3] Ibid.

There is genuine idealism in this; but even military settlement entailed some loss of tribal lands. British Kaffraria, however, was a fertile land, capable in Grey's opinion of supporting a dense population, and in an eloquent exposition of his policy before the Cape Parliament he argued that it was more realistic than 'the idea of maintaining a vacant tract of territory, intervening between ourselves and a barbarous race beyond it, who are to be left in their existing state'.[1] His speech was well received by the Cape Parliament and press.[2] His namesake the Secretary of State acknowledged his December dispatch in approving, though general, terms;[3] and Lord John Russell, to whom it fell during his short tenure of office to give the considered judgement of the Imperial Government upon the proposals, gave Grey credit for his breadth of vision and responded with an equally broad statement of the objectives of Imperial policy.

Let me, in the first place, declare explicitly that it is for no object of dominion or extention of territory that Great Britain wishes to maintain possession of British Kaffraria. So far as the interests of this empire are concerned, British Kaffraria might be abandoned and the eastern districts of the Cape colony left unprotected, without injury to the power of the United Kingdom, and with a considerable saving to its finances. But such considerations have not been allowed to prevail. The performance of an honourable duty to British colonists, the maintenance of a position acquired at great cost both of men and money, and lastly, views of comprehensive and vigilant humanity induce Her Majesty's Government to take a very different course.

But whilst approving of Grey's general policy Russell pointed out that there were serious obstacles in its way.

At the root of these obstacles lies the difficulty of supplying British Kaffraria with a sufficient European population to vanquish in arms and conquer by civilization the native tribes. . . . I fear that in British Kaffraria you will find it difficult either to stock the country with emigrants, or to procure from our limited body of pensioners a

---

[1] Governor Grey to Sir G. Grey, Bart. (17 Mar. 1855) (No. 39), Enclosure 1, Address to Legislative Council and House of Assembly (10 Mar.), ibid., p. 57.
[2] *South African Commercial Advertiser*, 17 Mar. 1855; *Grahamstown Journal*, 24 Mar. 1855.
[3] But he thought an absolute pledge about withdrawal of troops 'more than could properly be given': Sir G. Grey, Bart. to Governor Grey (12 Mar. 1855, No. 12, and 10 Mar. 1855, Private), CO48/361.

sufficient number of men fulfilling your conditions, and willing to embrace the prospects you hold out to them. Still, what is difficult is not impossible, and I will do all in my power to forward your design.

£40,000 would be granted and pensioners sent if they could be had; but Russell entered a caveat.

I must frankly tell you ... that perseverance in these measures must depend on the willingness of the Colonial Legislature to assist and promote your views. We cannot undertake to help the Cape colony unless the Cape colony is ready to take its proper share in the task.

This warning was reinforced in a private letter:

Her Majesty's Government will expect that by keeping up a force of Militia in British Caffraria, or by contributions of money to maintain garrisons in that territory the Cape Colony will contribute to its own defence. For Great Britain will not defray the expense of another war in British Caffraria.[1]

In the final paragraphs of the dispatch Russell showed that he realized the importance of the issues at stake.

If we succeed, we secure the colony of the Cape from invasion, we civilize savage tribes, we open a vast territory to the influence of Christianity, we give an example of an African nation adopting the peaceful habits and social improvements of an European community. If we fail, the parliament of the United Kingdom will give up its work in despair; border wars will be perpetuated, and the Cape colony, even with the assistance of Her Majesty's troops, will find it difficult to bear the cost and repel the danger of repeated incursions of savage tribes.[2]

Sir William Molesworth did not share his colleague's enthusiasm. 'I do not believe in Sir G. Grey's plans,' he wrote,' but there can be little harm in letting him try them.'[3] This latter line was the one he took when it fell to him, as Russell's successor, to defend the Kaffrarian vote against critics in the House of Commons: he pointed out that it was only 1 per cent of the expenditure of a

---

[1] Draft to Sir G. Grey in the Russell Papers, P.R.O. 30/22: 12. The letter does not appear to be in the Grey Coll. but even if not sent it illustrates Russell's attitude.

[2] Russell to Grey (3 June 1855) (No. 23): P.P., 1854–5, xxxvii [1969], 72–3. There is a draft in Russell's own hand in CO48/365. An extract from the dispatch is printed in Bell and Morrell, op. cit., pp. 536–8.

[3] Minute of Molesworth (n.d.), CO48/365.

single year of war in South Africa.[1] The vote was agreed to without a division.

Meanwhile Sir George Grey characteristically (but not without notice to the Imperial Government) had gone ahead with his plans in anticipation of Imperial approval, securing an advance of £20,000 from the commissariat chest for the purpose. There was a special reason for haste in the ravages of an epidemic of lung sickness among the Xhosas' cattle.[2] Some hundreds of Gaikas were employed, at 6d. a day and rations, on public buildings at Dohne, on roads and irrigation furrows: they all, Brownlee reported, 'seek employment for a specific purpose, such as obtaining blankets, cattle, horses and goats, some having in view the accumulation of property for its own sake, others for the purpose of obtaining wives'.[3] An army surgeon by his cures began to interest the Gaikas in European medicine and early in 1856 an Irishman, Dr. J. P. Fitzgerald, who had been one of Grey's collaborators in New Zealand, was appointed Superintendent of what came to be called the Grey Hospital in King William's Town, a post which he held with great skill, devotion, and influence over his patients for thirty-five years.[4] The missions welcomed the assistance given to their schools. The Lovedale Institution, founded by the Glasgow Missionary Society mainly to train schoolmasters and evangelists, opened an industrial department with four master tradesmen, a carpenter, a mason, a wagonmaker, and a blacksmith, with regularly indentured apprentices.[5] The Wesleyan Methodist station at Healdtown (a Fingo location) also had an industrial school. The first Anglican Bishop of Grahamstown, John Armstrong, received a grant of £4,000 towards the cost of school buildings at Kreli's, Sandile's, and Umhala's kraals, at the Fingo location at Keiskammahoek, and on the outskirts of Grahamstown itself.[6]

[1] House of Commons, 31 July 1855: *Hansard*, 3rd Ser. cxxxix. 1579-82.
[2] Grey to Russell (19 July 1855) (No. 103), P.P., 1856, xlii [2096], 8-9.
[3] Memo. of Brownlee (11 Dec. 1855), ibid., p. 37. The number employed was about 500.
[4] Grey to Labouchere (18 Aug. 1856) (No. 80), P.P., 1857, Sess. 1, x [2002], p. 51. On Fitzgerald, see *Grahamstown Journal*, 14 Feb. 1857 (British Kaffrarian correspondent) and *Dictionary of New Zealand Biography*.
[5] R. H. W. Shepherd, *Lovedale, South Africa: The Story of a Century, 1841-1941* (Lovedale, 1941), pp. 131-4. Printing and bookbinding were added in 1861.
[6] Armstrong to the Revd. E. Hawkins (10 Feb. 1855): T. T. Carter, *A Memoir of John Armstrong* (2nd ed., London, 1858), pp. 314-15. In private letters in the

In the course of 1855 Grey also offered the Kaffrarian chiefs monthly stipends to be paid by Government, to replace the revenues they received from 'smelling out' offenders under customary law.

> The alleged offence of witchcraft (a public crime) [he explained] subjects a person found guilty of it to torture and death and the total confiscation of his property. No sooner therefore does a person grow rich, than he is almost certain to be accused of this offence.... It is impossible that a people subjected to such a system can ever advance in civilization.

All fees and fines for public offences were henceforth to become part of the revenues of the Crown. The chiefs and their councillors (who were also to be paid) were still to sit and hear cases; but they were to be assisted in their deliberations and sentences by European magistrates—mostly serving officers—who would also be 'constantly moving through their districts, acquiring a knowledge of the country and its inhabitants . . . exerting themselves to the utmost to encourage industry, agriculture and to promote civilization'.[1] Grey had overridden the strong objections of Maclean, who thought he was going too fast. 'The Kaffir', he wrote, '. . . clings tenaciously to his old customs and habits'; as for the chiefs, 'this present plan, striking, as according to their ideas it does, at the very essence of chieftainship, will appear to them, or may readily be made to appear to them, as adopted solely for the purpose of destroying it and their independence together.'[2] Brownlee also thought the presence of European magistrates as assessors and advisers would be disliked and objected to, but he was less dogmatic in his opposition.[3] The Colonial Office, however, was still being swept along by Grey's enthusiasm. Even Molesworth, now dead, had been inclined to give him his chance, though 'altogether incredulous as to the prospects of

Grey Coll., Auckland, Armstrong complains of the jealousy of the Wesleyans. He died in 1856, but his projects were carried on.

   [1] Grey to Molesworth (18 Dec. 1855) (No. 46, H.S.) with Enclosure, Grey to Maclean (26 July), P.P., 1856, xlii [2096], 14–17.

   [2] Maclean to Liddle (4 Aug. 1855), ibid., pp. 18–19.

   [3] Brownlee to Maclean (6, 8, and 23 Aug. 1855), ibid., pp. 20–4. Brownlee also said that the stipends Grey proposed to pay—£75 per annum to Sandile and Umhala with less for lesser chiefs—were 'far below the revenue of the chiefs'. They were later increased.

success'.[1] His successor, Labouchere, though he thought Grey might have communicated with the Office beforehand, gave the scheme cautious approval.[2]

The new system was soon to be tested. The cattle-sickness was weakening the Xhosa tribes; and they were also unsettled by garbled reports of the Crimean War. Captain Reeve, the magistrate with the Christian chief Kama, was much questioned by his people about the war. A Fingo gave, perhaps to Currie of the frontier police, a curious report of the rumours that were circulating: 'They say . . . that it is a lie which has been told about the Russians being a white nation. Their opinion is that they are all blacks, and were formerly Kaffir warriors who have died or have been killed in the various wars against the colony.'[3] Two or three miles east of the Kei mouth, the little river Gxara makes its way to the sea through a curving tree-lined lagoon. Hereabouts, in the early months of 1856, a young Galeka girl, Nonqause, niece and adopted daughter of Umhlakaza, councillor of a relative of Kreli, began to see visions. We may allow her to tell her own tale:

It commenced after my having reported to Umhlakaza that I had seen about ten strange Kaffirs in the gardens. . . Umhlakaza told me not to be afraid of them. . . . He told me to . . . ask them what they were doing there. I did so. They replied 'We are people who have come to order you to kill your cattle—to consume your corn—and not to cultivate any more'. Umhlakaza asked them through me, 'What are we to eat when we kill our cattle. . . ?' They answered, 'We will find you something to eat.'

They reappeared another day with a similar message. Umhlakaza began to kill his cattle and spread the news. These men then said:

You must all be quick in killing your cattle, as in seven days the people will rise.' I asked them what people. They replied 'The same people as ourselves and they will rise at the different kraals; . . . they

---

[1] Minute of Ball (Parliamentary Under-Secretary to Molesworth and then to Labouchere) (15 Mar. 1856) on Grey to Molesworth (18 Dec. 1855), CO48/368. This is borne out by other minutes of Molesworth, e.g. of 6 Aug. 1855 in CO 48/366.

[2] Labouchere to Grey (20 Mar. 1856) (No. 45), P.P., 1856, xlii [2096], 46.

[3] Deposition (10 Apr.) in Grey to Labouchere (24 Apr. 1856) (No. 32), P.P., 1857, Sess. 1 [2202], 22. Sir George Cathcart, it may be relevant to note, had been killed by the Russians at Inkerman on 5 Nov. 1854.

would have cattle, corn, guns and assegais; and . . . they would drive the English out of the country and make them run into the sea'.[1]

Kreli and his councillors, Sandile, Macomo, and other chiefs, according to Nonqause, frequently visited Umhlakaza. It is clear that Kreli countenanced these prophecies and hoped to use them, but not so clear that he inspired them as some believed. Nonqause gave her evidence freely in 1858 (in Xhosa, of course) and seemed intelligent: she may be believed when she said Umhlakaza, who had since died, often blamed Kreli as the sole cause of the cattle-killing; but her account of her visions appears spontaneous. The Southern Nguni tribes, of whom the Galekas are one, have, we are told, 'an intense domestic cult of patrilineal ancestral spirits':[2] to a highly strung girl, brooding over their hopes and fears (for the Galekas had not yet lost their lands) such visions might naturally come. There had been similar prophecies in the past. Nxele, a Ndhlambi, had made one in 1818 after hearing a sermon on the resurrection from the dead at Dr. Vanderkemp's Hottentot mission.[3] Umlanjeni's prophecies had unsettled the Gaikas before the war of 1850. Modern anthropologists have invented the name 'cargo cult'—more appropriate in the Pacific Islands than in South Africa—for the phenomenon. But Sir George Grey had no such store of knowledge to draw upon: the *Pai-marire* cult among the Maoris lay in the future.[4] He had to act according to his lights.

At first Grey discounted the alarmist reports of Lieutenant-General Jackson, inspired by Commandant Currie, that Moshesh, Sandile, and other chiefs were entering into a combination to attack the Colony, though he believed Moshesh, threatened with attack by the Orange Free State, might encourage such an attack as a diversion.[5]

---

[1] Examination of Nonqause before the Chief Commissioner (9 Apr. 1858), *British Kaffraria Government Gazette*, reprinted in *Grahamstown Journal*, 1 May 1858. See also Cape Parliament V. & P., 1858, G. 38. This corresponds in general with Brownlee to Maclean (28 June 1856), quoted by J. A. Chalmers, *Tiyo Soga* (Edinburgh, 1878), pp. 107–8. Brownlee mentions the Gxara mouth as the site. I visited the site in 1951 and paid for it with an attack of tick fever.

[2] B. W. Brokensha, 'The Political Institutions of some Southern Nguni Tribes' (Univ. of Oxford B.Litt. thesis, 1950), p. 71.

[3] J. H. Soga, *The South-Eastern Bantu* (Johannesburg, 1930), pp. 161–3. Nxele was also known as Makana and (by Europeans) Lynx.     [4] See below, pp. 331–2.

[5] Grey to Labouchere (24 Apr. 1856) (No. 32), P.P., 1857, Sess. 1 [2202]. This dispatch enclosed the Fingo report about the Russians, cited earlier. On the threatened Basuto war see below, pp. 103–5.

At the Lieutenant-General's instance he sent for a regiment from Mauritius, and he felt that further reinforcements might be required. But by the middle of August he was constrained to admit that the prophecies, which he now for the first time reported, had led Kreli's Galekas to slaughter their cattle or other stock or dispose of them at nominal prices; that the road parties were breaking up; that the delusion, despite efforts of the chiefs to check it, had spread widely in British Kaffraria. The prophet was saying that if the destruction was accomplished by the end of the month, there would be a day of darkness on which the ancestral spirits would assume human form and appear with a new race of cattle immune from sickness and a numerous army of Russians. Grey believed that Kreli and Moshesh were acting in concert, and that unless the delusion was checked, the tribes would 'by the time fixed be left in such a state of poverty and starvation that they will be ready for any desperate enterprize'.[1] Later that month he went up to the frontier, visited the leading chiefs and failed to detect any hostile intentions; and reports came in that 'the cattle killing and waste of corn has in great measure ceased'.[2] In September the arrival of reinforcements from England encouraged Grey's hopes that war might be averted. Having received information that Kreli had sent messages to Sandile and Umhala urging them to kill their cattle, he warned Kreli that if starvation, thieving, and disturbances followed, 'I shall consider you as the guilty party, and will punish you as such.'[3] The crisis in fact had not been averted but merely postponed, and it is hard to resist the conclusion that Kreli, whether or not self-deluded, was manœuvring to postpone it until more and more of the tribes were driven to desperation.[4] In his answer to the Governor he denied sending messages to Sandile and Umhala and added that if a force went into his country to kill him, he would not fight.[5] But if this is to be taken seriously it can only mean that he was too deeply involved in the cattle-killing to stop. Some of the Ciskeian

---

[1] Grey to Labouchere (16 Aug. 1856) (No. 76), P.P., 1857-8, xl [2352], 4-6.
[2] Maclean to Grey (21 Aug. 1856), ibid., p. 19.
[3] Grey to Kreli (27 Sept.) in Grey to Labouchere (27 Sept. 1856) (No. 94), ibid., p. 30.
[4] J. C. Warner reported on 23 Sept. that cattle-killing was spreading among the Tambookies (Abatembu): Enclosure in Grey to Labouchere (29 Sept. 1856) (No. 95), ibid., p. 31.
[5] Grey to Labouchere (20 Oct. 1856) (No. 105), ibid., p. 47.

chiefs were now cultivating their gardens, but Sandile, Macomo, Umhala, and Pato had thrown in their lot with Kreli.[1]

The crisis came to a head in February 1857 and Grey went up to the frontier again to cope with it. On or about 8 February Kreli visited the prophet, four or five thousand of his followers remaining about half a mile off. He returned with a changed countenance 'that betokened disappointment and chagrin' but with orders from the prophet

that they were to kill everything with the exception of a cow and a goat, and that eight days were to be given them to do this . . . ; that the cattle and people would rise, perhaps on the eighth day but certainly on the ninth; that the sign would be that the sun would not rise until half-past eight, and then it would turn and go back, when darkness would follow; or otherwise a very heavy storm with thunder and lightning and darkness would warn them that the prophecies were about to be fulfilled.[2]

Hitherto Kreli and his people had held back. Now they killed most of their cattle and hides became a drug on the market at the trading stations. At last, on 18 February, the great day dawned for which the deluded people had waited.

They rethatched their huts in the most careful manner [said Grey in his despatch], that they might resist the expected hurricane; and finally, on the Wednesday, shut themselves up in them, awaiting the wonderful events which were to take place. On the Thursday they came out of their huts, downcast, destitute and in many instances desperate.

There was deep division in the land between the believers (*Amatamba*), some of whom continued to hope for fulfilment of

---

[1] Grey to Labouchere (28 Oct. 1856) (No. 106), P.P., 1857–8, xl [2352], 50. Brownlee later (13 Jan. 1957) admitted to Maclean that his advice to Sandile to cultivate was 'publicly adopted but privately subverted'; ibid., p. 64. There was another girl 'prophetess' at Umhala's kraal, instigated by him.

[2] King William's Town correspondent in *Grahamstown Journal*, 24 Feb. 1857 —a circumstantial, but probably not first-hand, account. Mr. E. A. Dowsley in 'An Investigation into the Circumstances relating to the Cattle-killing Delusion in Kaffraria, 1856–57' Univ. of South Africa, M.A. thesis, 1932), a detailed study I have read with profit, notes (p. 72) that 'the special magistrates, who one and all wrote most detailed accounts of all that happened . . . did not any of them describe the dramatic happenings of "the day"'.

the prophecy, and the *Amagogotya* or unbelievers. 'The destitute believers', Grey reported, 'were forming themselves into bands of robbers, and preparing to pillage their unbelieving country-men and the Europeans.' After an officer and a soldier had been murdered, he issued a warning proclamation that robbery under arms would be punished with death. Crowds of women and children were digging up roots for food. Before Government relief could reach the more distant parts, large numbers were bound to die of dysentery, fever, and other effects of famine. Most of the chiefs had no means of subsistence left but their salaries as Native magistrates, which made them entirely dependent on the Government, and their influence with the people they had led to disaster was naturally shaken. This was one great effect of the cattle-killing. Another effect was that many sought employ-ment on public works and even more made their way into the Colony with their families to find work as farm servants. 'These offers', Grey wrote, 'are being accepted, and we are marching them into the colony to places where they can find employment, feeding the men and their families by the way.'[1] The population of British Kaffraria was estimated to have declined from 104,721 on 1 January 1857 to 37,229 on 31 July. Between twenty and thirty thousand were thought to have entered the Colony, twenty or twenty-five thousand to have died.[2]

In opening the parliamentary session on 7 April, Grey charac-teristically expressed a hope that he could turn the situation to advantage:

A restless nation, who for years have harassed the frontier, may now to a great extent be changed into useful labourers. . . . I hope, indeed, that I may be able to devise means which will not only enable the Government to fill up the vacant portions of British Kaffraria with a European population sufficiently large to maintain itself, and to exercise a powerful influence for good upon the Kaffir race, but which will also enable it to establish a European settlement in Kaffraria Proper sufficiently strong to control and keep in check those tribes beyond the Kei who have manifested a hostile spirit, and to encourage

---

[1] Grey to Labouchere (6, 12, and 25 Mar. 1857, Nos. 25, 31, and 39), P.P., 1857–8, xl [2352], 67–70, 84–5.
[2] The detailed figures are in P.P., 1857–8, xl (H.C. 389), 31. The others are estimates from various sources.

and support our friends and allies in that quarter, whilst their presence
... will give a great impulse and assistance to the colony of Natal.[1]
This was not idle talk: Grey was already planning to bring more
immigrants into British Kaffraria and to punish Kreli. A recurrence of cattle-killing in May and June intensified the famine and
placed the chiefs more than ever at Grey's mercy. A Tembu
chief, Fadana, who collected a band of desperate men and made
raids into the Colony, was captured by Currie and his border
police on a punitive expedition in September and he and an alleged confederate, Quesha, were tried and imprisoned.[2] Macomo,
whose people killed an unbelieving minor chief, Vusani, was
arrested and sentenced to a long term of imprisonment.[3] Many
members of Kreli's family fled across the Bashee into Bomvanaland.

Grey's border system had proved its value in the cattle-killing
crisis. Brownlee in particular had ridden round the Gaika district
trying to break the spell, denying the truth of the prophecies until
he acquired the nick-name *Napakada* ('Never') and attempting to
organize the leading men among the unbelievers. When he gave
up the Gaika Commissionership in 1867 the chief Fynn said to
him 'You became a wall of partition—you divided us as a tribe
and you saved part of us.'[4] The other magistrates, notably Major
Gawler with Umhala, also served as a rallying-point with unbelievers, and no doubt Grey's pensions fortified chiefs like Siwani,
Toise, Anta, Oba, and Jan Tzatzoe, who exercised their influence
against the killing and kept most of their people loyal.[5] Grey's
own patience, firmness, and humanity, his refusal to take any provocative measures, showed him at his best. Precipitate action in the
early stages, before the tribes were weakened by hunger and
disease, might well have led to war.

Grey was no doubt encouraged by the arrival of reinforcements from England—which evoked some ill-timed criticism,

[1] Speech at Opening of Fourth Session of Parliament in Grey to Labouchere
(8 Apr. 1857) (No. 45), P.P., 1857–8, xl [2352], 90–1.
[2] Grey to Labouchere (3 Oct. 1857) (No. 148), CO48/384.
[3] C. Brownlee, *Reminiscences of Kaffir Life and History* (Lovedale, 1896), p. 165.
[4] Ibid., p. 151 and *passim*. On Brownlee's activities see also Chalmers, op. cit.,
p. 106.
[5] The Christian chief Kama also remained loyal but was supported only by a
minority of his tribe. Xhosa tribes had fissiparous tendencies and in this crisis
unbelieving minorities often joined loyal chiefs. On this see J. Rutherford, *Sir
George Grey* (London, 1961), pp. 357–8.

before the crisis was over, by Adderley in the House of Commons[1] —and especially by the realization of his plan of strengthening the frontier by military settlement in British Kaffraria. His pensioner scheme, though favoured by Lord John Russell, was severely criticized in detail by Benjamin Hawes, Under-Secretary at the War Office, whose years as Parliamentary Under-Secretary for the Colonies under Lord Grey added weight to his criticisms;[2] and in any case Colonel Tulloch, Military Superintendent of Out Pensioners, found the men unresponsive.[3] Sir William Molesworth, Russell's successor, was sceptical of this as of all Sir George Grey's schemes and, in telling him of the failure to enrol the pensioners, expressed his doubt whether any alternative plan was likely to attract able-bodied, energetic emigrants from England to the South African frontier.[4] Grey, who was already preparing for the pensioners, thought Molesworth misinformed about the prospects and much too pessimistic, and in 1856 his hopes were revived by a suggestion that men of the German Legion raised for service in the Crimea, in whose future Queen Victoria took a personal interest, might 'be established on the frontiers of the British possessions in South Africa'.[5] Major Grant, an officer sent out by special steamer to discuss the scheme with Grey, arrived in South Africa in May. Grey at once welcomed the scheme, sent a message to the House of Assembly asking for a vote of £40,000 with a further sum from a reserved schedule for churches, schools, and auxiliary services (both of which votes were duly passed) and then set out with Grant for the frontier to inspect the proposed sites. He suggested that 8,000 officers and other ranks, with wives and families where possible, might be sent; and pointed out that

---

[1] House of Commons, 25 Aug. 1857: *Hansard*, 3rd Ser., cxlvii. 2079-80. Labouchere stoutly defended Grey. Five regiments were sent from England.

[2] Hawes to Ball (n.d.—c. 11 June 1855), CO48/370.

[3] On 5 July Tulloch reported to the War Office: 'I cannot find a sufficient number to meet the demand for employment even at double the rates of pay which Sir George Grey offers.' Later 107 volunteers were reported, of whom he thought 20 unsatisfactory in character or likely to withdraw: ibid.

[4] Molesworth to Grey (12 Aug. 1855) (No. 9), P.P., 1856, xlii [2096], p. 43. Based on Molesworth's own Minute of 6 Aug. in CO48/370.

[5] Labouchere to Grey (25 Mar. 1856) (Confidential), P.P., 1857, Sess. 1, x [2202], 59. The Queen had written twice to Lord Panmure, on 11 and 14 Mar., about these men, many of whom had lost their nationality by entering her service and trusted they would be 'provided for in the Colonies': *The Panmure Papers* (ed. Sir G. Douglas and Sir G. Dalhousie Ramsay) (London, 1908), ii. 150-3.

prompt action should prevent the threatened disturbances.[1] By mid July Grey and Grant had selected a number of sites, chiefly existing military posts, and drawn up a detailed plan. Early in November Labouchere was able to inform Grey of the detailed terms of settlement that had been adopted and also of the fact that Baron Richard von Stutterheim, Commander of the Legion, would himself go out to South Africa as leader of the military settlement.

The legionaries were to go out as soldiers. They were to be disbanded on arrival but were liable to serve for seven years to resist attack or in aid of the civil power, were to muster every Sunday for church parade and to have thirty days' exercise in the first three years and twelve days in the last four. They were to have free passages, arms, accoutrements, uniforms, and camp gear, and free rations or the equivalent in money for a year after their location. The pay of the privates was to be 6d. a day, rising for non-commissioned officers up to 1s. 2d. for a colour-sergeant, with an advance of £5 for cooking utensils and tools, a free building lot, and, if it was in a village or new settlement, an acre of garden in addition. They would be required to build a cottage and keep it in good repair and would receive an allowance of £18-20 for the purpose: it would be rent-free and, if they fulfilled the conditions, would become their property after seven years. Wives, families, and fiancées would also receive free passages and a year's rations. There would be 20 officers for every 1,000 men. These would receive half-pay and an allotment at least double that of the rank and file, much larger building allowances (£100-200 according to rank) and substantial remissions of purchase-money if they bought land. They would forfeit these privileges if they returned within three years but after seven their allotment became their property.[2] But of the 8,000 Grey had been led to expect, only 2,362 accepted these terms; and whereas Lord Panmure had expected that the greater number would have wives and children, only 361 wives and 191 children came to South Africa. Moreover some of the women, picked up and

---

[1] Grey to Labouchere (30 May 1856) (Confidential), P.P., 157, Sess. 1, x [2202], 33-4.

[2] Conditions for the Formation of a Military Settlement in British South Africa (24 Sept.) in Labouchere to Grey (5 Nov. 1856) (No. 110), P.P., 1857, Sess. 1, x [2202], 65-8. These were modified in some details: E. L. G. Schnell, *For Men must Work* (Cape Town, 1954), pp. 260-3.

hastily married in English ports (52 in one day on H.M.S. *Britannia* at Portsmouth), were 'not of the best class'.[1]

Labouchere, indeed, privately admitted to Grey that 'these German recruits are not the most orderly and well conducted men in the world'.[2] He was aware that Cathcart's frontier settlement was in the melting-pot. Were there any European inhabitants in British Kaffraria? he asked. 'Is it not contrary to the Policy on which that district was set aside for special purposes that there should be any?'[3] But as the settlement scheme gained momentum and the cattle-killing moved on to its crisis, the point was lost sight of. The arrival of the Legion in January and February 1857 just as the crisis reached its culmination seemed providential. The men moved to their allotted sites and built huts; and Stutterheim in October, when he resigned for family reasons, took pride in the fact that 'eighteen villages, some more advanced, some less, have arisen from the ground, and marks of cultivation are seen everywhere about them'.[4] But his insistence that the settlement was a success was premature. There had in fact been a radical change of plan. Partly because of the Kaffrarian crisis and partly to discipline these men without women, Grey had kept the settlers under arms on full pay. Moreover he had virtually left the Colonial Office to find out for itself that he was so doing. He might have pleaded the emergency and the loyal Labouchere would almost certainly have found no fault with him;[5] but now he had placed himself on the defensive when there were other grounds for uneasiness. In February 1858 Lord Panmure instructed the Lieutenant-General Commanding that 'the Military Chest is not to be drawn upon for any extra pay on account of these settlers' after 31 March.[6] Grey pointed out that six regiments had now been dispatched to India; that the posts along the main roads formerly garrisoned by

---

[1] Schnell, op. cit., p. 72. Dr. Schnell's book is the only full treatment of the whole subject of German emigration to South Africa.

[2] Labouchere to Grey (26 Mar. 1856) (Private), Grey Coll. Auckland. Adderley had a more kindly recollection of the legionaries: *Life of Lord Norton*, p. 148.

[3] Labouchere to Grey (14 July 1856) (Private), ibid.

[4] Stutterheim to Grey (13 Oct. 1857) (Separate), P.P., 1857–8, xl (H.C. 389), 28–9. Some were to have been settled in the Queenstown district, but with the diminished numbers this idea was dropped: Lombard, op. cit., pp. 94–5.

[5] Cf. Minute of Barrow (n.d.) on Grey to Labouchere (30 Oct. 1857) (No. 154), CO48/384.

[6] Storks to Merivale (4 Feb.) in Labouchere to Grey (5 Feb. 1858) (No. 305), P.P., 1857–8, xl (H.C. 389), 48. What particularly annoyed the War Office was a reference to the high cost of living as a reason for keeping the Legion on full pay.

soldiers had now 'in great measure' become the locations of the settlers; that 'if they are abandoned now, all that has been done will be lost, and the country must be reconquered'. 'I shall do my best', he concluded, 'to induce the Lieutenant-General to refrain from fully acting on the recent orders, until we can hear again from Her Majesty's Government.'[1] But the War Office was also very critical of details of Grey's proceedings—the formation of a corps of 160 dragoons from among the military settlers, the issue of 2,000 pairs of boots—and, in a fit of petulance, Grey claimed to detect in their letters a note of 'personal illwill': 'whether . . . signed by Lord Panmure, Major-General Peel, or Mr. J. R. Godley, their severe tone, their style and the expressions used in them are the same.'[2] The German settlers were still on full pay and the outbreak of the Basuto war gave him a new excuse. He persuaded General Jackson to set the War Office instructions aside in no uncertain manner.

Your Excellency is aware that, in accordance with the instructions Her Majesty has herself issued to me, despatches from the Secretary for War have no force or authority for the Governor of this Colony except in so far as they are compatible with the good of Her Majesty's services.[3]

General Peel not unnaturally complained to the Colonial Office. Elliot was scandalized.

He treats the Secretary of State's despatches to the General as so much waste paper, or at best as suggestions for the consideration of the Governor which the latter may adopt or reject as he thinks proper, and all this he says in terms which appear to be studiously offensive, and in fact rebellious against the powers vested in a Minister by the Crown.

Nor did this letter stand alone. Grey, Elliot thought, 'ought to receive the severest rebuke which can be suitably administered'. Merivale's point of view was different. He found Sir George Grey's expressions, setting aside the tone, 'to a great extent justified': having just written to his superior that he considered 'a

---

[1] Grey to Labouchere (22 Mar. 1858) (No. 27), ibid., pp. 37–8.
[2] Grey to Lytton (25 July 1858) (No. 150), CO48/390. This shaft was no doubt aimed at Godley, with whom Grey had been at odds in New Zealand. Grey to Lytton (6 Jan. 1859) (No. 2) explained that the cavalry were to replace the Cape Mounted Rifles, who were below strength, CO48/393.
[3] Storks to Merivale (17 Nov. 1858), CO48/391.

certain mixed military and political measure' indispensable, he is told by the General that '*his* superior . . . has peremptorily ordered its discontinuance'. Carnarvon took Merivale's point a stage further. Grey had certainly used 'ill-considered and unbecoming language': but it was 'the not unnatural result of the existing system'.

> The old arrangement under which the Secretary for the Colonial office was war minister made such a conflict . . . impossible. . . . When the unity of command which was the feature of advantage of the old system, so far as the Army in the Colonies was concerned, was removed by the creation of the War Department, the first and main condition of success consisted in securing a complete understanding and communication in all military-colonial matters between this office and the War Department. This as far as I can understand has never yet been done.

Since it was unlikely that the War Office could be persuaded to resign any of its responsibilities, he suggested that duplicates of dispatches from commanding officers on matters other than discipline and military routine should be sent via the Governor to the Colonial Office by the same mail.[1] Bulwer Lytton, the Secretary of State, sent this suggestion to the War Office, which concurred.[2] But this did not prevent worse difficulties from arising when Grey went back to New Zealand as Governor. Meanwhile he escaped from his *faux pas* with a mild reproof from Bulwer Lytton.

> You were mistaken in assuming the existence of any illwill towards yourself, and it only remains for me to beg of you to understand that the despatches of the Secretary of State for War to the Lieutenant-General . . . contain the decisions of the Secretary of State himself and to convey to you my wish that the discussion of this subject may cease.[3]

By this time the financial difficulty had been eased by Grey's decision to let officers and men of the German Legion volunteer for service in India, as about 1,000 did. Lytton, with perhaps unconscious irony, remarked, 'I have no doubt that their removal

---

[1] Minutes of Merivale (26 Dec. 1858) and Carnarvon (1 Jan. 1859) on Storks to Merivale (17 Nov. 1858), CO48/391.
[2] Hawes to Merivale (3 Feb. 1859), CO49/399.
[3] Lytton to Grey (15 Jan. 1859) (No. 84), G.H. 1/55, Cape Archives.

from the Cape will be an advantage.'[1] The mere fact that these military settlers were kept on full pay so long—they were taken off in March 1860—was no doubt detrimental to their improvement of their allotments; but these were in any case small, often on poor soil and remote from any market, and most of the men were not of the stuff of which settlers are made.[2] Only about a third made good. But their three regiments reinforced the Cape frontier at a critical time, helped to extricate the Imperial Government from an embarrassing commitment and enabled Sir George Grey to send six regiments to India in the crisis of the Mutiny.

One of the grave weaknesses of the German military settlement had been that so few of the men had wives and families. Even before their departure for South Africa a German professor at the Royal Military College, Sandhurst, Demmler, had proposed to supplement it 'by diverting to the Cape a part of the regular yearly stream of emigrants which pours from Germany through Hamburg to America'—in all 150,000 each year. He suggested that he and an officer of the Legion, Baron von Gerber, who had been an emigration agent, should form an agency to carry out the plan. Without such support, he forecast that the legionary settlement 'must necessarily end in a signal failure'.[3] The Colonial Office and the Emigration Commissioners were sceptical: the emigrants most likely to be diverted to the Cape, the Commissioners thought, would be those without capital, who 'would multiply the number for whom the Government must find either labour or food'.[4] But the plan was referred to Sir George Grey and Grey welcomed it. He suggested that 1,000 heads of families, with their wives and children, should be given a free passage from Germany and a building allotment with an acre of land in the neighbourhood of some of the German military villages. At the same time, on Baron von Stutterheim's recommendation, he suggested that the agency be given not to Demmler but to

[1] Lytton to Grey (15 Jan. 1859) (No. 84), G.H. 1/55, Cape Archives. 386 of these men returned to South Africa, but only 43 rejoined the German military settlers: Schnell, op. cit., p. 268.

[2] Mills to Southey (13 Mar. 1860), Southey Papers, Acc. 611/5, Cape Archives. Wynyard to Newcastle (30 Jan. 1860, No. 15, and 17 Mar. 1860, No. 51) with Enclosures and Minutes, CO48/401 and 402. Newcastle to Grey (5 May 1860) (No. 129), G.H. 1/56, Cape Archives. And, of course, Schnell, op. cit.

[3] Demmler to Panmure (3 and 13 Nov.) in Labouchere to Grey (13 Dec. 1856) (No. 138), P.P., 1857-8, xl (H.C. 389), 2-3.

[4] Emigration Commissioners to Merivale (27 Nov. 1856), ibid., pp. 4-5.

J. C. Godeffroy & Son of Hamburg, the largest shipowners in Germany, with a firm in Frankfurt and Churchward & Co., a London firm which had assisted in the emigration of the Legion.[1]

Both Elliot and Labouchere took fright at this suggestion, estimating its cost, for passages, transport, and accommodation at both ends, and houses, at £100,000. 'I assure you', wrote Labouchere privately, 'that a demand upon Parliament for the means of sending out a large German Colony for their [the Legion's] sakes to Caffraria at the charge of this Country would not be listened to for a moment.'[2] He promised, however, to do what he could to send out 'a supply of young women of good character': he suggested Ireland as the most likely source, and in November a shipload of Irish girls duly arrived at the Buffalo Mouth (East London). Grey in his turn was horrified at the idea of having them 'thrown . . . into the country in such a manner that they must have married, from necessity, foreigners collected by chance from some of the worst continental seaports with whose language they were unacquainted, whose religion was different from their own, and many of whose habits and manners were repulsive to them.'[3] He hurried the Irish girls, 'under the guidance of good and trustworthy people', through Kaffraria into Cape Colony, whose Parliament in the previous session, at Grey's instigation, had voted £50,000 for immigration. In the meantime Grey had proceeded with his own plan. The original idea, he declared, had the support of the Secretary of State for War. 'I reported so strongly in its favour, indeed, upon the absolute necessity of the measure, that, backed as I was with the recorded opinion of the Secretary for War, I never doubted but that the measure would be carried out and made all my arrangements accordingly.' He painted one of his idyllic pictures. Reinforced by an emigration of German families, the military villages would become permanent locations: with the German officers as country gentry, with clergymen, schools, and medical attendants of the

---

[1] Grey to Labouchere (25 Mar. 1857) (No. 38), ibid., pp. 11–12.

[2] Labouchere to Grey (5 June 1857) (Private), Grey Coll., Auckland. See also Minute of Elliot (28 May) on Grey to Labouchere (25 Mar. 1857), CO48/381. This formed the basis of Labouchere to Grey (5 June 1857) (No. 204), P.P., 1857-8, xl (H.C. 389), 5–6.

[3] Labouchere to Grey (5 June 1857) (No. 205), P.P., 1857-8, xl (H.C. 389), 6–7. Grey's comment was part of his case against the discontinuance of the Godeffroy immigration: Grey to Stanley (12 June 1858) (No. 71), CO48/389.

same nation, they would constitute a harmonious society, 'which might readily attain to a great degree of prosperity'. 'The only difficulty', he continued; 'was to obtain the funds for conducting such an emigration; but I yesterday received a letter from a German house, stating that they have consented to conduct the proposed emigration for me at the rate of at least two thousand souls a year, the first vessels sailing from Germany in April next.' The military settlers were encouraged to make applications for their relatives to come out. The cost over the first two years would be £50,000 but the emigrants would repay the passage-money in instalments, the Kaffrarian Government raising a loan at 6 per cent in the meantime. The annual charge of £3,000 would be more than paid by the increased receipts from the augmented population. The emigrants would be entitled to land but would pay for it, building up by degrees a considerable land fund. Thus within a few years British Kaffraria would 'cease to be a cause of anxiety and expense to Great Britain'.[1]

The sedate Elliot was horrified at Grey's cavalier treatment of the Imperial Government's decision. Instalment payments by emigrants had failed everywhere they had been tried. The proposed loan was to be raised on the security of the revenues of British Kaffraria, towards which Parliament was making a grant of £40,000 a year.

We already see by a letter from the Hanse Towns Minister that German Merchants are not quite so easy as Sir G. Grey has been led to suppose, and that they want to know whether the Queen's Government will in any way make themselves answerable for the contract or guarantee the Colonial Loan.

Both these requests ought to be declined.

If Sir George Grey is so convinced that he is right and Her Majesty's Government wrong as to disobey their express orders, at least his plan should be left to its own merits and there is no excuse for burthening the funds of this Country with the risks of experiments which the Government has already disapproved.[2]

Chichester Fortescue thought more kindly of Grey's anxiety 'to obtain young unmarried women of good character, who may

---

[1] Grey to Labouchere (26 Dec. 1857) (No 206, CO48/381 and P.P., 1857-8, xl (H.C. 389), 13-15.
[2] Minute of Elliot (15 Feb. 1858), CO48/385.

become wives for the German soldiers'.[1] So did the Emigration Commissioners who found

great force in Sir George Grey's representation of the unprofitable nature of the expenditure now incurred in the occupation of Kaffraria, of the greater economy and more enduring effect of an increase of the European population and of the danger of allowing matters to take their course ... without an effort to raise up a permanent barrier against the encroachments of the Kaffirs.[2]

Lord Carnarvon, when the papers came to him, was broad-minded enough to remark that 'as regards the German firm it seems to me to be a matter of Colonial Finance with which we are not directly responsible.'[3] But, as so often, the economy-minded House of Commons was the determining factor in states-men's minds. Lord Stanley took fright at Godeffroys' suggestion of guarantees: 'I do not think the House of Commons which already looks with great distrust on any further expenditure on account of the German Legion would sanction so large an outlay. I am sure it ought not to do so.'[4] He concurred in Labouchere's conclusion. The arrangement with Godeffroys, he noted, was concluded on 25 August, after Grey had received Labouchere's disapproving dispatch, and it was not until four months after-wards that Grey wrote to Labouchere informing him that his decision had been set aside. Stanley doubted if the scarcity of wives for the Legion would 'be cured by sending out a number of married couples from Germany, accompanied by children as young as most of them must be if the majority of the parents be of an age to contend with the difficulties of a new settlement'. The expenditure also, he thought, had been seriously underestimated. He had accordingly instructed Messrs. Godeffroy that the emigration must be discontinued.[5]

This veto brought the head of the firm hot-foot to London. Herr Godeffroy, Stanley wrote to Grey, told him

that in full reliance on the agreement concluded with you as High

---

[1] Minute of Fortescue (16 Feb. 1858) on Grey to Labouchere (26 Dec. 1857) (No. 206), CO48/385.
[2] Murdoch and Rogers to Merivale (17 Mar. 1858), CO48/391.
[3] Minute of Carnarvon (12 Apr. 1858), ibid.
[4] Minute of Stanley (16 Apr. 1858), ibid. Expenditure on the German Legion had been criticized by Adderley and Sir de Lacy Evans on 22 May 1857: *Hansard*, 3rd Ser. cxlv. 753–65.
[5] Stanley to Grey (4 May 1858) (No. 23), P.P., 1857–8, xl (H.C. 389), 7–8.

Commissioner of British Kaffraria that Messrs. Godeffroy had entered into arrangements, and signed contracts, for procuring and sending out four thousand adults; that some of them had been actually despatched, and that ships were named for the conveyance of others; that contracts had been made for their provisions, that numerous agents in various German states had been retained; and in fact that . . . the Messrs. Godeffroy had signed and circulated all over Germany notices which not only would render them legally liable for any damage proved to be suffered by any individual, but would seriously compromise their good name unless they were able to satisfy all equitable claims, and to prevent complaint.

Stanley had gone too far. He agreed to let 1,600 adults be sent out in the course of the year and £5,000 of the Kaffrarian vote be 'paid to the contractors to cover all expenses which might fall upon them from the abandonment of the remainder of the contract'.[1] Grey defended himself in spirited fashion. He believed he was 'aiding Her Majesty's Government and helping them in a very serious difficulty' since 'they had pledged themselves to the Colony that if it would receive the German Legion containing so many doubtful characters, it should be accompanied by a large proportion of females'.[2] Three years later he told the Duke of Newcastle that these Germans were most valuable settlers, 'most industrious and self-dependent', making good in face of difficulties (indeed hardships) that could have disheartened most immigrants.

The Queen has no better or more grateful subjects than these Germans become. No antipathy exists between themselves and the British race. To be afraid to admit such Germans into a vast waste country, gaping for population such as this is, is to my mind simply to admit that we feel unequal to the task of governing.[3]

This verdict was endorsed by a Kaffrarian deputation which interviewed Sir Philip Wodehouse, Grey's successor, in 1864. The spokesman of the deputation contrasted their lot with the 'wretched' condition of the German Legion: 'The Prussian emigrants

[1] Stanley to Grey (20 May 1858) (No. 33), P.P., xl (H.C. 389), 9. Godeffroy had asked for a much larger sum. The episode cannot have increased the friendliness of Godeffroys to British interests in the Pacific Islands, where they had just opened an agency in Samoa.

[2] Grey to Stanley (12 June 1858) (No. 71), CO48/389.

[3] Grey to Newcastle (22 Mar. 1861) (No. 38), CO48/407.

were most thankful to Sir George Grey for having brought them out, and were perfectly contented with their condition, with the single exception that they would like more land.'[1] Sir George Grey would have been content with that vindication.

The combined effects of the cattle-killing and the German immigration was to make British Kaffraria very different from the military frontier province Cathcart had planned.[2] Grey, who had originated the decisive change of policy, had also skilfully adapted himself and constrained the Imperial authorities, willy-nilly, to adapt themselves to changing circumstances which no one could have foreseen. In 1858 he initiated further changes, concentrating the Xhosas in villages on sites selected by the special magistrates, levying a hut tax and a tax on houses (and at first on cattle, sheep, and goats). He also made grants of land on trust to the sons of chiefs, laying it down that 'no chief's son ought to have less than three hundred acres of good land' (many had much more).[3] A large number of those who had sought and found work in the Colony, where they had somewhat outstayed their welcome, returned as conditions improved to Kaffraria, where they settled on the locations of 'unbelieving' chiefs such as Kama, Toise, and Tzatzoe, which soon became densely populated. But the cattle-killing had broken down the isolation of the Ciskeian tribes and given a new impetus to Grey's plans of interspersing European and Xhosa settlement. The shrinking population and diminishing military expenditure after the cattle-killing made business in British Kaffraria and especially King William's Town dull. Grey's decision, after Stanley had stopped the German immigration, to offer lands on liberal conditions to farmers from the Colony was very welcome. The country between East London and King William's Town was to be laid out in farms of 1,500 acres at a quit-rent of £3, 200 being offered in the first instance. Applicants were not to be over forty unless they had grown-up sons, were to reside and do burgher duty and to show

[1] *Grahamstown Journal*, 18 May 1864. See also extracts in Schnell, op. cit. The immigrants were mostly peasants from Pomerania and the Uckermark.

[2] In 1856 British Kaffraria had had a European population (exclusive of military) of only 1,200 (626 of them in King William's Town) as against perhaps 90,000 Xhosas: P.P., 1857–8, xl [2352], 36.

[3] On all this see A. E. du Toit, 'The Cape Frontier: A Study of Native Policy with special reference to the Years 1847–1866', *Archives Year Book of South African History*, xvii. vol. i (Cape Town, 1954), 105–6. I read this in typescript in 1951.

they had capital to stock and improve their farms.[1] Prospects were bright, and the *Grahamstown Journal* remarked ruefully 'Albany has been weakened to strengthen a line further in advance.'[2] Was this the end of the advance? No, for early in 1858 Sir George Grey carried out his resolve to punish Kreli for his share in the cattle-killing and the intrigues later alleged against him. Kreli, a fine figure of a man, tall, well-featured, dignified, pleasant, astute, weighty in counsel, but embittered by misfortune, commanded the respect and love of his people like no other Xhosa chief.[3] His father had been killed in the war of 1834–5 while trying to escape from British hands, but though he had had a British Resident at his kraal until 1856, and Christian mission stations in his territory, Kreli had never been subject to British authority, and in ordering the dismissal of M. B. Shaw for meddling in inter-tribal conflicts, Molesworth, Secretary of State at the time, had expressed serious doubts of 'the expediency of employing residents beyond our boundaries'.[4] The cattle-killing episode, however, had shown that Kreli wielded great influence within colonial boundaries. Various incidents—an escape of prisoners, including chiefs of rank, from King William's Town and Cape Town gaols, unsettling rumours of the Indian Mutiny in circulation among the tribes and information that Kreli 'looked forward to a speedy time when his people would be able to renew hostilities against the English'—led Grey to determine on a sharp, sudden, and decisive blow.[5]

He sent Major Gawler and Commandant Currie, with a detachment of the border mounted police, a party of frontier burghers, and a Hottentot levy, to occupy the country between the Kei and the Bashee and capture Kreli or else drive him into exile beyond the Bashee. The country was then to be occupied by the remnants of Umhala's tribe, under Gawler as magistrate, 'until

---

[1] Regulations of 12 July 1858, *Grahamstown Journal*, 20 July 1858.

[2] Ibid., 18 Dec. 1858.

[3] J. H. Soga, *The South Eastern Bantu* (Johannesburg, 1930), pp. 239–42. For a European view, D. B. Hook, *With Sword and Statute* (Cape Town, 1907), p. 223. The historian Theal also speaks kindly of Kreli as a man, *History of South Africa* (reprinted 1964), viii. 209.

[4] Minute of Molesworth (7 Oct.) on Grey to Russell (25 July 1855) (No. 24 H.C.), CO48/367. Grey had expressed similar doubts in a separate dispatch of 1 Aug., ibid.

[5] Grey to Labouchere (11 Feb. 1858) (No. 9) and 13 Feb. 1858 (Private) G.H.23/27, Cape Archives.

such time as it may be filled up by English colonists'.[1] The Galekas once or twice attempted a stand, but by 26 February Kreli and his people—no numbers are mentioned—had fled across the Bashee into Bomvanaland. Gawler, and after his departure to join his regiment in India, Lieutenant George Pomeroy Colley, remained in charge of the country as special magistrates. 'It certainly bears a little the aspect of a "filibustering" expedition,' wrote Colley to his brother, 'as the country we are invading is at peace with us, and does not in any way owe allegiance to us. . . . But I leave all that on the Governor's conscience.'[2] It did not trouble Grey's conscience at all. He explained and defended his policy when he opened the Cape Parliament shortly afterwards, adding new details. In addition to the Ndhlambis, considerable numbers of Fingoes were to be removed from their locations on or near the frontier to new locations near Butterworth. The introduction of 'a large European population' was foreshadowed but not discussed in detail. There was criticism in the Cape Parliament, notably from Saul Solomon, of the use of the border police 'at a distance from the Colony in wars of aggression', but an amendment of Molteno approving Grey's use of the police was carried by 28 to 5.[3] What is more surprising is the Imperial approval of Grey's measures.[4] They had cost the Imperial Exchequer nothing and there is little indication that their full bearing was understood.

The main aim of Imperial policy after the withdrawal from the Orange River Sovereignty, as Labouchere reminded Grey in more than one private letter, was to cut the costs. 'It is much to be feared', he wrote, 'that as long as they can look to England for assistance on every occasion of danger or alarm . . . the Colonists will not exert themselves vigorously to provide for their own defence, especially as the expenditure caused by an increased military establishment must be very acceptable to large classes of the Community.'[5] This was hardly fair to the Cape, for in the

[1] This phrase is from Colley's letter to his brother (Feb. 1858): Sir W. F. Butler, *The Life of Sir George Pomeroy Colley* (London, 1899), p. 42. Currie had been sounded in October as to whether he thought he could capture Kreli: Southey to Currie (17 Oct. 1857), Southey Papers.

[2] Butler, loc. cit. It was now that the Bomvana chief handed over Nonqause to the British authorities.

[3] Governor's Speech at the Opening of Parliament (10 Mar.), *Grahamstown Journal*, 16 Mar. 1858. House of Assembly, 27 Apr., ibid., 8 May 1858.

[4] Stanley to Grey (29 Apr. 1858) (No. 21), G.H. 1/54, Cape Archives.

[5] Labouchere to Grey (14 July 1856) (Private), Grey Coll., Auckland.

previous year its Parliament had passed an Act for the organization of a 'burgher force' (though it is true that the reluctance of
the Western Province to run the risk of being called upon to
serve 600 miles from their homes led to its being locally organized
for the internal defence of its twenty-one divisions);[1] and the
Frontier Armed and Mounted Police under Currie steadily
increased in strength and efficiency.[2] In spite of his adjurations on
self-defence, however, Labouchere and the War Office made
generous provision for the defence of the frontier during the
cattle-killing crisis and this in its turn, when news of the Indian
Mutiny arrived after the crisis had passed its peak, gave Grey an
opportunity of displaying his qualities of instant decision by
immediately dispatching to India the whole garrison of Cape
Town and a battalion under order for New Zealand, with a
promise that more would follow.[3] The promise was kept: the
force destined for China was re-routed to India and six regiments
in all were sent from the Cape. The strength of the frontier police
was increased to 600 men, which meant a cost to the Cape of
£60,000 per annum. The saving to the Imperial Exchequer which
this involved and the reduction of the Kaffrarian vote, which
always led to sniping in the House of Commons,[4] to £20,000
no doubt caused the Imperial authorities to look kindly on purely
local operations.

The gradual assimilation of British Kaffraria to the Cape
Colony in its pattern of settlement inevitably raised the question
of assimilating their systems of government. Grey ruled Kaffraria
as High Commissioner and the Cape Parliament was apt to take
offence at his attitude 'that British Kaffraria is a kingdom of his
own which it cannot touch'.[5] He had refrained from promulgat-

[1] The burgher law was No. 16 of 1855. There were still petitions against it but
it was vigorously defended by a Select Committee of the House of Assembly
(Molteno chairman) in 1857; see *Grahamstown Journal*, 6 June 1857.

[2] Hook (op. cit., p. 202) says of Currie: 'He was a born fighter—as hard and
tough as possible. He could ride with or without saddle, go with or without boots,
but he couldn't move along without adjectives.' He was knighted in 1860,
presumably for his exploits in saving Imperial money.

[3] Grey to Labouchere (7 Aug. 1857) (No. 115), CO48/383.

[4] Cf. *Hansard*, 3rd Ser., cxlvii (5 Aug. 1857), 1113–16. The vote was carried
by 135 to 6, but Grey made an indignant defence against the criticism in
Grey to Labouchere (26 Nov. 1857) (No. 173), P.P., 1857–8, xl (H.C. 389),
35–6.

[5] The occasion was a Kaffrarian Witnesses Bill to facilitate attendance of witnesses and apprehension of criminals: see *Grahamstown Journal*, 4 May 1858.

ing the Royal Charter of 7 March 1854 which erected British Kaffraria into a separate and distinct government with an Executive Council. This, he maintained, would have cost £5,000 per annum and been of no assistance to the High Commissioner. He was afraid that two differing sets of laws would arise, with a chain of customs houses, whereas the true policy was 'to let British Kaffraria at the earliest possible period lapse into the Cape Colony'.[1] The Colonial Office found Grey's calculated neglect irritating. It might, Merivale thought, 'raise doubts as to the validity of many of his own proceedings'. It was founded on a misapprehension, for the Charter expressly reserved legislative powers to the Governor and High Commissioner. If, however, he had no use for an Executive Council, a short supplementary Instruction might be issued empowering him to suspend the operation of his former Instructions relating to the Executive Council.[2] The real difficulty was perhaps twofold. Parliament and the Colonial Office were perpetually complaining of the lack of accounts of expenditure of the Kaffrarian vote: 'Parliament', wrote Elliot in a Minute, 'is liberal enough to give the money in the dark, but will it allow it to be spent in the dark?'[3] Grey, immersed in an atmosphere of almost continuous crisis, doubtless felt he should have a free hand and evaded requests for information. The more formal the machinery of government, the more difficult it would have been to withhold it. There were also difficulties about 'letting Kaffraria lapse into the Cape Colony'. Not only would it raise the recurrent question of the separation of the Eastern Province, with which British Kaffraria had common interests it did not share with the Western Cape; but it would mean the end of the Kaffrarian vote, which Grey felt he could not yet do without. Late in 1857 he asked that it be continued at the full rate beyond the original three years and he wanted five more militia regiments (to save all further military expenditure) into the bargain. Merivale was not impressed by Grey's ingenious arguments, but Labouchere and Fortescue thought Parliament

---

[1] Grey to Labouchere (8 Dec. 1857) (No. 192), G.H. 23/27, Cape Archives.
[2] Minute of Merivale (10 Feb. 1858) on Grey to Labouchere (8 Dec. 1857) (No. 192), CO48/385.
[3] Minute of Elliot (1 May) on Grey to Labouchere (20 Mar. 1858) (No. 24), CO48/388. The Kaffrarian accounts for 1855 had been sent but the Colonial Office had not been informed: Rutherford, op. cit., p. 393. Further accounts were sent on 19 Jan. and 25 Mar. 1857.

should be asked for the £40,000.[1] The Government, however, fell: Stanley, on looking into the matter, took the view, which was of course the Treasury view also, that the programme of reduction after three years should be adhered to. He left it to Sir George Grey's discretion 'to effect the requisite reduction of expenditure . . . in the manner you may deem most desirable'.[2]

Sir George Grey, with the German military settlers still on his hands and the Godeffroy immigrants, without resources of their own, in the initial stages of settlement, was hard put to it. It may be said he had brought these difficulties on himself. But you had to take Sir George Grey as you found him. He had been sent to South Africa to save Great Britain from future wars by 'attaching the Kaffirs to our rule'. He needed a large measure of discretion and it had at first been given him. Then his defects came into prominence. He had little head for financial detail and underrated its importance in parliamentary and official eyes. He was self-willed and secretive: he was sparing of information it did not suit him to give, disobeyed instructions when it suited him, and manipulated facts to make out a plausible case for doing exactly what he wanted. He changed a policy of containment on the eastern frontier into one of expansion but was careful not to be explicit about how far he meant to go: he simply led the Colonial Office, or rather perhaps the Secretaries of State, step by step along with him. Molesworth, the Secretary of State most inclined to rebel, was dead. Grey's settlement of British Kaffraria—the Ciskei as it is now called—seems disputable policy in the light of history. If this fertile region could have been retained for the Xhosas, the Bantustans of apartheid would have had a broader base.[3] But how could it have been kept for them when they poured into the Cape Colony after the cattle-killing? In any case Grey thought apartheid wrong in principle, though his type of 'amalgamation' may not commend itself in our eyes either. With all his defects, he saw further into the future than Molesworth or Stanley.

[1] Grey to Labouchere (30 Dec. 1857) (No. 212) with Minutes of Merivale, Fortescue, and Labouchere (Feb. 1858), CO48/388.
[2] Stanley to Grey (5 May and 3 June 1858) (Nos. 24 and 43), G.H. 1/54, Cape Archives. The vote was passed by 177 to 30: Hansard, 3rd Ser. cli. 1420.
[3] According to Alice Werner (quoted by Shepherd, op. cit., p. 37 n.) it was Grey who suggested to Dr. W. H. J. Bleek the name Bantu for the group of languages spoken by the South African tribes—an interesting illustration of his scientific interest in aboriginal peoples.

Witness his defence of his actions in the crisis of the Indian Mutiny:

> The British Empire is so vast and so unwieldy, that it is all important that the world should see it has not overgrown its strength, but that it possesses quite as much energy, vitality and power of action at its extremities as at its centre, and that if any vital portion of it is seriously endangered, all parts of it can, without communicating with the centre, simultaneously stir themselves to meet the emergency. . . . All here now feel that they are useful members of a great body corporate, in which they have that personal interest which arises from having made sacrifice to promote the common good of the whole.[1]

Rutherford describes this as 'an eloquent flourish of patriotic sentiment'.[2] It was more. It implicitly rejected the idea that the Empire needed to be run by a centralized bureaucracy. In a moment of romantic vision, Grey had glimpsed afar off the many-centred Commonwealth of the twentieth century. No wonder he was not understood by myopic officials in Downing Street.

[1] Grey to Labouchere (7 Aug. 1857) (No. 115), P.P., 1857–8, xlii [2298], 14–16.
[2] Rutherford, op. cit., p. 373.

# IV

## NATAL: THE BASUTO MEDIATION: SCHEMES OF FEDERATION AND EXPANSION

SINCE the Trekkers' Republic of Natal had collapsed and most of them had moved back over the Drakensberg, Natal had appeared untouched by the main currents of South African history. But it stood within the wide, if undefined, limits of the High Commissionership instituted in 1846.[1] Sir George Cathcart had been asked to report on Natal, but he had been prevented by his various preoccupations and Sir George Clerk, on whom the responsibility at first devolved, excused himself on account of an injury in a riding accident. Assistant Commissioner Owen, to whom the task fell, was a man of less authority. Before his arrival, early in 1854, the immediate difficulty, the friction between the able, astute, ambitious Lieutenant-Governor, Benjamin Pine, and his senior officials had been resolved; in particular, Pine and Theophilus Shepstone, who with the curious title of Diplomatic Agent was in charge of Native affairs, had made up their personal quarrel. But there remained a more serious problem, what to do with the continuing influx of Zulus and others into Natal. The Location Commission of 1846–8 had recommended their concentration in large 'locations'. But in 1848–51 considerable numbers of European settlers arrived in Natal.[2] Their demand for land interfered with these plans and the Government resumed and broke up some of the locations. Pine's idea was cautiously to take small portions of the locations, give part of them to individual Natives and their families and form European settlements out of the remainder, so that they might be 'gradually intersected, as

[1] On the annexation of Natal see *inter alia* my *British Colonial Policy in the Age of Peel and Russell*, pp. 139 ff. On the High Commissionership see Fryer, op. cit., ch. vii.

[2] On this see the definitive work of A. F. Hattersley, *The British Settlement of Natal* (Cambridge, 1950).

they should be, by white settlements'.[1] Later, to gain 'a little comfortable breathing time', Pine appointed a representative Native Management Commission, to report on the problem. The Commission fell into the hands of its settler members. Professor Hattersley is no doubt justified in saying that 'it is unfair to suggest that the colonists were concerned to reduce the native population to the status of the squatters and servants';[2] but the bias of the report, which was mainly the work of Walter Macfarlane, an immigrant of 1849 and a future Speaker of the Legislative Council, was strongly against the existing system and the whole Shepstone policy. It summed up its criticism in one sentence: 'The fatal error has been committed of providing for the subsistence of a great Kafir nation within the District, and of creating rights in their favour, instead of merely satisfying the wants of a limited number of aborigines and refugees.' Law, clearly defined and enforced, should replace persuasion and personal influence. A Secretary for Kafir Affairs, with the necessary staff, should be invested with the powers of Paramount Chief, held by the Lieutenant-Governor under an ordinance of 1849. The Resident Government Agent should be the supreme authority in each location and the chiefs should exercise a delegated power only and be paid a salary. Young men should be trained in 'habits of industry' through a Government Industrial School in each location and a scheme of five years' apprenticeship 'at the usual wages of the country'.[3] Pine took his time to comment on this voluminous report, but when he did so expressed regret that

in discussing the important subject of the government of the Natives the Commission have allowed its direct bearing on the interests of the white Colonists, more especially as to the supply of native labour, to hold too prominent a place. . . . To expect a people whose past avocations have been war and the chase, suddenly or in any short space of time to subside into regular agricultural labourers is to expect an alteration in the natural laws which govern the world.

He did not advise much direct Government interference in labour

[1] Pine to Smith (1 Nov. 1851) (No. 31), P.P., 1852–3, lxii [1697], 22–5.
[2] Op. cit., p. 288.
[3] Proceedings and Report (26 Oct. 1853) of Commission on the Past and Present State of the Kafirs . . . in Natal . . ., Natal Archives. See also L. Young, 'The Native Policy of Benjamin Pine in Natal, 1850–1855', *Archives Year Book for South African History*, 1951, vol. ii, ch. viii, and E. W. Smith, *Life and Times of Daniel Lindley*, pp. 300 ff.

matters; though magistrates should exert moral influence to induce Natives to go into service, they should have free choice of masters.[1] On one important point, however, the Commission, Pine, and Owen were agreed. Shepstone had revived a scheme of the short-lived Trekker Republic for removing a large number of the refugees from Zululand and elsewhere to the country between the Umkomanzi and Umzimkulu, the colonial boundary, or even beyond the latter river. This experiment seemed worth trying and Shepstone was willing to take charge of it himself. Fortified by Owen's support and not unwilling, perhaps, to let a difficult subordinate have his own sphere of influence, Pine allowed Shepstone to take the preliminary step of negotiating with the Pondo chief Faku for permission for tribes from Natal to occupy part of his territory.[2]

Despite this concurrence of views on the spot, Merivale doubted the practicability of the Shepstone scheme. 'It seems to me that a much better plan would be to attempt the real *government* of these people in Natal itself: which has never yet been attempted. But this is hopeless without a stronger Civil and above all Military Force, and therefore without expence to the mother-country, which will not be tolerated.' In this dilemma it might after all be 'good policy thus to weaken those whom we cannot manage'— but not to promise them British protection, as Shepstone wished to do at least in the initial stage. 'Whenever white population multiplies, the district in question will be subjugated and annexed, either to the Orange River Territory, to British Kafraria, or to Natal. Until then, I would in no way meddle with it unless compelled.' But he saw military force as the key to the whole problem. So long as Natal needed military protection on a considerable scale, no prospect of self-government—which the Commission wanted as a stimulus to immigration—should be held out. If this line of policy was not possible, the force should be reduced to a mere detachment, 'which will drive the Europeans into self-defence, to be accompanied by self-government, and . . . they should be left to manage their own affairs and controul or negociate with the natives as they best may'.[3] The Secretary of

---

[1] Pine to Sir G. Grey, Bart. (5 Sept. 1854) (No. 58), CO179/35.
[2] Pine to Newcastle (12 Mar. 1854) (Separate) and Owen to Newcastle (6 Mar. 1854), ibid.
[3] Minute of Merivale (15 May) on Pine to Newcastle (12 Mar. 1854) (Separate), loc. cit.

State, however, saw another alternative:

> The natives may leave Natal if they please, but if they go, no obligation must be incurred by the Government in regard to them. . . . We cannot undertake to keep up a military force there on a scale sufficient to protect the European population from all risk to which they are liable from the great disproportion between their numbers and those of the Natives. If practicable I should be disposed to look to the withdrawal of the European population as the best solution of the admitted difficulty of the case.[1]

But after all the Government had just appointed to South Africa a new High Commissioner, whose aims in Native policy approximated to Pine's and had appeared to be successful in New Zealand.[2] The obvious course was to place the papers in Sir George Grey's hands and ask for an early report.

In July 1855 Sir George Grey announced his intention to proceed to Natal 'immediately'; but a second visit to the eastern frontier and a mediation between the Orange Free State and the Basuto (which will be discussed below) delayed his arrival until October. From the first he had disliked Shepstone's scheme. He feared that it would produce a chain reaction of intertribal wars.[3] He was opposed on principle to territorial segregation. But he relied a good deal on a characteristic (and ungenerous) argument *ad hominem*.

> The proposition . . . is nothing else than that Great Britain should establish a new kingdom in South Africa . . . make Mr. Shepstone the King of the country,—guarantee him the security and integrity of his dominions,—give him a pension of £500 a year,—and agree that he is to have despotic powers in governing the country . . . No guarantees are exacted from him.

Already, acting on Pine's authority, Shepstone had secured the cession of the territory to himself, subject to the approval of the Imperial Government; but Grey directed the Government of

---

[1] Minute of Sir G. Grey, Bart. (8 Aug. 1854), ibid.
[2] Merivale notes the analogy in his Minute of 15 May, though he points out that 'Sir G. Grey had a considerable military force'.
[3] Grey to Russell (19 July 1855) (No. 22), Cape Colony Parliamentary Paper (Apr. 1857), p. 13. M. B. Shaw, in a report to Maclean enclosed in this dispatch, had pointed out that Faku was likely to use the scheme 'as an instrument to compel his people to move higher up the country'.

Natal to take no further steps pending instructions from home.[1] Grey's report killed the scheme. Labouchere, now Secretary of State, was 'disposed to look at this important question through Sir G. Grey's eyes' and approved of his directions to the Government of Natal, though Pine, in England now at the end of his government, cleared himself of the charge of 'committing Her Majesty's Government to a course of policy still under consideration'.[2]

The other main question before Sir George Grey on his visit to Natal was the memorial of some 200 of the inhabitants in 1852 for a government 'assimilated in principle and form to that of Great Britain'—in other words, representative institutions. Pine, a clever man but prone to set popularity before principle, supported the plea without even discussing the arguments against it —though he claimed that by a property franchise accessible to Natives who possessed the qualification and professed Christianity, he was 'providing for their ultimate admission to a direct share in the government'.[3] Maybe he was hoping to rally support against the official clique with whom he was then at odds.[4] Neither Merivale nor Newcastle opposed representative institutions for Natal in principle, but they were more conscious than Pine appeared to be of the difficulty posed by 'the enormous preponderance in numbers of the Native Races'.[5] A decision was delayed by the necessity of settling the Cape constitution first and then by Sir George Clerk's inability to go to Natal. Owen did not think Natal ready for representative institutions, though he suggested as a compromise that each County Council might elect one member to be added to the existing Legislative Council. Merivale thought this was likely to sharpen rather than soften

---

[1] Grey to Russell (3 Dec. 1855) (No. 41), CO179/37. After his first meeting with Grey, Shepstone had written to a friend: 'I am afraid he will not let me go—he says the whole of the frontier politicians are opposed to the scheme as dangerous to them': Young, op. cit., p. 314.

[2] Minute of Labouchere (8 Feb. 1856), CO179/37. Pine to Ball (22 Feb.) in Labouchere to Grey (3 Mar. 1856) (No. 35), Cape Parliamentary Paper (Apr. 1857), pp. 202–3.

[3] Memorial of 231 Inhabitants of Natal to the Queen (2 Aug.) in Pine to Pakington (25 Aug. 1852) (No. 38) and Pine to Pakington (28 Sept. 1852) (No. 55), P.P., 1852–3, lxii [1697], 77–81.

[4] A. F. Hattersley, *More Annals of Natal* (London, 1936), p. 185.

[5] Minutes of Merivale (18 Dec.) and Newcastle (4 Apr. 1853) on Pine to Pakington (28 Sept. 1852) (No. 55), CO179/22.

antagonism.[1] Newcastle had sanctioned Pine's proposals for local self-government for the European settlers but, as Merivale foresaw, this did not appease the advocates of representative institutions: indeed there was opposition in some quarters, especially from Dutch farmers. By the time of Grey's arrival Pine had gone to England on leave of absence, and the Imperial authorities thought that the remainder of his term was too short to justify his return to Natal.

Considered in the light of his attitude in New Zealand, Grey's recommendations were surprisingly favourable to the settlers. These included, he said, a considerable number of English gentlemen of good education and intelligence and immigrants of similar calibre from the Cape, who had long considered South Africa as their home and were well acquainted with its problems. 'A European population thus composed ought . . . to have a voice in the government of their country.' But they numbered only 8,500 and 'mixed up with them, is a population of about a hundred thousand Zulu Kafirs, refugees from the tyranny of their chiefs, and anxious to feel that they are ruled by the British Government, as thereby having a claim on its protection'. It was important that they 'should feel that they are not altogether separated from the Government, and unrepresented in the legislature'. He therefore recommended a Legislative Council of four officials and twelve or more non-official members elected on the same franchise as the County Councils—that is, ownership or occupation of property of £50 or annual rental of £10. The Council should elect its Speaker: throwing this honourable office open to competition should be an inducement to the best class of men to take an interest in public affairs. The salaries of the leading officials should be reserved in a civil list, which should also include £5,000 for Native purposes. The plan, Grey maintained, was essentially an adaptation of the prudent and moderate views of the settlers and was capable of 'modification by easy stages as the colony advanced in wealth and population'. No doubt in due course, in order to enlarge their control of affairs, they would relieve Britain of military and other charges.[2]

---

[1] Owen to Newcastle (6 Mar. 1854) and Minute of Merivale (15 May), CO179/35.
[2] Grey to Russell (24 Nov. 1855) (No. 34), Cape Parliamentary Paper (Apr. 1857), pp. 35–41.

Merivale and the Parliamentary Under-Secretary, John Ball, hardly shared Grey's optimistic assumptions about the settlers, but Secretary Labouchere 'inclined to the adoption of Sir G. Grey's proposals *in toto*'.[1] His scheme of direct election was wisely preferred to indirect election by the local councils which Pine was now urging at home—an expedient which had been decisively rejected by local opinion when suggested in the Australasian colonies. The Charter of Natal (15 July 1856) was thus essentially Sir George Grey's work. Natal now became for the first time a separate colony, though in certain respects still subordinate to Sir George Grey as High Commissioner. Her Majesty's Government, Grey was informed, 'regard the affairs of the Native Tribes adjoining to and inhabiting that District to be so nearly connected with those of the Tribes immediately bordering on the Colony, that whatever authority is conveyed by that Commission extends over Natal also, as far as the nature of the case admits'. The new Lieutenant-Governor, John Scott, was therefore instructed to co-operate with him and defer to his paramount authority in respect of these special duties.[2]

In two other matters Sir George Grey's short visit changed the course of policy in Natal. He broke with the system of selling land at 4s. an acre which, since most of the Boer trekkers had gone back over the mountains, had left millions of acres of Natal unoccupied because unsaleable. He authorized the Officer Administering the Government to dispose of waste lands in farms varying in size from 1,500 to 3,000 acres according to soil and locality at a quit-rent subject to occupation, military service, and non-alienation for three years—the usual Cape Colony system in its Queenstown variant.[3] The Emigration Commissioners still preferred sales, but Labouchere and his advisers did not feel disposed to overrule Sir George Grey on a subject like this;[4] and the

[1] Minute of Merivale (31 Jan.), Ball, and Labouchere (11 Feb. 1856) on Grey to Russell (24 Nov. 1855) (No. 34), CO179/37.

[2] Labouchere to Grey (5 Aug. 1856) (No. 87), Natal Archives, G.H. 6. Extensive extracts from the Charter are printed in G. W. Eybers, *Select Constitutional Documents of South African History, 1795–1910* (London, 1918), pp. 188–94.

[3] Grey to Molesworth (13 Dec. 1855) (No. 44), Cape Parliamentary Paper (Apr. 1857), pp. 73–9.

[4] Labouchere to Grey (16 May 1856) (No. 62) enclosing Report of Murdoch and Wood (26 Apr.), ibid., pp. 211–13.

new Legislative Council, though considering the military service condition unsuited to Natal, adhered to the quit-rent system with modifications.

These regulations applied to the grass veld which covers so much of Natal: conditions in the sub-tropical coastlands were quite different. On the coast the problem was to find the crop best suited to Natal's circumstances. Cotton, coffee, arrowroot, tobacco, and indigo were all tried, but in the end sugar was the most favoured crop. Though an application of the Natal Sugar Company in 1853 for a grant of 20,000 acres for cane cultivation, lease to small growers, a central works, and grazing ground for horses and oxen was disallowed by the Secretary of State and fell through, individual planters were by this time beginning to grow cane successfully.[1] Mauritius, ten degrees of latitude north of Durban, was the source of the cane and most of the experience: the cane matured more slowly in Natal, but the soil was less stony and more suited to ploughing.[2] The difficulty was labour, especially at crop time. 'The Caffre', a cotton-planter's wife complained, 'gets his month's wages, tells you he is going to his kraal for an indefinite period, and leaves you at a day's notice.'[3] Deputations and individuals waited upon Grey, but his dispatch suggests that he needed no convincing that the solution of the problem was to be found in India. Rawson, Secretary to the Cape Government, who had served in Mauritius, wrote to the Government of India explaining Natal's circumstances and asking to be informed of the arrangements under which emigration would be sanctioned.

The immigrants [he explained] would not be brought together in large numbers on isolated estates, where they will be treated as a separate class, but will be located in small detachments, chiefly in villages, among a European population of whom a considerable proportion are engaged in the cultivation of small plots of ground, where the immigrants and their families will be rather treated as members of the household, and will consequently have a better

---

[1] Pine to Newcastle (31 Mar. 1853) (No. 16) and Newcastle to Pine (11 July 1853) (No. 29), P.P., 1852–3, lxii [1697], 100–2, 139.
[2] Hattersley, *The British Settlement in Natal*, pp. 235–43.
[3] E. W. Feilden, *My African Home* (London 1887), p. 268—quoting letter-diaries of the mid 1850s. Sugar-planters had the same problem.

chance of profiting by instruction and enjoying other civilizing influences.[1]

Early in 1856 the Acting Lieutenant-Governor, Lieutenant-Colonel H. Cooper, sent home an ordinance empowering the

MAP 2. THE BASUTO AND THEIR NEIGHBOURS

Lieutenant-Governor to make regulations for coolies introduced into Natal.[2] Labouchere raised no objection, though he suggested recruiting at Bombay rather than Calcutta or Madras, where Natal would be competing with Mauritius and the West Indies; and the Court of Directors informed the Board of Control that they proposed to authorize the Government of India to pass a

[1] Enclosure in Grey to Russell (17 Nov. 1855) (No. 32), Cape Colony Parliamentary Paper (Apr. 1857), pp. 30–4.
[2] Cooper to Molesworth (26 Jan. 1856) (No. 10), ibid., pp. 34 ff.

law permitting the emigration on whatever terms might be deemed just and expedient.[1] No immigrants arrived from India until 1860; but Grey had set the machinery in motion.

It was the Government which had ratified the Bloemfontein Convention that appointed Sir George Grey to South Africa, but he soon made it clear that he thought the Convention a mistake. He opposed the appointment of an Agent to the Basuto. The Orange Free State Government would be jealous and would attribute any differences with Moshesh to British intrigues.[2] Differences seemed unlikely under the regime of President Hoffman, in whom Moshesh expressed his confidence as a man 'intimately acquainted with our laws and customs'.[3] The complaints made were against minor chiefs, Witsi and Letelle. But this brief honeymoon ended when Hoffmann promised Moshesh a keg of gunpowder and was forced to resign. In informing Grey of his resignation, he warned the High Commissioner that 'a strong feeling prevails that there will be a war with Moshesh' and suggested he should 'cause the Volksraad to understand that should such war break out . . . Your Excellency will hold them responsible for all the consequences'.[4] Perhaps this letter was responsible for the note of anxiety about the future of the Republics which Grey sounded in his speech to the Cape Parliament a few weeks later. He pleaded for generosity towards them, 'to convince them that their interests and our own are, in fact, identical' and proposed an annual payment of £5,000 by the Cape to the Free State in consideration of the revenues received from the passage of its trade through colonial posts.[5] But no such vote passed the Assembly. As usual Grey trusted mainly to personal diplomacy. On his way to Natal he was present at a rather unsatisfactory public interview between Moshesh and Hoffman's successor J. N. Boshof, who incidentally had been summoned from Natal to the Presidency. Next morning (6 October) Grey saw

[1] Court of Directors to India Board (20 Mar.) in Labouchere to Grey (2 Apr. 1856) (No. 47), ibid., p. 206. This is not the place to discuss the cumbersome machinery by which the government of India was conducted before 1858.

[2] Grey to Sir G. Grey, Bart. (9 Apr. 1855) (No. 9), CO48/366, printed in *Basutoland Records*, ii. 142.

[3] *Friend of the Sovereignty*, 18 Mar. 1854: *Basutoland Records*, ii. 106.

[4] Hoffman to Grey (27 Feb. 1855), ibid., p. 140.

[5] Address to Legislative Council and House of Assembly (15 Mar.) in Governor Grey to Sir G. Grey, Bart. (17 Mar. 1855) (No. 39): P.P., 1854–5, xxxviii [1969], 59–63.

Moshesh in the presence of his sons and three or four of his principal chiefs: he urged upon the chief 'the absolute necessity of his forthwith coming to a friendly understanding with the Government of the Free State' and Moshesh promised to see the President and adjust all their differences—which he did in the course of the day.[1] But within six months Boshof was writing to inform Grey of a proposed commando against Witsi and to express his fear of a war with Moshesh over the boundary question and his hope that the High Commissioner might 'feel the inclination or have the power to interfere to prevent the calamities which I foresee from such an event'.[2] Moshesh disclaimed sympathy with the turbulent Witsi and the commando, accompanied by two of his younger sons, passed off successfully. But he remained firm in his objections to Major Warden's boundary line of 1849 and said Sir George Clerk had agreed that it was unfair to the Basuto.[3] Grey hinted to Labouchere that he might have to interfere to prevent a war on the border and pointed out that 'these difficulties must, in some degree, be attributed to ourselves, as they may all be more or less traced to the fact of our having left the Orange Free State without having in any way defined or settled the boundaries between that state and the Basutos on the one side and between it and the Griquas on the other.'[4] Boshof and Moshesh were peaceably inclined; but the differences were deep-seated and the British position was uneasy. 'I fear that as long as the treaties stand, which virtually prevent us from entering into treaties with the native tribes to the north, and from supplying them with arms and ammunition, whilst we are bound to permit the European States to procure these, we shall not be regarded in the light of sincere friends by the natives.'[5] Moreover the Free State Government, conscious of its deficiency in numbers, was anxious that Cape colonists should be allowed to serve as volunteers if war should come.[6] Burnet, the clear-sighted Agent on the border, saw it coming.

[1] Grey to Russell (17 Nov. 1855) (No. 31): *Basutoland Records*, ii. 165–6.
[2] Boshof to Grey (7 Apr. 1856), ibid., pp. 180–1. Also in P.P., 1857, Sess. 1, x [2202], 23–4.
[3] Moshesh to Boshof (21 Mar. 1856), *Basutoland Records*, ii. 177–8.
[4] Grey to Labouchere (7 June 1856, No. 54 and 14 July 1856) (No. 60), P.P., 1857, Sess. 1, x [2202], pp. 42, 47.
[5] Grey to Labouchere (16 Aug. 1856) (No. 74), P.P., 1857–8, xl [2352], 1.
[6] Boshof to Grey (7 Apr. 1856), loc. cit.

It appears to me that there is something hollow and deceptive in the present negotiations between the Free State and Moshesh. The great object which these Frontier Boers have in view and at heart, and what they are trying [to get] their Government to insist upon, is at bottom *the new line*. This cattle matter serves to introduce the subject, and to talk about as a great grievance, but the grand point to be gained is the Land. ... The Basutos are equally resolved that they will not be driven back or lose the lands they occupy. .... These people have no other country to fall back upon, and they fancy at present that it will be better to die defending it than to die of want, or be dispersed afterwards.[1]

President Boshof seems to have wanted to declare war on Moshesh at once but to have been unable to carry the Volksraad with him, so that on 6 November 1856 there was another parley, at which Moshesh undertook to hand over a number of cattle (which he did in excess) and of horses (in which he fell far short). More important, no doubt, was the decision of the Volksraad to stand firm on the Warden line.[2] But Moshesh clearly did not want to fight just yet—which suggests a doubt whether he was behind Kreli in the cattle-killing affair, now approaching its climax.

Meanwhile Sir George Grey was trying to secure freedom of action by an alteration of the Conventions with the Boer Republics. In a dispatch with many enclosures bearing on the tension between the Basuto and the Orange Free State, he argued:

When a great and powerful nation like England binds itself by a convention not to enter into treaties with numerous coloured races in the vicinity of her own possessions, and to act as a police for another nation, to prevent these coloured races from obtaining arms and ammunition with which they might defend themselves, I think she should at least preserve such control over the proceedings of the nations whom she thus benefits at the cost of others that they used these vast advantages justly, and well for others, and in a manner which did not compromise the interests or safety of British territories.[3]

In December he returned to the attack, with particular reference to a petition circulating among the Boers of the Klip River and Weenen districts of Natal for independence like that of their neighbours in the Orange Free State and the Transvaal.

[1] Burnet to Grey (15 Sept. 1856), *Basutoland Records*, ii. 288.
[2] J. H. Ford to Grey (5 Nov. 1856), ibid., p. 253. Also Translation of an Agreement between Moshesh and Messrs. G. P. Visser and J. J. Hoffman, ibid., p. 254.
[3] Grey to Labouchere (27 Sept. 1856) (No. 94), P.P., 1857-8, xl [2352], 27.

Her Majesty was made to say in the Convention entered into with certain delegates from the Orange Free State, that when arrangements for making over that Territory should have been completed, its inhabitants should then be considered as free. Hence it is argued that the Queen admits that Her subjects are not free, and the dissatisfied argue that they should be made free.

The independent Republics, he argued, were more fertile than the territories Great Britain had retained and must before long surpass them in population (they already had nearly a fourth) and in prosperity. A federal union under British rule would have built up a great state in South Africa: 'the policy has however been adopted of splitting the country up into small Republics with no bond of union between them, each of which in pursuit of its own interests hurries into disputes with Native Tribes . . . without regarding the interests of its neighbours.' If Great Britain intended to abandon no more territory, she should say so or the tendency to disintegration would continue.[1] Three months later, an attempt by President Pretorius of the Transvaal to claim and take possession of the Orange Free State and an inquiry by President Boshof whether Her Majesty's Government would be willing to enter into an alliance with the Free State, in effect against Pretorius, led Grey openly to advocate a reversal of the policy of withdrawal from the Orange River Sovereignty.

I am not aware whether or not Her Majesty's Government would be disposed to retrace this step, but I think, from the terms of the letter from the government of the Free State, and from other communications . . . that the inhabitants of that country would be gladly united with this colony under a federal union, leaving to Her Majesty if such a thing was desired, the appointment of the Governor, together with any of the principal officers, and I believe that it is by a federal union alone these South African Colonies can be made so strong and so united in policy and action that they can support themselves against the native tribes.[2]

The officials at the Colonial Office never much cared for Grey's highly coloured dispatches and grandiose plans. Grey's December

[1] Grey to Labouchere (20 Dec. 1856) (Separate); CO49/377. Queen Victoria sympathized with Sir George Grey's desire for 'the reabsorption, if possible, of the Orange Free State': see *Queen Victoria's Letters*, 1837-61, iii. 225.
[2] Grey to Labouchere (20 Mar. 1857) (No. 34), P.P., 1857-8, xl [2352], 71-2. Boshof to Grey (27 Feb. 1856) [1857], *Basutoland Records*, ii. 171-3.

dispatch, said Merivale, 'raises questions too important and various to be disposed of in the space of a Minute'.

I would only venture [he continued] to suggest that no eagerness on Sir G. Grey's part ought to hurry Government into any premature or ill-considered declaration of policy. If you are prepared to maintain in South Africa permanently, and at the cost of this country, a military force sufficient to enforce obedience within and keep off danger from without, then you may declare a 'permanent' policy in connexion therewith. So, if you are prepared to reduce the military force, and to leave the colonists and independent borderers to manage their own affairs and fight the natives as they best may. But any intermediate policy must be, as it always has been, a succession of shifts and expedients—under which we are not unlikely to attain our object by watching events quietly and suiting measures to meet them, but which is quite incompatible with positive declarations of policy, which another Secretary of State may probably revoke. It is a fault of Sir G. Grey that he is always finding fault with the past, and in his dislike for what he considers vagueness and weakness of policy, always asking for more positive instructions than he is at all likely to get—his very eagerness on these subjects is one of his elements of success.[1]

Labouchere, who always gives the impression of being friendly disposed personally towards Grey, urged him to be more specific about the modifications that he desired in the Conventions.[2] No course could be more detrimental to British interests than to take part with the Native tribes in collisions between them and their white neighbours, nor should any part be taken against them unless colonial interests were threatened. Even qualified interference as an arbitrator should be avoided unless there was a distinct invitation to act in that capacity by the disputants on both sides. As far as possible, the inhabitants of the British possessions should be discouraged from engaging as volunteers in these contests. On two points Labouchere was quite specific:

Her Majesty's Government [he declared] do not entertain the intention of abandoning any portion of Her Majesty's present dominions in South Africa. . . . But . . . the independence of the two republics must be scrupulously respected by us, not only for the sake of

---

[1] Minute of Merivale (20 Mar. 1857) on Grey to Labouchere (20 Dec. 1856) (Separate), loc. cit.
[2] Labouchere to Grey (7 Jan. 1857) (Private), Grey Coll., Auckland. A similar request is made in Clarendon (for Labouchere) to Grey (10 Aug. 1856) (No. 89), G.H. 1/52, Cape Archives.

consistency in our policy, but also from the higher motive of regard for our treaty engagements, so long as the engagements entered into on their part also are faithfully observed.[1]

Absorption of the Free State by the Transvaal would, Merivale admitted, 'try the principle of non-intervention to the uttermost'.[2] But, he and Labouchere agreed, no alliance could be made with the Orange Free State.

Even the danger of one of these states being annexed by the other through fraud or violence would not furnish sufficient reason for any interference on the part of the Cape Government, otherwise than by proffering the interposition of its good offices. . . . It will be for Her Majesty's Government [should the union be effected] to consider how far they will hold themselves bound by all the stipulations of conventions which were made with those states under wholly different circumstances as separate and independent communities.[3]

With the disclaimer of any further withdrawals and the discretion left him by this and other dispatches, Grey had to be content. Pretorius's enterprise was in fact a fiasco: a split occurred between his Volksraad at Potchefstroom and Commandant-General Schoeman at Lydenburg.[4] But President Boshof lost prestige by the episode and, perhaps in the hope of recovering it, while Grey's attention in 1857 was engrossed by Kaffraria, he took a stronger line with the Basuto. Early in March 1858 two field cornets, Olivier and Fouché, told three minor chiefs that if they did not remove from two Free State burghers' farms within two days they would be driven off by force. Moshesh's son Nehemiah, who had tried to play a peacemaker's part, argued that the Boers concerned were subjects of Moshesh, since he had given them ground. On the other side there was some talk of Letelle, one of the chiefs concerned, becoming a subject of the Free

[1] These points are made in three dispatches—Labouchere to Grey (31 Dec, 1856, No. 143) (volunteering) 5 Mar. 1857, No. 157, 5 June 1857, No. 203). P.P., 1857–8, xl [2352], 98, 100–1, 104. The declaration against further withdrawals is omitted from the dispatch (No. 203) as there printed, but is in G.H. 1/53, Cape Archives.
[2] Minute of Merivale (28 May) on Grey to Labouchere (20 Mar. 1857) (No. 34), CO48/381.
[3] Labouchere to Grey (5 June 1857) (No. 206), P.P., 1857–8, xl [2352], 104–5.
[4] See on this episode, E. M. Attree, 'The Closer Union Movements between the Orange Free State, South African Republic and Cape Colony, 1838–1863', Archives Year Book for South African History, xii, vol. i (Cape Town, 1949).

State.[1] It was just the kind of impasse likely to arise on a disputed boundary, and a conference between President Boshof and four members of the Volksraad on one side and Nehemiah, assisted by one of the French missionaries, Cochet, on the other could find no way out. Then Moshesh's brother Poshuli invaded what the Free State regarded as its territory with a considerable armed force, 'without the knowledge, consent or aid of the authorities in Basutoland proper'.[2] On 11 March Boshof had sent Moshesh a series of demands for the coercion of Poshuli and Letelle's son Lebenya, payment of compensation and arrears, and acceptance of the Warden line, requesting an answer by the 19th. When none arrived, a proclamation was issued on 19 March declaring that 'no other course is now open for the State than to assert its rights against the guilty Basuto tribes by force of arms.'[3]

On receiving the news, Grey issued a proclamation of neutrality, as he was bound to do, though he pointed out to the Secretary of State that it was one-sided. 'We permit one party, in procuring arms and ammunition, to obtain the means of destroying the other'—which was not permitted by the terms of the Convention to purchase them.[4] In spite of this advantage, the Free State commando, after some inconclusive fighting and the partial destruction of two mission stations, Beersheba and Morija, came to a stand before Thaba Bosigo. Essentially a mounted force, it shrank from an assault on this stronghold, and soon the men dispersed to look after their families and friends, whose farms were being raided by parties of Basuto.[5] Boshof was in a tight corner. Denied the volunteers from the Cape for whom he had hoped, he had appealed early in April to President Pretorius of the South African Republic (as the Transvaal was now called) for help.[6]

    [1] On the drift to war, see *Basutoland Records*, ii. 267–328. In a dispatch of 5 Mar. 1858 (No. 14) Grey speaks of a Commission to define the boundary: loc. cit., pp. 304–5 and CO48/388. But there is nothing about such a Commission in the *Basutoland Records* and Sir G. Lagden, *The Basutos* (London, 1909), i. 211, says categorically 'Nothing of the sort had occurred'.

    [2] Lagden, loc. cit. Lagden, a former Resident Commissioner in Basutoland, may, I think, be taken as authoritative on this point.

    [3] *Basutoland Records*, ii. 328.

    [4] Grey to Labouchere (25 Mar. 1858) (No. 31), ibid., pp. 334–5 and CO48/388.

    [5] For details of the war see *Basutoland Records*, ii. 332 ff. and (a brief account) Tylden, op. cit., pp. 72–6. On the break up of the commando see *Grahamstown Journal*, 22 May 1858.

    [6] Boshof to President and Commandant-General, S.A.R. (9 Apr. 1858) (in Dutch): *Basutoland Records*, ii. 342. Boshof warned Pretorius that parties in the

Pretorius used this appeal to further his own political ambitions. He offered to mediate, but Moshesh refused his mediation and Boshof, unwilling to accept Pretorius's conditions, appealed to Grey. 'Anything which Your Excellency may be able to do', he wrote, 'would be thankfully acknowledged as a humane and Christian act.'[1] Grey communicated this request to the Cape Parliament, no doubt hoping that its approval would strengthen his hand in case the Imperial Government raised any questions. Both Houses approved, though not without debate as to the form any mediation should take. The House of Assembly adopted Solomon's amendment expressing the opinion 'that, in case of either power declining to accept His Excellency's mediation, His Excellency should not further interfere, or take any step which might, either directly or indirectly, involve or compromise this Colony in the differences existing between the Free State and the Basutos'. The Legislative Council's approval was less qualified.[2] In any case both President Boshof and Moshesh accepted the proffered mediation. Grey at the same time suggested a suspension of hostilities, and this was arranged between Moshesh and deputations of the Orange Free State and the South African Republic (Paul Kruger being one of the latter) on 18 June.[3] Grey thought Boshof's conduct in appealing to the South African Republic had been disingenuous and believed it probable that the two Republics would agree to union and perhaps continue the war on that basis. If so, he wanted instructions 'as to which of the stipulations of these conventions are to be regarded as still binding'. He took occasion to reiterate his view that 'nothing but a strong Federal Government which unites within itself all the European races in South Africa can permanently maintain peace in this country, and free Great Britain from constant anxiety for the peace of her possessions here'.[4]

Bulwer Lytton, who was now Secretary of State, approved of

Cape might 'implore the British Government to take the land again into possession, which may a kindly Heaven prevent'.
[1] Boshof to Grey (27 Apr. 1858), *Basutoland Records*, ii. 353.
[2] Extracts from *Votes and Proceedings of Legislative Council and House of Assembly*, 5 May 1858, ibid., pp. 354–7.
[3] Peace Agreement between Deputations of the O.F.S. and S.A.R. and the Chief Moshesh (18 June 1858), ibid., p. 399.
[4] Grey to Stanley (9 June 1858) (No. 66), ibid., pp. 395–6 and CO48/389. This dispatch was written before Grey knew that the Free State Volksraad had accepted his offer of mediation.

Grey's offer of mediation. Both he and his Under-Secretary, Carnarvon, were uneasy at the one-sidedness of the Convention provisions about arms and ammunition. When the question of the union of the Republics was raised, Carnarvon thought 'it would be a very good opportunity for placing our relations on a simpler and fairer footing'. Lytton was even more outspoken, thinking the Convention's terms 'most objectionable'. 'Can we not get rid of the Treaty even if there be no union? Neutrality [he added] is our present policy—confederation may be wise hereafter—but now it seems to me that we should have much more to lose than to gain by it.'[1] If Lytton thought Grey's suggestion of federation premature, Merivale was 'entirely against any such federation or union with the Free Republics, whatever seductive shape the project may assume'.[2]

The minute just quoted was a comment on a brief dispatch from Grey enclosing a draft memorial said to be circulating among the inhabitants of the Orange Free State praying for a federal union with the 'parent colony', and asking for instructions on the reply he should make to any such application.[3] Lytton's public dispatch in reply was a categorical refusal: 'it is . . . my duty to state that Her Majesty's Government continue thoroughly persuaded of the sound policy of maintaining the absolute separation of the Orange Free State from the British Dominions.' The main ground stated was financial: 'it requires very little familiarity with past South African History to be certain that if the Territory were once more subjected to the Crown . . . a fresh and very heavy outlay would inevitably follow.'[4] But at the same time, in a long private dispatch, Lytton raised much wider questions. Having reviewed the main principles, as he saw them, of recent British policy towards the Republics, the Cape, and British Kaffraria, he asked:

Do you think that the time has happily arrived when the military force, maintained by this country in South Africa may be substantially and permanently reduced? . . . Supposing you to be of opinion that the present force, or something approaching to it, must be maintained —Do you think it would be safe and expedient to unite British

[1] Minutes of Carnarvon (24 July) and Lytton (27 July) on Grey to Stanley (9 June 1858) (No. 66), CO48/389.
[2] Minute of Merivale (24 Aug.) on Grey to Stanley (5 July 1858) No. 116), ibid.
[3] Grey to Stanley (5 July 1858) (No. 116), P.P., 1860, xlv (H.C. 216), 1–2.
[4] Lytton to Grey (6 Sept. 1858) (No. 33), GH 1/54, Cape Archives.

Kaffraria with the Cape Colony, placing it under the same Constitution the same Parliament and the same Executive? Do you think it would be practicable to carry the extension further, so as to include Natal? In the event of the Cape Colony being thus extended, where should the seat of Government be?

Are you of opinion, on the other hand, that the present unity of the Cape Colony is likely to be long maintained: or do you think the separation of the eastern and western provinces, which has often been urged by local interests on Her Majesty's Government, a better and a probable solution? And, if you think this disruption an event to be looked for, do you consider that it may be practicable to establish a federal union? And, if established, to make such a union, under a free Government, consistent with the maintenance of a British military force, and with the consequent necessity of keeping in the hands of the British Governor, as an Imperial officer, the relations with the frontier tribes?

Are your opinions in these subjects in any way modified by consideration of the policy to be adopted towards the free states?

And what is the permanent line of policy which you would recommend towards those states, consistently always with the maintenance of public faith pledged by the existing treaties?

He hoped for an answer 'before the meeting of Parliament next winter' and wished it 'to be written in the fullest sense, and with whatever explanation or comment you may deem it discreet to distinguish as confidential'.[1]

Lytton was apparently trying to draw Grey out. He had recently expressed a wish that he 'could get all the views of Sir G. Grey more collected and less in vague snatches and hints'.[2] But it was not unnatural that Grey should conclude that the whole future of South Africa was under discussion. He had warned sympathizers in the Free State that 'no federation could be brought about otherwise than through the intervention of your Volksraad and of the Parliament of the Good Hope'. Merivale noted the absence of any reference to the sentiments of Her Majesty's Government. Federation, he thought, 'certainly means one or other of two things: either enormous expense to the mother country or the independence of S. Africa'. Lytton noted 'the Governor's pertinacity in this proposal of federation, the popular favour it is pretty sure to obtain in flattering the national pride . . . the

---

[1] Lytton to Grey (6 Sept. 1858) (Private), P.P., 1860, xlv (H.C. 216), 31–3.
[2] Minute of Lytton (13 Aug.), CO48/389, cited by Rutherford, op. cit., p. 415.

certainty that the question will be largely discussed in Parliament'
and wanted the arguments against it 'clearly and forcibly placed
on record'. His own opinion coincided with Merivale's.

> It seems to me at the first blush, that in federation with this Dutch
> republic we have much to risk and nothing to gain—we reverse in it
> the old story of the giant and dwarf, in which the dwarf got the
> wounds and the giant the profit—the Dwarf would be thrusting his
> Dutch Nose into all sorts of black squabbles from which the British
> giant would always have to pull him out with the certainty of more
> kicks than halfpence.

But Grey had not had time to answer his earlier dispatches. It was
a case for caution 'not to take the shape of rebuke'.[1]

Meanwhile Sir George Grey had brought his mediation in the
Basuto war to a successful conclusion by the treaty of Aliwal
North on 29 September. Moshesh did not appear in person:
according to Tylden, 'one of his diviners had warned him not to
meet Grey'.[2] But Grey had gone to Morija to see him and persuaded him to send counsellors of standing to Aliwal. The Warden
line was confirmed as far south as Jammerberg Drift on the Caledon: from that point to the Orange River, the new line was more
favourable to the Basuto. According to Boshof, thirteen occupied
farms and thirty-seven unoccupied at the time of the take-over
were lost to the Boers.[3] Moshesh on the other hand gave up the
Beersheba lands except for 6,000 acres which the mission might
retain if it wished. All his subjects were to withdraw from the
Free State side of the line, all Free Staters from the Basuto side,
without compensation. Letelle and others who had gone over to
the Free State were not to be molested; but if they remained in
Moshesh's territory were to return to or come under his allegiance. Basuto hunting parties were to obtain permission from the
landdrost through their chief. There were the usual provisions
about cattle thefts and delivery of thieves. Moshesh was very
unwilling to accept these and the article about hunting, which he
declared unenforceable in times of scarcity. He finally signed the
copy of the treaty Burnet took to Thaba Bosigo, mainly for fear

---

[1] Minutes of Merivale (5 Oct.) and Lytton (6 Oct.) on Grey to Lytton (14 Aug.
1858) (No. 156), CO48/390.
[2] Op. cit., pp. 77.
[3] Extracts from Speech of Boshof at opening of the Volksraad (22 Nov. 1858),
*Basutoland Records*, ii. 499–500.

of antagonizing Sir George Grey. But he and his people were in an arrogant mood which was to cost them dear later on.[1]

The success of this mediation, however, and the apparent weakness of the Free State seemed to Grey a heaven-sent opportunity to press his federation scheme. He treated Lytton's private dispatch—as in a sense it was—as an invitation to make the best case he could for an all-embracing South African federation. This he did in what, with all its faults, must be called a masterly dispatch of 19 November. He began with an account of 'the policy ... of dividing South Africa into many states', true in substance but highly coloured in its ascription of motives. One consequence in particular of the Conventions, with their restrictions on the supply of arms, was 'a belief amongst the native tribes that Great Britain had determined to bring about, indirectly, their ultimate extermination, and that nothing but a general combination amongst themselves could prevent this result'. A country so divided 'must always be at war in some direction'. He forecast, eventually with justification, that the lands north of the Orange River 'must, in products, resources and numbers of inhabitants, far surpass the united colonies of the Cape of Good Hope and Natal'. They maintained close ties with the Cape and had the same origin, language, religion, laws, and customs. 'The only bond of union which at present holds together these states, European and native, is the High Commissioner.' These countries were increasingly valuable; their people did not want wars and were fully aware of the much greater advantages of peace; they were willing to contribute largely to defence 'and would do so much more largely if they were allowed to take a more direct share in the administration of the affairs of this country'. He recommended that an Act of Parliament be passed to 'permit of the several states and legislatures ... forming amongst themselves a federal union'. The Governor should be assisted by a responsible Ministry possessing the confidence of the General Legislature. Under such a system it was 'very improbable that any large native war would again take place': but if it did, the people could not say that it had been brought on by the mismanagement of a High Commissioner or

---

[1] Treaty of Peace . . . between the Orange Free State and the Basuto Chief Moshesh, *Basutoland Records*, ii. 476–8. Moshesh to Grey (15 Oct. 1858) with Notes of Burnet's Mission to Moshesh, ibid., pp. 486–95. See also Tylden, op. cit., pp. 77–8, and Lagden, op. cit., i. 175.

the Home Government and would enter upon it with enthusiasm. He did not promise immediate relief to Great Britain from all military charges, but a federal union would at once tend to diminish them and would ultimately greatly reduce them. It would also offer new openings to talent and promote economic prosperity. He did not think Lytton's alternative of a union between Natal, Kaffraria, and the Cape was practicable without the Orange Free State, but he believed that 'if the several legis-latures of the Cape of Good Hope, Natal and the Orange Free State were empowered to form a federal union, embracing Kaf-fraria within their limits, and adopting into the union, either now or hereafter, all such states as might see fit to join them, including even native states, they would accept such a measure'. Finally Grey touched on the 'frequently expressed determination of Her Majesty's Government' to avoid any changes in their policy.

I think the answer that should be made to any objections raised to reopening these questions should be, that the arrangements now in force in South Africa were not only necessarily made without the sentiments of its inhabitants being consulted, but even against their well-known wishes; and that now that they have representative bodies and have become used to self-government, it is at once a generous and a prudent line of policy to readjust these, in conformity with their well-ascertained desires, fortified as these would be by local knowledge and experience.[1]

Sir George Grey's dispatch was indeed a 'classic statement of the advantages of closer union and the dangers of disruption';[2] what has been less often noticed is that he based his case also on the creative power of self-government.[3] Self-government, if the Imperial authorities had the vision to grasp its possibilities, could heal the ills of South Africa. But vision was a gift not bestowed on the mid Victorian Colonial Office. Merivale's precise mind fastened on Grey's misrepresentation of the past rather than his vision of the future: 'the facts are so distorted, or so loosely stated as to be worthless, the motives (I speak from knowledge of the views of successive Secretaries of State) purely imaginary.'[4]

---

[1] Grey to Lytton (19 Nov. 1858) (Separate), P.P., 1860, xlv (H.C. 216), 4–10. Printed in full in Bell and Morrell, op. cit., p. 181–91.

[2] E. A. Walker, *History of Southern Africa* (London, 1957), pp. 270–1.

[3] But cf. de Kiewiet, op. cit., pp. 132–3.

[4] Minute of Merivale (1 Jan. 1859) on Grey to Lytton (19 Nov. 1858), CO48/390.

Carnarvon was more teachable, but judged that such a federation was not 'a practical measure which under present circumstances at all events any English Minister could propose to Parliament'. Nor had he any faith in federation as a cure for friction.

What rational probability is there [he asked] that the several members of the Federation will not quarrel as soon as they are brought into relationship? . . . If we leave the settlement to them we ought to know what provisions can be made for a federal Government with a stronger executive than most federal Governments possess—if on the other hand the Crown—i.e. the Colonial Minister—undertakes the task, it is obvious that the difficulties of composing the differences of Colony with Colony are evidently much greater than in the case of conflicting parties in the same Colony.

Moreover, as he said with truth, 'there are several great lines of policy to which every administration at home has adhered, which are unalterably laid down by public opinion here, and which it would be almost impossible either to abandon or to leave to chance'. His chosen example, the kidnapping of Native children, could only be alleged, however, against the Transvaal, which lay outside Grey's immediate purview. But an allusion to the reserved fund in Natal helped him to his conclusion: 'I am disposed to think . . . that the present separation and consequent sense of individual weakness is the best safeguard for fairness towards the native tribes and for peace on the frontier.'[1]

Maybe Carnarvon was right and Grey was wrong: the point at issue between them was never tried. Lytton, who thought Grey's dispatch 'a great waste of ability', did not even argue it but simply informed Grey that 'after weighing the arguments which you have adduced, Her Majesty's Government are not prepared to depart from the settled policy of their predecessors by advising the resumption of British sovereignty in any shape over the Orange Free State'.[2] But the matter did not rest there. Grey had never concealed his view that federal union was the appropriate system of government for South Africa: in September he had addressed a gathering of Free State burghers at Beersheba on the Basuto border with some effect.[3] A memorial with 750

[1] Minute of Carnarvon (7 Jan. 1859), loc. cit. and Bell and Morrell, op. cit., pp. 191–4.
[2] Lytton to Grey (11 Feb. 1859) (Separate), P.P., 1860, xlv (H.C. 216), 34. In Bell and Morrell, p. 194, n. 1, we overlooked the existence of this dispatch.
[3] *Grahamstown Journal*, 26 Sept. and 2 Oct. 1858.

signatures was presented to the Free State Volksraad in favour of federation: President Boshof, examined in Committee, came out clearly in its favour and against union with the South African Republic:[1] and the Volksraad carried, though only by 12 to 11, a resolution that a union or alliance with the Cape, federal or otherwise, was desirable, and asked the President to ascertain, by correspondence with the Governor, whether the Cape Parliament was disposed to such a union and willing to meet a Commission from the State to discuss terms.[2] Encouraged by this resolution, Grey promised to recommend the Cape Parliament at its ensuing session to take the proposal into consideration;[3] and when his Parliament met on 17 March he told members that 'you would, in my belief, confer a lasting benefit upon Great Britain, and upon the inhabitants of this country, if you could succeed in devising a form of federal union'.[4]

Grey was of course well aware that any such union would need the sanction of the Imperial Parliament. No doubt the approval of the Cape Parliament would have strengthened his case. He had just announced his intention to take the six months' leave he had been granted on the score of Lady Grey's ill health[5] and conceivably he hoped to carry his point by personal persuasion. If so, it only shows how completely he had lost touch with English opinion. He had talked of resigning when the Godeffroy immigration had been summarily discontinued by Lord Stanley. But though the political heads of the office were inclined—more so than the officials—to condone his tendency to act too much on his own responsibility,[6] this disobedience to instructions on a point of high policy could hardly be overlooked. He was sharply rebuked for having given President Boshof 'not that answer which you were instructed to give by Her Majesty's Government but a different answer, in accordance with your own views and not

---

[1] *The Friend*, 6 Dec. 1858, reprinted in *Grahamstown Journal*, 8 Feb. 1859.

[2] Resolution of 7 Dec. 1858 (in translation) in Grey to Lytton (13 Jan. 1859) (No. 8), P.P., 1860, xlv (H.C. 216), 11. For the majority, see *Grahamstown Journal*, 18 Dec. 1858.

[3] Grey to Boshof (13 Jan. 1859), P.P., 1860, xlv (H.C. 216), 12.

[4] Speech at opening of First Session of Second Parliament in Grey to Lytton (21 Mar. 1859) (No. 45), ibid., pp. 15–16.

[5] Grey to Lytton (18 Feb. 1859) (Separate), CO48/393. Stanley on 5 Mar. 1858 had granted leave if the state of the frontier permitted.

[6] See especially Minute of Carnarvon (18 Aug.) on Grey to Stanley (23 June 1858) (Separate), CO48/387.

with theirs'.[1] On hearing the news of his speech to the Cape Parliament Lytton reserved his decision until the next mail. Soon afterwards he received Grey's defence of his answer to Boshof: more ingenious than convincing, it rested on the statement that many inhabitants of the Free State, having refused to abandon their allegiance, held that 'they cannot, against their own consent, be deprived of the rights to which, as British subjects, they are, in point of law and as of right entitled', and that even Lytton's narrower federation would admittedly have required the assent of the Cape Parliament.[2] Lytton swept aside this flimsy defence and pointed out, with some justification, that he had often acted on his own responsibility 'by incurring heavy liabilities . . . and leaving the Secretary of State to choose between the difficult alternatives of repudiating your proceedings, or supporting you in that which he could no longer prevent'. But this could go on no longer. He informed Grey that the Government had come to the conclusion that 'you have so far compromised them, and endangered the success of that policy which they must deem right and expedient in South Africa, that your continuance in the administration of the government of the Cape can no longer be of service to public interest'.[3] Even now Grey was not reduced to silence. In an 'able and temperate defence' he argued at great length that 'I did not disobey your orders'. He claimed that Lytton's dispatches showed that he had not made up his own mind and that his clear duty 'was to keep the question an open one until the final decision of Her Majesty's Government was made'; that the attitude of the Cape Parliament, which he was trying to ascertain, was the key to the attitude of the Orange Free State; and that if he had erred 'it was from the sanguineness which springs from overzeal, not from intentional disobedience'. He again defended his policies on German immigration and Kaffrarian finance and insisted a Governor of the Cape must have wide discretion.[4]

The tone of injured innocence does not altogether ring true, especially when it relates to Grey's dealings with the Orange Free State, but his plea for the widest possible discretion in his varied

[1] Lytton to Grey (5 Mar. 1859) (No. 108), P.P., 1860, xlv (H.C. 216), 34.
[2] Grey to Lytton (19 Apr. 1859) (No. 58), ibid., pp. 17–18.
[3] Lytton to Grey (4 June 1859) (No. 147), ibid., pp. 35–7.
[4] Grey to Lytton (20 July 1859) (No. 128), ibid., pp. 18–26. The characterization of his defence is in a minute of Newcastle (3 Sept.), CO48/396.

responsibilities and the need for 'overstepping the duties of an ordinary British Governor' has great force.

It was Newcastle, not Lytton, who received this dispatch, for the Derby–Disraeli Ministry had fallen on 10 June. Lytton had asked Sir John Lawrence to succeed Grey, but he had declined.[1] It was therefore possible for Newcastle to write to Grey endorsing Lytton's disapproval of his conduct but offering to reinstate him 'upon one condition . . . that you feel yourself sufficiently free and uncompromised, both with your Legislature and with the inhabitants of the Orange River Free State, to be able personally to carry into effect the policy of Her Majesty's Government, which is entirely opposed to those measures, tending to the resumption of sovereignty over that state, of which you have publicly expressed your approval'.[2] This dispatch crossed Sir George Grey at sea, but a copy was sent him on his arrival in England. He had an interview with the Duke on 21 October and a few days later wrote to say he thought it was his duty 'to the Queen, to your Grace, who originally sent me to South Africa and who has since treated me with so much consideration, and to the people of that country' to return to the Cape.[3] This reference to the people was no empty formula. All over Cape Colony meetings were held deploring his recall and in many cases asking for his reinstatement. Petitions poured in not only from such meetings but from 'the coloured people of the Graham's Town Location' and from the Fingoes.[4] No previous Governor had reached such heights of popularity.

Meanwhile South Africa was not standing still. As part of his wider scheme, Grey had invited the Cape Parliament to consider the incorporation of British Kaffraria into the Colony; but Saul Solomon, Chairman of a Select Committee on the subject, moved on 14 June a resolution stating it was 'highly undesirable' thus to enlarge the limits of the Colony. This was carried with an addendum by the Attorney-General raising no objections to the restoration of East London, temporarily annexed to the Colony in 1848,

[1] Lytton to Adderley (21 Oct. 1859): Childe-Pemberton, *Life of Lord Norton*, pp. 172–3. Lytton dissuaded Adderley from moving a vote of censure on the Government for reinstating Grey.

[2] Newcastle to Grey (4 Aug. 1859) (No. 13), P.P., 1860, xlv (H.C. 216), 38. See also Newcastle to Grey (5 Aug. 1859) (Private), Grey Coll., Auckland.

[3] Grey to Newcastle (29 Oct. 1859), P.P., 1860, xlv (H.C. 216), 39.

[4] Ibid., pp. 27 ff. *Grahamstown Journal*, 26 July 1859 and *passim*.

to British Kaffraria.[1] With the collapse of the federation scheme, the Imperial authorities had to fall back on the plan, which had always been more popular in Kaffraria itself, of constituting it a separate colony, with a Lieutenant-Governor of its own.[2]

But what were the limits of British Kaffraria to be? In evidence before the Committee of the Cape Assembly in 1859, Commandant Currie frankly expressed the view that the territory from which Kreli had been driven was 'a country to be occupied by Europeans. . . not to be kept vacant. . . . It cannot be left in that way; either the Kafirs or private individuals—Europeans—will occupy it.'[3] A dispatch of 8 October, signed by Lieutenant-General Wynyard but originating with Maclean, proposed that this territory be occupied by a mixed European and Xhosa population under Government control—that is, on the British Kaffrarian plan. Sir George Grey, who was still in England on leave, warmly supported the idea but broadly hinted that the plan was premature and that the Cape Parliament should have been consulted first.

My intention was to have let the measures I had adopted continue to work for a little time longer and develop their results, until the question of the future occupation of the country between the Cape Colony and Natal had been more discussed and was better understood both in South Africa and England, when I think it might have been readily adjusted without any expense to Great Britain, and with the intelligent consent of all parties concerned, to whatever race they belonged.[4]

Merivale, in his minute on this letter, took his usual cynical view of Grey's methods and policies.

What he now recommends . . . appears to be the annexation (though the word is not used) of the country between the Kei and Natal and its Government after the fashion of British Kaffraria. I have sometimes thought that a good deal of our expenses and difficulties would have been saved in South Africa, if we had always been careful about

---

[1] *Grahamstown Journal*, 25 June 1859.

[2] This was announced by Sir G. Grey on his return, in his Prorogation Speech of 17 July 1860: Cape of Good Hope V. & P., L.C., 1860.

[3] Examination of Currie (27 Apr. and 2 May) by Select Committee of House of Assembly: *Grahamstown Journal*, 21 June 1859.

[4] Wynyard to Newcastle (8 Oct. 1859) (No. 22) and Grey to Merivale (Jan 1860), Cape of Good Hope, Annexures to V. & P., L.C., C39–'61. Grey was in fact 'grievously annoyed' with Wynyard: Wynyard to Southey (28 Sept. 1861), Southey Papers.

looking to the immediate future, i.e. the next move, which the move
now contemplated must needs produce. The annexation of independent Kaffraria will necessitate the reannexation of the Orange River
Territory. It would really be somewhat harsh, as well as scarcely
politic, to cut these people off from the coast and overlap them from
all sides and still refuse to govern them if they wish it. . . . No doubt
there is much to tempt the imagination in such a proposal. I cannot
but fancy the obstacles which would have impeded it formerly are
very much diminished. The Kafir power seems broken—and we seem
to know the limits of it.

Merivale was still an anti-expansionist. He still thought it possible,
'though difficult and unpopular', to adhere to the policy of non-
annexation: 'but one thing is certain—such a policy cannot be
carried out by an unwilling agent, whose ambition aims at
greater things.'[1] But Newcastle's minute shows that, whether by
Grey's persuasive tongue or in some other way, he had been won
over to the idea that an extension of South African frontiers was
inevitable.

A glance at the map and a knowledge of the habits of our Country-
men must at once convince anybody that the whole of Kaffraria must
in a few years become British. It is really a question of time. We are
not free agents in the final issue. The power of the Kafir is departing
—his savage nature is yielding to a great extent to the influence of
civilization. Annexation is an ugly word, and ugly deeds have been
done under it—but the word need not frighten us and the deeds by no
means be repeated. If Englishmen will take capital into Kaffraria and
the Natives will work for them for hire (as is beginning to be the case)
some form of Government is sure to follow. Can it be a Republic
between the two English Colonies—Cape and Natal? Must it not
inevitably be before long absorbed? Mr. Merivale thinks that the
consequence must be the reannexation of the Orange River Sovereignty.
I do not think this inevitable. I hope it may be avoided, but I would
leave this question to the progress of events and the results of experience.[2]

Newcastle informed Wynyard of Sir George Grey's views and
of his own concurrence in them, but he was if possible to postpone action upon them until the Governor returned to South
Africa.[3]

[1] Minute of Merivale (25 Jan.) on Grey to Merivale (Jan. 1860), CO48/406.
[2] Minute of Newcastle (28 Jan.) on Grey to Merivale (Jan. 1860), CO48/406.
[3] Newcastle to Wynyard (4 Feb. 1860) (Confidential), G.H. 1/56, Cape
Archives.

These projects of expansion into Kaffraria inevitably raised the question of Natal's future in South Africa. Its new status as a colony with a representative constitution naturally heightened the self-importance of the settlers. The new Lieutenant-Governor, John Scott, a high-principled but sensitive and retiring man, soon perceived that 'my duties here will be carried on under continued pressure of a democratic party'.[1] The Legislative Council resented the reservation of £5,000 for Native purposes and in an Address to the Queen at its first session asked 'that the control of all expenditure of the public revenue for native purposes should, like all other public expenditure, be vested in the Legislature of the Colony, and not entrusted solely to the Executive Government'. Such a reservation of control, it argued, 'might lead to the continuance of a crude and experimental and ever changing management of this interesting people, thus retarding their progressive improvement'[2]—a derogatory reference to the Shepstone system. The Council emphasized its grievance by striking the vote for six Native magistrates with their staff out of the estimates, leaving them to be provided for out of the Reserve Fund. Scott would not agree to this and defended the Reserve Fund as an act of justice to the unrepresented Native population, who contributed, through the hut tax, nearly half the total taxation of the colony.[3] Another Council Bill prohibited any coloured person from possessing not only firearms and gunpowder (which Scott thought fair enough) but assegais, horses, mules, and asses; and also required the permission of a Government officer for tribal or public meetings, the traditional dances of the first-fruits and war dances. Scott thought the Bill harsh, unjust, and in any case unenforceable, and reserved it.[4] 'This discreditable Bill', wrote Fortescue, 'shows the difficulty of working popular institutions when they are confined . . . to a small white population in the midst of an uncivilized native race.'[5] Labouchere for his part remained convinced that the principle of the Reserve Fund must

[1] Scott to Labouchere (10 Nov. 1857) (Private and Confidential), G.H. 298, Natal Archives.
[2] Address from Legislative Council (28 Apr.) in Scott to Labouchere (2 June 1857) (No. 44), P.P., 1860, xlv (H.C. 596), 1–2.
[3] Scott to Labouchere (3 June 1857) (No. 46), ibid., pp. 3–6.
[4] Scott to Labouchere (7 Sept. 1857) (No. 76), P.P., 1860, xlv (H.C. 596), 25–9.
[5] Minute of Fortescue (7 Dec.) on Scott to Labouchere (7 Sept. 1857) (No. 76), CO179/46.

be maintained in Natal 'while so large a military force is necessarily maintained there'.[1] On both points, therefore, Scott had been upheld.

But the Legislative Council at its next session renewed its efforts to secure control of Native policy. It asked for an alteration in the Royal Instructions, which tended 'needlessly to load a Governor with the feeling and dread of official responsibility'; and it passed a reserved Bill altering the section in the Charter which reserved the £5,000 for Native purposes. In the meantime, as a gesture, it passed the estimates as presented to it.[2] Lytton, who was by this time Secretary of State, maintained the ground on which his predecessor had stood. 'The Governor', he wrote, 'should be exhorted and encouraged by all means in his power to make the handful of whites more sensibly aware that to attempt to subjugate the Natal Kaffir in the various ways at which they aim could scarcely be successful even with a large military force.'[3] Feeling that some deference was due to the representative principle, he nevertheless offered a compromise.

If the Legislative Council are disposed to increase the sum to such an amount as may, in your opinion as well as theirs, really suffice to meet the exigencies of the native service, and will consent to place this annual sum in a permanent shape in the accounts . . . so that it cannot be diminished except by law and with your assent, then Her Majesty's Government are prepared, unless you see objections, to consent to having this larger sum expended with the consent and by the authority of the Legislative Council.

But Her Majesty's Government were not prepared to hand over 150,000 Natives to 8,000 white colonists.[4] After a Committee of Council had waited on the Lieutenant-Governor to discuss Lytton's compromise offer and refused to accept his interpretation of it, the Legislative Council declined to increase the amount voted for Native purposes and resolved

[1] Minute of Labouchere (2 Dec.) on Scott to Labouchere (3 June 1857) (No. 46), CO179/45.
[2] Scott to Labouchere (28 Apr. 1858) (No. 36) with Enclosures, P.P., 1860, xlv (H.C. 596), 40–4.
[3] Minute of Lytton (24 July) on Scott to Labouchere (28 Apr. 1858) (Nos. 35 and 36), CO179/49.
[4] Lytton to Scott (19 Aug. 1858) (No. 18), P.P., 1860, xlv (H.C. 596), 88–9. The sentence quoted was added by Merivale to a draft by Sir George Barrow. The figures are in a later minute of Merivale (5 Mar. 1859), cited below.

not to proceed with public business.[1] The underlying difference still was not so much the Council's desire for greater freedom of legislation and greater control over expenditure as the divergence of views about the objectives of Native policy. The Council's aim, said Scott, was 'the dispersion of the natives among the colonists in the capacity of servants working for wages, which necessarily involves a breaking up of the locations'. This, he maintained, was 'injust, impolitic and indeed impracticable'. It would be regarded as a breach of faith and awaken the dangerous elements in the Native character, which were now dormant, since existing policy had secured the colony unbroken peace since the first establishment of the government, with a military force never reaching 1,000 and now only some 500 men.[2] The legislative deadlock, however, was inconvenient and Lytton decided to renew his compromise offer. Even though Merivale had 'little hope of a satisfactory issue',[3] the dispatch was mainly of his drafting.

It is due in our opinion to the natives that a certain sum should be liberally and *bona fide* spent on their behalf and we consider that the maintenance of this principle is even more due to the colonists, inasmuch as we are convinced that this is the cheapest method of ensuring the security of themselves and of civilized institutions in the midst of a barbarous population, outnumbering many times their own. . . . The British Government will not furnish troops to support a policy of which it disapproves, and to act in the defence of those who insist on a counter policy which it believes to be fraught with serious danger.[4]

A dissolution had produced some changes in membership but no substantial change of principle, though the new Council declared it inexpedient to take Lytton's dispatch into consideration late in the session and therefore passed the estimates. In 1860 Scott was on leave in England, and the Council, though it continued the argument, did so in less aggressive tone.[5]

---

[1] Scott to Lytton (28 Dec. 1858) (No. 84) with Enclosures, P.P., 1860, xlv (H.C. 596), 55–61.
[2] Scott to Lytton (30 Dec. 1858) (No. 88), ibid., pp. 67–74. There were occasional punitive expeditions against refractory tribes.
[3] Minute of Merivale (5 Mar. 1859) on Scott to Lytton (30 Dec. 1858) (No. 88), CO179/50.
[4] Lytton to Scott (24 Mar. 1858) (No. 42), P.P., 1860, xlv (H.C. 596), 91–2. The sentences quoted closely follow Lytton's minute of 12 Mar., CO179/50.
[5] Report of Committee of Legislative Council (17 July) in Williamson to Newcastle (2 Aug. 1860) (No. 39), CO179/53.

One contribution to the relaxation of tension may have been the prospect of securing immigrants from India, since the Council at its first session had backed the request made at Sir George Grey's instance in 1855. Naturally the Mutiny year was not one in which immigrants could be hoped for; but in 1858 Sir George Clerk, now at the India Board, informed the Colonial Office that the Board concurred with the Court of Directors in thinking the experiment of emigration to Natal might be tried since 'it will be unjust to it and to the Indian Labourers to refuse to allow such Labourers to go to the Colony if they can be prevailed upon by legitimate offers to do so'.[1] Labour was admittedly in short supply on the coast, and after inquiry by a Select Committee the Legislative Council in 1859 passed three immigration laws. The most important, No. 14, 'to provide for the Immigration of Coolies into this Colony at the Public Expense and for the regulation and government of such Immigrants' was based on a St. Lucia ordinance sent out by the Colonial Office. Scott did not think many were required, but if a small number were introduced 'they would supply a body of constant and reliable labourers now wanting, their example of daily and steady industry would act beneficially on the Natives and that continual cry now being made for a change in the present condition of the Natives would moderate.'[2] Customs duties (notably on articles of African consumption such as beads, blankets, and hoes) were increased to provide the funds, though employers were to repay three-fifths of the passage money. The Indian Act sanctioning the emigration (No. XXXIII of 1860) came into operation on 7 August and within a few months a Special Agent had dispatched three ships from Madras and two from Calcutta, with 1,029 male adults. The Acting Lieutenant-Governor reported the Indian labourers to be 'well satisfied with the Colony, and the Colonists with them'.[3]

[1] Clerk to Merivale (1 June 1858) quoting a Government of India letter of 31 March, CO179/50.
[2] Scott to Lytton (28 June 1859) (No. 51), CO179/51. Ordinances No. 13 and 15 dealt with possible immigration from other sources, e.g. Java, and with immigration by private individuals at their own expense. They were based on Mauritius ordinances.
[3] Williamson to Newcastle (29 Nov. 1860) (No. 77), CO179/56. The Special Agent was the Natal Postmaster-General, W. M. Collins. On the whole subject see L. M. Thompson, 'Indian Immigration into Natal, 1860–1872', *Archives Year Book for South African History*, xv, vol. ii. (Cape Town, 1952).

For the moment, however, the problem overshadowing all others in Natal was the disputed succession in Zululand. Panda had not followed the usual custom of selecting the wife who was to bear the future chief, but had divided his kingdom between his sons Cetywayo and Umbulazi. In December 1856 they fought a battle, in which Cetywayo was victorious. Umbulazi was killed, but two of his brothers, with some of their followers, fled across the Tugela into Natal, two others into the Transvaal. Cetywayo was reputed to be unfriendly to Natal, and Scott asked for reinforcements;[1] but the Indian Mutiny prevented their being sent. In 1859 civil war broke out again. In the following September, while Scott was in England, Sir George Grey visited Natal with Queen Victoria's sixteen-year-old son, Prince Alfred. It was no doubt on this journey that he hatched a plan, based on the belief that the Imperial Government was now prepared to annex all Kaffraria, which he disclosed in February 1861 in a dispatch to Newcastle.

Natal [the dispatch continued] must thus become our real frontier, and I think its position is, and will be, most critical. Beyond it lies the numerous Zulu race, whom we leave in entire barbarism, and in a state of chronic internal war. . . . I think that all these dangers might be remedied permanently by making an arrangement with Panda, by which portions of his territories were given over to the government of his sons, to descend to them after his death, whilst a portion of his country abutting on Natal was given over to our rule, and was placed at present under the care of such a person as Mr. Shepstone, in order that some of the Zulus might be removed from Natal and be located in the country beyond the Tugela, which now lies nearly vacant. Europeans would accompany them to some parts of the country.

Panda and his sons might also be persuaded to establish, with the assistance of British officers, a system of taxation and police.[2]

Scott gained an inkling of Grey's plans through his Colonial Secretary, Erskine, and forestalled him with an alternative plan for annexing to Natal the territory between the Umzimkulu and Umtamvuna, which had been ceded by Faku in 1850 but left unoccupied.[3] Elliot much preferred this scheme to Grey's: 'the

---

[1] Scott to Labouchere (16 Dec. 1856) (No. 9), CO179/44.

[2] Grey to Newcastle (9 Feb. 1861) (No. 10), CO48/407. Printed in Annexures to V. & P., L.C., C.-44'61.

[3] Scott to Newcastle (21 Nov. 1860), CO179/57. Erskine is mentioned in Barrow to Grey (5 Nov. 1860) (Private), Grey Coll., Auckland.

natural growth of this Colony should be, it would seem to an ordinary observer, *towards* the Cape and *not* away from it.' Newcastle thought the two schemes ought not to be mixed up and was prepared to sanction Scott's, as he did by a dispatch of 26 December, leaving Sir George Grey's when it arrived, 'to stand on its own merits'.[1] Grey, however, was less favourably disposed towards Scott's scheme. He did not regard the treaty of 1850 as valid and had an eye on Faku's territory as a place where he could settle Adam Kok's Griquas. When Scott called at Cape Town on his way back to South Africa, therefore, Grey asked him to defer acting on Newcastle's instructions pending a further reference home and a report which Sir Walter Currie was making on Kaffraria.[2]

When Grey's own scheme was received in England, Newcastle was somewhat taken aback at its scope, though he thought it 'a great mistake to look upon it as a scheme originating either in the ambition or wilfulness of Sir George Grey'. He (or perhaps his Cabinet colleagues) deemed it advisable to apply the brakes.

I am of opinion [he wrote] that it would be most beneficial to the natives, and most conducive to peace, but I cannot help fearing that the tendency of your plans may be to an extension of frontier, and Her Majesty's Government would deprecate such a result, where it is not absolutely necessary for the safety of the settlers and the peace of the colonies in South Africa.

Newcastle also instructed Grey, if he made any approach to Panda and his sons, to act in conjunction with Scott.[3]

But Scott, acting no doubt partly from pique but partly on the promptings of Shepstone, had already torpedoed Grey's policy of *divide et impera*. On the plea that the nomination of a successor might end the chronic disturbances in Zululand, Scott, without informing the High Commissioner, abandoned the policy of non-intervention and in April sent Shepstone to Panda's kraal to 'offer the friendly advice of this Government'. On 16 May Panda formally proclaimed Cetywayo as his successor. The Zulu heralds

---

[1] Minutes of Elliot (30 Nov.) and Newcastle (19 Dec.) on Scott to Newcastle (21 Nov. 1860), CO179/57.

[2] Grey to Newcastle (19 Feb. 1861) (No. 16), CO48/407. On the development of the Griqua plan see below, pp. 134–6.

[3] Newcastle to Grey (4 May 1861), Annexures to V. & P., L.C., C.–44'61. See also Minute of Newcastle (22 Apr. 1861), CO48/407.

thereupon demanded the return of Panda's sons from Natal and Shepstone promised to convey this message, though not of course compliance with it.[1]

Scott concealed the knowledge of what he had done as long as he could, but a rumour, supported by a message from Panda himself that Cetywayo with his 15,000 men contemplated a foray into Natal, forced him to come into the open. There was panic on the border and he had to ask Sir George Grey for reinforcements. To do him justice, he did not succumb to panic himself: he erred rather in the opposite direction, thinking that 200 of the Cape Corps, with the Natal volunteers, 'could scatter any Zulu force that dared to appear on our table lands'.[2] But Grey was justifiably annoyed and hardly troubled to conceal his annoyance in a message he sent to the Cape Parliament. He also claimed that Scott when on leave had so alarmed the Colonial Office that he had been deterred from taking the preliminary steps to ascertain whether his plan was feasible. But he was unrepentant. 'It will not do to sit still and let events take their course.'

If it is said that the Policy I advocate must ultimately lead to some extension of the limits of the Empire, the answer I think is, that this is unavoidable. The European race and the coloured race will increase:—will hold intercourse with each other;—will pass within each other's limits;—and they will either do this in such a manner as to promote their mutual advantage, or to kindle mutual animosities and inflict ceaseless injuries upon each other.

To try to prevent British subjects from spreading 'as their wants render necessary, on such conditions as the strictest justice to the Native Races will sanction and require' was in his belief 'a serious offence against the welfare of the human race'.[3] If Cetywayo did not invade Natal (and it soon became clear that he would not) it would be advisable 'to pass into the Zulu country to punish him' and make 'such a complete and final settlement of the affairs of the Zulu Nation and of our border on that side as will place the Colony of Natal in perfect safety for the future'.[4]

[1] Scott to Newcastle (5 July 1861) (No. 43), CO179/59. Message of Grey to Cape Parliament (30 July), *Grahamstown Journal*, 6 Aug. 1861.
[2] Scott to Grey (15 July 1861) (Private), Grey Coll., Auckland.
[3] Grey to Newcastle (21 July 1861) (Separate), CO48/408. The dispatch is particularly interesting because Grey knew he was soon to leave South Africa.
[4] Grey to Newcastle (31 July 1861) (No. 111), ibid.

Rogers, who had now taken over the Under-Secretaryship, was impressed by Grey's representation of the danger from Cetywayo.

It seems to be certainly for our interest [he wrote] and probably for the interest of humanity that he should be put down . . . and I cannot . . . understand how Mr Scott could take the responsibility of aiding to set him up. It seems to me to have been a generous error. Sir G. G. seems to see his way in these matters much more clearly than the Lieutenant-Governor. But then it must be admitted that Sir G. G's plans invoke the employment of troops in earnest and the extension of our protectorate. But I do not consider this worse than the continued existence, on the other side of the Zulu frontier, of an army composed of 'embodied' and 'disembodied' regiments of savages who with their chief are simply waiting for an opportunity to attack us.[1]

Others in the Office, however, felt that Scott had been hard done by. Sir George Grey was treating him as if he had interfered with a 'settled line of policy' whereas his plans for Zululand, although the Office had indirectly come to hear of them, had merely been maturing in his own mind until he put them forward in February.[2] On 5 December Newcastle sent Scott a propitiatory dispatch, reaffirming the policy of non-interference in Zululand and assuring him that Grey's successor would be instructed to consult him on these problems.[3]

Grey delayed his departure for New Zealand until 15 August, when he knew the Zulu crisis had passed. It was time for him to leave. He had made a marvellous recovery from his recall in 1859. He had certainly turned his English leave to good account. He (it must surely have been he) had converted the Duke of Newcastle to an acceptance of the logic of expansion in South Africa. His brain was still seething with plans of expansion. If he could not re-annex the Orange Free State, he would hem it in by British territory to the south-east. He would wage preventive war with

[1] Minute of Rogers (1 Oct.) on Grey to Newcastle (31 July 1861) (No. 111), CO48/408.
[2] Minute of Barrow (2 Nov.) on Scott to Newcastle (30 Aug. 1861) (No. 61), CO179/59. Minute of Elliot (30 Nov.) on Scott to Newcastle (21 Nov. 1860), CO179/57.
[3] Newcastle to Scott (5 Dec. 1861) (Confidential), G.H. 11, Natal Archives. Newcastle also assured Scott of Her Majesty's Government's opposition to the reported Transvaal plan of securing a corridor through from Utrecht to the sea at St. Lucia Bay.

Cetywayo and settle the fate of the most dangerous tribe in South Africa. Then wars would cease and British and Dutch, Xhosa and Zulu would live together in harmony—with the British, of course, as the ruling element. The extraordinary mixture of idealist and *Realpolitiker* in Grey can still evoke half-reluctant admiration. He had South African opinion behind him, with some reservations perhaps in the Western Cape. But his weaknesses were gaining on him. He had offended an important subordinate. The senior officials in Downing Street remained suspicious, especially of his carefree attitude towards finance; and Parliament and public opinion in England had still to be won over. He had changed the mind of the Duke of Newcastle, but he had not changed British colonial policy.

# V

## SIR PHILIP WODEHOUSE: BRITISH KAFFRARIA: THE TRANSKEI: BASUTOLAND

S IR G EORGE G REY, for all his ability and energy, had left many unsettled questions behind him. The Imperial appointment, to please Lord Derby, of an undistinguished Civil Commissioner, E. M. Cole, as Auditor-General over the head of the much abler Richard Southey, who had been acting in the office, had revived the demands of Western Province politicians for responsible government, muted by Grey's personal popularity. Rawson, the Colonial Secretary, himself thought the time for responsible government had arrived.[1] Molteno's motion in the Assembly in 1860 failed, but only by two votes against a delaying amendment that the country be consulted.[2] Grey himself pointed out that the irresponsible Executive was constantly threatened with financial difficulties by the passage of motions for expensive local works and the rejection of proposals to increase taxation.[3] The Western move for responsible government in its turn, along with a wool tax and public works grievances, led to the formation in October 1860 of an Eastern Province Separation League; but a Bill drafted at a League Convention was defeated by 22 to 15 at the Assembly of 1861.[4]

From the Imperial point of view, however, the most urgent question was the future of British Kaffraria, which remained dependent on a parliamentary vote the Treasury was continually trying to bring to an end. Reluctantly yielding to Colonial Office

[1] See in particular an interesting letter from Rawson to Gladstone (18 Aug. 1859): Gladstone Papers, B.M. Add. MS. 44263.
[2] House of Assembly Debates, 25 May, *Grahamstown Journal,* 29 May 1860. Rawson and Porter both spoke in favour of the motion.
[3] Grey to Newcastle (21 June 1861) (Private), J. Martineau, *Life of Henry Pelham Fifth Duke of Newcastle,* p. 309.
[4] House of Assembly Debates, 11 June, *Grahamstown Journal,* 22 June 1861.

pressure to vote £15,000 for 1861 instead of halving it as at first proposed, the Treasury insisted that this must be the last vote.[1] The Duke of Newcastle hoped that the grant might nevertheless be tapered off for two more years; but in conveying this information to the colony he also pointed out that the annexation of the territory between the Kei and the Bashee, which he had sanctioned, 'would add very materially to the Local Revenue by the disposal of public lands, of which there would seem to be a very limited quantity remaining in British Kaffraria'.[2] This dispatch was in fact the outcome of discussions between the Duke and Grey's successor, Mr. Philip Edmond Wodehouse, 'a tall, thin, aristocratic-looking man' of fifty, who had risen through the Ceylon civil service and had 'no public reputation' but had won the high esteem of the Colonial Office as Superintendent of British Honduras and Governor of British Guiana.[3] Sir George Grey had thought it might be best to incorporate British Kaffraria in a great eastern colony stretching eventually as far as Natal, and Wodehouse even before his departure for the Cape realized that this proposal had a bearing on the responsible government question. In the Western Province responsible government might work 'neither better nor worse than in the other Colonies into which it has been introduced'. But in the proposed new Eastern colony 'the management of our relations with the Kaffirs must be so inseparably blended with its whole administration, as to render it indispensable that the Executive Authority possessing the control over the Troops and subject to the direction of the Home Government should have a substantial power of influencing and directing the general machinery of the Government'.[4]

Wodehouse's first important public pronouncement was his speech opening the Cape Parliament on 26 April 1862. He had by no means been convinced by the separation agitation in the Eastern Province. He had found no trace of any definite plan dealing with such questions as the apportionment of the public debt,

---

[1] Treasury to Colonial Office (4 May and 29 June 1861), CO48/410.

[2] Newcastle to Wodehouse (5 Dec. 1861) (Nos. 378 and 380), G.H. 1/57, Cape Archives.

[3] Parliamentary correspondent, *Grahamstown Journal*, 3 May 1862. By 1868, however, Wodehouse had become 'moderately stout, ruddy complexioned' and his hair was 'frosted with time'; ibid., 17 Apr. 1868. Wodehouse was made K.C.B. in 1862.

[4] Wodehouse to Newcastle (9 Oct. 1861) (Confidential), CO48/411. See also Grey to Newcastle (22 July 1861), NeC11028, Newcastle Papers.

the cost of military defence, the customs duties, or the civil service establishments. 'I have', he declared, 'been forced to the conclusion that the advocates of separation have to some extent shrunk from encountering fairly the great difficulties involved in the execution of their scheme.' He accordingly proposed the incorporation of British Kaffraria in Cape Colony but with a measure of administrative devolution to meet Eastern grievances, especially the appointment of two resident judges and a Solicitor General; and he suggested that Parliament should meet alternately in Cape Town and Grahamstown.[1] The speech was favourably received by the *Grahamstown Journal*, the most influential Eastern newspaper. The first reaction in British Kaffraria, or at any rate King William's Town, was unfavourable; but Wodehouse, aware of the Treasury's determination to end the Kaffrarian vote, paid a personal visit and claimed some success in making them see the need for 'an equitable arrangement' with the Cape.[2] His efforts were in vain, however, for the Western members, wanting responsible government and fearing new military burdens would follow incorporation, killed the Incorporation Bill by a vote of 19 to 14 on 30 June. Wodehouse fell back on the idea of a federation, in due course to be extended to include Natal.[3] The Duke of Newcastle thought Wodehouse had been too hasty and regarded federation as a 'very dangerous and unsatisfactory expedient'; but Chichester Fortescue persuaded him to ask Wodehouse whether a simplified version of the New Zealand provincial system might meet the case.[4]

All these plans were being made on the assumption that the Transkei would be annexed at least as far as the Bashee. Sir George Grey had sent Currie to prepare the way with Kreli and Faku. Currie suggested to Kreli, in February 1861, that he should move from the left bank of the Bashee beyond the Umtata, 'there to be located under regulations calculated to advance himself and

---

[1] Governor's Speech (24 Apr.): *Grahamstown Journal*, 29 Apr. 1862. Newcastle had already thrown cold water on the separation proposal in receiving a deputation on the subject on 14 Nov., *Cape Frontier Times*, 21 Jan. 1862.

[2] Wodehouse to Newcastle (22 May 1862), Private Correspondence of Sir P. E. Wodehouse, 1861-9, Colonial Office Library.

[3] Wodehouse to Newcastle (17 July 1862) (No. 95), CO48/414. For the debates see *Grahamstown Journal*, 5 and 6 July 1862.

[4] Minutes of Newcastle and Fortescue (9 and 16 Sept.) on Wodehouse to Newcastle (17 July 1862), loc. cit. See also Newcastle to Wodehouse (5 Nov. 1862) (Private), Newcastle Papers, NeC10886.

his people in the scale of civilization'.[1] Kreli asked for time to talk this over with his people, though Currie suspected his real object was to rally his tribe for one more bid to regain his old country by force.[2] Drought, however, forbade any such enterprise. In February 1862 Currie saw Kreli again at the Idutywa: 'with fear and trembling he came, tendered his submission, accepted the offer made a year ago'—and Currie arranged to locate him on his way back from Faku's country.[3] But when he same back in April, the chief failed to keep his appointment. He sent a message saying 'that the country did not belong to the Government, that he was afraid to go there, and that he would prefer remaining where he was, that what he had said to me at our late meeting was from the lips only . . . what he now said was from the heart.'[4] Wodehouse of course disclaimed any desire to move him against his wish, provided he behaved himself, but warned him that his old country was forfeit. The interviews with Faku took the same course— apparent success in 1861, when the chief expressed a wish to have his boundaries limited and to relinquish the rest to the British Government, followed by a change of mind a year later on the plea that his authority over the inland territory was disputed by other tribes.[5] Wodehouse had also inherited the dispute with Natal about this territory. Currie had been instructed to meet the Surveyor-General of Natal, Dr. Sutherland, with a view to the location of Adam Kok and his people in the upland parts of Faku's territories, but their co-operation had broken down. All Wodehouse's patience was needed to unravel this tangled skein.

Sir George Grey and Wynyard after him had committed the Government to finding a home for the Griquas in this Nomans-land. They reminded successive Secretaries of State that Sir George Clerk had left the Griquas without any safeguards against the steady whittling away of their lands by unauthorized sales to Free State burghers. Merivale had imbibed (possibly from Clerk) a strong prejudice against Adam Kok, whom he regarded as 'a mere impostor and lay figure kept up by certain missionaries and

[1] Currie to Grey (29 July 1861), Annexures to V. & P., L.C., C. 39-'61, pp. 4-5.
[2] Currie to Southey (9 Nov.) in Wynyard to Newcastle (22 Nov. 1861), Cape Archives.
[3] Currie to Southey (22 Feb. 1862), Southey Papers, Cape Archives.
[4] Currie to Military Secretary (12 Apr. 1862), Annexures to V. & P., L.C., G. 53-'62, p. 20.
[5] Currie to Grey (29 July 1861), Annexures to V. & P., L.C., C. 39-'61, p. 6

others for the purpose of working on the British Government through supposed faith of treaties'.[1] Grey may have been over-colouring the picture when he said that the Griquas were 'a good, moral, Christian people and would bring a large amount of capital to their new location: they farm on European principles, not as Natives do, and live in regular villages with well-built houses, exactly like a European community.'[2] But the historian of the Cape Coloured people endorses his description of Kok as 'an intelligent and wealthy man' and we may sympathize with Grey's desire to help a chief, with whom Great Britain had a treaty, to hold his people together. He had complicated the question, however, by his tacit permission to Nehemiah Moshesh to settle with his followers in this region in 1858–9, when they were hard pressed for food. Nehemiah professed to be 'on very friendly terms' with his nearest neighbours, the Amabaca and Amapondo-misi,[3] but clashed with the Pondomisi chief Jumba in 1860 and protested strongly when he heard that he might be placed under the chieftainship of Adam Kok.[4]

But this was a minor difficulty compared with the ambitions of Natal. If Sutherland's line was accepted, Currie thought it would be impossible to find enough land south of the Quath-lamba range to locate the Griquas.[5] Wodehouse felt bound to request Scott to postpone annexing the territory ceded by Faku until the negotiations with Adam Kok had been completed;[6] and urged on Newcastle the necessity of his being 'unmistakably recognized by Her Majesty's Government as the chief authority primarily responsible for the policy of the whole of South Africa'.[7] Adam Kok had made a preliminary trek into the new country in 1859. In 1860–1 his Griquas, despite opposition in some quarters, disposed of the 500,000 acres which still remained to them

[1] Minute of Merivale (5 Mar.) on Grey to Lytton (12 Jan. 1859) (No. 5), CO48/393.
[2] Memo. of Grey (1 Aug. 1861), V. & P., Cape Parliament, 1861, Appendix I, A.–118–'61, pp. 22–4. See also Marais, *The Cape Coloured People*, pp. 56–62.
[3] Nehemiah Moshesh to Grey (3 Mar. 1859), *Basutoland Records*, ii. 517–18.
[4] Nehemiah Moshesh to Wodehouse (n.d.–1862), Annexures to V. & P., L.C., G. 53–'62, p. 16.
[5] Report of Currie (19 Mar. 1862), ibid., p. 15. The Quathlamba is an alternative name for part of the Drakensberg.
[6] Wodehouse to Scott (13 Feb. 1862), Annexures to V. & P., L.C., G. 53–'62, pp. 8–9.
[7] Wodehouse to Newcastle (19 Feb. 1862), Private Correspondence of Sir P. E. Wodehouse.

and began to move with their wagons and stock to a rendezvous at Hanglip, a mountain near the Orange River, just inside the Basuto border. There they spent most of the year 1862, unfortunately a year of intense drought, which proved fatal to many of their stock. In May Wodehouse had authorized Kok to move 'into the land bounded on the north by the Drakensberg Mountains, on the west by the Umzimvubu, on the south by the Ingela range'.[1] Nehemiah was to be left undisturbed on the west bank of the Umzimvubu and was not to be subject to Adam Kok.[2] A wagon road had to be made across the Drakensberg, but in the summer of 1862–3 the Griquas reached their promised land and Nomansland became Griqualand East. Newcastle could hardly do other than back Wodehouse, not only on the ground he had urged, but also because Natal would undoubtedly look on Adam Kok's new location with a jealous eye.[3] The southern part of the territory ceded by Faku still remained available for annexation; but Scott wanted it to be under the sole control of the Lieutenant-Governor for a time and could not guarantee that the Legislative Council would vote the necessary funds.[4]

Meanwhile legal difficulties had arisen in the Transkei. Wodehouse visited the region in 1862, conferred on the magistrate at Idutywa, W. B. Chalmers, authority to punish petty offences, and had a British Kaffrarian ordinance passed to provide for the punishment of persons sentenced in the territory between the Kei and the Bashee. Letters Patent had been issued on 13 March 1862 annexing this territory, without any formal definition of its boundaries, to British Kaffraria; but Wodehouse had not promulgated them, since annexation while British Kaffraria remained a separate colony would necessitate the removal of the Cape

---

[1] Wodehouse to Scott (15 May 1862), G. 53–'62, pp. 12–13. On the move to Griqualand East see Revd. W. B. Philip, 'The Griquas and their Exodus', *Cape Monthly Magazine*, v (December 1872), 321–37; on the opposition, *Cape Frontier Times*, 2 Mar. 1861.

[2] Wodehouse to Moshesh and Nehemiah (13 May 1862), G. 53–'62, p. 18. In 1865 Nehemiah and his people fled before a commando of Adam Kok into the Wittebergen Reserve (Cape) and then to Basutoland; Report of Burnet (10 Apr. 1865), *Basutoland Records*, iii. 345–6.

[3] Newcastle to Scott (2 Sept. 1862) (No. 249), G.H. 12, Natal Archives. The Natal Legislative Council was still objecting to the Griqua settlement in 1863: Scott to Cardwell (26 Oct. 1863) (No. 73), CO179/68.

[4] Scott to Newcastle (4 Dec. 1862) (No. 143), CO179/65. On the final annexation of the County of Alfred see below, p. 192.

Armed and Mounted Police from the Transkei.[1] The Law Officers came to the embarrassing conclusion that the Transkei now formed part of British Kaffraria but that the High Commissioner had no power to authorize magistrates to try offences.[2] On their advice, the British Kaffrarian ordinance was not confirmed. The Duke of Newcastle got Wodehouse out of his hole by two Acts empowering the Governor of the Cape to commission magistrates outside its boundaries and providing that Letters Patent relating to the colonies be not deemed to have taken effect until they were promulgated;[3] but the episode illustrated the anomalous situation of the Transkei.

Wodehouse was also in difficulties with his Parliament. The drought of 1862 brought crop failures, stock losses, commercial depression, and revenue deficiency, and of the taxation proposed in the Governor's Speech of 1863 little more than a quarter was granted.[4] The Assembly, however, rejected a motion of Molteno for responsible government and requested the Governor to summon the next session in the East. This measure of appeasement paid dividends. When the new Parliament met at Grahamstown in 1864, it approved stamp duties, a succession duty, and a duty on bank notes, raised the tariff, and authorized a new loan, though this was delayed by the state of the London money market. But financial equilibrium had been attained only by rigorous economy and at the price of some unemployment among recent immigrants and a 'large emigration' to New Zealand. The atmosphere was not propitious for the discussion of the interrelated issues of colonial defence, the Transkei, and British Kaffraria.

As early as 1860 the War Office, prompted by Godley, had proposed that 'as the force which we keep at the Cape is entirely employed in the defence of the lives and properties of the people of the Cape', the Colony should pay at least half its

[1] Wodehouse to Newcastle (18 Feb. 1863) (No. 17) (an answer to the Law Officers), CO48/417.
[2] Atherton and Roundell Palmer to Newcastle (24 Dec. 1862) in Newcastle to Wodehouse (2 Jan. 1863) (No. 573), G.H. 1/59, Cape Archives. The problem had not arisen with Chalmers's predecessors, who as military men could exercise authority under martial law.
[3] Newcastle to Wodehouse (6 July 1863) (No. 661), ibid. The Acts were 26 & 27 Vict. cc. 35 and 76 respectively.
[4] Prorogation Speech of H.E. the Governor (28 July): *Grahamstown Journal*, 4 Aug. 1863.

cost.[1] It was true that the Cape, with one twenty-ninth of the total population of the British colonies, accounted for more than a fifth of the forces stationed in the colonies and more than a quarter of colonial military expenditure;[2] but the new plan, as Newcastle and his officials saw, could never be 'abruptly and rigidly enforced'.[3] Imperial military expenditure in South Africa was of the same order of magnitude as the total Cape budget. Besides, most of the force was not in the Cape but in British Kaffraria. But in view of the trend of opinion in the House and the country, Newcastle instructed Grey to consider reductions, and economy was still the order of the day under Wodehouse. Military opinion favoured fewer posts, transference of headquarters from Grahamstown to King William's Town, and a reduction in strength of the Cape Mounted Rifles, which had lost some of its point as the frontier moved east and the Armed and Mounted Police effectively took over day-to-day defence.[4] The castle at Cape Town was to be sold to the Colony for £65,000, which was to pay for buildings at King William's Town. But the Cape Parliament would not play. As the *Grahamstown Journal* succinctly put it: 'It has not the money and, if it had, it has not the mind.'[5] The Duke of Cambridge (Commander-in-Chief) objected to any interference with the Cape Mounted Rifles,[6] but was persuaded to withdraw his objections and let an alternative defence scheme of Wodehouse's go forward. This was to settle 1,000 European farmers in the Transkei on military tenure and raise a new force of Irregular Horse of the same type as the Cape Armed and Mounted Police. The Commander of the Forces, who would be Lieutenant-Governor of British Kaffraria, would control this force.[7] The 'uncompromis-

---

[1] Lugard (War Office) to Merivale (10 Feb. 1860), CO48/406. Newcastle minuted (14 Feb.): 'It is impossible not to remark the variance between the War Office Letters of 31 December and 10 February. They are both signed by Sir E. Lugard but the latter is no doubt the production of Mr Godley'; ibid.

[2] Memo. of Elliot (28 Jan. 1860) in Report of Committee on Expense of Military Defence in the Colonies, P.P., 1860, xli (H.C. 282), 17.

[3] Minute of Newcastle (14 Feb. 1860), loc. cit. See also Minutes of Elliot (6 Feb.) and Merivale (13 Feb.), ibid.

[4] See especially Wodehouse to Newcastle (19 June 1863) (No. 70), CO48/417. Extracts printed in V. & P., Cape Parliament, Appendix I, G. 32–'65.

[5] *Grahamstown Journal*, 10 Mar. 1864.

[6] Newcastle to Wodehouse (5 Dec. 1863) (Private), Newcastle Papers, NeC10887.

[7] Wodehouse to Newcastle (19 June 1863) (No. 70), CO48/417 and (13 March 1864) (No. 23), CO48/422.

ing, comfort-loving' Sir Percy Douglas, who succeeded General Wynyard in 1863, reluctantly accepted the decision of his superiors and on 3 June 1864 Cardwell conveyed to Wodehouse Her Majesty's Government's sanction of a first instalment of the plan, by which 200 Irregular Horse would be substituted for half the Cape Corps.[1]

Wodehouse announced the plan in opening Parliament at Grahamstown on 28 April. The terms of settlement were published on 3 June. Farms, varying in extent from 1,000 to 3,000 acres, were to be held on an annual quit-rent of £1 per 100 acres: personal occupation was required for three years and settlers were to maintain and equip one able-bodied European adult for every 500 acres held. The Transkeian territory would form part of British Kaffraria. The Imperial Government would bear the cost of the Irregular Horse maintained for its defence for the first five years: afterwards the Imperial contribution would diminish.[2] 'A much vexed question has ... been answered,' said the *Grahamstown Journal*, 'and in a manner which no one can complain of.'[3]

But the plan went awry. The terms of occupation were thought too onerous, and there were only a few score applications.[4] Modifications, made later, reduced the quit-rent to 15s. and relaxed the requirement about able-bodied Europeans;[5] but these came too late. At the very time when the fate of the Transkei was in the balance, there came a report, originating with the principal detective of the police post on the Bashee, that Kreli intended to cross the river 'to-morrow' in an attempt to recover his lost land. Currie immediately left Grahamstown for the Bashee and next day the Commander of the Forces, warned by telegraph, set out with a regiment from Cape Town. The Transkeian magistrate, Chalmers, however, wrote to his superior not only expressing disbelief in this report but alleging that 'the police

[1] Douglas to Horse Guards (10 Mar. 1864) and Cardwell to Wodehouse (3 June 1864) (No. 765), V. & P., Cape Parliament, Appendix I, G. 32–'65, pp. 20–5. The epithets are from du Toit, op. cit., p. 194.

[2] *Grahamstown Journal*, 3 June 1864.

[3] Ibid., 29 Apr. 1864. This was a comment on the Governor's speech before the details of the plan were known.

[4] Only 30 by 15 July, according to the *Grahamstown Journal*. See also J. S. Dobie, *South African Journal, 1862–6* (ed. A. F. Hattersley) (Van Riebeeck Society, No. 26, Cape Town, 1945), p. 161.

[5] *Grahamstown Journal*, 26 Aug. 1864.

are playing some game which I will sift out and let you know'.[1] Maclean backed his man, Chalmers, but Currie, who had no confidence in Chalmers and little in Maclean, repeated his conviction that Kreli, who had refused to come to the frontier post to meet him, was meditating war and urged that he be forestalled and driven beyond the Umtata by a force of troops and five or six hundred burghers, 'those who are to have Farms in this Country'.[2] But if, as seems likely, Currie and the police were trying to force the Governor's hand, the result was the opposite of what they intended. Wodehouse, rightly believing that 'Her Majesty's Government would view with extreme dissatisfaction an aggressive movement on our part, if made without distinct provocation,' refused to act on Currie's advice.[3] Later, at Kreli's request, he sent Warner, the experienced Tambookie Agent, to see the chief. Kreli mustered his available strength of 1,500 men. According to a later article by Warner, 'he said that *I* knew *he* would do *me* no harm, but *he* was not quite sure that I might not have a Commando at my heels to capture him'. He claimed to have sent word to Currie by the trader Crouch 'that he had no other message than the one he had been constantly sending ever since he was driven into the "Bush", namely "begging the Government to have mercy upon him, and give him back a small portion of the country he formerly occupied, as it was impossible for him to subsist where he was"'.[4] He convinced Warner of his friendly intentions and Warner convinced the Governor. Mastering the prejudice he had inherited from Grey or imbibed from Currie, Wodehouse sent Kreli a message through Warner that he would be taken back into favour, allowed to reoccupy part of the territory from which he had been expelled in 1858, and paid an allowance of £100 a

[1] Chalmers to Brownlow (26 May 1864), Southey Papers: quoted by du Toit, *The Cape Frontier*, p. 183.

[2] Currie to Wodehouse (4 June) in Wodehouse to Newcastle (11 June 1864) (No. 37), CO48/422.

[3] Wodehouse to Newcastle (11 June 1864) (No. 37), loc. cit. In a letter to Southey (12 June), quoted by du Toit, op. cit., p. 188, Currie says: 'The statement made by [Sub-Inspector] Wylde *was not on Oath* and between you and me Wylde behaved very well, for what he told Chalmers was not the T-th but a L-e, he was obliged to deceive, otherwise expose all my detectives.'

[4] J. C. Warner, 'Five Years Sojourn in the Transkei', *Grahamstown Journal*, 13 June 1870. Warner, an 1820 settler who had become a Wesleyan missionary, replaced Chalmers, in whom Wodehouse had lost confidence since his reports had leaked to the *King William's Town Gazette*; Wodehouse to Cardwell (19 Dec. 1864) (No. 135), CO48/424.

year. His country would remain outside British territory but Warner as British Agent would exercise some supervision over him.[1]

The war scare also had a profound effect on Cardwell, especially when considered with the objections of Sir Percy Douglas to any reduction of his force if he was to be expected to defend the remote frontier of the Bashee. Was it really necessary or desirable to proceed with the occupation of the Transkei? If a change of policy was consistent with engagements towards intending settlers and would not have a bad effect on Kreli, Wodehouse was authorized to withdraw the frontier behind the Kei.[2] In a private letter Cardwell was much more outspoken. He had brought the subject before the Cabinet, whose only object was 'to obtain a safe and tranquil frontier: . . . we explicitly disavow all desire for extension of territory in Kaffraria'. It was bad enough to have to persuade the House to guarantee a New Zealand loan.

A proposal to extend our frontier to the Bashee, coupled with Sir W. Currie's suggestions of going to the Umtata and your just criticism on those suggestions that the same reasons would hereafter justify any other extension,—I say this proposal coupled with a new vote for a police force for the territory so occupied would have been as unacceptable a proposal as it would have been possible for any Minister to make.[3]

Wodehouse was prepared for Cardwell's decision. He had told a friend in the War Office, who was to show the letter to Lord de Grey and Cardwell, that he did not want Douglas's army on the Bashee: 'rather than do this, I would make arrangements . . . for abandoning the idea of occupying the Transkeian Territory and allowing it to fall back into Native occupation.' If the Home Government were not satisfied with his present policy, let them say so and he would do his best to extricate them from the entanglement.[4] He was quick to adapt his frontier measures to the

[1] Wodehouse to Cardwell (14 Aug. 1864) (No. 79), P.P., 1865, xxxvii [3436], 13–14.
[2] Cardwell to Wodehouse (5 Aug. 1864) (No. 784), P.P., 1865, xxxvii [3436], 23–4.
[3] Cardwell to Wodehouse (4 Aug. 1864), Private Correspondence of Sir P. E. Wodehouse, 1861–9. The Times reported the war scare on 20 July and on 22 and 25 July E. Warner, Arthur Mills, and Lord R. Cecil asked questions in the House: Hansard, 3rd Ser. clxxvi. 1905, 2018–19.
[4] Wodehouse to Talbot (15 June 1864), quoted by du Toit, op. cit., p. 189. Du Toit gives the fullest account in print of these transactions.

change of policy. It would not do to leave the Transkei empty, nor should the whole of it be restored to Kreli, 'from whom it was taken as a punishment for his persevering hostility to us'. He asked permission accordingly 'to authorize as many of the chiefs of British Kaffraria as desire it to proceed with their followers over the Kei and to establish themselves beyond our actual rule, but under the general supervision of Mr. Warner'. They would have more land and some of their present allowances, which might be an inducement to keep on friendly terms with the Government and restrain their followers from depredations on colonial farmers. Those who preferred to stay in the Ciskei would presumably be individuals with some property who could be brought under the ordinary law.[1] Cardwell accepted this plan, hinting a doubt 'whether any danger is to be apprehended in locating those chiefs in closer contiguity with their paramount chief Kreli' but deferring to Wodehouse's judgement and local knowledge.[2]

Even now Wodehouse met with some setbacks. He proposed that Sandile, Anta, and Oba should be invited at once to move with all the Gaika tribe to a location across the Kei.[3] At a great meeting on 16 March Brownlee, the Gaika Commissioner, addressed the tribe, pointing out that the chiefs and headmen would still get their Government money, that the tribesmen would be relieved of hut tax, that Sandile would not be interfered with but would be able to do as he liked. He himself would be Resident with Kreli. Sandile at once protested: 'what had he sinned that Charles [Brownlee] should be taken from him?' Towards sunset, after consulting his chiefs and councillors, he gave his final answer:

I do not know the land beyond the Kei. I have not grown up there. When we separated from our common ancestors, we came here with the game as hunters, and since that time we never returned back to that country. We like to die here. We do not care if the land beyond the Kei is large or small, we are satisfied with the land in which we live, though it is sour. . . . I am satisfied with my Chieftainship I have here, and if it is small I do not care so long as I am taken care of by the

---

[1] Wodehouse to Cardwell (3 Oct. 1864) (No. 106), P.P., 1865, xxxvii [3436], 18–20.

[2] Cardwell to Wodehouse (9 Jan. 1865) (No. 826), ibid., pp. 27–8.

[3] Wodehouse to Graham (21 Feb. 1865), V. & P., Cape Parliament, 1865, Appendix I, G. 32–'65, p. 39.

English Government. But the chief reason for not going over is, that many of my people will not go with me, and those that are going will join Kreli, and I will be there a common Kafir.[1]

Warner was only partially successful with the Abatembu. He held no tribal meeting. The paramount chief, Gangelizwe, who lived on the upper Bashee, supported him; but the old regent Nonesi, a formidable character, opposed any move, first secretly and then openly, and was joined by Fadana, inopportunely released from Robben Island. Warner still thought that if the chiefs were kept to their bargain and not hurried too much, the move would be made. But Southey (now Colonial Secretary) told him it was to be a matter for individual choice, not collective decision.

I must plainly tell you [replied Warner] that the moment I let them know that none will be forced to go, but that those who remain will have to submit to Colonial law etc., the whole of these thirty thousand Kaffirs will probably say they will remain where they are. . . . The Tambookies have now been upwards of sixteen years nominally within the Colonial Boundary, but what do they know of the restraints of Colonial law?[2]

Four leading chiefs, with their followers, moved over the Indwe to join the main body of the tribe. Next year 'two or three kraals almost daily' were still crossing the river.[3] In 1868 Nonesi, stripped now of her authority as regent, herself crossed. But enough remained to keep Glen Grey, the Queenstown location, still a Tembu reserve.

It was the Fingoes who saved Wodehouse's Transkeian settlement. Their locations were admittedly overcrowded and Currie, swallowing the disappointment he felt when he was ordered back from the Bashee and his plans were shelved, threw himself into the task of moving them into the vacant territory before Kreli could occupy it. He did not get the full co-operation of some of

[1] *Grahamstown Journal*, 22 Mar. 1865.—From *King William's Town Gazette*. There is some mystery about Brownlee: Wodehouse had hoped he would go with the Gaikas and would also be acceptable to Kreli.

[2] Warner to Southey (4 and 12 May 1865), Southey Papers, Cape Archives. See also *Reminiscences of Sir Walter Stanford* (ed. J. W. Macquarrie), vol. i (Van Riebeeck Society, No. 39, Cape Town, 1958), esp. pp. 24–5.

[3] Report of Warner (16 Mar. 1866), V. & P., Cape Parliament, 1867, Appendix I, A. 14–'67.

the magistrates. One chief alleged that Currie had promised them Government protection and choice of their own magistrate, which he denied.[1] Wodehouse gave a clear ruling on some doubtful points.

First, the Fingoes will continue British subjects, and receive support and assistance so long as they prove themselves deserving. Second, they will not be required to pay hut tax. Third, certificates of citizenship are of no value beyond the Colony, but arrangements will be made to enable them to visit their friends. Fourth, a British officer will live with them to administer justice, and it will be their duty to support him. Fifth, being in arrear with hut tax should not hinder removal.[2]

About 40,000 Fingoes made the move. 'So far as they are concerned,' wrote Southey some years later, 'the move has been a great success.'[3] In Wodehouse's mind the Transkeian settlement was only a second best. He knew it would be unpopular in the Colony because it had been made 'in utter disregard of colonial views and of colonial hopes'.[4] To the Colony it seemed a step backward: British sovereignty had been relinquished and the tribes were to be ruled by their own chiefs and according to their own customs. The primary purpose was to secure the frontier: Wodehouse hoped that 'sufficient precautions have been taken against any future coalition of the Native Tribes in opposition to British power'.[5] So far as sovereignty was concerned, the retreat was temporary. Kreli, by an attack on the Fingoes, precipitated a new war in 1877; and this brought to a head the pressure that had been building up for annexation of the Transkei to the Cape. Fingoland, the Idutywa reserve, and Griqualand East were annexed by Act No. 38 of 1877, which was not, however, proclaimed until 1 October 1879. The Imperial Government delayed its sanction of other annexations pending the preparation of a code of law. This was done by the Cape Native Laws and Customs

[1] Currie to Southey (28 July 1865), V. & P., Cape Parliament, 1867, Appendix I, A.–14'67, p. 5.
[2] Wodehouse to Civil Commissioner, Grahamstown (25 July 1865) (telegram), ibid., p. 6.
[3] Southey to Grey (7 Oct. 1872), Grey Coll., Auckland.
[4] *Grahamstown Journal*, 24 Mar. 1865. The reference is to the offer to Sandile, but could be applied generally, except to the Fingo settlement.
[5] Wodehouse to Cardwell (11 Oct. 1865) (No. 99), CO48/428.

Commission of 1881–3 and Tembuland, Galekaland, and Bom-vanaland were annexed by Act No. 3 of 1885.[1] It still remained to annex Pondoland, the last independent chiefdom, ceded by the chiefs in March 1894. But in the main, the Transkei was left to the Xhosa tribes—a decision which proved to be better grounded than many in South African history. For once the Imperial Government had intervened in South Africa to good purpose.

With the miscarriage of Wodehouse's plan to incorporate the Transkei in British Kaffraria, his hopes of making that colony self-supporting fell to the ground. The idealistic impulse which had led the Imperial Government to sanction the parliamentary vote in 1855 had exhausted itself. The vote was now seen as 'in reality an Imperial contribution to the ordinary expenses of the Crown Colony of British Kaffraria'. The Cape Parliament had naturally refused to 'forgo the advantage which we had given them in placing the bulk of the troops for their protection against the Kaffirs within the limits of another Colony and thus making it impossible, or at all events very difficult, to call upon them for a military contribution'.[2] Now, however, the Cape Parliament forced Wodehouse's hand by resolutions in favour of a redistribution of electoral divisions on the basis of a census to be held in 1865. Such a redistribution would make the annexation of Kaffraria more difficult, as upsetting the new balance between East and West. Wodehouse did not feel strong enough to act himself, but urged that an Imperial Act be passed. The 'noisy agitation' in British Kaffraria would then come to an end and the Cape Parliament would apply itself to bringing British Kaffraria into the representative system.[3] Fortescue, admitting the awkwardness of forcing a union upon two colonies which did not want to be united, thought the Governor's recommendation should be accepted: British Kaffraria 'was created for the purpose of enabling the Imperial Government to fulfil more efficiently the duty which it had undertaken of protecting the frontiers of the Cape Colony, and the Imperial Government may fairly decide

[1] See W. B. Campbell, 'The South African Frontier, 1865–1885', *Archives Year Book for South African History*, xxii, vol. i (Cape Town, 1959); *Reminiscences of Sir Walter Stanford.*

[2] Minute of Chichester Fortescue (2 May) on Wodehouse to Newcastle (13 Mar. 1864) (No. 23), CO48/422.

[3] Wodehouse to Cardwell (13 July 1864) (No. 50), P.P., 1865, xxxvii [3436], 8. The census was the first held in Cape Colony.

how long the arrangement is to last'.[1] Cardwell was more guarded. Would it not be necessary to specify how many seats should be assigned to each part of the united colony? What about compensation for loss of office? Might not Kaffrarians complain of loss of land revenue or increased taxes?[2] Privately he added, 'the argument against it . . . will be the example of New Zealand and the difficulty into which the Imperial Government may be thrown by having a territory, in which Native difficulties are likely to arise, subject in any degree to the authority of the Cape Parliament'.[3] Wodehouse met this last point squarely:

> It has occurred to me that Her Majesty's Government, with the recent occurrences in New Zealand fully present to their minds, may view with apprehension a proposal to bring the Natives of British Kaffraria within the limits of a Parliamentary Government. They may shrink on the one hand from conferring political privileges on the Kaffirs, or on the other from rendering them subject to such a Colonial Legislature. No doubt there are serious objections, but perhaps the proper time for considering them has long since gone by. They existed in all their force when Parliamentary Government was first established here; and I cannot imagine that those who were then instrumental in effecting so great a change could for an instant have contemplated the separate existence of this little spot of British Kaffraria. We have now been dealing for several years with the large masses of Fingoes and Tambookies within the Colony, and I really do not see any reason to believe that we may not be equally successful with the Kaffirs, more particularly if you should approve of my proposal to encourage a large number of them to migrate over the Kei.

He reminded the Secretary of State that there was no responsible government at the Cape and that its advocates had lost support in recent years. The other difficulties in the way of annexation he made light of.[4]

The dispatch confirmed a decision the Imperial Government had virtually taken already. It would introduce into Parliament

[1] Minute of Fortescue (31 Aug.) on Wodehouse to Cardwell (13 July 1864) (No. 50), 48/423.

[2] Cardwell to Wodehouse (5 Oct. 1864) (Separate and Confidential), P.P., 1865, xxxvii [3436], 26. These questions are also raised in a preliminary way in the private letter of 3 Sept. cited below.

[3] Cardwell to Wodehouse (3 Sept. 1864), Private Correspondence of Sir P. E. Wodehouse, 1861–9.

[4] Wodehouse to Cardwell (14 Dec. 1864) (Separate and Confidential), CO48/424. The passage quoted was omitted from Command Paper 3436.

a Bill enabling the Queen by Order in Council to annex British
Kaffraria to the Cape Colony; but the Governor was to attempt
to obtain the concurrence of the Cape Parliament to the incorporation on terms 'to which, as the Representative of the Crown,
you will be able to assent on the part of British Kaffraria'.[1] The
Bill, giving the Governor power to proclaim the Act but also
empowering the Cape Parliament to incorporate British Kaffraria
by local legislation, was duly introduced and passed into law with
hardly any discussion on 27 March.[2]

This Imperial action was fiercely denounced in the Cape,
especially in the Western press. The King William's Town
papers, on the other hand, were 'significantly silent': opinion
there had been more divided than the newspapers had allowed.[3]
The Cape Parliament did not mince words. Solomon, member
for Cape Town, introduced resolutions which, even when toned
down by amendments moved by Rutherfoord, one of the members
for Graaff Reinet, denounced the Imperial Act as an 'arbitrary
interference with our rights as British subjects', which had been
passed 'without our having had any opportunity of making ourselves heard', and disclaimed any responsibility for it or for any
larger share of the expense of frontier defence. The House of
Assembly resolutions also expressed the opinion that Sir Philip
Wodehouse's policy 'in reference to the Annexation and Native
Questions generally' was 'calculated to deprive him of that degree
of the confidence of the House and of the country which is so
essential to the proper conduct of affairs in a Colony in which
Representative Institutions have been established'.[4] But Attorney-
General Porter, in the course of the debates, made some telling
points in defence of the Governor's policy.

British Kaffraria [he said] was created for the purposes of this

[1] Cardwell to Wodehouse (9 Jan. 1865) (No. 826), P.P., 1865, xxxvii [3436], 27.
[2] The British Kaffraria Act was 28 & 29 Vict. c. 5. Arthur Mills (who in 1864
had presented an anti-annexation petition from British Kaffraria) asked Cardwell
'whether, if the Imperial Government took upon itself . . . to unite these two districts against their will, he thought he would have a good ground for appealing
to the Cape Government hereafter to protect its frontier in the event of any
disturbances': *Hansard*, 3rd Ser. clxxvii. 1093.
[3] The phrase quoted is from the *Grahamstown Journal*, 14 Apr. 1865. A farmers'
deputation headed by the future Cape Premier Gordon Sprigg had waited on
Wodehouse the previous September urging annexation as 'the only measure
which can save Kaffraria from bankruptcy and ruin': ibid., 28 Sept. 1864.
[4] V. & P., Cape Parliament, 1865, House of Assembly, 22 and 23 May.

colony; it was kept up for the purpose of the colony; it was really, though not in theory, part of the colony and an unrepresented part of the colony; and it being clear that the smaller body would naturally gravitate towards the larger, the period of absorption became closer every day. . . . Is the colony of the Cape of Good Hope a self-defending colony of the British Crown? Alas! Sir, it is not. If it were so, I could well excuse that we should look big and talk big and wear our shoulders high. . . . On the contrary, of all the colonies of the British Crown . . . not one single colony costs the mother country, in time of peace, anything like the amount cost by the Cape of Good Hope. . . . I want to know upon what constitutional principle—by what principle of right or reason—it can be urged that the Imperial Government is not entitled to have a voice potential in reference to incorporation.[1]

The Governor defended himself with dignity in his Prorogation Speech some months later:

When I considered the many demands I had been compelled to make on the confidence of both Houses, and the many important measures which at the suggestion of the Government had become law, I was bound to recognize the value of the support that had been given, and should not on slight grounds have put in jeopardy its continuance. But there may be occasions on which the Governor of these Colonies, entrusted with large executive powers, and bound with regard, not only to their interests but also to those of the great Empire to which they are attached, cannot avoid exposing himself to the expression of Parliamentary dissatisfaction.[2]

By this time, after fierce parliamentary battles, obstructionist tactics, all-night sittings, and frequent calls of the House, the Annexation Bill and the Increase of Representation Bill, fused into one for fear that the first might pass without the second, which recognized the principle of equal representation of West and East, were finally passed without substantial change. Sir Philip Wodehouse might well feel that his policy had been justified by the event. The first election at King William's Town was turned into a protest against annexation;[3] but opinion was soon reconciled to the *fait accompli*.

[1] House of Assembly, 23 May: *Grahamstown Journal*, 2 June 1865. Porter on 15 May had foreshadowed his approaching resignation partly on the score of his age but partly on the score of his 'views respecting the position of the Executive Council': G.H. 28/83, Cape Archives.

[2] Prorogation Speech of H.E. the Governor, 10 Oct., V. & P., Cape Parliament, 1865.

[3] *Grahamstown Journal*, 3, 6, 9, and 13 Apr. 1866.

The incorporation of British Kaffraria in the Cape marked the end of any idea of confining the Cape Colony to Dutch burghers, English settlers, and their Cape Coloured servants, all under colonial (i.e. Roman–Dutch) law. The need of the expanding East for farm servants, the influx of Fingo refugees, the presence of the Tambookies in the north-east had weakened the principle. The aftermath of the cattle-killing made nonsense of it. But policies associated with this idea, in particular the pass laws, died hard. Frontier opinion was restive when refugees from the cattle-killing, after five years' service, became entitled (under Act No. 27 of 1857) to 'certificates of citizenship' like the Fingoes. The pre-vailing dearth increased the temptations to theft of cattle and sheep.[1] The Cape Parliament in 1864 passed Acts for the repression of stock thefts and for tightening up the issue of certificates of citizenship. Next year Wodehouse made a bid to liberalize the pass system:

It seems to be impossible in a country where public functionaries, employers and employed, are scattered over such vast tracts—where the employers are dependent on the native foreigners, not only for agricultural labour, but also for domestic service, to carry out such restrictions. The principle of the pass rules is restriction of intercourse. The desire of the farmer is to obtain labourers when needed and to discharge them when no longer required, without restriction.

Was it not time the Colony 'cast off rules so calculated to estrange all classes from each other'?[2] Wodehouse also thought it time the Colony came to terms with Xhosa custom in matters of marriage and inheritance. He saw the custom of *Ukulobola*, by which a 'bride-price' was paid in cattle by the bridegroom's father to the parents of the bride, as simply one example of the fact that 'at all times and by all Races the disposal of females in marriage has formed the groundwork of pecuniary arrangements'. He withdrew a circular issued by Maclean, at the instance of the missionaries, forbidding British Kaffrarian magistrates to entertain pleas for the recovery of cattle from parents of deserting wives.[3] The Duke of Newcastle saw

[1] *Grahamstown Journal*, Feb.–Apr. 1863, *passim*; Circular to Magistrates (9 Mar. 1863), V. & P., Cape Parliament, 1863, Appendix I, A47–'63.
[2] Governor's Speech (27 Apr.), V. & P., Cape Parliament, 1865. Act No. 22 of 1867 abolished passes, substituting provisions against vagrancy.
[3] Wodehouse to Newcastle (12 Sept. 1862) (No. 152), CO48/414.

'nothing immoral in the practice' and supported him. Interference would not be only 'highly impolitic if not dangerous' but
contrary to the Royal Instructions.[1] Wodehouse also tried to
relieve Fingoes owning property from disabilities arising because
the civil law did not recognize marriages by tribal custom as valid
or their issue as legitimate.[2] The Native Affairs Commission of
1865 declared that this Act had 'met with almost universal disapproval'; but few would now question its wisdom. On the other
hand, the Commission was in advance of the Government in
urging the creation of a Native Department under a Secretary for
Native Affairs in view of the rapid increase of the Native population, the need for attention to their wants and circumstances and
for 'uniform action in their superintendence'.[3] No such department was created, partly for economical reasons but partly
because Southey, the Colonial Secretary, claimed to be *au fait* with
Native affairs.

Straitened finance was the main theme of the Governor's
speech in 1866. When a Select Committee recommended large
reductions in establishments, he raised the question 'whether the
time has arrived for introducing a system of Government dependent on the support of a majority in Parliament, by means of which
all the colonial establishments and arrangements could be brought
into a condition acceptable to the colonial representatives'.[4] The
hint was not taken and next year Wodehouse turned the tables by
suggesting that a bicameral Parliament was an unnecessary burden.
One House of eighteen members elected by six electoral circles,
along with three officers of Government, could do the work.[5]
This time Molteno moved that responsible government was now
'both expedient and desirable', but he was once again defeated,
by 29 to 22.[6]

The time was not propitious for Lord Carnarvon to raise the

---

[1] Newcastle to Wodehouse (11 Nov. 1862) (No. 563) (draft), CO48/414.
[2] Wodehouse to Cardwell (13 Dec. 1864) (No. 131), CO48/424. A similar
ordinance (No. 10 of 1864) was passed for British Kaffraria. The Cape law, however, proved inoperative and another measure in 1868 was rejected.
[3] V. & P., Cape Parliament, 1865, Appendix 2, vol. i, p. xxvi.
[4] Message No. 38 (15 Nov.), V. & P., Cape Parliament, 1866, Appendix 2,
A. 3-'66.
[5] Governor's Speech (13 Apr. 1867), P.P., 1870, xlix (H.C. 181), pp. 8–13
See also Wodehouse to Carnarvon (19 Jan. 1867) (No. 6), CO48/436.
[6] House of Assembly, 28 May, *Grahamstown Journal*, 5 June 1867.

question whether the maintenance of over 4,000 troops at the Cape 'for objects which may be said to be on the whole more or as much Colonial as Imperial' was not 'open to great objection if not indefensible'.[1] He proposed gradual reduction and increasing payment. The five battalions would be reduced to four, one being divided between St. Helena and Natal. In 1868 two battalions would be furnished without cost, £40 per man being payable for the third; in 1869 all but one battalion would be chargeable. Payment at the Australian rate of £40 per infantryman and £70 per artilleryman would then continue until 1872, when the arrangement would be reviewed.[2] Wodehouse thought the time ripe for some reduction but did not like the financial arrangement and pointed out the difficulties which would arise in the event of responsible government.[3] The Eastern majority in the House of Assembly was critical and urged that the Colony was a special case. The Legislative Council argued that the frontier was an Imperial one: the 1820 settlers were placed there for Imperial purposes. The Council's final point cut deeper. It considered it to be Britain's duty to aid in civilizing the Native tribes: it was 'essential to the national honour that an impartial and efficient check should be interposed to that wild justice which ever accompanies the unrestrained avengement of private wrongs'.[4] Wodehouse agreed with the Council.

To me it appears inconsistent with sound policy, and opposed to a judicious administration of affairs, that in a colony inhabited by antagonistic races—where the whole political power is concentrated in the hands of one of them—where the war of races is familiar to the minds of all. . . the amount of military force, the sufficiency of military protection, should be made dependent on a pecuniary bargain between the white race in the colony and the mother country . . . by which that protection and force must be provided.

The Cape was no more ready for responsible government than in 1854; but the Governor could not hold the balance between the races without troops. 'Her Majesty's Government must either

---

[1] Carnarvon to Wodehouse (26 Nov. 1866), Private Correspondence of Sir P. E. Wodehouse.
[2] Carnarvon to Wodehouse (26 Jan. 1867) (No. 39), P.P., 1870, xlix (H.C. 181), 1-2.
[3] Wodehouse to Carnarvon (17 Jan. 1867), Private Correspondence of Sir P. E. Wodehouse.
[4] V. & P., L.C., 11 July 1867, P.P., 1870, xlix (H.C. 181), 7.

avoid diminution of the power of the Governor and keep
sufficient troops or force the colony to set up responsible government and withdraw them'. He urged the retention of a moderate
garrison even though the Colony was unable to pay the desired
contribution.[1] A short debate in the House of Commons showed
that the Cape had scant sympathy there;[2] but Wodehouse's
arguments impressed Elliot; and the Duke of Buckingham, now
Secretary of State, found another argument against withdrawal.
'Imperial purposes require that such a force be maintained as will
secure the permanent holding against foreign enemies of the
anchorage and naval station,' but this would be of little use to the
colonists and they could not fairly be asked to pay. The true basis
of contribution would be one which left the Imperial Government
free to control the location and employment of the troops.[3] He
sent a conciliatory dispatch which, without abandoning Carnarvon's general principles, alluded to the financial difficulties of
the Cape and trusted the Legislature's efforts to retrieve its finances
would enable the Colony to contribute its fair proportion towards
the expenses of the Imperial garrison.[4]

The first half of Sir Philip Wodehouse's term had been dominated by the problems of Kaffraria: the second half was dominated
by the Basuto question. We must now go back to 1860, when
Marthinus Pretorius was elected by an overwhelming majority
as President of the Orange Free State. This did not unite the two
Republics, for the Transvaal Volksraad, declaring that no one
could be President of both at once, forced him to choose. He
thereupon resigned the Presidency of the Transvaal. These political
changes affected Cape Colony only indirectly, but the Free State's
relations with the Basuto could not be ignored. As President of the
Free State, Pretorius signed, on 4 May 1860, a treaty with
Moshesh providing for the establishment of a joint court on cattle-
thefts and other issues between the two 'nations', to be aided by

[1] Wodehouse to Buckingham (16 July 1867) (No. 64), P.P., 1870, xlix (H.C.
181), 3–6.
[2] House of Commons, 4 June 1867, Hansard, 3rd Ser., clxxxvii. 1596–1603.
P. Vanderbyl, Liberal M.P. for Bridgewater, moved an Address asking that Her
Majesty's forces be not withdrawn from the Cape. Receiving no support, he
withdrew his motion.
[3] Minutes of Elliot (7 Sept.) and Buckingham (28 Oct.) on Wodehouse to
Buckingham (16 July 1867), CO48/437.
[4] Buckingham to Wodehouse (9 Dec. 1867) (No. 79), P.P., 1870, xlix (H.C.
181), 13–14.

border police.[1] But this remained virtually a dead letter, despite further meetings. There was constant friction on the border, especially between Moshesh's brother Poshuli and Jan Letelle, a Free State protégé. Moshesh was reported from more than one quarter to be anxious for British protection. Just before his departure for New Zealand, Sir George Grey sent J. M. Orpen on a special mission 'carefully to listen to his wishes, and after a conference with him which must from his manners and habits be a long one, to take down in detail his requests, in order that they may be thoroughly understood and then sent on to the Home Government'.[2] The outcome of Orpen's visit was a formal request by Moshesh, in December, to become a British subject. He feared another attack.

> Can the Queen suffer Her children to be attacked again with their hands bound, while those who attack are furnished with cannon and guns and ammunition by Her Government? . . . I still trust in Her justice and humanity, therefore I now ask to be recognized as Her subject, and that my subjects the Basutos may, on account of and through my chieftainship, be Her subjects too.

He did not wish to involve the Government in wars: he only wanted security and some guarantee 'that the land of the Basuto should continue to be recognized as mine, as it remains at present'.[3]

This request, along with news of a raid by Letelle on Poshuli and a projected counter-raid, faced Wodehouse on his arrival in South Africa. He found it hard to believe that Moshesh, or his tribe, realized the full implications of his request, such as the assumption by the British Government of responsibility for his administration, or at any rate for his relations with other States.[4] With the backing of his Executive Council, he favoured a less decisive course. He warned President Pretorius (with Letelle's raids in mind) that if war arose from malpractices of tribes within the Free State and subject to its laws, Her Majesty's Government would 'feel bound . . . to set aside existing treaties and enter upon new arrangements for the preservation of the peace of the country'. He also told him he was sending Burnet and Orpen to

[1] Treaty between the O.F.S. and the Chief Moshesh (4 May 1860) (in Dutch), *Basutoland Records*, ii. 555–6.
[2] Grey to Newcastle (14 Aug. 1861) (No. 121), P.P., 1868–9, xliii [4140], 1.
[3] Moshesh to Wodehouse (6 Dec. 1861), ibid., pp. 3–6.
[4] Minute of Wodehouse (23 Jan. 1862) (Extract), ibid., p. 7. In full in *Basutoland Records*, iii. 126.

ascertain by personal conference whether his relations with the
Cape Government could be placed on a more satisfactory footing.[1]
Pretorius was somewhat resentful that the Governor had 'adopted
so threatening a tone . . . before becoming acquainted with both
sides of the question'. Letelle's forays were reprisals on Poshuli.
A Commission had found British subjects as well as burghers
implicated in a trade in stolen stock and arms and ammunition.
He requested, finally, 'that Your Excellency will not finally enter
into any arrangements with the Chief Moshesh before allowing
me an opportunity of expressing my opinion on the terms of such
agreement and offering suggestions therein.'[1]

Meanwhile Burnet and Orpen were laboriously conducting
their negotiations with Moshesh. The old chief reiterated his
desire to be 'taken care of by the Government of the Queen as all
people are taken care of by it'.

What I desire is this, that the Queen should send a man to live with
me, who will be her ear and eye, and also her hand to work with
me in political matters. He will practise the Basutos and gradually
teach them to hear Magistrates, while he is helping me in political
matters. He will show them how these things are done in the Colony.

He wished to govern the people 'by our own laws', but if the
Queen wished to introduce other laws, he would be willing,
provided they were submitted to and accepted by the council of
the Basuto.[3] It is difficult to see how the chief could have gone
further in accepting the implications of British sovereignty; and
Burnet and Orpen reported that, so far as they could ascertain,
'the most influential of Moshesh's sons and chiefs, and the great
majority of his people, coincide with him in these views and
wishes'.[4] But the Duke of Newcastle, in approving the instructions to Burnet and Orpen, warned Wodehouse to 'avoid committing Her Majesty's Government in any way' and Wodehouse
had anticipated this caution. He confined himself to suggesting
that a judiciously selected Agent be stationed with Moshesh.[5]

---

[1] Wodehouse to Pretorius (27 Jan. 1862), *Basutoland Records*, iii. 129.
[2] Pretorius to Wodehouse (17 Feb. 1862), ibid., pp. 135-6.
[3] Minutes of Conference between Moshesh and Burnet and Orpen (11-21
Feb. 1862), ibid., pp. 141-8.
[4] Report of Burnet and Orpen (22 Feb. 1862), ibid., p. 151.
[5] Newcastle to Wodehouse (5 Apr. 1862) (No. 451) and Wodehouse to Newcastle (19 Apr. 1862) (No. 53), ibid., pp. 161-3. An extract from the former
dispatch is printed in P.P., 1868-9, xliii [4140], 83.

This was approved at home, even though Newcastle mistakenly thought that 'the access to our Market for Arms and Ammunition seems to be his only motive, and this we certainly cannot give him'.[1] But no appointment was made. The President and State Secretary confidentially informed Wodehouse that 'the probability of such a step being taken . . . has caused much anxiety in the Free State'.[2] An Agent in Basutoland who antagonized the Free State might do more harm than good. Wodehouse held his hand.

Yet the Free State itself could not avoid drawing the British Government into Basuto affairs. Pretorius and a representative of Moshesh had beaconed off a boundary between Jammerberg Drift on the Orange River and the sources of the Modder in April 1861, but the northern boundary gave trouble and, at the very time when they were taking exception to the appointment of an Agent, the Free State Government asked the High Commissioner to appoint a Commission 'for the purpose of pointing out to the Chief Moshesh the Winburg and Harrismith boundary line as defined by Sir Harry Smith during British supremacy'.[3] Wodehouse asked for Moshesh's assent but did not get it: he insisted on direct negotiation with the Free State Government in the first instance. But when the Free State appointed a Commissioner in November 1862 Moshesh alleged that the Basuto were too busy with their gardens to attend. A reappointment of the Commission in the following February led to meetings, but no agreement. Meanwhile the Basuto were peacefully encroaching on farms claimed by the Free State and gradually squeezing the farmers out.[4] Pretorius resigned the Presidency in April 1863 and went back to the Transvaal. A memorial was circulated in Dutch (eventually with 1,550 signatures) suggesting a return to British sovereignty. The Volksraad and the Dutch language should be retained, 'but instead of a state President let a Lieutenant-Governor be appointed by the Queen'.[5] Wodehouse took this sufficiently seriously to ask for instructions and, though he saw difficulties in

[1] Newcastle to Wodehouse (4 June 1862) (Private), Newcastle Papers, NeC 10886. Rogers to Wodehouse (5 June 1862), *Basutoland Records*, iii. 169.

[2] Wodehouse to Newcastle (19 July 1862), ibid., p. 175.

[3] Pretorius and Allison to Wodehouse (17 July 1862), ibid. p. 174.

[4] *Basutoland Records*, vol. iii, *passim* (esp. Gordon to Landdrost of Winburg, 31 May 1863, p. 210).

[5] *Grahamstown Journal*, 22 May 1863.

fitting it into the British structure of government, admitted that 'it is probable that the greater security would be given by the State being again brought under our control'.[1] Newcastle, however, was discouraging. Wodehouse must 'take care not to commit the Home Government to any approval of reannexation'.

I am unwilling without knowing more of the reasons which induce both the State and the Cape Colony to wish it to say positively that nothing would induce me to consent, but at present I see no reason whatever to change the views which induced me to cause the separation in 1854 and to adhere to that policy in 1859.[1]

In any case the Volksraad rejected the memorial when it came before it. But this did not deter the Acting President, J. J. Venter, from again soliciting the High Commissioner's intervention in the vexed question of the boundary.[3] He did not accept at the time, perhaps because of the political uncertainty in the Free State; but when the new President, elected in November, J. H. Brand, a well-known member of the Cape Parliament, renewed the invitation in the New Year, he was forthcoming. He stipulated, however, that the Free State Government should consent, provided Moshesh did the same, to such modifications of the 1858 boundary as he might consider 'just and reasonable and calculated to ensure the maintenance of peaceful relations';[4] and it was not until 4 May that the Volksraad, in special session, unanimously accepted these terms and not until October that he was free enough of Transkei problems to come up and mark the boundary in person.[5]

President Brand expressed the admiration of all at 'seeing your Excellency in the saddle from early morn until late in the evening and outstripping all in ascending the high peaks of Wodehouse Kop, Sikonyela's Head, Langeberg and other mountains'.[6] Broadly speaking, Wodehouse's award followed the Warden line of 1849, but it involved the displacement of many Basuto who were now squatting on Free State farms. 'The decision', he

[1] Wodehouse to Newcastle (20 June 1863), Private Correspondence of Sir P. E. Wodehouse.

[2] Newcastle to Wodehouse (3 Aug. 1863) (Private), ibid.

[3] Ventor to Wodehouse (7 Aug. 1863), *Basutoland Records*, iii. 229.

[4] Wodehouse to Brand (26 Feb. 1864), ibid., pp. 258–9.

[5] *Basutoland Records*, iii. 280. Wodehouse informed Brand on 16 May that he hoped to reach the disputed territory by the end of October.

Brand to Wodehouse (4 Nov. 1864), ibid., p. 310.

wrote to Cardwell, 'is no doubt favourable to the Free State, but I am convinced not unduly so.'[1] He told Moshesh he was satisfied that the Warden line had done 'no more, except in one portion, than preserve the farms for which British certificates have been given' and that it had not been disputed up to the time of the Aliwal treaty in 1858; the 'lawless system of appropriation' which had gone on since could not be countenanced by anyone called upon to mediate.[2] Moshesh was 'much hurt and disappointed'; but the real difficulty was that the very idea of a fixed boundary was 'utterly foreign' to the Basuto: 'the notion that a man should have the exclusive right to a bit of grazing land was to them monstrous.'[3] Wodehouse advised Brand to 'allow the chief full time for the removal of his people from the farms on which they are living';[4] but Brand, fearing that they would not move at all unless hustled, gave them only a month—and that in a rainy season when it was almost impossible to get building materials for huts.[5] Moshesh and his sons nevertheless declared their willingness to abide by the Wodehouse award, and a large burgher force, assembled in case of trouble, returned from the border.

Some of the burghers, however, had refused to allow the Basuto to harvest their corn, and this no doubt contributed to the atmosphere of mutual exasperation. Lesaoana, a petty chief residing on Free State territory near the border and a son-in-law of Moshesh, took advantage of the confusion to indulge in some cattle-stealing which brought on him a demand for a fine and an order to withdraw his people from the Free State. Moshesh promised co-operation, but his persuasions had no effect on Lesaoana. Three months after the original demand Brand notified him that the Free State would chastise Lesaoana: any assistance to him would be regarded as a breach of treaty.[6] On 25 May a

[1] Wodehouse to Cardwell (26 Nov. 1864), ibid., p. 320.
[2] Wodehouse to Moshesh (28 Oct. 1864), ibid., pp. 306–8. Whether Wodehouse's judgement about the Warden line was correct is another question.
[3] J. van der Poel, 'Basutoland as a Factor in South African Politics, 1858–1870', *Archives Year Book for South African History*, iv, vol. i (Cape Town, 1941), 190. On Moshesh's attitude see Burnet to Wodehouse (7 Nov. 1864), *Basutoland Records*, iii. 312.          [4] Wodehouse to Brand (28 Oct. 1864), ibid., pp. 308–9.
[5] E. W. Smith, *The Mabilles of Basutoland* (London, 1939), p. 142.
[6] Brand to Moshesh (18 May 1865), *Basutoland Records*, iii. 350. An attack by Paulus Moperi's people on two Free State burghers was now added to the original complaint about Lesaoana.

commando attacked Lesaoana, who after a short engagement took refuge with Molapo, a chief hard hit by the boundary award. A fortnight later Brand declared war and summoned the burghers 'to arms, in the name of God, for the defence of your rights and the protection of your homesteads and property, and for the suppression of the arrogance and violence of the Basutos'.[1]

The Free State forces, better led than in the previous war, not only overran but annexed large areas of Basuto territory.[2] They were clearly determined to humble Moshesh. They (or perhaps in the first instance their Barolong allies) sacked the houses of four French missionaries. Again held up at Thaba Bosigo, they made two attempts to storm the stronghold and came near success, but lost heart when in the second assault their leader, Wepener, was killed. Wodehouse had proclaimed neutrality, but it was an uneasy neutrality. The sympathies of the Cape colonists were with their Free State neighbours. A raid by Lesaoana on the Klip River district in Natal added a further complication. Wodehouse demanded reparation of Moshesh but declined to send reinforcements to Natal and urged restraint on the authorities, who were being pressed by the newspapers to join in the war.[3] But the affair added to his exasperation at the way in which 'this weak state' on the Orange River was enabled by the terms of the Bloemfontein Convention 'to expose all these regions, more or less . . . to the risk of hostilities with the Native Tribes'. He inquired whether, if overtures for reunion were renewed, the Imperial Government would 'still regard this as an Imperial question, to be dealt with as they may desire, or whether they would be disposed to leave the decision to the Local Government and Legislature, on the understanding that the consequences, whether for good or evil, must rest on themselves.'[4] Elliot in the Colonial Office was sympathetic to the view implied in Wodehouse's dispatch: it would 'undoubtedly deserve mature consideration whether the Governor should not be encouraged to take advantage of any fair opening that the progress of events

[1] Proclamation (9 June 1865) in *Basutoland Records*, iii. 360.
[2] Proclamation of Acting Commandant, General Wepener (31 July 1865), ibid., p. 423.
[3] Wodehouse to Civil Commissioner, Grahamstown (12 July) (with instructions for Burnet) and to Douglas (then in Natal) (15 July), ibid., pp. 394, 397–8.
[4] Wodehouse to Cardwell (12 July 1865) (Confidential), CO48/427.

may afford, for once more bringing them [these Boers] within the control of the only responsible and civilized Government in South Africa'.[1] Not so Cardwell, who was still an anti-expansionist: 'unless it should be called for by some overruling necessity,' he told Wodehouse, 'it is the wish of Her Majesty's Government not to enlarge the boundaries of the present British Colonies nor to extend the area of our responsibilities in South Africa.'[2] He approved of the demand for reparation for the cattle taken from Natal, but warned the Acting Lieutenant-Governor that it would be 'equally unjust and inexpedient' to take advantage of Moshesh's difficulties 'with any view of territorial acquisition'.[3]

Meanwhile the Free State had laid siege to Thaba Bosigo and demanded that it be surrendered and that the Basuto chief govern his people in future under the supervision of a Free State magistrate.[4] Moshesh again appealed to Wodehouse:

I will never do so [he wrote]. I consider myself subject to the British Government and I hope Your Excellency will take an interest in my cause and come to establish peace as soon as possible. . . . I am therefore giving myself and my country up to Her Majesty's Government under certain conditions which we may agree upon between Your Excellency and me.[5]

He sent his son George to Aliwal North to make representations on his behalf. Wodehouse did not reply directly but sent Burnet to Thaba Bosigo 'to ascertain Moshesh's position and views and to impress upon him that the Government is quite in earnest in declining to accept his overtures without previous proof of his sincerity by a settlement of the question with Natal'. He was not thinking of annexation but of 'the establishment at Thaba Bosigo of a British Agent, invested by consent of all parties, with authority to settle disputes on cattle thefts, and such matters, arising between the people of the Free State and the Basutos'.[6] But Burnet thought the position of the Basuto desperate.

[1] Minute of Elliot (17 Aug. 1865), ibid.
[2] Cardwell to Wodehouse (8 Sept. 1865) (Confidential), G.H. 1/61, Cape Archives.
[3] Cardwell to Bisset (27 Nov. 1865) (No. 97), G.H. 15, Natal Archives.
[4] Terms and Conditions of Peace in Brand to Moshesh (25 Aug. 1865), *Basutoland Records*, iii. 449.
[5] Moshesh to Wodehouse (29 Aug. 1865), P.P., 1868–9, xliii [4140], 10.
[6] Wodehouse to Cardwell (13 Oct. 1865) (No. 105), ibid., pp. 493–4.

Moshesh is done mentally. All is disorganization and jealousy among the greater Chiefs, who as well as the petties find the reins slipping from their hands. The great mass of the people are tired, worn out by the oppression and bad government of the Chiefs; and I am persuaded that the whole of Basutoland is ripe, rotten ripe for falling into the hands of the Queen's Government.[1]

Letsie, Moshesh's eldest son, who was making an effort to collect the cattle for Natal, reinforced his father's plea for British protection as 'the only hope we have of living in peace and quiet'.[2] All this impressed Wodehouse, but he warned Burnet that 'the Home Government have an intense horror of additional responsibility which to them means money and soldiers'. He still would not in the first instance attempt more than accepting the Basutos' friendly overtures and placing with them a Resident Agent as adviser and mediator.[3] By the New Year, however, the logic of Burnet's arguments had carried the Governor further. He urged upon the Secretary of State that by accepting the offered allegiance of the Basuto 'we should do great good, not only to the Basutos but to all three regions'. It should be done 'whenever the state of their relations with the Free State will allow of our intervention without giving offence to that Government'. He believed the people of the Free State would be glad to see it as soon as they were forced to admit the expediency of making peace.[4] Privately he assured Cardwell: 'I am not adding to the liabilities of the Mother Country—quite the reverse.'[5] The Basuto could easily provide the funds for the two or three magistrates or Residents and small body of Native police that would be required.

Wodehouse, however, had underrated the determination of the Free State President. Brand had been obliged to raise the siege of Thaba Bosigo, but managed to keep some forces in its neighbourhood, whom he tried to reinforce (to Wodehouse's annoyance) by recruiting volunteers in Cape Colony through an English resident of the Free State and enlisting a body of Fingoes through

[1] Burnet to Wodehouse (6 Nov. 1865), P.P., 1868–9, xliii [4140], 510.
[2] Letsie to Wodehouse (17 Nov. 1865), ibid., pp. 527–8.
[3] Wodehouse to Burnet (3 Dec. 1865), Basutoland Records, iii. 538.
[4] Wodehouse to Cardwell (13 Jan. 1866) (No. 6), P.P., 1868–9, xliii [4140], 13–15.
[5] Wodehouse to Cardwell (15 Jan. 1866), Private Correspondence of Sir P. E. Wodehouse.

a former superintendent of one of the Fingo locations.[1] When Wodehouse informed Brand of the Basuto overtures, offered his services in negotiating a peace, and hinted that acceptance of the chiefs' allegiance was the best chance of future good relations, the Volksraad declined his offer. Early in March, after a successful raid into the Drakensberg by Commandant-General Fick, first Molapo and then Moshesh, threatened with famine by the Boers' destruction of their crops, asked the Free State for peace. On 3 April 1866, under the shadow of Thaba Bosigo, President Brand signed a treaty with Nehemiah (Sekhonyana) and Mopeli, representing Moshesh, who was ill. The Basuto ceded the territory west of a line from Pampoenspruit on the Orange River northwards to the Caledon, which then became the boundary as far as its tributory the Putiatsana. Molapo and his people were to become Free State Subjects and to dwell in a proclaimed territory between the Putiatsana, the Caledon, and the Drakensberg.[2] 'The Basutos', said the *Grahamstown Journal*, 'are no longer a nation. They have lost union, prestige and land. . . . This victorious result of the war is likely to settle the question of the permanent independence of the Dutch Republics.'[3] Wodehouse's bid for peace without victory had failed. Would his bid for Basuto allegiance fail also? Forster, now Parliamentary Under-Secretary, thought the arguments in favour 'plain enough' but those against stronger. Quite apart from Parliament's suspicions of territorial acquisition, 'the Basutos though anxious now to be British subjects may hereafter dislike our rule, which we should have to enforce even at the cost of war'. As soon as they became British subjects, we should be responsible for their government and for the suppression of barbarous practices. 'Our aims', Forster suggested, 'ought . . . to be influence, not sovereignty.'[4] Cardwell adopted Forster's arguments in his dispatch. Whilst he would gladly accept any 'safe and practical exertion of your moral authority' such as an Agency, he still shrank from extending British rule in South Africa 'without some overruling necessity, such as has not yet arisen,

---

[1] Wodehouse to Brand (7 Nov. 1865), *Basutoland Records*, iii. 511–12. See also later correspondence at pp. 522–3, 530–1, 535–6.

[2] Treaty of Thaba Bosigo (3 Apr. 1866), ibid., pp. 649–51.

[3] *Grahamstown Journal*, 13 Apr. 1866. A prescient remark, I think, on the independence of the Republics.

[4] Minutes of Forster (21 Feb. and 8 Mar.) on Wodehouse to Cardwell (13 Jan. 1866) (No. 6), CO48/431.

and cannot be anticipated, I think, as likely to arise in the present case'.[1]

Wodehouse, however, was a persistent man, and Moshesh had not ceased to count as some observers supposed. Annoyed at the President's conclusion of peace without reference to him, the High Commissioner warned Brand of the unsatisfied claim of Natal against Moshesh and his tribe and broadly hinted that the peace was too severe and therefore impolitic.

It is now in contemplation, apparently, to drive the Basutos out of large portions of their finest lands, to coop them up within very narrow limits, and to place this comparatively distressed and very dissatisfied population in the closest proximity to the farms about to be given out, and upon which there is every reason to suppose a pressure will be brought to bear far exceeding that which was sufficient to drive the farmers on the old border to give up their farms in despair.[2]

He also hinted to Cardwell that Molapo, as a Free State subject, might easily pick a quarrel with his Basuto brethren or the Xhosa chiefs and the Free State then might 'with very little risk to itself push its power into the heart of Kaffirland and ultimately to the sea'.[3] 'You will therefore', he wrote privately, 'no doubt approve of my endeavour to buy from the Chief Faku just so much territory as will command the navigation of the St. John's.'[4] These hints and warnings produced little effect. Brand informed the High Commissioner that a plan was being devised 'by which such Basutos as are unable to find a livelihood in Basutoland will be permitted to enter the Free State to seek service under our burghers'—which was no doubt one of the objects of putting pressure on them.[5] Cardwell fell from office. Carnarvon discouraged Wodehouse from proceeding with his plan for a Resident Agent with the Basuto and, though he saw that the peace terms might

[1] Cardwell to Wodehouse (9 Mar. 1866) (No. 21), P.P., 1868–9, xliii [4140], 84–5.
[2] Wodehouse to Brand (21 and 30 Apr. 1866), Basutoland Records, iii. 661–2 and 678–80.
[3] Wodehouse to Cardwell (12 May 1866) (No. 43), ibid., p. 639 and P.P., 1868–9, xliii [4140], 15. He had made the same point in his private letter of 15 Apr., cited below.
[4] Wodehouse to Cardwell (15 Apr. 1866), Private Correspondence of Sir P. E. Wodehouse. Cardwell's reply of 9 June was discouraging and Port St. John's was not ceded until 1878.
[5] Brand to Wodehouse (16 May 1866), Basutoland Records, iii. 693–4.

lead to further complications, suggested no course of action to deal with them.[1]

The Free State soon found that it was one thing to sign a peace treaty and another thing to execute it. Instead of acquiescing in the loss of their lands, the Basuto, paying no attention to the Survey Commission, returned to them, cultivated, hunted, even threw up fortifications. 'The fact is', said the *Grahamstown Journal*, 'the Free State deserves to lose the whole of the land it has been so quick to annex but so tardy in occupying.'[2] By January 1867, according to the Smithfield correspondent of the *Friend*, of some 300 farms granted and sold, possession had not been taken of 50.[3] In March a commando was ordered to clear the conquered territory: only about half the men turned out and 'the Basutos would not be cleared'.[4] Many of their gardens were destroyed, but they were unwilling to retire behind the swollen Caledon. On 19 July martial law was introduced on account of murders, theft, and threats in the conquered territory.[5] In August war was resumed.

A year earlier, Moshesh, blithely ignoring the Treaty of Thaba Bosigo, had made a secret overture to Natal. He had given Paulus Mopeli (one of the signatories) authority 'to deliver up into the hands of the representative of Her Majesty's Government at Natal the whole government of the Basuto nation'.[6] Shepstone found that the leading chiefs had discussed this for five days:

Hitherto Moshesh had wished to retain his own supremacy over his people; he now finds, however, that to save his people it is necessary that he should surrender his supremacy, and he has with the full consent of his people resolved to do so in good faith.

'The control of Basutoland', Shepstone agreed, 'would ... place in the hands of the Government the key to all South African politics so far as natives are concerned.'[7] Colonel Bisset, the

[1] Carnarvon to Wodehouse (25 and 28 July 1866), ibid., pp. 716–18 and P.P., 1868–9, xliii [4140], 85–6.
[2] *Grahamstown Journal*, 24 Aug. 1866.
[3] Ibid., 15 Feb. 1867. Burnet reported on 18 Feb. 'that there is not a single purchaser or grantee east of the Caledon': *Basutoland Records*, iii. 747.
[4] *Grahamstown Journal*, 31 May 1867. See also *Basutoland Records*, iii. 762.
[5] *Basutoland Records*, iii. 790–1.
[6] Moshesh to Shepstone (15 July 1866), P.P., 1868–9, xliii [4140], 101–2.
[7] Shepstone to Erskine (Colonial Secretary, Natal) (5 Sept. 1866) enclosing his Memo. of 4 Sept., ibid., pp. 101–3.

Acting Lieutenant-Governor, in forwarding the documents to Wodehouse, made the additional point that large numbers of starving Basutos were flocking into Natal.[1] Wodehouse nevertheless feared that in view of the decided objections of the Imperial Government 'it is our imperative duty to reject the present overtures'.[2] But Carnarvon was less negative than Cardwell. He asked Wodehouse for his views and the High Commissioner had no hesitation in stating them. He believed Moshesh had made his overture to Natal only because his direct approaches to the Governor of the Cape and High Commissioner had failed. 'Circumstances may again afford an opening for effecting an arrangement with Moshesh,' he wrote, 'and . . . I am still of opinion we ought in that case to take advantage of it.'[3]

The opening soon came. On 16 May Moshesh made a fresh appeal to the new Lieutenant-Governor of Natal, R. W. Keate, to be taken under British protection.[4] Letsie and his subordinate chiefs and soon afterwards Paulus Moperi were received as Free State subjects on similar terms to Molapo; but it is pretty clear that they were throwing dust in the eyes of the Free State Government. Meanwhile Wodehouse's dispatch was having its effect. Adderley was already converted. 'I am strongly of opinion', he wrote, 'that as our mistaken abandonment of the Orange has thrown between us and a foreign Power a weak debateable land and isolated Natal we should take these Basutos'offer and so tend towards one South African British Government including Natal.'[5] Buckingham was also disposed to accept the offer; though his first inclination was towards annexation to the Cape,[6] which was certainly Wodehouse's opinion also. He was trying his best to keep things quiet until he heard again from the Secretary of State.

[1] Bisset to Wodehouse (8 Sept. 1866), P.P., 1868-9, xliii [4140], 103-4.
[2] Wodehouse to Bisset (19 Sept. 1866), *Basutoland Records*, iii. 728.
[3] Wodehouse to Buckingham (3 May 1867) (No. 41), P.P., 1868-9, xliii [4140], 15. Carnarvon, who had asked for Wodehouse's views in his dispatch No. 38 of 9 Jan., had resigned on 2 Mar.
[4] Moshesh to Keate (16 May 1867), P.P., 1868-9, xliii [4140], 104. Moshesh (and Letsie) renewed the request through a messenger in August. Perhaps this second request turned the scales with Buckingham.
[5] Minute of Adderley (28 June) on Wodehouse to Buckingham (3 May 1867) (No. 41), CO48/436.
[6] Minute of Buckingham (? 2 Oct.) on Keate to Buckingham (4 June 1867) (No. 5), CO179/83. In an earlier Minute of 10 July (in CO48/436) the Duke had expressed no preference as between the Cape and Natal.

He did not hear again until the New Year and then, curiously enough, the Duke plumped for annexation to Natal.

Her Majesty's Government [he wrote] consider that the residence of a British agent with Moshesh would not accomplish a permanent settlement of the difficulties which have to be met. . . . They have therefore come to the conclusion that the peace and welfare of Her Majesty's possessions in South Africa would be best promoted by accepting the overtures made. . . . They feel no doubt that the best and most obvious arrangement would be the annexation of Basutoland to the Colony of Natal.

He assumed that the Legislative Council would readily acquiesce and accordingly authorized the High Commissioner to treat with Moshesh for the recognition of himself and his tribe as British subjects on this basis. The arrangement should include a boundary settlement with the Free State.[1]

A similar but confidential dispatch was sent to Keate and he and his officials naturally welcomed it; but the Duke had placed the negotiations in Wodehouse's hands. He began by conveying the purport of it to Moshesh and to President Brand; one received it with gratitude, the other with surprise. The President could not coincide in the High Commissioner's view that the course proposed would tend to the peace of South Africa. He could not agree to Wodehouse's request to suspend hostilities, until certain murderers had been handed over and the annexed territory cleared of Basutos.[2] Wodehouse was indignant. He considered moving a strong detachment of frontier police into Basutoland and notifying the Free State that no further injuries to Basutos would be permitted.[3] He also hinted to the President that the cessions demanded from the Basuto had been excessive and that the boundary should be modified.[4] This merely stiffened Brand's attitude. Without directly replying on this point, he informed Wodehouse that 'the Basutos have quite sufficient land'.

Our Government cannot conceive that a neutral and friendly power will enter into any arrangement or adopt a course of action having the tendency however remotely, to embarrass the Government of the Orange Free State in obtaining satisfaction from . . . Moshesh . . .

[1] Buckingham to Wodehouse (9 Dec. 1867) (No. 78), P.P., 1868–9, xliii 4140], 86–7.
[2] Brand to Wodehouse (31 Jan. 1868), ibid., pp. 26–8.
[3] Wodehouse to Buckingham (18 Feb. 1868) (No. 15), ibid., pp. 25–6.
[4] Wodehouse to Brand (11 Feb. 1868), ibid., pp. 28–9.

at a time too when the Government and people of the Orange Free State have very nearly succeeded in vanquishing our enemy.[1]

Wodehouse's reply was crushing. He reminded the President that Moshesh, at the request of Sir George Grey, had forgone his advantage over the Free State in its hour of weakness. Brand's present policy, 'if successful, must inevitably drive the population of Basutoland, in a state of beggary and destitution, into the Cape Colony on the one side and to the borders of Natal on the other'. The President's attitude, he declared, indicated an unfriendly feeling towards the British Government which absolved him from observing the terms of the Bloemfontein Convention. He would prohibit all issues of ammunition to the Free State and take such further steps as he considered 'conducive to the good government of the country'.[2] Two days later, on 12 March 1868, he issued a proclamation declaring the Basuto tribe to be British subjects and their territory British territory.[3] He then sent Currie and his police up to Basutoland. Currie was to lose no time in informing the Free State commandants and people that the Basuto had become British subjects and that he had been directed to support them against any further attacks; but he was also to inform the Free State officers 'that this Government is still fully disposed to enter into friendly negotiations for the settlement of all questions in dispute'.[4]

Wodehouse's proceedings did not please the Duke of Buckingham. He thought the High Commissioner had been premature in informing Moshesh that his overtures had been accepted: 'this acceptance was . . . conditional upon the satisfactory completion of the negotiations with the Free State and of the acceptance by Natal.'[5] He was seriously disturbed lest his policy towards the Free State should lead to embarrassment or even 'expensive contests'.[6] When the news of the annexation arrived, he gave Wodehouse credit for his effort to save the Basuto from destruction, but still impressed on him the importance of avoiding any

[1] Brand to Wodehouse (3 Mar. 1868), P.P., 1868–9, xliii [4140], 41–3.
[2] Wodehouse to Brand (10 Mar. 1868), ibid., pp. 38–9.
[3] Proclamation (12 Mar.) in Wodehouse to Buckingham (18 Mar. 1868) (No. 24), ibid., p. 40.
[4] Wodehouse to Currie (14 Mar. 1868), ibid.
[5] Buckingham to Wodehouse (26 Feb. 1868) (No. 108), ibid., pp. 87–8.
[6] Buckingham to Wodehouse (27 Mar. 1868) (No. 116), P.P., 1868–9, xlii [4140], 88.

conflict with the Free State and still looked for the incorporation of Basutoland into Natal.[1]

Wodehouse powerfully defended his policy in two dispatches
of 2 May. He was convinced that Paulus Mopeli had gone much
further in his overtures to Natal than his instructions warranted.
At any rate Moshesh, whom he had seen at Thaba Bosigo in
mid April, now decidedly objected to the proposed union. What
he wished was to have Basutoland made a Native Reserve dependent on the High Commissioner. This change of intention had
caused inconvenience but was surely no 'ground for abandoning
the measure itself'. He did not himself think immediate union
with either Natal or the Cape desirable. Union with the Cape
would mean 'the sudden introduction of Cape Colonial Law':
the Natal legislature was inclined to press heavily on the Natives,
to raise money. He had not interpreted his authority to receive
the Basutos as subject to the prior assent of the Natal legislature.
The arrangements would have taken more than one session, raising the hopes of the Basuto and leading to remonstrances by the
Free State. 'The policy of leaving virtually to the decision of the
Natal Legislature whether the Basutos should become British
subjects or not is of very doubtful expediency.' To make their
fate depend on a negotiation with the Free State was to leave it to
'their most bitter enemies, who now desire nothing so much as
their complete ruin'. If this was insisted on he must resign. He
appealed for confidence, pointing out that 'not a shot has been
fired in war by a British soldier during my Government'.[2]

His arguments convinced Elliot. If it were desired to temporize,
matters might well have been left to the Free State and Natal;
'but . . . if it were desired really to do something . . . the only
effectual course was to act by one authority . . . the Queen's
Government, represented by Her Majesty's High Commissioner.'
A high and successful officer on the spot was justified in disregarding 'very qualified and guarded' instructions from home and
taking a more direct responsibility. Adderley thought Wodehouse
'needlessly querulous' but did not object to his plan; but the

---

[1] Buckingham to Wodehouse (24 Apr. 1868) (No. 127), ibid., pp. 88–9.
[2] Wodehouse to Buckingham (2 May 1868) (Nos. 328, 33), ibid., pp. 55–9.
No. 32 encloses a letter from Moshesh of 21 Apr. Wodehouse supplemented his
dispatches with a private letter to Barrow (9 May) warning against half measures:
'There must be full confidence or none.' Private Correspondence of Sir P. E.
Wodehouse.

expenses, so far as Basutoland was not self-supporting, should 'wholly fall on the Cape. . . . Not one shilling should fall on the English taxpayer for an object mainly concerning their peace and extension of communications with the interior.'[1] Buckingham, who mattered most, rose to the occasion magnanimously. Sir Philip Wodehouse had 'rightly judged of the spirit and object of the Government' in its instructions. Their purpose was 'to secure peace around the frontier and put an end to the constantly recurring strife between the Basutos and the Orange Free State provided that such an arrangement involved no liability on the Mother Country. . . . Sir Philip Wodehouse took a large responsibility on himself but I see no reason for any censure or withdrawal of confidence.'[2] A dispatch on these lines was sent to him a few days later.

The Free State was still very sore, and negotiations were coming to a deadlock. A proposal of Wodehouse to place 300 farms within the 'conquered territory' on sale and pay over the proceeds to the Free State as compensation gave deep offence, for the Free State was still hoping for the Thaba Bosigo boundary and still keeping its commandos in the field. His renewed complaints of breaches of the Bloemfontein Convention were a further irritant.[3] The Volksraad decided to drop the negotiation and appeal to England over Wodehouse's head by sending delegates to remonstrate with Her Majesty's Government in person. The Duke of Buckingham, with Adderley and Rogers, received the delegates (the Revd. G. van de Waal and Commandant de Villiers) at Stowe. He found them 'very shrewd and well able to maintain their case but intensely obstinate'. They pressed for a Special Commission to be sent out, but the Duke told them 'that could not be': Sir Philip Wodehouse was 'fully empowered and trusted'.[4] Any negotiation must be with him, and he had been instructed to negotiate a new Basuto–Free State boundary, since

[1] Minutes of Adderley and Elliot (30 June) on Wodehouse to Buckingham (2 May 1868) (No. 33), CO48/441.
[2] Minute of Buckingham (3 July), ibid. The dispatch, No. 149 of 9 July is in P.P., 1868–9, xliii [4140], 90. Keate (to Buckingham, 6 Aug. 1868, No. 71) and the Natal Legislative Council still argued for annexation to Natal, but of course in vain, ibid., pp. 114 ff.
[3] The correspondence is enclosed in Wodehouse to Buckingham (9 Apr. 1868) (No. 29), ibid., pp. 44–50.
[4] Buckingham to Wodehouse (24 Aug. 1868), Private Correspondence of Sir P. E. Wodehouse.

the Treaty of Thaba Bosigo had been superseded by the war which followed it.[1]

In spite of the deadlock, there were hopes in some quarters that the frontier might be advanced further beyond the Orange River. Sir Philip Wodehouse spoke his mind on this subject to the Cape Parliament.

What is to be hoped for, in my opinion, is the creation, beyond the River, of a large and well-organized Government, bound to this colony only by a common allegiance, by the ties of kinship, by congenial laws, by just covenants and by a common desire to extend the blessings of Christianity, peace and civilization to all within their reach.

But any such territorial arrangements must be essentially colonial, executed and maintained by colonial agency; though it might be adopted and sanctioned by the Imperial Government, 'it would be self-deception . . . to reckon on the British Government assuming to itself any substantial responsibility.'[2] Sir Philip Wodehouse was returning to the ideas of Sir George Grey. What is surprising is to find the Duke of Buckingham responding to them.

The Orange Free State and the Vaal Republic have never enjoyed any permanent peace with the native tribes in their vicinity since their formation as Free States, and having in consequence been not only embarrassed in the conduct of their own affairs, but a source of embarrassment and danger to their neighbours, it appears to me possible that the interest of our colonies in that quarter and the maintenance of peace in the countries round them may render it politic to take into consideration any overture which may be made to bring these States in some form or another under British authority.[3]

These questions, however, were for the future. The immediate question was to reconcile the Free State to the new regime in

[1] Buckingham to Wodehouse (9 Nov. 1868) (Confidential), P.P., 1868–9, xliii [4140], 92–3.
[2] Governor's Address proroguing Parliament, 2 Sept., *Grahamstown Journal*, 7 Sept. 1868.
[3] Buckingham to Wodehouse (23 Nov. 1868) (No. 194), P.P., 1868–9, xliii [4140] 92. This was apropos a memorial asking for the resumption of British authority over the Free State and a protectorate over tribes desiring it; but the Aliwal North negotiations gave Wodehouse the impression that only a minority in the Free State desired the restoration of British rule (to Granville, 14 Apr. 1869, No. 13), CO48/445.

Basutoland. With the failure of the appeal against Wodehouse, Brand saw that he had no choice but to come to terms, as he did after some further sparring, in the convention signed at Aliwal North on 12 February 1869. The new boundary followed the line of the Langeberg and Jammerberg from the Orange River to the Caledon and thence along that river to the Putiatsana; if Molapo, in writing, requested the Volksraad to relieve himself and his people from their subjection to the Free State, the Volksraad was to comply, and the boundary would then run up the Caledon to its source. The land south of the Caledon of more practical value to the Basuto had been kept, Wodehouse claimed: what they surrendered was 'very flat and open, is unsuited to their habits of life and has never been occupied by them'. North of the Caledon it was different, but it was better to accept the natural boundary of the river than to break off the negotiation. Two French mission stations now on Free State territory could be retained if desired. Careful provision was made for handling such matters as cattle thefts. The Free State claim to compensation for territory ceded at Thaba Bosigo was to be submitted to arbitration. Nothing in the treaty was to be construed as setting aside or invaliding the Bloemfontein Convention.[1]

The Convention of Aliwal North did not pass without question at home. The evangelical conscience had been aroused by the treatment of the French missionaries and by a self-appointed deputation to England consisting of D. D. Buchanan, a former editor of the *Natal Witness* and for a time an adviser of Moshesh, the French missionary Daumas, and Tsekelo, 'a disreputable son of Moshesh'.[2] Seventeen members of Parliament (who said that many more agreed with them) appealed to Lord Granville, now Secretary of State, not to ratify the Convention. It was a surrender to aggression and would mean 'the total ruin of the Basuto nation'.[3] Under-Secretary Monsell was inclined to argue against ratification as being unjust to the Basuto. Granville, on the other hand, saw the practical objections to any other policy: Wodehouse, if thrown over, would resign and if the Free Staters were not

[1] Wodehouse to Granville (14 Apr. 1869) (No. 13) with Convention enclosed, P.P., 1870, xlix [C. 18], 6–8, 17–18.
[2] Tylden, op. cit., p. 104. De Kiewiet (op. cit., pp. 23–6) agrees about Tsekelo's character.
[3] Hon. A. Kinnaird *et al.*, to Granville (recd. 23 June 1869), P.P., 1870, xlix [C. 18], 67–8, Granville had received a deputation on 2 June.

'frightened by our brag' we must either fight ourselves or effectually arm the Basuto.[1] He temporized, seeking more information about the compensation provisions and some assurances that the land left to the Basuto was sufficient for their maintenance.[2] Wodehouse defended himself vigorously. The land was not 'the private property of British subjects', as the deputation alleged, but tribal territory. He had got back all the really valuable land except a small angle north of the Caledon. The compensation, if payable, would be raised on the security of the farms to be sold, whose quit-rents would be more than enough to pay the interest. If he was to be supported, let it be done at once. If not, 'let the Convention be vetoed,—let the proclamation of the Basutos as British subjects be revoked,—set them free. . . . I believe it would be bad for them, bad for the Free State, bad for this Colony, but it would be better than to have it supposed in any quarter that Her Majesty's Government considered the Tribe to have been overreached and betrayed by me.'[3] Granville was satisfied except on the compensation article and Brand now consented to its being expunged.[4] Ratifications of the Convention were duly exchanged on 19 March 1870. Moshesh had died on the eleventh of the month. He had achieved the great object of his later life. The Basuto were subjects of the Queen, incorporated neither in the Cape nor in Natal.

This decision was reversed in 1871, but in 1884, after difficult negotiations, Basutoland returned to the direct rule of the Imperial Government. Wodehouse's policy was thus vindicated by time and prepared the way for the independence which, a century later, the Basuto now again enjoy. The Duke of Buckingham deserves credit for the crucial decision to back Sir Philip Wodehouse, but the fate of the Basuto was settled by the man on the spot. Caring nothing for popularity, whether with the colonists or his superiors, he 'intervened on behalf of these people at the time of their greatest distress, partly from a sense of duty to this Colony [the Cape], partly from what some would term a sentimental sympathy for the tribe'.[5]

[1] Minute of Granville (c. 20 June) on Wodehouse to Granville (14 Apr. 1869) (No. 13), CO48/445.
[2] Granville to Wodehouse (24 June 1869) (No. 50), P.P., 1870, xlix [C. 18], 37–8.
[3] Wodehouse to Granville (30 July 1869) (No. 45), ibid., pp. 27–30.
[4] Brand to Wodehouse (11 Nov. 1869), ibid., p. 35.
[5] Wodehouse to Granville (30 July 1869) (No. 45), loc. cit.

# VI

## RESPONSIBLE GOVERNMENT FOR THE CAPE: THE DIAMOND FIELDS: NATAL

WITH the advent of the first Gladstone Ministry in December 1868 the question of withdrawing Imperial troops from South Africa, which Wodehouse had induced the previous Ministry to postpone, was raised once more. The moving spirit was Cardwell, who came to the War Office determined to carry this reorganization through. On New Year's Day 1869 he wrote to Lord Granville, Secretary of State for the Colonies, to let him know that

notice has been given to the Cape Colony that unless a contribution equal to that paid by the Australian Colonies shall be paid by the Cape to the Imperial Exchequer, Her Majesty's Government will proceed to withdraw the greater portion of the troops, and will be guided exclusively by Imperial, as distinguished from purely Colonies considerations if they shall retain any of them within the Colony.[1]

On 24 March Granville informed Wodehouse that one of the three regiments at the Cape would be at once withdrawn unless provision had been made or he had clear grounds for believing that it would be made by the Cape Parliament at its next session. Another would be withdrawn in 1870 unless payment was made at the Australian rate. The third regiment would remain at Simonstown, which was to be regarded as an Imperial station.[1] Wodehouse made no further plea for postponement; but in his reply he urged 'the necessity for a definitive settlement of a scheme of government for these territories'. His position was becoming embarrassing; he was coming to the end of his term; and his

[1] Cardwell to Granville (1 Jan. 1869), Gladstone Papers, B.M. Add. MS. 44119. The letter also outlines the general scheme of colonial defence.
[2] Granville to Wodehouse (24 Mar. 1869) (No. 23), V. & P., Cape Parliament 1869, Appendix I, vol. ii, C. 1-'69.

successor would 'stand in even greater need of a clear explanation of the authority and responsibility attaching to him'.[1]

The session he had opened a week earlier (on 24 June) was filled with wrangles and recriminations about finance. The Governor again brought forward his plan of 1867 for a single chamber of fifteen elected members and three officials. It would save the colony £11,000 a year and would 'both afford the people ample control over the Government and tend to retain its expenditure within reasonable bounds'.[2] But his Constitution Amendment Bill was rejected by 39 to 22. On the other hand, Molteno, as leader of the responsible government party, which saw the remedy for financial difficulties in sweeping reductions in civil service salaries, failed to carry the increased tariff which he proposed as an alternative to the Government's tax proposals: the Bill was defeated in the Legislative Council. The frustrated Governor sought by a dissolution to get the country to face squarely the need for some constitutional reform.

Wodehouse's reply to Granville had called forth an interesting minute from Rogers. He thought the Cape ready for responsible government. He did not think the Native question need interfere. The Colony was 'large enough to have a public opinion not wholly dominated by those in contact with border natives and to be capable of defending itself at its own cost against any such partial outbreaks as must be expected from time to time'. But Natal was at a different stage of its development.

To give the Settlers power of governing the natives and at the same time to retain the sense of safety derived from the presence of British Troops would lead to an exacting native policy—dissatisfaction—quarrels and a native war. To withdraw the Troops would place the settlers so much at the mercy of the tribes that encroachments, thefts and general lawlessness might soon become intolerable. . . . The questions arise (1) how far one system can be pursued at Natal and another at the Cape and (2) whether the foreign policy of South Africa ought not to be in the hands of a Governor of a semi-Crown Colony who fairly represents the Home Government and has some military force

[1] Wodehouse to Granville (2 July 1869) (No. 39), P.P., 1870, xlix (H.C. 181), 15. Wodehouse was clearly referring not only to the constitutional difficulties but to the Natal Legislative Council's criticism of the High Commissioner's control over Natal's relations with tribes beyond its borders: see Keate to Buckingham (24 Sept. 1868) (No. 101), P.P., 1869, xliii [4140], 127–8.

[2] Message No. 11 (2 Aug.), *Grahamstown Journal*, 9 Aug. 1869.

at his disposal [rather] than . . . The Governor of a Colony who is at the mercy of his responsible Ministry.[1]

Monsell, on the other hand, thought that 'the Cape ought to have responsible government', and Granville after three months' delay, possibly waiting on the results of the Cape session, came down on the same side.

> If the colonists will not allow themselves to be governed—and I am far from blaming them for desiring to manage their own affairs, or from questioning their capacity to do so, which is seldom rightly estimated till it is tried,—it follows that they must adopt the responsibility of governing.

He also saw no reason for altering the arrangement which placed the foreign policy of South Africa under the control of the High Commissioner, through it should be exercised with great reserve as regards Natal.[2]

Granville's dispatch was not to Wodehouse's liking. He did not conceal his conviction that responsible government was unsuited to the Cape and 'applicable only to communities fast advancing to fitness for absolute independence'.

> I cannot satisfy myself of the justice or humanity of handing over this large native population to the uncontrolled management of a Legislature composed of those whose habits, interests and prejudices are so entirely different.

He therefore proposed to carry on with his plan of placing the two alternatives before the newly elected Parliament.[3] But although the constitutional reform plan, with a larger chamber than in the first version, won considerable support, especially in the East, and local and personal factors clouded the issue, the new House of Assembly defeated Wodehouse's Parliamentary Reform Bill by 34 to 26. It did not follow that all opponents of the Bill were supporters of responsible government; but, as the views of the Imperial Government were now known in the colony, it

---

[1] Minute of Rogers (8 Sept.) on Wodehouse to Granville (2 July 1869) (No. 39), CO48/445. Did he mean that the Governor of Natal should be High Commissioner?

[2] Granville to Wodehouse (9 Dec. 1869) (No. 104), P.P., 1870, xlix (H.C. 181), 15–17.

[3] Wodehouse to Granville (17 Jan. 1870) (No. 7), P.P., 1870, xlix (H.C. 187), 17–18.

must have been clear to most members that it was likely to come soon. This did not deter the Assembly, however, from adopting an Address to the Queen asking for the moral support of an Imperial garrison until the success of the Basuto and Transkeian experiments had been tested and the Colony was in a position to provide effectual protection for its frontier. Sir Philip Wodehouse supported the Address, arguing that 'the troops can be maintained here for as little money as at home, perhaps for less'.[1] The withdrawal was in fact being made more slowly than at first suggested, but the Imperial Government was not to be deflected from its policy and Lord Granville would not hold out any hopes of further delay.[2]

One argument in the Cape's armoury, the plea of poverty—which had never carried much weight with the Imperial Government[3]—was weakened by the discovery of gold and diamonds in the interior. The gold reef discovered in 1867 on the Tati in the Bamangwato country was too remote to be immediately remunerative, but the discovery awakened expansionist ambitions in President Pretorius. After an unsuccessful approach to the Bamangwato chief Matsheng, on 29 April 1868 he issued a proclamation extending the boundaries of the South African Republic westward to the twenty-second parallel, northward to Lake Ngami and almost to Moselekatse's kraal at Bulawayo and eastward to Delagoa Bay, where he was negotiating with a Scottish adventurer, Alexander McCorkindale. Matsheng, made uneasy by the Transvaal overture, appealed (through his missionary, John Mackenzie) to Wodehouse to 'come and occupy the gold country, in so far as it is at my disposal, and . . . govern the gold-diggers in the name of the Queen of England.'[4] Wodehouse's first request was for more information; but about the same time he received new ammunition against the Transvaal, in the shape of renewed

---

[1] Wodehouse to Granville (2 Apr. 1870) (No. 33) with Address of Legislative Assembly to the Queen, ibid. (H.C. 181–II), 3–6.
   [2] Granville to Wodehouse (23 May 1870) (No. 148), ibid., p. 5.
   [3] Granville to Wodehouse (7 Apr. 1870) (No. 138), ibid. (H.C. 181–I), p. 6. An Eastern petition enclosed in Wodehouse to Granville (3 Feb. 1870) (No. 17) alleged that defence would cost 10s. per head of the European population; Granville said it cost 15s. per head in England.
   [4] Macheng to Wodehouse (29 Mar.) and Wodehouse to Macheng (2 June 1868), *Grahamstown Journal*, 20 July 1868. In his *Ten Years North of the Orange River* (Edinburgh, 1871), p. 455, Mackenzie denied that Matsheng was advised by him, directly or indirectly, to write to Wodehouse.

complaints of the kidnapping of the African children for apprenticeship. 'It is for Her Majesty's Government to decide', he
declared in a characteristic outburst, 'how long we shall observe
the iniquitous terms of the Convention with the Republic, and
go on supplying it with ammunition to be used against the
Natives without making the slightest enquiry (which might be
troublesome) as to the merits of the quarrel.' He suggested 'a firm
but temperate remonstrance with the Republic, and efforts to
bring about a better understanding between it and the Natives'.[1]
But Matsheng's appeal and a memorial from Pietermaritzburg
requesting that an embassy be sent to Moselekatse provided him
with the text for a deliverance, on the same day, on a favourite
theme, Great Britain's paramount power in South Africa.

I am perfectly alive to the determination of the people of England
to resist all extension of their responsibilities by Territorial acquisitions.
. . . But it is quite consistent with that policy and with those views to
admit the equally self-evident fact that the British possessions in South
Africa, as possessing the whole accessible Sea-board, must inevitably
take part in and control, in a greater or less degree, the relations and
transactions of all the communities of the Interior; and that all the more
as circumstances may bring the latter out of the darkness of sheer
barbarism.[2]

He was well prepared therefore to deal with Pretorius's boundary
proclamation, and his reaction was sharp. Delagoa Bay he regarded, with Owen's annexations of 1823 in mind, as 'British
Territory': 'with regard to the Western encroachments it will be
proper for me to intimate that if they be persisted in, our Treaty
obligation with the State will be held to be at an end.'[3] Moreover
he had an ally in Adderley, who remarked in a minute on his
June dispatches: 'It is inevitable that a nation like the English,
mixed with more dogged Dutch, must possess practically the
whole of that country so far as climate permits. But . . . they must

[1] Wodehouse to Buckingham (3 June 1868) (Confidential), CO48/441. The
information came from J. H. Roself, editor of the *Transvaal Argus*. On the general
question see W. Kistner, 'The Anti-slavery Agitation against the Transvaal
Republic, 1852–1868', *Archives Year Book for South African History*, xv, vol. ii (Cape
Town, 1952); J. A. I. Agar-Hamilton, *The Native Policy of the Voortrekkers* (Cape
Town, 1928); de Kiewiet, op. cit., ch. xv.
[2] Wodehouse to Buckingham (3 June 1868) (No. 44), CO48/441.
[3] Wodehouse to Buckingham (9 Oct. 1868) (No. 100), CO48/442. McCorkin-
alde's base, Inyack (Inhaca) I had been annexed on 5 Nov. 1861.

do so entirely by their own strength and at their own risk.'[1] Buckingham had then expressed no opinion. But he was clear that the boundary proclamation could not be recognized as valid. Moreover, 'as that proclamation must be held to be evidence of an intention by the Transvaal to endeavour to annex and take possession of extensive districts notoriously occupied by native tribes', the High Commissioner must be given discretion to prohibit the supply of arms and ammunition to the Transvaal, which seemed to be countenancing slavery.[2] Great Britain must keep the 'missionary road' to the North open.

The gold discovery not only made Great Britain more alive to the possibilities of the North. It attracted prospectors from Australia. When a stone picked up at Hopetown in 1867 was identified as a diamond, they joined in the search for diamonds, which extended in 1869 to the lower Vaal. There they began 'panning' for diamonds and, towards the end of the year, an Australian party began digging for them.[3] These diamond fields were in territory claimed by the Griqua chief Nicolaas Waterboer, to whom the Cape Government paid a subsidy of £150 a year. In 1863 his agent, David Arnot, an able, pushing man of mixed ancestry, had reasserted his claims, which were disputed by the Orange Free State on the strength of a purchase from Henry Harvey as agent of Adam Kok and his uncle Cornelis Kok. Wodehouse had offered to arbitrate, but the Free State would only agree to arbitration on the lands north of the Vaal and Waterboer therefore declined.[4] The Transvaal also had claims to the land between the Vaal and its northern tributary the Harts. These disputes were still unsettled when a rush to the diggings on both sides of the Vaal in the winter of 1870 made a settlement urgent. President Brand and Waterboer held an abortive conference in August. On its breakdown, Waterboer on 25 August, followed

[1] Minute of Adderley (8 July) on Wodehouse to Buckingham (3 June 1868) (No. 44), CO48/441.
[2] Minute of Buckingham (22 Nov.) on Wodehouse to Buckingham (9 Oct. 1868), CO48/442. Embodied in dispatch No. 195 of 24 Nov. Questions on the 'enslavement' of children in the Transvaal were asked in the House of Commons on 19 Feb. 1869: *Hansard*, 3rd Ser. cxciv. 128–33.
[3] W. P. Morrell, *The Gold Rushes* (London, 1940), pp. 314 ff.
[4] On these involved claims see the carefully objective studies of J. A. I. Agar-Hamilton, *The Road to the North* (London, 1937) and W. B. Campbell, 'The South African Frontier, 1865–1885: A Study in Expansion', *Archives Year Book for South African History*, xxii, vol. i (Cape Town, 1959).

by Brand on 29 August, each proclaimed his right to the fields; and Brand appointed O. J. Truter, a Free Stater with Australian goldfields experience, as Commissioner. Wodehouse had now left for England, but his temporary successor Lieutenant-General C. C. Hay, influenced undoubtedly by his strong-minded, expan-sionist Colonial Secretary, Southey, who was in touch with Arnot, promptly issued a warning notice to British subjects and foreshadowed the appointment of a magistrate under the Cape of Good Hope Punishment Act 1863.[1] This was welcomed by the colonial press and by the executive committee of the Klipdrift diamond diggers, who wrote to Southey: 'No act of Government was ever more opportune than this.'[2] But Truter continued to officiate at Pniel, on the opposite bank of the river. Brand stood firm on the 'Vetberg line', fixed by Adam Kok in 1855, allegedly at Waterboer's request.[3] Correspondence between Brand and Hay continued, but was obviously leading nowhere; and on 19 November Hay transmitted and recommended a petition from Waterboer, no doubt engineered through Arnot by Southey, requesting the Queen to proclaim her authority over Griqualand West and extend to the Griquas the protection and privilege of British subjects.[4]

The Imperial Government had already sought and received Sir Philip Wodehouse's advice.

As a matter of right [he wrote] the native tribes are fairly entitled to that tract of country in which, for the present, the diamonds appear to be chiefly found. That they will be able to retain control of it, if these discoveries extend, is very improbable, but . . . it is unlikely that Boer Governments would prove equal to its management; and I certainly think that before very long British authority will in some form have to be established.[5]

In other words, Britain should base her action not so much on Waterboer's sovereignty, which was fast becoming a fiction, as on British paramountcy in South Africa. Lord Kimberley, who

[1] Hay to Kimberley (19 Sept. 1870) (No. 25), P.P., 1871, xlvii [C. 459], 36–7. The magistrate (J. Campbell) did not arrive till 13 Dec.
[2] Klip Drift Diggers Executive Committee to Southey (3 Oct. 1870), ibid., p. 64.
[3] Brand to Hay (24 Sept. 1870), ibid., p. 48.
[4] Hay to Kimberley (19 Nov. 1870) (No. 46), with Enclosure, ibid., pp. 86–90. On Southey's influence with Arnot, see Campbell, op. cit., pp. 181–2.
[5] Wodehouse to Kimberley (1 Oct. 1870), P.P., 1871, xlvii [C. 459], 45–6.

had now succeeded Granville, was not willing to go so far. His instructions to the new High Commissioner Sir Henry Barkly, given when a petition from Waterboer was expected but had not yet arrived, show that he was still thinking of the rights of the Griquas rather than the requirements of the diamond diggings. Barkly was to renew and press Wodehouse's proposal to settle the disputed claims by arbitration. He was to discourage, by all means short of force, any combination of Dutch Boers and English diggers to dispossess the Griquas.

> Her Majesty's Government have no wish, if it can be avoided, to extend the South African Colonies and they entertain special objections to any such extension in the present anomalous and unsatisfactory condition of the Government of the Cape Colony; but the case might be altered if that Colony should be willing to take upon itself the full responsibilities of Government . . . provided that the white immigrants concurred with the natives in desiring that the Griqua territory should be united to the Cape Colony.

He was not to annex the territory, however, or pledge Her Majesty's Government to annex it, without instructions from home.[1] Everything seemed to Rogers to point now to annexation —'but at the expense and under the conduct of the Cape Government'.[2]

Rogers was mistaken. President Brand told Barkly on his arrival at the end of the year that 'the Governor of the Cape Colony could no longer be regarded as an impartial or disinterested arbiter'.[3] Lands within the Vetberg line, he said, had been in the undisturbed occupation of Free State subjects for twenty years. But, according to Barkly, the registry of deeds showed that most of the sales or grants by Cornelis Kok (whom Waterboer did not in any case recognize as an independent chief) had been made to Griquas; and in any case sales of land did not involve transfer of sovereignty.[4] Barkly suggested the appointment of a Joint Commission, free from local influence, but in

---

[1] Kimberley to Barkly (17 Nov. 1870) (No. 35), ibid., pp. 65–6. The passage quoted was added by Kimberley to Rogers's draft in CO48/451.

[2] Minute of Rogers (24 Dec.) on Hay to Kimberley (18 Nov. 1870) (No. 43), CO48/451.

[3] Barkly to Kimberley (18 Jan. 1871) (No. 9), P.P., 1871, xlvii [C459], 100–1. Barkly saw Brand for three hours on 3 Jan.

[4] Barkly to Brand (23 Jan. 1871), ibid., pp. 128–9.

vain. All that Brand was willing to recommend to the Volksraad
was a reference to the arbitration of the President of the United
States or the King of Holland of two questions—first 'whether
under the convention of 1854 Her Majesty has the right to accept
Waterboer's allegiance', and secondly, the validity of the Orange
Free State's title to the 'Campbell grounds' north of the Vaal.[1]

By this time Barkly was up at the diamond fields. He could not
annex them in the face of Kimberley's explicit instructions, despite
the appeals of Waterboer and 'thousands of British diggers', but
he made it pretty plain where his sympathies lay. 'It appeared to
me that the British Government had already gone too far to admit
of its ceasing to support the cause of either Waterboer or the
diggers,' he wrote, 'and it was quite clear that any appearance of
faltering on my part would only encourage the Free State and
Transvaal Republics in upholding their claims.'[2] He won an
important success with the Transvaal. President Pretorius, whose
territorial claims had offended the chiefs and whose concession to
a speculative company had antagonized the diggers, agreed that
Campbell, the Cape magistrate, and O'Reilly, landdrost of Wak-
kerstroom, should meet to consider the boundary questions in
dispute between the Transvaal and the Barolong, Batlapin, and
Bangwaketse chiefs as well as Waterboer and submit a joint statement to the arbitration of Lieutenant-Governor Keate of Natal.[3]
But the main effect of Barkly's visit was to convince him of the
need to end the period of uncertainty at the fields. He asked permission to annex them at once 'in the probable event of the Cape
Parliament . . . agreeing by formal resolutions to take upon itself
the first responsibility of Government, with the burden of maintaining any force that may be necessary'.[4] President Brand for his
part was not idle. He called out a commando 'for the protection
and maintenance of the Vetberg', though in reply to Barkly's
protest he disclaimed any idea of using force to compel the diggers
to take out licences from the Free State Government.[5] Even
Gladstone now saw that annexation was on the way. 'If, as

[1] Barkly to Kimberley (8 Mar. 1871) (No. 25), P.P., 1871, xlvii [C. 459], 132–3.
[2] Ibid.
[3] Ibid. On the concession to the South African Diamond and Mineral Company
see Foreign Office to Colonial Office (28 Nov. 1870), ibid., p. 93.
[4] Barkly to Kimberley (8 Mar. 1871) No. 25), loc. cit.
[5] Barkly to Kimberley (17 Apr. 1871) (No. 36) with correspondence of Brand
and Barkly enclosed, ibid., pp. 154 ff.

appears, the parties be willing and the resolution of the Cape Legislature unequivocal, I do not object', he told Kimberley, 'to the proposed annexation of the Diamond Fields, while I regret the necessity which brings it about.'[1]

But this made the Imperial Government all the more eager to change the Cape constitution, 'which places an insuperable power of obstruction in the hands of a Legislature not responsible for the conduct of affairs',[2] for responsible government. Sir Henry Barkly, the initiator of an experiment in partially responsible government in Jamaica and a successful Governor under the responsible system in Victoria, seemed just the man for the job.[3] But even Barkly had his doubts. Would it be acceptable if the troops were withdrawn? Could frontier defence remain an Imperial duty? If the Cape took over Basutoland, would it be 'administered unreservedly as the Local Legislature may see fit and its Kafir inhabitants subjected, without their own consent, to the same laws and regulations as the rest of the population', or would the Queen's representative retain special powers, as at first in New Zealand?[4] Kimberley's instructions to Barkly answered these queries. Another regiment would be left at the Cape to see it through the constitutional difficulty and perhaps a little longer, to give time for the organization of an adequate colonial force. But no troops could be maintained permanently in the Colony unless required for Imperial purposes. The defence of the frontiers could not be separated from the internal affairs of the Colony. If the Cape adopted responsible government and Basutoland was annexed to it, the Cape Government would exercise the same control over it as over the rest of the Colony, but he agreed with Lord Granville that it would probably be better annexed to Natal. Until responsible government was introduced, Her Majesty's Government was unlikely to agree to any further extension of the South African colonies.[5] Kimberley also suggested that to obviate

---

[1] Gladstone to Kimberley (11 May 1871), Gladstone Papers, B.M. Add. MS. 44540. Kimberley sent a dispatch on these lines on 18 May.
[2] Kimberley to Barkly (17 Oct. 1870), P.P., 1871, xlvii [C. 459], 46–7.
[3] On Barkly in Jamaica see below, Ch. XII; on Victoria, see G. Serle, *The Golden Age . . . the Colony of Victoria, 1851–1861* (Melbourne, 1963).
[4] Barkly to Kimberley (28 Oct. 1870), P.P., 1871, xlvii [C459], 53–4.
[5] Kimberley to Barkly (17 Nov. 1870) (Confidential), ibid., pp. 66–7. Gladstone was consulted about these instructions, Gladstone Papers, B.M. Add. MS. 44539. The last reference was clearly to the diamond fields. Barkly left for the Cape on 24 Nov.

agitation for the removal of the seat of government 'local authorities should be invested with a greater share of legislative and administrative power'—in other words, there should be a federation of the Canadian type.[1]

*Le mieux est l'ennemi du bien.* This was too large a morsel of reform for the Cape to digest at once. The officials, led by Southey, did not want either responsible government or federation. They deprecated 'any change which shall reduce the influence of the Crown in this Colony, which we regard as the chief bond by which its heterogenous elements are held together'. Federation would 'present the very greatest, if not insuperable difficulties'.[2] The House of Assembly adopted Molteno's responsible government resolution, with a rider asking for a Commission to report on the federation proposal, by 31 to 26; but de Villiers, the future Chief Justice, who made the best speech on the winning side, 'did not think the Responsible Government party would be wise in mixing up Federation with Responsible Government'.[3] Porter, now senior member for Cape Town, then drafted a Responsible Government Bill, which passed its second reading by 34 to 27; but the Council rejected it by 12 to 9—mainly, according to Barkly, because Eastern members feared they would not be safe under a responsible ministry located in Cape Town.[4] Barkly disagreed with Lord Kimberley's preference for linking Basutoland with Natal and induced the Cape Parliament to pass a Bill annexing it to the Cape, with provision for a special system of administration and legislation, in effect continuing the existing system.[5] In his opening Speech he had also said that 'virtually . . . it rests with this Parliament to determine whether West Griqualand shall be annexed to this Colony or not' and Molteno's move to give precedence to responsible government was defeated. But

---

[1] Barkly's Speech on Opening Parliament (27 Apr. 1871), P.P., 1871, xlvi [C459], 170. See also Kimberley to Barkly (17 Oct. 1870), ibid., pp. 46–7.

[2] Memos. enclosed in Barkly to Kimberley (31 May 1871) (No. 53), ibid. pp. 173 ff.

[3] House of Assembly, 1 June, *Grahamstown Journal*, 9 June 1871. The vote was taken on 10 June.

[4] Barkly to Kimberley (20 June 1871) (No. 65), P.P., 1871, xlvii [C. 459], 187 See also No. 79 of 31 July 1871, ibid., pp. 197–8.

[5] Act 12 of 1871: Extracts printed in Eybers, op. cit., pp. 61–2. Colonel C. D Griffith of the F.A.M.P. was appointed Governor's Agent and soon raised Basutoland Mounted Police. A hut tax was levied and a code promulgated for the government of the country.

the margin was narrow, and when the Responsible Government
Bill was finally defeated in the Council Barkly withdrew the
Griqualand Annexation Bill because the Executive Council saw
no chance of carrying it so late in the session.[1] All he got from the
House was a resolution 'that pending the adjustment of the boundary disputes, and the passing of a law for the annexation of the
Diamond fields to this Colony . . . the Governor should be
requested to adopt such measures as may appear to him to be
necessary and practicable for the maintenance of order . . . the
collection of revenue and the administration of justice'.[2]

The main reason why the Cape Parliament fought shy of
annexation was the boundary dispute with the Free State. Cape
opinion was not shocked by the burghers' encroachment on
Waterboer's lands: after all 'it was the process by which a great
deal of South Africa had already passed into the possession of the
whites.'[3] There was general agreement that whatever territory
really belonged to Waterboer ought to be annexed but no such
agreement on what belonged to him.[4] The dispute continued; but
the Imperial Government's firm refusal to agree to foreign arbitration strengthened Barkly's hands.[5] On 30 September he informed
Kimberley of his intention 'to act on the application of Captain
Waterboer and his Raad . . . so soon as arrangements for simul-
taneously extending the laws and institutions of the Colony to the
large tract of country thus annexed, can be properly matured'.[6]
He drew further encouragement from the award of Lieutenant-
Governor Keate, made on 17 October. The conference of the
Cape and Transvaal officials at Bloemhof, carefully watched by a
Committee of the Volksraad, had broken up in mid June and the
documents were submitted to Keate as umpire. His award
accorded substantially with the claims of the Barolong, Batlapin,
and Bangwaketse and wholly with those of Waterboer.[7] The

[1] Barkly to Kimberley (15 Aug. 1871) (No. 87), PP., 1872, xliii [C. 508], 4.
[2] House of Assembly, 5 Aug., V. & P., Cape Parliament, 1871.
[3] De Kiewiet, op. cit., p. 281.
[4] Theal, *History of South Africa* (1965 reprint), viii. 367–71.
[5] Kimberley to Barkly (3 June 1871), No. 83, and 20 July 1871 (No. 100),
P.P., 1871, xlvii [C. 459], 183, 195.
[6] Barkly to Kimberley (30 Sept. 1871) (No. 115,) P.P., 1872, xliii (C. 508), 14.
[7] Barkly to Kimberley (31 Oct. 1871) (No. 121) with Award of Keate (17 Oct.)
enclosed, ibid., pp. 25–6. On the award see especially Agar-Hamilton, *The Road
to the North*, ch. v. The reactions on Bechuana tribes were important in the 1880s
but do not concern us here.

Transvaal Volksraad repudiated the award and President Pretorius, who after some vacillation had promised to comply with it, resigned. But this did not deter Barkly. He at once prepared an annexation proclamation and on 17 November the diamond fields of Griqualand West were proclaimed a British territory.[1] Other proclamations dealt with the boundaries, the erection of a High Court and the regulation of diamond digging, and confirmed rights and titles granted by the Free State or the Transvaal, reserving for special inquiry those granted since 1 January 1870.

Barkly had hoped to settle with Brand once annexation was a *fait accompli*.[2] But Brand appealed to the Imperial Government over Barkly's head through the astute Hamelberg, who was leaving South Africa for health reasons. Kimberley saw Hamelberg unofficially and made a small concession. If the Free State would refer the boundary question alone to two Commissioners, as the Transvaal had done, 'it might be open for consideration whether some impartial person unconnected with South Africa might not be appointed as umpire'.[3] Brand took advantage of this opening and suggested that the Dutch Ambassador in London name some distinguished European, not a British subject.[4] Other ambassadors were later suggested as alternatives. Brand still insisted that the Free State could in no circumstances formally waive all claims under the Convention of 1854; but this obstacle did not seem insuperable. Barkly went up to the diamond fields in September 1872 in hopes of going on to Bloemfontein and arranging terms with the President. But Brand was so ill that he had handed over his powers to a Commission of three members of the Volksraad, with whom Barkly found agreement impossible. He noted, however, that the Free State press seemed now 'to desire pecuniary compensation rather than restitution of territory'.[5]

An alternative suggestion commanded a good deal of support in

[1] The proclamations (Nos. 67–72) were enclosed in Barkly to Kimberley (31 Oct. 1871) (No. 123), P.P., 1872, xliii [C. 508], 31–4.
[2] Barkly to Kimberley (18 Aug.) in Kimberley to Granville (25 Sept. 1871), P.R.O. 30/29, 55.
[3] Kimberley to Barkly (2 Nov. 1871) (No. 133), P.P., 1872, xliii [C. 508], 43–4.
[4] Brand to Barkly (25 Mar. 1872), P.P., 1873, xlviii [C. 732], 38.
[5] Barkly to Kimberley (4 Nov. 1872) (No. 124), ibid., p. 134. The dispute was settled on this basis in 1876 for a payment of £90,000.

South Africa, in the House of Commons, and in the Colonial Office itself. Might not the Orange Free State be admitted into a South African federation? There was no great desire in the Cape, Barkly reported, to bring in Natal, with its great Native population, or the Transvaal.

With regard to the Orange Free State, however, the feeling is widely different, there being scarcely a family in the Colony which has not a brother, or son, or cousin there, whilst no reflecting politician can fail to perceive that either for good or for evil, the progress of settlement on the opposite bank of the Orange River is destined to exercise a most important influence over the future fortunes of the Colony.

He asked for instructions, leaving it to Kimberley to say whether the Imperial Parliament should be asked to pass a permissive Bill or whether the responsible government question should first be settled and a formal resolution of the Cape Parliament awaited.[1] Herbert, now Permanent Under-Secretary, favoured a permissive Bill next session if the Law Officers thought Imperial legislation necessary. The Parliamentary Under-Secretary, Knatchbull-Hugessen, though he believed every encouragement should be given to federation as 'the best possible solution of the present difficulty', was inclined to think Imperial legislation 'should follow and not precede Colonial action'; and Kimberley was definitely of that opinion.[2] Gladstone agreed, though as usual he wanted 'due precautions against extension of the responsibility of the Home Government'.

The States have been formed on principles of self-defence; their inception was, I think, due to our interfering with that policy, and I should see with regret any change which went to relieve them of what may be a burden but is also a duty and a source of strength and vitality. I also agree that the adoption of responsible government is to be looked upon as an essential preliminary.[3]

The dispatch to Barkly was framed accordingly. The Law Officers thought an independent state like the Orange Free State could be

[1] Barkly to Kimberley (30 Aug. 1871) No. 94), P.P., 1872, xliii [C. 508], 10–13. R. N. Fowler, Treasurer of the Aborigines Protection Society, moved a motion in favour of Confederation in the House of Commons on 3 Mar. 1871 and another on 28 May 1872. *Hansard*, 3rd Ser. cciv. 1275–95, ccxi. 806–10.
[2] Minutes of Herbert (17 Oct.), Knatchbull-Hugessen (19 Oct.), and Kimberley (30 Oct.) on Barkly to Kimberley (30 Aug. 1871), CO48/456.
[3] Gladstone to Kimberley (26 Oct. 1871), Gladstone Papers, Add. MS. 44540.

united with the Cape without an Imperial Act, though one would
be required to divide the Cape or unite it with Natal. Kimberley
favoured Imperial legislation in any case, but authorized Barkly,
if so requested, to make overtures to the Republics or Natal.

> There are two conditions [he added] which Her Majesty's Govern-
> ment regard as indispensable to their consent to any scheme of Federa-
> tion, namely (1) the adoption of Responsible Government and (2) that
> the United Provinces should undertake to provide for the maintenance
> of order within their territory, and for the defence of their frontiers.[1]

He went on to discuss details which were in fact premature, since
responsible government clearly had priority over federation.

Responsible government was now clearly imminent, though
Herbert admitted he felt anxious about Native affairs and was by
no means convinced 'that this country can relieve itself from
future obligation on that account by inducing the Colonists to
undertake their own government and defence'. Troubles might
arise which were not the frontier farmers' fault; if they became
dangerous 'British troops will have to be poured in and the constitution suspended.'[2] The Executive Councillors must not be
allowed to hold things up by opposing or declining to assist 'a
policy recommended by the responsible ministers of the Crown
at home and by their directions initiated by the Governor of the
Colony in which they hold . . . office.'[3] Sir Henry Barkly was
accordingly instructed to introduce the Bill again, though it was
left to his discretion whether or not to require the Executive
Councillors to introduce it.[4]

Barkly's task was eased by the illness of the Attorney-General:
Jacobs, who acted in his place and introduced the Bill (in the form
it had reached when thrown out by the Legislative Council) was
in favour of responsible government. The majority in its favour
in the House had now increased to ten (35 to 25) and three who
voted against it (presumably because of election promises) were

[1] Kimberley to Barkly (16 Nov. 1871) (No. 140), P.P., 1872, xliii [C. 508],
13–14.
[2] Minute of Herbert (14 July) on Barkly to Kimberley (31 May 1871) (No. 53)
CO48/455.
[3] Minute of Knatchbull-Hugessen (30 Sept.) on Barkly to Kimberley (14 Aug
1871) (Confidential), CO48/456.
[4] Minute of Kimberley (2 Oct. 1871), ibid. Embodied in confidential dispatch
of 20 Oct.

personally in favour.[1] The real fight was in the Legislative Council, which after twenty-one divisions passed the Bill by the narrowest possible majority—one on the second reading and the chairman's casting vote in committee. On 18 June it was reserved for the royal assent, which was of course a foregone conclusion.

But nothing came of the great federation scheme. The Cape Federation Commission appointed by Barkly took the view that until the Boer Republics and Natal showed a disposition to federate with the Cape and until Griqualand West and the Transkei at least up to the Bashee were annexed, federation was neither necessary nor expedient.[2] There was in fact renewed talk of bringing the Transkei under British rule: the 'emigrant Tambookies' under E. J. Warner and the Fingoes under Captain Blyth were in good order, but Kreli was restive, quarrelled with his agent Fynn, and later in the year attacked the Tembu chief Gangelizwe, whilst the disorders in Adam Kok's country led to the dispatch of a Commission which urged the annexation of Griqualand East with the least possible delay.[3] The Colonial Office itself now realized that this was the destiny of the Transkei but believed that responsible government must come first and other changes later.[4] The same considerations applied to the Griqualand West Annexation Bill, which had to be withdrawn after three days' debate. Almost all the Cape Dutch members sympathized with the Free State in the boundary dispute. Others said the diamond diggers wanted Free State rule because it gave them more power to coerce the Natives. The responsible government party did not want to offend the Dutch on the eve of taking office. The Conservatives wanted their revenge on Barkly for supporting responsible government.[5] He consoled himself for the loss of the Bill with the reflection that 'the reservation for the present of the Crown's prerogatives in the hands of its representative will decidedly facilitate the settlement

---

[1] *Grahamstown Journal*, 31 May 1872.

[2] Report of Federation Commission (20 Mar.) in Barkly to Kimberley (1 May 1872) (No. 44), P.P., 1873, xlviii [C. 732], 43–5. The Commission recommended the division of the Cape into three provinces. On obstacles to federation, cf. also *Grahamstown Journal*, 1 Dec. 1871.

[3] Barkly to Kimberley (23 Aug. 1872, Nos. 100, 101, and 102), CO48/461. Also various other dispatches and Cape Parliamentary Papers.

[4] Minute of Knatchbull-Hugessen (20 Nov.) and Kimberley (25 Nov.) on Barkly to Kimberley (23 Aug. 1872), loc. cit.

[5] *Grahamstown Journal*, 14 June 1872. An interesting analysis, confirmed by Barkly to Kimberley (17 June 1872) (No. 63) [C. 732], 50–2.

of affairs.'[1] Kimberley—underrating the urgency of action in 1871 if there was to be action at all—was now inclined to blame Barkly for annexing the diamond fields before the Cape Parliament had passed the Bill: 'it is for many reasons inconvenient that a territory which is practically a part of the Colony should not be formally incorporated with it.' But he felt bound to support him.[2] The Imperial Government was in fact paying the penalty of attempting too much at once. Molteno, who became the first Premier of the Cape on 1 December 1872, had worked for responsible government for many years and was right to concentrate on the Colony itself. As Barkly said many years later, his policy was 'not to seek to increase its responsibilities in connection with the rest of South Africa more than he could help'.[3]

It still remained to put the government of Griqualand West on a more permanent foundation. There was trouble, due largely to the beginnings of illicit diamond-buying, over the issue of digging or diamond-dealing licences to 'coloured persons'—in the early stages many Koranas in particular had dug for diamonds and Indians, presumably from Natal, were diamond buyers. Barkly spent three weeks there after the session, found 'a strong desire . . . for Representative Institutions and Local Self-Government', and recommended the appointment of Southey, who would leave office on the advent of a responsible ministry, as Lieutenant-Governor, with a constitution on the same lines as that of Natal.[4]

Southey was duly appointed; but the constitutional recommendation cannot have enhanced Barkly's reputation in the Colonial Office, for the constitution of Natal had been working badly. In 1861 (the year in which we last touched on the affairs of Natal) the Legislative Council had already asked for the recall of Lieutenant-Governor Scott 'from a scene of operations where his views differ so entirely from those of the inhabitants of the Colony'.[5] Adding insult to injury, it proposed to increase the salary of future Lieutenant-Governors, 'to afford a wider selection

---

[1] Barkly to Kimberley (17 June 1872) (No. 63), loc. cit.
[2] Kimberley to Barkly (27 July 1872), ibid., p. 80. Cf. Minute (22 July) on Barkly to Kimberley (17 June 1872) (No. 63), CO48/460.
[3] P. A. Molteno, *Life and Times of Sir J. C. Molteno* (London, 1900), ii. 457.
[4] Barkly to Kimberley (3 Oct. 1872) (No. 107), P.P., 1873, xlviii [C. 732], 119. The recommendation of Southey came later, on 18 Oct.
[5] Memorial of Legislative Council (9 Aug.) in Scott to Newcastle (21 Sept. 1861) (No. 90), P.P., 1862, xxxvi (H.C. 293,) pp. 6 ff.

from among men fitted by their experience to direct the affairs of a colony possessing a Representative Institution and composed of a mixed population'.[1] Scott for his part suggested a bicameral constitution with a nominated Legislative Council and an elected Assembly in which the Colonial Secretary and Attorney-General (as in the Cape) would have seats but no votes.[2] This proposal had some support in the Colonial Office, especially from Chichester Fortescue, who thought that under the existing constitution 'the unhappy four official members seem only to act as the red rag to the popular bull'.[3] But Rogers did not think Scott had made his case.

The true difficulty of the case seems to me insurmountable. A *certain amount* of legislative power has been given to the settlers, but the circumstances of the Colony render it impossible to give them *all*. On the other hand they will never be satisfied till they have all, and whether in one chamber or in two will (as it appears to me), always be struggling for what they have not got, except while they are accidentally pacified by some Governor who has tact and good management to make them trust him and be quiet. Sir G. Grey has accomplished this at the Cape in a good measure. . . . Mr. Scott would have a chance of managing the Legislature if he could identify himself with some popular wish (as that of utilizing the Zulus as labourers or obtaining an inordinate amount of military expenditure) but unless he can do this the Council will no doubt lead him an unpleasant life. . . . Will not . . . the Legislative Council take the place of the officials as 'red rag'? And shall we not find that we have only silenced controversy in the Assembly at the expense of chronic collision between the two branches of the Legislature?[4]

In any case Scott had dissolved the Council, and the Duke of Newcastle thought that 'we ought to have the experience of at least one session of the second Parliament under the Charter'; also before any change was made 'the remedial measure should be made the subject of discussion if not in the Legislature itself, yet

[1] Resolution of Legislative Council (12 Aug.) in Scott to Newcastle (19 Sept. 1861) (No. 89), ibid., p. 4.
[2] Scott to Newcastle (23 Sept. 1861) (No. 91), CO179/60.
[3] Minute of Fortescue (20 Dec.) on Scott to Newcastle (23 Sept. 1861) (No. 91), ibid.
[4] Minute of Rogers (23 Dec.) on Scott to Newcastle (23 Sept. 1861) (No. 91), ibid.

certainly among the persons whose interest is at stake'. He felt little confidence too in a Council composed exclusively of nominees of the Crown.[1]

Native policy remained the fundamental point at issue between Scott and the settlers. Here controversy centred on the desire of Scott and Shepstone to give greater security to the Natives' title to their locations by creating tribal titles for each tribe, to be vested in trustees, of which the chief should always be one. This ran counter to the Legislative Council's belief in individualization of title, which Shepstone for his part thought would be 'a reckless experiment, accompanied with very serious danger'.[2] Individualization of property in land was still believed in the Colonial Office to be an important objective; but Elliot for one saw that 'if the lands could be frittered away into grants to individual Zulus, they would . . . be soon defrauded of them by the Whites in return for petty gifts'.[3] Newcastle had no hesitation in supporting Scott, even though he looked to a gradual admixture of the races on a fair and friendly footing as a better guarantee of peace than complete segregation.[4] A Legislative Council suggestion that the Lieutenant-Governor, as being, under the Queen, paramount chief, should be constituted sole trustee paved the way to a compromise.[5] Later the Lieutenant-Governor and Executive Council for the time being were substituted for the Lieutenant-Governor alone and were constituted a corporation for this purpose by a Royal Charter of 1864.[6]

Scott and his Legislative Council also worked together to exempt Natives possessed of certain qualifications from Native law, to which all were subject under an ordinance of 1849, and to regulate the marriage of Natives by Christian rites and the descent of property owned by Natives; but the Council would only accept Scott's proposal to make an exempted Native with the requisite

[1] Minute of Newcastle (5 Jan. 1862) (No. 91), CO179/60. Newcastle to Scott (30 Jan. 1862) (No. 190), G.H. 11, Natal Archives.
[2] Memo. of Shepstone (23 Sept.) in Scott to Newcastle (21 Sept. 1861) (No. 90), P.P., 1862, xxxvi (H.C. 293), 17–20.
[3] Minute of Elliot (2 Dec.) on Scott to Newcastle (21 Sept. 1861) (No. 90), CO179/60.
[4] Newcastle to Scott (4 Feb. 1862), P.P., 1862, xxxvi (H.C. 293), 21–2.
[5] Report of Select Committee (5 Aug.) in Scott to Newcastle (4 Sept. 1862) (No. 128), CO179/65.
[6] Newcastle to Scott (5 May 1864) (Separate), Enclosure, G.H. 13, Natal Archives.

property qualification eligible for the vote in a form which he thought unduly restrictive and Cardwell would not accept.[1]

The fillip given to the economy of Natal by the arrival of 1,000 Indian immigrant labourers, mostly to work on the sugar estates, no doubt contributed to the political *détente* of the early sixties. The only drawback to the Indians from the planters' point of view was that they were very expensive. Most of the planters had to look to the banks for finance, since the law required 'an immediate and uncertain amount' to be repaid to the Government by employers of immigrants on their arrival, and the rate of interest was 12 per cent. A few Amatonga were introduced from beyond Zululand: they were much cheaper, but the supply was uncertain. So the planters turned to the Government to secure more liberal terms of immigration. After inquiry by a Select Committee, a new immigration law fixed the amount payable by employers at £12. 10s., to be paid in five yearly instalments.[2] Further legislation in 1864 extended the term of assignment from three to five years and authorized a loan of £100,000 for Indian immigration.[3] On this basis Natal applied for 2,844 male adults in 1863–4 and a permanent Natal Agency was opened in Madras. But the competition of the French colonies was severe and the order was not completed until 1866. Meanwhile the loan had run into difficulties on the London market. The supply of colonial securities, the Crown Agents reported, 'has for some time past been gradually outstripping the demand'. Not much more than a third had been taken up by the end of 1865 and that at prices slightly below par.[4]

By this time Natal had fallen into a depression. The prosperous years had seen some improvement in the port of Durban (until the

[1] Scott to Cardwell (25 Oct. 1864) (No. 72), CO179/72. Cardwell to Maclean (9 Mar. 1865) (No. 27), G.H. 14, Natal Archives. Professor E. H. Brookes in his *History of Native Policy in South Africa* (2nd ed., Pretoria, 1927), p. 60, regards this as 'a skilful and disingenuous attempt to maintain a political colour bar without saying so'.

[2] Scott to Newcastle (11 Aug. 1863) (No. 82), CO179/67. Professor L. M. Thompson in his 'Indian Immigration into Natal, 1860–1872', *Archives Year Book for South African History*, xv, vol. ii, shows that Scott was disingenuous in stating in this dispatch that the average cost was £17. 2s. 9d. per male assigned: the expenses incurred were at least £20. 6s. 2d. per male assigned and this excludes certain other expenses such as return to India of sick Indians, op. cit., p. 37. In 1864 expenses repayable by employers were increased to £15.

[3] Laws No. 15 and 17 in Scott to Cardwell (28 Oct. 1864) (No. 75), CO179/72.

[4] Julyan to Rogers (15 Dec. 1865), CO179/77.

contractor went bankrupt in 1864) but also speculative schemes for a railway up to Pietermaritzburg and even beyond it to the coal districts in the North, to be financed on the land grant system and fortified by a thirty-year monopoly of the right of search for minerals on all waste lands in Natal. The Colonial Office rejected the coal scheme out of hand and objected to the guarantee of interest suggested for the Natal Central Railway Company which was to construct the Durban–Pietermaritzburg line.[1] It was Scott's successor, Colonel Maclean, who received these dispatches. His short term of office was largely concerned with frontier problems—the effective occupation of the territory in the south-west ceded by Faku some years before, the seizure by the Transvaal of the 'Blood River territory' ceded by Cetywayo in 1861 but now disputed, and finally Lesaoana's cattle raid and the Basuto war.[2] Then in July 1865 Maclean, who had arrived at the end of the previous year a sick and much worried man, was totally incapacitated by a paralytic stroke.[3] A month later, after a short tenure by Lieutenant-Colonel Thomas, Lieutenant-Colonel J. J. Bisset, a former officer of the Cape Mounted Rifles, arrived to act as Lieutenant-Governor for a year and nine months. It was he who proclaimed the territory acquired from Faku as the County of Alfred on New Year's Day 1866. But it was also he who had to bear the first impact of the financial crisis precipitated by the collapse of Natal's 'overberg' trade owing to the Basuto war.[4] The annual treks of the Boers with their ox-wagons to trade in Pietermaritzburg stopped; the Free State courts were closed, so that debts were irrecoverable; large areas of land came into the hands of banks and trust companies, many of which became insolvent; the coastal planters were hard put to it to pay the instalments due on Indians already assigned to them and quite

---

[1] Cardwell to Maclean (27 Feb. 1865) (No. 70), P.P., 1865, l (H.C. 488), 68–9. Rogers had remarked in a Minute (29 Dec. 1865): 'A more reckless sacrifice of the future interests of the Colony to the possible advantage of a knot of shareholders than that which is embodied in the Coal Company's Ordinance was never within my knowledge submitted for the sanction of the Secretary of State', CO179/72.

[2] Maclean to Cardwell (27 Feb. 1865, No. 34, and 31 Jan. 1865, No. 28), CO179/74. On Lesaoana's raid see above, p. 158.

[3] Gawler to Grey (6 July 1866), Grey Coll., Auckland. Gawler explains that Maclean had been not only ill but heavily in debt. In 1868 he was granted a pension, backdated to Jan. 1867, when he ceased to receive any salary in respect of Natal, P.P., 1867–8, xli (H.C. 48).

[4] The crisis was aggravated by a fall in the price of wool.

unable to order more.[1] The Legislative Council typically tried to
tax the Natives rather than their own constituents by doubling the
hut tax of 7s.[2] Also, pending their claim to 'those full rights and
privileges of self-government which are now allowed to be the
birthright of every colony founded by Englishmen', the Council
asked for 'some admixture of a more popular element in the
Executive Council'.[3]

It was left to the new Lieutenant-Governor, R. W. Keate, who
had been Governor of Trinidad, to seek a way out of these difficulties. Under him, we are told, 'Government House for the first
time became a centre of gracious and impartial hospitality';[4] but
though Carnarvon tried to smooth his path by saying he would
not object to the appointment of two Legislative Councillors as
non-official members of the Executive Council, it was not long
before Keate was as much at odds with the Legislative Council as
ever Scott had been.[5] The session of 1867 was one of frustration.
Natal was trying to attract immigrants, with some capital if
possible, from England or the Cape; but it was difficult to offer
suitable land in large enough lots when the Imperial authorities
thought land had been granted too prodigally already.[6] The
diversion of the immigration loan of 1864 to public works helped
the Council to tide over. But next year the Council, after imposing stamp duties and levying fees on marriages according to
Native custom, concentrated on retrenchment. 'The elective
members', Keate reported, '. . . appear to be anxious to take the
opportunity of testing their power of subordinating all salaries,
whether fixed by the Charter of the Colony or by permanent
Laws, and whether the offices they remunerate are held during
pleasure or during good behaviour, to their annual vote.'[7] He
vetoed the Bill and dissolved the Council.

[1] On this see Thompson, op. cit., p. 40; Report on Blue Book for 1867 (9 Dec.
1868), CO179/90; Sir J. Robinson, A Life Time in South Africa (London, 1900),
p. 259.
[2] Bisset to Carnarvon (19 Dec. 1866) (No. 130), CO179/81. The Colonial
Office, after consulting Scott, referred this back but the increase was finally
agreed to.
[3] Report of Select Committee in Bisset to Cardwell (6 Aug. 1866) (No. 82),
CO179/80.
[4] Robinson, op. cit., p. 35.
[5] Carnarvon to Bisset (12 Oct. 1866) (No. 14), G.H. 16, Natal Archives.
[6] Cardwell to Bisset (9 May 1866) (No. 138), ibid.
[7] Keate to Buckingham (22 Sept. 1868) (No. 100), CO179/90.

In the new Council, however, as in the old, the elective members were in 'organized antagonism' to the official members.
They passed two Bills reducing civil list and other salaries,
which Keate reserved. A month later he sent home another Bill,
altering the Charter. It proposed to add four members chosen by
the legislature to the Executive Council, reduce the official membership to three and increase the elective, but not the official,
element in the Legislative Council.[1] This was a Bill the Imperial
authorities could not possibly accept. Their object, Rogers
thought, must be 'if possible to persuade the constituencies and
the members that Government really desire to govern in their
interests'. Lord Granville should take the opportunity of explaining his general policy in South Africa.[2] Granville acted on this
advice. The Bill altering the Charter, he told Keate, could not
receive the royal assent. The composition of the Executive Council should be left to the Crown and the circumstances of Natal
did not warrant a diminution of the power of the Crown in the
legislature.

British troops are for the present kept there almost entirely at the
expense of the Home Government in order to maintain order and
security. . . . It follows that the Home Government must retain the
management of Native policy and it is alike manifest from reason and
from experience that this is not really practicable unless the Crown
retains also an effectual control over the general administration of the
Colony.

But he was willing to have two non-officials from the Legislative
Council on the Executive Council as 'a mode of bringing the
feelings of the community to bear on the action of Government'.
He hoped that the Executive would not become 'an arena for
dispute' and that all classes, including the public service, would
bear their share of the necessary sacrifices.[3]

His hopes were disappointed. Without waiting for a reply,
the Legislative Council had made sweeping reductions in official
salaries and in establishments, amalgamating among others the

[1] Keate to Granville (23 Aug. 1869), No. 70 and 20 Sept. 1869, No. 75),
CO179/94 and 95.
[2] Minute of Rogers (13 Nov.) on Keate to Granville (20 Sept. 1869) (No. 75),
CO179/95.
[3] Granville to Keate (6 Dec. 1869) (No. 67), G.H. 18, Natal Archives. Natal
made a defence contribution of £4,000 annually.

offices of Colonial Secretary and Secretary for Native Affairs, presumably to squeeze Shepstone out. The Auditor-General was to become the servant of the Legislative Council.[1] The Imperial Government would never agree to this. Full concession, said Rogers drily, would mean 'New Zealand over again—a settlers' policy backed by Imperial troops'.[2] But the tone of Granville's dispatch (based on Rogers's minute) was still conciliatory. It was fair enough that Natives who owed their security and well being to British government should pay not only the expenses, military, and magisterial, which their presence in British territory involved, but also some equivalent for the advantages they received; but they should not be so burdened as to provoke discontent. He found little sign of 'care and impartiality' in the Legislative Council's reductions, and the export figures seemed to disprove 'any such depression as to justify a departure from the ordinary rules of justice and economy'. The Council had, he pointed out, agreed to a railway scheme involving a subsidy of £40,000 a year. He suggested an impartial inquiry into establishments.[3] This proposal the Council accepted, but the dispatch did not change the attitude otherwise, nor did the appointment, in May 1870, of two Legislative Councillors, Akerman of Pietermaritzburg and Goodricke, a Durban lawyer, to the Executive Council. The Council made some supplementary provision for 1869 and 1870, but it re-enacted its disallowed Bills. Keate thought it futile to submit estimates for 1871 to the Council and dissolved it, paid certain salaries without warrant and refused a Bill of Indemnity.[4]

This was going too far. Though Monsell favoured a return to Crown Colony government, both Rogers and Herbert, whilst rejecting the Council's demand for control of the executive as inconsistent with the fundamental principles of the constitution, thought yet another effort at compromise was called for.[5] Knatchbull-Hugessen, who had now succeeded Monsell, agreed with them in an interesting minute. Natal was not fit for responsible

[1] Keate to Granville (22 Oct. 1869, No. 100, and 18 Nov. 1869, No. 123), CO179/95 and 96.
[2] Minute of Rogers (9 Feb. 1870) on Keate to Granville (22 Oct. 1869), CO179/95.
[3] Granville to Keate (16 Mar. 1870) (No. 100), G.H. 19, Natal Archives. On the railway scheme, see below, p. 197.
[4] Keate to Kimberley (23 Sept. 1870) (No. 75), CO179/99.
[5] Minutes of Rogers (5 Jan.) and Herbert (20 Jan. 1871) on Keate to Kimberley (23 Sept. 1870), ibid. I have not seen Monsell's Minute, but Rogers refers to it.

government, which would be positively dangerous; but 'conciliation should be exhausted before stronger measures are taken'. All three, however, thought that the work of reconciliation 'should be in other hands than those of Mr Keate'.[1] In the meantime Kimberley merely informed Keate that the expenditure in question remained illegal 'until validated by a Law of indemnity'.[2] Twenty-two officials thereupon lost their employment. But when the Establishments Commission produced not one agreed report, but three, with the Speaker (Macfarlane) and the other Legislative Councillor still hammering away at their points of amalgamation of offices, abolition of Border Agents, magistrates' clerks, and the like, and Keate insisting that their real object was not economy but 'unchecked, unbounded and irresponsible power', Herbert thought the time for action had come.

Responsible government is impossible on account of the natives; retrogression to Crown government cannot be thought of in the absence of a demand for it from a decided majority. The present form of government must therefore be made to last until Natal is absorbed into the South African Confederation. But it has been very fully proved that this form of Government will not work in Natal unless as at the Cape . . . a sufficient sum of money to guarantee the steady working of administration is reserved from being voted by the elective members.

The Charter should therefore be amended to reserve a civil list of say £20,000. The Legislative Council could then be told that 'their general views had been accepted' and the Secretary of State would be prepared to consider proposals for the allocation of some of this to other public purposes.[3] Kimberley accepted Herbert's recommendations. The Supplementary Charter reserved £40,100 as a civil list, £28,100 for civil establishments being the approximate figure suggested by the Legislative Council. It was tactfully suggested that there were 'objections . . . of the most serious character' to entrusting a 'handful' of 13,000 white settlers with responsible government in the presence of a 'warlike native population' of 250,000–300,000.[4] The introduction of the new

[1] Minute of Knatchbull-Hugessen (28 Jan. 1871), CO179/99.
[2] Kimberley to Keate (18 Feb. 1871) (No. 60), G.H. 19: Natal Archives.
[3] Keate to Kimberley (24 Nov. 1871) (No. 107), with Enclosure and Minutes of Herbert (5 May) and Kimberley (11 May 1872), CO179/103.
[4] Kimberley to Musgrave (20 May 1872) (No. 189), Natal Government Gazette, 23 July 1872. Extracts printed in A. F. Hattersley (ed.), More Annals of Natal (London, 1936), pp. 216–19.

arrangements was entrusted to Anthony Musgrave, who had proved his quality as a conciliator in Newfoundland and British Columbia. Keate was appointed Governor of the Gold Coast, where he died in the following year.

Kimberley accompanied this dispatch by another giving approval in principle to an ambitious scheme of railway development put forward by a very persistent railway promoter named Welbourne, to whom the Legislative Council since 1869 had pinned its faith. The Colonial Office (with the possible exception of Knatchbull-Hugessen) preferred Government construction, but admitted that the state of Natal's finances would then limit construction to lines through the coastal sugar district and up to Pietermaritzburg. Even Knatchbull-Hugessen had qualms about the large land grants and the monopoly of coal and iron working which the scheme involved; and Kimberley asked how the proposed immigrants were to be prevented from going to the diamond fields.[1] But on reflection, while still suggesting modifications of the scheme and expert advice on the terms of the contract, he decided it would be politic to let the colonists have their way.

It is needless to say that the Secretary of State is always desirous to give effect, if he can properly do so, to the wishes of the colonists; and in most matters relating to the internal affairs of the Colony, he would be assuming a responsibility which he could not successfully discharge if, after fully explaining the reasons which appear to him to make one of two courses preferable to the other, he were to insist on opposing that course to which the colonists on mature reflection declare their adherence. . . . It appears to me that although I should undoubtedly have preferred a smaller beginning and a more gradual extension of the railway system I should not be justified in refusing to entertain the proposal that Natal should resort to . . . a subsidized Company.[2]

The settlers, as a body, still complained of their lack of labour and of the unwillingness of the Natives in Natal to supply it. In 1869 the Legislative Council passed a Bill 'to facilitate the obtaining of Native labour' which, Keate complained, would convert

[1] Minutes of Herbert (11 Mar.), Knatchbull-Hugessen (12 Mar.) and Kimberley (23 Dec. 1871), CO179/104.
[2] Kimberley to Musgrave (21 May 1872) (No. 190), P.P., 1872, xliii [C. 618], 42–4.

the magistrates' offices into servants' registry offices.[1] The Colonial
Office was at first inclined to ask why not? But when Keate replied
that advice to a chief of vacancies to be filled 'would take very
little to convert . . . into an order', the Office changed its line
entirely and expressed the opinion that 'the right which it appears
the Colonial Government possess of requiring from the Natives
forced labour on public works should be at once surrendered'.[2]
The Legislative Council had also suggested formal negotiations
for an influx of labour from the tribes to the north: contact with
the Amatonga, Amaswazi, and Amahlamini was in fact increasing,
and labourers were coming from those parts, but Keate rightly
thought that this should be left to private enterprise.[3] No doubt one
element in the situation was the increasing prestige of Shepstone,
to whom Sir John Robinson later paid a notable tribute.

Mr. Shepstone's inertia was qualified by legislative activity, and
though he was slow to move, in the end he did advance in the direction
of a more vigorous and enlightened policy. . . . Though I was usually
on the side of a progressive policy, looking back to those days in the
light of subsequent experiences, it seems to me now that the peace and
order that have so conspicuously marked the history of Natal have
been greatly due to this admixture of official conservatism with colonial
progressiveness.[4]

In the words of Natal's historian, in the seventies 'the problems
of railway development and of ensuring an adequate supply of
Indian labour for the sugar plantations dominated all other issues.'[5]
Reviving prosperity brought with it a new demand for Indian
labour. The five-year indentures of the second batch of Indians
were about to expire and many would not be tempted to stay on
the estates: others, who had been ten years in the colony, were
claiming the return passages to which they were entitled. In
1869–70 Keate's efforts to provide in the estimates for the introduction of more Indians, Government bearing one-third of the

[1] Keate to Granville (30 Oct. 1869) (No. 110), CO179/96.
[2] Granville to Keate (23 Feb. 1870) (No. 94) and Kimberley to Keate (13 Aug.
1870), G.H. 19, Natal Archives. Keate to Granville (19 May 1870) (No. 30),
CO179/98.
[3] Keate to Granville (30 Oct. 1869) (No. 110), loc. cit. See also D. Leslie,
Among the Zulus and Amatongas (ed. W. H. Drummond) (Glasgow, 1875).
[4] Robinson, op. cit., pp. 302–3.
[5] Hattersley, More Annals of Natal, p. 196.

cost, were foiled by the Legislative Council. Next year the Council was more co-operative: £20,000 out of a newly authorized
loan were allotted to Indian immigration.[1] But the complaints
made by the returning immigrants—nearly one-third of those still
alive of the 1860–1 immigration—had decided the Government
of India to forbid further emigration to Natal. According to the
report of the Madras Government 'they all complained that they
had been told, before leaving Madras and reaching Natal, that at
the end of their ten years' service, they would get £10 each on
leaving to return to India, but had not received any money at all.
Another general complaint was that they had not proper rations
of rice.' Some complained of cruelty, others of underpayment.[2]
Granville at once asked for an investigation and, not finding
Natal's first reply satisfactory, Kimberley sent a second dispatch.

This time the Natal Government persuaded Colonel B. P. Lloyd,
a Hindustani-speaking colonel in the Bengal Staff Corps who was
in Natal on sick leave, to serve on a Commission with the
Attorney-General, Gallwey. The Commission made an exhaustive inquiry and its report was a masterly survey of the whole
subject. There was evidence that recruiters in India had promised
a gratuity, but this was quite unauthorized. There was also evidence that many of the immigrants had been badly misled about
conditions in Natal. Wages did not appear unreasonable (by the
standards of those days); but 'complaints were frequent of deduc-
tions from pay . . . on account of sickness and absence without
leave'. The mealie meal (substituted for rice) of which some complained was liked by others. The most bitter complaints were
of treatment when sick: the Commission, whilst admitting the
healthiness of the climate, considered more frequent and regular
medical attendance and inspection desirable, though the Indians
appeared to prefer treatment in their own huts to hospitals.
Provision of schooling was almost negligible: it should be increased, and education might even be made compulsory. Resident
magistrates had neglected their duty of half-yearly inspection.
But, for all this, many Indians had prospered. The homesickness
of many could be remedied by increasing facilities for bringing

---

[1] Keate to Granville (23 Dec. 1871) (No. 131), CO179/104. See also Thompson,
op. cit., pp. 42–4.
[2] Proceedings of Madras Government (5 May) in Granville to Keate (9 Oct.
1871) (No. 11), G.H. 19, Natal Archives.

their wives with them and for marrying in Natal. Small grants of land might be offered in lieu of return passages. The appointment of a full-time Protector of Indian Immigrants (a term recommended instead of Coolie Agent) would provide better supervision; but the Indians had never been systematically ill-treated or oppressed, and Natal should seek to retain their 'industrial habits' and skill.[1] The Government adopted the report, and Musgrave urged the colony's claim to have emigration reopened.[2] Lloyd himself was appointed Protector of Indian Immigrants. Kimberley passed Musgrave's request on to the India Office, though he insisted that Government should not bear more than a third of the cost of an immigration which chiefly benefited one section of the colony.[3] Immigration was resumed in 1874. As Thompson says towards the end of his valuable study: 'Indians and Europeans were co-operating to their mutual advantage, without a hint of future clashes of interest.'[4]

The barometer in Natal seemed at last to be set fair. Musgrave had his difficulties. Influential politicians were irritated at the 'totally unexpected abridgment of their future power over the Establishments' by the revised Charter.[5] But, according to Lindley, he soon 'made the colonists happy by his open-hearted, friendly bearing towards them'.[6] The Colonial Office had had a hard task in keeping the Natal constitution afloat; but Kimberley seemed to have found the happy mean between intransigence and surrender. The conscientious scruples of the Imperial Government—and perhaps the sequel to the concession in New Zealand —made it impossible to allow the Natal colonists to manage their own Native affairs.

Even at the Cape, where Sir Philip Wodehouse's scruples had been overridden and responsible government conceded, it was already clear in 1872 that the limitation of British responsibilities in South Africa—the original aim of British policy—was not going to be achieved. The Afrikaners had not escaped the atten-

[1] Report of Coolie Commission (Aug. 1872) in Musgrave to Kimberley (20 Sept. 1872) (No. 18), CO179/107.
[2] Musgrave to Kimberley (20 Sept. 1872) (No. 18), ibid.
[3] Kimberley to Musgrave (5 Jan. 1873) (draft), ibid.
[4] Thompson, op. cit., p. 70.
[5] Musgrave to Kimberley (12 Aug. 1872) (No. 11), CO179/107.
[6] Smith, Lindley, pp. 376–7. An undated letter, obviously early in Musgrave term. Musgrave was appointed Governor of South Australia in 1873.

tions of the humanitarians by trekking north and now the discovery of diamonds was to involve them, willy nilly, in the toils of the financiers. Lord Kimberley and his successor Carnarvon thought they could discern a solution to all these problems in federation. But this in its turn proved to be a mirage.

# VII

## SELF-GOVERNMENT AND
## MAORI AFFAIRS
### 1853–1860

BRITISH policy towards New Zealand in its first twelve years as a British colony had culminated in the grant to it in 1852 of a liberal constitution. The sympathetic attitude of Earl Grey and his successor as Secretary of State for the Colonies, the Conservative Sir John Pakington, had contributed much to this achievement; at the same time the Governor, Sir George Grey, regarded the Constitution Act, with some justice, as mainly his handiwork, whereas in colonial eyes it was the outcome of a long struggle against Sir George Grey's obstructive tactics, nominally in the interests of the Maoris but really in defence of his own autocratic power.[1]

Thus, though the colonists welcomed the constitution, its passage was unlikely to put an end to their differences with the Governor. Many of them, to judge by the newspapers, looked to the first meeting of the General Assembly as an opportunity for settling old scores with Sir George Grey, to whom Pakington, in his covering dispatch with the official text of the Constitution Act, had entrusted the task of bringing it into operation. In a series of proclamations in February and early March 1853 Grey divided the colony into the six provinces constituted by the Act, divided the provinces into electoral districts, made provision for the election of Superintendents of provinces, members of Provincial Councils and of the House of Representatives, and for the registration of electors and the issue of writs; and proclaimed his own assumption of the powers vested in him by the Constitution Act. On 4 March, under powers delegated to him until the General

---

[1] On all this see my *British Colonial Policy in the Age of Peel and Russell*, chs. and xiii.

Assembly met, he issued regulations reducing the price of land throughout New Zealand, except the Canterbury and Otago Blocks, which were still governed by the regulations under which these settlements were founded. By mid-July, the end of the six months' period allowed after the proclamation of the Act, writs for the forthcoming elections had been issued. A series of financial circulars in August acquainted the nascent Provincial Governments with the arrangements the Governor had made to see them through until the General Assembly should make provision. The various Provincial Governments came into operation between July and October and the Provincial Councils, though delayed by the necessity of summoning them by proclamation in the Government *Gazette* at Auckland, all met before the end of the year.

But on the last day of the year Sir George Grey left New Zealand without summoning the General Assembly. As long ago as 30 July 1852 he had written privately to Pakington asking for 'leave of absence for eighteen months to enable me to visit Europe'—which he had not seen for a dozen years.[1] In February 1853 Pakington's successor, the Duke of Newcastle, wrote a dispatch granting him twelve months' leave. This reached him in May, though he did not acknowledge it until 1 August. It is clear that he never meant to meet the Assembly—though on his departure he recommended the Officer administering the Government, Colonel R. H. Wynyard, to summon it and Wynyard did so by proclamation of 18 January 1854. The postponement of the Assembly caused many protests and Grey's critics appealed to England. Adderley and Lord Lyttelton, who had been closely associated with the colonists in their campaign for the constitution, and even Sir John Pakington, lent a sympathetic ear, waited on the Duke of Newcastle, and criticized Grey's conduct in Parliament. Adderley, as we have seen, remonstrated against his appointment as Governor of the Cape. But Grey, on his arrival in England, supplied the Colonial Office with materials for his defence, stressing in particular the desirability of setting the provincial machinery in motion first. He convinced Merivale and Newcastle and was stoutly defended by his chiefs in Parliament. Once the Crimean War had begun there was small chance that Parliament

---

[1] Grey to Pakington (30 July 1852) (Private), Newcastle Papers (microfilm), NeC9555. His mother, whom he hoped to see, died on 5 May 1854.

would pay much heed to New Zealand grievances in any case. It was time its leaders looked to the future.[1]

There was no question what would be the great issue before the General Assembly, though it was not mentioned in the able speech written by the Attorney-General, Swainson, with which Colonel Wynyard opened the Assembly on 27 May. If responsible government had not been in the minds of the colonial leaders already, Edward Gibbon Wakefield, who had arrived in New Zealand in February 1853 and had been elected to the House of Representatives for the Hutt, was determined to bring it to the front. Henry Sewell's journal gives us a characteristic glimpse of his work behind the scenes as members gathered in Auckland for the opening. 'Wakefield's powerful mind goes about like a stockman driving in wild cattle and reducing them to order. He is the informing principle and mainspring of the whole. . . . The Otago and New Plymouth men for the most part follow him; and he has in fact by far the largest party in the House of mere followers. Nobody else has any followers at all.'[2] It was he who on 2 June moved the motion asking for the establishment of ministerial responsibility 'both as an essential means whereby the Central Government may rightly exercise a due control over the Provincial Governments, and as a no less indispensable means of obtaining for the General Government the confidence and attachment of the people'.

Faced with this resolution, which was carried after four days' debate by 29 to 1, Wynyard turned to his Attorney-General for advice. Basing himself on the Governor's commission and the Royal Instructions, Swainson concluded that

in the absence of special authority from Her Majesty's Government, it is not . . . within the power of the Officer administering the Government to take any measures for carrying into effect the resolution of the House of Representatives further than to prepare the way for opening

[1] I have discussed this question in *The Provincial System in New Zealand, 1852–76* (2nd ed., Christchurch, 1964), ch. iv. See also A. H. McLintock, *Crown Colony Government in New Zealand* (Wellington, 1958), ch. xviii (critical of Grey); J. Rutherford, *Sir George Grey*, pp. 252–62; and the judicious summing up of D. G. Herron, 'Sir G. Grey and the Summoning of the first General Assembly', *Historical Studies: Australia and New Zealand*, viii. 364–82. On the position at home see Godley to J. E. FitzGerald (9 Jan. and 20 Apr. 1854), *FitzGerald Letters*, Canterbury Museum.

[2] Journal of Sewell, 24 May 1854.

the principal offices of the Government to new men, and in the mean time, and as a temporary measure, to add two or three members of the Assembly to the Executive Council, for the purpose of establishing a recognized and responsible medium of communication between the Executive and the Legislative of the Government.[1]

But Wynyard did not send for Wakefield. Months before, Sewell, who knew Wakefield of old, had recognized that 'Wakefield will be the great moving power behind the scenes but will not do for ostensible leadership.'[2] Wynyard extricated himself from his dilemma by sending for J. E. FitzGerald, Superintendent of Canterbury, and Dr. Monro of Nelson, mover and seconder of the Address in Reply. Monro dropped out, disagreeing with FitzGerald on policy, and F. A. Weld and Sewell were invited to join the consultations. Then, on Sewell's initiative, Wakefield was brought in. But it was too late. He would not co-operate, and in any case Wynyard declined to add more than three to the Executive Council. Wakefield, 'affronted at being left out of active participation in the Government work', was 'fretful and dissatisfied'.[3] On 14 June FitzGerald, Weld, and Sewell were sworn in as Executive Councillors. Later they were joined by Dillon Bell; but he resigned after twelve days and was replaced by T. H. Bartley of Auckland, who was appointed to the Legislative Council.

By this time Wakefield had gone into opposition. 'His whole bent and aim', wrote Sewell, 'is now to destroy the Government which he has had a main hand in creating.'[4] Wakefield's first challenge was beaten off but further difficulties soon arose. FitzGerald wanted to go back after the session to his Superintendency in Canterbury. Sewell and Weld were willing to stay on but wanted a reinforcement in the person of E. W. Stafford, Superintendent of Nelson, who had first to get a seat in the House and made other conditions. Then, for the first time, the new Executive Councillors learned that Wynyard was not content merely to pension off the old officials. He would not take the responsibility of accepting their resignations, since they held their appointments

[1] Extract from Minutes of Proceedings of House of Representatives (6 June) and Opinion of Attorney-General (5 June 1854), P.P., 1854–5, xxxviii (H.C. 160), 2, 4.

[2] Journal of Sewell, 24 Feb. 1854.

[3] Ibid., 11 and 13 June, 1854. Sewell's Journal gives a fascinating 'inside history' of the Assembly of 1854.      [4] Ibid., 9 July 1854.

from the Crown. The advice of FitzGerald and his colleagues that the officials should be replaced by responsible Ministers as soon as an Executive Government Bill providing for pensions should be passed was rejected and they resigned on 2 August. They had expected Wynyard to yield to pressure and Sewell complains that 'the official memorandum prepared at the instance of Wynyard and Swainson, as a justification of concession, is made the ground of offence and is treated as coercion and menace'.[1]

Wynyard now, probably at Swainson's instance, turned to Wakefield for advice. A message to the Legislative Council, stating the case against the resigning Executive Councillors, was apparently prepared by him. On 17 August, amid disorderly scenes, Wynyard prorogued the Assembly for a fortnight. Wakefield was playing a deep game. He hoped to provoke a dissolution, secure from the Acting Governor a dissolution of the Provincial Councils also, and appeal to the electorate on a programme of free land for the working settler.[2] Sewell was clearly alarmed and so, probably, was Swainson. But Wakefield, after a conference with Swainson, realized that he could not bring off his coup and 'retired from the position of temporary adviser'.[3] On 31 August Wynyard opened the second session with a new set of Executive Councillors, Forsaith of Auckland—the one man who had voted against responsible government—Wakefield's son Jerningham, Travers of Nelson, and Macandrew of Otago. But a no-confidence amendment to the Address in Reply, drafted by Sewell but moved by Monro (presumably to restrict recriminations between old and new Executives) was carried by 22 to 11. The majority preferred to keep the old officials pending an appeal. On 2 September they adopted an Address to the Queen

to give effect to the principle of ministerial responsibility, in the conduct of legislative and executive affairs, by instructing His Excellency the Officer administering the Government to remove from their offices the . . . Attorney-General, Colonial Secretary and Colonial

---

[1] Journal of Sewell, 22 Aug. 1854.
[2] Sewell's Journal, *passim*, and Memo. of Wakefield (19 Aug. 1854) in Swainson, *New Zealand and its Colonization* (London, 1859), pp. 341–7. Wakefield's adoption of a land programme to appeal to the working settlers is examined in two unpublished University of New Zealand theses—the late D. G Herron's on 'The Course and Structure of New Zealand Politics, 1853–58' (Ph.D thesis, 1959) and P. A. Stuart, 'The New Zealand Career of E. G. Wakefield 1853–54' (M.A. thesis, 1959).          [3] Swainson, op. cit., p. 348.

Treasurer of this colony; and further to instruct His Excellency to give Your Majesty's Royal Assent to a Bill to be passed by the General Assembly for establishing the Executive Government on the basis of ministerial responsibility.

Such a measure of confidence in the people would be 'a sure means of uniting this distant dependency of Great Britain to its parent Empire by an indissoluble tie'.[1] After passing a Waste Lands Bill 'with the view of stopping the Governor from handing over the Waste Lands to Wakefield to be jobbed away in electioneering', the Assembly, whose southern members had been absent nearly four months from their distant homes, was prorogued on 16 September.

Wynyard's dispatch of 9 June, announcing his concession to the Assembly, reached the Colonial Office in mid-October. Frederick Peel, now again Parliamentary Under-Secretary, pointed out that 'when the Act of 1852 was passed it was clearly not contemplated that a seat in the Executive Council should depend on the votes of the House of Representatives'.[2] The General Assembly was not expected to meet often for some years to come. With the advent of the Duke of Newcastle to the Colonial Office the reservations of Earl Grey and the hesitations of Sir John Pakington had ceased to influence policy; but even the Duke of Newcastle had hesitations about New Zealand and did not send it a copy of his dispatch foreshadowing the introduction of responsible government in New South Wales.[3] He had left the Colonial Office, however, before Wynyard's dispatch arrived and his successor Sir George Grey had to handle the question. Merivale did not approve of Wynyard's concession. 'No one, I suppose, objects', he minuted, 'to the establishment of responsible government in New Zealand: I certainly think it very desirable: but this is not the way of doing it. Governors have invariably reserved the question for the Home Government however strong their own opinions in favour of the change.'[4] A dispatch was actually drafted, consenting to the concession and confirming the new

[1] Address of 2 Sept. in Wynyard to Newcastle (7 Sept. 1854) (No. 81), P.P., 1854-5, xxxviii (H.C. 160), 35.
[2] Wynyard to Newcastle (9 June 1854) (No. 48), Minute of Peel (28 Oct.), CO209/123. The earliest minute, by Elliot, was on 17 Oct.
[3] See above, p. 17.
[4] Minute of Merivale (11 Nov. 1854), CO209/123.

Executive Councillors' appointments, but censuring Wynyard's conduct. But the later developments made this unnecessary. On 8 December Sir George Grey wrote to Wynyard informing him that 'Her Majesty's Government have no objection whatever to offer to the establishment of the system known as responsible government in New Zealand. They have no reason to doubt that it will prove the best method for developing the interests as well as satisfying the wishes of the community.' The only condition was provision for retiring officials 'of which the necessity appears to be fully recognized by the General Assembly'. No legislative enactment was required to bring the change into operation.

In this country the recognized plan of Parliamentary government . . . rests on no written law, but on usage only. . . . If uncalled for, such legislation is objectionable, because the laws so enacted would probably stand in the way of the various partial changes which it might be necessary to adopt in the details of a system in its nature liable to much modification.[1]

The curious point in all these discussions is the absence of reference to the Maoris' position under responsible government. Grey in his early years as Governor had used the state of Maori feeling as an argument for postponing representative institutions and in his constitutional scheme of August 1851 he proposed to reserve to the Governor control over the expenditure of £7,000 'for Native purposes'. In 1853 he thought it one of his duties to 'explain to jealous Chiefs and easily alarmed tribes what were to be their duties under this new state of things and how their rights would be protected'.[2] But he did not contemplate responsible government as part of the 'new state of things'. The Constitution Act did not disfranchise Maoris as such and a few were placed on the electoral roll; but even a friend of the Maoris like Swainson thought them 'as a body . . . at present unfit to exercise the elective franchise with advantage either to themselves or to the country at large'.[3] Grey's personal influence had been great; but govern-

[1] Grey to Officer administering the Government (8 Dec. 1854) (No. 39), P.P., 1854–5, xxxviii (H.C. 160), 39. The Minutes of Merivale and Grey (6 and 7 Dec., CO209/124) on which this is based suggest that a Cabinet decision on the subject had been made in November.

[2] Grey, *Memorandum upon a Letter addressed by Lord Lyttelton to Sir G. Grey* (London, 1854), p. 15.

[3] W. Swainson, *New Zealand . . . Lectures on the Colonization of New Zealand* (London, 1856), p. 30. A few Maoris possessed the requisite qualifications; but

ment as such hardly touched the tribes of the interior. One or other of the missionary societies had reached most of them but the subsidized mission schools were not numerous and not uniformly successful; the resident magistrates' stations (Rotorua excepted) were on or near the coast; hospitals were few. The Maoris' chief contact with Government was as a land purchaser and resistance to land purchase was stiffening.

Taranaki was the danger point. It might never have been settled but for the devastating raid carried out by the powerful Waikato tribe, in the absence of most of the Atiawa chiefs, in 1834. The Waikatos carried off many slaves; others took refuge in the mountains. There was only a small remnant in Taranaki when representatives of the New Zealand Company in 1840 secured their signatures to a deed conveying certain lands to the Company, which signed another agreement with the Atiawa at Queen Charlotte Sound. A year later settlers arrived from England. Then in 1842 the Waikatos, under the influence of Christian teaching, liberated their slaves: they returned to find strangers in occupation of their land. They cut down the settlers' trees, refused to let them extend their cultivations, blocked their roads, threatened them with personal violence. Land Commissioner Spain thought absentees had forfeited their claims and awarded the Company 60,000 acres in 1844. This award was unenforceable. Governor FitzRoy came down, overruled Spain, and virtually repurchased 3,500 acres around New Plymouth. He also waived the Government's pre-emptive right over the remainder of the 60,000 acres in favour of the Company. 'As the Natives are, generally speaking,' he wrote, 'willing and anxious to sell the greater part of their lands, however tenacious of their right and choice, the Company's agent will not find it difficult to purchase portion after portion, for reasonable prices, provided that he does not injure his own market, by buying too much or too hastily.'[1] These expectations were not fulfilled. In 1848 Wiremu Kingi Te Rangitake, the most influential of the Atiawa chiefs, influenced in part no doubt by the increased security the settlers' presence

in 1859 the Law Officers of the Crown ruled that land held in common as tribes or communities did not qualify: Law Officers to Newcastle (7 Dec. 1859), CO209/152.
[1] Memo. (2 Dec.) in FitzRoy to Stanley (19 Dec. 1844) (Confidential), P.P., 1845, xxxiii (H.C. 369), 100-2.

gave, returned from Waikanae to his ancestral home at Waitara. Sir George Grey wished him to settle on the north bank of the river; but he defied the Governor, settled on the south bank and used all his influence to stop further land sales. There were some sales nevertheless. The Taranaki and Ngati Ruanui to the south were also resistant even to missionary influence. Doubt has been thrown, specially by Professor Keith Sinclair, upon the existence of a Maori Land League; but it is not easy to set aside the evidence of G. S. Cooper, Land Purchase Officer at New Plymouth, in a report to the Colonial Secretary on 29 April 1854:

The greatest obstacle to the acquisition of land in this province, and especially of late years, consists of a regularly organized and sustained opposition, or as it may be called an 'anti-land selling league'. This compact has been joined in by the Ngati Ruanui, Taranaki and a considerable portion of the Ngatiawa tribes and the league has been ratified and confirmed at several aggregate meetings, with various formulas and solemnities, a copy of Holy Scriptures having on one occasion been buried in the earth and a cairn of stones erected on the spot in attestation of the inviolability of the oath to oppose the sale of land by every means in their power, which has been taken by the confederated chiefs.[1]

Cooper thought that the League showed signs of breaking up and it seems that the meeting held about this time at Manawapou in the Ngati Ruanui country was not an unqualified success. But the Revd. Samuel Williams, in the letter on which Professor Sinclair mainly bases his argument, seems chiefly concerned to show that the 'southern chiefs' at Manawapou refused the hatchet offered them by the champion of the League.[2] The reported decision to leave each tribe to manage its own affairs certainly did not mean that opposition to land sales was ceasing. A few months later a minor chief, Rawiri Waiaua, whose influence had secured the Bell Block for the settlers, revenged himself for the destruction of one of his wheat fields by some of the young men of his old rival Katatore Te Whaitere by offering to sell a further block. Cooper, rather hastily, accepted the offer. On 2 August Katatore surprised

---

[1] McLean Papers 32/129, Turnbull Library. I owe this reference to Mr. E. Hill. The Revd. R. Taylor, *Te Ika a Maui* (London, 1855), pp. 277–8, seems an independent source, since Cooper's report was not published. T. Buddle, *The Maori King Movement* (Auckland, 1860), pp. 4–6, may be 'derivative' as Sinclair suggests. For his views see *The Maori Land League* (Auckland, 1950).

[2] The Revd. S. Williams to the Editor (7 Sept. 1860), *Southern Cross*, 28 Sept. 1860.

Rawiri and his men cutting the boundary and 'shot them down like dogs'.[1]

At first the settlers seemed to be taking the affair quietly. The Government at Auckland, feeling itself powerless to intervene even though Rawiri was a Native Assessor, urged the Superintendent and Resident Magistrate to 'keep the European population perfectly neutral ... endeavour to soothe the irritated feelings of the Natives' and check the spread of the trouble. When Donald McLean, Chief Land Purchase Commissioner, came down later, his emphasis was on strengthening the settlers' defences by a blockhouse and a stockade, training the militia and increasing the police force. The feud spread nevertheless. Wiremu Kingi supported Katatore. Arama Karaka, chief of Rawiri's *hapu*, came up from Kapiti to support his widow. The local authorities began to press for a detachment of troops, especially when the killing of a young Ngati Ruanui suspected of adultery by Ihaia, a friendly chief, brought the Ngati Ruanui into the quarrel. Early in 1855 Wynyard sent down the Native Secretary, Major Nugent, to report. Wiremu Kingi received him 'with marked civility' and he thought no danger to the settlers need be apprehended so long as they did not interfere and deprecated any 'active and armed interference of the government in these Native quarrels'. But late in March Wynyard was persuaded to come and see for himself and after interviews with all parties was persuaded that a force of two or three hundred troops ought to be stationed at Taranaki. At the same time he thought it the settlers' duty to 'lend their cordial aid' by raising a local force which he would arm. Before the troops actually arrived in August, the quarrel had been exacerbated by the ostentatious support of Ihaia by a rather self-important Wesleyan missionary, the Revd. H. H. Turton, which was counteracted by a visit and pastoral letter from Bishop Selwyn who, whilst condemning Rawiri's murder, pointed out that the settlers' partisanship was stiffening the back of Wiremu Kingi.[2]

[1] C. W. Richmond to C. Brown (3 Aug. 1854), *Richmond-Atkinson Papers* (ed. G. H. Scholefield) (Wellington, 1960), i. 151-2. See also *Taranaki Herald*, 9 Aug. 1854.

[2] Wynyard to Newcastle (15 Aug. 1854) (No. 76) and to Sir G. Grey (2 Nov. 1854, No. 119, 28 Dec. 1854, No. 138, 5 Feb. 1855, No. 12, 18 Apr. 1855, No. 41), P.P., 1860, xlvi [2719], 41-5, 58, 63, 72-5, 99-103; G. A. Selwyn, *Pastoral Letter ... to the Members of the Church of England in the Settlement of New Plymouth* (New

Wynyard's original non-interventionist line had the backing of the Colonial Office, though Merivale confessed he had 'hoped the Europeans had been strong enough to keep the peace instead of merely looking on at the wars of the Natives'.[1] But when Wynyard's visit to Taranaki led him to change his line, Merivale 'on the whole' approved.

The answer . . . which would most naturally occur would be, Follow the Acting Governor and Mr. McLean's suggestions: arm your militia: organize a police: stand on your own defence: and depend upon it, the Maoris will not meddle with you. Do not rely for defence on soldiers whom we have not to send, whom, we strongly suspect, you wish for more on account of their expenditure than for any other reason, and who after all would not serve you so well in this kind of warfare as yourselves, if armed. But the difficulty of using any part of this language is that hitherto we have used an opposite course of policy and, it must be said, very successfully. Lord Derby and Lord Grey met the demand from the colony by a very considerable supply of troops.

Sir William Molesworth, then at the Colonial Office for his tragically short spell as Secretary of State, did not find the point convincing.

When Lord Derby and Lord Grey were in office, New Zealand was governed from this country and therefore it was the duty of the Home Government to provide for its internal tranquillity. Since then New Zealand has obtained representative institutions and responsible government and, enjoying the sweets, it ought also to bear the burdens of self-government. One of the chief of those burdens is the preservation of internal tranquillity. I think the inhabitants of New Zealand ought to be told that they must prepare to rely upon themselves to defend themselves against the Natives—they must arm their militia—they must organize a police—they must keep upon good terms with the Maoris—and as the land has been made over to the local Government, all disputes with the Natives about land are *local* questions with which the Imperial Government has no concern, and to settle which disputes the Imperial Government cannot be expected to maintain a body of troops in the Colony.

Plymouth, 1855); *Taranaki Herald, passim.* The *Herald* was owned by the son of a Wesleyan missionary and Turton was a frequent correspondent.
[1] Minute of Merivale (7 Dec.) on Wynyard to Newcastle (15 Aug. 1854) (No. 76), CO209/124.

However, 'in existing circumstances and having the troops to spare', Wynyard had probably done right to send them.[1]

Early in September Colonel Thomas Gore Browne, who had been appointed Governor the previous November on promotion from St. Helena, arrived in New Zealand, just in time to make a prorogation speech to the General Assembly, which had met for a short session. He adopted Wynyard's policy in Taranaki and soon dispatched him there as Civil and Military Commissioner. He paid a brief visit himself on 24 October, declared his intention not to allow the troops to be used except to protect the settlement, and deprecated the injudicious zeal of Turton and the undue haste in beginning the survey which had led to Rawiri's death.[2] He had already discovered the difficulty of relying overmuch on the militia. 'In those places where it would be most required, the European population is thin and scattered, and as ordinary labourers can earn a shilling an hour, it is evident that it will not be easy to make it available and that any other force would be cheaper.'[3] An address from the Superintendent and Provincial Council of Taranaki put the point more bluntly. 'It would inevitably', they said, 'deprive us at once of a considerable portion of the working class, so rooted is their dislike to military service.'[4]

Gore Browne's primary task was the introduction of responsible government, but he had no clear instructions on how to carry it out. As he later explained to Sir George Bowen, then Governor of Queensland, 'the system was little understood even at the Colonial Office'. Lord Elgin, as Governor-General of Canada, had explained how he worked the system in private letters to Lord Grey rather than in dispatches to the Colonial Office. Gore Browne, when in England, saw Elgin and asked his advice.[5] We do not know what advice he received, but Elgin as Governor-General

[1] Minutes of Merivale (27 Sept.) and Molesworth (29 Sept.) on Wynyard to Sir G. Grey (19 Apr. 1855) (No. 43): CO209/129. This was a covering dispatch with a Memorial of the Provincial Council to the Queen asking that New Plymouth be garrisoned and the force in New Zealand be not reduced. A dispatch on the lines of Molesworth's Minute was drafted by 3 Oct. but became Labouchere to Gore Browne (28 Nov. 1855) (No. 28).

[2] Gore Browne to Russell (19 Nov. 1855) (No. 35), P.P., 1860, xlvi [2719], 176–8.

[3] Gore Browne to Russell (20 Sept. 1855) (No. 14), CO209/130.

[4] Address from Superintendent and Provincial Council in Gore Browne to Russell (14 Sept. 1855) (No. 5), pp. 144–6.

[5] Gore Browne to Bowen (17 Sept. 1864 and 22 June 1866), Gore Browne Papers 2/3, New Zealand Archives.

was certainly no cipher and Gore Browne did not intend to be one. He was impressed by the weakness of the power of the Crown in New Zealand with its elective provincial Superintendents, on whom large executive powers had been conferred, chiefly by the Provincial Councils' own Empowering Ordinances. He suggested that Parliament might amend the Constitution Act to make the Superintendents Crown nominees. The Imperial authorities, whilst agreeing that the Provincial Governments had arrogated to themselves undue power, did not think Gore Browne's remedy practicable.

I cannot doubt that the arguments in favour of greater concentration of government will acquire additional force with the progress of society. But whatever judgement Her Majesty's Government may form as to this subject, I must distinctly remind you that they have no disposition to impose their views upon the people of New Zealand.... Any political changes henceforth to be effected in New Zealand must be worked out with the free consent of the colonists themselves.[1]

Such was the verdict of Molesworth's successor, Labouchere. But Gore Browne's study of the situation and of the antagonistic interests of Maori and settler in the matter of land convinced him that he must make an important reservation:

In matters affecting the Queen's prerogative and Imperial interests generally, I should receive their [responsible ministers'] advice, but when I differ from them in opinion I should, if they desire it, submit their views for your consideration, but adhere to my own until your answer is received. Among Imperial subjects I include all dealings with the Native tribes, more especially in the negotiation of purchases of land. . . . The Governor alone is responsible for the tranquillity of the Colony, which would be endangered by the ordinary and inevitable change of opinion consequent on a change of my advisers.[2]

By general agreement, the General Assembly of 1855, summoned before Gore Browne's arrival and thinly attended, was not a suitable occasion for forming the first responsible Ministry. It was dissolved, and when the new Assembly met in mid April 1856, Gore Browne at once took the initiative and, as FitzGerald was ill with *angina pectoris*, sent for Sewell, his senior colleague of

[1] Labouchere to Gore Browne (21 July 1856) (No. 58), P.P., 1860, xlvi [2719], 457–8. The matter had been discussed in Minutes of Merivale (2 June) and Ball (19 June) in CO209/135.
[2] Gore Browne to Sir G. Grey (12 Mar. 1856) (No. 25), ibid.

1854. Sewell could not persuade Stafford to take office, but Dillon Bell, Whitaker of Auckland, and Tancred of Canterbury (a Legislative Councillor) accepted. Sewell explained to the House the arrangement he had reached with the Governor on the lines indicated in his dispatch. 'I think His Excellency is right in these reservations', he added, '. . . for this question of the management of the Natives is one of peace and war. It involves the interest of the Empire, which defrays the cost of our military defence. Are you prepared to take that on yourselves? I would not myself be responsible for advising you to that effect.'[1]

The firmness of the Governor, who insisted on two-thirds of their salaries as pensions for the retiring officials, secured the passage of this essential Bill; but the Sewell Ministry did not last long. William Fox, the leader of Wellington Provincialists, secured some support from Auckland members who distrusted Whitaker and from the Otago men, and carried a vote against them by a majority of one. He formed a Ministry, not without difficulty, and accepted the Governor's terms on Native policy, whilst telling the House that 'had this still been an open question, they might have asked to have a responsible voice in Native affairs'.[2] But Fox's position was precarious. His Auckland supporters began to move away and the arrival of two more Nelson members made it possible to turn him out in favour of a well-balanced Ministry headed by Stafford, who had proved himself an able, economical administrator. Of his colleagues, Sewell and Whitaker were astute lawyers and Sewell had good connections in England. C. W. Richmond, a Taranaki settler, an eloquent speaker, and afterwards a famous judge, was the finest character of them all. They stayed in office for five years.

The first point of the new Ministry's policy was a financial settlement. Auckland had a standing grievance against the clause of the Constitution Act which required one-fourth of the proceeds of land sales to be paid to the New Zealand Company in satisfaction of the lien on the land fund, to the amount of £268,000, granted to the Company by an Imperial Act of 1847. Auckland had not been colonized by the Company and rivalry between it and the Company's settlements had always been keen.

[1] House of Representatives, 25 Apr. 1856, *New Zealand Parliamentary Debates*, 856–8, p. 15.
[2] Ministerial Statement, 21 May 1856, ibid., p. 90.

In 1853 Sir George Grey, alleging this as his reason but influenced also by his personal hostility to the Company, had withheld from it £9,000 due from Auckland under this arrangement, leaving Wynyard to receive the inevitable disapproving dispatch from the Colonial Office[1]—though he took the matter up himself when he reached England. As Merivale pointed out to his political chiefs, the money would never be paid 'unless measures of a much more stringent character are adopted than it is now the fashion to use towards colonies; and there will soon be a demand of many thousands on the Treasury for the amount which the colony delays and objects to pay'.[2] Fortunately Adderley, representing the colony, persuaded the Company to take a realistic view. The directors agreed to relieve the colony of the charge on payment of £200,000, the nominal value of the Company's capital. The Imperial Government agreed, subject to certain conditions, to propose to Parliament a guaranteed loan of this amount.[3] These terms were accepted by the House of Representatives on 2 July. The House had already resolved in the second session of 1854 that the Company's debt should be borne by the South Island provinces in proportion to the amount of land available in each. Sewell now proposed to carry the bargain a stage further. The Imperial Government was to be asked to extend its guarantee to £500,000, so as to cover the existing debt of the General Government and to provide a capital fund of £180,000 for Native land purchase, the amounts being charged against the revenues of Auckland, Wellington, and Taranaki. Subject to these provisions, the land revenue was to be made provincial revenue. This statesmanlike settlement whose object was 'to destroy the old rancours and heart-burnings between the North and the South', came to be known as 'the compact of 1856' and lasted for eleven years. It depended, of course, on the willingness of the Imperial Government to enlarge its guarantee and at the end of the session Sewell went home to negotiate this.

Meanwhile a struggle had been going on behind the scenes over the control of Native affairs. The House did not like the arrange-

[1] Grey to Pakington (9 May 1853) (No. 50) and Newcastle to Grey (30 Dec 1853) (No. 99), P.P., 1854, xlv [1779], 234–6, 406–7.
[2] Minute of Merivale (5 June) on Wynyard to Newcastle (5 Feb. 1854) (No. 15) CO209/122.
[3] Russell to Gore Browne (4 July 1855) (No. 8), P.P., 1857, Sess. 2 (H.C. 171), 4

ment of April and was jealous in particular of the power it gave to Donald McLean. As Sewell noted in his journal,

> We go down to the House with proposals for voting large sums for Native expenses—Hospitals, schools, pensions, magistracies &c. &c. The House . . . asks what control is there over the Departments, on the expenditure of money? We answer—none. Then every member gets up to find fault with this or that item; in answer to which little can be said, for little is known, and nothing can be promised. It may be that sullenly and reluctantly they vote the money this year, upon the urgent importunity of Government with threats of stopping it next year . . . unless the House can exercise its ordinary control over it.[1]

After the session, as Ministers turned from parliamentary to administrative business, matters came to a head. To quote Sewell again,

> When we come to put the machine in motion we find difficulties— the Native Land Purchaser and Native Secretary set up a little ministry of their own. They have the Governor's private ear and possess him with the notion that it is essential for the peace of the Colony to keep up a little separate empire of their own. They refuse allegiance to Responsible Government, only they are constantly reminded of the disagreeable fact of its existence by the money difficulty. . . . The Governor gets restive and sore at finding himself pulled up by the reins of finance. . . . Everything threatens a final split and catastrophe.[2]

Finally Ministers resolved to place their views before the Governor and appeal home 'with the determination if the Home Government sided with the Governor to throw up Responsible Government as an impracticable thing'. On 24 August Whitaker and Sewell (Stafford was in Nelson, winding up his Superintendency) saw Gore Browne, having previously submitted a minute.

> We went into the practical working of our plan of conducting Native affairs showing him that whilst we secured for Responsible Ministers a full knowledge of everything, we did not mean to take from him his individual right of deciding questions. He gradually moderated his tone, listened, and at last assented, in short, gave in.[3]

[1] Journal of Sewell, 27 July 1856. On 11 Aug. the House resolved 'that it would greatly conduce to the peace and good government of the Colony if all departments of Government were placed under the ordinary control of responsible ministers, subject to . . . the rule laid down in the second paragraph of the Governor's memorandum of 15 April 1856': *Votes and Proceedings*, H.R., 11 Aug. 1856.
[2] Journal, 21 Aug. 1856.
[3] Ibid., 26 Aug. 1856.

The terms of the arrangement were embodied in the Governor's minute of 28 August. McLean was to be appointed Secretary for Native Affairs as well as Chief Land Purchase Commissioner. Correspondence was to go to him but he was to submit it with his opinion, if possible in writing, to a member of the Ministry—in practice Richmond, who was later made Minister for Native Affairs. McLean's opinion and Ministers' advice were both to be submitted to the Governor, with whom the final decision lay. McLean might also communicate with the Governor directly. But if a proposal involved expense it must not exceed the amount voted by the Assembly. Ministers might have their protest against any proposal referred home, but a difference of opinion on Native affairs was not to be regarded as a sufficient reason for resignation. This seemed to Ministers the best arrangement possible so long as Imperial military and naval forces remained indispensable. But they protested against the view that the colonists could not be trusted with the management of Maori affairs.

It must be admitted that the Imperial Government has a large direct interest in the preservation of peaceful relations with the aborigines; but on the other [hand] it cannot be denied that the colonists as a body have a far greater interest in the same object; not only their property but their lives are at stake.[1]

The Governor, in his correspondence with the Colonial Office, emphasized the importance of good relations with his Ministers when the colony contained 'a proud and independent race of savages, recognizing Her Majesty's supremacy but imperfectly and repudiating all authority except that of her representative'. 'The Maoris', he pointed out, 'are constantly advised and reminded of their power and the large amount they contribute to the revenue, by persons belonging to several classes and more than one nation, who are actuated by various motives, among which allegiance to Her Majesty is not always a prominent one.'[2]

[1] Minutes of Gore Browne (28 Aug.) and Sewell and Richmond (2 Sept.) in Gore Browne to Labouchere (21 Sept. 1856) (No. 94), P.P., 1860, xliv [2719], 360–4. The arrangement about McLean was apparently the outcome of conversation with Sewell and Whitaker: Minute of Gore Browne (25 May 1861), M.A. 1/2:61/58, N.Z. Archives.

[2] Gore Browne to Labouchere (21 Sept. 1856), loc. cit. The Governor had American whalers especially in mind: Gore Browne to Merivale (2 June 1856) (Private), CO209/159.

Merivale doubted whether the compromise would work. 'I do not', he wrote, 'think it possible, with advantage, to withhold native affairs from the cognizance of the responsible advisers, the matter being so closely connected with other points of domestic administration.'[1] But as it seemed improbable that a really strong responsible Government could be formed in New Zealand for some time, it might be advisable to adopt the Governor's view for the time being; 'the maintenance of so large a military force in the colony affords ample justification of such a measure'.[2] A few months earlier, when Gore Browne had detained the 58th Regiment on the eve of its departure, Merivale had even contemplated the possibility of going back, in view of 'the enormous difficulty of managing uncivilized nations along with responsible government . . . where those nations are numerous and quarrelsome'.

I believe [he wrote] by far the best thing for New Zealand would be to withdraw Auckland and New Plymouth back again under Crown Government, to increase the militia force there, and to leave the other settlements, which are under no apprehension from Natives, to govern themselves. And I daresay the European colonists would be content enough to submit to a 'suspending Act' for a limited time in exchange for greater security and greater military expenditure.[3]

But the time for such a step had passed, as his political chiefs saw. Labouchere, in a dispatch of 10 December, approved the Governor's policy. The presence of the military force was his main argument, though he also mentioned the Maoris' large contribution to the revenue, lack of representation in the legislature, and uneven distribution among the provinces.[4] The omens were none too favourable for Sewell's mission to secure further financial assistance from England. Indeed Labouchere bluntly informed the Governor early in 1857 that he had 'no expectation that Her Majesty's Government will entertain and

[1] Minute of Merivale (18 July) on Gore Browne to Sir G. Grey (12 Mar. 1856) (No. 25), CO209/135. Ball (Parliamentary Under-Secretary) shared Merivale's doubts: Minute (23 Feb. 1857) on Gore Browne to Labouchere (18 Oct. 1856) (No. 109), CO209/139.
[2] Minute of Merivale (4 Oct.) on Gore Browne to Labouchere (9 May 1856) No. 47), CO209/136.
[3] Minute of Merivale (30 May) on Gore Browne to Molesworth (14 Feb. 1856) No. 14), CO209/135.
[4] Labouchere to Gore Browne (10 Dec. 1856) (No. 90), P.P., 1860, xlvi [2719], 61.

recommend to Parliament the proposal to guarantee a loan of £500,000 to the Colonial Government'.[1] The Colonial Office was also disturbed to hear that the province of Wellington was raising a loan and that 'the local is so independent of the general government that the latter has no official knowledge of the fact'.[2] Such actions were bound to affect colonial credit and make Sewell's task more difficult. But he argued his case on very broad grounds:

It seems to have been overlooked in this colonization of New Zealand, that to govern a people who retain to themselves the permanent seigniory of the soil is simply impossible. Theoretically there is a plain and inseparable connection between territorial and political sovereignty —practically this is proved by daily experience in New Zealand.

It was essential to press on with the acquisition of Maori lands to meet the growing demands of incoming settlers. A capital fund must be raised for the purpose and without an Imperial guarantee the interest burden would press too heavily on colonial finances. He denied that land purchase harmed the Maoris. 'The policy of the Colonial Government is in fact to make Colonists of the Natives on their own lands'—that is, by giving them individual titles and making Crown grants to them, a policy almost universally favoured at this time by enlightened opinion in the colony.[3] Sewell supplemented his advocacy, oral and written, at the Colonial Office by skilful lobbying. He was in close touch with Adderley and with Godley, now established at the War Office. In a letter to Richmond he claims he has 'made a favourable impression on Sir John Pakington, and Lord John Russell and I think Gladstone are well disposed. Our success depends on getting help from this kind of man and it requires time and labour writing and preaching.'[4] Significantly, Adderley, Russell, and Pakington were among the nine members of the Select Committee

[1] Labouchere to Gore Browne (28 Feb. 1857) (No. 10), P.P., 1860, xlvi [2719] 463.
[2] Minute of Merivale (11 May) on Gore Browne to Labouchere (12 Feb. 1857 (No. 11), CO209/141.
[3] Sewell to Ball (8 May 1857), CO209/144. In his later evidence, Sewell quoted a letter from Chief Justice Martin in support of the policy of individualization and Crown grants. It was also supported by Bishop Selwyn, Swainson Dr. A. S. Thomson, and others.
[4] Sewell to Richmond (15 May 1857), Richmond–Atkinson Papers (ed. Scholefield), i. 265–6.

appointed by the House of Commons on 3 July, under Labouchere's chairmanship, to consider the loan proposal. The Committee examined two witnesses only, Merivale and Sewell, and Merivale's evidence shows strong traces of Sewell's original memorandum. He had done his work well. Though the questions of one Conservative member (J. W. Henley) had a sharp edge, the Committee's recommendation that the Imperial Government give a guarantee for the whole £500,000 had become a foregone conclusion.[1] There were a number of criticisms when the Bill came before Parliament, the most damaging from Sir John Trelawny, member for Tavistock, who took exception to the composition of the Committee, the weightiest from Sir James Graham. But Labouchere quoted Canadian and West Indian precedents for such guarantees and Sir George Lewis, Chancellor of the Exchequer, supported the Bill on the broad ground of Great Britain's interest in the colonial connection. The colonies, he said, were precluded

from pursuing the policy of independent nations by excluding English manufactures or establishing high prohibitory duties . . . In this manner the trade and productions of Great Britain were benefited, and, in order to insure the prosperity and good government of her colonies, financial advantages were afforded them—especially when they were young or in difficulties—at the expense of the mother country. It was upon that principle that he judged the plan now under consideration. . . . It must be borne in mind that the liabilities of the colony were for the most part owing to Imperial legislation and Imperial policy.[2]

These arguments proved effective. The Bill passed its second reading by the comfortable majority of 78 to 23 and became law on 17 August. Sewell had managed to tone down the original proposal that provincial borrowing should be prohibited by Act of the General Assembly into a provision that no New Zealand Act varying the security should be valid unless confirmed by the Queen in Council.[3]

[1] The Report (9 July 1857) is in P.P., 1857, Sess. 2, ix (H.C. 171).

[2] House of Commons, 30 July and 6 Aug. 1857; *Hansard*, 3rd Ser. cxlvii. 704–8, 1133–43. Henley, who had wanted the £180,000 for Native land purchase excluded, moved an amendment in committee to reduce the amount to £200,000.

[3] The Act was 20 & 21 Vict. c. 51. The Imperial authorities were at first inclined to ask for an amendment of the Waste Lands Act 1858 to recognize the lien on waste land revenue imposed by the Loan Act, but it was finally assented to; see my *Provincial System in New Zealand*, p. 105.

The Colonial Office took advantage of Sewell's presence in England to consult him on two other matters bearing on Native affairs. Sir George Grey's appropriation of the £7,000 reserved for 'Native purposes' by the Constitution Act to missionary bodies in aid of their schools was unpopular. The schools varied greatly in efficiency. As a Methodist missionary and trained teacher, the Revd. A. Reid, frankly admitted, the missionaries were 'not the most fitting persons to conduct schools'. A Board which reported in 1856 on Native land purchase and other matters recommended that the Governor appoint a Board of Education, including a paid inspector, to approve all teachers and distribute the available funds.[1] Only with difficulty was the House of Representatives persuaded to vote another £1,000 (less than the Governor had requested) for other Native purposes which he might feel 'imperatively necessary'.[2] The Governor's dispatch on this question had been put by for Sewell's opinion.

I think the leaning of the Governor's mind [he wrote] is in favour of a separation between the ordinary Colonial Government and Government for the Natives. . . . The effect of such a separation would I am confident, be mischievous in every way—and especially to the Natives themselves. Practically the Government would fall into the hands of irresponsible persons, who would be looked on with the greatest dislike and jealousy by the body of the Colonists, while the Natives would come to be regarded as a separate and antagonistic race.

He therefore favoured 'placing the management of Native affairs under the ordinary rule of Responsible Government'.[3] This view, however, was not yet generally accepted; and Gore Browne, after a private conversation with Richmond, offered a compromise on the education vote on the basis of a payment of say £7 per pupil. If Ministers were prepared to ask the Assembly to guarantee such a payment, subject to proper inspection, for seven years, he would recommend Her Majesty's Government to remove the schools from the civil list. They would be placed on the estimates, leaving the £7000 'available for the Native purposes to which it ought to be devoted'.[4] On applying for instructions, he was left to work

[1] Report of Board on the System of Land Purchase, etc. in Gore Browne to Labouchere (23 July 1856) (No. 71), P.P., 1860, xlvi [2719], 237–44.
[2] Gore Browne to Labouchere (22 Sept. 1856) (No. 95) and Enclosures, ibid., pp. 391–2.
[3] Minute of Sewell (18 July 1857), CO209/144.
[4] Memo. of Gore Browne (25 Aug. 1857), Stafford Papers, Turnbull Library.

out his own solution in the spirit of the 1856 arrangements. This proposal was the basis of the Native Schools Act 1858. Agreement was also reached on a detailed appropriation of the £7,000 reserved by the civil list.[1]

Sewell was also consulted on the Native Reserves Act 1856, which vested powers in the Governor and Executive Council and not in the Governor alone, and was given to understand that it would be allowed. It was passed, Ministers argued, on the understanding 'that the large powers thereby created should not be exercised otherwise than in conformity with the public opinion of the Colony as represented by Responsible Ministers'.[2] Ball noted the understanding with Sewell, but his own opinion was 'decidedly against yielding unless and until the Assembly are prepared to defray a large portion of the cost of military defence'.[3] Chichester Fortescue, his successor as Parliamentary Under-Secretary, held similar views. But Labouchere preferred those of Merivale:

The Governor's power without the aid of the Assembly is quite inadequate and the Assembly is moved by his responsible advisers. . . . In short, he must consult his advisers at every step and yet in theory he manages native affairs independently of them. That this seems to work fairly at present is, I really think, in great measure attributable to a considerate feeling and sense of responsibility on the part of the Councillors themselves. But this cannot be expected to continue to work.[4]

The Maori chiefs were far too intelligent not to notice that power was passing from the impartial authority of the Crown to representatives of the settlers who were acquiring their land and changing their whole way of life. The young Ngati Toa chief Tamihana Te Rauparaha, who had visited England, and his cousin Matene Te Whiwhi, an able chief who wore European dress and lived in a European house, became imbued with the idea of unifying the Maori districts under a single king. Te Whiwhi

[1] Minutes of Gore Browne (25 Aug. 1857 and 6 Mar. 1858), Stafford Papers. On the Native Schools Act see memo. by Responsible Advisers on Native Affairs (29 Sept. 1858), P.P., 1860, xlvii (H.C. 492), 31.
[2] Memo. of Responsible Advisers on Native Reserves Act in Gore Browne to Labouchere (20 Sept. 1856) (No. 93), CO209/137.
[3] Minute of Ball (22 Apr.) on Report of Murdoch and Rogers on Native Reserves Act (16 Apr. 1857), CO323/84.
[4] Minute of Merivale (1 Oct.) on Gore Browne to Labouchere (12 June 1857) (No. 50), CO209/141.

journeyed north in 1853 to spread the idea but was rebuffed by the powerful Tu Wharetoa chief Te Heuheu Iwikau. On reflection, however, this old warrior chief changed his mind and convened a meeting in the Taupo district in 1854 and another towards the end of 1856. In April 1857 Gore Browne encountered Te Heuheu on his way to yet another meeting at Rangiriri in the Waikato, convened by the Ngati Haua chief Wiremu Tamihana. He recounted his grievance with growing excitement.

He said that if the lowest Englishman chose to visit the Maori he was welcomed and received all the hospitality in their power to afford . . . but that if a chief of the highest rank visited Auckland he was refused admittance and neglected by all except the Governor and one or two of the officers of Government; that Englishmen among the Maoris were often men of desperate character; that they got drunk and ill treated both men and women; that their cattle trespassed on Maori lands, and that instead of compensation they received abuse . . .; and that for all this they could get no redress. That the English were by degrees obtaining the best of their lands, and that they would soon 'be eaten up and cease to be'. That for these reasons they were determined to have a King of their own and Assemblies of their own; that they would not interfere with the English in the Settlements, but that the laws they intended to make should be binding on all who chose to reside among the Natives.

Gore Browne replied that he was glad the Maoris had seen the need of laws. He 'would willingly aid them in framing such a code as would be binding on both races' and consult Te Whero Whero, whom Te Heuheu indicated as the future King; but he 'could not consent to any such election'. The Maoris, he realized, did not understand 'King' quite in the English sense; but 'though they constantly professed loyalty to Her Majesty the Queen, attachment to myself and a desire for the amalgamation of the races, they did mean to maintain their separate nationality'. The Governor had two long interviews with Te Whero Whero, who promised to be guided by his advice, and he for his part promised to send a magistrate to reside in the Waikato.[1] Even if he was 'inclined to shy at the name of "King" ', this seemed a promising beginning, especially as control of the movement was passing from the excitable Te Heuheu to the cool, clear-headed Wiremu

[1] Gore Browne to Labouchere (9 May 1857) (No. 40), CO209/141.

Tamihana Te Waharoa. Richmond, as an interesting letter to Sewell makes clear, was already thinking of legislation in 1858 to meet the Maoris' 'plainly expressed desire for better government'.[1] If this was met, he hoped the desire for independence would disappear. In July 1857 F. D. Fenton was dispatched to the Waikato as magistrate. Unfortunately Fenton, an able lawyer well qualified to draw up a code in Maori, cherished a grudge against McLean and the Native Office. He ignored and depreciated Te Whero Whero and built up a 'Queen's party' of younger chiefs. He was recalled early in 1858—and not replaced.[2]

Richmond's legislation, however, went forward. The Native Districts Regulation Bill provided for the constitution of such districts where Native title had not been extinguished and for local regulations on a variety of subjects—to be initiated, it was hoped, by Maori *runangas* and merely put into shape by Government. The Native Circuit Courts Bill, building upon the Resident Magistrates Ordinance of 1846, vested all the summary jurisdiction of justices and resident magistrates (in Native districts) in a circuit court composed of the resident magistrate and his Native assessor assisted by a jury, which could also be used in civil actions at the request of either party. Assessors might in certain cases hold courts with limited powers. Both measures vested executive powers in the Governor in Council, but Gore Browne raised no objection and gave his assent to the Bills.[3]

It was a different matter with Richmond's most ambitious measure, the Native Territorial Rights Bill. This empowered the Governor in Council, on application and after report, to issue certificates of Native title to tribes, communities, or individuals and to issue Crown grants for the benefit of individual Maoris. These might be made inalienable, but 10s. per acre was to be paid into the Colonial Treasury on alienation to Europeans where this was permitted. These grants were to be an experiment, for three years in the first instance, and no more than 50,000 acres was to be granted in any one year. The Bill was permissive only: its

---

[1] Richmond to Sewell (16 June 1857), *Richmond–Atkinson Papers,* i. 276-7.
[2] There is an interesting discussion of the Fenton episode in J. E. Gorst, *The Maori King* (ed. K. Sinclair) (Hamilton, Auckland, and London, 1959), pp 65-84. On the King movement see especially M. P. K. Sorrenson in W. T. G. Airey (ed.), *Studies in a Small Democracy* (Auckland, 1963), pp. 33-55.
[3] Native Districts Regulation Act 1858 (No. 41); Native Circuit Courts Act 1858 (No. 42); Richmond in *N.Z.P.D.,* 1856-8, 444-50.

object, Ministers claimed, was 'to place in the hands of the
Government a new and powerful instrument for the civilization
of the Natives, and by no means to increase the immediate
facilities for the acquisition of land by Europeans'. The proposal
to establish a voluntary registry of Native title was a statesmanlike
one; and the proposal to individualize title by degrees was, as
already noted, in accordance with most enlightened opinion at
the time. The permission to alienate such land to Europeans was
a concession to the 'direct purchase' agitation long carried on at
Auckland and in the far North, and a tax upon it, though likely
to be unpopular, could be defended as a substitute for a land fund,
the main resource of Provincial Governments for such works as
roads, bridges, and drainage. But though Ministers disclaimed
any desire to check the operations of the Land Purchase Department, there was perhaps some substance in McLean's claim that
'the change contemplated by this Bill would confuse the Native
mind, disturb existing treaties with them, cause new complications in reference to title, and very much increase the difficulty of
obtaining land in blocks of sufficient extent to promote systematic English settlement'; and he certainly understood better than
Richmond the difficulty of the task to which he had set his hand.

It is believed that the magnitude of such an undertaking is underrated; that the means for its prosecution are not at the disposal of the
Government; and that the question for present consideration is not
whether the Government should undertake the civilization of the race,
and the establishment of English institutions or abandon them to the
fate supposed to await them; but in what manner such funds as are
likely to be at the disposal of Government may be most judiciously
employed in developing and rendering more effective existing institutions.

But the Ministers' memorandum had also entered on the wider
question of control of Native policy.

Under the present system of Government in New Zealand it is vain
to expect that cases in which Europeans and Natives are in dispute can
be satisfactorily dealt with by irresponsible officials. . . . To insure the
success of comprehensive measures of native policy it is already most
desirable, and in future years will become essential, to enlist the support
of the settlers. It would consequently be the height of impolicy to
attempt to exclude from influences upon native questions the leading

public men of the colony, who are, many of them, well acquainted with the character and wants of the Maoris, and without distinction of party, anxious to promote their welfare. . . . All political parties using the new powerful instrument of public opinion would combine to assail the Government policy and to decry its agents. . . . It is fearlessly asserted that no such administration could long endure the pressure to which it would be subjected, or could possibly succeed in a charge so difficult as that imposed upon the Government of this Colony. In addition to all this, it is impossible that the relations between the Executive and a free Legislature could ever be satisfactory under such arrangements. The legislation which will be from time to time required upon native subjects can only be conducted by members of the Assembly representing the Government, and they only can obtain the necessary supplies. . . . In contradistinction to such a plan, Ministers desire to see the department of native affairs conducted by one of the Ministry as its acknowledged head, but subject to the supervision and control of the Governor, as fully as before the establishment of responsible Government, with a recognized right on the part of His Excellency to interfere, if need should arise, in even the details of administration: and of being authentically informed of the opinions . . . of the permanent officers of the department . . . with whom he would always be entitled to communicate personally.

In pushing on with their Bill despite Gore Browne's warning that he could not assent to it, Ministers were of course bringing the whole issue before the Imperial authorities. The arguments in the memorandum are cogent, but there were two powerful arguments on the other side which Gore Browne did not fail to use.

It may be asked . . . on what grounds one portion of Her Majesty's subjects could demand the right of governing another portion not allied to them by blood or interest, and who are unrepresented in their councils. It could not be because the Natives desire it, for it is well known that the Maoris refuse to recognize any authority but such as emanates directly from Her Majesty. The settlers desire that a large naval and military force should be maintained at the expense of the Imperial Government, for the purpose of restraining and keeping the Maoris in subjection; but Her Majesty could hardly be expected to retain them in the Colony for the sole purpose of coercing a part of her subjects who yield her a willing obedience and forcing on them a government which (with or without reason) they fear and distrust.

He proposed to act according to the arrangements of 1856 until instructed otherwise, and he reserved the Territorial Rights Bill for the royal assent. There were several provisions he did not like. He regarded his power to issue Crown grants as important and did not wish to be bound to consult his Executive Council. He had 'always considered the representative of the Crown in the light of a trustee for the Native race' and disliked the restrictions imposed upon their use of their land.[1]

When the Bills and accompanying correspondence reached the Colonial Office, Gairdner, the senior clerk in this department, struck by the 'marked exhibition of ability and subtilty on the one side and of clear, manly common sense on the other'; but the issue was not really in doubt. The Imperial Government was not yet ready to abdicate its responsibilities towards the Maoris. Moreover, Lord Carnarvon, basing himself on a report of the Colonial Land and Emigration Commissioners, found the Native Territorial Rights Bill 'open to various important objections'.

It is no doubt most desirable that the disputes of the Natives respecting the rights to land should no longer be settled by arms, and that the occupation of land in severalty by the Natives should be encouraged. But . . . I am bound to ask myself whether in case the decision of the Governor in Council on titles to land should be resisted by the Natives, the British Government are prepared to promise such a military force as may be sufficient to enforce them. If any such expectation could be held out, it would be clearly necessary that the decisions which imposed so much responsibility and expense on the Home Government, should be taken by an officer solely responsible to that Government, and not to the colonists. If (as is the case) no such expectation could be held out, it is more than questionable whether the moral influence of the European Government would not suffer by the issue of certificates of title which the Natives would be at liberty to disregard with impunity. It appears to me . . . in every respect better that the establishment of tribal and other titles, and the acquisition by individual Natives of property in severalty, should be facilitated not by the issue of formal documents, appearing to rest on the authority and involve the guarantee of the Government, but by the cautious enactment of rules respecting the occupation of land, which are contemplated in . . . Act No. 41.

---

[1] Native Territorial Rights Act 1858 (No. 80); Richmond in *N.Z.P.D.*, 1856-8, 526-8; Gore Browne to Lytton (14 Oct. 1858) (No. 102) with Memos. by Responsible Ministers on Native Affairs (29 Sept.) and by Native Secretary (13 Oct.), Gore Browne to Lytton (15 Oct. 1858) (No. 103), P.P., 1860, xlvii (H.C. 492), 17-65. Correspondence between Gore Browne and Richmond (May-June 1858), *Richmond-Atkinson Papers*, i. 399-407.

He expected that the Act, if allowed, would be speedily followed by a change from Government to individual purchase; but it was far more advisable that Government should purchase territories than that individuals should purchase properties, so that the line which separates the purchased lands on which European law is to prevail from the unpurchased on which the Native usages will continue to subsist, though always advancing, will be broad and unequivocal.

No doubt if the Imperial Government were prepared to transfer the management of Native affairs to responsible Ministers, the system of land purchase might be decided by colonial and not Imperial authority. But that time had not come.

Whilst Her Majesty's Government feel themselves constrained to justify to Parliament the large expense which every year is incurred for the maintenance of a military force in New Zealand for the defence of the colony, and for the better control and regulation of the Native race, they must retain in their hands the administration of those affairs which at any moment may involve the employment of those troops, and the consequences of an expensive conflict.[1]

Whilst the Imperial Government thus recognized its obligation to maintain troops in New Zealand as a safeguard for peace with the Maoris, the two Governments had been bickering about liability for barrack accommodation. Labouchere warned the colony that Her Majesty's Government might order the withdrawal of troops from districts in which adequate provision for their accommodation had not been made.[2] But when the Colonial Government ordered 'iron houses' costing £1,350 for the troops at New Plymouth, the frame building landed on the beach from Australia cost nearly £7,000.[3] The Government's exasperation can be imagined. Gore Browne thought the southern provinces would object in any case to paying for barracks in Auckland, Wellington, and New Plymouth; Stafford sent an elaborate minute of protest; Sewell, consulted in England, pleaded poverty.[4]

[1] Carnarvon to Gore Browne (18 May 1859) (No. 34), P.P., 1860, xlvii (No. 492), 171-3.
[2] Labouchere to Gore Browne (21 Oct. 1856) (No. 82), CO209/136.
[3] Journal of Sewell, 5 Aug. 1855.
[4] Gore Browne to Labouchere (11 May 1857) (No. 41) with Minute of Stafford (8 May); Minute of Gairdner (19 Sept.) referring to a private letter from Gore Browne; Minute of Stanley (8 Mar. 1858) referring to interview with Sewell, CO209/141.

In October 1857 Governor and Ministers agreed that it was desirable to send a detachment to Napier, but it was three months before Ministers consented to authorize expenditure from colonial funds for their accommodation.[1]

Now the War Office, with the Indian Mutiny on its hands, wanted to reduce the force in New Zealand to 1,000 men. Lord Stanley, the Colonial Secretary, was inclined to agree if the Admiralty would let the Colonial Government have a steamer to carry the troops from point to point.[2] The Colonial Government, on the other hand, was thinking in terms of reinforcement, not retrenchment. Katatore, who had killed Rawiri for offering a disputed piece of land for sale, had changed his mind and offered the same land to the Government. Ihaia, who had had a similar offer refused for lack of title, took his revenge by ambushing and killing Katatore, on 9 January 1858, on his way back, unarmed, from the town.[3] On 12 February Gore Browne, urged on by his Executive Council, issued a proclamation prohibiting armed assemblies in the settled districts and warning such that they would be 'treated as persons in arms against the Queen's authority'.[4] He did not think the danger so immediate as to justify application to Australia, but ordered the militia to be enrolled at New Plymouth and Wellington as it had been already at Auckland. But, as he had pointed out earlier, tradesmen, labourers earning high wages, and working settlers could not easily be persuaded to serve in the militia so long as danger seemed remote. In a few years' time the revenue would rise and the colony might fairly be required to contribute to the cost of defence; and it was 'to be hoped the Natives will be so far advanced as no longer to require special exemption from the control of the Assembly and may some way or other be represented in it'. But in the meantime, 'at the risk of appearing importunate', he was ready to back his Ministers' plea and urge that 2,000 men, a force sufficient to prevent any Maori outbreak, should be maintained in New Zealand.

---

[1] Minute of Executive Council (19 Oct. 1857), EC1/2, N.Z. Archives. Gore Browne to Labouchere (23 Jan. 1858) (No. 6), CO209/145.

[2] War Office to Colonial Office (22 Jan. 1858) with minute of Stanley (n.d.); Colonial Office to Admiralty (19 Mar. 1858), CO209/149.

[3] *Taranaki Herald*, 16 Jan. 1858 and 8 Jan. 1859; Gore Browne to Labouchere (22 Jan. 1858) (No. 5), CO209/145.

[4] *New Zealand Gazette*, 12 Feb. 1858.

Gore Browne's plea impressed Merivale, who, cool and detached as usual, suggested that 'the stimulus which the sense of security would give to occupation and production' in New Zealand would make such a force an excellent investment for Great Britain. But, he admitted, 'this is not the policy in vogue with Parliament or the country'.[1]

With Ihaia besieged in his pa by Wiremu Kingi with 600 followers and the settlers increasingly restive at the spoiling of their property and goods, Gore Browne came to feel that 'neutrality . . . would be more dangerous to the peace of the Settlement and perhaps that of the Colony at large, than active intervention'. He ordered the parties to stop their feud and offered to remove Ihaia to safety in the Chatham Islands.[2] Wiremu Kingi, who had threatened to fire on the troops if they interfered, submitted to this decision, but Ihaia, having received a small reinforcement from his friends and a promise of more, refused to go.[3] The feud died down for the moment; but the Taranaki Provincial Council felt justified in bringing the condition of the province formally to the notice of the House of Representatives in a memorial. They pointed out that the settlers, numbering about 2,500, occupied 11,000 acres of cultivated land and 32,000 acres of forest, another 20,000 acres of forested land remaining unsold in the hands of the Provincial Government, whereas some 3,000 Maoris occupied over 2,000,000 acres, 300,000 of these 'forming a belt of the richest arable soil in the colony . . . immediately available for the plough'. The present settlers, they claimed, 'can no longer find within the Province a field for future enterprise and the employment of their increasing families'. They also suggested a remedy. As against the present system of requiring the assent of every claimant before a purchase was made, the Provincial Council were of opinion that 'such of the Natives as are willing to dispose of their proportion of any common land to the Government should be permitted to do so, whether such Natives form a majority or only a large minority of the claimants' and an equitable division of such communal land among the claimants should

[1] Gore Browne to Labouchere (25 Feb. 1858) (No. 14) and Minute of Merivale 18 May), CO209/145. Gore Browne had twitted Richmond with the failure of the settlers to respond when the militia was called out, but they did respond now, nd a new Militia Act was passed in 1858; *Richmond–Atkinson Papers*, i. 348–51.
[2] Gore Browne to Labouchere (6 Apr. 1858) (No. 23), ibid.
[3] Gore Browne to Labouchere (17 May 1858) (No. 38), ibid.

be compulsory.[1] In Richmond's paraphrase, they should 'be able to deal with those who desire to sell land, and . . . should not be stopped by those who do not'.[2]

In view of what happened afterwards, it is interesting to find Gore Browne rejecting the suggestion of the Provincial Council.

> I foresee [he wrote] there can be no permanent peace until the Native title is extinguished (with exception of the necessary reserves) over all the land between the town and the Waitara River. To obtain this desirable object however I will never permit land to be taken without the consent of those to whom it belongs. . . . The whole of the Maori race maintain the right of the minority to prevent the sale of land held in common with the utmost jealousy.

He knew that Wiremu Kingi was the soul of the opposition; 'but I will not permit the purchase of land, over which he has any right, without his consent'.[3] At the Colonial Office, Elliot had no sympathy to spare for the settlers, who had 'from the first origin of the Colony been as willing to rush into rash disputes with the Natives as unwilling afterwards to fight them out manfully. . . . They are the last members of the Empire who can with any fair countenance seek to involve the national forces in difficult Native wars.'[4] The political chiefs—Bulwer Lytton and his Under-Secretary Carnarvon—took a less jaundiced view. Lytton was quite outspoken.

> It is impossible to wade through all these papers . . . without feeling that no part of Her Majesty's Dominions is more exposed to danger of a serious kind than New Zealand, that 2000 men are not one too many, that the maintenance of that force would be likely to save this Country vast expenditure and the Colony great loss of life.[5]

He thought the colony should pay for barracks; but soon afterwards an alternative proposal arrived from New Zealand, that the colony should contribute £5 annually for each man of the military establishment, and, though the Colonial Office thought the figure too low, it was accepted eventually—after a delay du

---

[1] The Memorial (19 May 1858) is in Appendices to Journals, H.R., 1858, G–
[2] House of Representatives, 2 June 1858, *N.Z.P.D.*, 1856–8, 487. Richmond did not express agreement but 'would not reproach them'.
[3] Gore Browne to Stanley (9 June 1858) (No. 45), CO209/145.
[4] Minute of Elliot (1 Nov. 1858), ibid.
[5] Minute of Bulwer Lytton (28 Oct.) on Gore Browne to Stanley (26 Jur 1858) (No. 51), ibid.

to the interdepartmental inquiry on the general question of the military defence of colonies.[1] But despite Bulwer Lytton, Gore Browne did not get his reinforcements. The departments were still discussing the question when the Derby–Disraeli Government fell and Palmerston returned to power and the Duke of Newcastle to the Colonial Office. Early in 1860, after Colonel Gold, Wynyard's successor, had written to the War Office direct, asking for more troops, Newcastle notified Gore Browne that the colony's only regiment, the 65th, would be brought up to its full strength of 1,200 rank and file and the Admiralty would comply with the colonial request for a gunboat as soon as possible. But the crisis Gore Browne feared had now come.[2]

Land purchase had been proceeding steadily in the North Island, despite the hardening opposition to it in the central districts. In three and a half years ending on 30 September 1859, 567,000 acres were acquired in Auckland (where about 1,500,000 had been purchased previously), 534,000 acres in Wellington, and 302,000 in Hawke's Bay.[3] In Taranaki, on the other hand, when the purchase of the block of forest land, variously estimated at 14,000 and 20,000 acres, which had cost both Rawiri and Katatore their lives, was finally completed early in 1859, it was the first for five years. The system of purchase based on the Crown's pre-emptive right under the Treaty of Waitangi and operated for many years by McLean, had long been criticized by the 'direct purchase' party in Auckland, who had had their innings under Governor FitzRoy; but a Board headed by the Surveyor-General, Ligar, reported it to be acceptable to the Maoris generally and on the whole the best, though capable of improvement in detail. The Board also gave its views on 'Native title':

It appears that the title or claim to land by tribes arise from occupation, dating sometimes from remote periods, and from more recent conquests, followed by occupation either by themselves personally or by remnants of the conquered people. That this title existed no longer than it could be defended from other tribes. That the boundaries were

[1] Minute of Stafford (8 Sept.) in Gore Browne to Lytton (9 Sept. 1858), O209/146. War Office to Colonial Office (2 Aug. 1860) with Minute of Rogers Aug.) and Treasury to Colonial Office (6 Sept. 1860), CO209/158.
[2] Admiralty to Colonial Office (13 Dec. 1859), Newcastle to Gore Browne 7 Jan. 1860) (No. 5), CO209/152.
[3] These figures are from P.P., 1860, xlvii (H.C. 492), 159. The figures for Wellington and Hawke's Bay cannot be distinguished until 1858.

in some cases clearly defined and admitted by adjoining tribes but that in many others they were quite the reverse. . . . That no tribe has in all instances a well-defined boundary to its land as against adjoining tribes; and that the members of several other tribes are likely to have claims within its limits.

Each Native has a right in common with the whole tribe over the disposal of the land of the tribe, and has an individual right to such portions as he or his parents may have regularly used for cultivations, for dwellings, for gathering birds and rats, or as pig runs. This individual claim does not amount to a right of disposal to Europeans as a general rule.[1]

The Ligar Report did not touch on the position of the chief; but some comments by Richmond in 1857 bear on this.

The right of putting a veto upon sales seems to be recognized as belonging to chiefs who do not possess the *dominium utile*. There is no such thing as a pure individual title. Every sale of land requires the assent of the whole tribe and sometimes of many tribes. . . . If we were stronger we might take cognizance of and settle questions of territorial right between the Natives. It would be politic (as *I* think it would be just) to support any who might demand to have the lands of the tribe partitioned and their own share allotted to them to deal with as they thought good. I am not without hope that we may by degrees take hold of such questions—but not by the strong hand.[2]

Soon after this, Richmond wrote to R. R. Parris, who had just been appointed District Land Purchase Commissioner in Taranaki, telling him he would receive formal instructions from McLean later.

In the meanwhile you cannot be wrong if you act on the established principle of not buying a disputed title. The Government will not have anything to do with land which it would require an armed force to keep possession of. . . . I should suppose it would be very impolitic to appear too anxious about the matter. If you could work by persuading the Natives to individualize their titles, abandoning the surplus to Government in payment for the necessary surveys, I think such a plan would certainly receive the Governor's approval. But a site for a town on the Waitara must be secured.[3]

---

[1] Report (9 July 1856), P.P., 1860, xlvi [2719], 237 ff. The other members of the Board were Major Nugent, C. W. Daldy, and T. H. Smith.

[2] Richmond to T. King (18 May 1857), *Richmond–Atkinson Papers*, i. 266.

[3] Richmond to Parris (6 July 1857), i. 282. McLean's very detailed instruction to Parris (26 Aug.) are in P.P., 1861, xli [2798], 77–8.

Two letters from Halse, Assistant Native Secretary, to McLean at the end of the year carry the matter a stage further.

A preliminary meeting was convened at Waitara last Saturday [28 November] by Teira and others favourable to the sale of a portion of the southern side of that river. Wiremu Kingi was in opposition but owing to the silence of the majority of the Natives present it is difficult to say what, if any, advance was made in that direction.

The second, more hopeful letter informed McLean that 'the Waitara question is to be again discussed after Christmas'.[1] There seems to be no more mention of Waitara in the McLean Papers for nearly a year—a year which saw Katatore's murder and a narrow escape from armed intervention. Then on 23 November Halse writes to McLean: 'Some warm discussions have taken place at Waitara about land during the past fortnight and more will be continually occurring until they put their heads together and resolve on selling it.' Parris, in more stilted language, writes next day: 'Some of the principal claimants to Waitara, who opened the subject for that place in December last, are I am glad to say steady adherents to their then determination and are now preparing for a favourable opportunity and gently initiating William King for the event. Te Teira has written to his friend at Arapawa, a claimant.'[2] Parris was also negotiating the sale of the Mangaoraka land, concluded early in 1859, and prospects seemed favourable for other sales.[3] Wiremu Kingi, on the other hand, remained as obdurate as ever. As he wrote, nominally to the Governor, actually to McLean:

These lands will not be given by us into the Governor's and your hands lest we resemble the seabirds which perch upon a rock. When the tide flows the rock is covered by the sea, and the birds take flight, for they have no resting place. . . . You, O Mr. McLean, are aware of that word of mine when you first came here and saw me . . . 'I will not give the land to you'.[4]

In March 1859 the Governor, hardening in his determination to make law prevail in Taranaki, paid the province a visit. On the

[1] Halse to McLean (1 Dec. and 21 Dec. 1857), McLean Papers 32/239.
[2] Halse to McLean (23 Nov. 1858), McLean Papers 32/240. Parris to McLean 24 Nov. 1858), ibid. 32/334.
[3] Parris to McLean (24 Jan. 1859), ibid.
[4] W. Kingi to the Governor (11 Feb. 1859), P.P., 1861, xli [2798], 324–5. The reference is probably to an overture by McLean when Wiremu Kingi returned from Waikanae in 1848.

8th through McLean as interpreter, he addressed a large gathering of Maoris. He advised them to sell the land they could not use themselves. 'He never would consent to buy land without an undisputed title. He would not permit anyone to interfere with the sale of land unless he owned part of it; and on the other hand he would buy no man's land without his consent.' After the Governor's address Teira rose, offered his land and pressed for an immediate answer. Gore Browne replied that if he could give a satisfactory title it would be accepted. Thereupon Teira laid a fine *parawai* mat at the Governor's feet. As he picked it up a cry was heard, 'Waitara is gone!' Wiremu Kingi, at whom some of Gore Browne's remarks were clearly aimed, then rose and said: 'I will not permit the sale of Waitara to the *pakeha*. Waitara is in my hands. I will not give it up, *ekore* [I will not]! *ekore! ekore!* I have spoken.' Then 'waving his hand, he and all his people marched off without any salutation.'[1]

There is an air of stage management about this dramatic scene, but not on the Governor's part. Teira's offer clearly came as a surprise to him—as it did to Richmond—but McLean had known for a year that the negotiation was in progress. Parris, and presumably McLean, must have known that Wiremu Kingi was actually living in a pa on the land Teira offered; but he had no cultivations there and he never put forward an individual claim, despite the special attachment to Waitara which he had inherited from his father. What he claimed was the right as chief to forbid the sale. Gore Browne denied any such right:

> The right to sell land belonging to themselves, without interference on the part of other chiefs (not having a claim to a share in it) is fully admitted by Maori custom; any recognition of such a power as that assumed by William King would therefore be unjust to both races because it would be the means of keeping millions of acres waste and out of cultivation.

He thought Kingi would back down, as he had done in 1858. But he was prepared if necessary to enforce obedience.[2]

---

[1] Gore Browne to Lytton (29 Mar. 1859) (No. 29) with Enclosures, P.P., 1860 xlvii [2747] (or P.P., 1861, xli [2798]—which is identical), 1 ff. On the cry 'Waitara is gone' see H. L. Gore Browne, *Narrative of the Waitara Purchase and the Taranaki War* (ed. W. P. Morrell) (Dunedin, 1965), p. 17 n. The last sentence is from 'Diary of Proceedings at Taranaki' (7–23 Mar. 1859) in the Gore Browne Papers 2/5 N.Z. Archives.

[2] Gore Browne to Lytton (29 Mar. 1859), loc. cit.

The Taranaki settlers thanked Gore Browne for his 'anxiety to promote the further acquisition of land from the Natives'. No doubt Parris's efforts to purchase land since his appointment in 1857 were an attempt to remedy the settlers' grievance, felt all the more acutely since the collapse of the Australian market for agricultural produce had caused a shift to pastoral farming; but there is no evidence that the Governor's response to this particular offer of 600 acres was influenced by settler pressure. He did not receive the settlers' deputation until he had met the Maoris.[1]

The Governor had promised that Teira's title would be investigated. Teira was not offering the land as an individual owner but on behalf of the Ngatihinga and Ngatituaho *hapu*:[2] it was never claimed that he was the chief of the *hapu*—according to some the chief was Te Patukariki, according to others Ropoama, who had lived for some years past at Queen Charlotte Sound. Te Patukariki was not a party to the transaction, but did not oppose it. Parris, of course, remained in Taranaki, trying to smooth the way for Teira rather than making new inquiries: presumably he felt he had discovered all the relevant facts during the year preceding the actual offer of the land, but did not venture to tell the Governor so. Investigations elsewhere depended upon McLean. He made it his business to visit Ropoama, whom he recognized as the chief of Teira's *hapu*, at Queen Charlotte Sound. By the end of April he was back in Wellington. He did not visit the Atiawa who were still living at Waikanae but went on to the Manawatu to complete negotiations for a block of 30,000 acres and then to Wanganui.[3] Gore Browne, whom he met there, alluded in a

[1] *Taranaki Herald*, 19 Mar. 1859. Gore Browne told the deputation that 'if he [Kingi] should have a joint interest in any land offered for sale, his claim will receive due attention, and the land will not be purchased without his consent'.
[2] It was stated later by Archdeacon Hadfield, and not denied, that Teira had a personal grievance against Wiremu Kingi: a girl who was betrothed to Teira's brother jilted him and married Kingi's son. This may well have been his motive for offering the land, and Kingi's objection to land sales was well known; but it does not affect the question of Teira's title. In 1866 three judges of the Native Land Court (Fenton, Rogan and Monro) investigated the case and found that Wiremu Kingi, as nearer in descent to the first traceable owner, had a superior claim to Teira. The Court, however, for reasons of policy, did not pronounce judgement: Evidence of Fenton in *A.J.H.R.*, 1885, I–2B, 1891, G–1, p. 46 (references I owe to Mr. Harold Miller). But Kingi did not assert this in 1860.
[3] McLean to Richmond (25 Apr. 1859), *Richmond–Atkinson Papers*, i. 455; *Wellington Independent*, 29 Apr. and 27 May 1859.

speech to the heavy demands on McLean's services and outlined his programme for the year.

He will accompany me to Napier, where I trust he will be able to acquire a much coveted block which the Natives now, for the first time, propose to alienate. He will then settle some disputed questions in the Wairarapa, after which he will return to Whanganui via the Manawatu and, as I hope, conclude the negotiations pending there and at the Waitotara. He will then go on to Taranaki, and after settling some purchases in that province (I trust to the satisfaction of the settlers) he will proceed to Auckland.[1]

McLean has frequently been blamed for neglecting the Taranaki negotiations, but this programme was a heavy one and it was not his fault that it was not carried out. He was detained in Hawke's Bay for three and a half months, but in that time he negotiated the purchase of several areas, bringing the land settled or available for settlement to 1,700,000 acres; but some time after leaving the province on 8 September he was struck down, at Castlepoint, by rheumatic fever.[2]

In mid July McLean's lieutenant, T. H. Smith, had dropped a hint that the Governor was 'getting a little fidgetty about your remaining so long at Hawke's Bay'.[3] Teira had been badgering Parris and the Governor to complete the purchase; they were playing for time, thinking McLean's presence in Taranaki 'indispensable to a proper management of the business'.[4] As McLean did not come, Richmond, on the Governor's prompting, urged Parris to 'press the matter as fast as is prudent'.[5] Though Wiremu Kingi remained 'doggedly opposed', Parris was convinced that 'Teira and his supporters are the principal claimants to the land on the South bank of the river. . . . The best argument in their favour', he told McLean, 'is that when they came to Waikanae, William King asked Tamati Raru (Teira's father)'s leave to build their Pas on the South side, thereby admitting that the land was theirs. Tamati Raru told William King for the first time a fortnight ago that it was only stubbornness on his part to oppose

---

[1] Speech at Wanganui dinner, 12 May, *Taranaki Herald*, 4 June 1859.

[2] The figure is from the Hawke's Bay correspondent of the *Taranaki Herald*, 15 Oct. 1859. McLean fell ill some time in October.

[3] Smith to McLean (13 July 1859), McLean Papers.

[4] Smith to McLean (26 Aug. 1859), ibid.

[5] Gore Browne to Richmond [27 Aug.] and Richmond to Parris (27 Aug. 1859), *Richmond–Atkinson Papers*, i. 484–5.

Teira in the sale of the land on the South side, that his (William King's) land was on the North.' He had received authority from the Governor to make a payment to Teira on account; 'but I shall do nothing until you arrive, unless things are more favourable than at present'.[1] But early in November news of McLean's illness reached the Governor. He wrote expressing his sympathy and added: 'At Taranaki they are growling steadily about Teira's land and I have directed Parris to make an advance if he sees no possible objection but to await your arrival before he surveys the boundary.'[2] On 29 November Parris paid Teira an instalment of £100. Kingi came to New Plymouth to oppose the sale. Parris asked him:

Does the land belong to Teira and party?—Yes, the land is theirs, but I will not let them sell it.
Why will you oppose their selling that which is their own?
Because I do not wish for the land to be disturbed; and although they floated it, I will not let it go to sea. . . . It is enough, Parris; their bellies are full with the sight of the money you have promised them, but don't give it to them; if you do, I won't let you have the land, but will take it and cultivate it myself.[3]

All Taranaki had been awaiting the outcome of this battle of wills. 'Had the attempt to prevent the sale succeeded', the *Taranaki Herald* declared, 'it is not too much to say that the purchase of land would for the future have been impracticable.'[4] But Wiremu Kingi had by no means given up the struggle. The Governor regarded himself as committed to the purchase and, in spite of rumours that the survey would be interrupted, he resolved, with the backing of the Executive Council, to proceed to a survey and, in case of resistance, to occupy the block by force.[5] On 20 February the survey party was interrupted by a number of old women, who threw their arms round the surveyors' necks and prevented them from carrying on their work. Lieutenant-Colonel Murray, the local commander, thereupon warned Wiremu Kingi

[1] Parris to McLean (3 Oct. 1859), McLean Papers 32/344. This letter seems to establish Parris's *bona fides*. Teira's is more doubtful: see below, p. 291.
[2] Gore Browne to McLean (7 Nov. 1859) and Gore Browne to Parris (25 Oct. 1859), ibid., 32/157.
[3] Parris to McLean (4 Dec. 1859), P.P., 1861, xli [2798], 321.
[4] *Taranaki Herald*, 3 Dec. 1859.
[5] Gore Browne to Newcastle (25 Jan. 1860) (No. 10), P.P., 1860, xlvii [2747], 5.

that if he did not desist he would take military possession of the land. Kingi sent a dignified reply to Colonel Murray's letter:

> You say that we have been guilty of rebellion against the Queen, but we consider we have not because the Governor has said he will not entertain offers of land which are disputed. The Governor has also said that it is not right for one man to sell the land to Europeans, but that all the people should consent. You are now disregarding the good law of the Governor and adopting a bad law. I have no desire for evil, but, on the contrary, have great love for the Europeans and Maoris.[1]

He did not call off the old women. Murray did not feel he could give the surveyors protection without reinforcements, but he used the authority he had been given to proclaim martial law on 22 February. This was an unfortunate step. The proclamation was intended as a preliminary to calling out the militia and volunteers;[2] but, translated into Maori, it read like a declaration of war. The Governor and Colonel Gold, commanding the troops, came down immediately from Auckland, and Gore Browne sent a message by Parris desiring Wiremu Kingi to come and see him. Kingi returned a temporizing answer, but never came.[3] On 5 March Gold with 400 troops marched to the Waitara, but with instructions from the Governor to avoid collision as long as possible since 'the first bloodshed is a matter to which the Natives attach great weight'. That night Kingi erected a pa commanding the road, but on a message from the Governor next morning that the troops would fire in twenty minutes if he did not evacuate it, he led his men out and the troops set fire to the pa.[4] The survey was now resumed. But on the night of the 15th Kingi's men built a pa within the newly cut boundary line. Next day 'they proceeded to pull up the survey sticks, dance war dances and light fires on the line'. Gold sent them a written summons but they refused to receive it.[5] Thereupon Gold marched up his men from

[1] Kingi to Murray (21 Feb.) in Gore Browne to Newcastle (27 Feb. 1860) (No. 21), P.P., 1860, xlvii [2747], 9. This is the nearest he came to asserting a claim.

[2] H. L. Gore Browne, op. cit., p. 19. Mrs. Gore Browne is virtually a first-hand authority on such details; her husband read and sometimes annotated her manuscript.

[3] Gore Browne to Newcastle (2 Mar. 1860) (Separate), P.P., 1860, xlvii [2747], 11.

[4] Gore Browne to Newcastle (12 Mar. 1860) (No. 24), ibid., pp. 12–13.

[5] H. L. Gore Browne, op. cit., pp. 20–1. See also Ronald's 'Diary of the Taranaki War' in *Richmond–Atkinson Papers*, i. 535.

the Waitara and on the 17th breached the pa with artillery. The Maoris returned the fire whenever the guns stopped: one soldier was killed and two were wounded. The pa only contained seventy men, but Gold did not attempt to storm it and the garrison evacuated it during the night. In this inglorious way the Taranaki war began.

It was not surprising that it had come to war. The desire of the Taranaki settlers to extend their narrow holding as their numbers grew was natural and the Government was anxious to satisfy it; but the war was not a mere land-grabbing operation engineered by the settlers. It is fashionable nowadays to believe that 'colonialism' is and always has been a great wrong, and presumably therefore that the United States of America, not to mention Australia and New Zealand, have no right to exist and that Siberia should still be in the hands of the nomad tribes the Russians found there. It is better, surely, to come to terms with history and to recognize that colonization ever since the days of ancient Greece, if not before, has been one of the great forces shaping the world we know. In any case the Waitara purchase was the occasion rather than the cause of the war in Taranaki. Gore Browne, a man with high principles and a sensitive conscience, never shrank from responsibility for the policy which led to the war. He hoped that a mere show of force would break a deadlock which threatened the peace of the whole colony. He underrated Wiremu Kingi's unyielding determination; but there is much truth in Professor Sinclair's epigram that he 'started a war by trying to stop it'. Wiremu Kingi's veto was an assertion of independence irreconcilable with British sovereignty. In the modern anthropologist's pattern of Maori society the *mana* of a chief tends to be illustrated rather than precisely defined. The recent events in Atiawa history—the Waikato conquest, the break-up of the tribe, the early European land purchases, the dissolving effect of pakeha contacts and customs—suggest that Wiremu Kingi's underlying purpose was not only to retain the tribal lands for their own sake but also to maintain his *mana* as chief against all challenges. Gore Browne can hardly be blamed for holding that submission to his veto would merely increase tension between the two peoples. Even Professor Sinclair, for all his criticism of Gore Browne and sympathy with Kingi, admits that 'his general bearing went far to confirm the Governor in his erroneous judgements'.

The expediency of the purchase is a different question. In this connection, McLean's responsibility needs to be examined. He knew that Teira's offer was impending: the Governor, in accepting it, obviously looked to him to see the matter through. There is a certain deviousness in his conduct. The promised 'investigation' never in fact took place—though the delay did give an opportunity for others to establish claims. The only satisfactory explanation seems to be that McLean and Parris thought they already knew most of the facts bearing on the case, but could not admit this without also admitting that Teira's offer had been stage-managed. The purpose of McLean's visit to Queen Charlotte Sound was to secure Ropoama's backing for Teira; Wiremu Kingi's attitude was already clear. The Governor clearly knew and approved of McLean's programme for the year, which was to end with a visit to Taranaki in the hope of wearing down Kingi's opposition and clinching the purchase. We need not assume that he purposely prolonged his visit to Hawke's Bay: land purchase negotiations were generally long drawn out and he may well have thought that 120,000 acres on the Ruataniwha plains deserved more time than 600 acres at Waitara. Then his illness inevitably postponed his visit and the final stages of the negotiations went on without him. He may have been jealous of Richmond's influence with the Governor; Matene Te Whiwhi told Archdeacon Hadfield that 'Mr. McLean expressed his regret that the Governor should have taken such a hasty and premature step as the forcible ejection of William King from Waitara, without further investigation'.[1] But, as he admitted, the Governor doubtless wished to avoid giving him unnecessary trouble or anxiety during his illness. In 1863, after Sir George Grey had given up the Waitara purchase, Featherston took McLean to task in a friendly letter: 'Say what you will, McLean, you will never convince me that you believed in the validity of the purchase from Teira. You simply from a spirit of chivalry backed up Browne after he had gone too far to recede.' McLean replied that a clash between Maori and European was inevitable. The 'paltry six hundred acres of land at Waitara' were certainly not the cause of it: 'I am as ignorant as can be of any valid grounds for giving up that land

---

[1] Letter of Hadfield in *New Zealand Spectator*, 10 Oct. 1860, O. Hadfield, *The New Zealand War: The Second Year of One of England's Little Wars* (London, 1861), pp. 49-50.

except that it has become fashionable in New Zealand for one party to reverse what another has done.'[1] Those who think the Waitara purchase a blunder or a crime can never prove that war would have been avoided; and all the probabilities are against such a conclusion.

In any case the colonists did not admit responsibility for the war. 'They have never', wrote Richmond, 'had the direction of Native policy; nor have they directed or even suggested the acts of the Imperial Government in its relations with the Natives; but they approve of the stand made by His Excellency in the Taranaki case, and are naturally willing . . . to risk life itself in the maintenance of the Queen's authority over the islands of New Zealand.' But the colony was unequal to sustaining a prolonged war: 'justice therefore and humanity require that England should freely recognize the onerous duties cast upon her by the colonization of New Zealand'.[2] As soon as hostilities began, in fact, the Governor estimated that New Zealand would need 3,000 troops, a steam gunboat, and a war steamer for some time to come.

[1] Featherston to McLean (13 June 1863) and McLean to Fetherston (17 June 1863), McLean Papers, 32/211.
[2] Memo. of Richmond (27 Apr.) in Gore Browne to Newcastle (27 Apr. 1860) (No. 40), P.P., 1860, xlvii (H.C. 492), 166–9.

# VIII

## THE TARANAKI WAR AND THE
## APPEAL TO SIR GEORGE GREY

A QUICK victory was the only hope of preventing the war from spreading; but Colonel Gold was not the man to win a quick victory and the Taranaki and Ngati Ruanui tribes, southern neighbours of Te Atiawa, were almost immediately involved. On 27 March, ten days after the first shots had been fired, three settlers and two boys, who had gone into the country to look after cattle, were murdered in the Omata district. Next day Taranaki and Ngati Ruanui tribesmen danced a war dance outside the Omata blockhouse, fired some shots at it, and built two pas nearby. Gold thereupon organized a force to relieve the block-house and bring in a clergyman and some settlers who had remained in the country. The militia and volunteers, who went by sea, were attacked immediately on arrival. The regulars, under Lieutenant-Colonel Murray, advancing along the main road, were less closely involved and, in blind obedience to Gold's orders to be back in town by dark, left the militia and volunteers to fend for themselves. A gallant and successful attack on a Maori pa by a landing party from H.M.S. *Niger* rescued them from their exposed position, but this Waireka affair inevitably led to bad feeling between regulars and colonial forces. Harry Atkinson, one of the volunteer officers, sharply criticized Murray's conduct in a letter to his brother-in-law Richmond.[1]

Gore Browne himself privately was critical of Gold's inability to move without cumbrous trains of commissariat carts.[2] An expedition of this kind into the Ngati Ruanui country in April demolished some pas and burnt or carried off Maori property but led to the destruction of abandoned farms by way of reprisal.

[1] H. A. Atkinson to C. W. and Emily Richmond (6 Apr. 1860), *Richmond–Atkinson Papers*, i. 552–3. cf. also *The Times*, 13 June 1860.
[2] Gore Browne to McLean (25 May 1860), McLean Papers 32/157. See also H. L. Gore Browne, op. cit., p. 22.

But the Governor, in his anxiety not to alienate the Waikato tribes, felt obliged to ask Gold in May not to interfere with Wiremu Kingi unless he himself began hostilities.[1] Even these restraining

MAP 3. TARANAKI AND WANGANUI

orders did not save Gold from a sharp reverse. Major Nelson, 'a fiery old field officer who longed for distinction', had arrived from Melbourne in command of a wing of the 40th Foot. He determined to attack Puketakauere pa, half a mile from the Wai-tara river, and Gold promised support. The morning of the attack, 27 June, was 'one of the wettest and stormiest of a wet and stormy winter' but Nelson carried on with his plans. An artillery sergeant apparently forgot to send up a pre-arranged rocket signal; per-haps Gold thought the weather had led to a postponement; it is said he was in bed with severe influenza when the firing was

[1] Gore Browne to Gold (17 May 1860), G36/3, N.Z. Archives.

heard. Troops were nevertheless marched out from New Plymouth; but the promised support never reached Nelson and his attack was heavily defeated.[1] Recriminations even extended to the columns of the London *Times*.[2] The Governor, relieved for a time of his anxiety about the Waikatos, had withdrawn his restraining orders and now urged the necessity of a 'decided and indisputable success'.[3] By a master stroke of the military machine Colonel Gold was promoted Major-General and thus made ineligible for his present command;[4] and his defeat led Major-General Pratt, commanding in Australia, to come to New Zealand with every man he could spare and take command himself.

Meanwhile no less a person than Bishop Selwyn had declared his opposition to the Government's war policy. Taking as his text a resolution of the Hawke's Bay Provincial Council thanking the Governor for his 'equitable and open declaration of policy', the Bishop sent a letter on 28 April to Tancred, one of the Ministers, protesting

because martial law was proclaimed at Taranaki before a single Native was known to have taken up arms against the Government, and when no offence had been given by the Natives beyond an obstruction of the work of the surveyors; because the persons described in the resolution as 'disaffected aborigines' were the faithful and efficient allies of the Government in the war at Port Nicholson and were always considered as among the most peaceful and industrious of the New Zealand tribes till they became entangled in the land questions raised by the English settlers at Taranaki.

He claimed that all questions of title to land should be investigated before a regular tribunal and furthermore that 'inasmuch as this colony was avowedly formed, not for the acquisition of territory for the English race, but for the protection of the New Zealanders, this primary object shall not be sacrificed to the aggrandizement of the English provinces'.[5] In an able memorandum Ministers

---

[1] Sir J. E. Alexander, *Incidents of the Maori War in New Zealand in 1860–61* (London, 1863), pp. 154–64; M. S. Grace, *A Sketch of the New Zealand War* (London, 1899), pp. 27–37. Grace was an assistant staff surgeon during the campaign; Alexander arrived in February 1861.

[2] *The Times*, 14 and 17 Sept. 1860. Letter of protest from Col. Gold, ibid., 19 Feb. 1862. Gold's statements denied by Nelson's brother ibid., 20 Feb.

[3] Gore Browne to Newcastle (20 July 1860) (No. 70), P.P., 1860, xlvii [2747], 87.          [4] He was gazetted on 10 July 1860: *Spectator*, 14 July 1860.

[5] Selwyn to Tancred (28 Apr.) in Gore Browne to Newcastle (25 May 1860) (No. 49), P.P., 1860, xlvii [2747], 48–9.

answered the Bishop point by point. The proclamation of martial law was a precautionary measure only. 'Actual force was not used until a fighting party of Kingi's people had erected a pa and danced the war dance upon the disputed ground, and had contemptuously rejected a summons by the officer in command to evacuate the pa.' Kingi's services against Rangihaeata were of questionable value and his attitude at Waitara had been 'one of pure hostility to the interests of the settlement'. There had already been an investigation of title in Taranaki, by Commissioner Spain, and the turbulent conduct of Te Atiawa had 'induced Governor FitzRoy to set it aside'. The methods of investigation of title to the Waitara block did not differ from those in the purchase of the Bell block, which the Bishop had approved. The Bishop's most fundamental point was categorically denied, 'successive Secretaries of State . . . having declared that the equal benefit of both races was the motive for assuming the sovereignty of the islands'.[1]

Archdeacon Hadfield, whose long residence at Waikanae had made him Wiremu Kingi's closest European friend and adviser, was also active. A memorial for the Governor's recall was circulating among Te Atiawa at Waikanae and though the Archdeacon denied that it originated with him it is difficult to believe that he was not cognizant of it and known to be in sympathy with it.[2] He wrote a pamphlet for publication at home and in conjunction with Bishop Abraham of Wellington addressed a letter to the Duke of Newcastle. When the General Assembly met on 30 July, the regular Opposition—the Wellington party led by Fox and Featherston with Carleton and others from Auckland—strongly criticized the Waitara purchase and pressed for a committee of inquiry into the circumstances of the war. The inspiration, however, came from Hadfield. He had won over Featherston, and then Fox, who in a letter to Godley had admitted his suspicions of Hadfield's bias, allowed his doubts to be swept away.[3] Carleton, as the son-in-law of Henry Williams and the brother-in-law of Hadfield, was a natural adherent of the mis-

[1] Memo. of Ministers (25 May) in Gore Browne to Newcastle (25 May 1860) (No. 49), loc. cit., pp. 49–53.
[2] Minute of Cox (30 Mar. 1861) on Gore Browne to Newcastle (17 Dec. 1860) (No. 135), CO209/157.
[3] Fox to Godley (5 May 1860), Correspondence of J. R. Godley, Canterbury Museum.

sionary party. Fox strongly criticized the Governor personally. After Dr. Monro had appealed to members to put some restraint on their tongues in this crisis, Sewell suggested as a compromise that Hadfield and McLean be requested to attend at the bar of the House and give evidence as to the causes of the war. Party leaders on both sides supported the suggestion and both men were heard on 14 August. Hadfield maintained that no one could alienate land without the consent of the tribe; the right even of a chief so to alienate any part of the territory of a tribe was questionable and it could 'scarcely be allowed to any chief of a *hapu* even if he should act in accordance with the various individuals of the *hapu*'. Teira, he declared, was not even a chief of a *hapu* but only an ordinary freeman or *tutua*. He admitted, however, that his information was chiefly derived from two Atiawa associates of his, Hohepa Ngapaki and Riwai Te Ahu, the latter of whom according to Richmond was 'well known to the Land Purchase Office as a small and very greedy claimant'. McLean for his part denied that there was any fixed rule guiding alienation of land: custom varied. Among Te Atiawa 'a family of three or four people had been regarded as empowered to dispose of its common property'. Neither Ropoama nor Patukakariki had raised objection. Sewell found McLean's evidence disappointing, considering the investigation of title to have been rather perfunctory; but Hadfield made an unfavourable impression on him.[1] Two days later Stafford moved

that, in the opinion of this House, the interference of Wiremu Kingi at Waitara, and his resort to force to prevent the survey of land there, rendered the measures adopted by His Excellency the Governor indispensable for the due maintenance of Her Majesty's sovereignty and that the welfare of both races of Her Majesty's subjects peremptorily requires a vigorous prosecution of the war to a successful conclusion.[2]

The motion was carried with only four dissentients, the Foxites abstaining; but Sewell noted in his journal that 'the House was so thin at last that the vote though carried was too shabby to be

---

[1] Evidence of Hadfield and McLean: *N.Z.P.D.*, 1858–60, pp. 285–306. Journal of Sewell, 19 Aug. 1860.
[2] *Journal of House of Representatives*, 1860, p. 32.

worth anything'.[1] The Legislative Council carried a motion in less specific terms assuring His Excellency of cordial support, but with three dissentients, among them the former Attorney-General, Swainson.

On one matter, however, all parties in the House were agreed. Featherston, referring to the crucial Executive Council on 25 January, inquired 'whether Ministers gave that advice with or without responsibility—whether they consider themselves responsible for the war'. Stafford in reply pointed out the incorrectness of supposing that Ministers were debarred from advising the Governor on Native affairs: 'they were not only not so debarred from advising His Excellency, but they were required to advise, both as responsible Ministers and as members of the Executive Council. . . . We are entirely and fully responsible for advising and concurring in the course taken by the Governor.'[2] But this did not mean that it was a colonial war: all parties agreed that the war was an Imperial one. Featherston, though he thought the Governor more sinned against than sinning, was 'not prepared to relieve His Excellency from the responsibility of this war, on the contrary, I hold him solely responsible for it'.[3] And Richmond told the House that he had avoided rather than sought intercourse with Maoris: 'I have always told them that I was only one of his [the Governor's] *runanga*. . . his ear to hear and report but not his mouth to speak and to decide—that I was, for all purposes of merely executive government as much the Governor's servant as were the officers of Government under the old system.'[4]

The need to bring the Maoris under more effective government was also generally accepted. They were nominal British subjects; but in the centre of the island at any rate they were left to themselves in matters of government. The Waitara purchase forced the question of Maori land titles to the front. The Maori King movement drew attention to the failure of the colonial Government to provide any institutions of Government beyond the resident magistrates, who as we have seen were virtually confined to the courts. Selwyn, in a memorandum for the Governor in May, suggested that one or more Maori provinces be constituted in the

[1] Journal of Sewell, 19 Aug. 1860.
[2] House of Representatives, 7 Aug. 1860, N.Z.P.D., 1858-60, p. 223; also in P.P., 1860, xlvii [2747], 388-9.   [3] 15 Aug. 1860, N.Z.P.D., 1858-60, p. 328.
[4] 9 Aug. 1860, ibid., p. 262; also in P.P., 1860, xlvii [2747], 411.

Central North Island.[1] In the course of long Assembly debates, the Government gained acceptance of its view that Richmond's Native Districts Regulation Act of 1858 was a convenient framework of policy; but only two districts, in the far north, had as yet been proclaimed. The general meeting of Maori chiefs which had been summoned to Kohimarama just outside Auckland, mainly to discuss the issues in the Taranaki war, might also develop into a regular institution. Of the fourteen resolutions which emerged from the Committee of the House on 14 September, seven dealt with land titles, one of them declaring 'that, as an essential preliminary to the individualization of Native Title, measures ought to be taken forthwith . . . for the ascertainment and registration of . . . Tribal Titles'. The most significant resolution was political and aimed at bringing McLean's private empire within the ordinary ambit of government.

that in the opinion of this House the present departmental arrangements for the management of Native affairs are open to grave objection, and that as a first and essential step towards a better system, the political administration of Native Affairs ought to be separated from the function of extinguishing the Native title to land, which should be administered by a separate department.[2]

But when the Governor had asked for a large Imperial force, the House naturally thought it inopportune to reconsider his relations with his Ministers in the conduct of Native affairs.

Before the House had concluded its debates on these matters, news arrived of a Bill Newcastle had introduced into the Imperial Parliament. This originated in a proposal of the Governor a year before to create a new Council to strengthen his hand against settler pressure—especially, it would seem from the context, at Auckland.

With the increase of the European population land has necessarily acquired an additional value; the Native race have seen the land they alienated for farthings sold for pounds; they feel that dominion and power, or as they term it 'substance' went from them with the territories they alienated, and they look with apprehension to the annihilation of their nationality. . . . The Europeans covet these lands and are

[1] Memo. on Native Affairs by the Bishop of New Zealand (8 May) in Gore Browne to Newcastle (22 May 1860) (No. 46), P.P., 1860, xlvii (H.C. 522), 2-8.
[2] J.H.R., 1860, pp. 92-3.

determined to enter in and possess them *recte si possunt si non quocunque modo*.[1]

He recommended that the Governor should be assisted by a permanent Council for Native Affairs, two of them nominated by responsible Ministers and five (three of them paid) by the Governor. He hoped that Bishop Selwyn and ex-Chief Justice Martin would accept seats: 'the presence of men so well known and so thoroughly trusted by the Maoris would secure to it an influence which no other European body could possibly acquire'. This body would handle land purchase, ensure ample reserves for the Maoris, regulate the allocation of part of the proceeds of sales for their benefit, and see that the conditions of purchase were fulfilled before handing over the lands for settlement in the usual way. He hoped such a system might induce the Maoris to sell their lands more freely. He left open the question whether it should be introduced by Imperial or colonial legislation; but he clearly preferred the former alternative and enclosed a Bill drafted by Sewell, who had resigned from the Ministry soon after his return from England early in 1859.[2]

Ministers did not like the scheme at all: they were 'decidedly of opinion that the union of these powers in a permanent Board could not fail to excite strong public dissatisfaction'.[3] The Colonial Office was in two minds about it. Merivale could not 'foresee any good from the establishment of two governments in the one colony'. 'It will', he added, 'be a difficult measure to pass, interfering so directly with self-government.' Rogers, who was soon to succeed him as Permanent Under-Secretary, pointed out that the Imperial Parliament could not constitutionally invest the Council with any power other than those reserved by the 73rd section of the Constitution Act, dealing with the purchase of Maori land: other powers could be conferred only with the consent of the colonial Government. On the other hand, it was on the British sovereign and not the legislature that the New Zealand

---

[1] So in the original; Gore Browne's Latin had grown rusty.
[2] Gore Browne to Newcastle (20 Sept. 1859) (No. 80) with Enclosures, P.P., 1860, xlvii (H.C. 492), 77 ff. Sewell had drafted the Bill by 3 July and had a long conversation with the Governor on the management of Native affairs on 4 Apr.: Journal.
[3] Remarks by Ministers on Mr. Sewell's Draft Bill in Gore Browne to Newcastle (20 Sept. 1859) (No. 80), loc. cit.

chiefs conferred the dominion of their country and the guardian-
ship of their interests, and it was hardly consistent with the honour
of the Crown to hand this trusteeship over to an authority which
had not acquired their confidence. On balance, therefore, Rogers
favoured the Bill, which he had been instructed to draft.[1]

Before the Duke of Newcastle as Colonial Secretary could
introduce the Bill in the House of Lords, news had arrived of the
outbreak of war in Taranaki. This gave the Duke a further
'reason why the management of the Natives should not be left to
the local Government; . . . if quarrels arose between them . . . and
if those resulted in an outbreak, it was upon the Imperial Government that the whole expense of quelling such an outbreak fell'.
Hence the Imperial interest in anything which would remove the
causes of quarrels.[2] But this did not abate the opposition to the
Bill, which came especially from New Zealand colonists in London. Within two days of Newcastle's introductory speech on
3 July, J. E. FitzGerald, the moving spirit of the opposition, produced a memorandum protesting against the passage, without
the knowledge of the colonists, of a bill which would 'entirely
supersede the General Assembly over two thirds of the North
Island. No ministry would take the responsibility of governing
the country with Native policy wholly beyond its grasp; not a
penny would be voted for Native affairs if they were taken out of
the Assembly's hands; the two races would be placed in a position
of antagonism just when their interests should be merged in a
common government.'[3] FitzGerald also saw many members of
Parliament he knew personally, urging them to oppose the Bill.
The Aucklanders, though most of them did not share FitzGerald's
exaggerated fears, agreed to join in petitioning both Houses for
delay.[4] The Bill passed the Lords, despite critical remarks from the
Earl of Derby and Lord Lyttelton, who, however, disappointed
the petitioners by not dividing the House. A few days before the
Bill was due to be read a second time in the House of Commons,
a deputation headed by three M.P.s (Arthur Mills, Roebuck, and

[1] Minute of Merivale (6 Feb.) on Murdoch and Rogers to Merivale (1 Feb.
1860), CO209/158. Draft dispatch by Rogers (20 Apr. 1860): CO209/159.
[2] House of Lords, 3 July 1860: *Hansard*, 3rd Ser. clix. 1326–8.
[3] Memo. of FitzGerald (5 July) in Lewis to Gore Browne (26 July 1860)
(No. 48), *A.J.H.R.*, 1860, E–No. 6B, pp. 5–8.
[4] W. S. Grahame to McLean (26 July and 23 Aug. 1860), McLean Papers.
FitzGerald wrote to Lords Derby, Stanley, de Vesci, and Naas and to Gladstone,
Pakington, and Lord Robert Cecil. All but Lord R. Cecil replied favourably.

Childers) but chiefly composed of New Zealand colonists saw
the Prime Minister. It must have made some impression, for
later that week Palmerston, who was at first inclined to go on,
saw Rogers and Chichester Fortescue, who as Under-Secretary
had charge of the bill in the Commons, heard what Fortescue had
to say, asked some pretty searching questions, and then told them
he would postpone the Bill.[1] On Tuesday, 21 August, Palmerston
announced to the House that the Bill would not be pressed any
further. 'We cannot wonder', said *The Times*, 'that the House of
Commons protested, almost as one man, against this ill-judged
measure.'[2]

By the time news of the Bill had reached New Zealand it had
been withdrawn, but the views of the House of Representatives, foreshadowed as they had been by the representations of
Fitz-Gerald and the New Zealand colonists in London, remain
significant. On 2 October Fox moved some resolutions of remonstrance and though Richmond 'did not think it was a time to fly
in the face of the Imperial Government' and was 'quite disposed to
meet the views of the Colonial Office more than halfway', the feeling of the House was clearly in favour of 'a protest against that
being done for New Zealand by the Imperial Parliament which the
Colonial Legislature could do for itself'.[3] Stafford suggested that
the resolutions should be referred to a Joint Committee of both
Houses and in due course Fox brought up its report, which adhered to the principle of his original resolutions but was more
constructive and less bellicose in tone. The Committee were of
opinion

that it is essential to the successful operation of any system which may
be established for the better administration of Native affairs that it
should have the cordial support of the local Legislature and that such
co-operation cannot be expected towards any system of Native administration imposed upon the colony by the actions of the Imperial
Parliament, taken without reference to the views or to the local knowledge and experience of the colonial Legislature.[4]

[1] Chichester Fortescue to Newcastle (27 Aug. 1860), Newcastle Papers,
NeC10931. Rogers to Lady Rogers (c. 20 Aug. 1860), *Letters of Lord Blachford*,
pp. 229–30.
[2] *The Times*, 23 Aug. 1860 (according to Fortescue, written by Lowe). *The
Saturday Review* (25 Aug.) regretted the loss of the Bill.
[3] Stafford's phrase. For the debate see *N.Z.P.D.*, 1858–60, pp. 610–25.
[4] 12 Oct. 1860, ibid., p. 656.

The Committee then suggested the formation of a Native Council but of a different kind from the one to be set up under the Imperial Bill. The Government should consult it on all important questions relating to the management of Native affairs and it should have the duty of submitting for consideration measures on certain specified matters; but having heard its advice, the Government should act 'at their own discretion and on their own responsibility'. A Bill was to be drafted on these lines by Whitaker and Richmond and when the new system came into operation the department of Native Affairs was to be placed on the same basis as the other departments of government.[1]

The Bill was read a second time and then amended to make ministers of religion, members of the General Assembly, and holders of provincial office ineligible for the Council and to limit its duration to seven years. The Legislative Council amended some of the clauses but a conference between the Houses compromised the differences. The House then requested the Governor's views upon its understanding that, if it passed the Bill, the ordinary control and departmental administration would be placed under responsible Ministers, 'subject . . . to the proper constitutional action of the Supreme Head of the Executive'.[2] On receipt of the desired message, both Houses passed the Bill. The Governor thereupon reserved it for the royal assent. But it was clear from his covering dispatch that he still doubted 'what right the Assembly has to govern and tax a race it does not represent, whose interests are not presumed to be identical with those of its own constituents, to whose lands it has not a reversionary right, and against whose aggression Her Majesty's Government is called on to protect the European settlers'. His support for the Bill was qualified.

I have not altered the opinions I have always expressed, viz. that the Crown is the rightful guardian of the Maori race, but if the Crown has not the means of acting in that capacity without aid from the Assembly of New Zealand, it is evident that any attempt to legislate in a manner not acceptable to that body must prove abortive. . . . . I believe this Act to be the best compromise which can now be made.[3]

[1] N.Z.P.D., 12 Oct. 1860, p. 657.
[2] J.H.R., 1860, pp. 247–9.
[3] Gore Browne to Newcastle (26 Nov. 1860) (No. 120), CO209/156. See also Journal of Sewell (4 Nov. 1860).

It was going to be difficult, however, to form a Council carrying any weight. Sir William Martin declined to serve; Selwyn was excluded by the terms of the Bill; Swainson was thought too unpopular; McLean and Nugent accepted seats, the former under pressure from the Governor after a first refusal; Dillon Bell was to be Secretary for Native Affairs.[1] But the plan never came to fruition.

> It looks and sounds [Chichester Fortescue wrote] as if it were a concession to the Imperial Government, while in reality I believe it would be a concession by the Imperial Government in the matter of Native Administration. . . . It seems to me that the present is the worst possible moment for such a concession . . . because it will appear to the Natives that the Queen is delivering them over to the rule of the Pakeha at the moment when the latter are flushed with victory and confident in their strength under the protection of the large force which will then be present in New Zealand.

It would also deprive the Imperial Government of its only possible bargaining counter in discussions of the Imperial contribution to the expenses of the war and the amount of force to be retained in the Colony.[2] Newcastle's views were similar. In face of the Treaty of Waitangi the Bill could not be sanctioned without injustice and bad faith to the Maoris.[3]

This did not mean that the Imperial authorities were satisfied with the existing arrangements. They admitted that the situation in New Zealand was 'extremely serious'. But they were uneasy at Gore Browne's demand for troops in addition to the reinforcements he was receiving from the Australian colonies and they did not like the colonists' disclaimer, voiced in a memorandum by Richmond, of all responsibility for the existing state of affairs and their insistence that it was an Imperial war. The Duke of Newcastle had left the country on 10 July to accompany the Prince of Wales on his tour of Canada and the United States. When the April dispatches with Richmond's supporting memorandum arrived, Chichester Fortescue suggested that they should

[1] Martin to Gore Browne (31 Oct.) and Gore Browne to C. W. Richmond (2 Nov. 1860), *Richmond–Atkinson Papers*, i. 646–9. Gore Browne to Newcastle (4 Dec. 1860) (No. 132), CO209/156.
[2] Minute of Fortescue (21 Feb. 1861) on Gore Browne to Newcastle (26 Nov. 1860) (No. 120), CO209/156.
[3] Minute of Newcastle (23 Feb. 1861), ibid. But this was not a decision communicated to New Zealand.

go to the Home Secretary, Sir George Lewis, who brought the matter before the Cabinet.[1] The outcome was a stinging rebuke to the colonial Government and the colonists generally.

England cannot undertake the defence, against a nation of warlike savages, of a number of scattered farms or villages, selected, not with a view to defence, but to the profitable pursuit of peaceful industry, and subject to the risks which necessarily attend the occupation of land in the midst of an uncivilized population. . . . Immediate and imminent dangers must be met as they arise. But a policy which requires the continual presence of a large force carries, in most cases, its condemnation on its face.

The colonists did not commit themselves to contribute to the expense of the troops; volunteering appeared to be confined to the particular localities threatened; the attempt to invest the Governor with larger powers was determinedly opposed.

I allude to these circumstances [the dispatch continued] not of course as relieving the Home Government from the duty of supporting the colony against a pressing danger, but because they must materially affect the disposition of the British Government and people to undertake that indefinite expenditure of blood and treasure to which Mr. Richmond invites them.[2]

In a dispatch a month later Chichester Fortescue asked the Governor for a full report on the alleged seigniorial right of the chief to assent to or forbid the sale of land belonging to members of the tribe and the extent to which such a right had been or ought to be recognized by the Crown.[3] This is a clear indication that the Colonial Office was exercised in mind about the rights and wrongs of the Waitara purchase as well as about the expenses of the war. It was inclined to reject Wiremu Kingi's claim. In a minute of 26 November Rogers subjects it to a careful analysis and concludes

---

[1] A deputation of colonists saw Lord Palmerston on 18 July and urged immediate aid to New Zealand: he promised to bring the matter before the Cabinet that day: W. S. Grahame to McLean (26 July 1860), McLean Papers. This perhaps dates the Cabinet.

[2] Lewis to Gore Browne (26 July 1860) (No. 48), P.P., 1860, xlvii [2747], 262–3. A Minute of Rogers (16 Aug. 1860) in CO209/154 makes it clear that he drafted this dispatch.

[3] Chichester Fortescue to Gore Browne (27 Aug. 1860) (No. 55), ibid., p. 264.

that the Governor was right in principle. But then he adds a postscript:

I have just spoken to a gentleman who assisted Sir G. Grey in his negotiations for the purchase of land at Taranaki. He says that in his time William King was held by common consent the undoubted chief of the Waitara country—and that no one would have dreamt of purchasing land without his concurrence or otherwise than through him.[1]

The gentleman, Sir Godfrey Thomas, was (though Rogers does not say so) the step-brother of Sir George Grey. Newcastle's dispatch next day still held to the view that 'the disloyal and defiant conduct of that chief when his claims were denied by the Government was such as to leave you no other alternative than an appeal to arms.'[2] But Rogers's doubts grew.

Gore Browne defended himself ably against Sir George Lewis's strictures. From the outset, 'English law was by a fiction assumed to prevail over the whole colony' but in fact it was a dead letter beyond the English settlements; for sheer lack of means, the Government had been 'driven to temporize and ignore aggression or crime which it could neither prevent nor punish'.

I venture to say, that when Her Majesty's Government declared New Zealand a colony and invited the industrious and law-loving classes to emigrate, an assurance of protection was certainly directly or indirectly given, and without it these men would never have left their native land.

In the matter of expense, a colony able to afford it might well pay half; but 'when the finances (as in the case of New Zealand) are unable to bear such a burden, they should be relieved of an additional percentage, subject to readjustment every three or five years'.

The Imperial authorities were under a misapprehension about a militia and volunteer force. It was useful in its own district.

But . . . it can never be sent out of that district without payment, which must be as much in excess of a soldier's pay as the settler's labour and his expenses are greater than those of an English labourer. . . . A large proportion of those who form the rank and file of volunteer corps are farmers, tradesmen and persons possessing stock or engaged

[1] Minute of Rogers (26 Nov.) on Gore Browne to Newcastle (4 Sept. 1860) (No. 95) and memo. of Thomas (26 Nov.), CO209/155.
[2] Newcastle to Gore Browne (27 Nov. 1860) (No. 89), ibid., p. 268.

in business which would be ruined by their absence for any length of time. . . . Except as an auxiliary to regular troops in the district in which it is raised, a colonial militia is therefore the most expensive force which can be employed; and though equal in bravery and perhaps superior in activity to Her Majesty's troops, it is not usually found to be so effective for continuous operations.[1]

A month later, with the assistance of Dillon Bell, he sent a voluminous dispatch answering Fortescue's query about seigniorial right.

Whatever may be the true theory of Native tenure . . . there is nothing more certain than that there exist among the native tribes themselves no fixed rules by which the practice of Government in its dealings with them for land could be guided. . . . There were a few tribes which had been so broken and scattered by conquest and otherwise, that with reference to them the British Government has from the first neither recognized the tribal right in case of alienation nor permitted the exercise of a veto on such alienation by the chiefs. Of these was the Ngatiawa of Taranaki.

The whole case was gone over in detail and the effect was to convince Newcastle and Chichester Fortescue, at least, of the 'substantial justice' of the Governor's case.[2]

But meanwhile the minority in New Zealand who were not so convinced were making their voices heard in England. The first criticisms came in private letters from missionaries and their wives, some of which were printed for private circulation. Bishop Selwyn declined suggestions that he should write to the Duke of Newcastle and Gladstone (whom he had known at Eton):[3] his colleague Abraham and Archdeacon Hadfield, as we have seen, had no such inhibitions. Fox wrote to Godley putting all the blame on Gore Browne and 'the experiment of reserving Native affairs from the control or interference of the colonists . . . to an extent far beyond what in my opinion the Constitution Act justified':

---

[1] Gore Browne to Newcastle (1 Nov. 1860) (No. 109), P.P., 1860, xlvii [2747], 159–61.

[2] Gore Browne to Newcastle (4 Dec. 1860) (No. 126), ibid., pp. 169–96. Fortescue to Gore Brown (26 Feb. 1861) (Private), CO209/159. This refers to Dillon Bell, whose share in the dispatch is mentioned in various other sources. See also Newcastle in *Hansard*, 3rd Ser. clxiii. 170.

[3] Lady Martin to Miss Palmer (28 Aug. 1860), *Extracts of Letters from New Zealand on the War Question* (printed for private circulation, London, 1861), p. 17.

but Godley did at least hear the other side.[1] More damaging no
doubt were the tendentious dispatches of the Melbourne correspondent of *The Times*, H. S. Chapman. Chapman, who had formerly been a New Zealand judge, according to Richmond
derived his information from his old colleague, Sir William
Martin. His messages were strongly biased in favour of the
Opposition and had a special animus against Governor Gore
Browne. One of them elicited a reply from Gore Browne's
brother, then Lady Margaret Professor of Divinity at Cambridge,
and this in turn drew a retort from Colonel Hadfield, brother of
the Archdeacon.[2] *The Times* did not merely echo its correspondent's opinions but, sensitive to the public opinion it professed to
lead, it began early in 1861 to change its tune. As one leading
article remarked:

> Had we shown more jealousy for the Queen's sovereignty and less
> haste in appropriating a desirable block of land, we might never have
> been placed in our present dilemma. England is too great to stickle for
> a plot of ground, if it can be shown that vested interests were not
> sufficiently respected in the purchase of it.[3]

The *Saturday Review*, in an article very possibly written by Lord
Robert Cecil (the future Marquis of Salisbury), had similarly said:

> The Governor has dealt with a Maori as he never would have dared
> to deal with an Englishman, and . . . has plunged us in a costly and
> perilous quarrel to uphold a paltry claim which, be it good or bad, has
> been advanced, prosecuted and carried out with very little regard for
> the most obvious principles of justice.[4]

The best-informed support of the colonists' case came from the
*Spectator*, which carried on its founder Rintoul's close interest in
New Zealand.

The critics, however, did not confine themselves to indirect
approaches to the British public. Hadfield appealed to it directly

[1] Fox to Godley (5 May 1860), Correspondence of J. R. Godley (typescript),
But cf. Stafford to Godley (28 May 1860), Kilbracken Collection, Canterbury
Museum.
[2] *The Times*, 14 Nov. 1860 ('From Our Melbourne Correspondent', 25 Sept.),
17 Nov. (Browne), 20 Nov. (Hadfield).
[3] Ibid., 14 Feb. 1861.
[4] *Saturday Review*, 3 Nov. 1860. On Lord R. Cecil's connection with the review
see Lady G. Cecil, *Life of Robert Marquis of Salisbury*, i (London, 1921), 82. Lord
Robert had visited New Zealand in 1852 and expressed similar views later in
Parliament.

in *One of England's Little Wars: A Letter to the Right Honourable the Duke of Newcastle*, a bitter attack on Governor Browne. 'The question at issue is simply this—Is a Native chief to be forcibly ejected from his land because an individual member of his tribe tells a subordinate land agent that it is his, and not the chief's, and that agent believes him?' The Governor's attack on Wiremu Kingi was not only 'a gross act of injustice' but 'an act of folly closely bordering on insanity'.[1] Professor Browne defended his brother, from the documents available to him, in *The Case of the War in New Zealand*, but was naturally handicapped by his lack of local knowledge. Fox in *The War in New Zealand*, published in Auckland but clearly intended for the British public, by implication demanded the recall of the Governor as the man responsible for 'an unjust war'. But the most weighty criticism, because less obviously biased, came from the former Chief Justice, now Sir William Martin, in a closely reasoned pamphlet avowedly 'for circulation among members of the Imperial Parliament and members of the General Assembly of New Zealand'. *The Taranaki Question* begins with the proposition: 'The present is a land quarrel'; and it was fair comment that 'the whole argument of Sir William Martin's pamphlet is based on the rules laid down by himself'. But the fact that the Government thought it needed answering by *Notes on Sir William Martin's Pamphlet entitled 'The Taranaki Question'*, published in January 1861, is a testimony to the persuasiveness of the argument. Martin traversed the ground, now becoming familiar, of 'tribal right' and asserted that in Kingi's letters there was 'a clear and unambiguous claim on behalf of his whole tribe'; he maintained that 'at the Waitara, for the first time, a new plan was adopted' of backing land purchase by force, that this necessitated a new practice of resort to a court, and that 'as there was no legal decision upon the Native rights, so there was no legal warrant for the Government to take the land'; he drew attention to the conspicuous failure of the Government to enforce the law and protect life and property in Taranaki and ended by saying that 'there was no place in New Zealand to which it was more evidently inexpedient to introduce any new elements of discord'.[2] This, of course, turned the Government's own argu-

---

[1] O. Hadfield, *One of England's Little Wars* (London and Edinburgh, 1860) pp. 5, 19–20. The pamphlet is dated Otaki, 29 May 1860.

[2] Sir W. Martin, *The Taranaki Question* (Auckland, 1860), *passim*.

ment upside down—it was precisely because of the discord that the Government had decided to make its stand in Taranaki—and Gore Browne could reasonably ask, on the court question, 'How came Sir William Martin to have been Chief Justice for so many years without having recommended such a Court?'[1] The controversy continued in New Zealand with a reply by Sir William Martin to the Government's *Notes*.[2] But the main point the critics were seeking to make had undoubtedly been made. The British public was made aware that the justice of the war was challenged in New Zealand.

Whilst this controversy was proceeding, General Pratt and his staff were developing a plan of campaign which, despite criticism from the Governor and from the Taranaki settlers, both of whom wanted a spectacular success, was perhaps the best calculated to wear down Te Atiawa and end the fighting.[3] A series of expeditions in September and October cleared Te Atiawa and Ngati Ruanui out of their pas in the open country north and south of New Plymouth. A force of about 800 from the Waikato, chiefly of Ngati Maniapoto and Ngati Haua, went down, fighting bravely, to defeat at Mahoetahi on 6 November, and its leader Wetini Taiporutu was killed. Te Atiawa held aloof from this action. At the end of the year Pratt began a systematic advance by sap against Te Atiawa's bush strongholds, consolidating his advance by redoubts as he went along. Meanwhile the Governor and various officials had been having talks with the northern chiefs about possible terms of peace. In March Wiremu Tamihana came down to Taranaki and three days' armistice was arranged, but he was hoping for a Parliamentary inquiry and the terms were unacceptable. The sap was therefore resumed. It was now within a hundred yards of Te Arei pa. Te Atiawa had had enough. On the morning of 19 March they hoisted a white flag. McLean was in charge of the negotiations at first, but a few days later the Governor arrived at headquarters, accompanied by two Ministers, Whitaker and Weld (who had replaced Richmond as Native Minister in the previous November) and the Maori chiefs Waka Nene and Tamati Ngapora. On 8 April Wiremu Kingi's fighting

[1] Note by Gore Browne in his personal copy of Sir W. Martin's *Remarks on Notes published for the New Zealand Government* (Auckland, 1861), N.Z. Archives.
[2] See previous note.
[3] The plan is ably defended by the Deputy Adjutant-General, Lieutenant-Colonel R. Carey, in his *Narrative of the late War in New Zealand* (London, 1863).

chief Hapurona signed the terms on behalf of Kingi's people. The
investigation of title and the interrupted survey at Waitara were
to be completed. The Governor was to dispose as he thought fit
of land occupied by the British forces. Te Atiawa were to restore
captured arms and plunder from the settlers. Those who had
borne arms against the Government were to 'submit to the Queen
and to the authority of the law and not to resort to force for the
redress of grievances real or imaginary'. Hapurona was to assist
in keeping the peace.[1] Wiremu Kingi 'consented' to it, but refused
to sign and retired to the Maniapoto country. The settlers, if the
*Taranaki Herald* truly interpreted their feelings, were lukewarm;[2]
but the Governor appeared to have gained his point. There were
soon complaints, however, that the terms were not observed; and
the Ngati Ruanui and Taranaki tribes had not submitted and still
occupied European land at Tataraimaka. Lieutenant-General
Cameron, who had arrived with a good reputation as a fighting
soldier to take command, wanted to carry the war into their
country. But Gore Browne thought that a settlement with the
Waikatos, who had returned home without taking part in the
negotiations, must have precedence.[3]

The Maori king, Potatau (Te Whero Whero), had died on
25 June 1860. He had dismissed a deputation from Taranaki but
could not prevent a war party from going to fight for Wiremu
Kingi, who for his part had handed over his land to the King as
a bid for his support. McLean and a number of missionaries had,
however, attended a great meeting of the King party at Ngaruawahia in May and McLean's defence of the Government's policy
had made such an impression that the anti-Government leaders
broke up the meeting without letting him complete his speech.
Gore Browne considered, but rejected, the idea of warning the
tribes that the election of a successor to the late King 'would be
viewed as an act of defiance';[4] and his colourless son Matutaera
(Methuselah) became the figurehead of a movement he was even

[1] Gore Browne to Newcastle (7 Apr. 1861, No. 47, and 12 Apr. 1861, No. 49),
P.P., 1862, xxxvii [3040], 35-9.
[2] *Taranaki Herald*, 6 and 13 Apr. 1861. On 23 Mar. the *Herald* had said of Kingi:
'He fought for a position to which he had some claim. His distinct failure in the
struggle, and the abandonment of his pretensions, may be as much as a powerful
conqueror ought to require.'
[3] Cameron to Military Secretary, Horse Guards (6 May 1861) with Enclosures
WO33/10 (Confidential Print FG41).
[4] Gore Browne to Newcastle (31 July 1860) (No. 78), CO209/154.

less able than his father to control. The Kingite chiefs were invited
to the meeting at Kohimarama in July, but few attended. Even
Wiremu Tamihana could not prevent the Ngati Haua young men
from joining the expedition of Wetini Taiporutu which ended in
disaster at Mahoetahi. Six hundred Waikatos, still in high spirits,
returned in February;[1] soon afterwards Wiremu Tamihana set
out on his peace mission, but he returned disappointed, with some
sore feelings against Sir William Martin and the missionaries who
had urged him to go.[2]

Now that a force of over 3,000 troops—two-thirds of them in
Auckland—was available, was the Governor to insist that the
Maori King acknowledge the Queen's supremacy? General
Cameron, at what he described as an Executive Council, strongly
recommended that the Waikatos be called to account and not
allowed more than a few days to make their submission.[3] But this
was too strong meat for the Governor or his Ministers to stomach.
Sir William Martin pleaded that the King question should not be
made a pretext for hostilities. The zeal of the King party, he
declared, was cooling: the weakness of the King and the jealousies
of the chiefs were daily undermining it. 'Nothing can sustain or
strengthen it but an attempt to suppress it by force.'[4] Nevertheless
the Governor went ahead with a Declaration to the Waikatos
which amounted to an ultimatum. 'An authority has been set
up', he maintained, 'inconsistent with allegiance to the Queen
and in violation of the Treaty of Waitangi.' The Waikatos had
interfered in Taranaki, levied war against the Queen, threatened
interference with the administration of justice, stopped the Royal
Mail, usurped jurisdiction over Her Majesty's European subjects.
He demanded 'submission without reserve to the Queen's
sovereignty and the authority of the law', restoration of plunder
and compensation for losses sustained by the Queen's subjects at
their hands. No other demand would be made (this implied that
renunciation of the King's title would not be insisted on) and the

[1] The Revd. J. Morgan to Gore Browne (8 Feb. 1861) (Private), Gore Browne
Papers 1/2.
[2] Morgan to Gore Browne (17 Apr. 1861) (Private), ibid.
[3] Cameron to Gore Browne (15 Apr.) in Cameron to Military Secretary,
Horse Guards (6 May 1861), WO33/10. Cameron notwithstanding, it cannot
have been a formal Executive Council for, though he took the oaths of office on
8 Apr., he did not take his seat in Council till 21 May, E.C. 1/2, N.Z. Archives.
[4] Memo. of Martin on our Relations with Waikato (3 May) in Gore Browne
to Newcastle (16 May 1861) (No. 74), P.P., 1862, xxxvii [3040], 50–1.

past would be forgiven.[1] The Executive Council approved the policy. McLean and his chief assistant, T. H. Smith, submitted a written protest; but Gore Browne, fortified by the Council's approval, adhered to his opinion[2] and Tamati Ngapora, the Maori King's 'contact man' with the Government, agreed to convey the terms to the Waikatos. But Wiremu Tamihana's reply, defending his Taranaki policy and criticizing the Governor's, showed a firm and unyielding front.[3]

Cameron still wanted to attack the Waikatos as soon as possible; but in the view of the Governor and of a Secret Committee of both Houses the force in the colony was not sufficient in view of the probability of 'a simultaneous attack . . . by their allies on some at least of the European settlements'.[4] Gore Browne thought he would need 'a moveable column of not less than three thousand rank and file' with a further force, for which militia would not suffice, to keep up communications with Auckland. He also asked for a royal proclamation to undeceive those Maoris who believed that he was not acting in accordance with the views and wishes of Her Majesty's Government.[5] From the point of view of the New Zealand Government it was a question of a pause to await reinforcements rather than of a change of policy.

The pause, however, was welcome to the Imperial authorities, who were more and more restive about the colonial assumption—supported up to a point by Gore Browne—that they should pay the cost of the war. Richmond even challenged the Governor's proposal that advances from the commissariat chest for pay, allowances, and rations to the Taranaki militia and volunteers should be recovered from the colonial Treasury. The sole direction of Native affairs and the resultant warlike operations, he urged, 'confessedly rests with His Excellency, acting under the

---

[1] Gore Browne to Newcastle (6 July 1861) (No. 97) with Enclosure: Declaration of the Governor to the Natives assembled at Ngaruawahia (21 May) (No. 74), P.P., 1862, xxxvii [3040], 69–72.

[2] Gore Browne to Maria Browne (26 May–6 June 1861): Gore Browne Papers 2/4. Minutes of Executive Council, 21, 22, 24 May 1861, E.C. 1/2.

[3] Memo. by Smith of Conversation with Tamati Ngapora (30 May) in Gore Browne to Newcastle (6 June 1861) (No. 82), P.P., 1862, xxxvii [3040], 58–60. Reply of Tamihana in Gore Browne to Newcastle (6 July 1861) (No. 97), loc. cit.

[4] Resolutions of Secret Committee of both Houses in Conference (5 July) in Gore Browne to Newcastle (6 July) (No. 97), P.P., 1862, xxxvii [3040], 76. Gore Browne to Maria Browne (22 June–5 July 1861), Gore Browne Papers 2/4.

[5] Gore Browne to Newcastle (6 July 1861) (No. 96) (Confidential), ibid., p. 69.

direction of Her Majesty's Secretary of State, the colony of New Zealand being for the purpose a Crown colony as completely as before the establishment of ministerial government'.[1] This lawyer-like argument raised the hackles of Rogers, who had been more and more coming round to the critics' view that 'the present war is notoriously the result of an act which has been pressed on the Governor by the settlers and has been adopted by him in their interest and (rightly or wrongly) against the interest of those whom it is the object of the Government to protect'. But the matter might be argued on a broader ground. 'The question is should a New Zealand war be paid for by the British taxpayer or by the Colonial taxpayer. The war in New Zealand is part of the government of New Zealand—and for whose benefit is the government of New Zealand carried on? Plainly for the benefit of those who inhabit it.' The fact that New Zealand was in part or in whole under the government of an officer of the Colonial Department was little to the purpose unless it could be said that the government was carried on with a view to British interests. 'It is true that the question is not one of dry justice. When bodies politic are so closely related to each other as England and its Colonies the stronger is under an obligation to help the weak— an obligation of generosity and wisdom as inevitable practically as one of strict justice.' England must pay 'in great measure' the expenses of the war but not the whole expense without giving the Governor much greater power than he actually had, or stood any chance of getting[2]—for very soon the Assembly's Native Council Bill, making the proposed Council advisory to the responsible Ministry and not the Governor, reached the Colonial Office. Gore Browne was instructed not to make any further advances from the commissariat chest for local forces 'except on a distinct pledge given by the Government of the Colony that all such advances will be repaid from colonial funds, so far as the Imperial Government shall require repayment'.[3]

Meanwhile the campaign against the Taranaki war was continuing in England. The Church Missionary Society presented a

[1] Gore Browne to Newcastle (29 Sept. 1860) (No. 100) and Memo. of Colonial Treasurer (3 Mar.) enclosed, P.P., 1860, xlvii [2747], 134–5.
[2] Minute of Rogers (12 Jan. 1861) on Gore Browne to Newcastle (29 Sept. 1860) (No. 100), CO209/155.
[3] Newcastle to Gore Browne (26 Jan. 1861) (No. 13), P.P., 1861, xli [2698], 70–1.

memorial to the Duke of Newcastle earnestly requesting Her Majesty's Government 'to make some authoritative declaration to the effect that the tribal rights, and the rights of the Chiefs in respect of land titles will be recognized as heretofore'; to explain to the Maoris that the 'proclamation of "Fighting Law" did not, and does not yet preclude the peaceable solution of the questions at issue'; and to adopt 'some mode of adjudication upon the particular case of the land at Waitara'.[1] Hadfield, in a letter published as a pamphlet after *The Times* had refused it, attacked Gore Browne in unmeasured terms and concluded: 'There is only one honourable course left to the Home Government. Governor Browne, who ought never to have been placed in the responsible post he has held, ought to be immediately recalled. His name is execrated throughout the land.'[2] This he followed up by a third pamphlet, if possible more offensive, in which he asserted: 'Nothing . . . can be clearer than that this war has been brought about by the offended pride of Governor Browne. . . . Of what account is a million of money, of what account are hundreds of human lives, of what account are the sufferings of thousands of ruined colonists when the dignity of a Colonial Governor is at stake?' As for McLean, he was 'under the influence of an undoubted bias and considerable pressure' and was 'an ignorant uneducated man'.[3]

Parliament did not descend to the level of this Christian clergyman; but on 11 April, on a motion to go into Committee of Supply, Sir John Trelawny, one of the critics of the Loan Bill of 1857, moved an amendment that

while this House is prepared to contribute all the aid in its power to the Executive in putting down rebellion in Her Majesty's Colony of New Zealand, yet, having regard to the Treaty of Waitangi, it would rejoice to hear that the difficult and complicated question of the title to the block of land at Waitara is to be the subject of inquiry before a special tribunal immediately on the reassertion of the Queen's authority.[4]

[1] *Memorial* [of C.M.S.] *to His Grace the Secretary of State for the Colonies together with a Memorandum on New Zealand Affairs* (London, 1861).
[2] O. Hadfield, *A Sequel to 'One of England's Little Wars'* (London and Edinburgh 1861), p. 15.
[3] O. Hadfield, *The Second Year of One of England's Little Wars* (London, 1861) pp. 16–17, 39.
[4] *Hansard*, 3rd Ser. clxii. 481.

Chichester Fortescue ably defended the Governor, taking his facts from his dispatch of 4 December and emphasizing Gore Browne's difficulties.

> Obliged to act under a constitution which appeared to have been framed in forgetfulness of the existence of large native tribes within the dominions to which it was intended to apply, he was the head of an ultra-popular government, in which the executive, where it ought to be strong, was essentially weak. He had not that command of funds enjoyed by Sir George Grey . . . for the purpose of conciliating the Natives and for promoting native objects . . . while his power was broken up and frittered away by the institution of provincial govern-ments.[1]

But the general tone of the debate remained critical. Bishop Selwyn's brother, member for Cambridge University, in a speech all the more effective for its moderation, paid tribute to Gore Browne as 'a sincere friend of the Natives': 'but he was not sufficiently firm in maintaining his own principles. . . . The Governor had fulfilled his own prophecy, his government yielded to the pressure from without.'[2] Robert Lowe made a counter-attack on the critics. Wiremu Kingi, by his 'absolute and unmiti-gated defiance', had put himself in the wrong. 'He spoke like a Sovereign to a Sovereign.' 'The meaning of the war', Lowe bluntly asserted, 'no one can misunderstand. It is a struggle for sovereignty and dominion.'[3] But, in spite of this and of depre-catory remarks by Adderley, the amendment was actually carried by 38 to 24, though in so thin a house this was not of much account. In answer to a question a week later, Chichester Fortescue said that the object of Government policy 'would be in co-operation with the local authorities to improve the administration of native affairs, and above all, to endeavour to introduce some system under which native titles to land should be subject to the decision of regular tribunals',[4] but on a later motion of Trelawny, charging the Governor with misusing Her Majesty's forces to deprive

---

[1] Ibid. 486.
[2] Ibid. 492. Selwyn's speech was reprinted 'for general information and especi-ally in support of the rights of interests of New Zealanders'—i.e. the Maoris. *Occasional Papers: printed for General Information* (Auckland, 1861), no. v.
[3] House of Commons, 12 Apr. 1861, *Hansard*, 3rd Ser. clxii. 532–7.
[4] House of Commons, 19 Apr. 1861, ibid. 829.

'several of Her subjects of certain property in land situate on the River Waitara', the House was counted out.[1]

The Colonial Office was, however, increasingly coming to doubt whether Gore Browne was quite the man for the crisis.[2] As the colonial Native Councils Bill showed, pressure was building up for the transfer of power in Native affairs to the colony. 'The only substantial check on the Colonial Government', wrote Rogers, 'would be the uncertainty what assistance they would get from England or how dearly they would have to pay for it in case of an appeal to arms.' If this objection was overruled he thought the Native Council might be accepted subject to certain safe-guards—notably that 'the Governor should retain a personal veto in all matters whether administrative or Executive' and that 'the Assembly should agree to vote a certain minimum sum for Native purposes for a period of years'.[3] But Newcastle was worried by the slow progress of military operations and the tendency of dis-affection to spread, and by the temper of the House of Commons. The courage of the Maoris had evoked admiration and unless they continued to be considerately treated, he felt that 'the recall of the Troops by a motion in the House of Commons is not a thing to be considered impossible'.[4] Gore Browne's term had nearly come to an end; and circumstances had placed at the disposal of the Government a man whose name would give him a power Gore Browne had never wielded. Early in 1861 Sir George Grey, restless and un-happy at the separation from his wife on his return to the Cape in the previous year, had volunteered to go back to New Zealand. Five days after the letter to Gore Browne just quoted, Newcastle wrote to Grey to prepare him for an acceptance of his offer —though 'it must depend on the news from that Colony before another month has passed and upon the decision of my col-leagues'.[5] On 28 May, whilst defending Gore Browne's policy

[1] House of Commons, 11 June 1861, Hansard, 3rd Ser. clxiii. 952–3. Trelawny was apt to empty the House: see 'Sir John Trelawny as Cassandra', Spectator, 27 Aug. 1864.

[2] As early as Aug. 1860 Chichester Fortescue had asked Grahame if Browne was quite the man for the emergency: Grahame to McLean (23 Aug. 1860), McLean Papers.

[3] Minute of Rogers (21 Mar. 1861) on Gore Browne to Newcastle (26 Nov. 1860) (No. 120), CO209/156.

[4] Newcastle to Gore Browne (26 Apr. 1861) (Private), Gore Browne Papers 1/1. This was before news of the cessation of hostilities had reached England.

[5] Newcastle to Grey (1 May 1861) (Private), Newcastle Papers, NeC10885. Or

against Earl Grey, whose criticisms indeed had been directed not so much against the Governor as against the grant of responsible government to a minority of European colonists, the Duke announced in the House of Lords that by the previous days mail he had instructed Sir George Grey to proceed to New Zealand as Gore Browne's successor.[1] He was to be the *deus ex machina* to resolve the problems which had been too great for a high-minded but at times impulsive Governor who had never fully grasped their complexity.

Grey's separation from his wife, see J. Rutherford, *Sir George Grey*, pp. 427–8.
[1] *Hansard*, 3rd Ser. clxiii. 177–8 (for the debate, 152–79).

# IX

## SIR GEORGE GREY AND THE
## WAIKATO WAR

SIR GEORGE GREY had volunteered to go to New Zealand 'in
any capacity—even under Colonel Gore Browne'[1]—but a Government which turned to him, before the cessation of fighting in
Taranaki was known, in justifiable anxiety about a possible
extension of the war, was bound to allow him wide discretionary
powers. The Imperial authorities considered delegating to him,
with or without an advisory council, wide law-making powers
within Maori districts to be constituted under section 71 of the
Constitution Act. But the Law Officers advised that this would require an Act of Parliament and the idea was dropped.[2] Newcastle
told the House of Lords, however, that he had given Grey
wider discretion than he would give any other Governor.[3] If the
Taranaki war had died down, the question of peace or war with
the Maori King still remained open. Newcastle in a dispatch to
Grey expressed his apprehension at the prevalent feeling that
'the King question must be settled once for all'. He deprecated the
use of armed force 'for the mere purpose of exacting from the
Maoris a verbal renunciation of the so-called King'. But perhaps
the same object might be attained by making use of the chiefs in
the government of their own districts in concert with the Queen's
officers. At the same time he pointed out that the distinction the
Maori leaders were inclined to draw between the authority of the
Queen and that of the Governor was inadmissible.[4]

[1] Shipley to Gore Browne (14 Feb. 1861), Gore Browne Papers 1/3.
[2] Law Officers to Newcastle (25 June 1861), CO209/166. Rogers commented
(10 July): 'This opinion is directly contrary to the opinions which I had understood to have been expressed by Sir R. Bethell [Attorney-General] when the subject was under the consideration of the Cabinet.'
[3] House of Lords, 26 July 1861, *Hansard*, 3rd Ser. clxiv. 1577.
[4] Newcastle to Grey (22 Sept. 1861) (No. 91), P.P., 1862, xxxvii [3040],
95–6. The phrasing was largely taken from a Minute of Rogers (?22 Aug.) on
Gore Browne to Newcastle (16 May 1861) (No. 74). Newcastle agreed that it
did not matter 'if they merely honour their King whether his name be Potato
or Brian Boru and commit no breach of the Queen's peace', CO209/162.

A new approach to the problem of the Maori King was also favoured by a change of Ministry in New Zealand. On 5 July, after three days' debate in the House of Representatives, the Stafford Ministry was defeated, by one vote, on a motion of no confidence and Fox and the 'peace party' were installed in office. In his policy statement Fox proposed negotiations with the Maori King, a suspension of land purchase and winding up of the Land Purchase Department, and the creation of a tribunal to investigate Maori land titles.[1] McLean's resignation of the Native Secretaryship cleared the way for a reorganization of his department and on 6 September, on the motion of Dillon Bell, the House resolved

that no such reorganization will be effectual or satisfactory to the country which does not, while fully recognizing and securing to the Governor both the initiative and the decision where imperial interests are concerned, place the conduct of the ordinary business of native administration under responsibility to the Assembly.[2]

When Grey arrived and took over the government at the beginning of October, Fox at once presented him with a memorandum referring to this resolution and stating that Ministers 'regard the existence of the Native Secretary's department, free as it is from all control on the part of the responsible ministry, as a very serious evil'.[3] In his first governorship Grey had been attacked, and by none more bitterly than Fox, as an autocrat. Now he seemed to have turned over a new leaf. In his characteristic off-hand way he informed the Duke of Newcastle at the end of November:

At the present crisis it is quite impossible that Her Majesty's Government could be advantageously carried on under such a system. I therefore immediately arranged to consult my Responsible Ministers in relation to Native Affairs, in the same manner as upon all other subjects, and in like manner to act through them in relation to all Native matters.

[1] House of Representatives, 16 July 1861, N.Z.P.D., 1861–3, pp. 172–5. Newcastle had warned Grey in a private letter of 5 June that 'you may find your old opponent, Mr. Fox, installed in power and have to inherit him as your Prime Minister', Newcastle Papers, NeC10885.

[2] J.H.R., 1861, pp. 203–6. This motion was apparently inspired by a fear that Grey might set up a dictatorship. It had at first been proposed that McLean should relinquish the office of Land Purchase Commissioner but it seemed that the Native Secretaryship might become a political office, so he preferred the alternative: M.A. 1/2:61/58, N.Z. Archives.

[3] Memo. of Fox on Machinery of Government for Native Purposes (8 Oct.) in Grey to Newcastle (9 Oct. 1861) (No. 3), P.P., 1862, xxxvii [3049], 2–3.

... Your Grace will, I have no doubt, inform me if you wish me to discontinue this arrangement, but I think it would be well to leave it permanently in operation until difficulties arise under it, which I do not see any probability of.

He believed that the Assembly by its proceedings towards the Native race had shown it was worthy of confidence.

Any attempt to set up either the Governor or any special body between the natives and the General Assembly, as a protective power for the natives against the presumed hostility of that body will, I fear, produce an ill effect upon the native mind, as making them regard the Assembly as their admitted natural enemies; whilst it will, perhaps, create in the minds of the General Assembly some prejudice against the natives.[1]

The shot was, of course, aimed at the projected Native Council, which now dropped out of sight. Grey knew he must keep on good terms with the General Assembly; he believed that his prestige and knowledge of the Maori would ensure that the policy was really his and that his skill as a dispatch-writer would carry the Imperial Government along with him.

He treated his predecessor with his usual personal courtesy but his dispatches dwelt on the great cost and small result of the Taranaki war and the inevitably greater cost of a war in the Waikato such as Gore Browne had contemplated: the colony could not possibly meet its liabilities under such a policy. Did the Imperial Government realize the state of the Waikato? 'Throughout the whole of that district during the continuance of hostilities and since their cessation, no outrage of any kind has been committed, and travellers, Government officers and others move with as much safety as the Queen's subjects can in any others part of Her Majesty's dominions.' A European could reside quietly in the midst of it, lease a piece of land despite the law, warn trespassers, and collect fines from them.[2] What was really needed was not negotiation with the Maori King, who had no power to bind others, but the establishment throughout the Maori districts of

---

[1] Grey to Newcastle (30 Nov. 1861) (No. 36), P.P. 1862, xxxvii [3049], 27–8.
[2] Grey to Newcastle (2 Nov. 1861) (No. 14), P.P., 1862, xxxvii [3049], 14–15. The man in question, James Armitage, was killed by the Maoris at the beginning of the Waikato war.

civil commissioners, each with a clerk, interpreter, district surgeon, Native magistrate or assessor, police, schoolmasters, clergymen, and a district *Runanga* as provided by the Native Districts
Regulation Act 1858. These would not only have power to make
by-laws but also to inspect and report on schools, erect and maintain gaols and hospitals, construct and maintain roads, adjust
disputed boundaries and recommended Crown grants to tribes,
*hapus*, and individuals. Money would be raised by court fees and
fines and by local taxation imposed by the *runangas*. There was
nothing particularly new in this scheme, in which Ministers
expressed their 'general and very cordial concurrence'. They
hoped that 'as Europeans find their way into the interior they will
gradually participate in working the system of government under
which they will be living'. They rightly attached importance to
beginning at the bottom and not at the top, and thought that
'even an instalment of what is proposed by His Excellency, if
successfully established, will suffice to reconcile Maoris to live
under one common government with the colonists'.[1] In this
atmosphere of mutual congratulation and optimism the Governor
hardly needed to explain that he did not mean to insist on Gore
Browne's terms to the Waikatos. He also told the Secretary of
State that he did not propose to repeat the experiment of the
Kohimarama Conference: the summons of such a 'Maori Parliament' was 'a proceeding very likely to keep alive and perpetuate the distinction now so unhappily prevailing between the
two races'.[2] The phrase shows that there were considerations of
*Realpolitik* in Grey's mind and not merely high-principled idealism; and Newcastle's minute shows they were in his mind too.
'I fear that the tyrant maxim *divide et impera* may be (humanely
used) more safely applied to the Maoris than our own more
civilized and constitutional notions of combination of wisdom
and power.'[3]

Especially characteristic of Grey was his suggested method of
financing this policy. The success of his first governorship had
been in no small measure due to the military and financial support

[1] Grey to Newcastle (2 Nov. 1861) (No. 15) and Memo. of Ministers on Sir G
Grey's plan (31 Oct.), ibid., pp. 15–21.
[2] Grey to Newcastle (30 Nov. 1861) (No. 35), ibid., pp. 25–7.
[3] Minute of Newcastle (26 Feb. 1862) on Grey to Newcastle (30 Nov. 1861)
(No. 35), CO209/165.

he had received from home, most notably from Earl Grey as
Secretary of State; as Governor of the Cape he had managed to
secure a parliamentary grant in aid of the government of Kaffraria;
now he announced that he had made 'an arrangement with the
New Zealand ministers' by which half the cost would be paid
from colonial funds—subject, Ministers noted, to the approval of
the General Assembly:

> I, upon behalf of the Imperial Government, undertook that the
> remaining half should be paid out of the sum of £35,000 which the
> Colony is required to provide in reduction of the expenditure incurred
> by Great Britain in maintaining troops in this Colony. The total sum
> which will in any one year be deducted . . . in pursuance of this
> arrangement will probably not exceed £25,000.

Within about seven years he expected the plan to 'defray its own
cost and yield some surplus' and 'at least in great part' do away
with an annual expenditure of £629,000, half a million of which
was military expenditure from Imperial funds. For some years yet
it would be necessary to maintain a large military force in the
country to show the Maoris that the peace policy did not arise
from weakness, but even in this short period the total annual
expenditure would 'not nearly equal the mere annual interest of
the capital which would be sunk without producing any annual
return whatever in the first year of a general war'. He also suggested that the troops might be employed, with the Maoris, in
road-making and some of the officers in civil posts under the new
system of administration.[1]

Newcastle had entrusted Grey with wide discretionary powers
and he had used these to abandon the main point in the Imperial
position—the continuing responsibility of the Crown, acting
through the Secretary of State and his instrument the Governor,
for the management of the Maoris. It was the most important
question relating to New Zealand that the Colonial Office had had
before it since the Assembly had demanded responsible government in 1854. Rogers, with the delicacy of a civil servant always
conscious that he was only an adviser, was restrained in his

---

[1] Grey to Newcastle (6 Dec. 1861) (No. 38) with Memos. by Grey (29 Nov.)
and by Ministers (5 Dec.), P.P., 1862, xxxvii [3049], 28–31. I cannot accept the
suggestion of Mr. Harold Miller in *Race Conflict in New Zealand* (Auckland, 1966),
p. 85 that the military officers were chosen for military purposes.

comments on this crucial point. It was the Parliamentary Under-Secretary, Chichester Fortescue, who was most outspoken.

> I believe the amount of Imperial control retained by the former arrangement was more nominal than real, and while it did not prevent the Governor from really acting under the influence of his Ministers it gave the Colonists good (apparent) grounds for calling the Native policy Imperial and the war growing out of it an Imperial war.

He believed that a strong Governor like Grey would have as much power under this system as the other and would be more likely to obtain funds. In short (and here Rogers agreed with him) the transfer of the Native Department to Ministerial control could not usefully be opposed.[1] Newcastle was of the same opinion and added some interesting comment.

> My bill two years ago attempted to place in the hands of the Governor some real and independent power. When that failed and when any attempt to induce the Colonial Legislature last year to do the same thing was given up it became evident that 'Native Affairs' must be under the same control as the rest of the Colonial system. It is useless to consider now which of the two plans is most just and most theoretically right—it is manifest that one way only is now practical and Sir G. Grey well knows that his enquiry whether I 'wish him to discontinue this arrangement' can only be answered in one way.

But the financial side of the arrangement left a nasty taste in his mouth.

> The financial part of Sir G. Grey's plan . . . is ingeniously contrived so as to throw the whole burden upon the Mother Country—for whilst we are to give up to the Colony £25,000 now payable for Soldiers they are to pay only the same sum they now pay (as I understand it) for Native purposes—and moreover our Soldiers and Officers are to do civil work as well as fight for them. I think we shall have to forgo the £25,000 for a few years to be applied to Native purposes, but it must be on strict conditions. . . . The whole Colony ought for a time to forgo measures of otherwise very proper improvements and extension for the double purpose of in part paying for the war which has ended and preventing that which may so easily be brought on.[2]

[1] Minute of Chichester Fortescue (21 Feb. 1862) on Grey to Newcastle (30 Nov. 1861) (No. 38), CO209/165.
[2] Minute of Newcastle (7 Mar. 1862), ibid.

There was also the question raised by Rogers, 'Can you get Parliament to vote money for such purposes?'[1]

It seems to me out of the question [Fortescue answered] to ask Parliament for a Vote, like the British Kaffraria Vote, for Native purposes —but that Parliament might consent to continue to provide the whole cost of Troops for say three years more, on condition of the Colony devoting to the cost of Native Government and improvement a sum fully equal to their present contribution towards the troops.[2]

Newcastle felt it necessary to ask for more details before putting the proposition to the Treasury. As he wrote,

While you . . . inform me of the concessions which you hope from Her Majesty's Government, you do not tell me by what sacrifices the colonists are prepared to meet these concessions. I do not understand, for example, to what extent they are willing either to impose on themselves additional taxation or to [re]appropriate existing taxes. . . . Nor do you indicate the amount of personal effort which the colonists are prepared to make in their own defence.[3]

Repayment of advances from the commissariat chest for militia and volunteers was a particularly sore point. Newcastle noted in March that 'considering the attention which the question of Colonial Expenditure in general and the expense of War in New Zealand in particular is just now attracting . . . any despatch to Sir G. G. definitively laying down what portion of the cost shall be borne by the Colony must be seen by the Cabinet before it is sent'.[4] The Treasury resisted for two months the proposal for 'the appropriation of the Colonial Military Contribution to Native Purposes instead of the Imperial Exchequer' before it finally relented.[5]

The consequence of this Treasury reluctance was that the dispatch on 26 May 1862 conceding the point at issue was written in a sharp 'snubbing style' bound to give offence both to the

[1] Minute of Rogers (20 Feb. 1862), (No. 38), CO 209/165. On Rogers's view that political considerations were 'above my level' see a Minute of 24 Jan. on Grey to Newcastle (2 Nov. 1861) (No. 16), CO209/164.

[2] Minute of Chichester Fortescue (21 Feb. 1862), loc. cit.

[3] Newcastle to Grey (26 Feb. 1862) (No. 14), P.P., 1862, xxxvii [3049], 73.

[4] Minute of Newcastle (20 Mar.) on Lugard (War Office) to Rogers (20 Feb. 1862), CO209/171. The reference is to the House of Commons Resolution of 4 Mar. 1862 (see above, pp. 8–9 and a Commons discussion initiated by Adderley on 13 Mar.; *Hansard*, 3rd Ser. clxv. 1441–9.

[5] Newcastle to Grey (26 May 1862) (Private), Grey Coll., Auckland.

Governor and to colonial opinion. The Duke feared that the colonial Government had 'no adequate apprehension . . . of the obligation under which the colonists themselves lie to exert themselves in their own defence'. It involved sacrifices, 'but this is exactly what the British Government has a right to expect from them'.

I am ready [the Duke continued] to sanction the important step you have taken in placing the management of the natives under the control of the Assembly. I do so partly in reliance on your own capacity to perceive, and your desire to do, what is best for those in whose welfare I know you are so much interested. But I do it also because I cannot disguise from myself that the endeavour to keep the management of the Natives under the control of the Home Government has failed. It can only be mischievous to retain a shadow of responsibility when the beneficial exercise of power has become impossible.

He held out no hopes that a large military force would be kept in New Zealand for any length of time: the Governor must expect a 'speedy and considerable reduction'. He doubted whether military officers could be seconded to serve as civil commissioners: if any were, their whole pay must be defrayed by the colony. Great Britain would bear no part of the expense of the militia and volunteers. The military contribution of £5 per man must be paid to the end of 1861; but for the years 1862–4 all sums in excess of the present £26,000 spent on Native purposes could be reckoned as military contribution.[1] In a private letter the Duke warned Grey that he would be 'utterly unable to obtain any further assistance from Imperial funds to other purposes than the expenses of the troops now in New Zealand and . . . you should know that both the Treasury and the House of Commons are growing very impatient of *that* expense'. It amounted to about a penny on the income tax and that 'at a time of great distress among the labouring classes'.[2] Goldwin Smith took this dispatch as the text of one of his famous letters to the *Daily News*.

If these carping comments were intended to shame the General Assembly into doing more, they missed their aim. In their

[1] Newcastle to Grey (26 May 1862) (No. 53), P.P., 1862, xxxvii [3049], 80–1. The phrase 'snubbing style' is from M. Richmond to Gore Browne (11 Aug. 1862), Gore Browne Papers 1/2.

[2] Newcastle to Grey (26 May 1862) (Private), loc. cit. The income tax in the United Kingdom at this time was 9*d*. in the pound.

arrangements of October Grey had taken Dillon Bell's motion as
their starting point, but the Assembly had hardly reckoned with
the financial implications. The dispatch of 26 May had not
arrived when the Assembly met in Wellington on 14 July, but the
short dispatch asking for more details and an accompanying
private letter from Chichester Fortescue (the Duke being ill) had
given the Governor and his Ministers a foretaste of its contents.[1]
The comments of Alfred Saunders, then a Foxite member of the
House, in his *History* a generation later, are interesting.

> The Government and the Opposition knew very well that the only
> dignified, the only right, the only respectable course was now to quietly
> accept what they had asked for, without attempting to formulate any
> resolution on the subject; but the Opposition, for mere party purposes,
> ... succeeded in getting Mr. Fox, in opposition to his own judgement,
> to bring in a resolution that it would be impolitic to carry and incon-
> sistent to oppose.[2]

This wordy resolution, while disclaiming 'exclusive responsibility for the cost of educating, civilizing and governing the
Native race' or 'liability for the principal share of the cost of
suppressing insurrections', approved the 'ordinary conduct of
Native affairs' by responsible Ministers. In moving it Fox deprecated any attempt to 'define too closely what was to be the Imperial administration and what the ministerial' and reiterated his
earlier criticism of the arrangements of 1856.[3] Featherston made
much the best speech on the Government side. He pointed out
that everything depended on the good sense, tact, and discretion
of the two parties concerned, the Governor, and his Ministers;
but he trusted that, as the Governor was asking the House 'to
share his grave responsibilities', the appeal would not be made in
vain. But the tortuous phrases of the resolution gave many openings for attack. FitzGerald criticized it as an evasion: 'they should
recognize the charge of the Native race as a peculiar trust left to
the colonists to manage to the best of their ability' and then ask
the Home Government for assistance in fulfilling their duty.
T. B. Gillies of Otago, on the other hand, criticized the Imperial
Government for handing over sovereignty of the Maoris before

[1] Chichester Fortescue to Grey (26 Feb. 1862) (Private), Grey Coll., Auckland
[2] A. Saunders, *History of New Zealand, 1642–1893*, ii (Christchurch, 1899), 34.
[3] House of Representatives, 25 July 1862, *N.Z.P.D.*, 1861–3, pp. 436–7.

it 'had fulfilled the terms of its treaty with them, civilized them, made them British subjects'. Stafford emphasized Sir George Grey's responsibilities, given the circumstances of his appointment. Domett thought 'we should start from the fact that both England and the colony are merely component parts of one Empire' and could not sympathize with any attempt to demand such a power with respect to Native affairs, in which peace and war were involved. Having given no clear lead, the Government could hardly complain if the debate ended inconclusively. On 28 July an Opposition member moved the previous question, and the vote resulted in a tie.[1] The Speaker (Dr. Monro) having voted with the noes, Fox resigned.

The Governor now had to look for a Ministry and the House for a policy. Stafford declined office, alleging that he and his friends had been held up as enemies of the Maoris and could not hope to govern with advantage to the Colony. FitzGerald, whose absence in England had withdrawn him to some extent from party politics, was next sent for but declined likewise. Grey then appealed to Domett, an official of his in Crown Colony days, and persuaded him to form a Ministry. Dillon Bell became Native Minister and for a time Treasurer; but within a fortnight the Ministry was reinforced, not with Fox's consent, by his Treasurer, Reader Wood, and two of his colleagues, Sewell and Crosbie Ward of the *Lyttelton Times*. The strong man in the Ministry, however, turned out to be Thomas Russell, Whitaker's law partner in Auckland and the principal founder of the Bank of New Zealand. While the Ministry was being formed the House filled the vacuum by debating some resolutions on Native policy moved in an eloquent speech by New Zealand's most ardent theorist on the subject, FitzGerald:

1. That in the adoption of any policy or the passing of any laws affecting the Native race, this House will keep before it, as its highest object, the entire amalgamation of all Her Majesty's subjects in New Zealand into one united people.

2. That this House will assent to no laws which do not recognize the right of all Her Majesty's subjects, of whatever race, within this colony to a full and equal enjoyment of civil and political privileges.

Both these were agreed to without a division; but when, in a third

[1] *J.H.R.*, 1862, pp. 32–7; *N.Z.P.D.*, 1861–3, pp. 436–76.

resolution, FitzGerald drew the practical consequences by asking the House to approve the appointment of Maori chiefs to the Legislative Council and 'a fair representation in this House of a race which constitutes one-third of the population of the colony', realism dictated a different course and the resolution was defeated by 20 to 17, many members abstaining.[1]

Domett now took up the invidious task of framing resolutions which, in face of Newcastle's dispatch of 26 May, would empower Ministers to advise the Governor on Native affairs whenever either party thought it advisable without accepting any responsibility or binding the colony to any liability 'beyond the amount authorized or to be authorized by the House of Representatives'.[2] His resolutions were carried on 19 August by 27 to 18, though members doubted whether they would have any influence with the Home Government and Grey in forwarding them said he was 'satisfied [that] whatever may be in theory the nature of the relations existing between myself and my responsible advisers, the practical result will be the same'.[3] In fact as long as Sir George Grey was Governor all this discussion of abstract principles was beside the point.

It was not beside the point, however, to join issue with the Duke of Newcastle, whose dispatch of 26 May had now arrived, and this the House proceeded to do in a long Address to the Queen moved by Domett on 13 September. The fundamental point was that 'the proposal of His Excellency was made without obtaining the assent of the General Assembly to accept the responsibility thereby imposed upon it'. The allegiance of the Maoris had never been more than nominal; and the transfer was proposed at a time when a large section of them were endeavouring to set up a separate nationality and 'when its duties must entail upon the colony expenses which it is not in a condition to bear and dangers it cannot successfully contend against without the aid of a considerable military force'. On military problems the Address made some telling points. It was not true that the colony was making

---

[1] N.Z.P.D., 1861–3, pp. 483–513.

[2] J.H.R., 1862, pp. 49–50, 79–81. See also Ministerial Minute (6 Aug. 1862) P.M. 1/2, N.Z. Archives.

[3] Grey to Newcastle (26 Aug. 1862) (No. 89), P.P., 1863, xxxviii (H.C. 177), In a private letter of 13 Aug. he had made the same point more explicitly: 'The new ministry take up the policy of the old one, which is my own', Newcastl Papers, NeC11090.

no sacrifices. War taxation amounted to £500,000 sterling, over £5 per head of the European population, and in Taranaki nearly the whole male population over sixteen had been on active service for two and a half years. Any attempt to exact compulsory service from settlers outside their own locality would simply depopulate the North Island for the benefit of the goldfields of Australia and Otago. Besides, the military ardour of the community was damped down by a system which placed local forces 'in a position of marked inferiority to the regular army, not only in the performance of military duties but also in the distribution of honours and rewards'. The colony had seen 'wars . . . needlessly prolonged, lives lost and treasure squandered' by incompetent commanders whom it had no power to remove. 'Any proposal to get rid of the divided responsibility hitherto existing in the colony and to unite the government under a single administration, is a proposal in name rather than in fact, unless the control of the military force be entrusted to Your Majesty's representative in the colony.' The Address ended with a plea that 'the youngest of Your Majesty's colonies may not be left to struggle unaided amid political and financial difficulties too great for its strength, but that Your Majesty may be pleased to deal with it as an integral part of the Empire to which we are proud to belong and one where peculiar troubles and dangers demand peculiarly liberal consideration'.[1]

The militia question was a sore point not only between the two Governments but between General Cameron and the colonial authorities. When an invasion of the Waikato had seemed imminent in June 1861, the General had drawn attention to the desirability of having militia available for such services as 'guarding depots of supply, escorting convoys, furnishing drivers to the transport service, and occupying the different posts which must be established along the line of march' and pointed out that the Militia Act limited their radius of service to fifteen miles from their homes. 'At this critical juncture, when every settlement in this island is threatened with attack', they had not even been called out except at Taranaki.[2] Gore Browne had backed his Ministers,

[1] Grey to Newcastle (6 Oct. 1862) (No. 98), Enclosure, ibid., pp. 4–6. *J.H.R.*, 1862, pp. 187–9. Grey had also written a complaining letter to Newcastle on the dispatch, but it does not appear to be in the Newcastle Papers: its purport may be gathered from Newcastle's reply of 26 Feb. 1863, Newcastle Papers, NeC10887.
[2] Cameron to Gore Browne (14 June and 1 July 1861) in Gore Browne to Newcastle (5 July 1861) (No. 95), P.P., 1862, xxxvii [3040], 67.

who pointed out that it was very expensive to call the militia out
for service. 'It must prevent their producing the revenue which
enables the colony to defray its share of the expenses of the war;
and if they are taken from their occupations, they must themselves
become dependent on resources which would fail for want of
their support.'[1] At the same time he had reminded the Assembly
that the Imperial Government expected full and cordial co-operation both in men and money—though he was prepared to sanction
advances from the commissariat chest of the money 'required
for organizing and maintaining the colonial forces in an effective
state'.[2]

Newcastle was 'by no means satisfied with these proposals'. In
his opinion the Imperial Government had done enough by sending
out 6,000 men: 'the colony can and ought to do the rest'.[3] The
Select Committee on Colonial Military Expenditure had recommended that assistance should still be given to the New Zealand
settlers but that 'their principal reliance ought to be on their own
resources';[4] and a leading article in *The Times* showed that public
opinion was moving in that direction. 'Let us signalize the return
of peace', it said, 'by the withdrawal of our troops from a position
in which they never ought to have been placed.'[5] The Fox
Ministry, by offering more liberal inducements, increased the
number enrolling and attending parades but questioned whether
colonial militia could ever 'satisfy the expectations of military
officers who have been accustomed to older and less sparsely-
peopled communities'. Grey for his part thought it doubtful
policy 'to enrol a militia force of European settlers for the purpose
of putting down the Native population'. He preferred a permanent armed police, composed of both Europeans and Maoris,
which was authorized by an Act of this session.[6] A forthright
speech of Atkinson's revealed some of the tensions that underlay

[1] Gore Browne to Newcastle (5 July 1861) (No. 95) and Memo. of Stafford
(2 July), P.P., 1862, xxxvii [3040], 66, 68.
[2] Message No. 2 (25 June) in Gore Browne to Newcastle (4 July 1861) (No. 92),
ibid., p. 65.
[3] Newcastle to Grey (22 Sept. 1861) (No. 89), ibid., p. 94.
[4] P.P., 1861, xiii (H.C. 423), vi. On this Committee see above, pp. 6–8.
[5] *The Times*, 30 Aug. 1861.
[6] Grey to Newcastle (24 July 1861) (No. 81) enclosing Memo. of Fox (12 July)
P.P., 1863, xxxviii (H.C. 467), 25–6. The Colonial Defence Force Act was No. 3?
of 1862, but it was not brought into operation until 5 May 1863—the day after th
Oakura ambush.

these discussions. The chief duty of a local militia, as he understood it, was to defend the lives and property of Her Majesty's subjects in their district. 'Not only were we, the Taranaki Militia, not allowed to defend our property, but . . . our property was wantonly destroyed by order of the military authorities.' One commander forbade them to export their stock; his successor upbraided them for not disposing of it, thus providing unlimited food supplies for the Maoris. Their fences were used to build a palisade round the town. A militia's first duty was obedience. They were 'required to reduce this maxim to practice by standing quietly by and seeing . . . their houses burnt, their stock driven away or slaughtered before their faces'.[1]

The Colonial Office paid scant heed to these complaints or to the fears of an exodus to escape militia service. The frankest expression of opinion was in a minute of Rogers. The colonial argument, as he saw it, was that, if the North Island was not to be depopulated, it must be defended by Imperial troops.

I should like to make them believe, if possible, that this is a mere provisional state of things and that

1. if they fail to place their own relations with the Natives and their own armed police force on such a footing as to maintain order and peace with a trifling amount of assistance from the Home Government they must be allowed to take the consequences of their failure, even if those consequences should be the depopulation of their Country. It is the same to the Imperial Government whether British immigrants prosper and consume British manufactures at Auckland or at Canterbury or Melbourne.

2. . . . . Imperial assistance can only be given at all on the condition that their dealings with the natives are just and Christian with a view to elevate not to subjugate or extinguish them.

These views, without the implied suspicion of colonial intentions, were embodied in a dispatch approving the proposed armed police.[2]

Meanwhile an uneasy peace continued. Grey visited the far north and the lower Waikato but had to admit that the Maoris had lost confidence in the Government and laughed at his promises: 'I am often quite at my wits end what to do with them and

[1] House of Representatives, 20 Aug. 1862, *N.Z.P.D.*, 1861–3, pp. 579–80.
[2] Minute of Rogers (15 Nov.) on Grey to Newcastle (24 July 1862) (No. 81), CO209/169. The dispatch was No. 106 of 21 Nov.

find this the most difficult duty I ever had in my life.'[1] His officers had some success in introducing the new institutions in the north and in Rotorua, the Bay of Plenty, Taupo, the east coast, and Manawatu; but the King tribes held stubbornly aloof and had a following in other tribes. They had their own *runangas* and were not prepared to give up their King, their flag, and all pretensions to independence. As a Maniapoto chief said to Gorst, Grey's emissary to the upper Waikato, 'we [the magistrates] were worms, baits that Sir George Grey was fishing with, and if we were suffered to remain, some of the tribes in Waikato would inevitably be caught.'[2] Gorst had the title of Resident Magistrate, but in these circumstances his chief value was as an intelligent observer. A report of his in June 1862 is the best account we have of the Waikato under the Maori King. Matutaera himself was a nullity and 'though now carefully secluded from the profane eye, might have been seen, not many months ago, smoking his pipe and digging kumaras like a common man'. His business was done by a *runanga* at Ngaruawahia, chiefly composed of relatives of his: 'Rewi, Thompson, Reihana, or any great men from the provinces on a visit to Ngaruawahia would sit with the regular members and take part in the deliberations.' Gorst admired their calm wisdom, good temper, and attention to business; but 'their wise resolutions are not often carried into practical effect. . . . Any conflict between the local and central authorities is at once settled by the latter quietly giving way.' There was no 'limit to the province of government; their regulations extend to the minutest details of private life. . . . The term "law" is applied equally to a piece of tattered paper pinned to a post, warning travellers not to cross a maize plantation, and to one of the Ten Commandments.' Only among Thompson's Ngati Haua was there an attempt to make a code of laws. Among Rewi's Maniapoto the young men were supreme, 'demoralized by the possession of Taranaki plunder, and . . . violently hostile to the Europeans and to the Government'. Several young men, armed and dressed in uniform, were drilling in companies and called themselves the King's soldiers. Economically the Waikato was in evident decline. Many European traders had left or ceased to trade.

[1] Grey to Newcastle (9 Jan. 1862), Newcastle Papers, NeC11085.
[2] Gorst to Fox (5 Feb.) in Grey to Newcastle (8 Feb. 1862) (No. 15), P.P., 1862, xxxvii [3049], 52.

The Natives in this neighbourhood, once the greatest wheat-growing district in the Waikato, are now planting scarcely any wheat; they have sold nearly all their horses and cattle, and most of their pigs; their houses have fallen into ruin; their clothes are ragged; their mills, ploughs and threshing machines are left to go to decay, while the owners are travelling about to *huis* and *tangis*, or spending their days sitting watching a boundary line that they may pounce upon stray cattle. . . . The education of the children is now totally neglected; they are left to run about the village with the dogs and pigs. . . . Not only has the number of children in the Mission schools decreased by more than half, but almost all those village schools which gave such promise a short time ago have come to nothing.

The King's Government, naturally, was hopelessly short of money. The chief sources of revenue were ferries, fees and fines, and voluntary donations. Attempts to tax wheat and potatoes sent down the river and ships entering Kawhia had been abandoned. 'The Maori King', Gorst concluded, 'is kept up by a feeling of distrust and opposition to the English Government; but it is the existence of this distrust, not its manifestation in the form of the Maori King, that is dangerous.'[1]

Sir George Grey and the colonial Government were faced with a dilemma. The only hope of improving relations and better government lay through increased intercourse between Maori and European. Roads were the primary means of communication, in Sewell's view 'the true solution of our native difficulties'; but could roads be made through lands over which the Native title had not been extinguished, without the tribe's consent? Sewell said yes, in virtue of the Crown's right of 'eminent domain', with compensation if necessary; the Imperial Government said no, it would be 'alike contrary to the principles of English and Native law' and 'Her Majesty's troops ought not to be employed in a war so originating'—thus, so Sewell complained, 'in fact shutting up the country in permanence'.[2] But one road stood on a different footing. So long as the country between Auckland and the Waikato river was covered by the dense Hunua Forest, the colonial capital

---

[1] General Report on the State of Upper Waikato (5 June) in Grey to Newcastle (10 June 1862) (No. 59), P.P., 1863, xxxviii (H.C. 467), 6–16. This Report, with some revision, is the basis of ch. xii in Gorst's book, *The Maori King* (London and Cambridge, 1864).

[2] Opinion of Sewell (22 Nov.) in Grey to Newcastle (18 Dec. 1862) (No. 130), P.P., 1863, xxxviii (H.C. 467), 99–100; Newcastle to Grey (22 Mar. 1863) (No. 20), ibid., p. 145. Journal of Sewell, 31 May and 7 June 1863.

lay open to surprise attack by the Waikato tribes. There had been alarms during the Taranaki war. Grey determined to employ the Imperial troops on making a 14-foot metalled road through the bush, clearing it for 30 yards on either side. Officers and men hated the job;[1] but it was done. The road could be justified as a precautionary measure, lessening Auckland's liability to attack by making a counterblow possible. But it inevitably sharpened Maori suspicion of Grey's intentions.

The most important legislative measure of 1862 was a Native Lands Act recognizing title by Native custom. As the judges of the Supreme Court, in a memorandum for Gore Browne, had expressed the view that the constitution and procedure of the Court were not well adapted for investigating and determining such titles,[2] the new Act set up a Native Land Court to ascertain Native title upon application of any tribe, community, or individuals and issue certificates to proprietors. This achieved the main objective of critics of the Waitara purchase, though it also was seen in course of time to be a move away from the long-term objective of most philo-Maoris, the issue of Crown grants to individual Maoris. There was doubt in some quarters of the competence of the General Assembly to pass a Bill on the subject of Native lands, especially when the Domett Ministry, in the person of Dillon Bell, proposed, as the Fox Ministry had not, to allow the persons named in any certificate to dispose of their lands by sale, lease, or exchange to any person or persons whatsoever. This clause swept away the pre-emptive right of the Crown, reserved by section 73 of the Constitution Act and ultimately traceable to the Treaty of Waitangi. Sewell thought the prime mover was Thomas Russell, 'a shrewd strong-willed man with distinct aims of personal and individual advantage to be got out of this bill'.[3] The Bill was reserved, but the Imperial Government had shifted its ground since its objections to the Native Territorial Rights Bill of 1858. Rogers in a long minute on the new Bill pointed out that 'the Home Government has steadily resisted until lately the permission of direct purchase'; but Sir George

---

[1] *Memoirs of General Sir George Richards Greaves* (London, 1924), pp. 79–80.
[2] Memo. of Judges of the Supreme Court (9 May) in Gore Browne to Newcastle (21 May 1861) (No. 77), P.P., 1862, xxxvii [3040], 53–4.
[3] Journal of Sewell. 6 Sept. 1862. Sewell took a close interest in this Bill and here are frequent references to it in his Journal.

Grey had been authorized, if he thought fit, under proper safe-guards to waive the Crown's right of pre-emption and it seemed to him that the law was 'conceived in a spirit of justice and capable of being worked cautiously and beneficially by Sir George Grey'. He advised that the royal assent be given and his advice was taken. But it could hardly be overlooked that the Ministers who passed an Act thus revolutionizing Native land policy were, in spite of their disclaimers, making themselves responsible for Native affairs.[1]

These disclaimers in any case won no sympathy from the Colonial Office. After a sarcastic allusion to 'these singular resolu-tions, so ambiguous in every respect except in the evident inten-tion of avoiding those powers and responsibilities which, until they were conferred by the Imperial Government, the Colonial Legislature and Ministries had repeatedly demanded', the great dispatch of 26 February 1863 laid down in lapidary phrases what Her Majesty's Government held to be 'the respective obligations of the mother country and the Colony with reference to the native race, especially with regard to the expense of native wars'.

If it be asked whether the expense of native government and of native wars in New Zealand is in its nature local or Imperial, or to speak with requisite accuracy, whether that expense should be defrayed by taxes imposed on the inhabitants of New Zealand, or by taxes imposed on the inhabitants of the United Kingdom, the first and most obvious answer is, that the cost of all war and government should be borne by those for whose benefit it is carried on, that is to say, in this case, by the inhabitants of New Zealand. . . . Nor if the question is viewed as one of dry justice would this answer be much affected by the circumstance that the native policy has been conducted subject to instructions from the Home Government . . .

I am aware . . . that the question cannot be dealt with as one of strict right. . . . When bodies politic are so closely related to each other as Great Britain and her Colonies, the stronger is under an obligation to assist the weaker, an obligation of generosity and wisdom as irresistible practically as one of technical justice, and unquestionably heightened in proportion to the amount of control exercised by the power which gives assistance over the affairs of the community which receives it.

[1] Minute of Rogers (n.d.—Feb. 1863) on Grey to Newcastle (31 Oct. 1862, No. 111, and 5 Nov. 1862, No. 113), CO209/170. The Native Lands Act (No. 42 of 1862) was enclosed in Grey's dispatch of 31 Oct.

In New Zealand the special circumstances of the acquisition of the sovereignty gave the British Government a special obligation to see that the rights of the British settlers were not used to the injury of the Maoris.

The Home Government has therefore been anxious to preserve an effectual authority in the management of native affairs, either until the amalgamation of the races had proceeded so far as to break down the sharp division of colour which at present exists, or until a system of government had taken root in the Colony which, by assigning to the Maoris some recognized constitutional position, would furnish some guarantee against oppressive treatment of the less educated race, and would thus at once satisfy and protect them.

But the powers retained by the Governor had proved inadequate for their purpose; an attempt to remedy this weakness had been abandoned in deference to colonial feeling; hence Sir George Grey's action in acceding to the colonists' demand for the abolition of the special power of the Native Department had been approved; and this relinquishment of responsibility did not require the consent of the colonists to make it effectual. In any case, the Waitara war was not an Imperial war.

The decision to complete, by force if necessary, the purchase of that land, was adopted at the advice not of the Native Department but of the Executive Council, and the proclamation of martial law was transmitted to the officer in command under the signature of the chief responsible ministers. It was under this pressure, with this advice, and through this agency, that Governor Browne took the steps which led to the war—steps which, although I thought it my duty to sanction them, were in a direction opposite to that which a purely Imperial policy would have dictated.

It was still the Governor's duty to prevent any step 'at variance with the pledges on the faith of which Her Majesty's Government acquired the sovereignty of New Zealand or in any other way marked by evident injustice towards Her Majesty's subjects of the native races'—for the colony was still defended by the Queen's troops maintained at the expense of Great Britain.[1]

This long dispatch was mainly Rogers's work. The Duke of Newcastle had criticized the first version as too didactic—'like

[1] Newcastle to Grey (26 Feb. 1863) (No. 22), P.P., 1863, xxxviii (H.C. 177), 9–16.

what they find fault with in Stephen—but better'. He wrote a second version, which was then revised by Fortescue, 'all of which took a good deal of the sting out of it, and, I half think, a little of] the coherency', he told his sister.[1] He believed that the Home Government must pull the colony through its troubles 'but in so doing . . . make the colonists feel or believe that when this is once done they will be left in a great measure to take the consequences of any false step which they may make'. To do this it was necessary to use 'strong and determined language which will make them angry'.[2] Indeed the dispatch had another purpose: it was 'an attempt to obtain from public opinion in England support against the public opinion of New Zealand'.[3] In another dispatch of the same date, Sir George Grey was told that the tone of dissatisfaction was not with his personal policy but with 'the proceedings of the Colonial Government and Legislature';[4] and this dissatisfaction had now led Rogers at least to adopt the views of the critics of the Waitara purchase and the Taranaki war. The alienation of feeling was becoming dangerous. The Imperial Government and sections of the British public felt that New Zealand was shirking her responsibilities: the New Zealand colonists felt that they were unjustly aspersed.[5]

This was the more serious because, before the Newcastle dispatch arrived, war had broken out again in New Zealand. It will be remembered that after the peace negotiations with Te Atiawa General Cameron had wished to strike a blow at the Taranaki and Ngati Ruanui tribes, who remained in occupation of the Omata and Tataraimaka blocks, but had not received Gore Browne's sanction in view of the threat to Auckland from the Waikato. Grey shared Gore Browne's view that it was not right to leave these tribes in occupation of European land which they could regard as a prize of war. As soon as the completion of the road to the Waikato exposed the King tribes to a counterblow if they should intervene, Grey and Cameron embarked for Taranaki. On

[1] Rogers to Miss Rogers (18 Mar. 1863), *Letters of Frederic Lord Blachford*, pp. 243–4. Some of the phrases echo his Minute of 12 Jan. 1861; see above, p. 265.
[2] Minute of Rogers (4 Jan. 1863), Newcastle Papers, NeC10908a.
[3] Rogers to Miss Rogers (18 Mar. 1863), loc. cit.
[4] Newcastle to Grey (26 Feb. 1863) (No. 24), P.P., 1863, xxxviii (H.C. 467), 143–4. Cf. also his private letter, cited on p. 281.
[5] Cf. *The Times*, 19 Jan. 1863, and Crosbie Ward, *Letter to the Right Hon. Lord Lyttelton on the Relations of Great Britain with the Colonists and Aboriginees of New Zealand* (London, Apr. 1863), esp. pp. 60 ff.

12 March 1863 they occupied Omata and on 4 April Tataraimaka, without opposition.[1]

This stroke was part of a wider scheme of which, characteristically, Grey did not breathe a word until he had carried it out. He had criticized the Waitara purchase before he returned to New Zealand, and may well have determined never to complete it. He explained his views in a dispatch of 24 April, through the words he puts into the mouths of Wiremu Kingi and his Atiawa followers:

They did not take up arms to prohibit the alienation of territory [to] the Crown, or to maintain any seigniorial rights, but . . . the people of the Waitara, without having been guilty of any crime, were driven at the point of the sword from villages, houses and homes which they had occupied for years.

This was well calculated to prepare the way for a reversal of policy, but it is a travesty of the real attitude of Wiremu Kingi in and before 1860. As Richmond, now a judge, commented in a letter to Mrs. Gore Browne:

If Wiremu Kingi had remained at his pah like a peaceable subject, and had come out when the chain reached his kainga and protested against its being included, the Governor was in no wise pledged to include it—on the contrary if any fair shew of title had been made he was pledged to exclude it. . . . The fallacy throughout is that we intended to seize a piece of land which we had bought, instead of which we merely insisted on ascertaining what Teira's party were rightfully entitled to sell.[2]

Domett for his part could not accept Sir George Grey's picture of the peaceful disposition of Te Atiawa. As he said:

No one who lived in New Zealand at the time can forget that for more than five years before the purchase from Te Teira the natives had been waging an incessant warfare among themselves, destroying each other's pas, ravaging each other's cultivations, and endangering the lives of the settlers, defying interference by the Government . . . and living in a state of hostility and misery alike fatal to themselves and disastrous to the English settlement.[3]

---

[1] Grey to Newcastle (6 Apr. 1863) (No. 37), P.P., 1863, xxxviii (H.C. 467), 121–3.

[2] C. W. Richmond to Mrs. Gore Browne (8 Nov. 1863), Gore Browne Papers 1/2 and *Richmond–Atkinson Papers*, ii. 70.

[3] Minute of Domett (20 Apr.) in Grey to Newcastle (24 Apr. 1863) (No. 39), P.P., 1864, xii [3277], 1–9. The Minute is at p. 6.

But his Native Minister, Dillon Bell, in a conversation with Teira,
elicited the fact that Wiremu Kingi's settlement on the south bank
of the Waitara had not been a personal concession by his father
Tamati Raru but the outcome of a tribal agreement in fear of a
raid by Ngati Maniapoto; and Ministers, though retaining their
opinion that the war had arisen on a different issue, agreed that the
purchase ought not to be completed without reserving the sites
of their pas. Moreover, in view of the dangers of divided counsels
and in the light of the resolutions adopted by the last Assembly,
they were willing to leave the decision to the Governor and assist
him in carrying it into effect 'so as to make it conducive to the
establishment of a permanent peace'.[1] So Grey proceeded with his
plans and on 11 May issued a proclamation abandoning and
renouncing all claim to the Waitara purchase.[2]

But Grey's attempt to involve Ministers in the responsibility
for his decision recoiled on himself. A Ngati Ruanui ambush at
Oakura, between Omata and Tataraimaka, on 4 May, in which
eight officers and men of a party conveying a military prisoner
were killed, destroyed any chance that the abandonment of Waitara would be interpreted as an act of belated justice. As a Maori
remarked to Arthur Atkinson a few days afterwards: 'We asked
the Governor to give us Waitara and he would not. . . . But when
he heard of these murders he said: "Ah! I must give up Waitara".'[3]
The murders at Oakura were avenged by General Cameron in
a sharp action on 4 June at Katikara, on the south-western boundary of the Tataraimaka block, in which a force of Ngati Ruanui,
Taranaki, and allied tribes was driven from a strong position with
heavy loss. But the repercussions of the Oakura ambush and the
Waitara proclamation did not stop there.

Grey's reversal of policy at Waitara did not take Rogers by
surprise. 'My own impression', he wrote, 'has long been that it
must and ought to come to an abandonment of Waitara.' The
Duke of Newcastle did not go so far. 'I confess,' he replied to
Rogers's minute, 'I cannot bring myself to the conclusion that
the purchase of Waitara was an act of injustice, though it may have

[1] Minute of Domett (30 Apr.) in Grey to Newcastle (5 May 1863) (No. 42),
ibid., pp. 11–13. Extract of letter from Domett to Crosbie Ward (9 May 1863) in
Gore Browne Papers 2/3. Domett to Stafford (6 Sept. 1863): Stafford Papers,
Turnbull Library.
[2] Proclamation (11 May 1863), P.P., 1864, xli [3277], 27.
[3] Journal of A. S. Atkinson (16 May 1863), *Richmond–Atkinson Papers*, ii. 43.

been improvident and impolitic.'[1] Both agreed, however, that they must support Sir George Grey.

But Waitara was overshadowed by Oakura. Before Tatarai-

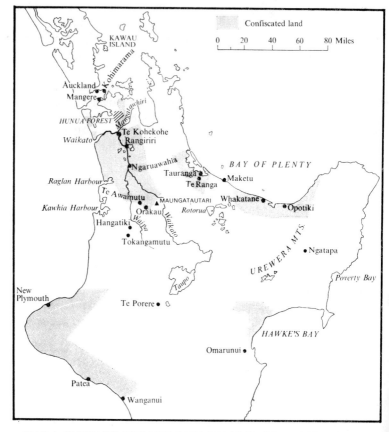

MAP 4. WAIKATO AND THE EAST COAST OF THE NORTH ISLAND

maka was reoccupied, there had come into Grey's hands a letter from the Kingites at Taranaki to the Tauranga chiefs boldly declaring that 'if we see that the Governor takes forcible possession of Waireka and Tataraimaka we will slay him at once'.[2]

[1] Minutes of Rogers (16 July) and Newcastle (20 Aug.) on Grey to Newcastle (24 Apr. 1863) (No. 39), CO209/172.

[2] Letter of *Runanga* of King Matutaera at Taranaki to Tauranga Chiefs (8 Dec. 1862) in Grey to Newcastle (14 Feb. 1863) (No. 16), P.P., 1863, xxxviii (H.C. 467), 108. There seems little doubt that they hoped to ambush Grey himself.

Information reached the colonial Government that the ambush had been instigated from the Waikato. Gorst believed it was Rewi Maniapoto's doing:[1] Grey, on the other hand, asserted that the message had been sent on behalf of a number of Waikato chiefs.[2] In any case the information gave him just the impetus he needed to set in motion a preventive war against the Waikato tribes. Early in the New Year he had visited Ngaruawahia and returned with the impression that 'the King party are daily becoming weaker and more reasonable, but that any untoward event may again rouse them into activity'.[3] They objected to his plan of placing a steamer on the Waikato river. They refused to allow Te Wheoro to build a school and 'other buildings' at Te Kohekohe: in the belief that these 'other buildings' were intended as barracks, a large party sent the timber down the river again.[4] These incidents occurred before the occupation of Tataraimaka. Afterwards all Europeans were compelled to leave the Waikato: Rewi attacked Gorst's office at Te Awamutu, confiscated his printing press, and theatened to kill him if he stayed. Rewi and Reihana appear to have planned an attack on Te Ia, where the Mangatawhiri stream joins the Waikato, if not a raid on Auckland itself. Rewi's plans were strenuously opposed by the King's sister Te Paea, Wiremu Tamihana, and other chiefs;[5] and the attack never took place. But the Government could not take it for granted that prudence would prevail. In Grey's words:

Was it to be expected that a civilized people, who knew that the question of whether they were to be attacked or not was discussed in runangas or councils . . . and was only decided in the negative by a small majority, which any night might become a minority, should delay for a day to take the requisite measures for the protection of their families and properties?[6]

[1] J. E. Gorst, *The Maori King* (ed. K. Sinclair), ch. xvii.
[2] Grey to Cardwell (30 Aug. 1864) (No. 129), P.P. 1865, xxxvii [3245], 110.
[3] Grey to Newcastle (6 Feb. 1863) (No. 5), P.P., 1863, xxxviii (H.C. 467), 101–2.
[4] Grey to Newcastle (30 Mar. 1863) (No. 32) with Enclosures, ibid., pp. 111–15. The original idea was a courthouse, modified (at Gorst's suggestion) into a station for (Maori) police. But Grey *had* thought it might be 'at any time turned into a military post': Grey to Cameron (30 June 1862), G36/3, N.Z. Archives—a reference I owe to B. J. Dalton, *War and Politics in New Zealand* (Sydney, 1967), p. 163.
[5] The Revd. A. G. Purchas to Bell (25 Apr.) in Grey to Newcastle (9 May 1863) (No. 45), P.P., 1864, xli [3277], 2a. Cf. Gorst, op. cit., chs. xvii and xviii.
[6] Grey to Newcastle (6 Jan. 1864) (No. 9), P.P., 1864, xli (H.C. 326), 3.

Within a few days of the ambush at Oakura, on the plea (supported by evidence) that there was reason to apprehend a general rising of the tribes, Grey asked for a reinforcement of three regiments, two to be of Sikhs.[1] Nothing could be done until General Cameron had read the Taranaki tribes a lesson at Katikara; but on 15 June part of the Auckland militia was called out for training, and on the 23rd a call was made for 400 volunteers from the militia for general service.[2] Grey was in fact returning, with more careful preparation, to the ideas of Gore Browne, on which he had at first poured so much scorn.[3] He was forcing the issue, with a view of relieving Auckland from all danger of attack and 'placing this part of New Zealand in a state of permanent security'.[4] General Cameron, whom Gore Browne had held in leash, was given his head. On 12 July, with a field force of about 1,300 men, he crossed the Mangatawhiri and occupied a position commanding the navigation of the Waikato.[5]

It may reasonably be argued that Sir George Grey's plan was defensive in purpose; but two items in the plan gave it the air of a war of aggression. There were a number of Maoris living in Auckland and the Commissioner of Police required them to remain indoors from dusk to daybreak; but on the evening of the 9th, aware no doubt that the soldiers of the garrison had left that morning for the front, 'a great many Natives, men, women and children, carrying with them their boxes, kept moving out from town'.[6] But this was not enough. If there was to be war, the clearance of potentially hostile Maoris from the district between Auckland and the Waikato, on the flanks of the new road, was an essential military precaution. General Cameron's plan was to send

[1] Grey to Newcastle (9 May 1863) (Nos. 44 and 45), P.P., 1864, xli [3277], 17–20. Newcastle at first favoured the idea of Sikhs, but Lord de Grey and Sir C. Wood (Secretaries of State for War and India) told him that 'according to precedent, any regiments serving with Indian regiments are placed upon Indian allowances' and for this and other reasons he dropped the idea: Martineau, *Life of Newcastle*, p. 326.

[2] *New Zealand Gazette*, 16 and 25 June 1863.

[3] See Whitaker (Attorney-General but not a member of the ministry) to C. W. Richmond (25 June 1863), *Richmond–Atkinson Papers*, ii. 52.

[4] Grey to Newcastle (4 July 1863) (No. 72), P.P., 1864, xli [3277], 32–3. Cf. also Memo. of Domett (24 June), P.P., 1864, xxxvii [3455], 8–9.

[5] Grey to Newcastle (28 July 1863) (No. 83), xli [3277], 33. Cameron had 145 officers and 3,717 soldiers with 1,668 militia and volunteers: W.O. 33/12, p. 121.

[6] *New Zealander*, 10 July 1863.

in detachments of troops, without notice, to disarm the Maoris and compel them to retire up the Waikato. The Government preferred to send magistrates round the *kaingas* to require an oath of allegiance, with removal as the alternative.[1] Almost all chose to leave. A number of European settlers were killed by the Maoris, and one influential Maori, Tamati Ngapora, a friend and confidant of Sir William Martin, a Christian pastor, and an uncle of Matu-taera, sadly left his home at Mangere to become in due course the ablest and most trusted adviser of the Maori King. Nor did the removal achieve its primary purpose. 'The bush is now so infested with these natives', Cameron complained, 'that I have been obliged to establish strong posts along our line of communication.' He thought it impossible to move up the Waikato until reinforcements arrived.[1]

If this operation was bound to embitter the Maoris concerned, public opinion in England was much more influenced by the Government's proposal to confiscate the territory of the Waikatos and fill it with settlers. This idea originated with Sir George Grey and was in fact an adaptation of the military settlement scheme he had carried out in British Kaffraria when High Commissioner in South Africa. He outlined his plan to the Executive Council (presumably) on 15 or 20 June.[2] When Cameron invaded the Waikato the Governor issued a proclamation to the Waikatos which was at once a declaration of war and a warning of what was to come.

Those who wage war against Her Majesty, or remain in arms, threatening the lives of her peaceable subjects, must take the consequences of their acts, and must understand that they will forfeit the right to the possession of their lands guaranteed to them by the Treaty of Waitangi; which lands will be occupied by a population capable of protecting, for the future, the quiet and unoffending from the violence with which they are now so constantly threatened.[3]

The proclamation was dated 11 July, but Gorst met the messenger carrying the first copies of the Maori version on the evening of the 14th, that is two days after the invasion.[4] By this time the

[1] Cameron to Secretary of State for War (30 July 1863), WO33/12, p. 5.
[2] Domett in his Memo. of 24 June refers to the plan as outlined by the Governor 'at a late meeting of the Executive Council', which had met on 15 and 20 June.
[3] *New Zealand Gazette*, 15 July 1863.
[4] Gorst, op. cit. (ed. Sinclair), p. 245.

Ministers knew they would have to accept the responsibility which Newcastle's dispatch had placed squarely on the shoulders of the colony; they were already committed by an act of the previous session to borrowing £500,000 for the reinstatement of Taranaki and the repayment of commissariat advances for the militia and volunteers; they must increase New Zealand's resources. A force of military settlers would enable the butchers, bakers, and other suppliers of the troops and the civilian population of Auckland to be withdrawn from militia service; and the lands in the Waikato not required by the military settlers could be sold to defray the expenses of the war.[1] The necessity of some such scheme was widely recognized. Sewell, who became one of its strongest critics, noted in his journal a few days after the Waikato proclamation: 'even as things are, with six thousand soldiers in the Colony, nothing will really restore peace but the occupation of the whole Waikato Country [by] Military settlers.'[2] There was also the point made by Domett in one of his memoranda:

> The natives are fond of war, and have but little to risk besides their land, and as the practice has hitherto been to give up that and allow them to keep all the plunder they could get, a feeling has sprung up that by war they have everything to gain and but little or nothing to lose. The only real punishment we could inflict has been hitherto scrupulously withheld.[3]

Not that it was proposed to deprive the Waikatos of all their land: hundreds of thousands of acres would still be left them. By 3 August Ministers had worked out a detailed scheme for enlisting 5,000 men, not over forty, chiefly from the goldfields of Victoria and Otago, with a promise of grants of 50-acre sections

---

[1] Memo. of Domett (24 June) in Grey to Cardwell (24 Nov. 1864) (No. 172), P.P., 1865, xxxvii [3455], 8–9. The dispatch of 26 Feb. arrived about 7 May. Domett in a Minute of 12 May, later withdrawn, said he never would have accepted office 'on any condition of accepting with it, particularly under circumstances which caused the special appointment by the Home Government of Sir George Grey, the direction of Native policy and the accompanying responsibility'. Bell concurred. Grey could not persuade them out of this attitude that they were bound by decision of the General Assembly, which on 6 Nov. passed a resolution 'cheerfully accepting' the responsibility. The Minutes are in P.M. 1/2, No. 34 N.Z. Archives.

[2] Journal of Sewell, 22 July 1863.

[3] Memo. of Domett (31 July) in Grey to Newcastle (29 Aug. 1863) (No. 109) P.P., 1864, xli [3277], 54–6.

and town allotments after three years' militia service. Sir George Grey approved it and Dillon Bell was sent to Australia to raise 2,000 men in anticipation of the approval of the Assembly.[1] As his biographer says, 'land acquisition was not Grey's primary objective';[2] but, of course, once he had launched the scheme— which, by the way, he now called his Ministers' plan—he had loosed a force he could not wholly control. The *New Zealander*, which was now losing readers through its very moderation, noted on 17 September:

There is . . . a general grievance throughout the whole of the local corps, which requires frank and immediate recognition on the part of the local government, and that is, an unmistakeable promise to confer, at the close of the war, a portion of land upon all those members of the Militia, Volunteers and other local corps who have been engaged on actual service but whose occupation will not permit them to enrol themselves under the 'military settlers' proclamation.[3]

Inevitably the war had become, to Aucklanders at least, a speculation. As Sewell reflected, 'The people of Auckland . . . have got effectual hold of the British army, the British Treasury and the Colonial Chest and they will not let them go till they have settled the Native difficulty and made themselves independent proprietors out of the Native Estate.' If they had to pay for this war, they would do their best to make a good thing out of it; and if they moved quickly the Imperial Government would be unable to withdraw its support from the confiscation policy because it would be committed to the military settlers.[4]

Actually the Duke of Newcastle thought the confiscation scheme justified in principle.

Any body of natives which takes up arms against Her Majesty, on such grounds as those which are alleged by the Waikatos, may properly be punished by the confiscation of a large part of their common property. I think that the lands thus acquired may properly be employed

---

[1] Grey to Newcastle (29 Aug. 1863) (No. 109), loc. cit.
[2] J. Rutherford, op. cit., p. 493.
[3] *New Zealander,* 17 Sept. 1863. W. C. Wilson withdrew from his partnership with John Williamson, who had founded the paper in 1845 to champion the rights of the Maori, and started the *New Zealand Herald* on 13 Nov. Next year Williamson gave up his paper.
[4] Journal of Sewell, 17 and 19 Nov. 1863. In the latter entry Sewell is interpreting Whitaker's views.

in meeting the expenses of carrying on the war; nor do I see any objection to using them as the site for military settlements.

But he pointed out the risk that friendly tribes might view the measure 'as a new and flagrant proof of the determination of the colonists to possess themselves of land at all risks to themselves and at any cost'; he feared that the Assembly might push the Governor further; and he dropped a broad hint that the Government must see to it that the policy was not so extended as to entail a prolongation of the war.[1]

This risk was increased by the revolt of Domett's colleagues against his indolence and propensity to act without consulting them and often in opposition to their views.[2] He resigned when the Assembly met, nominally on account of his inability to find a representative in the Legislative Council, and Fox was sent for. But what emerged from the consultations was essentially an Auckland Ministry in which the two law partners, Whitaker and Russell, were the leading spirits, though Fox, the bitter critic of the Taranaki war, was yoked with them, as one of his colleagues said, 'like a wild elephant between four tame ones'.[3] Whitaker, in his Ministerial statement, disclaimed any desire to drive the Maoris to desperation and the colony seemed to be more united this time than in the Taranaki war.[4] Even FitzGerald's organ, the Press, admitted that 'the Oakura murders and the expulsion of Europeans from the Waikato left us no option but that of fighting'.[5] But that did not deter FitzGerald, in the debates on the New Zealand Settlements Bill, from describing the confiscation policy as 'this great—. . . this enormous crime . . . to be perpetrated against a race to whom we have refused the right of representation in this House'.[6] The Bill passed both houses with little opposition, but FitzGerald's speech, Sir William Martin's Observations on the Proposal to take Native Lands under an Act of the Assembly, which questioned the legal power of the Assembly to take such lands

---

[1] Newcastle to Grey (26 Nov. 1863) (No. 104): P.P., 1864, xli [3277], 104–5. In a private letter of the same date, Newcastle tells Grey 'I have written a despatch which may strengthen your hands for resistance if you find it necessary', Newcastle Papers, NeC10888.
[2] H. A. Atkinson to A. S. Atkinson (8 Nov. 1863), Richmond–Atkinson Papers, ii. 69–70.
[3] T. B. Gillies to C. W. Richmond (9 Nov. 1863), ibid., p. 73.
[4] Legislative Council, 3 Nov. 1863, N.Z.P.D., 1861–3, p. 756.
[5] Press, 3 Aug. 1863.
[6] House of Representatives, 5 Nov. 1863, N.Z.P.D., 1861–3, pp. 783–9.

without their owners' consent, and Sewell's reference to 'panic legislation' in a published *Letter . . . to Lord Lyttelton*—all of them written in highly emotive language—gave a handle to critics in England.[1] Dr. Pollen, in a speech in the Legislative Council, actually expressed 'hopes . . . that the statesmen of England would stand between us and the Natives and, if need be, prevent the wrong which might be inflicted under the powers this Bill proposed to give'.[2]

An important aspect of the military settlement scheme was that it involved borrowing on an unprecedented scale. The £500,000 loan approved in 1862 had not been raised; Crosbie Ward, who had gone home on behalf of the colonial Government to negotiate for a guarantee with the Imperial authorities, had not been able to come to terms,[3] and in any case the renewal of the war had made the amount inadequate. Parallel with the New Zealand Settlements Act and an Act, based on an Irish precedent of 1798, giving the Government exceptional powers for the suppression of rebellion, was a Loan Act authorizing a loan of £3,000,000— mainly for the expenses of the war and the settlement scheme, including £100,000 for compensating loyal Maoris.[4] The Government's hopes of an Imperial guarantee of this new loan, to be negotiated by the Colonial Treasurer, Reader Wood, placed it more than usually at the mercy of English opinion. The active and willing service of the colonial militia and volunteers made a good impression in England; and *The Times* and the *Spectator* remained sympathetic to the colonists. But, to judge from the trend of events in 1864, *The Times* cannot safely be regarded as a barometer of opinion on this particular issue. It was also a serious blow to New Zealand when the fatal illness of the Duke of

[1] Martin's *Observations* in Grey to Newcastle (6 Jan. 1864) (No. 9), P.P., 1864, xli (H.C. 326), 4–17. Sewell, *The New Zealand Rebellion* (London, 1864).

[2] Legislative Council, 16 Nov. 1863, *N.Z.P.D.*, 1861–3, p. 872. Pollen objected to the wide terms of the Bill rather than its principle.

[3] Newcastle to Grey (27 July 1863) (No. 75) with Enclosures, P.P., 1864, xli [3256], 3 ff. Crosbie Ward wanted New Zealand's liabilities scaled down to £150,000; the Imperial authorities stood out for £200,000. Reader Wood thought this should have been accepted, and Newcastle told Grey 'Mr. Crosbie Ward has made a great mess of his mission'; Newcastle to Grey (27 July 1863) (Private), Newcastle Papers, NeC10887.

[4] New Zealand Loan Act (No. 11) and Loan Appropriation Act (No. 12) and Memo. of Wood in Grey to Newcastle (6 Jan. 1864) (No. 10), P.P. 1864, xli (H.C. 326), 31–2.

Newcastle forced him to resign the Colonial Secretaryship in April
1864. Gore Browne had complained of his 'coldness and reserve'
in correspondence;[1] but the dispatches which had given offence
had generally been of Rogers's drafting, and his Olympian detachment had its advantages. He had refused to budge from his original
stand on the Taranaki war and he had recently given his approval,
with some qualifications it is true, to the confiscation scheme.
Moreover he still had confidence in Sir George Grey, whom he
had after all been responsible for appointing. The colonists were
not likely to find his successor Cardwell—'able but hard and
didactic'[2]—so sympathetic to their case. Moreover Cardwell was
very sensitive to the prevailing political breeze, and this was
blowing hard against the colonies in matters of defence expenditure.

Cardwell saw Reader Wood, who had now arrived in England,
and conferred with his two Under-Secretaries, Rogers and Chichester Fortescue, on the problem. Rogers, though he considered
legal arguments 'out of place', went 'along with Sir W. Martin
in his arguments from policy, good faith and natural justice'. The
Settlements Act seemed to him 'a thoroughly bad one'; and he
was sceptical of the success of the military settlement scheme.
Chichester Fortescue, on the other hand, thought the views of
Martin and Gorst 'very one-sided'. Because the Maoris were not
foreign enemies, they could not be deprived of portions of their
territory without legislation. Because the war might spread, the
Act could not be confined to the districts actually in rebellion.
Everything depended on the spirit in which it was carried into
effect. The Governor should be instructed to satisfy himself of the
justice and propriety of every proceeding taken under it.[3] This was
the course Cardwell took. In a private letter to Grey, he accepted
Reader Wood's explanation of the Act's sweeping terms, but he
still found it open to 'very grave objections' and vindicated the
right of the Mother Country, which had sent 10,000 men, to
make her voice heard. Moreover he warned Grey there was no
hope of a Parliamentary guarantee of anything like £3,000,000.[4]

[1] Gore Browne to Maria Browne (3 Feb. 1861), Gore Browne Papers 2/4.
[2] *Spectator*, 2 Jan. 1864: and see above, pp. 23–4.
[3] Minutes of Rogers (n.d. and 8 Apr.) and Fortescue (16 Apr.) on Grey to
Newcastle (6 Jan. 1864) (Nos. 9 and 10), CO209/178. An extract from Fortescue's
Minute has been quoted above, p. 20.
[4] Cardwell to Grey (26 Apr. 1864) (Private), Grey Coll., Auckland.

His dispatch described the Act as 'a rapid expansion of the principles in which the Duke of Newcastle acquiesced with so much reserve'.

It renders permanently insecure the tenure of native property throughout the Islands and is thus calculated to alarm our friends. It makes no difference between the leaders and contrivers of rebellion and their unwilling agents and allies and is thus calculated to drive to despair those who are but half our enemies. The proceedings by which unlimited confiscation of property is to take place may be secret without argument and without appeal; and the provision for compensation is as rigidly confined as the provision for punishment is flexible and unlimited.

The status of the Maoris was anomalous: nominally British subjects, they were virtually independent. All the more was it incumbent on the Imperial and colonial Governments to make it clear that 'their European rulers are just as well as severe'. Cardwell did not dispute the colony's right to sell confiscated lands to help defray the expenses of the war; but Great Britain, having borne most of the expense, had a right to require that confiscation should not go further than was consistent with permanent pacification or national honour. The Act would not be disallowed; but Her Majesty's Government would much prefer a cession of land imposed by the Governor and the General. If this was not possible, the Act should be limited in duration to two years and the discretion of the Court should be enlarged. The extent and location of the confiscations should be made known as soon as possible and a Commission appointed to inquire what lands might properly be forfeited; the Governor should withhold his concurrence unless 'personally satisfied that the confiscation is just and moderate'. These measures should be accompanied by a general amnesty excluding only those concerned in murders of unoffending settlers or other heinous offences. There could be no guarantee for the part of the loan to be applied to the settlement scheme. The dispatch concluded by foreshadowing a reduction of the Imperial forces and the requirement of 'a much more adequate contribution' for military assistance in future.[1]

This confiscation dispatch, like the dispatch on responsibility fourteen months earlier, was clearly written with one eye on the

---

[1] Cardwell to Grey (26 Apr. 1864) (No. 43), P.P., 1864, xli (H.C. 326), 48-53.

House of Commons. On the day it was sent Arthur Mills moved for papers on the confiscation policy. 'He was not appearing', he said, 'as the advocate of the Natives; he wished only to present to the House a fair and impartial view of the case.' But this did not deter him from acid comment on the merchants of Auckland 'whose fortunes were to be built upon the ruins of the Maori race'. The only alternatives, he declared, were to disallow the Acts or 'to throw upon the Local Legislature the entire responsibility of the course it was taking'. Buxton, his seconder, attributed the war to land hunger and neglect of the Maoris: 'that hunger after land had become inflamed beyond all self-control by the furious hatred of the Natives engendered by the war.' We had no right over the Maoris except that conferred by the Treaty of Waitangi and our part of that Treaty had been 'utterly unfulfilled'.[1] The speech of Cardwell himself contrasted with these bitter criticisms of the colony. He paid a notable tribute to Gore Browne, whom he knew personally: 'I believe a more upright and honourable man never served the public.' He pointed out the objections to disallowing the first use by New Zealand of the newly granted power of controlling Native policy; but he did not defend the 'wide and sweeping' language of the Settlements Act and emphasized the British Government's power, by instructions to the Governor, 'to restrain and prescribe the operation of this statute within the limits dictated by justice and equity'. He was trying to hold the balance even between the Maoris and 'those who, of the same race as ourselves and settled in that distant part of the world, live in apprehension for the safety of their families and themselves'.[2] The tone of the debate continued to be critical, though tempered by the confidence expressed on all sides in the wisdom and moderation of Sir George Grey.

Cardwell went part of the way to meet Reader Wood in the matter of the loan. He offered a guarantee of £1,000,000 on condition that the debt of nearly £500,000 to the Imperial Treasury was paid out of it, that New Zealand paid for all but one regiment at the Australian rate of £40 per infantryman and £55 per artilleryman and that £50,000 annually continued to be applied to 'Native purposes'.[3] In conveying this offer, however, Cardwell

[1] *Hansard*, 3rd Ser., clxxiv. 1625–41.
[2] Ibid. 1642–50.
[3] Rogers to Hamilton (Treasury) (2 June 1864), P.P., 1864, xli [3356], 16–17.

imposed an onerous responsibility on Sir George Grey in his dealings with his Ministers.

> If unfortunately their opinion should be different from your own as to the terms of peace, Her Majesty's Government expect you to act upon your own judgement, and to state to your Ministers explicitly that an army of ten thousand English troops has been placed at your disposal for objects of Imperial concern, and not for the attainment of any merely local object; that your responsibility to the Crown is paramount; and that you will not continue the expenditure of blood and treasure longer than is absolutely necessary for the establishment of a just and lasting peace.[1]

Fox exaggerated in saying that this 'gave effect to the will of the colonial minority over the will of an almost unanimous majority';[2] but its suggestion that Sir George Grey was trusted but Ministers were not was a blow at responsible government.

The Loan Guarantee Bill had a rough passage. Arthur Mills moved its rejection, declaring that

> the question now was, not whether the mother country should tax the colonies, but whether the colonies should tax the mother country. Here was a colony, with a revenue of £700,000, nine-tenths of which was derived from customs or in other words, by the imposition of high duties on British manufactures, which jealously resented as an outrage the slightest attempt at Imperial interference, which possessed the fullest power of self-government, and yet which came . . . asking for the credit of the Imperial Parliament in order to obtain a loan to carry on a war, as to the righteousness of which the people of this country had serious misgivings.[3]

Cobden asked what interest the English people had in the matter: 'if we have any generosity to spare, it is wanted by our countrymen—the taxpayers of this country.' When Cardwell pointed out that, when the loan was put on the market at $5\frac{1}{2}$ per cent, the tenders were so few that the attempt was a failure, J. B. Smith, member for Stockport and a Manchester cotton merchant, replied that 'the real difficulty . . . was that the colony was not prepared to pay a sufficiently high rate of interest'.[4] The Government

---

[1] Cardwell to Grey (26 May 1864) (No. 65), P.P., 1864, xli [3356], 15–16.
[2] W. Fox, *The War in New Zealand* (London, 1866), p. 156.
[3] House of Commons, 14 July 1864, *Hansard*, 3rd Ser. clxxvi. 1471–5.
[4] Julyan, one of the Crown Agents for the Colonies, wrote to Southey at the Cape on 5 July: 'The money market seems paralysed here, at all events so far as Colonial Securities are concerned', Southey Papers, Cape Archives.

brought up its heaviest guns, Gladstone and Palmerston. Gladstone went part of the way with Mills: 'the inhabitants and the Legislatures of free colonies must learn self-reliance.' But he pointed out that 'the policy which led to the war had not been exclusively that of the colony. The Home Government had approved it, and were so far responsible for it.' The colony was also paying 'a very large proportion of the expenses of the war'. Palmerston's support was unqualified. Opponents were arguing that, after New Zealand had been colonized in the expectation of British protection, 'we ought to deprive it of the assistance of the Crown in bringing the war to a conclusion'. The House would surely not force the colony to borrow at 7 or 8 per cent when the guarantee would make it 4 per cent. Mills's amendment was defeated by 92 to 55; but in committee a concession was made to the critics.[1] The guarantee was not to operate until the Governor certified that the conditions —repayment of Imperial advances and appropriations for military contributions and Native purposes—had been adopted by the General Assembly. It was a gesture of distrust.

Why was the general tone of these debates so critical of New Zealand? Perhaps because, on issues like this, the humanitarian strain in the English character, the ingrained sympathy with the underdog, could unite with the anti-colonialism of the Manchester School. Exeter Hall influences still made themselves felt. A publication of the Aborigines Protection Society, bitterly critical of the confiscation policy, demanded that the colonial Government be deprived of the management of Native affairs.[2] But such a policy had few supporters, apart from isolated figures like Earl Grey (who was no Exeter Hall man). The Manchester liberals, on the other hand, were approaching the peak of their influence. Their newspapers were gaining at the expense of *The Times*. Goldwin Smith had seized on the confiscation issue as an occasion for another scathing letter to the *Daily News*: 'In rapacity and atrocity we have had many equals—perhaps not a few superiors; in pious rapacity and sanctimonious atrocity we may

[1] Twenty speakers took part in the second reading debate: *Hansard*, 3rd Ser. clxxvi. 1471–1522. There was a further debate in Committee on 18 July. The Act is 27 & 28 Vict. c. 82.

[2] *The New Zealand and the Maori War of 1863–64 with especial reference to the Confiscation of Native Lands and the Colonial Ministry's Defence of their War Policy* (London, 1864). See also K. Sinclair, 'The Aborigines Protection Society and New Zealand' (Univ. of Auckland, M.A. thesis, 1946).

look through history for our peers in vain.' He did not want to
be too hard on the colonists, he said. 'They did not make the laws
which have disinherited them, with the rest of the English people,
of the soil of their own country and driven them out to seize upon
the land of others. But I doubt whether their house will flourish
with a murdered man beneath its hearthstone.'¹ The knowledge
of the New Zealand situation displayed in the debates was not
great. Apart from the Government spokesmen, only Adderley
in the Commons and Lyttelton in the Lords could be called well-
informed, though Lord Alfred Churchill, having visited New
Zealand, was able to deny that there was 'any general desire on the
part of the colonists to exterminate the Natives'.² Most members
must have derived their information from the blue books, supplemented by newspapers, books, and some private letters.
Arthur Mills had two brothers-in-law in Canterbury, but they
were remote from the Maori war: perhaps his reference to the
Auckland merchants came from a private source. Once again the
critics stated their case better than the colonial Government.
Nothing on the colonial side was comparable with Gorst's fascinating account of the Waikato Maoris, sympathetic to the point
of being tendentious, in his book *The Maori King*, published in
March 1864.³ Moreover General Peel, Secretary of State for War
in two of Lord Derby's administrations, quoted in the debates a
private letter from an officer, highly critical of the colonial
Government and its tendency 'to use British troops for the purpose of taking the land of Native British subjects'.⁴ The Duke of
Cambridge, the Commander-in-Chief, in the Lords hotly protested 'against the impression getting abroad that any of Her
Majesty's troops . . . perform the services on which they are sent
with the slightest disgust';⁵ but he was soon to be proved wrong.

¹ Goldwin Smith to the Editor of the *Daily News* (18 Feb. 1864): quoted in the
Christchurch *Press*, 16 May 1864. But there was an able criticism of this 'impatience
of Empire' in *The Economist*, 23 July 1864.
² *Hansard*, 3rd Ser. xlcciv. 1653. Nevertheless Grey in more than one letter in
1863 remarked on the bitterness and exasperation of the settlers, especially at
Taranaki, Newcastle Papers, NeC11091.
³ The sub-title of *The Maori King* was *The Story of our Quarrel with the Natives
of New Zealand*. For an estimate of the book see K. Sinclair's Introduction to the
1959 edition. Gorst had also written to the newspapers, e.g. *The Times*, 24 Dec.
1863.
⁴ *Hansard*, 3rd Ser. clxxvi. 1683.
⁵ Ibid., 1992.

The admiration of the troops for the bravery and skill of the Maori warriors was another fact which must not be left out of account as forming English opinion.

These debates occurred at a time when General Cameron appeared to have carried his Waikato campaign to a victorious conclusion. Communications were his chief problems.

Some fifteen hundred horses toiled incessantly at the task of hauling waggon-loads of stores from Auckland along the forty miles of road to the river, running the gauntlet through the flanking column of marauding Natives who had got to the rear of the General's main force and being assailed by ambuscade parties as the transport corps dragged its slow length along.[1]

A steamer specially built in Sydney to operate on the Waikato proved too unwieldy for river work. It became unmanageable at a critical point of the attack on the Maori stronghold of Rangiriri, which nevertheless surrendered at daylight on 21 November. After this Ngaruawahia, the seat of the Maori King, was occupied on 8 December without opposition and Sir George Grey reported to the Secretary of State that 'the neck of this unhappy rebellion is now broken'.[2] But no submission followed, though possibly Grey and his Ministers missed a chance of peace by their inability to agree whether the Governor should go to Ngaruawahia with the General alone or whether his Ministers should accompany him.[3] After a pause to bring up supplies, the war was carried into the territory of the warlike Maniapoto early in 1864. The decisive encounter was at Rewi's pa of Orakau. After three assaults had been repulsed, the brigadier in command drew a cordon of troops around the place and approached it by sap. On 2 April Cameron arrived and summoned the pa to surrender, in vain. An assault began and penetrated an outwork. Even the official account then rises to eloquence:

The enemy suddenly came out of the entrenchment on the open, and in a silent and compact body moved without precipitation. There was something mysterious in their appearance, as they advanced towards the cordon of troops, without fear, without firing a shot, or a single

[1] Fox, *The War in New Zealand*, p. 75.

[2] Grey to Newcastle (9 Dec. 1863) (No. 182), P.P., 1864, xli [3355], 13.

[3] 'I do not think that I am to form one of a commission with every consecutive ministry as they come rapidly on, following one another. . . . In this manner I lose all character for consistency of action or views': Grey to Cameron (19 December 1863), G 36/4, N.Z. Archives.

cry being heard even from the women, of whom there were several among them. They had already been more than two days without water; they had no food but some new potatoes; an overwhelming force surrounded them, and all hope of relief failed but still, with an extraordinary devotion to their cause, calmly, in the face of death, [they] abandoned their position without yielding.[1]

They broke through the cordon, but the fire of the troops took heavy toll before they reached the *manuka* scrub. Their mountain stronghold of Maungatautari was abandoned.

One of Grey's great anxieties had been that the war might spread to other tribes. But Cameron's successes had their effect and Grey's resident magistrates, not only in the North but in such districts as Wairarapa and the Manawatu, no doubt had a tranquillizing influence. The important chief Wi Tako Ngatata, who had for a time been inclined to support the King, thought better of it, and under the influence of Featherston and Fox, made a formal declaration of allegiance to the Queen early in June. On the other hand, on a report that the east coast tribes were coming up to join the Kingites, Cameron had detached a force to Tauranga in January and after Orakau he moved his headquarters there. Eight days later, his troops, who had gained a footing in the Gate pa outside the town, were dislodged by the Maoris after the loss of most of their officers, and retired in disorder. Fortunately the loyal Arawas had defeated a war party from the east coast tribes at Maketu on the previous day; and Colonel Greer wiped out the Gate pa defeat at Te Ranga, a few miles further east, on 21 June. Early in August all but a few of the Ngai Terangi, the Tauranga tribe, submitted and surrendered their arms. But even now the war was not over. On the contrary there arose in Taranaki a prophet, Te Ua Haumene, who saw a vision of the Maoris as a chosen people, who could be made invulnerable by incantations to the *Atua Pai marire*, the good and peaceful God. When a foraging party was ambushed near Oakura on 6 April, the smoke-dried heads of the officer and six soldiers killed were sent round the tribes to enlist recruits; and on 30 April a party of 200 fanatics attacked a redoubt at Sentry Hill in broad daylight. The attack failed with heavy loss, but their leader attributed the failure

[1] Journal of Deputy Quartermaster-General Gamble (4 Apr. 1864), WO33/16. This is a valuable source on the whole campaign.

to lack of faith. Whilst the Maori King and his advisers sulked in the Upper Waipa Valley, a new, embittered phase of the war was beginning.[1]

Undoubtedly many Imperial officers were now sick and tired of the war and unsympathetic towards what appeared to be its objects. We have already referred to one private letter; but Deputy Quartermaster-General Gamble in his official journal looked forward to 'the termination of a war which is accompanied by more than ordinary difficulties for us and which, though it has assumed large dimensions, is not, in its result, really identified with Imperial so much as with Colonial interests'.[2] We do not know what the private soldier thought, as he pocketed his meagre pay. But even *The Times*, after the repulse at the Gate pa, asked what the soldiers were fighting for and answered: 'Just to clear off some poor fellows from their own native land and obtain the title clear of encumbrance for the speculators at Auckland.'[3]

The colonists could not fail to be aware of these officers' views.

Could it well be supposed [the *Nelson Examiner* asked sarcastically] that officers in 'crack' regiments recently sent to New Zealand from China, India and elsewhere, arrested too when on the eve of returning to England, could like a campaign in New Zealand? No quotable glory or honour results from a victory over those who are described as savages only half-armed and half-naked . . . while there is a constant risk of being defeated by these same savages.

It hinted that they were jealous because no land had been allotted to them.[4] The colony resented Cardwell's didactic dispatches. The *Wellington Independent* interpreted them, incorrectly, as a deliberate attempt to hamper the policy of the colonial Ministry and resume the control of Native affairs;[5] and, with greater truth, claimed that 'the Imperial Government distrusts the colonists and has set up Sir George Grey as an independent power between them and the natives'.[6] Fox answered the criticisms of the Aborigines

---

[1] This paragraph is based on Grey's dispatches in P.P., 1864, xli [3355] and [3386] and 1865, xxxvii [3425]; Journal of Gamble, loc. cit.; and J. Cowan, *The New Zealand Wars* (2 vols., Wellington, 1922).

[2] Journal of Gamble (8 June–7 July 1864), loc. cit., p. 124.

[3] *The Times*, 15 July 1864. Cf. Whitmore in 1869: 'The country was panting for peace, and was terrified at the idea that the immense burdens it had undertaken would not restore peace': N.Z.P.D. v. 365.

[4] *Nelson Examiner*, 3 Nov. 1864.    [5] *Wellington Independent*, 12 July 1864.

[6] Ibid., 30 July 1864. In a private letter, Gladstone had written: 'Three cheers

Protection Society in a memorandum printed for Parliament. Confiscation, he declared, was a custom recognized by the Maoris themselves: 'they never do consider themselves conquered unless their lands are taken.' The chief object of the Government was 'neither punishment nor retaliation but simply a material guarantee against the recurrence of . . . uprisings against the authority of law and the legitimate progress of colonization'. It was never proposed to leave the Maoris without ample land for their future use.[1] The respected Bishop Williams of Waiapu made an able and dispassionate defence of the war in a letter to the Church Missionary Society.[2] But what was wanted now was not so much an appeal to England as a change of policy in New Zealand.

The unity of purpose in the colony at the outset of the Waikato war was now giving way to unedifying quarrels. Cardwell's appeal to Grey to exercise his independent judgement had succeeded only too well. The Governor, still in his early fifties and ambitious of further promotion, determined to play the Imperial game. Fox, a man of generous impulses but prone to suspicion, had been prejudiced against Grey ever since the struggle for self-government in his first term of office. He and the subtle, tenacious Whitaker proved no mean antagonists in the fierce and prolonged controversy with the Governor which FitzGerald dubbed the 'memorandummiad'.

The first round of the quarrel was fought over the Maori prisoners taken at Rangiriri, who were held on a hulk in Auckland harbour. Ministers had hoped that the fall of Maungatautari would end the war and enable them to be released. Grey still wished them and especially the chief Tioriori, an associate of Wiremu Tamihana, to be released on parole, as a move towards peace. After three months of argument about the prisoners' health, the conditions of their confinement, and the responsibility for the treatment of prisoners taken by Imperial troops, their custody was transferred early in July to the Governor, who sent

for [dispatches] No. 43 and No. 65, which the responsible advisers do not like': (to Cardwell, 3 Nov. 1864), Gladstone Papers, B.M. Add. MS. 44118.

[1] Memo. of Fox (5 May) in Grey to Newcastle (5 May 1864) (No. 67), P.P., 1864, xli [3386], 33–5.

[2] The substance of this letter was repeated in W. Williams to the Colonial Secretary (30 Apr.) in Grey to Newcastle (6 June 1864) (No. 86), P.P., 1865, xxxvii [3425], 33–4. Some letters of Fox to his brother, the Revd. G. T. Fox, were reprinted as *The Revolt in New Zealand* (London, 1865).

them to his newly acquired island of Kawau—from which, in September, they escaped. Despite Cardwell's support of Grey on the question of responsibility, this may be called a drawn battle. Ministers protested against Cardwell's attitude 'as prejudging the case unheard and as infringing the principle of Responsible Government'; but by this time the controversy had merged in other issues.[1]

A more important dispute had arisen over a proposed proclamation to the Waikato tribes, offering an amnesty and land to all who would give up their arms and obey the Queen's law. This had existed in embryo ever since Ministers had wanted to go up to Ngaruawahia with the Governor and the General in December and the terms of a possible proclamation had been discussed. Grey objected to the draft submitted by Ministers on 30 April, especially to the stipulation that arms must be given up. 'Only to pardon those who came in with guns and ammunition in their hands', he declared, 'will be regarded as a declaration of lasting war against those who do not comply.'[2] The proclamation was not issued, partly on account of this difference of opinion and partly for tactical reasons after the defeat at the Gate pa. But early in September, fortified by Cardwell's instructions of 26 April and 26 May Grey took a new initiative and transmitted to his Ministers a draft proclamation offering pardon to those implicated in rebellion (unless they were concerned in certain murders) if they came in before 22 October, took an oath of allegiance, and ceded 'such territory as might in each instance be fixed by the Governor and Lieutenant-General'. It was now Ministers' turn to object. The old difference over the surrender of arms and ammunition re-appeared and Ministers would be no parties to a declaration constituting the Governor and the General sole arbiters of what should be deemed a satisfactory cession of territory.[3] Grey rightly judged that in the matter of disarmament he could count on the backing

[1] This quarrel can be followed in a number of dispatches, with innumerable Enclosures, in P.P., 1864, xli [3380] and [3386] and 1865, xxxvii [3425]. The most important are Cardwell to Grey (27 June 1864) (No. 76) in [3880], 19 and Memo. of Fox (n.d.) in Grey to Cardwell (29 Sept. 1864) (No. 134) in [3425], 128–31.

[2] Grey to Newcastle (7 May 1864) (No. 71) with twelve Enclosures, one of them dated as late as 25 May, P.P., 1865, xxxvii [3425], 1 ff. A draft of 22 Apr with a note by Fox of 18 May on the Governor's vacillations, is in P.M. 1/3 N.Z. Archives.

[3] Grey to Cardwell (7 Oct. 1864) (No. 143) with Enclosures, ibid., pp. 135–41

of the Secretary of State. As Rogers pointed out when the papers arrived:

It is worth while for the Colonists to impose a considerable additional period of war on the Imperial Government and on themselves rather than give up the cardinal point of disarmament. . . . The interest of the Imperial Government lies in an immediate pacification, even on terms which will not ensure the Colonists against further trouble so long as that pacification is substantial. . . . Sir George Grey's credit is concerned in bringing about a speedy peace having, in the eyes of the English public, an appearance of justice and consideration for the natives. His object therefore coincides with that of the Home Government— and I therefore should rely on his judgement as against that of the Ministry.[1]

The question of cessions of territory, which it will be remembered Cardwell thought preferable to confiscation, raised the whole issue of confiscation policy. It became clear, as time went on, that Governor and Ministers had different views on this. Ministers, according to their own account, had always aimed at a line running from Raglan or Kawhia on the west coast to Tauranga on the east, with further confiscations in Taranaki and between Waitotara and Patea. On 17 May they submitted a draft Order in Council to Grey and urged the importance of locating the military settlers in the Waikato as soon as possible. Grey stalled: first he pleaded lack of information on Ministers' intentions in detail, then he professed to favour piecemeal rather than general confiscation. Reader Wood, when he returned from his mission to England, declared that he never would have accepted the mission had he not felt assured, on the basis of a conversation with the Governor before his departure, that he was in accord with the Ministry on the subject of confiscation. Now he was told by the Governor that the attitude of Ministers over confiscation and the amnesty proclamation was 'prolonging the war and closing the avenue to peace'.[2] Not unnaturally, when he reported this conversation to his colleagues, at the end of September, they submitted their resignations next day.

[1] Minute of Rogers (16 Dec.) on Grey to Cardwell (7 Oct. 1864) (No. 143), CO209/183.
[2] Memo. of Reader Wood (29 Sept.) in Grey to Cardwell (24 Nov. 1864) (No. 172) and Grey to Cardwell (7 Oct. 1864) (No. 143), P.P., 1865, xxxvii [3425], 136 and [3455], 5–6.

Events had been moving that way for some time, especially since the arrival of Cardwell's dispatch of 26 May.

> His Excellency the Governor [wrote Ministers on 2 August] has recognized negative powers, and he is bound to judge for himself as to the justice and propriety of employing Her Majesty's troops, but he is not entitled, without the advice of his Ministers, to deal with any question of Native policy; and if the policy they recommend for his acceptance appears to him clearly disastrous, he may appeal to the General Assembly and from the General Assembly to the constituencies. The Governor's constitutional position with regard to his administration is the same in regard to Native as to ordinary constitutional affairs. His Excellency's Responsible Advisers . . . do not claim the right to enforce their policy with Imperial troops; but His Excellency's advisers do insist that the Governor has not the right to carry out a policy of his own, irrespective of his Responsible Advisers.

This seems sound constitutional doctrine; and Grey's argument that 'the sessions of the General Assembly are . . . not only short but by far too infrequent to enable them to exercise such a control over public affairs as is exercised by the Parliament of Great Britain'—suggesting that Ministers were in practice irresponsible —is not at first sight at all convincing. He was no doubt speaking more from the heart when he complained of the lack of 'facilities for procuring a new ministry' in New Zealand.[1] We may well imagine that many of the exchanges between Governor and Ministers were with a view to cutting a good figure before a future General Assembly—and, in Grey's case, before Parliament and the Colonial Office. Moreover Grey was a shrewd observer and was no doubt aware that opinion in New Zealand was turning against the Ministry. It was in fact high time Ministers resigned. They said in so many words that responsible government in New Zealand would never work under Sir George Grey; and Whitaker wrote to Richmond in mid October that it was 'now nearly two months, perhaps more, that neither Fox nor I have seen him on business'.[2]

Grey did not at once accept the resignations. On 3 October Ministers defined (for the first time, according to the Governor)

---

[1] Grey to Cardwell (26 Aug. 1864) (No. 124) enclosing Memo. of Whitaker (2 Aug.), P.P., 1865, xxxvii [3425], 99–108.
[2] Whitaker to C. W. Richmond (17 Oct. 1864), *Richmond–Atkinson Papers* ii. 127–8.

the area they deemed sufficient for cession or confiscation: 1,000,000 acres in the Waikato and 600,000 acres in the Taranaki–Wanganui region. The Governor then on 25 October, on his own responsibility, issued a proclamation granting pardon to 'all such persons implicated in the Rebellion, as may come in on or before 10 December next, take the Oath of Allegiance, and make the cession of such Territory as may in each instance be fixed by the Governor and Lieutenant-General Commanding'. He had, he said, undertaken 'that care should be exercised to take any cessions of land in a manner which should unequivocally exhibit the Natives who made them, in the position of defeated rebels; and further, that no arrangement for the cession of any land should be concluded until the advice tendered by my Responsible advisers had been fully considered'. He had also carried out Cardwell's instructions not to bring the Settlements Act, with its confiscation provisions, into operation until the way of cession had been tried and failed.[1] He must have known by this time that it would fail.

On the whole Grey had in every point at issue taken the more humane line and the motives of Whitaker and Russell, at least in their confiscation policy, were not above suspicion. With 10,000 Imperial troops in the country, Ministers could hardly expect an active-minded Governor like Grey to be content with a negative role, especially in the prevailing climate of opinion in England. It was idle for Ministers to complain that Sir George Grey took to himself all powers in matters of importance, leaving those of little or no account to them. This was not entirely Sir George Grey's fault: it was the natural result of the presence in New Zealand of a large Imperial army backed by a strong-minded Secretary of State and a critical public opinion. But there is no doubt that Grey, who was after all the originator of the military settlement scheme, changed his views, or at least his tactics, on confiscation, trimming his sails to the wind; and there is a grain of truth (even if some exaggeration) in his Ministers' charge that he would do the colonists an injustice 'in order to secure a character for clemency at their expense'.[2] He sent home information when

[1] Grey to Cardwell (27 Oct. 1864) (No. 151) with Enclosures, P.P., 1865, xxxvii [3425], 166–7.
[2] A phrase in Whitaker's Memo. of 22 Sept. enclosed in Grey to Cardwell (7 Oct. 1864) (No. 143), P.P., 1865, xxxvii [3425], 139–41.

he chose: a Ministerial memorandum of 30 May on the proposed confiscation proclamation was not transmitted until 3 September and Reader Wood's damaging memorandum of 29 September on his conversation with the Governor before his departure for England was not sent home until 24 November, the day the Assembly met. He was playing to the gallery in England, but he overplayed his part. The Colonial Office clerks, though they leaned to Grey's side, grew heartily sick of these prolonged wrangles. 'I have read these papers,' wrote Rogers after Ministers' complaints of the delays in transmission, 'but the effect is rather to produce a state of confused stupor than anything else.'[1] Chichester Fortescue in particular did not acquit Grey of a share of the blame for letting the machinery of government run down as it had done by 'separating himself from his ministers and negotiating with them in diplomatic fashion rather than endeavour to guide and influence them in Native affairs from day to day by requiring constant information and taking constant part in their Native administration'.[2] He had vacillated; he had temporized; he had changed his ground; he had not played fair. Grey had his revenge on his Ministers, for the Waikato settlement scheme did not pay and fell far short of their hopes. But the Ministers had theirs, for these quarrels wore Grey down until he became intolerable and wrecked his own career. One other point had emerged clearly. Cardwell's reliance on Grey as an instrument of Imperial policy had been a hopeless failure; and if Grey with all his experience and finesse could not impose an Imperial policy, no one else could.

[1] Minute of Rogers (n.d.) on Grey to Cardwell (7 Nov. 1864) (No. 162), CO209/185.

[2] Minute of Chichester Fortescue (21 Dec.) on Grey to Cardwell (7 Oct. 1864) (No. 143), CO209/183; Minute of 17 Jan. 1865 on Grey to Cardwell (7 Nov. 1864) (No. 162), loc. cit. Cf. also Cardwell to Grey (26 Dec. 1864) (No. 139), P.P., 1865, xxxvii, [3425], 200–1.

# X

## THE WELD MINISTRY AND SELF-RELIANCE

THE existence of serious differences of opinion between Sir George Grey and his Ministers could not be concealed for long, and the New Zealand public was inclined to side with the Ministers, both from personal distrust of Sir George Grey and from dislike of the terms of Cardwell's dispatches, which he was endeavouring to implement. The *Wellington Independent*, which stood close to Fox, argued that 'the instructions given to Sir George Grey were inconsistent with constitutional privileges.'[1] Even FitzGerald's organ, the Christchurch *Press*, which had always doubted whether the policies of Domett, Whitaker, and Fox would win the assent of the Imperial Government, remarked that 'if there is one subject upon which a New Zealand colonist may be forgiven for losing his temper a little, it is at the attitude in which it is endeavoured to make Sir George Grey stand to the Colony'. 'War may have been necessary,' it admitted in a later article. 'But we protest against his accepting the honour due to a peacemaker.'[2] On the other hand, the South Island, which paid two-thirds of the expenditure of the General Government, was uneasy at the heavy expenditure that was going on in the North without any apparent prospect of achieving the end in view. In an article which might have been written by an English newspaper about New Zealand, the *Press* declared that 'there is no state so deplorable as that in which the community are living by the profits of a war which is mainly, almost exclusively, paid for by others'.[3] Though the price of wool was good, the failure to negotiate the £3,000,000 loan had embarrassed provincial as well as general finances: Otago,

---

[1] *Wellington Independent*, 8 Oct. 1864.
[2] *Press*, 5 Sept. and 5 Oct. 1864. On 6 Dec., after the correspondence had been published, the *Press* admitted that 'by all independent men his [Grey's] faults will be forgiven when compared with those of Ministers'.
[3] Ibid., 23 July 1864.

whose goldfields had passed their peak, was forced to retrench and Southland, which had hoped to tap Otago's wealth, subsided into ignominious bankruptcy. Why, the southern provinces asked, should Auckland be colonized at their expense? For this, they said, was what the great military settlement scheme amounted to: 'not a condition is imposed on the expected emigrants which might not have come from any provincial immigration office.'[1] Weld summed up the situation, in retrospect, in 1869: 'The colony had neither money nor credit, its debentures were unsaleable, its account largely overdrawn, large bodies of immigrants from different parts of the world were encamped in tents in Auckland and its environs and were receiving a pittance of Government aid'[2]—because no land for the military settlers had yet been confiscated.

Otago was inclined to go for separation of the islands and leave the North to stew in its own juice. The *Otago Daily Times* ever since 1862 had been urging this course and winning support from the gold rush immigrants, most of them from Victoria, who knew nothing about the Maoris and had no interest in the war. Canterbury, or at any rate its leaders, took a wider view. Of all the provinces it had the closest links with England. Its leaders kept in touch with Englishmen who counted like Lord Lyttelton and Adderley and were well aware of the trends of English thinking on colonial problems and in many ways—not all—sympathized with them. On 13 October a number of Canterbury members of both Houses dined together at the Christchurch Club. The next step was to ask the Superintendent (Samuel Bealey) to call a meeting in Christchurch Town Hall for Friday, 21 October at 7 p.m. It was a cold, wet, stormy evening, but the hall was crowded. Weld, who had ridden in from his estate at Brackenfield thirty miles north of Christchurch, moved the first resolution, a colourless one welcoming His Excellency's announced intention of summoning the General Assembly. It was his speech, not his resolution, that gave the desired lead.

We were now in a position of having apparently lost our credit at home, and of being involved in immense expenditure and financial difficulties, with an enormous army for which we pay one million or one million and a half a year. . . . In England we were at present in very bad odour. . . . He took up the English newspapers and he saw them filled with attacks upon the colony and charges against us of being greedy and desirous of getting the lands of the natives. . . . As far as he could see, there was one course left to us. We were, for the first time in the history of New Zealand, in the position of being able, if we asked it, to obtain entirely the government of our own affairs. He believed it was never offered us before, and he would say he did not look without deep regret upon the circumstances in which it was offered to us now, in a fit of economy of the English nation. He believed if we said to the English Government 'We will entirely take the whole charge of local affairs upon ourselves, take the whole expense of Maori questions and will deal with them as we like, and keep up our own forces', they would close with the bargain. . . . He was for such a course, at the earliest practicable moment, which . . . was now.[1]

Weld was no orator to sweep a meeting off its feet and it did not go entirely his way. Ollivier, a prominent figure in provincial politics, thought he had not gone far enough and moved a series of resolutions strongly condemning the Whitaker–Fox Ministry's financial policies and hinting at the expediency of separation, which clearly had a number of supporters at the meeting. Weld's and Ollivier's resolutions were put separately and both declared carried. But Weld's had far wider repercussions.

Weld's initiative met with a response everywhere except in Auckland. Even the *Otago Daily Times* changed its tune:

The time for separation has gone by. . . . Neither the North nor the South is in a position now to ask for separation, simply because they are under obligations to third parties, who would not be willing to relieve either from its joint liabilities. . . . It is not to separation that the South Island has now to address itself. Its policy, we may say its necessity, is to bring the North Island within its control.[2]

On the other hand, the threat of separation could be held *in terrorem* over the heads of North Islanders. The Otago Provincial

[1] *Press*, 22 Oct. 1864. See also *Nelson Examiner*, 27 Oct. 1864 and Stafford's Address to his Constituents, ibid., 7 Jan. 1865; C. C. Bowen to H. S. Selfe (15 Oct. 1864), Selfe Papers, Hocken Library. Weld had bought about 1,000 acres of the Broomfield run in 1861 and built on it a sixteen-roomed house: D. N. Hawkins, *Beyond the Waimakariri* (Christchurch, 1957), p. 81.
[2] *Otago Daily Times*, 29 Oct. 1864. On the separation movement in the South, see my *Provincial System in New Zealand* and A. H. McLintock, *History of Otago* (Dunedin, 1949).

Council shortly afterwards, having passed a series of resolutions deploring the financial burdens cast upon the province, resolved to seek the concurrence of the other South Island provinces in a financial and political separation of the islands 'unless some measures can be taken which shall lead to the early termination of the war on terms consistent with the honour of the colony and the safety of the Northern settlements'.[1] Wellington was on the whole receptive of Weld's ideas. In a leading article headed 'A National Policy for New Zealand', the *Wellington Independent*, though more inclined to blame the Colonial Office than the Ministry or the people of Auckland, hailed with satisfaction 'the appearance of what we may term a national spirit'.[2] A 'numerous and influential' meeting at New Plymouth, at which Atkinson was the principal speaker, passed a resolution favouring the withdrawal of the Imperial forces 'if necessary to effect the object aimed at'—namely 'the real and absolute government of New Zealand placed in its hands alone'.[3] Weld visited other provinces, possibly Otago, certainly Marlborough and Wellington, to canvass for support. By the time the *Phoebe* had reached Auckland with most of the southern Members of Assembly on board, the essential preparatory work had been done. Whitaker, who had been asked to advise the Governor whom he should send for, approached Stafford first; but Stafford, not without *arrière-pensées* which became apparent later, yielded precedence to Weld, who, he agreed, was the man of the hour.[4]

Weld put his terms in writing. His policy was, in a word, self-reliance. He wished above all to put an end to 'the system of double government by Governor and Ministers'; but he recognized the right of the Home Government to insist upon it 'so long as the Colony is receiving the aid of British troops for the suppression of internal disturbances' and would accordingly recommend the Assembly 'to request the Home Government to withdraw the whole of its land force', which would be replaced by a small, specially trained colonial force. The Home Government would then be requested to issue instructions to the Governor

---

[1] 10 Nov. 1864, *Votes and Proceedings*, Otago Provincial Council, Sess. xix, pp. 91–2.

[2] *Wellington Independent*, 1 Nov. 1864.

[3] *Taranaki Herald*, 26 Nov. 1864. The meeting was on the previous Saturday, 19 Nov.

[4] Stafford's Address to his Constituents: *Nelson Examiner*, 7 Jan. 1865.

to be guided entirely by his constitutional advisers except on matters directly concerning Imperial interests and the prerogatives of the Crown. There were two other important points. Sufficient land should be confiscated without delay to fulfil engagements to the military settlers and the seat of government should be at once removed from Auckland to Wellington, the site on Cook Straits recommended by an Australian Commission in terms of a resolution passed by the General Assembly in 1863.[1] Sir George Grey promised to 'aid to the best of his ability in carrying out' these propositions if the Assembly concurred in them and Weld met the Assembly on 24 November with a well-balanced team of Ministers—Sewell, Fitzherbert of Wellington, Atkinson of Taranaki, and Major Richardson of Otago.[2]

But when he laid his policy before the House, Weld ran into difficulties. Auckland, sore at losing its position as capital, felt it was being thrown to the wolves. Its alternative policy, placed by the Superintendent of the province, Robert Graham, before the Lower House and by Whitaker before the Upper, was a temporary separation of the islands, with Imperial control of Native affairs in the North. More serious for Weld was the split in his own following on the question of immediate withdrawal of the Imperial troops. Under pressure from a strong deputation comprising Stafford, Featherston, FitzGerald, and Jollie (member for Timaru) he toned down his resolution on this subject to read:

That the resources of New Zealand have been already heavily burdened and their development retarded by the great sacrifices that have been entailed upon the colony by the Native insurrection. That, nevertheless, the colony is resolved to make every further possible effort to place itself in a position of self-defence against internal aggression, with a view to accept the alternative indicated by the Home Government—namely, the withdrawal of Her Majesty's land forces at the earliest possible period consistent with the maintenance of Imperial interests and the safety of the colony.

After Graham's amendment had been rejected by 35 to 18, the amended resolutions were agreed to without a division.[3]

---

[1] Mr. Weld's Propositions (22 Nov.) in Grey to Cardwell (24 Nov. 1864) (No. 173), P.P., 1865, xxxvii [3455], 13–14. For the Assembly resolutions on moving the seat of government to 'some suitable locality in Cook's Straits' to be chosen by a Commission see *J.H.R.*, 1863, pp. 70–1, 86–8.

[2] W. B. D. Mantell joined the Government as Native Minister on 16 Dec.

[3] Weld moved the original Resolutions on Native Affairs (which were not

The session, though it lasted less than three weeks, also enabled Weld to carry through his policy of removing the seat of government to Wellington and to make a beginning of restoration of New Zealand's finances. 'It required no prophet', said Fitzherbert, the Colonial Treasurer, 'to foretell that it could not be long before we should be driven out of the fool's paradise that consists in the belief that war can be regarded as a profitable venture.'[1] The House authorized the raising of £1,000,000 by Treasury bills at 8 per cent, advanced the rate of interest of the remainder of the £3,000,000 loan from 5 to 6 per cent and increased the customs duties. At the same time it rejected the Imperial offer to guarantee £1,000,000 of the loan. The requirement that the territorial revenue should be included in the security 'would be incompatible with subsisting arrangements with the provinces and would prejudice the securities for provincial loans'.[2]

Weld's success, in short, was qualified. Stafford told his constituents, with a touch of malice, that 'the large majority of the House . . . could not accept the principal article of what has been termed the Canterbury programme, which it is understood was arranged at a comfortable dinner at the Christchurch Club, where some say it was even styled "the voice of the country".'[3] The War Office soon instructed General Cameron to make arrangements for sending home five of his ten regiments. But there was bound to be an awkward transitional period, especially with Cardwell pressing for payment of the increased contribution of £40 per head for the remaining troops.[4]

Still the adoption of a self-reliant policy led to an immediate improvement in the tone of the English press. FitzGerald, in a letter to Adderley which was printed in *The Times*, stated the two alternatives: 'The Home Government must absolutely

debated) on 30 Nov., Atkinson an amended series on 5 Dec.: *J.H.R.*, 1864. pp. 15, 26–7, 32–3. For the debates see *N.Z.P.D.*, 1864–6, pp. 92–100, 113–42 (House), 107–12 (Council). There is an interesting message on the whole matter from an Auckland correspondent in the *Nelson Examiner*, 15 Dec. 1864.

[1] *A.J.H.R.*, 1864, B No. 1A (Financial Statement). The Treasury bills were to tide over until the market for the loan was more favourable.

[2] *J.H.R.*, 1864, p. 58. See also Memo. of Sewell (3 Jan.) in Grey to Cardwell (6 Jan. 1865) (No. 7), P.P., 1865, xxxvii [3480], 7–8.

[3] *Nelson Examiner*, 7 Jan. 1865.

[4] Cardwell to Grey (27 Feb. 1865) (No. 16), P.P., 1865, xxxvii [3455], 22–3. He had warned Grey privately on 26 Jan. that Parliament would expect a reduction of the force in New Zealand.

abstain from any interference with the Colonial Government, and must leave us to work out the problem as best we may, or you must take the Northern Island into your own hands and govern it . . . as you like.' *The Times* naturally thought the nation would prefer self-reliance to 'the profitless offer of a mountainous island, with a war settled on it by way of mortgage'.[1] There was also a new note of friendliness in the parliamentary debates of 1865, not only from enthusiasts for self-government and self-defence like Mills and Adderley, but also from the humanitarian Buxton. He had now arrived at a more balanced view of the origins of the war.

The Natives were in dread of the colonists, and the colonists were in dread of an attack from the Natives. Some acts of violence inflamed the irritation and anxiety of men's minds, and thus by degrees both sides drifted into war without its being possible to say that either party had wished or intended to draw the sword, or could be fairly blamed for having at length taken up arms.

He was thus able to overcome his former hesitations about leaving the colonists to deal with the Maoris in their own way. Cardwell himself had been struck by the colonists' kindliness and generosity towards the Maoris in private communications.[2] 'The Imperial Government', said *The Times*, summing up this debate, 'no longer aims to destroy the Natives or to rescue them, or to improve them or Christianize them, or to see that they have their rights, or to see that they do not push their claims too far, or to obtain from them land or titles to land. It no longer aspires to either a humane or a vigorous policy. It leaves all this to the colonists.'[3] Unfortunately this was not true. There were still troops in the country, and the Imperial Government was not prepared to leave everything to the colonists.

The confiscation policy was still a great barrier to understanding. On 17 December—a week after the amnesty offer of October had expired—Sir George Grey, on the advice of his new Ministers,

---

[1] FitzGerald to Adderley (14 Nov. 1864) and leading article, *The Times*, 25 Jan. 1865. FitzGerald had written this letter on the eve of his departure for the General Assembly.

[2] House of Commons, 10 Mar. 1865, *Hansard*, 3rd Ser. clxxvii. 1481–1517.

[3] *The Times*, 13 Mar. 1865. Cf. also Gladstone to FitzGerald (20 Apr. 1865): 'The tone and spirit of your declarations, and if I understand them rightly of Mr. Weld's, are such as really to form an epoch in Colonial History', FitzGerald Papers (typescript), ii. 112.

had confiscated an area of about 1,200,000 acres in the Waikato and foreshadowed further confiscations in the country between Wanganui and New Plymouth and in the province of Taranaki. The land of Maoris who had adhered to the Queen would be secured to them and those in rebellion would be given land if they submitted at once.[1] Cardwell saw no reason to object to this proclamation on the score of justice, though the area was larger than he had expected; but he reminded the Governor that 'Her Majesty's Government will not consent to the confiscation of territory, however justly forfeited by rebellion, which would render necessary the employment of an Imperial force to protect the new occupiers against the former owners of the land.' He saw in the proposed confiscations in the Taranaki–Wanganui region the seeds of a new war; and if the confiscated territory had to be defended, it must be defended by a colonial force.[2]

The country between the Taranaki settlement and Wanganui had not yet been occupied. It was the seat of the troublesome Ngati Ruanui and their allies. The Whitaker–Fox Ministry had suggested its occupation by a line of blockhouses in the winter of 1864, after the conclusion of the Tauranga campaign: General Cameron, however, had maintained that the winter rains and the poor communications in the area made the Ministerial plan impracticable and Sir George Grey had sided with the General.[3] The idea of the new Ministry was to make a road through the region, with the help of friendly Maoris and troops who would otherwise be idle. There would be guard posts to cover the road parties, but they did not want 'the gigantic apparatus of an Imperial Army'. But Cameron said an army would be needed, and the Governor backed him. The Ministers then modified their proposals. They insisted that they did not want by any operations of theirs to hinder the reduction of Imperial forces in the colony. They proposed to raise a colonial force of 1,500 men and dispense with the troops as soon as the state of the country permitted. They also proposed to issue a proclamation confiscating a strip of land ten miles wide along the coast from Taranaki to Wanganui, so as

[1] Proclamation in Grey to Cardwell (7 Jan. 1865) (No. 13), P.P., 1865, xxxvii [3480], 17–18. Also *New Zealand Gazette*, 5 Jan. 1865.
[2] Cardwell to Grey (27 Mar. 1865) (No. 20), ibid., pp. 20–1.
[3] Grey to Cardwell (29 July 1864) (No. 109) with Enclosures, P.P., 1865, xxxvii [3425], 89–93.

not to hold undefined threats over the Maoris' heads. The Governor approved of this idea and sent it on to the General. The General declared a confiscation on so great a scale would mean a renewal of the war. The Ministers denied it, saying that the whole area was no more than 500,000 acres, from which the land held by friendly Maoris and grants to rebels making submission would be deducted. But Cameron would not budge. Thereupon Grey, 'frightened by the General's threats to represent the whole thing as a mere land-raid', withdrew his assent to the proclamation.[1]

Thus Cameron found himself committed to operations on terms satisfactory neither to him nor to the Ministers. He conducted them so half-heartedly that the Maoris nicknamed him the lame sea-gull—for he kept well away from the bush. He had a force of nearly 3,000 in the Wanganui district and over 1,500 in Taranaki; but after the first check at the newly formed camp at Nuku-maru on 25 January, he recommended the Governor to 'apply by the first opportunity for a reinforcement of at least two thousand men'.[2] He knew he would never get them. 'I suppose', he said in an uninhibited letter, 'that as long as a hundred men can be collected together we shall be required to carry on this miserable war for the profit and gratification of the colony.' He then went on to speak of the Waitotara, through which the road was being made. 'I have made inquiries about the purchase of the Waitotara block, and have reason to believe that it was a more iniquitous job than that of the Waitara block.... The Government at home ought to be made acquainted with the true history of the business.'[3] So far Grey had been going along with the General. Whatever his professions to Weld, he did not really believe in the self-reliant policy: he was reluctant to leave Auckland and in fact stayed on there for a time, much to the prejudice of Government business. He preferred the alternative of separation of the North, keeping the troops and with them the authority their presence gave him. But Cameron was losing control of his temper. He was continually finding fault with Ministers and with Colonel Warre,

[1] Journal of Sewell, 31 Dec. 1864, 6, 7, and 15 Jan. 1865; Memo. of Atkinson (5 Jan.) in Cameron to de Grey (7 Jan. 1865), P.P., 1865, xxxvii [3480], 23–4. But on 7 Jan. this Memo. was 'cancelled and withdrawn', ibid., p. 25.
[2] Cameron to Grey (29 Jan.) in Cameron to de Grey (Secretary of State for War) (6 Feb. 1865), P.P., 1865, xxxvii [3495], 17.
[3] Cameron to Grey (28 Jan.) in Grey to Cardwell (27 Apr. 1865) (No. 53) P.P., 1866, l [3601], 50. On the Waitotara purchase, see below, p. 328.

commanding in Taranaki, who had been willing to meet Ministers' wishes. He considered his force 'insufficient to attack so formidable a work as the Weraroa Pah', which Grey regarded as the key to any further advance along the coast.[1] The friendly Maoris of Wanganui wanted to attack it. Would this interfere with the General's operations, Grey inquired? Treating the Maoris' offer as 'mere bounce', Cameron asked if the Governor wanted him to attack the pa, notwithstanding the risk.[2] Grey had had enough. He moved over to the Ministers' side and disclosed to them the imputations Cameron had made against them. In a formidable memorandum, which was published in New Zealand and of course sent home, Weld made his counter-attack. He indignantly denied that the war was carried on for the profit or gratification of the colonists, but did not confine himself to denials.

Ministers cannot but admit that it would have been for 'the profit' of the Colonists if the Lieutenant-General Commanding had found it possible, by vigorous action, so to carry on the war in the headquarters of fanaticism as to have ensured the submission and then put a stop to a rebellion which has incalculably retarded the progress of New Zealand, which has depreciated the value of property throughout the country districts of the Northern Island and which has placed both islands of New Zealand in a state of the greatest financial embarrassment. . . . Ministers would further state that, though they believe that the repression and punishment of the rebel tribes of this district, and the opening and occupation of their country, is an absolute necessity, regard being had to the safety of the neighbouring settlements, and the peace of the Island generally, they nevertheless have advised His Excellency to oppose the demand for reinforcements from England, nor will they advise any operations to be undertaken which may involve the retention of Imperial forces in the Colony.[3]

Shortly afterwards Cameron let fly against the Ministers in a letter on the subject of the Weraroa pa: 'What is it to Mr. Mantell or to any other Colonial Minister how many British officers and soldiers we lose in any operation they recommend, so long as the policy they advocate is carried out?'[4] Even Grey was now becom-

---

[1] Cameron to Grey (28 Jan.), loc. cit.
[2] Cameron to Grey (17 Mar.) in Grey to Cardwell (27 Apr. 1865) (No. 53), P.P., 1866, 1 [3601], 56. This dispatch had 58 Enclosures.
[3] Memo. of Weld (20 Mar.) in Grey to Cardwell (1 Apr. 1865) (No. 36), ibid., pp. 9–10.
[4] Cameron to Grey (30 Mar.) in Grey to Cardwell (27 Apr. 1865) (No. 53), ibid., p. 61.

ing a convert to the view that the colony must rely on itself: 'If otherwise subjected to such imputations as those contained in some of your recent letters, it would be better that it should attempt to extricate itself from its difficulties by relying on its own resources, energies and courage.'[1] He also began, less wisely, to complain that the General was maligning him in confidential letters to the Secretary of State for War. Such conduct 'must irretrievably damage the position of the Governor and weaken his influence'.[2] Ministers for their part complained that Cameron's instructions and conduct of operations were nullifying the policy of self-reliance. 'It is clear', Weld declared, 'that so long as the Imperial forces remain in New Zealand the Colony is and will be precluded from exercising that control over measures essential to its defence and safety, the attainment of which was one of their main objects in assuming office.' Ministers could not be expected to recommend or the Assembly to authorize the payment of £40 per head for Imperial troops in such circumstances. When the Assembly met on 24 July, they proposed to tender their resignations 'because an irresponsible authority, unknown to the Constitution, is maintained, which only leaves to the Colony a nominal responsibility and a large money liability, whilst it effectually deprives it of self-government'.[3] The Governor told Ministers that he would resign too.[4]

This threatened crisis was averted. Weraroa pa had become in a curious way the key not only to the military but to the political and constitutional position in New Zealand. The militia and the Native Contingent which had now been formed at Wanganui were still itching to take it; and the Maori garrison at one stage offered to surrender it to them. But the commander of the troops, Brigadier-General Waddy, forbade the militia to take any action and when a force of regulars appeared on the scene the Maoris refused to surrender to the troops.[5] In Grey's view action against the pa was urgent. A small force at Pipiriki, higher up the Wanganui

[1] Grey to Cameron (1 May) in Grey to Cardwell (27 Apr. 1865) (No. 53), ibid., p. 66.
[2] Grey to Cardwell (23 May 1865) (No. 73), P.P., 1866, l [3601], 105–6.
[3] Memo. of Weld (12 July) in Grey to Cardwell (13 July 1865) (Separate), ibid., p. 130.
[4] J. C. Richmond to Mary Richmond (28 July 1865), *Richmond–Atkinson Papers*, ii. 171. Richmond had joined the Ministry on 26 June.
[5] J. C. Richmond to Mary Richmond (28 June 1865), ibid., p. 167.

river, was dangerously exposed. In mid July the Governor himself came to Wanganui and took charge of operations. On the night of 20–1 July a position commanding the pa was taken, with fifty prisoners, and at daylight of the 22nd, Grey's mixed colonial and Maori force occupied the pa, the garrison having escaped down the cliff during the night. The presence of the Imperial troops had given 'moral support' but they had not taken part in the action.[1] Four days later in Wellington, in high spirits at this exploit, Grey told the General Assembly he would 'now at once issue orders for the return to England of five regiments'.[2] Ministers had now withdrawn their resignations. There was a further reason for the *détente*. General Cameron in February had asked to be relieved, as his health had been impaired by his arduous and harassing duties, and on 1 August he sailed home, never to return.[3]

The damage done by the quarrel did not end with the General's departure. Cameron's officers supported him. The official journal of Deputy Quartermaster-General Gamble, whilst praising the capture of Weraroa pa, regretted that it afforded a 'further and more notable exemplification of the spirit which has of late manifested itself in depreciating the services, and acting independently of the opinion, counsel and authority of the Officer Commanding Her Majesty's Troops'.[4] The quarrel had in fact become 'a quarrel . . . between the whole army and the whole colony'.[5] It was highly embarrassing to the Imperial government. The General was technically in the wrong in neglecting to furnish the Governor with copies of his dispatches to the Secretary of State for War in accordance with a circular of 1859 which he had overlooked;[6] but the Governor, by siding with his Ministers, had lost whatever sympathy he had previously had in the Colonial Office. As Rogers minuted:

It is quite absurd to suppose that the General is not to write confidentially to his superiors. The true remedy is that Sir G. G. should

<hr/>

[1] Grey to Cardwell (19 July 1865, No. 92, and 22 July 1865, No. 94), P.P., 1866, l [3601], 149–52, 160.

[2] *N.Z.P.D.*, 1864–6, pp. 189–90.

[3] For a defence of Cameron see Dalton, *War and Politics in New Zealand*. do not find it convincing.

[4] Journal of Gamble (7 Aug. 1865), WO33/16, pp. 174–5.

[5] Minute of Fairfield (26 Apr. 1870), CO209/212.

[6] Cameron to War Office (14 Nov. 1865), WO33/16, p. 515.

write more confidentially to his superior and not confine himself to writing despatches which are all communicated to and therefore in a measure written for his ministers and the Colony.[1]

Cardwell was inclined to support the view of Grey and his ministers that a chastisement of the tribes between Taranaki and Wanganui was 'just in reference to the past and politic in reference to the future', always provided it did not delay the departure of the troops. But he deprecated the publication in the colonial newspapers of the minutes of Grey and his Ministers as tending to impair the influence of the commander of the troops with the New Zealand public.[2] This was in answer to Grey's long dispatch on the quarrel of 27 April, with its voluminous enclosures; but as the controversy continued Cardwell and Lord de Grey resolved not to permit it to continue an hour longer than they could help. On 23 September a telegram was sent to Major-General Sir H. K. Storks, an officer who had done distinguished service in charge of British military establishments in Turkey during the Crimean War and was now Governor of Malta, instructing him to hold himself in readiness to proceed to New Zealand. He was to supersede both Sir George Grey and Sir Duncan Cameron and to unite in his own person 'civil and military power for the purpose of carrying into effect the policy embodied in certain Resolutions adopted by the New Zealand Assembly in December last'.[3] With the news that General Cameron was on his way home and Grey had announced to the Assembly the impending withdrawal of the five regiments the emergency passed and Sir Henry Storks was available to take charge of another colony in crisis, Jamaica. But Grey continued his polemic against Cameron in dispatches home even after the General's departure; Cardwell accompanied his congratulations on the capture of Weraroa pa with a warning that the Governor's personal assumption of command raised some awkward questions; and friction continued on financial issues. The goodwill which had greeted the advent of the self-reliant Ministry was being frittered away.

[1] Minute of Rogers (n.d.) on Grey to Cardwell (23 May 1865) (No. 173), CO209/190.
[2] Cardwell to Grey (26 July 1865) (No. 50), P.P., 1866, l [3601], 218–20.
[3] Cardwell to Storks (26 Sept., Private, and 1 Oct. 1865), Cardwell Papers, P.R.O., 30/48. But as late as 12 Oct. Cardwell told Gladstone 'I have Storks on the leash, ready to be slipped': Gladstone Papers, B.M. Add. MS. 44118.

On one of the issues Cameron had raised, the Waitotara purchase, Grey and his Ministers made a successful defence. Cameron, in a dispatch to the Secretary of State for War—an extraordinary document to come from a military commander in a self-governing colony and only to be excused by the virtually complete cessation of personal intercourse between him and the colonial Government —gave a full account of the transaction as related to him by 'a very respectable settler'.[1] Cardwell thereupon very properly asked the Governor for a report. Grey had in fact referred the matter to his Ministers early in March—that is, before his open breach with Cameron—with a suggestion for an inquiry. Ministers expressed willingness to ask Sir William Martin to undertake this, but first wished the Governor to specify the source of his information.[2] Presumably at this stage he wished to shield Cameron and, when this motive no longer operated, he remained unaware who Cameron's informant was. Finally in 1866 Featherston, who as Superintendent of Wellington had completed the Waitotara purchase in May 1866, provided a definitive report showing that many of Cameron's allegations were based on misinformation.[3] Even to Rogers's suspicious mind his statement 'read . . . like an honest and conclusive one'; and on Rogers's advice Lord Carnarvon, who was then Secretary of State, closed the matter as 'one over which the Imperial Government now claims no control'.[4]

The question of the withdrawal of the five regiments was much more complex, involving as it did both the principle and the timing of self-reliance. In the first instance it was General Cameron himself who was most prominent in opposition. At a meeting of the Executive Council in January 1865 he 'derided the notion of withdrawing the troops from the Colony' and laughed at the Ministers' idea that a colonial force of 1,500 would suffice to

[1] Cameron to Secretary of State for War (7 July) in Cardwell to Grey (22 Sept. 1865) (No. 76), P.P., 1866, 1 [3601], 231. Cameron's informant was a Wanganui civil engineer, H. C. Field, who had a bee in his bonnet, the 'monstrous system of Government land purchase monopoly'. General (then Major) Greaves also was involved in this matter: his information was from a Maori source, Memoirs pp. 111–12.
[2] Memos. by the Governor (4 Mar.) and Weld (18 Mar.) in Grey to Cardwell (12 Dec. 1865) (No. 157), P.P., 1866, 1 [3695], 17–18.
[3] Featherston to Stafford (3 May) in Grey to Cardwell (8 May 1866) (No. 41) P.P., 1866, 1 [3750], 4–6.
[4] Cameron to Grey (21 Aug. 1866) (No. 13), ibid., p. 21. Minute of Rogers (n.d.) on Grey to Cardwell (8 May 1866) (No. 41), CO209/196.

replace them.[1] On the other hand, the Imperial Government stood firmly by its policy of withdrawing the regiments. It left the General some latitude with respect to the time of withdrawal, but looked forward to further reductions in due course and reminded the Governor that the troops 'must be considered as a reserve to come to the protection of any district against a sudden and unexpected danger, and not as the permanent force by which the safety of any district is to be secured in ordinary times'. Cardwell also insisted on the repayment of past advances from the Imperial Treasury and on the stipulated contribution in future towards the cost of the force retained.[2] The Weld Ministry met the first point by handing over debentures for £500,000 with a view to the adjustment of the debt; but in the atmosphere generated by the quarrel with Cameron, the discretion left to him seemed to make responsible government a farce. 'Practically in leaving to the General the decision of the Military Policy', Sewell writes, 'the Government of the Colony is left with him.'[3] Grey taunted Cameron with saying that he could afford to send away five regiments but could not spare enough men to expel two or three hundred Maoris from Weraroa pa.[4] The controversy however, fortified the Ministry in its belief that the Colony must take care of itself and get rid of the General and the troops. 'They are paralysing all our efforts; emboldening the Natives by their inaction and wasting our resources by an extravagant and absolutely profitless expenditure', wrote Sewell.[5] This was the policy with which they met the Assembly on 26 July.

The complementary policy was the organization of a colonial force. One had been raised under the Colonial Defence Force Act 1862 and had done good service in the Waikato campaign; and in Major G. S. Whitmore, who had for a time been Cameron's Military Secretary, it had an able Commandant. But this force seems to have lost its identity in the military settlement scheme. The new proposal was to form an armed constabulary of 1,350 Europeans, enlisted if possible from among the regular regiments, and 150 Maoris. The cost was estimated by Weld at £187,000

[1] Journal of Sewell (14 Jan. 1865).
[2] Cardwell to Grey (27 Mar. 1865) (No. 20), P.P., 1865, xxxvii [3480], 21–2.
[3] Journal of Sewell (21 June 1865).
[4] Grey to Cameron (19 May) in Grey to Cardwell (13 July 1865) (No. 89), P.P., 1866, l [3601], 136.
[5] Journal of Sewell (21 June 1865).

per annum as against the expenditure of nearly £60,000 a month during the Wanganui–Taranaki campaign.[1] No appropriation had been made for the purpose during the short session of 1864. Ministers had hoped that 'a short, quick and decisive campaign would finish everything in a few weeks' and give them a breathing space. Besides, money was short and, as Atkinson explained to the House, 'We have not pressed for the enlistment of permanent forces, because we have at the present time on pay about 2200 men whom we cannot get rid of until we get land for them, principally in Auckland.'[2] But the Assembly afforded Auckland members another opportunity of voicing their disbelief in self-reliance and arguing that the proposed colonial force would be both too expensive and too small. Stafford also expressed scepticism about the departure of the troops.[3] He probably knew that Grey, unlike his Ministers, still wanted to keep them.

On 2 September, on the advice of Ministers, Grey issued two proclamations. In one of them the area to be confiscated from Taranaki to the Wanganui river was for the first time defined. In the other the Governor announced that 'the war which commenced at Oakura is at end'. Weld explained in a memorandum that Ministers did not aim at expelling any part of the tribes who now or lately occupied the confiscated land. 'Their purpose is to apportion without delay ample allowances of land to all rebels who come in within a reasonable time, and to give back to the loyal inhabitants as nearly as possible the exact land they are entitled [to].' Commissioners would be sent forthwith into the Taranaki–Wanganui country and into the Waikato to carry out this policy. The peace proclamation also announced that 'the Governor is about to call a meeting of all the great chiefs to consult with his Government as to the best means whereby the Maori people may be represented in the General Assembly, so that they may henceforth help to make the laws which they are called upon to obey'.[4] In the Waikato, in fact, a real pacification appeared to be at hand.

[1] Memo. of Weld (20 Mar.) in Grey to Cardwell (1 Apr. 1865) (No. 37), P.P., 1866, l [3601], 11–13. The question of New Zealand military forces during the Maori wars is much in need of detailed study.
[2] House of Representatives, 18 Aug. 1865, N.Z.P.D., 1864–6, pp. 327–32. On Weld's hopes see his Notes on New Zealand Affairs, p. 41.
[3] Address in Reply debate, H.R., 1 Aug. 1865, loc. cit., pp. 209–29.
[4] N.Z. Gazette, 2 Sept. 1865. Memo. of Weld (2 Sept. 1865), Grey Coll., Auckland. Notes on New Zealand Affairs, pp. 27 ff.

On 27 May Wiremu Tamihana had made his submission to Brigadier Carey and signed a document in the name of the King and himself which declared that 'We consent that the laws of the Queen be laws for the King, to be a protection to us all for ever and ever.'[1] Matutaera remained at Hangatiki and made no submission on his own behalf, but both he and Rewi were quiescent. On the other hand, a Maori messenger carrying the proclamation was killed between Weraroa and Patea on 22 September and shortly afterwards a European interpreter was killed.

If the chiefs were submitting, in short, the prophets and fanatics were not. The headquarters of the fanatical new religion of *Pai marire* or Hauhauism (from the short barking cry uttered by its adherents) had survived the loss of one of its leaders at the Sentry Hill redoubt and another in battle with the friendlies at Moturoa island on the Wanganui River. It spread alarmingly along the east coast and into the Bay of Plenty, where by Christmas 1864 it was endangering the recently concluded Tauranga peace. The tenets of the new religion were a curious mixture of Christian beliefs and the characteristics of the 'cargo cult', a belief that its adherents would be given power to drive the whole European population out of New Zealand and that 'immediately the Europeans are destroyed and driven away men will be sent from heaven to teach the Maori all the arts and sciences now known by Europeans'.[2] An Italian priest, from conversations with missionary priests and extensive reading, argued that it was 'the direct result of the teaching of the Protestant missions' with their teaching of the individual's right to interpret the Bible.[3] It was, of course, true that the wars had dealt heavy blows to Maori Christianity. Despite his courageous championship of the Maoris at the time of the Taranaki war, Bishop Selwyn's service with the troops as chaplain in the Waikato campaign was misinterpreted. In the mind of the Maoris those who were not with them in this crisis were against them. The lengths to which the fanatics were prepared to go were shown by the hanging of a devoted German missionary, the Revd. C. S. Völkner, close by his own church at Opotiki on 2 March

[1] Carey to Cameron (28 May) in Grey to Cardwell (30 May 1865) (No. 76), P.P., 1866, 1 [3601], 108–9.
[2] J. White (R.M., Whanganui) to Colonial Secretary (29 Apr.) in Grey to Newcastle (26 May 1864) (No. 80), P.P., 1865, xxxvii [3425], 23.
[3] P. Ottavio Barsanti, *I Protestanti tra i selvaggi della Nuova Zelanda ossia Storia del Pai Marire* (Turin, 1868).

1865. This was accompanied by a cannibalistic orgy: his head was cut off, his body thrown to the dogs, his brains were eaten, and his eyes were swallowed by Kereopa, one of the *tius* or Hauhau emissaries. According to his fellow-missionary Grace, who was held prisoner but afterwards rescued, Völkner was charged with 'going to Auckland as a spy for Government'—a charge which has found some credence but is hard to accept.[1] The murder produced a revulsion of feeling among some at least of the Ngati Awa and Ngati Porou. The friendly elements in the East Coast tribes were encouraged by visits of warships until a punitive expedition of the colonial forces, with Maori assistance, turned the scale against the Hauhaus among the Ngati Porou and another landed in September at Opotiki and drove the Hauhaus back into the hills.

In spite of the Hauhau propaganda, pacification had proceeded far enough for the Native Land Court foreshadowed by the Act of 1862 to be brought into operation. As Sir William Martin said in a paper 'on the best mode of introducing and working the Native lands Act', the political aspects of the problem were now giving place to the administrative and social aspects.[2] A new Native Lands Bill introduced by FitzGerald, who had just replaced Mantell as Native Minister, provided that the Court should consist of a Chief Judge, other judges and Maori assessors to be appointed from time to time. The purchase of Native lands with certificates of title was still permissible, but the Court might recommend restrictions on alienability. In Dr. Sorrenson's view 'it seems likely that the main reason for the new Act was to simplify the procedure of the Native Land Court and of direct purchase'.[3] But FitzGerald seems miscast as the inaugurator of a policy of direct purchase; and though the Weld Ministry fell before the

[1] Grey to Cardwell (6 Apr. 1865, No. 42, and 27 Apr. 1865, No. 55) with Enclosures, P.P., 1866, 1 [3601], 20 ff., 74 ff. *Tiu* = Jew. As the other *tiu*, Patara, said to the trader Levy: 'The Jews were once a grand people, but were now reduced to a very small one, through the persecutions they had gone through—the Maoris believing themselves to be undergoing the same'; ibid., p. 28. Kereopa was executed after trial in 1871.

[2] Enclosure (30 June 1865) in Grey to Cardwell (2 Feb. 1866) (No. 20), P.P., 1866, 1 [3695], 81–90.

[3] M. P. K. Sorrenson, 'The Purchase of Maori Lands, 1865–1892' (Univ. of Auckland, M.A. thesis, 1955), p. 22. The Act (No. 71 of 1865) 'created a good deal of satisfaction among the Northern Maoris' but worked harshly on them elsewhere.

Bill passed its final stages, it was Weld who appointed Fenton, the draftsman of the Bill, as Chief Judge of the Native Land Court.

The Weld Ministry also attacked the question of Maori representation. The difficulties were obvious. If a few chiefs were appointed to the Legislative Council, others would take offence: if too many were appointed, the Council itself would take offence. If the Maoris had separate representation in the House, other members might feel less responsible for Maori affairs. If they were given the franchise in existing electoral districts, the franchise itself would have to be reconsidered.[1] The Government at first leant in that direction but finally decided to invite a number of chiefs to Wellington and provide for a Commission, part European but predominantly Maori, to consider the problem. The Commission was to report on the most expedient mode of defining an electoral franchise, pending the conversion of customary into Crown titles, upon persons of Native race and 'generally as to the most advisable mode in which persons of the Native race may be admitted to the practical exercise and enjoyment of equal political rights with others of Her Majesty's subjects'.[2] FitzGerald's appointment as Native Minister shows it was no mere window-dressing. No immediate good might come but, as J. C. Richmond told the Council:

The present movement was a corollary of the Native Lands Act. The two were essentially the abandonment of the system of protectorate, or dry-nursing. The Colonial and Home Governments confessed alike that they had failed. They were throwing the Maori on to the world to take his lot with other subjects, and they must remove all disabilities.[3]

Weld and his colleagues had shown a very different temper from their predecessors and given new meaning to the idea of the unity of the colony. The Auckland Provincial Council had petitioned the Queen to separate the province from the South 'by itself, or with such other portions of the North Island as may be deemed expedient', the Imperial Government exercising control over Native affairs; and Sir George Grey told Cardwell that in his opinion 'unless some such arrangement . . . is carried out, it

[1] Journal of Sewell, 4 June 1865.
[2] Native Commission Act 1865 (No. 12,) P.P., 1866, l [3695], 144.
[3] Legislative Council, 1 Aug. 1865, N.Z.P.D., 1864–6, p. 206.

will be impossible to bring to a satisfactory termination the difficulties prevailing in this country'.[1] But in spite of the known sympathies of the Governor and before news had arrived of the rejection of the petition, Weld defeated, by 31 to 17, a motion of Russell, supported by the Auckland members and five Otago separationists, in favour of a separation of the islands and the temporary appointment of a Deputy-Governor for the province of Auckland.[2]

The vulnerable point of the Ministry was its finance. It had inherited a bad financial situation: the military settlement scheme had produced some good military material but few successful settlers and large sums had been spent without ending, still less paying for, the war. Grey on its behalf had asked the Imperial Government for pecuniary aid 'either by covering the remainder of the three million loan by Imperial guarantee or by making to the Colony an annual grant in aid of the extraordinary expenditure for the next four or five years'. He did not conceal his own opinion that an additional million, or even two, beyond the million still left of the loan, would be needed to set New Zealand on its feet.[3] Cardwell's answer was a firm no. Parliament would never listen to such a proposal.

I should be told that since 1 April 1863 the sums charged upon the Imperial Treasury for the service of New Zealand had fallen very little short, if at all, of two millions of money; that a loan, which at the request of the then Colonial Treasurer the Imperial Parliament had consented to guarantee had been refused by the Colony; but that in contending for that guarantee I had laid before the House of Commons on behalf of the Colony the statement of a balance of receipts over expenditure, which was scarcely consistent with my present application for Imperial aid on the score of a deficient colonial exchequer. I should be reminded that, in stating that balance, I had not included the portions of land confiscated in this war which would be available for sale, nor for the increasing revenue to be derived from customs or excise on articles consumed by the new settlers on those portions of the confiscated lands which might be devoted to purposes of military settlement. I should be told, I fear with irresistible force, that I had failed to establish a sufficient case for that which must always be regarded as

---

[1] Grey to Cardwell (5 Jan. 1865) (No. 3) with Enclosures, P.P., 1865, xxxvii [3480], 5 ff.
[2] J.H.R., 1865, pp. 113–14, 122.
[3] Grey to Cardwell (8 Apr. 1865) (No. 49), P.P., 1866, l (3601), 42–3.

in the highest degree exceptional, viz. a vote of the Imperial Parliament in aid of the expenditure of an established and in the main a flourishing and advancing colony.[1]

Grey's suggestion that a guarantee would cost the Imperial Exchequer nothing was ignored. Cardwell had shown himself more familiar with Domett's optimistic forecasts of 1863 than with the realities of 1865. The sale of confiscated lands to date had only realized £22,500. 'What would we not give', wrote Sewell, 'to be well quit of this *damnosa haereditas*, part of that legacy of evil left to us by the late Government?'[2] A letter of Gladstone to Lord Lyttelton, a week before this dispatch was sent, adds an interesting footnote to it.

It seems to me that if Mr. Sewell's tone represents that of the New Zealand colonists in general, they are too much afraid of pecuniary difficulty. They seem to think that paying 8 per cent. (and what if it were 10 or 12) for three or five or some small number of years is too much for an Englishman to face. Why, what are we to say of the Italian Government which is undertaking to pay 8 per cent. upon its funded debt, or of the fact that England herself in the Revolutionary war borrowed scores of millions at from 6 to 7 per cent., with condition of never redeeming except at £100 the obligation which brought only *48 or 50.*[3]

The old grievance of advances from the commissariat chest for militia pay and rations continued to rankle. 'I incline to think', wrote Gladstone, 'that a governor with a key to our chest in his hand, and with responsible ministers around him, is in an utterly false position, and the greatest charity to him so far as orders on paper are concerned is to take away the key.'[4] Cardwell thought it questionable policy to 'screw down a safety valve which your printed regulations leave unscrewed'; but he once again instructed

---

[1] Cardwell to Grey (26 July 1865) (No. 50), ibid., pp. 219–20. Sewell had some reason to complain of the 'cold, sneering, unsympathetic spirit' of this dispatch, which also dealt with the Grey–Cameron quarrel—an unfortunate concatenation for New Zealand, Journal of Sewell, 8 Oct. 1865.

[2] Journal of Sewell, 27 Mar. 1865. But the figure on sales (£22,469) was given by Fitzherbert in his Budget: *A.J.H.R.*, 1865, B No. 1A.

[3] Gladstone to Lyttelton (19 July 1865), Turnbull Library. Gladstone may have been shown Sewell's journal, which he 'sent home for circulation'.

[4] Gladstone to Cardwell (9 Oct. 1865), Gladstone Papers: B.M. Add. MS. 44535.

Grey to discontinue resort to the chest.[1] He and Gladstone, in short, gave Ministers little credit for the honesty of their intentions and refused to believe that New Zealand could not extricate itself from its financial difficulties by a united effort. So did General Cameron, who in a last fling before his departure remarked that 'the Colony appears to have experienced no difficulty in raising funds to remove the seat of Government from Auckland to Wellington, to purchase new Government buildings, Government Houses, residences for Ministers, increasing the number of Ministers and augmenting their salaries, paying large sums as compensation to Taranaki settlers, and entering into a costly new postal service to England in addition to the existing one'—an excursion into politics which provoked a sharp Ministerial retort.[2]

But the unity of New Zealand was an aspiration rather than a fact. It was governed provincially, and many of the provinces were in difficulties and Auckland in open revolt. With only £600,000 of the loan left and much of that committed, with no help from the Imperial Government and Treasury pressure still being applied, the Ministry had no choice but to find the finances for its colonial force from current revenue. Fitzherbert proposed to readjust charges between the General Government and the provinces, taking away their treasured rights to three-eighths of the customs revenue, to permit the sale below par of the balance of the loan, and to raise £75,000 by stamp duties.[3] The provinces were in fact being asked to sacrifice something of their financial independence. A direct attempt to defeat the Budget on this ground was unsuccessful. But as the session wore on, Weld fell ill and lost his grip. 'He alone could hold the party together,' wrote his colleague Richmond, 'and his forced and frequent absences from the House caused supporters to become languid and work to become disorganized.'[4] Some members from Fitzherbert's own province of Wellington began to waver. 'Wellington

---

[1] Treasury to Colonial Office (25 July) in Cardwell to Grey (26 July 1865) (No. 54), P.P., 1866, l [3601], 221. Cardwell to Gladstone (12 Oct. 1865), B.M. Add. MS. 44118.

[2] Memos. of Cameron (26 July) and Weld (12 Aug.) in Grey to Cardwell (14 Aug. 1865) (No. 108), [3601], 177–80.

[3] Financial Statement (30 Aug. 1865), A.J.H.R., 1865; B No. 1A. Crosbie Ward defended his defection from Weld on the ground that stamp duties would not in any case raise enough (to Selfe, 15 Mar. 1866), Selfe Papers.

[4] J. C. Richmond to Mary Richmond (19 Oct. 1865), Richmond–Atkinson Papers, ii, 191.

had got all it wanted,' said the *Press* sarcastically; 'the seat of government was removed and the Panama contract settled.'[1] On 11 October Julius Vogel, an able, ambitious young Otago member, moved that the revenue from the stamp duties should be placed on the same footing as the customs and distributed in part to the provinces.[2] The Ministry was saved from defeat by the Speaker's casting vote, but the ailing Weld had had enough. He resigned and advised the Governor to send for Stafford who had taken no part in the division but had never wholeheartedly supported the Ministry and had a reputation as a tried and economical administrator.

The self-reliant policy had been an intelligent response to carping criticism in England and separationist propaganda in New Zealand. But such a revolution in colonial habits of thought and action could not be brought about by one touch of an enchanter's wand, and Weld was no spell-binder. His ideas, or perhaps one should say rather the ideas of FitzGerald and of Godley before him, commanded respect in England; but his transparent honesty was obscured by the distrusted figure of Grey, with whom he co-operated only too loyally. Cameron's petulant procrastination blurred the picture further. An able but unimaginative Secretary of State could not perceive the advantage of a generous gesture of temporary aid to see this Ministry, which had adopted the policy of self-reliance, so long preached at home, through the inevitable difficulties of the transition. It is no doubt also true that the self-reliant policy was, as Stafford said, the work of a few leaders rather than the voice of the country. But the country had responded to this act of national leadership. It was only when the one trusted leader lost his grip that the rank and file of the House relapsed into their usual provincial jealousies and electoral preoccupations and refused the new taxation that was needed to make self-reliance a reality.

[1] *Press*, 17 Oct. 1865. Two of the three members in question got into difficulties with their constituents; the third declared that he did not know an important division was pending (he was absent on private business) and would have voted with the Government, *Wellington Independent*, 14–17 Oct. 1865.

[2] *J.H.R.*, 1865, p. 223.

# XI

## THE WITHDRAWAL OF THE TROOPS

WELD'S resignation, Sewell tells us, had been partly based on a calculation of chances.

> We anticipated one of two results. Either that Stafford would be able to form a presentable Government, and do battle with us fairly upon the principles of a Policy adverse to our own. If successful, the new Government would be fairly entitled to its position. If, however, upon testing the House it appeared that Stafford could not form such a Government with such a Policy, then the result would be that we should return to office with the certainty of carrying our measures.[1]

The calculation went astray. Stafford could not persuade any of the leading men to join him. His colleagues, Colonels Haultain (Auckland) and A. H. Russell (Hawke's Bay), and James Paterson, an Otago merchant, were none of them men of weight. But Sir George Grey, despite his professions of regret at parting from the Weld Ministry, spiked Weld's guns by promising Stafford a dissolution, if necessary without supply. The bond of union between Sir George Grey, Stafford and his colleagues, and the Auckland members who provided the solid core of their supporters was a common opposition to the withdrawal of the Imperial troops. Stafford's boasted economy was false economy—saving £25,000 in the Native Department, reducing the colonial forces, above all avoiding payment for the troops. Weld and his colleagues knew such a policy would not get Imperial approval: 'by return of mail', wrote Sewell, 'he will receive such a stunning rebuke from the Home Government as will effectually put that Policy to silence.'[2] Stafford's friends did not agree: 'they say the Home Government cannot help itself, and Sir George Grey is so powerful at home that it is idle to think of resisting him.'[3] This was a delusion. Sir George Grey's prickliness and his undignified quarrels, first with Whitaker

---

[1] Journal of Sewell, 21 Oct. 1865.
[2] Ibid., 15 Oct. 1865. Cf. also Weld to Gore Browne (15 Jan. 1866), Gore Browne Papers 1/3.
[3] Journal of Sewell, 21 Oct. 1865.

and Fox and then with General Cameron, had ruined his credit in England and brought him to the brink of recall. But Sewell for his part underrated the wily gamesmanship of Grey and Stafford. Stafford's policy was to avoid if possible any head-on collision with the Imperial Government and not to disavow self-reliance, in the hope, no doubt, that the war would peter out and thus resolve the difficulty. On taking office, he expressed himself as 'entirely contented with the position as we now find it'—that is to say, one regiment on the point of embarking and orders issued for the immediate dispatch of four more. 'We do not propose', he added, 'to tender to His Excellency any advice adverse or in opposition to the instructions of the Imperial authorities.'[1] When the Legislative Council passed a motion regretting that the previous Assembly's resolutions in favour of the speedy withdrawal of the Imperial troops had not been carried into effect, all Stafford asked of the House was retrospective approval of the Governor's protest against General Cameron's proposal to remove some of the troops in the previous May.[2]

Meanwhile Cardwell was doing his best to keep the colony up to the mark. He warned Grey privately on 25 August that it was the Government's intention to let no troops remain except on the terms of the Loan Act 1864.[3] In response to Grey's speech opening the Assembly, he sent instructions to place at the disposal of the General Commanding, 'with a view to their early removal from New Zealand', all troops for whom no appropriation on the new terms had been made.[4] A month later, on receipt of the peace proclamation and of Fitzherbert's Financial Statement making no provision for the £40 capitation charge, the Secretary of State announced the Government's decision to reduce the regular force in New Zealand at once 'to a strength not exceeding three battalions of infantry and one battery of artillery'. Even this would not remain unless Ministers undertook to propose the required capitation charge to the Assembly. The Governor was also to see to it that the troops were concentrated and not left in distant and isolated posts.[5] On the surface, everything was going smoothly.

[1] Ministerial Statement (19 Oct.) in Grey to Cardwell (10 Nov. 1865) (No. 135), P.P., 1866, l [3695], 2.
[2] J.L.C., 1865, p. 124; J.H.R., 1865, pp. 288–9.
[3] Cardwell to Grey (25 Aug. 1865) (Private), Grey Coll., Auckland.
[4] Cardwell to Grey (26 Oct. 1865) (No. 86), P.P., 1866, l [3601], p. 252.
[5] Cardwell to Grey (27 Nov. 1865) (No. 97), ibid., p. 259.

Grey immediately notified Cardwell that he was complying with his instructions: 'Nothing remains for me but to place at the disposal of General Chute Her Majesty's forces in New Zealand with a view to their early removal': but he would advise him only to allow one regiment to leave every two months.[1]

The advent of the 'vigorous, downright' General Chute gave a much needed fillip to the morale of the troops. We can well believe the words of Colonel Haultain, a former regular officer himself, when he wrote to Gore Browne: 'General Cameron's tactics, prompted by hostility to the Governor and to the Colonists, had completely demoralized the troops and they could not be brought to face the bush if it was suspected that Maoris were in it.'[2] In the early weeks of 1866, after taking a couple of pas, Chute, accompanied by Dr. Featherston, led a force right through to New Plymouth by 'the difficult, almost unknown Maori trail through the dense forest on the east side of Mount Egmont' and back round the mountain to Patea.[3] As Featherston said in an election speech:

> That General Cameron has wasted two millions of the Colony's money is proved beyond a doubt by General Chute's having achieved, with a flying column of some three hundred regulars, and about the same number of Colonial forces, pakeha and Maori, what General Cameron, with some five or six thousand men, dared never even to attempt.[4]

There were, it is true, some repercussions later. The expedition put out of court Weld's plan of sending Parris as a Commissioner to conciliate and settle the Ngati Ruanui and their neighbours; Chute did not discriminate very carefully between hostile and friendly Maoris; and the Native Contingent and *kupapas* had a short way with tribal enemies.[5] When military settlers occupied

---

[1] Grey to Cardwell (13 Jan. 1866) (No. 13), P.P., 1866, l [3695], 73. In No. 6 of 8 Jan. he had forwarded a long memo. of Stafford arguing that the increased contribution was unreasonable in view of the strain the long and costly war imposed, ibid., pp. 57–61.

[2] Haultain to Gore Browne (22 Jan. 1866), Gore Browne Papers 1/3.

[3] J. Cowan, *The New Zealand Wars* (reprinted, Wellington, 1956), vol. ii, ch. 6.

[4] Quoted by A. Saunders, *History of New Zealand*, ii. 192.

[5] Weld wrote in 1869: 'I should have resigned rather than permitted it', *Notes on New Zealand Affairs*, p. 48. On *kupapas*, Maori guerrillas distinct from the Native Contingent, see R. I. M. Burnett in *Journal of the Polynesian Society*, lxxiv (1965), 227–30.

the land later on, the embers of disaffection were found to be still smouldering.

It now seemed possible to carry the withdrawal of the troops a stage further. General Chute was instructed, unless provision had been made for payment of the capitation charge, to send away every soldier, whether infantry or artillery, except for one regiment, which would be retained on condition that the colony devoted £50,000 a year to Native purposes; and he was reminded that this should not be left in isolated posts.[1] Meanwhile, however, new friction had arisen between the Governor and the military authorities. In a letter to his brother, a clergyman, Colonel Weare, commanding the 50th Regiment, made some serious accusations against the colonial authorities in connection with the shooting of certain Maori prisoners. 'Since the leaving of Sir Duncan,' he alleged, 'the true sentiments of the governor and his government have come out towards the Maoris in their urging General Chute to all these atrocities of killing and no prisoners.'[2] His brother sent this letter to the Colonial Office, which in accordance with the recognized procedure forwarded it to Sir George Grey. Exasperated beyond endurance, Grey burst out into bitter complaint of this defamation of Governor and colonists by military officers, which prejudiced people in England against the colony and its Government.

The result of this system was, for the Empire, great and unnecessary loss of life and expenditure of money; for the Colony almost ruin. For those who pursued it a large participation in honours and rewards; for myself, repeated censures, at least implied, and an absence for years of that public sympathy, from those in authority, so requisite to enable a man to struggle with cheerfulness and hope against great difficulties.[3]

He tried to turn the charge of condoning brutality against Chute, with whom he was already at odds over his refusal to transfer his headquarters to Wellington. It was impossible for him to make arrangements for reducing the posts, returning the troops, and cutting down the military expenditure without frequent personal communications. Pending such discussions, he asked the General

---

[1] Cardwell to Grey (25 June 1866) (No. 68), P.P., 1866, l [3695], 141.
[2] H. E. Weare to the Revd. T. W. Weare (13 Jan. 1866) in Cardwell to Grey (26 Apr. 1866) (Confidential), P.P., 1867–8, xlviii [4019], 1.
[3] Grey to Cardwell (30 June 1866) (Separate), P.P., 1867–8, xlviii [4019], 10.

to suspend execution of his orders to reduce the forces and stop the issue of rations to local levies.[1] He urged the Imperial authorities to withdraw their orders to the General 'to reside at Auckland, fifteen days' distance . . . from myself and from the seat of the disturbances which are again breaking out'.[2] But even after the egregious Colonel Weare had withdrawn his remarks with abject apologies and Lord Carnarvon had succeeded Cardwell as Secretary of State, the tone of Grey's dispatches could not pass unnoticed.

It is wholly impossible [wrote Carnarvon] that the government of the Colonies can be carried on if such language as you have addressed to my predecessor is to be applied on such grounds as you have alleged, by an officer representing Her Majesty . . . to the Minister whose function it is to communicate to him Her Majesty's commands.[3]

Grey accepted this rebuke and begged that, if the language was deemed improper, he might be allowed to withdraw it and offer 'the fullest and most unreserved apology'.[4] But the Colonial Office had come to the conclusion that Grey was unjustifiably delaying the withdrawal of the troops and Carnarvon took note of his remark 'that if all Her Majesty's troops are withdrawn from the outposts to the chief towns they would be entirely useless to the Colony'.

It is not with the object of being useful that they are now in New Zealand. The Colony has long since adopted the duty of protecting itself and Her Majesty's troops are no longer there for the purpose of protecting it, but merely remain, or ought merely to remain in default of the transports necessary for sending them away.

The Governor had also been remiss in the matter of information: most of it had come in letters transmitted through the War Office. The only way of avoiding further misconceptions and delays was to place the removal arrangements under the exclusive control of General Chute. He would not require the Governor's authority to move the troops. It would rest with the colonial Government to face the consequences of the withdrawal. It was, after all, an

[1] Grey to Chute (10 May) in Carnarvon to Grey (27 Aug. 1866) (No. 16) P.P., 1866, 1 [3750], 23.
[2] Grey to Carnarvon (15 Oct. 1866) (No. 104), P.P., 1867, xlix [3833], 10. A colonial trooper had recently been murdered at Ketemarae, South Taranaki.
[3] Carnarvon to Grey (1 Nov. 1866) (No. 41), P.P., 1867–8, xlvii [4019], 3–5.
[4] Grey to Carnarvon (12 Jan. 1867) (No. 11), ibid., pp. 16–19.

agreed policy, 'on the faith of which Her Majesty's Government has entirely ceased to interfere with their native policy'. There was one exception, however, a single regiment might still be retained if the vote of £50,000 for Native purposes was continued. But this regiment must be concentrated in accessible places with adequate barrack accommodation and not dispersed or employed virtually as a frontier police.[1] A dispatch a month later reinforced this one. Lord Carnarvon complained that Sir George Grey's own dispatches showed 'how little you recognize any continued responsibility to the Imperial Government for the conduct of the war': the Imperial authorities were left to learn from the newspapers of actions on the west coast and in Hawke's Bay.[2]

The Office thought that rebukes such as this, coming so soon after the withdrawal of control of the troops, might lead Sir George Grey to resign.[3] But, playing up to his new role of defender of the colony against Imperial criticisms, he did not. He and Stafford were hand in glove; and though a motion of no confidence in the Stafford Ministry was carried on 15 August 1866, the outcome was the formation of a much stronger Ministry, including Weld's former colleagues, Fitzherbert, Richardson, and J. C. Richmond, under the same head.[4] With this new Ministry at his back, Grey could plausibly claim to be doing his best to implement the self-reliant policy and defended himself stoutly. He laid the blame for the lack of information on Chute's insistence on residing at Auckland.

I feel keenly the disgrace to which your Lordship has seen fit to subject me, in requiring me virtually to serve under my junior officer, by ordering me to give him every facility in carrying out the duties the performance of which Her Majesty entrusted to me, and which for so long a series of years I have carried out to Her Majesty's satisfaction;

---

[1] Carnarvon to Grey (1 Dec. 1866) (No. 49), P.P., 1867, xlix [3833], 44–6. The last sentence no doubt referred to a report of the Wellington correspondent of *The Times* that it was proposed to station this regiment at Taupo: *The Times*, 30 Oct. 1866.

[2] Carnarvon to Grey (28 Dec. 1866) (No. 56), P.P., 1867, xlix [3833], 50–1. The two engagements, at Pungarehu and Omarunui, had been reported in the *N.Z. Gazette* on 11 and 26 Oct. Grey had reported the second on 3 Nov. ([3833], p. 19) but not the first, though he was in this district from 24 Oct. to 10 Nov.

[3] Minute of Rogers (25 Mar.) on Grey to Carnarvon (12 Jan. 1867) (No. 11), CO209/200.

[4] *J.H.R.*, 1866, pp. 90–2; *N.Z.P.D.*, 1864–6, pp. 889–95.

but it will be my pride to try to serve Her Majesty as carefully in disgrace as in prosperity.

Only three regiments and a wing of a fourth (and that against his wish) remained;[1] and this great reduction had been 'so effected, in a country still in rebellion in parts, that no injury has accrued to Her Majesty's possessions or subjects'. Since General Chute was in command of the colonial as well as the regular forces, he could not move these except by Chute's orders. It was to these complications and Chute's reluctance to come to Wellington that he attributed any delays. He predicted that the colonial Government would refuse the terms for keeping the last regiment:

> I do not doubt from the present state of feeling in this country that the General Assembly will continue to provide large funds for the native race; but I think the Local Government will argue, that if a regiment is retained here, it is quite uncertain where the officer in command may choose to reside . . .; and that as he will have the command of the local forces as well as of the regular forces . . . the Local Government may, to a certain extent, lose its control over the forces it raises and pays, and thus not have the means of providing for the safety of portions of the Colony on any sudden emergency.[2]

This forecast was verified a month later in a memorandum of Stafford which Grey duly sent home:

> Ministers . . . decline to accede to the proposed conditions after having been informed by Lord Carnarvon that the Imperial troops are not to be useful to the Colony. Ministers are indeed unable to conceive on what grounds Lord Carnarvon could have supposed that after such an intimation the Colony would consent to agree to conditions, or to impose on itself obligations in connection with a force which would occupy the position of the force of a foreign power, rather than that of one having interests to guard and duties to perform common to the Empire of which New Zealand is a part.[3]

There was one difficulty which Stafford did not mention in his minute or Grey in his dispatches. Where was the trained colonial force which Weld had proposed to raise to replace the Imperial troops? The taxation which his Ministry had proposed to finance

---

[1] By 12 April the 57th had embarked; the 12th was concentrating for embarkation at the end of the month; a wing of the 50th awaited embarkation orders: Report of Chute, G 16/12, N.Z. Archives.

[2] Grey to Carnarvon (12 Feb. 1867) (No. 22), P.P., 1868–9, xliv (H.C. 307), 4–11

[3] Memo. of 15 Mar. in Grey to Carnarvon (4 Apr. 1867) (No. 30), ibid., p. 19

it had brought about his downfall; and a year later, after Jollie's Financial Statement, a motion of FitzGerald that 'this House . . . does not perceive the necessity for creating a permanent military force of the magnitude contemplated by the Government', though itself lost, had precipitated the no-confidence motion which enforced a reconstruction of the Stafford Ministry. Nor was the Micawber-like attitude of the House towards finance the only difficulty in the way of creating an adequate colonial force. Colonel Haultain, Minister of Defence, wrote to Stafford early in 1867 on a report that the Ureweras were about to attack Whakatane: 'There are about two hundred men now there—but as they have just been receiving arrears of pay . . . if the Ureweras were to take that opportunity, they would probably find not one-fifth of the men capable of resisting them.'[1] Colonel Gorton, who commanded the Wanganui militia district from 1865 to 1869 tells us that a camp at Waihi, 170 strong, kept three canteens going which, though supposed to stock everything a soldier would require, stocked nothing but liquor.[2]

However that may be, New Zealand's relations with the Imperial Government had again become strained. The old argument about advances from the commissariat chest and colonial failure to repay them monthly was exacerbated by an unnecessary gibe of the Deputy Commissary-General that the Imperial troops were 'actively engaged in an aggressive warfare': the colonial Government retaliated by alleging 'extraordinary carelessness' on the part of commissariat officers and consequent overpayments to contractors, which the colony was then required to refund, and suggesting that the Deputy Commissary-General was aggrieved because he had been given no grant of land whereas the Inspector-General of Hospitals had.[3] Sir George Grey no longer tried to bring the two Governments into harmony: he was too busy prosecuting his quarrel with General Chute. The Colonial Office had entirely lost confidence in him. Rogers put the main point in a minute:

Even if it be granted that Sir G. G. is influenced by purely public

---

[1] Haultain to Stafford (8 Feb. 1867), Stafford Papers. See also 'Our Wellington Correspondent' in *The Times*, 16 May 1867.

[2] E. Gorton, *Some Home Truths re the Maori War* (London, 1901), p. 68.

[3] Strickland to Treasury (8 Nov. 1866) in Carnarvon to Grey (1 Feb. 1867) (No. 9), P.P., 1867, xlix [3833], 53–4. Memo. of Stafford (16 May) in Grey to Buckingham (8 June 1867) (Separate) and Strickland to War Office (18 Oct.) in W.O. to C.O. (8 Nov. 1867), P.P., 1868–9, xliv (H.C. 307), 43–6, 460.

motives, it is clear that in weighing Colonial safety and prosperity against Imperial expenditure, his scale of measurement is not the Imperial scale—he evidently considers that the Imperial resources ought to be made use of in aid of the Colony to an extent to which the Home Government has decided that they ought not to be made use of. . . . He makes an effective statement by making much of the possible disaster to the Colony and making little of the risk and expense to Great Britain—but at bottom his argument is a declaration that he will continue to carry out a Colonial and not an Imperial policy.[1]

The refusal of Lord Carnarvon's terms was 'grounded on a misapprehension of Lord Carnarvon's despatch'. The withdrawal of the troops from the Governor's authority and the declaration that they did not remain available for defence did not apply to this last regiment. But, Rogers added, 'I trust that the rejection of the offer will be closed with at once.'[2] The quarrel between Grey and Chute made it desirable to get both of them 'out of New Zealand as soon as practicable without expressing censure on either'.[3] In any case Sir George Grey's six-year term was coming to end. Carnarvon, whose dispatch had stirred up this new controversy, had since resigned. It was his successor, the Duke of Buckingham, who closed a dispatch declining to continue the controversy on the control of the troops with a dry announcement that by the next mail he hoped to 'be able to inform you of the appointment of your successor in the Government of New Zealand, and of the time at which he may be expected to arrive in the Colony'.[4]

This was certainly an implied censure but it was not the dismissal which Grey in his touchy, aggrieved frame of mind interpreted it to be.[5] The belief that he was being censured for defending the colony's interests made him for the first time really popular in New Zealand. Both Houses adopted addresses attributing the Imperial action to the systematic defamation of Governor, Government, and colonists by unnamed persons.[6] We may concur

---

[1] Minute of Rogers (16 Apr.) on Grey to Carnarvon (19 Feb. 1867) (No. 22), CO209/200.
[2] Minute of Rogers (27 May) on Grey to Carnarvon (4 Apr. 1867) (No. 30), CO209/201.
[3] Minute of Rogers (16 Apr. 1867), loc. cit.
[4] Buckingham to Grey (19 June 1867) (No. 37), P.P., 1868–9, xliv (H.C. 307), 408.
[5] Buckingham to Grey (17 Nov. 1868), Grey Coll., Auckland. Cf. Bowen to Stafford (24 June 1868), Stafford Papers.
[6] J.L.C., 1867, pp. 74–5; J.H.R., 1867, pp. 159–60.

with Rutherford's judgement that 'Grey had been set an impossible task and had not quite succeeded in performing it';[1] but he had outlived his usefulness as Governor. He could not have continued in office with any benefit to New Zealand, still less to Imperial interests. His successor, Sir George Ferguson Bowen, Governor of Queensland, though more of a scholar than a man of action, at least tried to reduce friction. The tendency of Grey's actions in the later part of his term was to increase it.

The settlement of the long-standing question of liability for the expenses of the war also reduced friction. In 1866 the New Zealand Government appointed Major Richardson to examine the accounts with the Imperial representative, Commissary-General Jones. The Imperial claim of £1,304,963 was reduced by £500,000 when the debentures sent home in 1865 were at last realized at par. Jones avoided personal discussion and left for England without waiting for the colonial counter-claim, finally set by Richardson at £906,856.[2] Though the Treasury defended Jones, the Colonial Office clearly thought his abrupt departure unjustifiable. Rogers was inclined to shrug his shoulders and say: 'They do not intend to pay us a farthing—and I am not aware that we have any means of making them do so.' Buckingham's approach was more statesmanlike. He would cry quits and make a fresh start with the new Governor.[3] Fitzherbert, when he took the matter up in England, found him 'very sympathetic', though the Chancellor of the Exchequer (Ward Hunt) and the officials of the Treasury and some at the Colonial Office were less so.[4] Buckingham's view prevailed. His dispatch of 1 April announced the Imperial Government's willingness 'to close these accounts by a mutual release, waiving the claim which they consider might be established against the Colony'.[5] One ticklish problem was

[1] Rutherford, op. cit., p. 569. His 'Review of Second New Zealand Governorship' (ch. 36) is well worth reading.

[2] Memo. of Richardson (1 Apr.) and Report (1 July 1867), A.J.H.R., 1867, B. Nos. 5 and 5A. Gore Browne had complained to Cameron (8 Aug. 1861) of Jones's unnecessarily offensive references: G36/3, N.Z. Archives.

[3] Minutes of Rogers (17 Sept.) and Buckingham (20 Sept.) on Grey to Buckingham (17 July 1867) (No. 65), CO209/202.

[4] Fitzherbert to Stafford (27 Feb. 1868), Stafford Papers. Fitzherbert decline an offer to settle for £150,000; see Treasury Minutes of 28 Mar. in Treasury to Colonial Office (28 Mar. 1868), CO209/209.

[5] Buckingham to Officer administering the Government (1 Apr. 1868) (No. 34), A.J.H.R., 1868, A. No. 1A.

thus out of the way before the colony was plunged into a new crisis.

Despite the efforts of J. C. Richmond (who performed the duties of Native Minister in Stafford's reconstructed Ministry, but without the title) and of Parris to appease the Ngati Ruanui chiefs by marking out liberal reserves on the confiscated block, one of the chiefs, Titokowaru, who had lost an eye in the Sentry Hill attack, began in April 1868 to attack isolated settlers on the confiscated land. Lieutenant-Colonel McDonnell, commanding the Armed Constabulary which had been formed under an Act of 1867, failed in an attempt to arrest those responsible. In June four settlers were murdered. On 12 July Titokowaru surprised a redoubt at Turuturumokai, killing ten and wounding six of its garrison of twenty-two before relief came. A few days earlier Te Kooti Rikirangi, a Rongowhakaata tribesman who, in circumstances still obscure, had been deported in 1866 to the Chatham Islands with some Hauhau prisoners, had seized a visiting schooner, escaped with nearly 300 followers and landed near Poverty Bay. They refused to surrender their arms when challenged by the Resident Magistrate, Major Biggs, and, after a sharp skirmish with a scratch force led by Colonel Whitmore on 8 August, retired into the bush. The Government, reluctantly yielding to McDonnell's demand for reinforcements, had by now opened recruiting offices for the Armed Constabulary. A month later, on 7 September, McDonnell attacked Titokowaru's bush stronghold of Te Ngutu-o-te-Manu. The Maoris were no stronger than at Pungarehu in 1866, the colonial force was nearly three times as strong but virtually untrained. The attack was repulsed and the hastily gathered force simply disintegrated.[1] McDonnell resigned in disgust and Whitmore, an abler and more knowledgeable soldier and a tougher disciplinarian, was brought from the east coast to succeed him. On 16 September McLean, now Superintendent of Hawke's Bay, moved in the House of Representatives 'that this House views with alarm the position in which the

---

[1] Bowen to Buckingham (6 July 1868, No. 57, 8 Aug. 1868, Nos. 78 and 79, 6 Sept. 1868, No. 91, and 7 Oct. 1868, No. 99), P.P., 1868–9, xliv (H.C. 307), 158–9, 197–200, 218–19, 245 ff., 267 ff. On the campaign against Titokowaru see T. McDonnell, *An Explanation of the Principal Causes which led to the Present War on the West Coast of New Zealand* (Wanganui, 1869); T. W. Gudgeon, *Reminiscences of the War in New Zealand* (London, 1879); and Cowan, op. cit. On Te Kooti see G. H. Ormond Wilson, *War in the Tussock* (Wellington, 1961).

Colony is being placed by the action of the Government in relation to defence and Native affairs'. His particular grievance was
the transfer of the Napier division of the Armed Constabulary
from the east coast to the west. Stafford ridiculed McLean's suggestion that the fortunes of the whole colony were involved
in the transfer of fifty-seven men; but there was no effective
reply to the attack by Atkinson, who had quite lost confidence
in Haultain, on the Ministry's failure to train a permanent
force, and it was saved from defeat only by the Speaker's casting
vote.[1]

Meanwhile, official discussions had been proceeding in England
about the withdrawal of the last regiment, the second battalion
of the 18th (Royal Irish), in view of the colonial Government's
refusal of Lord Carnarvon's terms. The War Office, inspired perhaps by the Duke of Cambridge at the Horse Guards, was inclined
to think its withdrawal 'very prejudicial to Imperial interests'.
Some troops were required in those seas. Why not station them
in New Zealand? Rogers, who had long ago made up his mind
that 'there would be no quiet for ourselves or safety for the natives
until our troops were recalled', did not accept this War Office
argument. 'New Zealand . . . is the worst place in the world for
a depot, because it may easily happen that the moment when they
are wanted elsewhere may be a moment when the circumstances
of the Colony make it hazardous to withdraw them.' Regular
troops, moreover, had been found 'extremely ill fitted for Maori
warfare'. Finally there was the point that 'after the positive and
repeated statements of the New Zealand Government that they
do not want and will not pay for them it would I should think
be very difficult to justify their retention in the House of Commons'.[2] The Duke of Buckingham was inclined to defer a decision
until Sir George Bowen had arrived and made a report. But, said
Rogers, the Colonial Government had now accepted responsibility for the security of the colony and 'the question whether
Imperial interests require a regiment to be stationed in New
Zealand after the Colony has undertaken its own defence is a
matter on which the Imperial Government is better able to judge

[1] N.Z.P.D., 1868, iii. 374–8, 572–4; iv. 32.
[2] On Rogers's long-term policy see *Letters of Lord Blachford*, p. 298. On the
official discussions, see his Minute (8 Jan.) on War Office to Colonial Office
(7 Jan. 1868) enclosing Horse Guards to War Office (28 Dec. 1867), CO209/209.

than the Governor'. Adderley, who was now Parliamentary Under-Secretary, also deprecated 'asking the Governor his opinion about Imperial interests of which we are the judges'. 'The House of Commons', he added, 'expects and approves of the last soldier leaving.' The Duke of Buckingham suggested that Bowen be reminded of an earlier dispatch on this subject and told that the War Office now proposed to arrange for the regiment's removal. He must understand that any postponement 'should be as short as possible and should not be allowed at all except on clear and conclusive grounds of Imperial interest which would be satis-factory to Her Majesty's Government and to Parliament'.[1]

This left but a small loophole, and Sir George Bowen warned Stafford that 'the only possible justification for me in taking any further step, in the face of the positive orders from home, would be an Address from the Colonial Legislature to the effect that the conditions proposed by the Imperial Government were accepted, and a memorandum from Ministers advising me to endeavour to delay the departure of the 18th Regiment'.[2] This note was written before the repulse at Te Ngutu-o-te-Manu. The Legislative Council had debated, but rejected, a motion that it was expedient that at least one Imperial regiment should continue to be stationed in New Zealand; and though it had later passed a resolution asking the Governor to defer the departure of the last regiment, Stafford did not 'propose to depart from the course which . . . has been consistently pursued for the last three years'.[3] But the revelation of the weakness of the existing colonial force caused him to shift his ground. He moved, and Fox, the Leader of the Opposition, seconded a motion requesting the Governor to delay, pending reference to the Imperial Government, the departure of the regi-ment, when its removal 'would tend to increase the excitement and confidence of the rebellious Maoris and to discourage those friendly to Her Majesty's Government'. The motion also, how-ever, stated, somewhat disingenuously, 'that the Colony has, for many years past, constantly fulfilled, and is virtually fulfilling, the condition on which the retention of an Imperial Regiment in New

[1] Minutes of Rogers (20 Apr.), Adderley, and Buckingham (21 Apr.) on War Office to Colonial Office (16 Apr. 1868), CO209/209.
[2] Bowen to Stafford (20 Aug. 1868), Stafford Papers.
[3] *J.L.C.*, 1868, p. 26. Memo. of Stafford (8 Aug.) in Bowen to Buckingham (8 Aug. 1868) (No. 80), P.P., 1868–9, xliv (H.C. 307), 227.

Zealand was sanctioned in the despatch of Lord Carnarvon'.[1]
Dillon Bell, who had the reputation of being a weathercock, on
this occasion showed to better advantage. 'If the Imperial Government has . . . treated us in a shabby and scurvy way, we on our
part', he admitted, 'treated that Government with constant deceit,
shuffling, and evasion. We were constantly pretending we were
going to perform a duty, the performance of which we have as
constantly evaded.' He appealed to Stafford to drop the pretence
that he was carrying on the self-reliant policy.[2] But, whatever
the variety of opinion on the expediency of self-reliance and the
extent to which it was being carried out, the large majority of the
House was in favour of Stafford's motion and Bowen, regarding
it as 'a case of urgent necessity' in terms of the Colonial Regulations, proceeded to act upon it. He moved a detachment of Imperial troops to Wanganui, where its presence restored the morale
of the militia and friendly Maoris and deterred Titokowaru and his
followers from their threatened attack on the town; and he
referred the whole case home.[3]

Its reception at the Colonial Office was far from sympathetic.
Rogers expressed his views in a long and bitter minute.

This is of course a serious matter—but not, I should say, quite so
serious as it is made to look by Sir G. Bowen. The Colonists of New
Zealand have made a bargain—they have been allowed in pursuance
of that bargain to conduct native affairs in a manner which was likely
to produce resentment and destitution among large masses of the
Maoris. They have been warned that their confiscation policy was one
which the Home Government disapproved and distrusted and which
they (the Home Government) would absolutely have arrested but for
the engagement on the part of the Colonists to provide for their own
defence. They have been warned emphatically that the Home Government would not help them through the foreseen consequences of an
oppressive or imprudent policy. . . . Notwithstanding all this they have
been pushing forward settlement into the confiscated lands. . . . They
have reduced their military force. They have refused to keep a regiment
on the terms on which (unfortunately as I think) it was offered them
—and (though this is of less importance) they have so contested our

[1] J.H.R., 1868, pp. 178–80. See also Bowen to Buckingham (8 Oct. 1868)
(No. 100) and Enclosures, ibid., pp. 276–8.
[2] House of Representatives, 2 Oct. 1868: N.Z.P.D., iv. 111–12. See also
pp. 105–32 passim. The motion was carried by 33 to 13.
[3] Bowen to Buckingham (7 Oct. 1868, No. 99, and 7 Nov. 1868, No. 113):
P.P. 1868–9, xliv (H.C. 307), 267, 278–80.

pecuniary claims on them as to force us to abandon much of these claims for peace' sake.

Now, what we have warned them of happens. And they propose—not to change their policy and draw in their settlements—not to give the Home Government the old control (imperfect and delusive enough) over the causes of war (which indeed would be impracticable if they did offer it)—not to pay towards the expenses of any troops left in New Zealand—but only that the regiment should be left because the Colonial Government has in fact for the last few years performed what Lord Carnarvon required and they (most fortunately as I think) rejected as a condition of keeping that regiment. I think that they ought not to receive that encouragement to carry out their past and present policy which the retention of this regiment will give them.[1]

The Duke of Buckingham agreed with Rogers and, in a dispatch adopting his arguments in less aggressive tone and recalling Stafford's quite recent refusal to accept the Imperial conditions, Bowen was told that the troops were to leave as soon as the troop-ship arrived. 'I find it difficult', the Duke concluded, 'to imagine any such change in the state of affairs as can render it necessary for you to adopt the responsibility of detaining the troops after the receipt of these instructions.'[2] This dispatch was dated on the day of Disraeli's resignation; but Lord Granville, on succeeding to the Colonial Secretaryship a few days later, hastened to inform Sir George Bowen that he agreed with his predecessor.[3]

The change in the state of affairs which the Duke of Buckingham found so difficult to imagine, however, actually occurred. Colonel Whitmore restored the morale of the west coast force, which was reinforced by some good material from the Thames goldfields, but was less successful with the *kupapas*, though about 100 joined him under the command of the formidable warrior Kepa Te Rangihiwinui (Major Kemp). His first attack on Tito-kowaru's position at Moturoa, some twenty miles west of Wanganui, on 7 November met such strong resistance that he drew off his force, perhaps prematurely.[4]

[1] Minute of Rogers (27 Nov.) on Bowen to Buckingham (7 Oct. 1868) (No. 99), CO209/208. This suggests that Rogers was one of the officials whom Fitzherbert found unsympathetic to the financial settlement.
[2] Buckingham to Bowen (1 Dec. 1868) (No. 127), P.P., 1868-9, xliv (H.C. 307), 422-3.
[3] Granville to Bowen (18 Dec. 1868) (No. 3), ibid., p. 424.
[4] Bowen to Buckingham (17 Nov. 1868) (No. 116), ibid., pp. 283 ff. For details see Cowan, op. cit., ii. 244-62.

The force remained in good shape, but many settlers and their families took refuge in Wanganui. Close on the heels of this reverse came news that Te Kooti, on the night of 9–10 November, had swooped down on Poverty Bay, killing thirty-three Europeans, including the Resident Magistrate Major Biggs, and thirty-seven Maoris. The west coast force was ordered to stand on the defensive whilst Whitmore, with 280 of the constabulary, returned to the east coast to take command against Te Kooti. The real ground for alarm was that the war might spread. The militia in Taranaki and Wellington were called out; block-houses were built in the Hutt and Wairarapa; recruiting for the constabulary was carried out in every town in the colony and an officer was sent to raise recruits in Melbourne.[1] Sir George Bowen informed General Chute, who had transferred his head-quarters to Australia, that a general rising of the King tribes was 'only too probable';[2] and in a confidential dispatch home he expressed concern at the moral effect of removing the Imperial garrisons in New Plymouth, Wanganui, and Napier whilst war was still raging.[3] Sir David Monro, Speaker of the House of Representatives, in a letter to a newspaper suggested the dispatch of a Commission with power to suspend the constitution in the North Island, a policy which had some support in Auckland, whilst even FitzGerald, now Controller-General and thus out of politics, though opposed as ever to an appeal for aid in men, wanted aid in money.[4]

Early in February 1869 the Duke of Buckingham's last dispatch arrived. Stafford professed uncertainty 'whether it is not still left open to the Colony to retain the single regiment on the new condition of payment of a subsidy of £40 per man', but he was still unwilling to pay for the services of Imperial troops because 'those services are expressly not available for carrying out a Colonial policy'. At the same time he took exception to the statement in the dispatch that Imperial non-interference in the confiscation

---

[1] Bowen to Buckingham (7 Dec. 1868) (No. 125) and Enclosures, P.P., 1868–9, xliv (H.C. 307), 269 ff. Two hundred recruits were raised in Melbourne, but 'nearly all . . . landed at their destination drunk': 'Our Melbourne Correspondent', *The Times*, 24 Feb. 1869.

[2] Bowen to Chute (2 Dec. 1868), (H.C. 307), p. 310.

[3] Bowen to Buckingham (7 Dec. 1868) (Confidential), ibid., pp. 312–18.

[4] Monro to the Editor, *Nelson Examiner*, 24 Nov.; FitzGerald in *Wellington Independent*, 17 Dec. 1868. Both enclosed in Bowen to Buckingham (7 Jan. 1869) (Confidential), (H.C. 307), pp. 327–34.

policy 'was conditional on being totally relieved from any responsibility in respect to the military defence of the settlers'. He pointed out that 'the confiscation policy of 1863 was allowed before the announcement of the withdrawal of the army'.[1] It was true that the Colonial Office had changed its ground. The rather hesitant approval of Newcastle had been forgotten under the influence of Sir Frederic Rogers, who under successive Secretaries of State had held firmly to the policy of withdrawing the troops and at the same time had become increasingly critical not only of New Zealand's neglect of self-defence but of its general policy towards the Maoris. This had become decidedly more liberal. Weld and his successors had been more generous in their interpretation of the confiscation policy than Whitaker and Russell; though their proposed Commission on Native representation had come to nothing, McLean as a private member had introduced a Bill giving the Maoris four members in the House of Representatives in 1867 and it had duly passed into law; another Act of 1867 enlarged the responsibilities of the state in the field of Maori education, hitherto left to state-subsidized Christian missions.[2] But this new spirit passed unnoticed in the Colonial Office. Retaining the image of New Zealand it had formed from reading the innumerable special pleadings of Sir George Grey and the disingenuous memoranda of Stafford, it discounted the alarmist dispatches of Sir George Bowen and held to its course.

Actually, however, the transport *Himalaya*, which arrived in February, left the troops stationed at Auckland and Wanganui behind. The captain had received at Point de Galle, Ceylon, a telegram ordering him not to go on to New Zealand but to embark a regiment at various Australian ports direct for England. General Chute induced him to embark one wing of the 18th nevertheless, but Captain Lambert, Commodore of the Australia and New Zealand station, who had come to New Zealand on his own initiative, sent him on from Wellington to Brisbane in accordance with his telegraphed instructions; and General Chute, after a visit to New Zealand, agreed to the Governor's request that

---

[1] Memo. of Stafford (12 Feb.) in Bowen to Buckingham, (8 Feb. 1869) (No. 18), (H.C. 307) pp. 351–2.
[2] Native Schools Act 1867 (No. 41). The initiative was left to the Maoris: if a majority at a meeting duly called were willing to provide a proportion of the expense, an educational district was to be constituted and a committee elected. No grant was payable unless English was taught.

the remaining wing of the regiment be left.[1] The Colonial Office
had not heard of the restraining telegram. Rogers believed that
the orders sent out from the Horse Guards, which did not conceal
its dislike of the policy of withdrawal, 'had a rather uncertain
sound' and that Commodore Lambert had used them as a pretext,
believing in fact that the troops could not safely be sent away.[2]
However that may be, this concession tided over the immediate
emergency. Whitmore's stern discipline and skilful, energetic,
hard-driving leadership had overcome the personal unpopularity
he incurred by his overbearing temper and made the colonial
force under his command, for the first time, a highly efficient
instrument of war. With his Ngati Porou and Arawa allies, Whitmore beleaguered Te Kooti in his hill fortress of Ngatapa. Te
Kooti escaped down a cliff on the night of 4–5 January but was
pursued, and 136 of his small force were killed. Back on the west
coast, Whitmore before the end of March harried Titokowaru
into a swamp refuge from which he escaped without any taste
for further military adventures. Then a foray by Te Kooti and
his allies the Urewera mountaineers against the thinly settled Bay
of Plenty led to a three-pronged invasion of the practically unknown Urewera country under Whitmore's general command.
This did not go quite according to plan and Whitmore had to be
invalided out, but Te Kooti moved away into the Taupo district
in the heart of the island.[3]

The news of the Poverty Bay massacre did not deflect British
policy from the course on which it was set. On New Year's Day
1869 *The Times* devoted a long leading article to the subject.

Even such a tragedy is still only a consequence which was to have
been anticipated from the conduct pursued by the Colony itself.
A cry may very likely, we fear, be raised on behalf of making vengeance
for the atrocities of these savages an Imperial concern. The sentiment
that no matter where Englishmen suffer it is equally the duty of England to see that right is done is so natural and generous that we should

[1] Bowen to Granville (8 Mar. 1869) (No. 28), P.P., 1868–9, xliv (H.C. 307),
364–7.
[2] Minute of Rogers (c. 17 May) on Bowen to Buckingham (8 Feb. 1869)
(No. 18), CO209/210.
[3] Bowen to Buckingham (10 Jan. 1869) (No. 5), to Granville (20 Mar. 1869,
No. 37, 29 Mar. 1869, No. 41), P.P., 1868–9, xliv (H.C. 307), 337 ff., 380 ff.
Bowen to Granville (5 June 1869) (No. 65), P.P., 1870, l [C. 83], 4. Sir G. S.
Whitmore, *The Last Maori War in New Zealand under the Self-Reliant Policy*
(London, 1902), *passim*; Gudgeon, op. cit., Ormond Wilson, op. cit.

gladly feel free to refrain from discouraging the tendency. But, if only in the interest of Colonial self-government, we must protest against such interference. The agency which has produced the calamity is the almost incredible negligence of the Colony itself, and the Colony is best left to deal by itself with the effects of its own culpable inertness.[1] This policy of non-interference was apt, however, to be accompanied by well-meant suggestions on how best to fight the war. There was quite a correspondence in *The Times* on this topic. Lord Granville for his part warned Bowen that 'Her Majesty's Government have no intention of permanently retaining any Imperial troops in New Zealand, still less of increasing the force there; nor can I lead you to expect that the regiment now in the Colony will remain beyond May next.' But at the same time he suggested that it might 'deserve the consideration of your Government whether a more perfect organization might be introduced among the Native Contingent by a large infusion of European commissioned and non-commissioned officers' and thought 'clearly judicious' two suggestions of Bowen in a confidential dispatch—the prohibition of outlying settlements and some modified recognition of the Maori King—though he recognized that these were 'evidently for the decision of the Local Government'.[2] Another dispatch drew the Governor's attention to the report that the Chatham Island prisoners 'had been taken there with the expectation, if not the promise, that they should be brought back to New Zealand after a given time'; that this unfulfilled promise led to their escape; and that 'they did not offer any violence to the settlers till attempts were made to hunt them down'.[3] Two months later Granville drew attention to a newspaper report that Richmond had offered £50 for the head of a certain Nikora and that large rewards had been offered for Titokowaru and Te Kooti dead or alive.[4] Satisfactory explanations were given on all these points, but they naturally provoked irritated comment in New Zealand, passed on to the Imperial Government by Sir George Bowen, who was clearly irritated himself.

I am informed that there appears to be a very general determination to resist the active interference of any Imperial authority in the internal

[1] *The Times,* 1 Jan. 1869.
[2] Granville to Bowen (26 Feb. 1869) (Confidential), P.P., 1868–9, xliv (H.C. 307), 427–8.
[3] Granville to Bowen (26 Feb. 1869) (No. 30), P.P., 1870, l [C. 83], 184.
[4] Granville to Bowen (20 Apr. 1869) (No. 43), P.P., 1869, xliv (H.C. 307), 430.

Government of New Zealand, now that the Imperial Government has transferred the entire control and management of Native affairs to the Colonial ministers for the time being, and has absolutely declined to give any assistance, or to incur any responsibility in the suppression of the existing Maori rebellion. . . . It is naturally very painful to be subjected to censure, both in England and in this Colony, for the actions of other men, when all power of direct control has been taken out of the hands of the Governor, and he has also been deprived of all physical force by the entire removal of the Imperial troops.

He would be careful not to identify himself with any illegal or cruel measures but did not believe any public men desired to adopt them.[1]

Meanwhile Stafford had reopened the question whether the troops should be entirely withdrawn by a number of pointed inquiries.

Will one regiment be allowed to remain if the Legislature bind itself to accept the conditions specified in Lord Carnarvon's Despatch No. 49, of 1 December 1866, namely that a grant of £50,000 per annum for Native purposes be continued?

If not, then what payment per head for each officer and man would be required; and would more than one regiment be left if paid for by the Colony?

If troops are retained, could they, when directed by the Governor be employed in active service in the field to suppress insurrections?

If not allowed to be employed in the field, would they be allowed to occupy in sufficient numbers positions to act as supports to colonial outposts, though not required to take part in active operations, and would the Governor be empowered to determine at what posts they should be stationed?

He then proceeded to name a number of posts.[2] Rogers regarded these inquiries as mainly a delaying move. He saw three possibilities.

1. To withdraw the troops relentlessly (though it may be with a little delay) on some such excuse (not of principle) as Commodore Lambert has devised.
2. To take the war on our backs and send out troops in plenty and military officer to replace Sir G. B. as Governor—requiring from

---

[1] Bowen to Granville (7 July 1869) (No. 83), P.P., 1870, l [C. 83], 56–7.
[2] Bowen to Granville (11 Mar. 1869) (No. 30), Enclosure, Memo. of Stafford (11 Mar.), P.P., 1869, xliv (H.C. 307), 371.

the Colonial Government certain assistance and absolute submission in military matters to our officer.

3. To retain in the colony a small number of troops to garrison
   certain towns, the defence of which and nothing else is to be
   placed under the charge of our military officers—who will not
   be interfered with there, or interfere with Colonial forces in the
   field.

Surprisingly, Rogers was 'disposed to Number 3'. But he took it
for granted that Lord Carnarvon's offer would not be renewed. The
£50,000 a year for Native purposes was no compensation for the
cost of a regiment, and 'would involve us, if it is not to be illusory,
in continual conflicts with the colonists on the question what is
a native purpose'. Only one regiment should be retained, at
Australian rates, and it should not be stationed on confiscated
territory or at Taupo, 'the probable centre of military operations'.[1]

If Rogers was for once inclined to compromise, Granville saw
'nothing in these papers to induce me to change the policy which
has already been decided upon'.[2] He consulted Cardwell, now
Secretary of State for War, and of course the Prime Minister.
Both agreed with his line. 'I am satisfied', Cardwell wrote, 'that
nothing will do but either a relentless removal of the troops as
suggested by Rogers, or an arrangement . . . to separate off the
North Island for a time, to permit an equitable settlement with
the Natives during that separation—and for the aggregate Colony
to pay the cost of it.'[3] Both commented on the 'slipperiness' of
Stafford's memorandum. 'Did he think it a question of the safety
of the colony,' Gladstone shrewdly observed, 'he would not bargain about terms for the moment but leave them to be settled.'[4]
So Granville's reply was a *non possumus*: 'It is needless to repeat
how much Her Majesty's Government sympathize with the
settlers in their misfortunes. But these considerations, however
painful, cannot affect the course which Her Majesty's Government
believe it to be desirable to pursue, in the best interests of both the
Mother Country and the Colony.' Stafford had given 'not . . . the

[1] Minute of Rogers (18 May) on Bowen to Granville (11 Mar. 1869) (No. 30),
CO209/210.
[2] Minute of Granville (19 May), ibid.
[3] Cardwell to Granville (19 May 1869), P.R.O. 30/29: 53.
[4] Minute of Gladstone: CO209/210. The word 'slipperiness' is Cardwell's in
a Minute of 20 May, ibid.

slightest indication of the sacrifices which the Colony is prepared
to make or he to advise'. It would be for the colony to consider
whether it could rely on the superiority of Whitmore's troops 'to
enforce the submission of the Maori nation or whether attempts
should not be made towards a peaceful solution'.[1] Rogers for one
favoured the second, not the first alternative. As he wrote a few
days later:

We think that they are absolutely mistaken in this policy—because
(1) we cannot imagine that they can possibly raise or pay a sufficient
force of men to give effect to it (2) because they cannot possibly expect
the Imperial Government to carry on at its own expense a war which
as between colonists and the Empire is for purely colonial objects and
as between the colonists and the Maoris (both assumed to be British
subjects) is of doubtful justice and doubtful necessity.[2]

The Gladstone Government was not going to help Stafford's
Government out of its difficulties. It still kept up a bold front. The
Governor's speech to the General Assembly on 1 June proposed
a new loan, if possible with an Imperial guarantee, 'for the conquest of a permanent peace'. But the Ministry's attempt 'to carry
out the self-reliant policy at all hazards' (to quote the Wellington
correspondent of *The Times*) was losing its support in the colony.
'The error', the correspondent added, 'is the result either of a
failure to comprehend the gravity of the crisis, or of a dogged
determination to maintain an "idea", notwithstanding the proof
that they have not the means to maintain it accumulates every hour.'[3]
The Ministry sealed its fate by withdrawing McLean's powers as
Government Agent on the east coast when he detained the Ngati
Porou chief Ropata Wahawaha, who was under orders to proceed to the west coast. McLean's management of the east coast
Maoris pointed to him as the man most likely to bring about the
peace the colony needed; and when Fox moved a vote of no
confidence on 15 June he could count on McLean's support. Fox
attacked the Ministry's 'half and half sort of self-reliance' and
assumed that the Imperial Government would at least leave the one
regiment if only the colony asked for it.[4] Ministers were better

[1] Granville to Bowen (21 May 1869,) P.P., 1868–9, xliv (H.C. 307), 433–4.
[2] Minute of Rogers (29 May 1869), CO209/210.
[3] 'Our Own Correspondent', Wellington (12 Mar.), *The Times*, 17 May 1869.
[4] *N.Z.P.D.* v. 95–100.

acquainted with the true state of the case. Hall and more especially J. C. Richmond, in a speech of remarkable philosophic detachment, believed the course was set for independence.

> We have been as it were winged out of the nest by the Mother Country. . . . It has seemed to the Imperial Government that we have been playing fast and loose with the Empire. That is an excuse for a harshness which I should otherwise think unpardonable; but on other questions the present Government of Great Britain do not deserve to be sneered at as ungenerous or illiberal. What is generosity in a Legislature or Executive Government? I doubt if in such a body such sentiment ought to exist. They deal not with their own but with other people's means . . . not . . . with the money of the rich and powerful alone, but with the bread and butter of the poor and helpless. . . . We know that the day must have come when we should have demanded those powers now forced upon us . . . and we do ill to scold because we have been anticipated. . . . I believe that before long we may have to meet here as a Constituent Assembly.[1]

It was no wonder the majority preferred the easier path of asking for Imperial assistance. On 24 June Fox carried his motion by the comfortable margin of 40 to 29 and Stafford resigned. Within a few days Fox, with Vogel as Colonial Treasurer and McLean as Native and Defence Minister, was installed in office.[2]

Fox proposed a complete change of defence policy, once again largely on financial grounds. 'The amount of wear and tear and the costliness of these operations . . .', he declared, clearly with the Urewera campaign in mind, 'is such that it is impossible for this country to face it.' His Government would stand on the defensive as far as possible, reducing and demilitarizing the colonial forces. The Armed Constabulary would be reorganized on the principles of the Royal Irish Constabulary by St. John Branigan, who had made a reputation as Commissioner of Police in Otago in the days of the gold rush. But the Ministers also made it 'a cardinal point of their policy to endeavour to obtain from the Imperial Government assistance in men'.[3] The defence debates were lengthy and at times confused, but the candid discussion of the defects of the colonial forces and the searchings of heart about New Zealand's

[1] N.Z.P.D. v. 191–202, esp. pp. 194–5.
[2] Two new appointments were made on 2 July—Dillon Bell and W. Gisborne (Under-Secretary), who was appointed to the Upper House to take the Colonial Secretaryship.
[3] Ministerial Statement, 29 June 1869, ibid., p. 315.

relations with the United Kingdom make them unusually interesting. The merits of the self-reliant policy were much canvassed. The Auckland members remained unrepentant opponents. Creighton declared that it had always been given a one-sided interpretation: 'honourable members had looked upon it as meaning that the North was to provide the men and its quota of money; that it should do the fighting, and that the South should lend its credit.'[1] Richmond and Hall in the House and Whitmore and others in the Legislative Council defended the policy. Hall in particular pointed out that Imperial troops meant Imperial interference, Exeter Hall influence, officers writing letters to the newspapers: the evils likely to arise from the retention of the regiment were greater than the advantages. Stafford distinguished himself by his bitter sneers:

This war is looked on by the people in England as a street row or an Irish riot on a fair day, in which England ought not to entangle herself. . . . It is not so much a question of money as of avoiding these little wars which are a nuisance to them, and as to which most troublesome motions are made in Parliament. . . . There is no Imperial Government. There is a British Government, sitting in Downing Street, managing affairs in the United Kingdom very badly, but no Imperial Government.[2]

But on the whole there is no doubt that the Ministry carried the House with it in its appeal for Imperial assistance. It was clearly willing to pay whatever sum the Imperial Government might think appropriate for the troops, and during the debates the idea emerged of sending Commissioners to England to make representations personally.[3]

During the progress of these debates there came a moment of acute anxiety. Te Kooti with sixty of his own followers, accompanied by the Tuwharetoa chief Te Heuheu and a party from Taupo, arrived at Tokangamutu, now the headquarters of the Maori King. Early in 1868 word reached the Government that the King party had determined not to renew hostilities but to maintain strict isolation, refusing to admit surveyors or to sell or lease land. About the same time the King renounced his baptismal

[1] 6 Aug. 1869, ibid. vi. 339.

[2] 3 Aug. 1869, ibid. pp. 211–12. Stafford's bitterness as an Irish Protestant landowner at Gladstone's Irish policy may be in evidence here.

[3] The dispatch of commissioners was mentioned in the resolutions on defence moved by McLean on 3 August: *J.H.R.*, 1869, p. 117.

name of Matutaera and took the name of Tawhiao.[1] A year later Sir George Bowen sent a conciliatory letter to Tawhiao, which was followed up by a semi-official letter from Sir William Martin to the King's uncle and chief counsellor Tamati Ngapora, offering on behalf of the Government to make the district in which the King was living a separate district with its own laws and to give back part of the Waikato to law-abiding Maoris. Early in June an influential Auckland settler, J. C. Firth, on his own initiative held an interview with Tamati Ngapora or Manuhiri, as he was now known, but found him intransigent: 'we must have all of Waikato,' he declared.[2] Te Kooti's arrival put the King's policy to the test. Fox urged that the removal at this juncture of the last Imperial regiment, which had recently been ordered to concentrate at Auckland, would precipitate a conflict and invite the King to join forces with Te Kooti and put the Maori cause to the arbitrament of war.[3] The House unanimously passed an address to the Governor requesting him to urge General Chute to use his discretionary power to retain the regiment pending further references to the Imperial Government.[4] Dr. Featherston was dispatched to Melbourne with this message. His mission was successful. On 14 August General Chute notified the War Office that he had agreed to retain the regiment in New Zealand pending further instructions.[5] It had in fact been an unnecessary alarm. Te Kooti's presumptuous demands for greenstone ornaments and heirlooms and recognition as a prophet had antagonized Tawhiao, and even Rewi, though he escorted Te Kooti to the borders of the Ngati Maniapoto country, declined to involve himself in his desperate guerrilla war.[6] Te Kooti attacked posts in the Taupo district, but in a sharp action at Te Porere on 4 October he was defeated and

[1] Bowen to Buckingham (5 Mar. 1868) (No. 15), P.P., 1868–9, xliv (H.C. 307), 114–17.

[2] Bowen to Granville (12 Mar. 1869) (No. 32), ibid., p. 377. *Mr. J. C. Firth's Conference with Tamati Ngapora and the King Natives at Orahiri* (Auckland, 1869). See also Bowen to Granville (20 June 1869) (No. 70), P.P., 1870, l [C. 83], 19.

[3] Memo. of Fox (22 July) in Bowen to Granville (5 Aug. 1869) (No. 103), P.P., 1870, l [C. 83], 79–80. Fox had already, on 6 July urged the Governor to take steps to delay the regiment's departure, but Bowen had declined, ibid., pp. 44–5.

[4] J.H.R. 1869, p. 89. The Legislative Council carried a similar resolution by 19 to 2.

[5] Chute to War Office (14 Aug. 1869), P.P., 1870, l [C. 83], 212.

[6] Memo. of McLean (6 Aug. 1869), ibid., p. 87. Rewi's speech at Pahiko (9 Nov.), ibid., p. 181. On Te Porere see Wilson, op. cit.

wounded and became a fugitive in the bush. Te Heuheu surrendered and the last crisis of the Maori war was past.

The crisis in New Zealand's relations with the United Kingdom, however, had not yet been resolved. The censorious tone of much press comment and of many of the Colonial Office dispatches printed for Parliament and the General Assembly, gave deep offence. Richmond, in a letter apropos of *The Times*'s New Year leading article, made some telling points.

I see the Colonies are in England called 'touchy'. Well, if true, that is a fact which a statesman ought not to overlook. . . . If we are no longer to look for any benefit from England which is not accorded to foreign nations, we ought in future to meet the courtesy used towards foreign nations, and despatch writers ought to drop the pedagogic style. . . . The very principle which induces Great Britain to abdicate the management of the affairs of distant colonies should make her statesmen and public writers modest in their criticisms. . . . Only one English statesman, Mr. Chichester Fortescue, and only two or three public writers show that they substantially realize the condition of New Zealand. Most of them do not even faintly apprehend the difficulty of governing such a population in such a land under such a Constitution.[1]

Sir George Grey, who had now carried his vendetta against the military authorities home to England, had probably ceased to carry any weight with English public opinion. But Weld and his Minister of Colonial Defence, Atkinson, were also in England. Weld, though he still did not want Imperial troops, urged that assistance be given in the form of a guaranteed loan and complained that the press was 'taunting Colonists with supposed deficiencies instead of criticizing in a friendly spirit'.[2] Atkinson, in opposing immediate removal of the last regiment, declared that 'there is a very strong belief among the rebel Maoris that the Queen disapproves of what the Colonists have done and are doing, is angry with us, and will not let the soldiers help us any more'. He also saw John Bright and Under-Secretary Monsell.[3] The former Speaker, Sir Charles Clifford, wrote to Pollen:

New Zealand is making a great stir in England just now and there is

---

[1] J. C. Richmond to the Editor, 12 Mar., *The Times*, 26 May 1869. The *Saturday Review* (5 June) thought Richmond's complaint justified.

[2] Weld, *Notes on New Zealand Affairs*, p. 7.

[3] Atkinson to Sir G. Grey (17 Mar. 1869) (forwarded by Grey to Granville, 19 Mar.), P.P., 1868–9, xliv (H.C., 307), 515–16. On Atkinson's interviews see *Richmond–Atkinson Papers*, ii. 285.

every reason to believe that Government will do something for us.
. . . I know that the Ministry are alarmed lest before they have done
anything another massacre should occur that would raise a greater
feeling of sympathetic indignation throughout England and compel
them to do more than they wish to do.[1]

New Zealand, as the most recently settled British colony and one
with many settlers of high social standing at home, was better
placed than any other to sway a public opinion becoming uneasy
about colonial policy. As Monsell told the House, no doubt with
some exaggeration, 'there was hardly a gentleman in that House
who had not a friend or a relation in New Zealand'.[2]

When Viscount Bury on 22 July called the attention of the
House of Commons to recent events in New Zealand, the tone
of the debate, which was confined to back-bench members,
showed a feeling in some quarters that a policy sound in principle
had been too harshly pressed. And Sir Charles Adderley, in expressing the hope that the Government would 'give its hearty support
to the self-reliant party in the colony', chose to ignore the fact
that four members of the self-reliant Ministry—Weld, Atkinson,
Richmond, and Sewell—were in one way or other critical of the
prevailing policy of the Imperial Government.[3] 'We shall not be
surprised', The Times remarked next day, 'if the later and sterner
dogmas of the Colonial Office be abandoned, and the settlers
gratified with a modicum of Imperial assistance.'[4] A few days later,
in the House of Lords, Carnarvon, in a sympathetic speech,
deplored existing misunderstandings and suggested that 'some one
on the spot, accredited by Her Majesty's Government, enjoying
their confidence and also the confidence of the colonists, and
armed with whatever powers the Government might think fit
to entrust to him might make inquiries and offer suggestions
which might bring about a better state of things.' Selwyn, now
Bishop of Lichfield, begged the Government if only on the ground
of the obligations to the Maoris under the Treaty of Waitangi,
to 'pause before they refused all further aid to the colony'.[5]

[1] Quoted by Pollen to Stafford (30 Apr. 1869), Stafford Papers.
[2] Hansard, 3rd Ser. cxcviii. 479.
[3] Ibid. 456–92. Magniac, an East India and China merchant, Sir H. Selwin-Ibbetson, and R. R. Torrens, a former Premier of South Australia, expressed
sympathy with the colony.          [4] The Times, 23 July 1869.
[5] Hansard, 3rd Ser. cxcviii. 778–95. Carnarvon's suggestion of a commissioner
won support from the Saturday Review.

Outside Parliament a group of colonists attempted to carry on the struggle by bringing other colonial governments to the assistance of New Zealand.[1]

In mid-September Bowen's dispatch of 5 August, with the documents covering the appeal to Chute to delay withdrawal, reached England. Even Rogers saw 'the possibility that the retention of the Troops may lead Tamati Ngapora to recede from his demand for the whole of the Waikato and so hasten peace'. Granville for a moment considered a surprising alternative: 'I have a plan,' he wrote to Cardwell, 'which Rogers doesn't like, and which may possibly make you a little seasick. Take away the regiment and having removed the only dangerous instrument, send Sir G. Grey to replace Bowen, who is clearly a pompous donkey.' But Cardwell believed that Grey had lost his influence and was distrusted by colonists and Maoris alike, and Granville let go of his trial balloon.[2] 'I think we must harden our hearts,' he told Rogers. 'If you and Monsell agree about the terms, do not refer again to me.'[3] Cardwell, however, was having his difficulties at the War Office.

Northbrook, Lugard and Storks urge upon me . . . their opinion that, if any serious calamity recur in New Zealand, there will be a great revulsion of feeling in this country [he told Granville]. How far would you be disposed to retard for a fixed period—say twelve months—the removal of the Regiment on condition that the Colony at once proceed upon your suggestions and attempt 'a peaceful solution of existing complications by a prohibition of outlying settlements, and by a modified recognition within certain limits of the so called Maori King on a plan similar to that formerly suggested by Mr. Fox'?[4]

But Granville, with the backing of Gladstone, stood to his guns.

If the active employment of British Troops in a Colony, in which Responsible Government has been established under ordinary circumstances, is fraught with difficulties, it is still more objectionable when

[1] Youl, Sewell, and Blaine to Fox (13 Aug. 1869), *A.J.H.R.*, 1870, A. No. 6. On this proposal see above, pp. 36–7.
[2] Minute of Rogers (13 Sept.) on Bowen to Granville (5 Aug. 1869) (No. 103), CO209/212. Granville to Cardwell (23 Sept.) and Cardwell to Granville (25 Sept. 1869), P.R.O. 30/48, 5/28.
[3] Granville to Rogers (29 Sept. 1869), CO209/212.
[4] Cardwell to Granville (5 Oct. 1869), P.R.O. 30/48, 5/28. Lord Northbrook and Sir E. Lugard were Under-Secretaries, Sir H. Storks Controller-in-Chief at the War Office.

the presence of these Troops is calculated to encourage the Colonial Government in a policy which the Home Government have always regarded as pregnant with danger. . . . Large concessions . . . are unavoidable to appease a pervading discontent, with which the Colony is otherwise unable to cope; and still larger concessions will be required, unless a Force is kept on foot capable of commanding the respect of the Natives when the Queen's Troops are withdrawn. But the abandonment of land, the recognition of Maori authority, and the maintenance of an expensive Force, however indispensable some or all of these may be, are distasteful remedies, which will not be resorted to while the Colony continues to expect assistance from this country.

Having thus proved to his own satisfaction that the removal of the troops was in the best interests of New Zealand itself, the Secretary of State informed the Governor that Sir Trevor Chute would have strict instructions not to delay further the execution of the order to remove them.[1] Granville knew, of course, that this dispatch, which was promptly published, would meet with criticism. 'If you, Gladstone, Lowe, Bright and Childers cannot defend me in the Commons,' he wrote light-heartedly to Cardwell, 'you deserve to be sent to New Zealand yourselves.'[2] *The Times* now took Granville's part, but the *Saturday Review* said truly 'Lord Granville seems unaccountably to have forgotten that a logical triumph is a poor set-off for the possible slaughter of British colonists and the certain alienation of colonial feeling.'[3] The *Spectator* even more outspokenly denounced Granville's policy as 'likely to force New Zealand, as soon as possible, into cutting a knot which only entails upon her embarrassment, humiliation and wearisome as well as dangerous suspense and is utterly fruitless of any substantial result of good'.[4]

The Fox Ministry's policy had been shaped on the assumption that a frank appeal for help and a willingness to pay for it would achieve the object which Stafford's evasive tactics had so notably failed to achieve. All the more bitter were the disappointment and anger at the terms of Granville's dispatch. The *Press* was unique in hailing it with relief. Most newspapers thought very differently. The *Daily Southern Cross* appealed from the English Cabinet to the English people. The *Lyttelton Times* argued that if Great Britain

[1] Granville to Bowen (7 Oct. 1869) (No. 115), P.P., 1870, l [C. 83], 196–7.
[2] Granville to Cardwell (9 Oct. 1869), P.R.O. 30/48, 5/28.
[3] *Saturday Review*, 16 Oct. 1869. Cf. *The Times*, 14 Oct. 1869.
[4] *Spectator*, 16 Oct. 1869.

refused all aid she automatically renounced the right to interfere in New Zealand affairs: 'New Zealand could therefore no longer be a Colony and must not delay in declaring itself an independent state.'¹ 'It would be idle', *The Times* Wellington correspondent wrote on the reception of the dispatch, 'to gloss over the fact that but one feeling with regard to the document prevails in New Zealand and that is one of profound and undisguised indignation.'² Ministers' feelings were expressed in a memorandum drawn up by the Colonial Secretary, Gisborne. He quoted Gladstone's remark in the 1864 debates that 'he did not see how England could with justice throw the whole responsibility of the war on the Colony'. 'That war', said Gisborne, 'has not yet ceased.'³

Nowhere more than in New Zealand does there exist a stronger feeling of loyalty to the Crown, and of devotion to Her Majesty, or a higher value attached to its position as an integral part of the Empire, and Ministers feel assured that throughout the Colony there will arise universal feeling of regret that the tone and purport of Earl Granville's despatch (written at a time when he must have known the Colony to be in the greatest distress) are scarcely susceptible of any other explanation than a desire to abandon this country and to sever its connection with the Empire.⁴

Fortunately by this time Dillon Bell and Featherston, the Commissioners appointed under an Act of 1869 and charged, among other things, with 'the re-establishment of cordial relations between the Imperial and Colonial Governments', had arrived in London. They wisely refused to enter into controversy about the past. In their first conversation at the Colonial Office with Robert Meade, then Lord Granville's private Secretary, they were handed a letter from Granville conveying the decision of the Cabinet that it would not be expedient to cancel the orders given for the removal

¹ *Lyttelton Times*, 3 Jan. 1870: quoted by R. T. Hunt, 'Independence Agitation in New Zealand, 1869–1871' (Univ. of Otago, M.A. thesis, 1950), pp. 94–5. Mr. Hunt's general conclusion is that the New Zealand colonists as a whole did not desire independence.

² 'Our own Correspondent', Wellington (21 Jan.), *The Times*, 23 Mar. 1870. According to the *Spectator* (29 Jan.) 'the bills of the New Zealand Government, before floating easily, became quite unsaleable when the contents of the despatch were known'.

³ Granville commented in the margin: 'Yes it has. It ceased about the beginning of 1866 [1865?]. If the Colony had then acted wisely it would not have been renewed.'

⁴ Memo. of Gisborne (7 Jan.) in Bowen to Granville (13 Jan. 1870) (No. 7) with Notes by Granville, CO209/216.

of the troops. Featherston thought it was still not too late to countermand the orders. 'It was difficult', Meade noted, 'to gather from Mr. Dillon Bell what his final opinion was'; but he argued that the heavy demands of the wool trade on shipping in the summer months ruled out the embarkation of the troops by mid January as the War Office expected.[1] A month later, in their first official report to the New Zealand Government, the Commissioners declared themselves convinced 'that Her Majesty's Government have absolutely made up their minds on the question, and that nothing we can say has any chance of inducing them to reconsider their resolution'. On the other hand, their discussions were making it clear that no 'recognition of Maori authority' such as Lord Granville's dispatch appeared to suggest could take place through executive act or legislation in New Zealand and that the Imperial Government was 'by no means prepared to propose any surrender of the Queen's sovereign rights'.[2] This contentious issue therefore disappeared from the agenda and the Commissioners were free to concentrate on the question of a loan guarantee.

Weld had favoured this form of aid and FitzGerald, another proponent of the self-reliant policy, said bluntly, in a letter published early in 1870: 'The question is *one of money*. . . . The Colony is paying at present the utmost amount of taxation which it can bear.'[3] Lord Carnarvon had argued in a letter to *The Times* the previous November that 'even from a material point of view a small outlay now may be found to be ultimately the best economy'. A recent guarantee to the new Dominion of Canada had been 'money well laid out'. New Zealand's case was different, but a guarantee 'would only do for our own flesh and blood in an English colony what we have done for far less deserving foreigners all over the world and . . . would not entail upon us any appreciable risk'.[4] He now raised the general question in the House of Lords on 7 March.

<hr/>

[1] Memo. of Conversation with the N.Z. Commissioners (28 Jan. 1870) (R.M.), CO209/220.

[2] New Zealand Commissioners to Gisborne (25 Feb. 1870): *A.J.H.R.*, 1870, A. No. 9. A dispatch (No. 24) of the same date from Granville to Bowen informed him in conciliatory terms of the Government's inability to reverse its decision, CO209/212.

[3] *The Self-Reliant Policy in New Zealand: A Letter by J. E. FitzGerald* (London, 1870). In a letter of 1 June, FitzGerald thanks Selfe for printing it, Selfe Papers.

[4] Carnarvon to the Editor (2 Nov.), *The Times*, 3 Nov. 1869.

It is not the part of England to stand entirely and indifferently by when a great Colony is involved in such disasters and dangers as those in which New Zealand is involved; and . . . however wise and right your policy may be on paper, you cannot administer the affairs of a great Empire on a cut and dried rule, worthy rather of a pedant than of a great minister of this country.

Fitzherbert's request for a guaranteed loan had been referred to the Treasury 'without one word of commendation'.

Heavily pressed as we are in the race of international competition, are our fortunes so well assured that we can afford to throw away the affection, the loyalty, and the warm feelings of the colonists as if they were merely so much idle lumber?[1]

Carnarvon, however, had made a tactical error in concentrating on the settled point of the withdrawal of the troops. In a clever debating speech Granville claimed that he was merely carrying on the policies of the Duke of Buckingham, attributed the heat of the controversy to the trouble-making propensities of Sir George Grey, and twitted Carnarvon with the fact that his 'whole official career was one long continuous epistolary wrangle with the Governor, the Government and the Legislature of New Zealand'. Lord Grey was still pursuing the high aim of interposing an impartial authority between the colonists and the Maoris by the impracticable means of securing the colonists' assent to a modification of the constitution. Only Lord Lyttelton referred to the guarantee question, saying that he could not perceive 'the danger of this country giving the aid of its credit to a Colony of substantial resources during a time of difficulty'.[2]

Unofficial discussions were proceeding, but the prospects did not seem hopeful. Harry Atkinson in a letter to his brother said he had seen Featherston several times: 'he is in a horrible state of savageness and disgust with the Home Government.' The Chancellor of the Exchequer, Lowe, 'in his nasty way' had remarked that if the colonists were as weak as they said, they had no business in New Zealand, to which Featherston had retorted:

[1] *Hansard*, 3rd Ser. cxix. 1324–33.
[2] Ibid. 1336–62. Granville in referring to Sir George Grey doubtless had in mind a protest made by him with Clifford, Sewell, Atkinson, and Logan Campbell against the recent policy of the Colonial Office, which was reprinted in New Zealand newspapers.

'That argument will apply to Ireland, if you are so weak that you can't protect life and property what right have you there?' Granville had denied that his dispatches were meant to drive New Zealand out of the Empire, but Rogers had not upheld him. Featherston was coming to the conclusion that there was 'no other course open to us' but separation.[1] But by 9 May the ice had begun to break, and Featherston and Bell were consulting Granville on the wording of a telegram to be sent to catch the mail steamer at Point de Galle. They presumed they might refer to their offer 'if the Government would give substantial aid to emigration and the opening up of the country by roads and public works, to accept it on behalf of the Colony as a measure of conciliation which would be taken as proof of the continued goodwill of the Imperial Government and of its desire that the relations between the Imperial and Colonial Governments should be maintained on the most friendly footing.' They had asked for £1,000,000, spread over a period of years, as 'the least amount with which the objects in view could be really secured'.[2] The Imperial Government was opposed in principle to state aid to emigration and considered guarantees to colonial loans objectionable. But Granville was willing to consider the New Zealand request 'an exceptional one coming at the close of long financial relations between the Imperial Government and the Colony and at a period when for the first time the Colony has, on its own resources alone, made a gallant and successful effort to meet the difficulties to which it is exposed'. But the amount of the guarantee was still in dispute: Granville offered £500,000 only.[3] The Commissioners said it would be refused and resisted pressure to recommend its acceptance. So the telegram went without such a recommendation.[4] But Gladstone was now having second thoughts. 'It is I suppose too late', he writes to Granville on 12 May, 'to discuss the question between the million and the half and no one would say the separation of a Colony ought to turn on so small a question. But I hardly

[1] H. A. Atkinson to A. S. Atkinson (25 Mar. 1870), *Richmond–Atkinson Papers*, ii. 302–3.
[2] Featherston and Bell to Granville (9 May 1870), *A.J.H.R.*, 1870, A No. IA, p. 35.
[3] Minute of Granville (n.d.—May 1870), CO209/220. Rogers's reply to the Commissioners of 10 May, based upon this Minute, helps to date it.
[4] For the telegram (11 May) see *A.J.H.R.*, 1870, A. No. 9B. See also H. A. to A. S. Atkinson (18 June), *Richmond–Atkinson Papers*, ii. 306.

think it can.'[1] By 14 May the Cabinet had changed its mind. Featherston and Bell were able to send a second telegram: 'The Imperial Government will, under proper conditions as to repayment, guarantee loan of one million. . . . We have accepted this offer on behalf of Colony.'[2] In writing later to Gisborne, the Commissioners recorded their belief that 'nothing but the most sincere desire on Lord Granville's part to give the settlers assistance of a substantial kind could have overcome the objections of the Cabinet to a grant of any guarantee whatever.' They also acknowledged the cordial assistance of Monsell and the willingness of Stansfeld, Financial Secretary to the Treasury, to put the matter in the form 'most satisfactory to the Assembly'.[3] Writing to Granville to accept the guarantee, they said, with truth:

It is not a mere matter of money that has been arranged—a lasting tie has been made between the two Governments, by their engaging together in objects in which the nation has a common interest with her dependency: in the peopling of a new country which is one of her great off-shoots, in the opening up of that country by roads, in the reward by the steady and permanent employment of those Native allies who have so faithfully served the Crown, above all in the weaning of the turbulent and disaffected tribes from warlike habits to peaceful industry.[4]

This loan guarantee was not only an essential element in the success of Vogel's great public works policy, launched in his budget some forty days later. The solution of the New Zealand problem, one of the most long-lasting and contentious issues of the 1860s, contributed to make the years 1869–70 one of the turning points in the history of British colonial policy.

The reception of the settlement was mixed. *The Times* thought it a bad precedent. Self-governing colonies should develop their own resources. 'It is as certain as any economical proposition can be that every million guaranteed by this country affects our borrowing power and lowers the price of Consols, though it may be freely admitted that our loss falls infinitely short of the gain to

[1] Gladstone to Granville (12 May 1870), A. Ramm (ed.), *The Political Correspondence of Mr. Gladstone and Lord Granville, 1868–1876* (Camden, 3rd Ser. lxxxi London, 1952), p. 99.
[2] Bell and Featherston to Fox (14 May 1870), *A.J.H.R.*, 1870, A. No. 9B.
[3] N.Z. Commissioners to Gisborne (14 June 1870), ibid., A. No. 9C.
[4] Featherston and Bell to Granville (9 May 1870), ibid., A. No. 1A, p. 36.

New Zealand.'¹ The *Spectator*, on the other hand, in an article headed 'The Death-Bed Repentance of the Colonial Office' congratulated the Government 'on its tardy conversion to the belief which for so many years we have professed, through little but evil report from all our Liberal contemporaries, that the nation is proud in its heart of hearts of our Colonial Empire'.² In New Zealand the settlement was for a while prejudiced by continuing soreness over the withdrawal of the troops. Their departure on 24 February had evoked an indignant memorandum from Fox. The protestations that they were being removed for the benefit of the colony were merely 'a civil disguise of the fact that it is considered necessary to sacrifice the Colony to Imperial policy'.

Indeed it might be laid down as a principle, that whilst a colony remains a part of the Empire, and is governed by a nominee of the Crown, it has the right to look for assistance to the Imperial country in any emergency with which it is beyond its own power to cope. To satisfy the theories of Lord Granville as to responsibility, New Zealand must cease to be a part of the Empire, and that is one reason why the Despatch in question may be regarded, as urged by Sir George Grey, as a hint to that effect.³

Rogers considered this memorandum an illustration of

the 'Spenlow and Jorkins' policy which I have always considered especially characteristic of that Colony. While Dr. Featherston and Mr. Bell have come to an amicable settlement on the strength of the guarantee of a million, the minister on the spot is heating the furnace, threatening separation, charging the Imperial Government with indefinite liabilities and denouncing its policy.⁴

Fox was still writing in the same vein early in June, shortly before the meeting of the General Assembly; and when the Assembly met, members of both Houses echoed his denunciations of Imperial policy. But though no less a person than Sewell, now Minister of Justice, was still thinking in terms of preparing to face the question of independence, others avowed their belief in self-reliance without drawing this conclusion and deprecated this

¹ *The Times*, 17 May 1870.
² *Spectator*, 21 May 1870.
³ Memo. of Fox (28 Mar.) in Bowen to Granville (2 Apr. 1870) (No. 39), *A.J.H.R.*, 1870, A. No. 1, pp. 86–8.
⁴ Minute of Rogers (30 May) on Bowen to Granville (2 Apr. 1870) (No. 39), CO209/216.

continual harping on grievances.[1] Even the news of the guarantee, received on 13 July, did not silence criticism. The Wellington correspondent of *The Times* reported 'a strong feeling in and out of Parliament that the Colony would best consult its own honour by refusing it'.[2] But this feeling of pique did not last. The Legislative Council adopted a harmless series of resolutions regretting the course adopted by the Home Government but looking forward to a restoration of friendly feeling; and a private member's motion in the House declaring that 'the Imperial Government has failed in its duty to the Colony' was withdrawn.[3]

A certain amount of naval assistance had been given to New Zealand from time to time during the wars; and Admiralty orders in July 1869 that two ships of war should cruise off the New Zealand coasts were no doubt designed to soften the blow of withdrawal of the troops. But when Fox in September 1870 expressed a hope that Her Majesty's Government would maintain 'as large a naval force as possible in New Zealand waters', Rogers took alarm. 'Here we have a fresh attempt to fasten on us part of the responsibility of defending the Colony against native troubles. This steady system of encroachment makes me so impatient that I distrust my own judgement as to the terms of the answer.' Monsell wisely preferred a short answer, simply saying that 'Her Majesty's Government had no intention of withdrawing the instructions given to the Commander of the squadron stationed at New Zealand for Imperial purposes "to protect the colonists in the event of disaster occurring" '.[4] There was another flutter in April 1871 when H.M.S. *Virago* was inadvertently ordered home, before her place had been filled, just when the Maori King's refusal to give up the murderers of a surveyor had caused fresh excitement. Fox, who was on his farm in Rangitikei near a Hauhau settlement, sent an alarmist telegram declaring that if the Imperial Government intended 'to withdraw the countenance afforded by the presence of a Naval force', it would be difficult for 'the best affected' to retain their 'feeling of attachment to the

[1] For Sewell's speech in the Legislative Council, 13 July see *N.Z.P.D.* vii. 363–71.

[2] Wellington correspondent (4 Aug.), *The Times*, 29 Sept. 1870.

[3] Legislative Council, 21 July, *J.L.C.*, 1870, pp. 23–4, 39–40, 44–6. House of Representatives, 27–8 July, *J.H.R.*, 1870, p. 94

[4] Memo. of Fox (19 Sept.) in Bowen to Kimberley (24 Sept. 1870) (No. 123) with Minutes of Rogers and Monsell (3 and 5 Dec.), CO209/217.

parent country'.[1] Lord Kimberley, now Secretary of State, explained the mistake but expressed regret at the tone and language of Fox's telegram and Fox apologized for it.[2] The Colonial Office was in fact doing its best to secure more and better warships for the Australian station, though it could not promise that these would 'always be at hand on the far extended coasts of the Australasian colonies'. New Zealand was free if it liked to establish its own navy in terms of the Colonial Naval Defence Act 1865.[3]

As this episode showed, New Zealand's relations with the Imperial Government were moving into smoother waters. Though Granville's attitude towards the loan guarantee redeemed his record, Kimberley had not been involved in the controversies of the past and soon became more seriously interested in colonial questions than Granville had ever been. But Granville had taken his cue from Rogers and Rogers's sympathies became so deeply engaged with the Maoris that his retirement in 1871 was in itself a contribution to better relations between New Zealand and the Imperial Government. Rogers never quite reconciled himself to the fact that colonization implied a displacement of Maoris by colonists on much of the land of New Zealand. Sooner or later the state would be strong enough to halt the process and insist that the Maoris should not be entirely deprived of their lands. But government in New Zealand in the fifties and sixties was weak, decentralized, too much absorbed in colonizing the country to see how this looked from the Maori side. The Colonial Office tried to remain above the battle, but its well-meant advice only succeeded in irritating the colonists without benefiting the Maoris. It had handed over responsibility for Maori affairs without really trusting those to whom it was handed over. It may be said that the New Zealand leaders brought this distrust upon themselves by asking for control without seeing its implications and by trying to evade the implications when these were brought

[1] Telegram of Fox to Bowen (12 Apr. 1871), A.J.H.R., 1871, A. No. 1, p. 10. See also Vogel to Kimberley (1 May 1871) with Minutes of Rogers and Kimberley (5 and 7 May), CO209/225.

[2] Minute of Kimberley (20 July) on Bowen to Kimberley (1 May 1871) (No. 39), CO209/221. For Fox's apology see Memo. of 28 Sept. in Bowen to Kimberley (25 Sept. 1871) (No. 91), A.J.H.R., 1872, A. No. 1, pp. 11–12.

[3] Minute of Holland (6 Sept.), Herbert (8 Sept.), and Kimberley (9 Sept.) on Bowen to Kimberley (6 July 1871) (No. 55), CO209/222.

home to them. But there were faults on both sides. When a New Zealand Ministry formulated the policy of confiscation and military settlement as a means of financing the war, the Imperial Government gave it at least qualified approval and then imposed upon Sir George Grey the impossible task of checking it in mid-career. A quarrel was then inevitable. And if the Waikatos had not lost their lands by confiscation after defeat, most of them would have been lost by the processes of negotiation, sanctioned by the Land Court, which were described by the Native Land Laws Commission of 1891.[1] 'No possible action or line of policy by our Government', wrote Judge Maning in 1868, 'could have had the slightest effect whatever in averting this war; the natives were determined to try their strength with us, and do not in reality blame us for having inflicted loss and suffering on them '[2] This is an exaggeration. The defeated tribes long remained sore at the loss of their lands. The Hauhaus in their bitterness and frustration revived savage customs which had been disappearing. But the Maoris in general fought not only bravely and skilfully but chivalrously, in a way which could not fail to win the respect of the Pakeha. Whatever might be said in the more scurrilous newspapers, the colonial leaders had never hated the Maoris. There is no evidence that the course of policy in the later war years and afterwards—the institution of the Land Court, the grant of representation in the General Assembly, the introduction of Government schools, McLean's patient and tactful pacification and tacit acquiescence in Maori authority in the 'King Country'—were affected by Imperial advice. These policies were due to the pressure of events on the spot.

The course of the war was certainly affected by the presence of Imperial troops. The main campaign of 1863–4 could never have been undertaken without them. The controversies arising out of their presence produced, in reaction, the self-reliant policy. But the practical difficulties of self-reliance were never understood in England. *The Times* once remarked that 'our New Zealand colonists do not pretend that they are too weak or too few to compete with the savages around them: they are only too rich

---

[1] On this see Sorrenson, op. cit.

[2] Report of Maning (29 Mar.) in Bowen to Buckingham (23 July 1868) (No. 65), P.P., 1868–9, xliv (H.C. 307), 163–4. Maning, a judge of the Native Land Court, wrote in *Old New Zealand* and *The War in the North* classic descriptions of Maori life in pre-colonial and early colonial days.

and too busy'.[1] But the colonists could not neglect colonization to concentrate on defence: only the wealth produced by colonization could provide the sinews of war when Imperial assistance was withdrawn. Great Britain's own difficulties in finding recruits for the army and reviving the militia during and after the Crimean War might have been expected to produce a greater understanding of New Zealand's problem.

It was, however, the manner rather than the substance of British colonial policy that was most at fault. It was right and proper that Colonial Office dispatches should uphold Imperial interests in just treatment of the Maoris and avoidance of undue dependence on Imperial troops and the Imperial treasury. But Richmond was justified in complaining that colonial leaders were treated as if they were not yet out of the schoolroom. They were mature and able men, steadily widening their experience in the act of government. Stafford was disingenuous and had the Irishman's 'chip on the shoulder' about England, Fox was impulsive and hot-tempered; but the missions of Fitzherbert, and later of Featherston and Bell, showed how colonial leaders responded to frank and courteous treatment. Free and friendly negotiation, with a steady advance towards equality of status if not of power, could alone ensure a continuing connection between the Imperial Government and self-governing colonies. The risk of alienation had been real. But the progress of pacification and economic recovery, stimulated by the guaranteed loan, soon diverted New Zealand's attention to the exciting questions of public works, immigration, and national development. Delicate questions might still arise between the Imperial and colonial Governments—possible commercial negotiations with foreign Powers, intercolonial preferential tariffs, aspirations in the Pacific Islands—but they were settled more and more by a dialogue between the two Governments and less and less by *fiat* of the Imperial power.[2]

---

[1] *The Times*, 18 May 1869.

[2] On foreign relations see Minutes of Rogers, Monsell, and Kimberley (13–19 July) on Bowen to Granville (9 May 1870) (Confidential), CO209/216. On intercolonial preferential duties, see memos. of Vogel and circulars of Kimberley in *A.J.H.R.*, 1871–3, A. Nos. 1 and 1A; Minutes of Rogers (10 Apr.) on Board of Trade to Colonial Office (27 Mar. 1871), CO209/224; P. Knaplund, *Gladstone and Britain's Imperial Policy* (London, 1927) and C. D. Allin, *Australasian Preferential Tariffs and Imperial Free Trade* (Minneapolis, 1929). On New Zealand and the Pacific Islands, see A. Ross, *New Zealand Aspirations in the Pacific in the Nineteenth Century* (Oxford, 1964).

# XII

## FIRST STEPS IN
## CONSTITUTIONAL REFORM

In the twenty years preceding our period the British West Indies had passed through a double crisis, in fact had undergone a social revolution. The Abolition of Slavery Act, passed by the Imperial Parliament in 1833, had come into operation a year later and the system of apprenticeship, designed to ease the transition from slavery to freedom, had been prematurely brought to an end by the colonial legislatures, under pressure from home, in 1838.[1] Hardly had the West Indies begun to adjust themselves to the new order of things when they were faced with the loss of the protected market for their principal export. The Sugar Duties Act 1846 proposed to diminish their preference by stages and equalize foreign and colonial rates of duty in 1851. Sugar prices collapsed early in 1847 and a general financial panic, to which other causes contributed, soon followed. The West Indies obtained some relief. Though the majority report of Lord George Bentinck's committee of 1848 in favour of a protective duty of 10s. a hundredweight for six years was not acceptable, the Russell Ministry agreed to postpone equalization of duties until 1854. Trinidad and British Guiana, with the aid of an Imperially guaranteed loan, could begin increasing their labour force by a thousand or two indentured immigrants a year from India. In some other colonies, notably Barbados but also Antigua and St. Kitts, shortage of land forced most of the Negroes to continue working on the estates and they maintained or even increased their sugar production. In a few islands—Antigua, Nevis, St. Lucia, Tobago, Grenada—we hear of Negroes growing sugar on a share-cropping system, not very successfully. Even in comparatively fortunate British Guiana, many estates changed hands. In Jamaica and many of the smaller

---

[1] See W. L. Mathieson, *British Slavery and its Abolition, 1823–1838* (London, 1926) and, especially, W. L. Burn, *Emancipation and Apprenticeship in the British West Indies* (London, 1937).

islands planters in the less favoured areas, overburdened by debt and irregular labour supply, simply abandoned their estates.[1] Whilst the Negroes generally were content to cultivate the provision grounds allowed them in the days of slavery, the more enterprising of them bought small lots or squatted on the abandoned estates, became small farmers producing for the local market, and prospered.[2]

The Christian missionaries, especially perhaps the Baptists in Jamaica, had become leaders of the people in the last days of slavery and during the apprenticeship, but their influence had declined since. Separatist Afro-Christian sects were growing at their expense. Little was done for public education, despite the efforts of Governors like Lord Elgin in Jamaica and Lord Harris in Trinidad: there were religious as well as financial difficulties. The health of the Negroes received less attention than in the days of slavery, when many estates had weekly visits from doctors under a contract system. Terrible epidemics of cholera and small-pox revealed the appalling sanitary condition of the towns. The once dominant planters were not only financially stricken but seemed to have lost all their energy and most of their public spirit.[3]

Most of the West India colonies still lived under the old representative system of Governor, Council, and elective Assembly which had originated in the seventeenth century before sugar was king. The colonies taken from the French in the Seven Years War and retained at the Peace of Paris—Tobago, Grenada, St. Vincent, and Dominica—were given these institutions and Tobago received them again when, after being returned to the French in the Treaty of Versailles, it was retaken in 1793. St. Lucia and Trinidad, acquired later, became Crown Colonies. Lord Hawkesbury, it seems, drew a moral from what happened in Grenada: 'by not establishing in that Island a Government agreeable to the

---

[1] On all this see my *British Colonial Policy in the Age of Peel and Russell*, chs. vii and xi, and W. L. Mathieson, *British Slave Emancipation, 1838–1849* and *The Sugar Colonies and Governor Eyre* (London, 1932 and 1936). There are useful tables of sugar imports into the United Kingdom from the various colonies in P.P., 1856, lv (H.C. 209) and 1863, lxvii (H.C. 272).

[2] On this subject see especially D. Hall, *Free Jamaica, 1838–1865: an Economic History* (New Haven, 1959).

[3] Details in the Parliamentary Papers support the conclusions of P. D. Curtin's penetrating sociological study, *The Two Jamaicas: the Role of Ideas in a Tropical Colony, 1830–1865* (Cambridge, Mass., 1955).

inhabitants, they were all of them gradually driven out of the Island.'[1] The proliferation of boards and committees of the Assemblies, which carried on many of the functions properly belonging to the executive, had seriously curtailed the powers of the Governor in the 'chartered' colonies; and the concentration on sugar and the recent decline of the white population had made oligarchies of all of them. Now that the sugar economy had been undermined by slave emancipation and free trade, the electorate, except in the Bahamas, which had never been a sugar colony, nowhere numbered more than a few hundred and the number voting was even smaller. In Barbados, where there were 1,359 electors in 1854, only 78 had voted at the last poll: many seats were uncontested.[2] In recent elections in St. Vincent, Lieutenant-Governor Eyre reported, 18 members had been returned by 10 voters or less: 'in one instance, a single voter actually returned two of the nineteen members composing the whole House of Assembly.'[3] In Jamaica, some of the poorer voters used to let their taxes fall into arrears and then make the candidates pay their taxes in order to get their votes; the *Morning Journal* denounced the 'open and shameless purchase and sale of votes at elections'.[4] The planters were losing power and the coloured petty bourgeoisie of Kingston and other towns gradually acquiring it.[5] The lack of information about the racial composition of the other Assemblies perhaps testifies to the comparative quiescence of racial feeling, but there were certainly coloured Assemblymen in Montserrat and Dominica and probably in St. Vincent, where the Speaker delivered himself in scathing terms on the incapacity of the large majority of members. 'During the time I have been speaker,' he wrote, 'it has scarcely been possible to find a member who could, as chairman, conduct the business of a Committee of the House. Very many cannot read a manuscript at all—some cannot read a manuscript law bill at all—and on one occasion a gentleman in

---

[1] Draft Commission of 1794, quoted by D. J. Murray, *The West Indies and the Development of Colonial Government* (Oxford, 1965), p. 51.

[2] Colebrooke to Newcastle (20 Mar. 1854) (No. 15), P.P., 1854–5, xxxvi [1919], 67 ff. In Antigua 234 voted out of 1,200, in Nevis 76 out of 500.

[3] Eyre to Colebrooke (2 May) in Colebrooke to Russell (19 May 1855) (No. 28), P.P., 1856, xlii [2050], 88.

[4] Sir C. E. Grey to Pakington (28 Apr. 1852) (No. 39), P.P., 1852–3, lxvii (H.C. 76), 145–6.

[5] See especially Sir C. E. Grey to Pakington (26 June 1852) (No. 53), P.P., 1852–3, lxvii (H.C. 76), 157–62.

the chair could neither read nor write.'[1] As there was 'no law in
existence for the furtherance of education' in St. Vincent, this
state of affairs is not perhaps surprising.[2]

But the strongest impression left on the mind of the historian is
of the informality, one might say the amateurishness, of government in the smaller islands. The business was conducted in the
principal town. Members would come in on the day appointed
for a committee meeting with other affairs besides its business to
transact. 'If there be occasion for special calls,' writes Sir William
Colebrooke, Governor of Barbados and the Windward Islands,
'the Boards meet on other days, but as the Legislative Bodies are
always in session and usually meet for a day at intervals of a fortnight or a month throughout the year, this is not generally
required.'[3] In Grenada, where the Assembly was chiefly composed
of planters who could not afford more than two days' absence
from home, 'the business of the House', we are told, 'generally
commences late on the first day and by two or three o'clock on
the following day most of the country members are anxious to
return home.'[4] Officials had to be maids of all work. In St. Kitts,
some years later, there was no Colonial Secretary; his duties were
performed by the private secretary of the Lieutenant Governor;
there was an Island Secretary, but his duties as 'registrar of deeds,
clerk of the Crown, clerk of the courts, etc.' occupied his whole
time.[5] The Colonial Secretary in St. Vincent was also clerk of the
Privy Council, clerk of the Legislative Council, clerk of the
Crown, secretary of the Supreme Court, and Registrar of Wills
and Deeds.[6] It is hardly necessary to labour further the point that
the old representative system by the 1850s was very ill calculated
to produce a sense of political or financial responsibility or a
coherent, constructive body of legislation.

The Imperial Parliament had compensated the slave-owners,

[1] Choppin to Eyre (22 June) in Colebrooke to Russell (3 July 1855) (Private
and Confidential), CO260/83.
[2] Eyre to Colebrooke (2 May) (No. 52) in Colebrooke to Russell (19 May
1855) (No. 28), P.P., 1856, xlii [2050], 89.
[3] Colebrooke to Newcastle (22 Dec. 1853) (Gen. No. 8), CO28/178. This
refers to Barbados but he speaks of 'a similar method' in other islands.
[4] Kortright to Hincks (16 Apr.) in Hincks to Stanley (10 May 1858) (No. 19),
P.P., 1859, Sess. 2, xxi [2567], 79.
[5] Pine to Hamilton (1 Oct.) in Hamilton to Newcastle (22 Oct. 1861) (No. 89),
P.P., 1862, xxxvi [2955], 76-7.
[6] Memo. of Eyre (13 Feb. 1855), P.P., 1856, xlii [2050], 100.

though most of the compensation actually went to their creditors. It had also advanced £500,000 in Exchequer bills to Jamaica planters in consideration of their losses in the last slave insurrection and a similar sum to sufferers from hurricanes in Barbados, St. Vincent, St. Lucia, and Dominica;[1] and planters in arrears with interest and instalment payments on these loans were given extensions of time.[2] On the other hand, Disraeli deeply disappointed West Indian hopes when in his December Budget in 1852 he declined to arrest the process of equalizing the sugar duties. He was willing to allow the colonies to refine their sugar in bond for home consumption—that is to let the duty be paid on refined rather than raw sugar; but his Budget lapsed with the defeat of the Conservatives and Gladstone in the following April announced that he had found this concession impracticable.[3]

In any case the trend of British colonial policy in the West Indies as elsewhere was towards the limitation of Imperial responsibilities. Sir John Pakington drew the attention of the Governor of the Windward Islands to the expense entailed by the numerous military outposts in the islands and instructed him to report whether their number could be reduced; and despite Colebrooke's statement of their value as 'sanitary stations for the troops during the prevalence of epidemics', the Duke of Newcastle in the following October announced that the Government had decided to withdraw the garrisons from St. Vincent, Grenada, and Tobago in the Windward Islands and from St. Kitts and Dominica in the Leeward group.[4] This policy was maintained despite protests from the island Assemblies, alarmed by a recent disturbance on Tortola, one of the Virgin Islands, which had had to appeal to

[1] The main Act was 2 & 3 Gul. IV, c. 5; 5 & 6 Gul. IV, c. 51 brought Dominica within the scheme.

[2] P.P., 1854-5, xxxvii (H.C. 159), *passim*. Another relief measure was the Encumbered Estates Act 1854 (17 & 18 Vict., c. 117), modelled on the Irish Act, to facilitate the sale of such estates in colonies which adopted the Act: see Barkly to Newcastle (26 Feb. 1854), Newcastle Papers, NeC9553; and House of Commons, 7 Aug. 1854, *Hansard*, 3rd Ser. cxxxv. 1377-83. But this Act was slow to win acceptance. St. Vincent (1857) was the first to adopt it; Jamaica and Antigua eventually used it most; see R. W. Beachey, *The British West Indies Sugar Industry in the Late Nineteenth Century* (Oxford, 1957), ch. i.

[3] *Hansard*, 3rd Ser. cxxiii. 848-53 (Disraeli); cxxv. 1357-8 (Gladstone).

[4] Pakington to Colebrooke (25 Aug. 1852) (No. 2—Military), Colebrooke to Pakington (22 Nov. 1852) (No. 50—Military); Newcastle to Colebrooke (21 Oct. 1853) (No. 4—Military) and to Mackintosh (Leeward Islands) (21 Oct. 1853) (No. 2), P.P., 1854, xli (H.C. 177), 1-2, 5, 57.

the Danish island of St. Thomas for help. The troops were concentrated at Barbados, which was given a steamer to move them if required, and a small garrison was left at Antigua.[1] Parliament was also told in 1853 that expenditure on the stipendiary magistrates who had supervised the transition from slavery to freedom would be discontinued as vacancies arose.[2] But Gladstone's Budget did contain a glimmer of hope for Jamaica. If its Assembly would amend its 'vicious constitution' and make possible 'a strict control over expenditure', then Her Majesty's Government would 'employ the credit of this country in the way of guarantee' on its behalf.

This was the outcome of a constitutional crisis which had faced Newcastle soon after he took office. Disappointed of its hopes of 'some extensive and liberal measures of relief' from the Conservative Ministry, the Jamaica Assembly resolved to insist on a 20 per cent cut in every salary, annuity, or grant paid out of the public chest, with a few exceptions, and a corresponding reduction of import duties and certain taxes. When the Council rejected these Bills, the Assembly refused to do business with it. As the increasingly influential 'coloured party' adhered to the practice of making 90 per cent of the revenue depend upon annual votes, the expiry of the Revenue Bills on 30 April reduced the colony to acute financial straits. Governor Sir Charles Grey, who was nearing the end of his term, left the problem to the Imperial Government.

Let the civil establishment be reduced on the principle of moderate but fair compensation to a scale suited to the circumstances of the island, and let a sufficient portion of the revenue be made permanent to provide securely, and without annual bickerings, for that establishment, and let the Governor . . . be authorized to appoint from time to time three members of the Assembly to bring in Government Bills, and I really think that all would go on quietly enough. But I utterly despair of the Assembly being induced to effect these obvious improvements itself, and whether they ought to be effected by immediate intervention of the Imperial Parliament, similar to the Act of 1839, and aided perhaps by a commission from England and the superintendence of Her Majesty's Privy Council, I will abstain from discussing.[3]

---

[1] P.P., 1854, xli (H.C. 177) *passim* and House of Lords, 23 Feb. 1854; *Hansard*, 3rd Ser. cxxx. 1137–43. The Antigua detachment was later withdrawn but had to be sent back in 1858.
[2] House of Commons, 20 May 1853, *Hansard*, 3rd Ser. cxxvii. 445.
[3] Grey to Newcastle (10 May 1853) (No. 40), P.P., 1852–3, lxv [1655], 5–9. On

A fortnight later, Sir Charles suggested a suspension of the constitution and temporary government by a Commission.[1] Newcastle believed that the Jamaica deadlock was due to no fault of Sir Charles Grey but to 'that ill constructed frame of polity which so long as it endures, will defy and paralyse the soundest and best intentioned plans for the regeneration of her Government and people'.[2] But, warned by the fiasco of 1839, he believed the deadlock could best be broken not by the intervention of the Imperial Parliament but by good management under a new Governor. In Henry Barkly, with his parliamentary experience, West Indian interests, and record as a conciliator in British Guiana, he thought he had a man well fitted for the task. A confidential memorandum by Henry Taylor was circulated to the Cabinet;[3] and Newcastle outlined the plan in the House of Lords, where it received the support of Lord Derby (who said his Government had contemplated action on similar lines) and Lord Grey.[4] Barkly was to secure a reform of the civil list, with some reduction of officers and salaries when opportunities arose, and Crown initiative in money votes; and the Government must also have one or more organs in the Assembly, in short some approximation to responsible government.

Whether the organs of the Government in the Assembly should be so far the organs of a majority of the Assembly also, that they should lose their offices and official seats at the pleasure of that majority or on ceasing to carry with them the votes of that majority, is a question which I am unable to determine without much more local knowledge than I possess. That responsible government should be established is the first thing necessary; but what form that responsibility should in the first instance assume, depends chiefly upon the composition of the Assembly and the materials which it affords for what has been termed party government, as also upon the control which public opinion may be likely to exercise over such a government and over the majority of the Assembly.

the background of this crisis, see my *Colonial Policy in the Age of Peel and Russell*, ch. xi, esp. pp. 260-2.

[1] Grey to Newcastle (26 May 1853) (No. 50), P.P., 1852-3, lxv [1655], 16-17.

[2] Newcastle to Grey (13 June 1853), CO138/70.

[3] This is an inference from the presence of this memo. of 30 June 1853 in the Cardwell Papers: 7/44. Cardwell, who was not a member of the Aberdeen Cabinet, may not have seen it until 1865. But the essential decision to link constitutional reform with financial guarantee had been taken before 18 Apr.

[4] House of Lords, 30 June 1853, *Hansard*, 3rd Ser. cxxvii. 947-76.

If such measures were adopted, Her Majesty's Government would guarantee a loan to redeem the whole island debt except that owing to Great Britain. Newcastle also warned an Assembly based on so narrow a franchise of the consequences of rejecting the reforms: 'it would be vain to expect that a body so little in harmony with the spirit of the times as the Assembly of Jamaica can be long maintaincd in the exercise of irresponsible power.'[1]

We can follow the course of the political struggle in detail in a fascinating series of private letters from Barkly to Newcastle and to Henry Roberts, recently Commissioner of Education for Jamaica and now Newcastle's private secretary. The Governor's opening speech, laying his programme before the Assembly, received a courteous reply, which, however, stressed 'the peculiar privileges and practice of this House' as being 'among the most precious of the . . . trophies . . . won in the cause of civil and religious liberty'.[2] Some of these privileges, especially in finance, were among the main obstacles to reform, and the House, though forgoing the old privilege of leaving individual members free to initiate financial proposals, transferred this power to a Finance Committee of nine members which the Governor thought might give rise, being irresponsible, to even greater evils. 'I never', he told Newcastle, 'had a more unaccountable or less to be depended upon set to manage in my life.'[3] He tried the planters' party but found its most moderate leader, Westmorland, curiously afraid of coming out publicly in support of his opinions. He discussed a scheme of responsible government with two leaders of the coloured party, Jackson and Heslop: 'but as soon as this became known the fiercest jealousy was manifested both by their own friends and by what is called the Government Party.'[4] Eventually he got an unobjectionable Revenue Bill passed by a majority of two: 'how that majority was acquired,' he wrote, 'how I got the term of the Bill extended at the eleventh hour to the end of next year by threatening to reject it on any other terms etc. it is better

---

[1] Newcastle to Barkly (16 Aug. 1853) (No. 1), P.P., 1854, xliii [1806], 115–21.
[2] Barkly to Newcastle (18 Oct. 1853) (No. 3) with Enclosures, ibid., pp. 11 ff.
[3] Barkly to Newcastle (10 Nov. 1853), Newcastle Papers, NeC9553.
[4] Ibid. This 'Government' party was not the planters' party nor the 'coloured party' with which it is identified by Curtin (op. cit., p. 182). Barkly to Newcastle (10 Dec. 1853) (Private) is not very specific about it but I presume it consisted of officials and hangers-on of Government, Newcastle Papers, NeC9553.

you should not know!'[1] The next item of the programme was constitutional reform: three plans were propounded in the Assembly, 'that of the Jackson party . . . advocating responsible Government *a l'outrance*'. He saw objections to bringing forward a scheme of his own.

First of all it would have put Government in a false position had I urged anything short of 'Responsible Government', which nevertheless is quite unsuited to the circumstances of the Island. Secondly, neither the Planters, the Jews, the Browns, nor the old King's House Party, were strong enough by themselves to carry any scheme I could have proposed through the House.

But he expected, through the hopes and fears of these various sections, to secure very much the scheme he would himself have recommended. One powerful lever was the anxiety of public creditors to be paid: 'I have taken care to let all my Hebrew Friends in particular know that I will not commit the Crown to any increase of the debt of Jamaica, until I see the Constitution reformed in a way which I think will be satisfactory to Her Majesty's Government.' He was taken aback by the revelation that colour dominated Jamaican politics.

It was openly avowed by Mr. Jackson that those of his colour would not allow a white Ministry to be formed, and that they claimed in fact for themselves a preponderating influence in the State. . . . Not only did Mr. Osborn and other coloured men who usually support the Government give their votes on this basis, but every official who had the slightest tinge of African blood in his veins, abandoned his usual political connexion and voted the same way. . . . Though it is the extent of prejudice in the Whites which has almost forced them into this combination, it is not the less likely to prove formidable to the future peace of the country.[2]

However, after a reference back, a Committee of the Assembly produced, just before Christmas, an agreed report on political reform. The Assembly then adjourned for a month's recess. As Barkly explained to Roberts:

Even if a House could have been got together sooner, there would have been danger in proceeding without the Planters, who would certainly have remained to commence their Sugar Crops, as my

---

[1] Barkly to Roberts (26 Nov. 1853) (Private), Newcastle Papers, NeC9553.
[2] Barkly to Newcastle (10 Dec. 1853), ibid.

coloured friends might have upset the Coach without the drag which
the pressure of the former constitutes upon their go-ahead propensities.[1]

The Bill drafted during the recess by Bryan Edwards, leader of
the Bar, leant towards the policy of the planters' party, proposing
'to confer far greater powers on the Representative of the Crown
. . . than he could have ventured to ask for himself and to reduce
his organs in the Legislature to mere ciphers'.[2] The Bill had a
rough passage. Whilst the Chief Justice, Sir Joshua Rowe, 'in the
Railway and elsewhere' spoke of it as unconstitutional, the leaders
of the coloured party adopted Fabian tactics, hoping to prolong
the struggle until the country members grew weary and went
away.[3] But on 10 March Barkly reported that the third reading
had passed the House by 15 to 3.

The fact is the coloured Party have found out on calmer reflection
that, in aiming a great blow at the Council by diminishing official
influence in it, and in creating as they imagined at the same time a
number of snug Ministerial Berths for themselves, they have given up
more than they are likely to gain, by having included in the measure
a cession of their powers of misappropriating the Revenue, and a great
increase of the power of the Representative of the Crown.[4]

They now hoped the Council would reject the Bill. But the Chief
Justice was persuaded out of his original intention to move sweeping amendments. The Council's amendments were so moderate
that Jackson could only resort to procrastination: the House met
only five times in three weeks and Westmorland was so disgusted
that he left for the country. But the long battle was bad for business and the press began to abuse the Assembly for its delays.
Jackson and his party changed their tactics and 'set to work in real
earnest to pass the Bill indeed but to make its rejection by the
Council certain' by moving to reduce judicial salaries. But the
Council sprang a 'countermine', engineered we may guess by
Barkly himself. Though the 'half-frantic' Chief Justice seconded
the motion of the coloured party leader, Jordon, for rejection of
the amended Bill, the Council passed it on 6 April by a majority
of one.[5]

[1] Barkly to Roberts (26 Dec. 1853), (Private), Newcastle Papers, NeC9553.
[2] Barkly to Roberts (10 Jan. 1854), ibid.
[3] Barkly to Roberts (26 Jan. and 10 Feb. 1854), ibid.
[4] Barkly to Roberts (10 Mar. 1854), ibid.
[5] Barkly to Newcastle (25 Mar.) and to Roberts (9 Apr. 1854), ibid. The
figure inserted for judicial salaries was £9,800. Jackson had wanted £7,000, the

The 'Act for the better Government of this Island' enlarged the Council by providing for the appointment for life of such persons, having freehold property with a clear annual income of £300 or paying £30 in taxes, as would enlarge the present membership to seventeen, and separated it from the Privy Council. The Governor might appoint not more than three members of the Assembly and one member of the Legislative Council to be the organs of Government in the Assembly and Council and to assist him in his executive duties and in the management of the colony's finances. The right of every member of the House of Assembly to propose a vote of money was to cease. The Act set aside £25,000 as a civil list and £30,000 annually to liquidate the public debt at an interest rate of not more than 4 per cent. It was not to come into effect until it received the royal assent and the Imperial Parliament passed a Loan Guarantee Act.[1]

'It appears to me', wrote Taylor, 'that the substance of what the Government required is so nearly accomplished by the Act as to leave no doubt that it should be accepted and confirmed.'[2] Newcastle was of the same opinion and Parliament passed the Loan Guarantee Act without debate.[3] Early in September, on receiving the Order in Council confirming these Acts, Barkly dissolved the Assembly. Local and personal issues predominated and there was no substantial change in membership.[4] When the formal instruments, delayed by 'the absence from London of all the personages who had to co-operate in the preparation of the new Letters Patent and Royal Instructions',[5] arrived in the island, Barkly, on 22 November, proclaimed the Act and the new Executive Committee took office. It comprised the planter Westmorland as Minister of

Assembly had raised this to £8,000. The Chief Justice wanted no reduction. The statement quoted by Hume Wrong in his *Government of the West Indies* (Oxford, 1923), p. 65, that 'the Bill was neither introduced by the local government, nor matured under its auspices' is technically correct, but misleading.

[1] Barkly to Newcastle (10 Apr. 1854) (No. 46) and Act (16 & 17 Vict., c. 29) enclosed, P.P., 1854, xliii [1906], 89–109.

[2] Minute of Taylor (4 May) on Barkly to Newcastle (10 Apr. 1854) (No. 46), CO137/323.

[3] The 'Act to guarantee the Liquidation of a Loan or Loans for the Service of the Colony of Jamaica' of £500,000 was 17 & 18 Vict., c. 54.

[4] Barkly to Sir G. Grey, Bart. (19 Oct. 1854) (No. 107), CO137/324. Of the 47 members of the House of Assembly, nearly half were of British descent, 'a third more or less of African extraction', and a fifth of Jewish descent.

[5] Minute of P. Smith (12 Dec.). Sir G. Grey (9 Oct.) had commented on 'the very slow progress of these documents', CO137/324.

388 FIRST STEPS IN CONSTITUTIONAL REFORM

Agriculture, Public Works, and Finance, Bryan Edwards as Minister of Justice, and Edward Jordon, whom Barkly persuaded to transfer from the Council to the Assembly, in charge of the 'duties more immediately connected with the intellectual and physical welfare of the emancipated Peasantry'.[1] On the death in 1855 of the Attorney-General, Barkly appointed Alexander Heslop, a coloured barrister of the Inner Temple, to hold the office on a political tenure. The Executive Committee, after a short honeymoon, found it difficult to pass their legislation in face of opposition concerted by 'a small knot of disappointed office-seekers'; but Barkly remained convinced that they possessed more of the confidence of the House than any alternative combination and 'if . . . the new form of Government . . . works but indifferently in a legislative point of view it promises to be invaluable in an administrative one'.[2] Merivale in the first year of Barkly's successor put his finger on the difficulty: 'it is the old story of constitutional government without party, and without patronage whereby to consolidate a party.'[3] Sir Henry Barkly, by a remarkable combination of patience, firmness, and finesse, had converted a hopelessly inefficient and irresponsible form of government into a constitution which could work, given good leadership at the top, harmony in the Executive Committee, and a modicum of public spirit in the Assembly. But it was a transitional constitution only. It stimulated rather than satisfied the ambitions of the 'coloured party'.

The constitutions had worked with less friction in the smaller islands than in Jamaica: their weakness lay rather in their inefficiency as instruments of government. Sir William Colebrooke, a very experienced Governor, thought the committee system of carrying on business natural in the circumstances of the islands, but admitted that it had the defect that 'the Governor . . . having no recognized organ in the Assemblies . . . has been unable to

---

[1] Barkly to Grey (19 Oct. 1854) (No. 107), loc. cit. Hosack succeeded Westmorland in 1855 and G. Price (a councillor) replaced Edwards on the latter's appointment as Chief Justice in 1856. There are some interesting remarks on Jordon's earlier career in P. Abrahams, *Jamaica* (London, 1957), pp. 77–81.

[2] Barkly to Labouchere (9 Apr. 1856) (Confidential), CO137/331. The Legislative Council was responsible for the rejection of 'bills for the establishment of permanent systems of education and sanitary improvements', so that it was not only a question of coloured opposition.

[3] Minute of Merivale (30 July) on Darling to Stanley (10 June 1858) (Private official), CO137/337. Darling had arrived on 24 July 1857.

advise with those bodies in questions of public interest'. The withdrawal of many resident proprietors accentuated this defect. To obviate it, he thought it advisable 'to appoint a separate Executive Council in each island, which should include with the members of the Legislative Council a certain number of members of the Assembly, with which body the Governor would thus be placed in relation'. He did not see this as a move in the direction of responsible government.

The principles of responsible or party government are so obviously inapplicable in these small communities, that it should be distinctly understood that the appointment of members of the Executive Council did not alter the relations of that body to the Governor as his advisers or divest him of the responsibility for the measures which he might adopt with their advice.

He coupled this with a proposal to create a General Legislature for Barbados and the Windward Islands with a Legislative Council and General Assembly chosen by the Governors and Assemblies from among the members of the island legislatures, supplemented by an Executive Council selected by the Governor-in-Chief and possessing the sole right of initiating money votes.[1]

Taylor, with his long experience of the West Indies, dismissed the idea of a General Legislature as impracticable: 'it could only be effected by the concurrence of the respective local Legislatures, whose concurrence is rarely to be obtained for any purpose and could never be brought about for a purpose in which so many personal and local feelings would be brought into collision.' He was even doubtful whether they could individually be persuaded to adopt Colebrooke's Executive Council scheme or something on the lines of the Jamaican reform: 'the less the ostensible interference of the Crown Authorities the more likely in my opinion is it that some reforms may be effected.'[2] Taylor's influence is evident in the reply Newcastle sent to Colebrooke just before leaving office. These reforms, he said, were likely to promote good government: 'it must rest however with the local Legislature to

---

[1] Colebrooke to Newcastle (20 Mar. 1854) (No. 15), P.P., 1854–5, xxxvi [1919], 67–71.
[2] Minute of Taylor (21 Apr.) on Colebrooke to Newcastle (20 Mar. 1854) (No. 15), CO28/180.

devise such reforms of their Political Institutions as may appear to them to be expedient.'[1] In fact Colebrooke's successor, the Canadian Francis Hincks, did not share his views except on the desirability of widening the franchise somewhat, and no change was made in Barbados.

The Lieutenant-Governor of Tobago, Willoughby Shortland, had, however, been receptive of Colebrooke's ideas. He introduced two Bills, one to authorize the selection of members from the two Houses to sit in a General Assembly to be convened at Barbados, the other to separate the Legislative and Privy Councils and to authorize the appointment of one member of Council and two members of the Assembly as an Executive Committee. The Assembly rejected the first but passed the second, it is true without a clause reserving the initiative in money votes to the Crown but on the understanding that this would be covered by a standing order.[2] The Act was duly confirmed and, so Shortland reported next year, 'tended to remove many of those hindrances to good government before found so difficult to surmount'.[3]

The path was not so smooth in the other colonies of this government. MacDonnell in St. Vincent, like Colebrooke, favoured an Executive Council of officials, Legislative Councillors, and members of Assembly, though he wanted a few independent members also—'far too numerous a body for executive purposes', Taylor commented. The existing Council, said MacDonnell, 'has its own President and its own peculiar privileges, so much so that the Lieutenant-Governor cannot discuss with its members measures of the most urgent importance connected with the Legislative business of the Colony without causing more or less jealousy, kept, it is true, within respectful limits'.[4] Newcastle gave this scheme a qualified approval, provided membership did not exceed ten, but hinted that a further change, on Jamaican lines, might be advantageous.[5] MacDonnell got an Act authorizing the Officer administering the Government 'to select any one of the members of the General Assembly . . . to be an organ of communication

---

[1] Newcastle to Colebrooke (12 June 1854) (No. 72), CO29/39.

[2] Shortland to Colebrooke (22 Jan. 1855) (No. 7), CO285/70. The 'Act for the Better Government of the Island' was No. 455 of 1855.

[3] Shortland to Hincks (16 June 1856) (No. 56), P.P., 1857, x [2198], 124–6.

[4] MacDonnell to Colebrooke (14 Mar.) in Colebrooke to Newcastle (28 Mar. 1854) (No. 12), CO260/79.

[5] Newcastle to Colebrooke (12 June 1854) (No. 38), CO261/16.

between him and that branch of the Legislature';[1] but he left soon afterwards for South Australia and E. J. Eyre, his successor, reported that this measure had not achieved its object. 'There is no leader in the House', he declared, 'of sufficient influence or ability to carry any decided influence with the majority and the mere fact of one member undertaking to act as the Government representative appears to have the effect of placing him in strong antagonism to all the others.'[2] Yet St. Vincent was 'without many of the most essential laws and the most necessary institutions'—an education law, a law for the management of inter-state estates, a public hospital, a refuge for the destitute or for orphans, a mental asylum. The only remedy Eyre saw as efficacious was to consolidate the two Houses in a single mixed chamber. An independent Executive Council was only a second best. St. Vincent, he thought, was too impoverished to afford a paid Executive Committee.[3] Taylor confessed he could see no way out of these difficulties. The parliamentary guarantee had helped Jamaica to find one.

I conceive that the mere rottenness and old ill-working of the same polities in the smaller Islands, without any violent crisis to allege, would not enable the Government to succeed in obtaining from Parliament the same sort of assistance to enable them to modify and somewhat qualify (for it is nothing more in Jamaica) the evils of their systems of Government.

Action by the legislature was required to set up an Executive Committee, and the Assembly could not be expected 'to protect the public against their own corruption'.[4] Russell, just before leaving office, suggested that Colebrooke should be brought home and consulted on possible action by Parliament;[5] but this suggestion was not followed up. Eyre persevered, however, and in 1856 secured an Act, limited to three years, authorizing the appointment of an Executive Council of five Legislative Councillors and five members of the House of Assembly. In spite of

---

[1] MacDonnell to Colebrooke (10 Aug.) in Colebrooke to Sir G. Grey (28 Sept. 1854) (No. 67), CO260/87.
[2] Eyre to Colebrooke (2 May) in Colebrooke to Russell (19 May 1855) (No. 28), CO260/82. This passage was omitted from the dispatch when it was printed in P.P., 1856, xlii [2050], 88–92.
[3] Eyre to Sir G. Grey (8 Jan. 1855) (Private) and Eyre to Colebrook (2 May 1855) (No. 52), CO260/82.
[4] Minute of Taylor (23 June 1855), ibid.
[5] Minute of Russell (18 July 1855), ibid.

technical objections to its restriction of the royal prerogative, this
was duly confirmed.[1] When the three years expired, Eyre went
one better and secured, by a *coup de main*, an Act for the appointment of a paid Administrative Committee. This measure was
pushed through all its stages in both Houses on a single day when
it was not expected to come on for another fortnight. The Committee, consisting of one member of Council and two of the
House of Assembly, was to administer the finances and initiate
all money votes and in due course took over other duties hitherto
performed by Assembly committees.[2]

Lieutenant-Governor Keate in Grenada, like Eyre in St. Vincent, thought a single mixed chamber desirable but unattainable
and an Executive Council selected from both Houses the next
best thing.[3] His attempt to convert the Joint Committee of Public
Accounts into a Finance Committee which would prepare estimates with the assistance of the executive, failed; but in May 1856
he secured an Act creating an Executive Council of ten, selected
in equal numbers from the two Houses, on the understanding that
a Tax Act would also be accepted. But the Colonial Office objected
to the Tax Act as imposing discriminatory taxation on the clergy
and public servants and it was disallowed accordingly.[4] A revised
Executive Council Act was passed towards the end of the year
and was confirmed.[5] Keate's successor Kortright found it 'an
immense improvement on the old system' but by no means perfect. Of the ten members only three resided in town; one of these
was a merchant seldom able to leave his business and another was
infirm. 'It is only', he reported, 'on such occasions as the meetings
of the courts of law or of the legislature that a full board can be
expected.' That the system worked at all was due to the public

---

[1] Eyre to Hincks (9 Apr. 1856) (No. 42) in Hincks to Labouchere (28 Apr.
1856) (No. 22) with Minute of Taylor (22 May) and Smith (Chief Clerk)
(27 May), CO260/85. Labouchere to Hincks (16 June 1856, No. 22, and 20 Aug.
1856), CO261/16.

[2] Eyre to Hincks (14 Mar. 1859) and Walker to Lytton (20 Apr. 1859) (No. 20),
CO260/92. One of the members of the new Administrative Committee was the
former Speaker, Choppin, quoted on pp. 379–80.

[3] Keate to Colebrooke (4 May 1854) (No. 40), P.P., 1854–5, xxxvi [1919],
92–4. Approved in principle by Sir G. Grey to Colebrooke (27 July 1854) (No. 2),
CO102/23.

[4] Labouchere to Hincks (12 Nov. 1856) (Confidential), CO102/23. See also
Labouchere to Hincks (23 Aug. 1856, nos. 25 and 26), ibid.

[5] The Act (No. 537) was allowed by Labouchere to Hincks (12 Feb. 1857),
ibid.

spirit of two members who lived some few miles away in the country. The obvious remedy was a paid Executive Committee with the initiative in money votes, but this was violently opposed in the Assembly as an encroachment on its privileges—though Kortright believed the real grounds were a 'personal feeling of enmity and dislike for some of the members of the Executive Council'.[1] Before the three-year term of the Act expired, Kortright submitted to the Assembly a Bill which continued it but also included provision for an Administrative Committee. The Assembly struck out these words wherever they occurred but left in other clauses intended to refer to this Committee, leaving the measure so defective that Newcastle declined to advise confirmation in its existing form.[2] As the Assembly stubbornly declined to amend it, the Executive Council Act was disallowed. Reform had miscarried.

In the Leeward Islands St. Kitts was the pioneer of reform. After one unsuccessful attempt, towards the end of 1857 Lieutenant-Governor Robinson passed through a newly elected Assembly an Act 'to authorize the appointment of an Executive Council and Administrative Committee for the Islands of St. Christopher and Anguilla'. The Executive Council was to consist of members of both Houses, was to have the advisory powers of the old Council, which had in fact ceased to be consulted except as a matter of form, and to hold office by a political tenure. The Administrative Committee of two members from the Assembly and one from the Legislative Council was to be paid and was to have the responsible superintendence of the finances and the sole initiative in money votes.[3] This Act was confirmed and towards the end of 1858 both Executive Council and Administrative Committee were duly constituted. Before long there was friction between the two bodies. Robinson clashed with the Administrative Committee over the question of a grant to the Roman Catholics towards restoration of a church and talked of appealing to the Executive Council.

[1] Kortright to Hincks (16 Apr. 1858) (No. 35), P.P., 1859, Sess. 2, xxi [2567], 78–9.
[2] Kortright to J. Walker (9 July) in Walker to Lytton (18 July 1859) (No. 26), CO101/115. Newcastle to Walker (16 Feb. 1860) (No. 21), CO102/23.
[3] Robinson to Hamilton (13 Dec. 1857) (No. 90) in Hamilton to Labouchere (7 Jan. 1858) (No. 3), CO239/101. This was Hercules, soon to be Sir Hercules, Robinson, the future Lord Rosmead, Governor of many colonies and twice High Commissioner in South Africa.

The Administrative Committee thereupon threatened to resign and Robinson gave way. The Committee also objected to bringing the Executive Council into discussions about payment for troops. It seems that the Lieutenant-Governor presided at meetings of the Committee, but in most respects they were in the position of Ministers, making the Executive Council, in Taylor's words, 'rather a superfluous body'. Merivale, who agreed with Taylor, thought Her Majesty's Government might indicate that 'the maintenance of the Executive Council is not in their view a necessary point of government.'[1] This was done; but the hint was not taken and we find Benjamin Pine, early in his long term as Lieutenant-Governor, urging the need of entrusting the executive government to 'two or at the utmost three adequately paid and permanent chief officers'.[2] The little island of Nevis quickly followed the example of its neighbour, passing an Act to authorize the appointment of an Executive Council and Administrative Committee in 1859.[3]

Antigua, noted for its comparative freedom from racial prejudice and the higher standards of its Assembly, had for some time had an informal arrangement whereby an Attorney-General who was a member of the House was recognized as the organ of Government; but this lapsed with the appointment of an Attorney-General who was a stranger to the island. Messages from the Governor were simply shelved, the Colonial Secretary complained: 'the time and energies of the Legislature are frittered away in the discussion of crude undigested schemes, to be applied at haphazard, according to the crotchets of some individual member, to the remedy of any evil which engages more especially his particular care.'[4] In 1859, however, the Assembly passed, without a division, an Act to authorize the appointment of an Executive Council and Administrative Committee; money votes were to be introduced only by a member of the Committee with the

[1] Price to Eyre (10 Sept.) and Eyre to Price (23 Sept.) in Eyre to Newcastle (26 Sept. 1859) (No. 134) with Minutes of Taylor (25 Oct.) and Merivale (26 Oct.) and Newcastle to Eyre (6 Nov. 1859) (Draft), CO239/102.

[2] Pine to Hamilton (1 Oct.) in Hamilton to Newcastle (22 Oct. 1861) (No. 89), P.P., 1862, xxxvi (2955), 75–9.

[3] Musgrave to Hamilton (23 Apr. 1861), ibid., p. 100. Musgrave reported that the usefulness of the new system was 'lessened by the distrust with which it is regarded'. The Act was No. 257 of 1859.

[4] Musgrave to Eyre (7 June) in Eyre to Lytton (8 June 1859) (No. 54), P.P., 1860, xliv [2711], 77–8.

sanction of the Executive Council.[1] Confirmation of this Act
was delayed by the tactlessness of Eyre, acting as Governor in the
absence of Governor Hamilton, in recommending for the Executive Council three violent opponents of Hamilton;[2] but it was
eventually confirmed, though there was some confusion at first
about the respective functions of Executive Council and Administrative Committee. On this point Newcastle intervened with
authority. It was the Administrative Committee, not the Executive Council, that was to hold office by a political tenure.

It is not to be supposed that it was the intention of the framers of
the Act or of the Legislature to run counter to the plain policy adopted
in every other Colony in which analogous Acts have been passed and
divorce these principal administrative functions from that of principal
advisers to the Government. . . . I should regard it as highly objectionable that the Executive Council should be a body removeable by a
vote of the Legislature, whilst even as regards the Administrative
Committee, it is desirable that frequent changes should be as far as
possible avoided.[3]

Hamilton soon reported that the new system had been 'received
with satisfaction' and was 'likely to be permanently beneficial to
the Colony'.[4] Thus some of the islands at least, under the guidance
of Governors discreetly supported by the Colonial Office, had
brought about better co-operation between executive and legislature in matters of administration and finance, paving the way,
it might be hoped, for much-needed improvements in legislation.

Other colonies sought rather to reform their legislatures. Montserrat in 1853 proposed to fuse the Council of seven and House of
Assembly of twelve members into a single chamber of twelve,
four nominated and eight elected.[5] Newcastle insisted on amendments making nominations subject to the sanction of the Crown
and preserving the Crown's right to confirm or disallow Acts.[6]
These amendments being rejected, the Act was not confirmed.
The Administrator, Rushworth, announced, however, to the

[1] Eyre to Newcastle (25 July 1859) (No. 67), CO7/112.
[2] Minute of Cox (28 Sept.) on Hamilton to Merivale (28 Sept. 1859), ibid.
Hamilton to Newcastle (10 Sept. 1859), Newcastle Papers, NeC11123.
[3] Newcastle to Hamilton (7 Dec. 1860) (No. 122), CO393/10. Newcastle was
taking exception to the Executive Council Minutes of 19 June.
[4] Hamilton to Newcastle (6 Aug. 1861) (No. 63), P.P., 1862, xxxvi [2955] 63.
[5] Mackintosh to Pakington (28 Jan. 1853), CO175/2.
[6] Newcastle to Mackintosh (23 June 1853) (No. 40), CO393/10. Taylor had
thought the Act a very beneficial one: Minute of 8 Mar., CO175/2.

Assembly that he would no longer assent to grants of money voted by simple resolution. The requirement that all grants should be included in Bills passed through both Houses in the ordinary way was at least one step to improvement.[1]

The Virgin Islands Assembly, frightened by the Tortola disturbances, passed in 1854 an Act substituting for the two Houses a single Legislative Council of three nominated and six elected members under the presidency of the Officer administering the Government.[2] The Duke of Newcastle had suggested an equally divided Council with a casting vote for the President, but the Act was confirmed.[3] The new Legislative Council, however, was disputatious and obstructive. In 1859, after a sudden dissolution, a more amenable Legislative Council was persuaded to meet the Imperial Government and pass a measure reducing the number of elective members from six to four.[4]

In British Honduras, where an irregular settlement of logwood cutters had grown gradually into a colony, a public meeting was the sole legislative authority. One such public meeting in 1851 asked for regular recognition as a colony, with a 'chartered constitution'. Sir John Pakington agreed with Superintendent Wodehouse that a single chamber of seven nominated and fourteen elected members would be more suitable.[5] The public meeting, however, preferred to constitute the Legislative Council of eighteen elected and only three nominated members. In spite of the departure from Pakington's suggestions, the Duke of Newcastle confirmed the Act.[6] The new constitution, with the Colonial Secretary, Public Treasurer, and Attorney-General as nominated members, was soon reported to be working smoothly.[7]

---

[1] Rushworth to Hamilton (27 Oct. and 15 Nov. 1855), CO175/4.

[2] Kortright to Hamilton (12 Mar.) in Hamilton to Labouchere (9 Apr. 1856) (No. 7), P.P., 1857, x [2198], 211–12.

[3] Newcastle had said that only on these terms would Her Majesty's Government assume the responsibility for law and order: No. 50 of 16 Sept. 1853 quoted by Sir G. Grey to Mackintosh (26 Jan. 1855) (No. 47), CO407/10.

[4] Price to Robinson (19 Mar.) in Robinson to Lytton (9 Apr. 1859) (No. 59), P.P., 1860, xliv [2711], 98–100.

[5] Pakington to Sir G. E. Grey (16 Nov. 1852) (No. 26), CO 124/7. The Governor of Jamaica was the official superior of the Superintendent of British Honduras. On all this see D. A. G. Waddell, *British Honduras: A Historical and Contemporary Survey* (London, 1961).

[6] Newcastle to Grey (15 July 1853) (No. 16), CO124/7.

[7] Stevenson to Bell (2 Mar.) in Bell to Labouchere (24 June 1857) (No. 34), P.P., 1857–8, xl [2403], 21.

British Guiana was a kind of half-way house between a Crown and a self-governing colony. It inherited from the Dutch regime a Court of Policy which had some of the functions of a Legislative Council and contained an element indirectly elected by a body known as the College of Kiezers; but in financial questions the Court of Policy joined with directly elected Financial Representatives to form a Combined Court.[1] The skilful management of Governor Barkly had extricated the colony from the impasse which followed the collapse of sugar prices and the defeat of Lord George Bentinck's relief proposals; and with the aid of Indian immigrants it began to get on its feet again.[2] An odd alliance of negrophil missionaries and a group of planters now proposed to replace the Court of Policy and Combined Court by an elective Council and Assembly; but this radical reform found no favour in London, where a meeting of interested planters and merchants proposed instead to reform the tenure and increase the numbers of the College of Kiezers and Financial Representatives. The Court of Policy in 1852, responding to this initiative, passed, over tenacious obstruction, a Bill equalizing the numbers of its official and non-official members, increasing the numbers of the College of Kiezers and Financial Representatives and replacing the Kiezers' life tenure by a three-year term.[3] Taylor doubted the wisdom of giving up the official majority in the Court of Policy as a civil list compromise was approaching its end; and Pakington thought two of the proposed changes inadmissible:

the one—that for excluding all but planters from seats in the legislature, as unduly favouring that portion . . . of the community, the other—that for constituting the elective section a majority in the Legislature, as unduly depriving the Crown of that authority which is essential for the welfare and protection of the unrepresented classes.

He pointed out that there were only 916 voters in a population of nearly 128,000. He was willing to assent to an amended ordinance; but any final settlement should include the civil list also.[4] Barkly reported the 'usual supporters of Government' to be disappointed 'both at the objections raised and at the allusion to the

---

[1] See Sir C. Clementi, *A Constitutional History of British Guiana* (London, 1937).
[2] *British Colonial Policy in the Age of Peel and Russell*, ch. xi.
[3] There is a detailed account of this episode in Clementi, op. cit., pp. 204–35.
[4] Minute of Taylor (10 Sept.) on Barkly to Pakington (8 June 1852) (No. 106), CO111/290. Pakington to Barkly (13 Nov. 1852) (No. 81), CO112/32.

renewal of the Civil List'; but the Civil List Ordinance of 1853 removed this question out of the way for another seven years.[1] When Philip Wodehouse took up the post of Governor of British Guiana in March 1854 interest in constitutional reform had died down. But an elected member of the Court of Policy reopened the question towards the end of the year, and Wodehouse asked for instructions. He was empowered to make changes, and his difficulty in filling vacancies in the Court of Policy and the uncertain and unsatisfactory relations between the legislature and the executive led him in 1855 to introduce a Bill allowing the Governor the sole initiative in money votes but giving up his double vote, abolishing the College of Kiezers, and making election of non-officials in the Court of Policy as well as of the Financial Representatives direct.[2] Most of these changes were admittedly improvements, but Taylor doubted if Wodehouse was wise to raise these questions 'without any obvious and immediate necessity'. He objected to giving up the Governor's casting vote—'any false step in giving up the rights of the Crown or conceding representative rights can never be recovered'—and it had never been intended to grant the Combined Court its powers in perpetuity without simultaneous grant of a civil list in perpetuity.[3] Labouchere (in spite of some doubts on John Ball's part) adopted Taylor's objections and asked for the Court's co-operation in a reform measure free from these objections.[4] But the 'Portuguese riots' of 1856 made the time seem inopportune for constitutional changes. The reform project was dropped; and the old institutions, which Taylor thought 'greatly to be preferred to the system of the other West Indian Colonies possessing Representative Assemblies' continued for another three generations.[5]

[1] Barkly to Pakington (25 Jan. 1853) (Confidential), CO111/293. The Civil List Ordinance was No. 5 of 1853. Ordinance No. 15 of 1860 continued the arrangement until 1 Jan. 1869.

[2] Wodehouse to Molesworth (19 Sept. 1855) (No. 131) enclosing Ordinance No. 19 of 1855, CO111/306.

[3] Minute of Taylor (1 Nov. 1855), ibid.

[4] Minute of Ball (12 Nov. 1855), ibid. Labouchere to Wodehouse (16 Feb. 1856) (No. 33), CO112/33.

[5] On all this see Clementi, op. cit. The Crown initiative in money votes was, however, recognized in 1858 and the College of Kiezers abolished in 1891. Taylor's comment was in a note on a Minute of Merivale (10 Nov.) on Wodehouse to Molesworth (19 Sept. 1855) (No. 131), loc. cit. On the Portuguese riots see below, p. 459.

# XIII

## THE JAMAICA CRISIS AND THE RETREAT FROM REPRESENTATIVE GOVERNMENT

CAPTAIN CHARLES HENRY DARLING, who was appointed Governor and Captain-General of Jamaica in 1857, appeared to be excellently qualified for the post. After a period as assistant private secretary to his uncle, Sir Ralph Darling, Governor of New South Wales, he had served as Military Secretary to Sir Lionel Smith in the Windward Islands and Jamaica, later as Agent-General for Immigration when Lord Elgin was Governor of Jamaica and then as Lieutenant-Governor of St. Lucia. In 1851 he had been sent in a similar capacity to the Cape of Good Hope to take charge at the seat of government whilst the military governors waged war on the frontier; and in 1855 he had been given the task of introducing responsible government in Newfoundland. He had experience therefore of different types of colonial institutions and knew the West Indies well. But he had quarrelled with one of his ablest officials at the Cape and his career in Jamaica showed him to be at once extremely sensitive to criticism and seriously deficient in the art of managing men.

The Executive Committee system Barkly had introduced could not be expected to work without some friction with a legislature so jealous of its privileges as the Assembly of Jamaica. Though it had given up, as part of the constitutional arrangements of 1854, the right of any member to initiate money votes, the Assembly still insisted on a member's right to move an address to the Governor requesting him to recommend a money vote and was critical of recommendations from the Governor which went into details as to the application of the money.[1] The numerous central or local government officials who were members of the Assembly

---

[1] The Crown Law Officers (Fitzroy Kelly and Cairns) in a letter to Lytton (23 Dec. 1858) upheld this right: CO137/341. See also Darling to Newcastle (10 Jan. 1860) (No. 3), CO137/348.

took their official responsibilities lightly: 'there is not one', wrote
Darling, 'upon whose steady and consistent support the Government can rely.'[1] The position of the Executive Committee itself
was equivocal. The Committee got into trouble for spending
more than the amount authorized on roads. In Darling's opinion
two at least of its three members were inclined to disavow all
responsibility to the Legislature and look upon their offices as
quasi-permanent, subject to removal only if the Governor were
dissatisfied with their conduct as his organs and assistants. He for
his part thought of their position as one of 'virtual responsibility
. . . to the majority of the Legislature'.[2] The intention of the Act
for the Better Government of the Island, he declared, was

to establish in Jamaica the main principle, at least, upon which responsible government in other colonies rests, namely that in all important
questions, which are of a purely domestic nature, the colony should
be governed according to the well-understood views and wishes of the
constituencies (assumed to be the people) as expressed by their representatives in the legislature.[3]

The Executive Committee, on the other hand, agreed that the
Assembly intended the Governor alone to be responsible: Hosack
declared that he had accepted office on the understanding that
the Governor would support his Executive Committee against
factious opposition.[4] The Governor, said the Committee, was
arguing for party government, on the assumption that the Executive Committee would then command a majority in the Assembly.
But this was only an assumption: the Assembly, in their opinion,
lacked the necessary cohesion. 'Each individual forms his own
opinion of every measure submitted to the Assembly and acts
according to the dictates of his own judgement.'[5] How were the
Governor's advisers, in the absence of party organizations, to
ascertain the views and win the support of a majority? 'It is surely
not intended that they should put themselves in communication

[1] Darling to Newcastle (28 June 1860) (Confidential), CO137/350. Darling
was particularly critical of the Clerks of the Peace, subsequently described as 'a
sort of local attorney-general', appointed by the Custodes of the parishes and
removable only with difficulty. At this time, of the 47 members, 11 besides the
Attorney-General were officials.
[2] Darling to Newcastle (23 Nov. 1860) (No. 156), CO137/351. Most, but not
quite all, of this dispatch was printed in House of Lords Papers (254) 1864, xiii.
[3] Minute of Governor for the Executive Committee (18 Sept. 1860), ibid.
[4] Minute of Jordon, Hosack, and Price (25 Sept. 1860), ibid.
[5] Minute of Jordon, Hosack, and Price (25 Oct. 1860), ibid.

with all or even a majority of the Legislature for the purpose of ascertaining their opinions upon every measure which is intended to be brought forward?'[1] Darling denied that he wished to establish party government: all he was contending for was 'that the Executive Committee should be so composed as adequately to represent from time to time the sentiments and views which prevail in the Legislature'. If it should appear that the Committee's opinions were not sufficiently in accord with those of the Legislature, 'the Committee should advise the Governor accordingly, with a view to their retirement from office'.[2] The Committee, which could claim to have given Jamaica six years of 'steady government', took the hint and resigned in November 1860.

The Colonial Office was inclined to sum up in favour of the Executive Committee in this controversy. Chichester Fortescue, in particular, noted 'the apparent absence of any sufficient reason why the Governor should have provoked discussions upon so critical a subject, of so theoretical a character, and in which the point at issue is so fine that at times the eye can hardly follow it'. The real point at issue, he thought, was one of practical politics:

*How* are the several acts and measures of the Government . . . to be defended by the members of the Executive Committee?—as the acts of the Governor?—of the Committee?—or of both?—Messrs. Jordon, Hosack and Price give the first answer—the Governor gives the second —the truth seems to lie with the third. The Executive Committee certainly have the letter of the Act of 1854 in their favour. . . . But their doctrine is opposed to the spirit of the arrangement, to the expressed intentions of all who entered into it, and to the relations which have practically prevailed under it between the Governor and his Executive Committee and between the latter and the Legislature.[3]

The controversy also drew from the Duke of Newcastle, joint author of the Act of 1854, an interesting comment on its objective.

That the Act . . . established the best possible Government *in theory* for Jamaica nobody pretended to suppose but it was intended to remedy great existing evils and to prevent the advent of still greater in the shape of Government by Party of mixed Races.[4]

[1] Minute of Jordon, Hosack, and Price (6 Nov. 1860), H.L. Papers No. 254, p. 29.
[2] Minute of Darling (19 Nov. 1860), ibid., p. 30.
[3] Minute of Chichester Fortescue (27 Dec.) on Darling to Newcastle (23 Nov. 1860) (No. 156), CO137/351.
[4] Minute of Newcastle (14 Jan. 1861), ibid.

The dispatch sent to the Governor on 29 January 1861 took the line suggested by Taylor and Chichester Fortescue. After an elaborate discussion of the responsibility of the Governor and the Executive Committee as the Office saw them, it concluded:

> No doubt the Governor's responsibility and that of the Executive Committee do substantially differ. The Governor is responsible to the Crown, in the sense of his being judged by his acts in Executive Committee according to their merit or demerit. The subordinate members of the Committee are responsible in the sense of a liability to consequences with reference not to merits only, and in some cases even not to merits at all, but to the question whether the acts done, be they right or wrong, or voluntary or constrained, have left the Committee capable of executing with advantage to the public service the particular functions for which their offices were constituted.

Unless Messrs. Jordon, Hosack, and Price had lost their ability to obtain support in the legislature, the Secretary of State regretted their resignations, provoked as they had been by an erroneous view of his position on the Governor's part: 'it is highly inexpedient that frequent changes should take place in the composition of the Executive Committee.'[1] But the hope of Stephen Cave, Chairman of the West India Committee, that this dispatch might induce the Governor to seek a reconciliation with the Executive Committee was disappointed. He had appointed a new one and was more concerned to justify his actions.[2] The Colonial Office, whilst admitting that it might have misconstrued some of Darling's language, stood its ground on the main point at issue: the measures of the Governor in Executive Committee were to be regarded as his measures 'to be concurred in and supported by the Executive Committee, and not the measures of the Committee, sanctioned by the Governor'.[3]

The Duke of Newcastle was justified in his fear that, by directing public attention to the question of responsibility, Darling might have 'raised Spirits which he cannot lay'.[4] Early in 1862 he

---

[1] Newcastle to Darling (29 Jan. 1861) (No. 232), H.L. Paper No. 254, pp. 92–3.
[2] Darling to Newcastle (22 Feb. 1861, No. 25 and 1 Mar. 1861, No. 31), ibid., pp. 42–7. He returned to the point in No. 168 of 26 Nov. 1861. For Cave's view see Cave to Newcastle (31 Jan. 1861), CO137/358. The new Committee comprised Baron von Ketelhodt, Raynes Smith, and Solomon.
[3] Newcastle to Darling (16 Apr. 1861) (No. 272): H.L. Paper No. 254, pp. 93–4.
[4] Minute of Newcastle (14 Jan. 1861), loc. cit.

went on leave, clearly with an eye to securing a better government. Eyre, who seemed to Taylor 'the best man available for stopping a gap in the Government', was appointed Acting Governor and found himself saddled with an inexperienced Executive Committee, who were even less successful than their predecessors in retaining the confidence of the Assembly.[1] The displaced Committee, joined by Westmorland, probably the ablest man in the House, was a formidable opposition; and Eyre, who was trying to avoid any change until Darling returned, thought it would be impossible to carry on for another session without at least bringing in Jordon 'as representative of the coloured section of the community'.[2] When the Assembly resumed, late in January 1863, the Committee was defeated on an important revenue Bill. Eyre asked Westmorland if he would let the main Bills before the House go through if the Committee brought forward no more: if so, he would prorogue the Assembly until Darling's return. Westmorland, after consulting his friends, declined. Eyre thereupon dissolved.[3] The new House at once passed a vote of no confidence in the Executive Committee, which in any case was divided against itself; and Eyre appointed Westmorland, Jordon, and G. L. Phillips, a Legislative Councillor and a leading member of the Jewish community, as his new Executive Committee.[4] Darling's appointment as Governor of Victoria removed the personal obstacle to their return. Newcastle warned Eyre that 'Her Majesty's Government will not yield to the attempt which is now [being] made to introduce party government into Jamaica'; but he defended his action effectively and explained to the members of the new Committee that their appointment was not a recognition of any party.[5]

[1] On Taylor's responsibility see his letter to Miss M. Spring-Rice (2 Dec. 1865), Sir Henry Taylor Papers, Bodleian Library, Oxford, M.S Eng. lett., d. 12.

[2] Eyre to Newcastle (23 Dec. 1862) (Confidential), CO137/368. Printed, but without the sentence about Jordon, in H.L. Paper No. 254. Darling did not concur in Eyre's view: Darling to Newcastle (27 Jan. 1863) (Confidential), CO137/377.

[3] Eyre to Newcastle (31 Jan. 1863) (No. 36), H.L. Paper No. 254, pp. 56–60.

[4] Eyre to Newcastle (8 Apr. 1863) (Confidential), CO137/371. Price and Hosack were 'studiously left out' but in July Price replaced Phillips.

[5] Newcastle to Eyre (16 Mar. 1863) (No. 568), H.L. Paper No. 254, p. 95. Based on Minute of Taylor (7 Mar.) on Eyre to Newcastle (31 Jan. 1863) (No. 36), CO137/370. For Eyre's defence see Eyre to Newcastle (8 Apr. 1863) (Confidential), CO137/371.

So far Eyre had managed well; but he got into difficulties when, towards the end of the year, he recommended the removal of the well-meaning but incompetent Agent-General for Immigration, Ewart, for neglect of his duty when heavy mortality occurred among Indian labourers on the Law Layton sugar estate.[1] In February 1864 a thin House censured Eyre for refusing to comply with its application for correspondence concerning the dismissal or to allow Ewart and others to give evidence before the House and one of its committees, and refused to proceed to any further business with the Lieutenant-Governor.[2] The crux of the question was that Ewart was a coloured man and married to the coloured daughter of the Receiver-General and that a white man had been provisionally nominated to succeed him.[3] A further difficulty, this time involving the Executive Committee, soon followed. The previous Executive Committee had perpetrated what can only be described as a 'job' in sanctioning a scheme for a tramway from Spanish Town to Porus through the parish of St. Catherine. The promoters were a Jamaica capitalist, David Smith, and the Colonial Engineer, Leahy; and they proposed to lay the tramway down the centre of the public road and thus secure a monopoly of traffic. Price, as Custos of St. Catherine and now a member of the Executive Committee, was well-informed about the job and in a position to stop it. Darling had allowed the Colonial Engineer to become a shareholder and Eyre said, probably with truth, that he had been misled by the interested representations of the Engineer.[4] G. W. Gordon, already coming into prominence as a leader of the more extreme wing of the coloured or 'town' party, attacked Eyre in the Assembly as 'grovelling, pretentious and prevaricating' and declared that it was 'time for the people to dethrone him'; and Eyre complained that the Committee remained passive and did not disavow such proceedings on the part of their friends and adherents. His own uncertain tenure of office, moreover,

[1] Eyre to Newcastle (20 Oct. 1863) (No. 238), CO137/375. Appointment and dismissal of this officer rested with the Secretary of State. A (Jewish) sub-agent was also removed for neglect of duty. The gaoler, who was removed for misconduct, had been 'a sort of electioneering Agent' for the 'coloured' party.

[2] Resolutions of House of Assembly (8 Feb.) in Eyre to Newcastle (9 Feb. 1864), H.L. Papers, No. 254, pp. 351–2.

[3] Eyre to Newcastle (27 Jan. 1864) (Confidential), CO137/378.

[4] Eyre to Newcastle (20 Feb. 1864) (No. 59) with Minute of Jordon, Westmorland, and Price (20 Feb.), H.L. Paper No. 254, pp. 70–4.

made him more vulnerable.[1] Cardwell removed this latter difficulty by recommending his promotion to the Governorship;[2] and
no doubt he concurred (as did Chichester Fortescue) in Taylor's
view that Eyre should 'take no notice of these idle blusterings in
the Assembly'.[3] Governor and Secretary of State were in fact
agreed that it was best to make do with the existing Executive
Committee. But Eyre soon had to remove Price, becoming convinced that he was privy to a 'very offensive notice of motion'
reflecting on the Governor's proceedings in relation to the tramway.[4] Before long he was involved in another difficulty, not of his
own making. The elderly Receiver-General was given sick-leave
and soon afterwards died. Jordon accepted the acting appointment, giving up the virtual certainty of the Speakership. But the
rule was not to appoint a local man to this financial office; and
Taylor thought it would be better to appoint H. W. Austin, who
had just been made Island Secretary as well as Governor's Secretary, to the Receiver-Generalship and Jordon, both an abler and
a more influential man, to the Secretaryship, the most important
office in the island.[5] Unfortunately the Assembly rejected the
Executive Committee's Bill to amalgamate the two secretarial
offices; and the Committee did not think it proper to carry
through the amalgamation by executive authority. Eyre accordingly recommended that Jordon be appointed Receiver-General.[6]
But Cardwell had offered the joint Secretaryship to Jordon, who
had accepted, and, with Taylor's backing, he refused to vary his
decision.[7] The Executive Committee (on which Hosack had
replaced Jordon) thereupon tendered their resignations; but they
were persuaded by Eyre to withdraw them.

These political squabbles and administrative complications must

[1] Eyre to Newcastle (23 Feb. 1864) (No. 73), CO137/379. Eyre to Newcastle
(18 Mar. 1864) (Separate), H.L. Paper No. 254, pp. 88–90.
[2] His appointment was foreshadowed in Cardwell to Eyre (6 Apr. 1864)
(No. 794) though his Commission was not forwarded until 30 July.
[3] Minute of Taylor (1 Apr.) and Fortescue (4 Apr.) on Eyre to Newcastle
(23 Feb. 1864) (No. 73), CO137/379.
[4] Eyre to Cardwell (21 May 1864, No. 155, and 23 May 1864, No. 157), H.L.
Paper No. 254, pp. 225–7, 232.
[5] Eyre to Cardwell (24 Oct. 1864) (No. 275) with Minute of Taylor (18 Nov.),
CO137/385.
[6] Eyre to Cardwell (23 Jan. 1865, No. 13, and 3 May 1865, No. 121),
CO137/387 and 391.
[7] Minutes of Taylor (6 June) and Cardwell (16 June) on Eyre to Cardwell
(3 May 1865) (No. 121), CO137/391.

have distracted attention from the state of the island. The Negroes remained an underprivileged, but hardly an oppressed, class. Few had the vote, fewer still sat in the Assembly; but as members of parish vestries, Road Boards, and Boards of Health and in the humbler position of rural constables, some took a share in the work of local government. There was no sign of the return of the Negroes to regular estate labour for which the planters hankered. In the years 1860–4, 4,635 Indian indentured labourers were introduced under the new law passed late in 1858 after much discussion with the Colonial Office and in the colony;[1] but their arrival did not substantially alter the picture of a stagnant sugar industry and a half-ruined planter class. In 1863 and 1864 the island was afflicted by a severe drought. Early in 1865 E. B. Underhill, lay secretary of the Baptist Missionary Society, who after a visit in 1859 had written a book on the West Indies, wrote a letter to Cardwell, the Secretary of State, drawing his attention to the 'continually increasing distress of the coloured population' as depicted in letters reaching him by every mail. The drought and the increased prices of provisions and clothing (due in part at least to the American Civil War) were the immediate causes, but the want of capital and employment were in Underhill's view the root of the trouble. He asked for 'a searching inquiry into the Legislation of the Island since emancipation, its taxation, its economical and material condition'.[2] Eyre considered Underhill's picture 'very exaggerated'. Hosack agreed: extreme poverty, in nine cases out of ten, was the result of sheer idleness or a preference for a dishonest mode of living rather than honest labour.[3] A circular sent out by Eyre produced a good deal of supporting evidence, though many of the eighty replies are stereotypes, summed up by Eyre in a characteristic sentence—'deterioration, decadence and decay are everywhere noticeable'. There was general agreement that crime was on the increase, though Richard

---

[1] Acts No. 4238 and 4239 of 1858, P.P., 1859, Sess. 2, xx (H.C. 31). There is much correspondence on the subject in this Parliamentary Paper.

[2] Underhill to Cardwell (5 Jan. 1865), P.P., 1866, i [3595], 1–2. Underhill had a personal introduction to Cardwell from his father, who had given him 'valued assistance at a general election' and had permission 'to write to him on any matter on which he could afford me assistance': E. B. Underhill, *The Tragedy of Morant Bay* (London, 1895), p. xi.

[3] Eyre to Cardwell (2 Mar. 1865) (No. 40); Remarks of Hosack (28 Feb.) in Eyre to Cardwell (7 Mar. 1865) (No. 45), P.P., 1866, li [3595], 7, 10–11.

Hill, a coloured Legislative Councillor, remarked that 'the Legislature for some years past has been converting . . . trespasses into
larcenies'. It is not surprising to find 'an opinion still prevalent
among the people that it is no crime for the poor man to help
himself [to] the property of the rich'; but this could hardly
excuse thefts from provision grounds whose owners were poor
men themselves.[1]

Underhill's letter inevitably found its way into the press and
became a text for political agitators. The Baptist ministers naturally desired to back up Underhill's statements. A collective report
from their chairman and secretary to the Governor was remarkably able and moderate; but the public meetings which Baptist
ministers initiated in many parishes were liable to lead to recitals
of wrongs and grievances and excited denunciations of the
Government. The Colonial Office contributed to the excitement
by a very ill-advised reply to a petition to the Queen got up by
some people at Ocho River in the parish of St. Ann's. Eyre was
instructed to inform the petitioners, as from the Queen, that their
prosperity depended on steady and continuous labour, which
would 'enable the planters to pay them higher wages for the same
hours of work than are received by the best field labourers in this
country'.[2] The words were, in fact, Henry Taylor's; and it is
extraordinary that with all his experience he should so misjudge
the state of affairs. 'The Queen's letter' indeed did harm, for Eyre
published it in the *Government Gazette* and later circulated no fewer
than 50,000 copies. We can well understand the statement of the
Baptist leaders that 'the effect has been to produce an amount
of irritation most painful to observe'.[3]

Others were not so restrained in their comment, notably G. W.
Gordon. Gordon, the son of a Scottish-born planter and one of his
slaves, was a talented mob-orator and political organizer. At one
stage a wealthy man, he had now, through his speculative temper
and carelessness about money, run deeply into debt. There was

[1] Eyre to Cardwell (19 Apr. 1865) (No. 90) with voluminous enclosures,
ibid., pp. 29 ff. Hill's comment is on p. 108, the other on p. 101. The Baptist
ministers' letter of 1 May (pp. 146–50) attributed the increase of larceny to irregular
employment, food shortage, and a growing vagabond class.
[2] Eyre to Cardwell (25 Apr. 1865) (No. 117) and Cardwell to Eyre (14 June
1865) (No. 222), ibid., pp. 135–9. Taylor's Minute of 3 June is in CO137/390.
[3] The Revds. J. E. Henderson, W. Dendy, and J. Reid to Secretary, Executive
Committee (4 Aug. 1865), P.P., 1866, li [3594], 54.

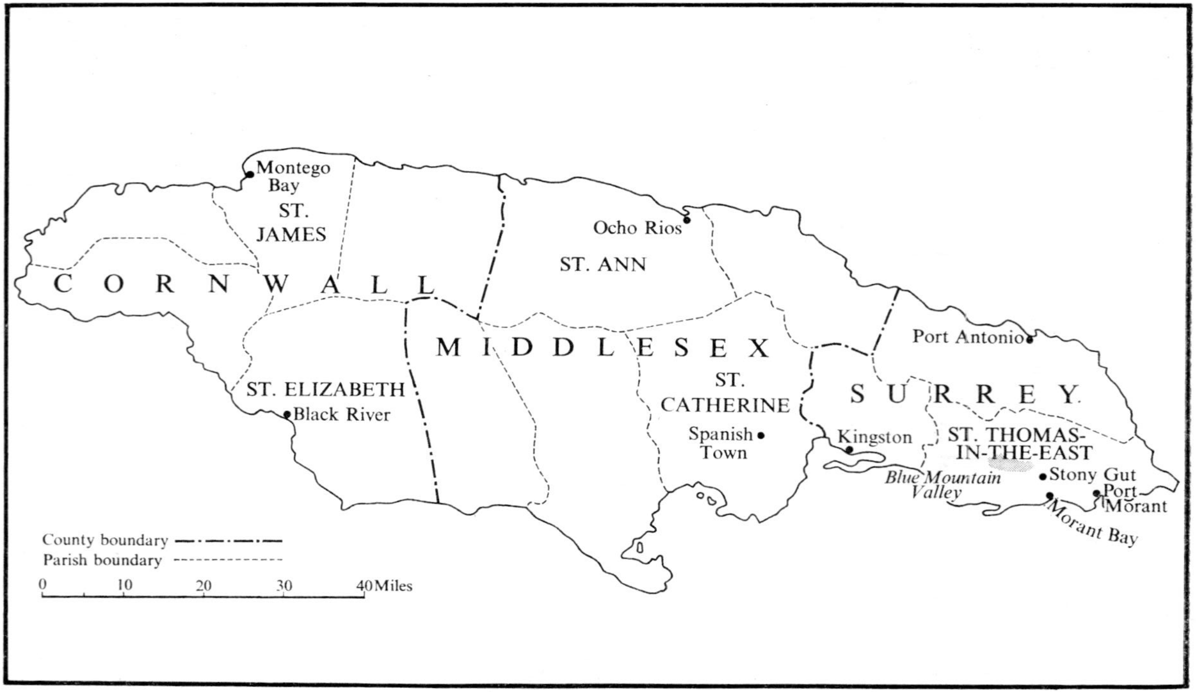

MAP 5. JAMAICA

a religious streak in his nature, but it is hard to believe that it was not political calculation rather than religious conviction which led him to identify himself, after various changes, with the Native Baptists. In 1862 he had complained of the state of the lock-up at Morant Bay in St. Thomas-in-the-East and at the same time alleged that the rector of the parish had unlawfully sent a poor, sick Negro there. Eyre had removed him from the commission of the peace for misrepresentation and declared that he could have remedied the condition of the lock-up as one of the justices himself.[1] Taylor found Gordon's statement more convincing than Eyre's defence. He might have been guilty of culpable neglect earlier, but he had rendered a public service by bringing the conditions of the lock-up to light. But he agreed that there had been 'wilful and deliberate misrepresentation' against the rector which justified the removal.[2] The Secretary of State's reproof and the continuation of the controversy by a memorial to the Queen from a public meeting no doubt did not endear Gordon to Eyre. His attacks on Eyre in the Assembly, already mentioned, widened the breach. Gordon was in the chair at an 'Underhill meeting' at Kingston, which called upon 'all descendants of Africa in every parish throughout the Island to form themselves into societies, and hold public meetings, and co-operate for the purpose of setting forth our grievances, especially now, when our philanthropic friends in England are leading the way'.[3] The Queen's letter roused him to new heights of rabble-rousing eloquence in a widely circulated address.

People of St. Ann's. Poor people of St. Ann's. Starving people of St. Ann's. Naked people of St. Ann's. You who have no sugar estates to work on, nor can find other employment, we call on you to come forth; even if you be naked, come forth and protest against the unjust misrepresentations made against you by Mr. Governor Eyre and his band of custodes. People of St. Thomas-in-the-East, you have been ground down too long already. Shake off your sloth. . . . It is your duty to speak and to act too.

After unbridled invective against the new Custos of the parish

[1] Eyre to Newcastle (8 July 1862, No. 41 and 7 Aug. 1862, No. 56), P.P., 1866, li (H.C. 88), 3-5, 18.
[2] Newcastle to Eyre (5 Sept. 1862) (No. 490), ibid., pp. 37-40. Based on a Minute of Taylor of 25 Aug.
[3] Resolutions of Public Meeting in Kingston (3 May) in Eyre to Cardwell (17 May 1865) (No. 132), P.P., 1866, li [3595], 191.

(Baron von Ketelhodt), the address proceeded: 'Can you and the inhabitants of St. Thomas-in-the-East longer bear to be afflicted by this enemy to your peace? . . . Try to help yourselves and Heaven will help you. More anon!'[1] All this may have been intended merely to produce a lively meeting, but it was inflammatory stuff.

Disaffection was also reported in the parish of St. Elizabeth in the west and Eyre thought it advisable to send a warship to Black River at the end of July. Shortly afterwards another was sent to Montego Bay in the parish of St. James, where there were rumours of resistance to the payment of taxes. The head constable who gave the information about Black River is said to have been poisoned later.[2] Eyre was on the whole less alarmist than some of the custodes and more clear-sighted than his Executive Committee about the prospects of the sugar industry and the planters generally, but he was not a popular man and was apt to complain of the tone of the press and the tendency of the Executive Committee 'to take their part with those to whom they look for support in the assembly [rather] than with the Crown which has appointed them to their offices and which looks to them for advice and co-operation'.[3]

On Saturday, 7 October the smouldering discontent among the Negro population broke out into violence. When a Negro was being tried for assault by the justice at Morant Bay, St. Thomas-in-the-East, a large body of peasants, 'armed with bludgeons and preceded by a band of music, came into the town and, leaving the music at a little distance, surrounded the Court-house, openly expressing their determination to rescue the man . . . if convicted'. One of the party created a disturbance in court: when his arrest was ordered, the mob rushed in, rescued the prisoner, and man-handled the police. Their leader, Paul Bogle, was a Native Baptist preacher and a friend of Gordon. The magistrates did not think it necessary to inform the Government but on Monday sent six policemen to Stony Gut, where Bogle lived, with a warrant against him

<hr>

[1] Address enclosed in Eyre to Cardwell (22 Aug. 1865) (No. 210), ibid., p. 259. A draft of this Address exists in Gordon's handwriting.
[2] Eyre to Cardwell (24 July 1865, No. 189, and 7 Aug. 1865, No. 198) with Enclosure, P.P., 1866, li [3595], 236 ff. On the poisoning see Eyre to Cardwell (Jan. 1866), P.P., 1866, xxx [3682], 2.
[3] Eyre to Cardwell (8 July 1865, Separate, and 20 July 1865, Confidential), CO137/392.

and twenty-seven other ring-leaders. When the police arrived on Tuesday morning a shell was blown and about 200 men appeared out of Bogle's chapel and an adjoining cane-piece, armed with guns, cutlasses, pikes, and bayonets, caught and hand-cuffed the policemen and made them swear on the Bible to desert the whites and join the men of their own colour. The Custos of the parish, Baron von Ketelhodt, arrived about noon and the magistrates persuaded him to ask the Governor for troops. Eyre received the letter at eight in the morning of Wednesday, 11 October.[1]

There were two regiments in the island, the 6th (Royals) and a West India regiment, about 1,000 men in all. After consulting the Executive Committee and the Attorney-General, Eyre re-quested the military commander, Major-General O'Connor, to get ready 100 men for transport to Morant Bay. They arrived on H.M.S. *Wolverine* on Thursday morning. They were too late to avert bloodshed. On Wednesday a crowd of about 400 Negroes had marched four abreast from Stony Gut on Morant Bay and were joined on the way by a contingent from another Negro settlement. They reached the town about half-past three, when a meeting of the parish vestry was nearly over. Seizing some arms at the police station, they approached the court-house, which was guarded by about forty volunteers. The Custos appeared on the steps, calling out 'Peace, peace!' The mob shouted 'War, war; we want no peace; colour for colour; kill them.'[2] As the Custos was reading the Riot Act, Captain Hitchins and others of the volun-teers were hit by stones and bottles. He was then allowed to give the order to fire and seven rioters fell. Thereupon they rushed on the volunteers: some were disarmed, others fled or took shelter. The magistrates had remained in the court-house, but about half-past five its shingle roof was set on fire. The occupants dashed into the neighbouring fort-house, but this too caught fire later, forcing them into the open. Several escaped; two doctors were spared; others, including Baron von Ketelhodt, were beaten to death.

---

[1] This paragraph is mainly based on Eyre to Cardwell (20 Oct. 1865) (No. 251), P.P., 1866, li [3594], 1–9. The substantial accuracy of Eyre's account was not challenged by the subsequent Royal Commission, whose report, however, supplies further details. The Blue Books on the Morant Bay rebellion total 2,595 pages.

[2] Evidence of A. Warmington to Royal Commission, P.P., 1866, xxx [3683–I]. Other versions differ slightly.

The mob marched back to Stony Gut, releasing fifty-one prisoners from the gaol on their way out of the town.[1]

On hearing the news on Thursday afternoon Eyre applied to the General for another 200 men and decided to dispatch a company from Newcastle along the Blue Mountain Valley to meet an expected advance of the rebels. On the advice of a midnight Privy Council and a Council of War next morning, he proclaimed martial law in the county of Surrey (the eastern third of the island) but excepted the town of Kingston. The same day he proceeded, on a chartered French packet, with Colonel A. A. Nelson as Brigadier, various officers of the militia and volunteers, and 50 more troops, to Morant Bay, on to Port Morant and, at daylight next morning, round the eastern tip of the island to Port Antonio. 'We arrived', he reported, 'just in time to save this settlement from the rebels, who were burning buildings and destroying property about twelve miles to the eastward and had already threatened to come in and destroy Port Antonio this very day.' The dreaded Maroons came down from the mountains to assist the authorities and were put under the command of their former Superintendent, Colonel Fyfe. Eyre believed that he had to deal with an incipient rebellion, which after five days he had contained within the line Morant Bay–Port Antonio; and he had also sent to Barbados for more troops, 'five hundred or as many as you can spare'.[2] Courts martial were already dealing out summary punishment; and the advance of Colonel Hobbs along the Blue Mountain Valley, not encountering the expected armed resistance, became a kind of punitive expedition.

Eyre now decided to return to Kingston, where the Executive Committee and the Custos (Dr. Bowerbank) wanted him to proclaim martial law in the town. He thought this inexpedient. But on his tour he claimed to have found unmistakable evidence that Gordon 'had not only been mixed up in the matter, but was himself, through his own misrepresentation and seditious language

---

[1] The main authority for this paragraph is the Report of the Royal Commission P.P., 1866, xxx [3683], 10–11. But a recent publication of the Jamaica Information Service, *The Morant Bay Rebellion* (Kingston, [1963]) adds some details, notably about the fort-house.

[2] Here we return to Eyre to Cardwell (20 Oct. 1865) (No. 251), loc. cit. On 16 Oct. a telegram was also sent via Havana to Nova Scotia for naval and military assistance. It was by this route that the first news of the rebellion reached England.

addressed to the ignorant black people, the chief cause and origin
of the whole rebellion'. He was now in Kingston and Eyre called
on the Custos to issue a warrant for his arrest. Declining his
friends' advice to flee, on 17 October Gordon gave himself up to
General O'Connor at his house. Eyre had him conveyed on board
the *Wolverine* to Morant Bay, where he was tried by court-
martial on 21 October and sentenced to death. He was hanged,
with seventeen others, at 7 a.m. on the 23rd.[1] Paul Bogle was
taken by the Maroons that day, and tried by court-martial and
hanged on the day following.

Eyre defended himself ably, 'My own impression', he told
Cardwell, 'is that the rebellion is *quite crushed* and that it will not
break out elsewhere.'[2] But any hesitation or delay might have
meant universal insurrection and perhaps loss of the colony. He
trusted that the Secretary of State would 'not regard the just
severity which has been exercised otherwise than as a merciful
substitute for the much larger measure of punishment which would
have had to be executed had the rebellion been allowed time to
gather head and extend itself'.[3] His defence of his treatment of
Gordon was summed up in a note to General O'Connor: 'were
condign punishment to fall only on the ignorant people who have
been misled into rebellion, and the educated coloured man who
led that rebellion to escape a very unfortunate impression would
be produced upon the public mind.'[4] He knew, of course, that his
action was illegal and must be covered by an Act of Indemnity:
but by thus stretching the executive power he had given a handle
to his critics then and ever since. He did himself further harm by
incriminating not only Gordon's associates Dr. Bruce and the
Jewish journalist Levien (though he had the sense to leave them
to the civil tribunals) but also 'a few Baptist missionaries who . . .
endorse, at public meetings or otherwise, all the untruthful statements or innuendoes propagated in Dr. Underhill's letter'.[5] On
30 October he proclaimed a general amnesty except to those

---

[1] Eyre to Cardwell (20 Oct. 1865) (No. 251) with postscript of 23 Oct., loc.
cit. On Gordon's friends' advice, see *The Morant Bay Rebellion*, p. 24.
[2] Eyre to Cardwell (23 Oct. 1865) (Private and Confidential), Cardwell
Papers, P.R.O. 30–48: 7/42.
[3] Eyre to Cardwell (20 Oct. 1865) (No. 251), loc. cit.
[4] Eyre to O'Connor (22 Oct. 1865), ibid., p. 24.
[5] Eyre to Cardwell (20 Oct. 1865) (No. 251), loc. cit. He named five missionaries, including the chairman, the Revd. J. E. Henderson.

actually guilty of murder or arson, or in arms, or with stolen property in their possession; but he continued martial law, perhaps because General O'Connor would not agree to the alternative safeguard of a wide distribution of troops.[1]

The excitement in Jamaica now began to subside, but the politically articulate classes—coloured as well as white—had been thoroughly frightened and confidence in the existing regime had been undermined. In Eyre's view there were two alternatives. Either the Imperial Government must suspend the constitution or the Assembly must be persuaded to alter it to 'one better adapted to the present state and requirements of the Colony . . . one in which union, co-operation, consistency and promptness of action may, as far as practicable, be secured'.[2] He himself favoured a Crown Colony constitution, but did not expect the Assembly would go so far. Nor did it, when it met on 8 November. The measure it passed by large majorities substituted for the two Houses a Legislative Council, half elected, half nominated for seven years. The franchise was at the same time raised: the qualifications were to be a freehold of an annual value of £30, a salary of £100, payment of property tax, or of £5 in export duty. Qualifications for election to the Council were substantially higher. The Queen was to appoint a Commissioner with financial experience at £3,000 to act with a member of the Chamber at the existing salary of £800 as an Executive Committee.[3] The Bill was a compromise with the country party in the Assembly. The Executive Committee shared Eyre's doubts about the Commissioner from England, designed in their opinion to keep them out of any share in the government.[4] Taylor and Rogers, though thinking the new measure 'a great improvement on the old constitution' were uneasy about the probable predominance of the planting interest in the new legislature. There was no harm, said Taylor, in making the Governor look to 'compromise and management' to secure the co-operation of the Chamber.

[1] See W. F. Finlason, History of the Jamaica Case (London, 1869), pp. 188 ff.
[2] Eyre to Cardwell (24 Oct. 1865) (Confidential) and Speech on the Opening of the Legislative Session in Eyre to Cardwell (8 Nov. 1865) (No. 284), P.P., 1866, li [3594], 50, 164. The quotation is from Eyre's Speech.
[3] Eyre to Cardwell (7 Dec. 1865) (No. 313) with 'Act to alter and amend the Political Constitution of this Island', ibid., pp. 196–214.
[4] Minutes of Westmorland, Hamilton, and R. W. Smith (8 Dec.), ibid., pp. 226–8.

In a community in which, for want of large educated Constituencies, the Crown, acting under the control of Parliament and English public opinion, is the best, or rather the only possible, representative of the people, it is desirable no doubt that the power of the Crown should be a prevailing power; but it is not desirable that it should be paramount to the silencing of such interests as can make themselves intelligently heard.

But he noted the absence of the Crown Colony Governor's casting vote.[1] If he thought the Act should nevertheless be confirmed, Forster (now Parliamentary Under-Secretary) believed the new Assembly would be worse than the old and Cardwell agreed with Forster.[2] In any case the Assembly itself had had second thoughts when confidentially informed through Taylor of the views of the Imperial Government.[3]

Cardwell's first reaction to the crisis was to commend Eyre's promptitude and vigour and the clear narrative of his dispatch of 20 October, which was published in the *Gazette* as 'the best antidote to that disposition to condemn your proceedings which a part of the Press seems to exhibit'.[4] Even at this stage he pressed Eyre for further details of 'the measures of severity to which you have felt it necessary to have recourse'.[5] But the reports from the military officers concerned and from the Arctic explorer Sir Leopold McClintock, who arrived at the end of October as Commodore of the West India station, and the accounts in the press led Cardwell to make more detailed and searching inquiries of the Governor, especially on Gordon's case.[6] News of 'a rebellion of the negroes' had reached England on 3 November by way of Nova Scotia: details from the *Jamaica Colonial Standard* were available on 13 November, but it was not until the 17th that full accounts were published. *The Times* accepted the idea of a conspiracy, with Gordon as the 'prime mover', and the intention 'to

[1] Minutes of Rogers (30 Dec.) and Taylor (9 Jan. 1866) on Eyre to Cardwell (7 Dec. 1865) (No. 313), CO137/396.
[2] Minutes of Forster (12 Jan.) and Cardwell (13 Jan. 1866), ibid.
[3] Minute of Taylor (to Fairfield) (26 Mar. 1871), CO7/143. I have not seen the private letter which Taylor, at Cardwell's instance, sent Eyre.
[4] Cardwell to Eyre (17 Nov. 1865) (Private) (draft in Cardwell Papers), P.R.O. 30/48, 7/42.
[5] Cardwell to Eyre (17 Nov. 1865) (No. 341), P.P., 1866, li [3594], 239.
[6] Cardwell to Eyre (23 Nov. 1865, Nos. 343 and 344, and 1 Dec. 1865, No. 356), ibid., pp. 240–2. No. 356 enclosed a letter from McClintock.

destroy the whole white population'.[1] The Liberal *Daily News*, on the other hand, whilst it 'rejoiced to find how limited the disaffection was, and how far in all its symptoms it fell short of revolt', declared that 'the accounts of the manner in which it was put down are such as must fill the English nation with dismay' and implored the Government 'to send out at once someone who can stop this horrible outbreak of insane passion'. Three days later it declared it to be 'the duty of Government instantly to supersede Governor Eyre'.[2] The *Spectator* asked what Eyre said in his dispatch to justify these 'astounding measures' and answered: 'As far as we can judge, absolutely nothing'.[3] It was not merely a question of Exeter Hall. The Englishman's dislike of cruelty, oppression, and intimidation was as strong as ever and had indeed been strikingly manifested among the working men of the north during the American Civil War.[4] The provincial press created by the repeal of the paper duties took the question up. Great meetings in Manchester, Leeds, Bradford, Newcastle, York, Shields, Rochdale, Blackburn, Derby, Plymouth, Reading, and Brighton denounced the proceedings in Jamaica. The Prime Minister, Earl Russell, told a Manchester deputation 'he was not in the least surprised that there should be great anxiety and strong feeling on this subject in the country', but pleaded for suspension of judgement pending explanations.[5] Soon afterwards sympathizers with the Jamaica Negroes formed the Jamaica Committee to continue pressure on the Government. Clearly some act of policy was necessary. On 6 December the Cabinet decided to appoint a Royal Commission to proceed to Jamaica under Lieutenant-General Sir H. K. Storks, Governor of Malta, who would also temporarily supersede Eyre in the government.[6]

As it happened, the facts revealed by Underhill's letter and Eyre's subsequent circular had led the Colonial Office to consider

[1] *The Times*, 17 Nov. 1865. *The Times* changed its attitude in March 1866 in the light of the evidence about the suppression of the rising reported by its special correspondent in Jamaica.

[2] *Daily News*, 17 and 20 Nov. 1865. To my regret, time did not permit me to scan other daily newspapers.     [3] *Spectator*, 25 Nov. 1865.

[4] This point is well made by B. Semmel, *The Governor Eyre Controversy*, (London, 1962).

[5] *The Times*, 1 Dec. 1865. Cardwell received deputations from the Baptist Missionary Society on 6 Dec. and the Anti-Slavery Society on 9 Dec.

[6] This was announced on 7 Dec. and conveyed to Eyre in Cardwell to Eyre (16 Dec. 1865) (No. 374), P.P., 1866, li [3594], 254–5.

the possibility of reforming the Jamaica constitution. Taylor had never concealed his belief that only 'an enlightened and beneficent Despotism' like that of British India could do much for Jamaica.

> It seems just possible [he added] that hostilities between the rural and civic Sections of the Assembly, the former being the majority, but the latter having the more power from residing on the spot, *may* lead to the sort of measure just adopted in Dominica, the abolition of the Assembly by its own act. There are often indications that way in the Jamaica newspapers.[1]

A month or two later Cardwell asked him for his views on the question of reforming the constitution by Act of Parliament. It seemed to him 'very important that there should be some not inconsiderable local party in favour of it'; and if the Crown showed any intention of pressing for increased power, inveterate habit would cause a local reaction against it. If any steps were to be taken in England, they should be 'so guarded as not to disclose the end to be aimed at'—the publication of the dispatches and reports arising out of the Underhill letter, followed by a Committee 'to be moved for by Mr. Buxton or some other friendly M.P.' But even so it was unlikely that English public opinion would be aroused to the extent of calling for the overthrow of the West Indian Assemblies. They were guilty not of cruelty and oppression but of neglect and mismanagement, and 'this is not the sort of misgovernment against which public opinion in England will revolt'. Moreover the example of 1839 showed that 'you cannot take up the case of Jamaica alone'. Nevertheless it might be worth while setting up a Committee, though this might lead to the question what specific measures the legislature had neglected and whether these had been enacted in the Crown Colonies of Trinidad and St. Lucia. They had not; but 'French and Spanish Roman Catholic Colonies cannot be dealt with by an English Protestant Government as easily as if they were English and Protestant'. Universal, compulsory education there would mean co-operation with foreign priests and heavy taxes for which 'the Government would be presently called to account by the Representatives of the West India Committee in the House of Commons'.[2] Some time after this inconclusive discussion Underhill

---

[1] Minute of Taylor (30 May) on Eyre to Cardwell (19 Apr. 1865) (No. 90) (the dispatch enclosing the replies to his circular), CO137/390.

[2] Taylor to Cardwell (29 July 1865), CO7/143. Taylor's insight into the ways

wrote another letter to Cardwell asking for a Royal Commission to be sent to Jamaica.[1] Taylor still preferred a parliamentary inquiry: Rogers had an open mind.[2] But by this time the Morant Bay outbreak had settled the point in favour of a Royal Commission and had also prepared the way for a radical reform of the Jamaican constitution. Eyre, who continued to defend his interpretation of the rising and his measures of repression with ability and moderation, was sore at his supersession; but, as Taylor told him, 'there was no way by which the public feeling could be prevented from running to an ungovernable excess but that of appointing a commission of enquiry'.[3]

The Royal Commission, in which Sir Henry Storks was reinforced by two highly respected lawyers, Russell Gurney, Q.C., M.P., Recorder of London, and J. B. Maule, Recorder of Leeds and a future Director of Public Prosecutions, examined 730 witnesses, not without encountering some difficulties, for much of the evidence of the Negroes was found to be contradictory and unreliable. The newly formed Jamaica Committee sent out John Gorrie (a Scottish barrister and future Chief Justice of Fiji) and J. Horne Payne of the English bar to represent it. Eyre was not cross-examined. Brigadier Nelson came well out of cross-examination, leaving the impression of being a clear-headed, humane man: so did Westmorland. His fellow-member of the Executive Committee, Hosack, did not come out so well; still less did Colonel Hobbs, commander of the Blue Mountain Valley column.[4] The Commission's report, submitted on 9 April 1866 after three strenuous months in the island, is a masterly and notably impartial document. Its conclusion that the rising was 'a planned resistance to lawful authority' but not a general conspiracy against the Government must be accepted. So must its view that the outbreak was due not so much to the admitted grievances of the labouring class (even though St. Thomas-in-the-East had an unusually high proportion of 'estate Negroes') as to the desire of

of English government reminds one he had written *The Statesman*. The reference (in the Antigua series) I owe to Miss G. J. Sellers, whose Oxford B.Litt. thesis 'Edward Cardwell at the Colonial Office' I examined in 1958.
    [1] Underhill to Cardwell (9 Oct. 1865), P.P., 1866, li [3595], 275-6.
    [2] Minute of Taylor (11 Oct.) and Rogers (12 Oct.) on Underhill to Cardwell (9 Oct. 1865), CO137/398.
    [3] Taylor to Eyre (31 Jan. 1866), Russell Papers, P.R.O. 30/22, 16.
    [4] Hobbs committed suicide on his way back to England.

the free settlers to obtain the so-called 'back lands' rent free. The more controversial parts of the report concerned Eyre's conduct and in particular his treatment of Gordon. The Commissioners reaffirmed Cardwell's praise of Eyre for 'the skill, promptitude and vigour which he manifested during the early stages of the insurrection'. They considered the declaration of martial law justified and the military arrangements 'prompt and judicious'. But the suppression of the outbreak had cost 439 lives, 354 of these after trial by court-martial, and not less than 600 floggings.[1] These punishments seemed to the Commission to have been 'far greater than the necessity required'. Much of this excess might in its view have been avoided if clear and precise instructions had been given to those engaged in the suppression and officers had been warned of their responsibilities. After the Governor's amnesty proclamation on 30 October, prisoners might have been handed over to the ordinary tribunals even though martial law was still retained. In the case of Gordon, which the Commissioners examined with meticulous care, they considered the evidence 'wholly insufficient to establish the charge [of high treason] upon which the prisoner took his trial'. But they by no means held him blameless. He knew how far he could go with safety and drew the line short of rebellion: 'but that would not be so easy to his ignorant and fanatical followers'.[2]

Storks's personal impression of Eyre was favourable. He gave the Commission no trouble: he was 'a gentleman . . . a very energetic and at the same time conscientious man', though 'very obstinate and in no sense a man of the world'.[3] But he soon saw that Eyre could not remain in Jamaica and urged the appointment of a man 'who brings with him the prestige of reputation and station'.[4] The appointment naturally had to await the conclusion of the Commission's labours. The senior officials at the Colonial Office were broadly in accord with its findings; but, as Rogers pointed out, if Eyre's repression had not been sufficient 'it is

[1] The Provost-Marshal, Ramsay, who had charged with the Light Brigade, was responsible for the worst floggings. He was afterwards tried, but a Grand Jury of 7 white and 7 coloured men and 1 Negro found no true bill despite the Judge's charge. Ramsay was clearly unbalanced.

[2] Report of the Jamaica Royal Commission (9 Apr. 1866), P.P., 1866, xxx [3683], 8-40.

[3] Storks to Cardwell (8 Jan. and 9 July 1866), Cardwell Papers, P.R.O. 30/48, 7/43.

[4] Storks to Cardwell (6 Feb. 1866), ibid.

utterly impossible to say (in the comparative absence of troops) what might have followed first in our West Indian Islands and next wherever any Africans are or have been held in slavery'. He 'ought to have seen that the officers employed received strong general cautions at once' and to have warned General O'Connor, even later, 'that subordinates should receive specific prohibitions and limitations as to the exercise of their powers'. But Eyre's paramount duty, as Taylor and Rogers agreed, was to place the colony in safety; and with all his energies concentrated on this object, there would almost necessarily 'be some failure of watch-fulness and thoughtfulness in other directions, at least for a time'. Besides the 'clear and precise instructions' of which the Commission spoke would have been difficult to give when Governor and commanding officers were without previous experience of martial law. Moreover, both Taylor and Rogers remained convinced that Gordon's execution was 'a just and necessary act'. Rogers confirmed this conclusion of Taylor in a striking image.

If a man occupies himself in singeing the end of a slow match and on being told that it communicated with a barrel of gunpowder replies that he 'knows how far he can go' . . . and if the barrel ultimately explodes . . . if he was himself sitting on the barrel I should think he was a madman. If his mortal enemy whom he had held up for execration and whose speedy destruction he had prophesied were sitting on it, I should think him a murderer.[1]

If Taylor and Rogers thought that Gordon had tried to blow up Eyre and been blown up himself, Forster was of a different opinion. He did not question the Commission's view that the proclamation of martial law was justified but thought it clear that 'the Disturbances were put down not by the punishments or terror of Martial Law but by the presence and the skilful disposition and handling of the troops. . . . Martial Law means and must mean "the Devil let loose" '. Forster held Eyre responsible for the unlawful execution of Gordon; for the lack of clear and precise instructions about martial law; for its long continuance and for eighty-nine unnecessary executions. He found it hard to believe that he did not put a different value on black and on white life.

After all men and above all men in authority must be held responsible for mistakes and for such a mistake as this by which the Governor has

---

[1] Minute of Taylor (c. 14 May 1866), with marginal comments of Rogers, on Report of Royal Commission, CO137/411.

deservedly stamped the reputation of this country with cruelty I cannot but think recall with blame is a mild retribution.[1]

Cardwell was not given to minute-writing; but he and the Cabinet leant rather to Forster's view than to that of Rogers and Taylor. A dispatch from Cardwell to Storks announced the general concurrence of the Cabinet in the conclusions of the Royal Commission. Making every allowance for Eyre's difficulties—the suddenness of the emergency, the atrocities committed at its outbreak, the disparity in numbers between the white and black populations, the inadequacy of his force, the civil war in nearby Haiti, they still thought martial law had been carried on too long, its severities being justified only when absolutely necessary for the re-establishment of public safety. Instructions should have been issued to officers which would have rendered abuse of its powers impossible. They also deplored and condemned the trial and execution of Gordon. Westmorland had apparently suggested at the time that he 'should be reserved for trial by a regular tribunal, with all the means of defence which are secured by the ordinary process of law to every subject of the Queen. This . . . would have been the proper course.'[2]

The Cabinet had already taken its main constitutional decision. Early in December Cardwell had told Eyre that, if the Jamaica Legislature wished to reconstitute itself by its own act, Her Majesty's Government would accept either a wholly nominated Legislative Council or a Council partly nominated and partly elective but not one 'in which a small number of elected members should have a majority of votes': for 'where there is no wide basis for constituent and representative power and responsibility to rest upon, there is no eligible alternative but to vest power and responsibility substantially in the Crown'. If the Legislature was unwilling to devolve its powers, Parliament would expect more information before legislating.[3] This contigency did not arise.

---

[1] Minute of Forster (22 May 1866) on Report of Royal Commission, CO137/411.

[2] Cardwell to Storks (18 June 1866) (No. 173), P.P., 1866, li [3681], 3–7. Gladstone, who saw the dispatch in draft, took a rather harsher view than Cardwell: 'The truth is, it is a most great and grievous offence, though with great and indeed extraordinary palliation': Gladstone to Cardwell (13 June 1866), Gladstone Papers, B.M. Add. MS. 44536.

[3] Cardwell to Eyre (1 Dec. 1865), P.P., 1866, li [3594], 250–1. This was the dispatch Taylor had sent Eyre in draft.

Though Eyre at first thought the Assembly would be unlikely to leave Her Majesty's Government a free hand in face of the Act recently passed, in fact it responded to his invitation to amend this Act and empower Her Majesty 'to create and constitute a Government for this Island in such form and with such powers as to Her Majesty may seem best fitting and from time to time to alter and amend such Government'. Eyre himself recommended a Legislative Council consisting of the Governor as President, six official and six non-official members and an Executive Council of the Governor and four officials.[1] On 15 February 1866 Cardwell moved for leave to bring in a Bill to make provision for the government of Jamaica. The intention, he told the House, was to give it a government similar to that of Trinidad; but the Bill would be in force for three years only. It was favourably received, and when Adderley moved in Committee that the limitation of its operation to three years be omitted, Cardwell readily agreed.[2] The most notable speech in the House of Lords came from Lord Grey. In a short time political ascendancy under the existing constitution would have passed into the hands of the Negroes. There was 'no peculiarity in the black race which will prevent their improvement' but for many years to come they would be unfit to exercise political power and the best thing therefore in the meantime was to give full power to the Crown.[3] The Act, which became law on 23 March, was an empowering measure only and left it to Her Majesty to frame a constitution by Order in Council.[4] After Storks had been consulted, this was forwarded by dispatch on 16 June. Jamaica thus became a Crown Colony. On the same day Storks was notified that Eyre would not be reinstated in the government. The new Governor was to be Sir John Peter Grant, recently Lieutenant-Governor of Bengal. He had taken the side of the ryots against the indigo planters and had been recommended by the Secretary of State for India, Lord Halifax. H. T. Irving of the West India department of the Colonial Office was to be his Colonial Secretary.[5]

---

[1] Eyre to Cardwell (8 Dec. 1865), P.P., 1866, li [3594], 234–5. Eyre to Cardwell (22 Dec. 1865) (Confidential), CO137/396. The Act was 29 Vict., c. 24 (No. 4544).
[2] *Hansard*, 3rd Ser. clxxxi. 581–2. See also ibid. 918–27 (22 Feb.) and 1173–7 (26 Feb.).
[3] House of Lords, 13 Mar. 1866, *Hansard*, 3rd Ser. clxxxii, 126–33.
[4] The Act was 29 & 30 Vict., c. 12.
[5] Cardwell to Storks (16 June 1866) (Private), Cardwell Papers, P.R.O. 30/48,

Eyre's recall was the logical consequence of the Government's acceptance of the Royal Commission's report. 'The Report and the decision of Her Majesty's Government upon it', wrote Cardwell in a farewell letter to Storks, 'have scotched the question here.'[1] Cardwell was mistaken. On 26 June, four days before he wrote this letter, the Russell Ministry had resigned. As Mr. Semmel says, 'even after the publication of the Commission report, the Radicals had refrained from embarrassing the Liberal government, most especially since it was involved in Reform legislation. But they were perfectly willing to assault Earl Derby's government'.[2] The Russell Ministry, Forster notwithstanding, had confirmed the Indemnity Act passed by the Jamaica Assembly.[3] This did not deter the Jamaica Committee from wanting to prosecute Governor Eyre for murder, though Charles Buxton resigned the chairmanship in protest. Buxton nevertheless on 31 July, in a well-documented speech, moved four resolutions in the House of Commons. The first and least controversial deplored the excessive punishments after the disturbances. The second declared categorically that

this House, while approving the course taken by Her Majesty's Government in dismissing Mr. Eyre . . . at the same time concurs in the view expressed by the late Secretary of State for the Colonies, that 'while any very minute endeavour to punish acts which may now be the subject of regret would not be expedient, still that great offences ought to be punished'; and that grave excess of severity on the part of any Civil, Military or Naval Officers ought not to be passed over with impunity.

The third and fourth dealt with compensation to property owners and to families of those put to death illegally and with remission of all further punishment on account of the disturbances. Adderley, now Parliamentary Under-Secretary for the Colonies, criticized Buxton for attempting to try the whole case over again: 'it is a question whether the Legislature ever does well needlessly

---

7/43. Later E. E. Rushworth, formerly President of Montserrat, was appointed Financial Secretary. On the indigo planters see R. J. Moore, *Sir Charles Wood's Indian Policy, 1853–66* (Manchester, 1966), esp. pp. 194–7. He does not, however, mention Grant.

[1] Cardwell to Storks (30 June 1866) (Private), Cardwell Papers, P.R.O. 30/48.
[2] Semmel, op. cit., p. 72.
[3] 29 Vict., c. 1 (Act No. 4534). Minute of Forster (9 June) on Law Officers to Cardwell (8 June 1866), CO137/409.

to step out of its usual functions and take part either in the judicial or the Executive proceedings of the country'. He for his part did not think the case against Eyre had been made out and moved the previous question, though this motion was later withdrawn. John Stuart Mill, who followed, had succeeded Buxton as chairman of the Jamaica Committee, and had already asked the Chancellor of the Exchequer (Disraeli) nine questions as to whether any steps had been or would be taken by the Government to bring to justice those concerned in illegal acts[1] and had given notice of an amendment committing the House to a prosecution of Eyre. Nothing, he declared, could be better for his cause than Adderley's speech.

If officers of the Government are to be allowed to take the lives of the Queen's subjects improperly—as has been confessedly done in this case—without being called to a judicial account and having the excuse they make for it sifted and adjudicated by the tribunal in that case provided, we are giving up altogether the principle of government by law and resigning ourselves to arbitrary power.

But Mill got no support except from his fellow committeeman Thomas Hughes and Eyre found some defenders. In particular Cardwell declared that 'there was a man who, among all these anxieties and alarms, did retain some portion of his self-possession and natural courage, and that was Governor Eyre'. Forster announced his intention to vote for the first and second resolutions but deprecated a prosecution. After Disraeli had wound up the debate, the House adopted the first resolution only. Buxton withdrew the others.[2]

The Jamaica Committee had failed to gain the sympathy of the Commons; but the excitement in the country about reform encouraged it to carry on its campaign, especially as Eyre returned to England a few days after the parliamentary debate. The Jamaica whites fêted him on his departure as the saviour of the colony. Even the missionaries of the Free Churches in Kingston deplored the unfair criticism in England and expressed their conviction that his 'general policy . . . was absolutely necessary to meet the exigencies of the case, and was dictated simply by a sense of duty'.[3] On his arrival in Southampton, he was given a dinner by a citizens'

[1] House of Commons, 19 July 1866, Hansard, 3rd Ser. clxxxiv. 1064.
[2] Hansard, 3rd Ser. clxxxiv. 1763–1838.
[3] Address from the Missionaries in Kingston (5 Jan. 1866), P.P., 1866, xxx [3682], 472–3.

committee, though the other party to the controversy put up
anti-Eyre posters and organized street demonstrations. Eyre made
a dignified speech and the affair encouraged his friends to form
an Eyre Defence and Aid Committee, engineered by his fellow-
explorer Hamilton Hume but headed by Carlyle. At the same time
it 'reinforced the determination of the Jamaica Committee not
to be satisfied with the Governor's dismissal'.[1] They were, as
Mr. Semmel admits, only a small minority of the educated and
articulate classes but the reform agitation enabled them to rally
a good deal of working-class support. Early in February 1867
James Fitzjames Stephen, on behalf of the Jamaica Committee,
filed an application in the Bow Street Police Court for warrants
against Colonel Nelson and Lieutenant Brand, R.N. (who had
presided at Gordon's trial) on a charge of murder. Eyre was
omitted as being beyond the Court's jurisdiction. Nelson and
Brand surrendered to the Court, were given bail and, after a preliminary hearing committed for trial at the Central Criminal
Court. Thus encouraged, the Committee applied to the Market
Drayton magistrates for a warrant against Eyre, who was living
at Adderley Hall;[2] but after hearing Hardinge Giffard (the future
Earl of Halsbury) the magistrates unanimously dismissed the case.
A fortnight later, on 10 April, the case of The Queen v. Nelson and
Brand came before Lord Chief Justice Cockburn and a Middlesex
grand jury. The Lord Chief Justice, in his charge, held that,
Jamaica being a settled colony, Eyre had no power to declare
martial law and that the whole proceedings against Gordon were
'altogether unlawful and unjustifiable': 'it was', he concluded,
'as lamentable a miscarriage of justice as the history of judicial
tribunals can disclose'.[3] The grand jury nevertheless ignored the
indictment and strongly recommended that martial law should be
more clearly defined by legislative enactment.

Fitzjames Stephen now advised the Committee to drop the
prosecution of Eyre, but Mill would not listen. Early in 1868,

[1] Semmel, op. cit., p. 96. Whilst I am much indebted to Mr. Semmel's full
account of the controversy, it seems to me that he exaggerates the extent to which
the active participants in it were influenced by the reform agitation. This was part
of the background. There is a useful contemporary book, with a different bias,
W. F. Finlason, History of the Jamaica Case.
[2] This was not, as might be supposed, the residence of Sir Charles Adderley,
but belonged to a Mr. Reginald Corbet.
[3] Charge of the Lord Chief Justice of England to the Grand Jury at the Central
Criminal Court in the Case of The Queen v. Nelson and Brand (London, 1867).

when Eyre had moved to London, Sir Robert Collier, on the Committee's behalf, applied for a warrant against him for murder. When this was refused, he applied to another magistrate for a warrant on the ground 'that he had issued an illegal and oppressive proclamation of martial law, and caused divers illegal acts to be committed under the same and . . . had unlawfully and oppressively caused the arrest, imprisonment and flogging of divers persons by virtue of the said illegal proclamation'. The magistrate committed Eyre for trial. When he was asked if he had anything to say, his statement moved the spectators to sympathetic applause. The case came before Mr. Justice Blackburn (a future law lord) on 2 June. He differed from the Lord Chief Justice's view of the law. In his view the Jamaica legislature had given the Governor power to proclaim martial law in special circumstances. After this dictum and the review of the facts which followed, it was doubly sure that the grand jury would throw out the indictment.[1] In some extra-judicial observations a few days later, the Lord Chief Justice reiterated his opinion that 'mere honesty of intention would be no excuse for a reckless, precipitate and inconsiderate exercise of so formidable a power, still less for any abuse of it in regard to the lives and persons of Her Majesty's subjects'.[2] But Eyre had won his case, and though he had still to face a civil action by a certain Phillips, turning on the question whether a colonial Act of Indemnity took away a right of action in England for unlawful imprisonment,[3] his legal vindication was complete. He felt sore that Nelson had been defended by the War Office whereas he had been 'left unaided and unsupported by the Government [he] had served';[4] but in 1871, after resistance in some quarters, £4132 was placed on the estimates to meet his expenses.[5] His hope of re-employment was, of course, vain; but an unbiased observer must surely feel that the Jamaica Committee could have found a a better way of championing the Jamaica Negroes than the persecution of Eyre. It was easy for Lord Olivier, for example, with

[1] W. F. Finlason, *Report of the Case of the Queen v. E. J. Eyre* (London, 1868), pp. 59–87. Cf. also Semmel, op. cit., and Finlason, *History of the Jamaica Case.*
[2] *Report of the Case of the Queen v. E. J. Eyre*: Appendix, pp. 104–5.
[3] *Phillips* v. *Eyre, The Times,* 24 June 1870.
[4] Eyre to Rogers (21 Jan. 1867) and to Buckingham (21 Mar. 1868), P.P., 1872, xliii (H.C. 56), 2–3. See also Minutes of Holland (25 Jan.) and Taylor (27 Jan.) on Eyre to Rogers (21 Jan. 1867), CO137/429.
[5] P.P., 1872, xliii (H.C. 56), 66. And see *Hansard,* 3rd Ser., ccxii. 798 ff. The vote was strongly contested but passed by 243 to 130.

the advantage of hindsight, to say there was no danger of a general rising in Jamaica:[1] it was by no means obvious to Eyre. Shameful things had been said and done by some officers in the heat of the moment; Eyre himself had made grave errors of judgement; but he had seen the issue as one between order and anarchy, not between black and white.

Meanwhile Jamaica had made a fresh start under the Crown Colony regime, to which the Colonial Office tried to impart a sense of purpose new to Jamaican government. In his instructions to Sir J. P. Grant, Carnarvon called attention to no fewer than ten immediate questions: 'the relief of the poor—the influence of the Church of England and other religious bodies—education—the administration of justice by the magistracy—the police—the repression of praedial larceny—the unauthorized occupation of land—the introduction of capital and labour—taxation—and official reform.' This was really Taylor's list, but Carnarvon added some sentences to his draft stressing the 'paramount neces-sity' of justice as a means of allaying 'the feeling of personal wrong and class triumph' after the events of the last twelve months.[2]

The aftermath of the rebellion raised some difficult issues. Should compensation be paid for damage done by the rioters or by the troops? The Imperial authorities said not from Imperial funds for the latter: colonial funds might pay half of the former.[3] Ought sentences to be reviewed? In some cases not, in others not for some time to come, said Grant: his general principle was 'not to interfere with the sentences of any of those who have shown a murderous mind, and to reduce all others to seven years, except in the case of Bogle'.[4] There was also some resistance to proprie-tors' attempts to enforce their rights of possession through Supreme Court writs, though the influence of a Baptist mission-ary, Dr. Philippo, secured squatters' acceptance of the terms that they should sign agreements acknowledging the proprietors' rights and pay rent.[5]

---

[1] Lord Olivier, *The Myth of Governor Eyre* (London, 1933).

[2] Carnarvon to Grant (1 Aug. 1866) (No. 32), P.P., 1867, xlix [3903], 88–95.

[3] Minutes of Taylor (7 Nov.), Holland (8 Nov.), Adderley (9 Nov.) and Buck-ingham (12 Nov.) on Grant to Buckingham (8 Oct. 1867) (No. 196), CO137/427. The decisive word against Imperial payment came from Buckingham.

[4] Grant to Carnarvon (9 Oct. 1866) (No. 23), P.P., 1867, xlix [3859], 4–10. 'Bogle' was H. T. Bogle, Paul's nephew.

[5] Grant to Carnarvon (9 Oct. 1866) (No. 22), ibid., pp. 2–3.

THE JAMAICA CRISIS AND THE RETREAT

In opening the first session of the new Legislative Council, Grant gave priority to a reform in the legal system of the colony. The deterioration in the administration of justice and the lack of confidence in it as the stipendiary magistracy declined in numbers and influence were generally acknowledged. Grant, with his Indian experience, saw the best remedy in the creation of perhaps a dozen district judges (barristers from Great Britain if possible) with both civil and criminal jurisdiction up to a certain limit, with a cheap form of appeal.[1] Next year he passed a law for the organization of a constabulary on the Irish model to replace the inefficient old police and in 1869 he supplemented this by a new rural police, under headmen who were resident householders, to deal particularly with the special Jamaican problem of thefts of growing produce and small stock.[2] Yet another reform was the replacement of the clerks of the peace, who were paid by fees and often executed their office by ill-qualified deputies,[3] by salaried clerks of petty sessions without the right of private practice.[4] A reform of prison discipline was also under discussion and in 1870 a young English barrister, R. S. Wright, was set to work on a new Criminal Code.[5]

The state of Jamaica's finances was a serious obstacle to reform. The financial results of the year 1865-6 were naturally bad, but this was only one of a series of deficits. Grant found the accounts as prepared for the Assembly so confused as to be almost unintelligible. The new Government had both to reduce expenses and to impose new taxation. This was done with some ingenuity. A tax of a penny an acre on all land, with registration of possession in return, was paid 'with remarkable cheerfulness': cottagers with land attached, hitherto not taxed at all, could hardly complain if they were taxed for the benefit of the poor of the parish; rum was

[1] Grant to Carnarvon (23 Oct. 1866, No. 31 and 26 Dec. 1866, No. 82), P.P., 1867, xlix [3903], 8-9, 37-9.
[2] Grant to Kimberley (19 Dec. 1870) (No. 250), P.P., 1871, xlvii [C. 334], 5. There was complaint in some quarters about whipping, but 'only about half a thief per cent. was ever whipped', Note of Taylor on Grant to Granville (5 Feb. 1870) (No. 23), CO137/447.
[3] Evidence of Mr. Justice Ker, Report of Jamaica Royal Commission, Minutes of Evidence, P.P., 1866, xxxi [3683-I], 291-2.
[4] Law 3 of 1870; see also Grant to Kimberley (4 Aug. 1871) (No. 103), P.P., 1872, xlii [C. 523], 4.
[5] Minute of Taylor (29 Mar.) on Grant to Granville (5 Feb. 1870) (No. 23), CO137/447.

a good choice for an increased duty. A system of licenses for trades and businesses was also introduced. The people of Jamaica, Grant reported, would still not be heavily taxed.[1] Buckingham and Adderley scouted the suggestion that Parliament might give further relief by guaranteeing £350,000 of unguaranteed debt; but the blow was softened by permission to apply the sinking fund to the purchase and cancellation of bonds of existing guaranteed loans, which reduced the debt burden considerably.[2]

Another reform, long desired in Jamaica, was the end of the ecclesiastical establishment. The Clergy Act, the last of a series dating back to the reign of Charles II, by which the stipends of rectors and curates were paid out of general taxation, expired in 1869. 'Her Majesty's Government', wrote Granville, 'are of opinion that the moral and religious culture of the subject-race, and not the ascendency of any one communion ought to be the object of your Government.'[3] But perhaps two-thirds of the people were unprovided with religious instruction and belonged to no Christian communion, and Grant found it went against the grain to say to them 'Subscribe for all your own religious wants, or go without religion, as you please.'[4] Taylor and Rogers shared his feelings. 'If the taxpayers of Jamaica were to be the judges of what is required for their welfare, I do not believe that they would make provision for education or the administration of justice any more than for their spiritual needs.'[5] But as many denominations were unwilling to accept State aid, all that could be done was to pass a law (No. 30 of 1870) 'to regulate the gradual Disendowment of the Church of England in Jamaica'. It also provided for a diocesan synod to frame a constitution.[6]

The improvement in education, based on grants in aid to schools of a certain standard according to the recommendation of the

[1] Grant to Buckingham (9 May 1867) (No. 90), P.P., 1867, xlix [3895], 58–62. A few details come from later dispatches.

[2] Grant to Buckingham (25 Feb. 1868) (No. 35) with Minutes of Taylor (24), Rogers (29), Adderley and Buckingham (31 Mar.), CO137/431. Treasury to Colonial Office (9 Dec. 1868), CO137/438.

[3] Granville to Grant (1 Mar. 1869) (No. 26), P.P., 1871, xlviii (H.C. 269), 3. The odd expression 'subject-race' was presumably inadvertent.

[4] Grant to Granville (23 July 1869) (No. 180), ibid., pp. 3–10.

[5] Taylor to Rogers (15 Oct.) with Minutes of Grant to Granville (23 July 1869) (No. 180), CO137/442.

[6] P.P. 1871, xlviii (H.C. 269), 19–21. There was a change from state supported establishment to religious equality in all the West Indian colonies, but the method varied. It cannot be discussed further here.

Inspector, who had a system of grading, was slow.[1] There were
other difficulties besides shortage of funds: of five schoolmasters
imported from England to teach in model schools, two were
intemperate, one absconded in debt, one was ineffective, and only
one satisfactory.[2] There was more progress with public health,
towards which the old Assembly had been apathetic. A Medical
Department, organized in 1868, was to cover the whole island
outside Kingston.[3] The number of doctors soon increased from
fifteen to thirty-five.

The question of the 'back lands', in the view of the Royal
Commission, had been at the bottom of the Morant Bay rising.
The great majority of the squatters were on lands to which it was
unknown whether any title existed except that of the Crown. As
Grant pointed out, people who had no confidence in the security
of their possessions would cultivate badly and would be disaffected
towards the law. He dealt with this by a law enabling the Crown,
after a suit in the district court, to enter upon the land provisionally on behalf of the owner, should one come forward within
seven years, and to grant seven years' leases at a fair rent either to
the former squatters or to other parties. By the end of the financial
year 1869–70, over 12,000 acres had been surveyed under this
scheme and considerable portions of them leased to willing tenants
without serious opposition. Only 189 squatters had been ejected.
A long-standing evil was thus in process of treatment by conversion of squatters into leaseholders.[4]

For the once dominant but now ailing sugar industry, the
experience of British Guiana and Trinidad appeared to indicate
that the appropriate treatment was Indian immigration. The
Assembly, after one experiment in 1845–7 before the sugar crisis
reached its height, had been reluctant to resort to it except on
terms too favourable to the planters to be acceptable to the
Colonial Office. Immigration had, however, been resumed in
1860–4, and in 1866 the Imperial authorities authorized a loan of
£12,000 'to cover an equal sum which in the last two years has

[1] Grant to Buckingham (24 Oct. 1868) (No. 248), P.P., 1868–9, xliii [4090], 14.
See also subsequent Colonial Reports.
[2] P.P., 1871, xlviii [C. 334], 18. This is a 'Blue Book' Report.
[3] Grant to Granville (8 Nov. 1869) (No. 264), P.P., 1870, xlix [C. 85], 12.
[4] District Courts Land Law (No. 7 of 1867). See Grant to Buckingham (23 Aug.
1867) (No. 165), CO137/425. Also Report on Jamaica Blue Book for 1870 in
Grant to Kimberley (4 Aug. 1871) (No. 103), P.P., 1872, xlii [C. 523], 15–16.

been diverted from the Immigration Revenue to general purposes'.[1] Nineteen hundred 'statute adults' were then ordered and
1,636 arrived in 1867. In the same year a Royal Commission
headed by Rushworth, the Financial Secretary, was appointed to
examine the immigration system. On its recommendation a new
law (No. 34 of 1869) was passed with more liberal provision for
rations (which were to be for the whole period of the indenture
instead of the first three months) and for wages and medical
treatment.[2] W. M. Anderson, Agent-General for Immigration
and a member of the Commission, was sent to India as Agent for
the colony and after an interruption in 1868 the flow of immigrants
was resumed. The fact that a good proportion of those entitled
to free passages took advantage of the alternative of commuting
these for land or money suggests that the Indians found Jamaica
congenial. Sir J. P. Grant did not agree with the Colonial Office
requirement of 40 women to every 100 men. 'The Agent', he
reported, 'is driven to collect and despatch the lowest dregs of the
Indian seaport bazaars.' He suggested a reversion to the former
figure of 25 per cent. But the Colonial Office was not to be moved.
'It does not follow', said Taylor, 'that any additional evil will be
created by transferring the fifteen prostitutes from the one place
to the other'; and he had heard that women of questionable
character in India sometimes led good lives in the West Indies.[3]
Grant was prepared to defend the system as a whole against the
criticism of the Anti-Slavery Society and to argue against the
Colonial Office for the defrayal of part of the cost by the state.[4]
Nor was this because he could not look beyond sugar. On the
contrary, he welcomed the beginning of a new export trade to
North America in bananas and other fruit and predicted a great
future for it.[5]

Grant's able, firm, and fair-minded administration, which came
to an end in January 1874, had seen Jamaica well on the way to
recovery from the crisis of 1865. He was lucky in one respect:

[1] Carnarvon to Grant (10 Oct. 1866) (No. 62), CO138/73.
[2] Grant to Granville (7 Sept. 1869) (No. 220), CO137/442. Also Grant to
Kimberley (19 Dec. 1870) (No. 250), P.P., 1871, xlvii [C. 334], 7–8.
[3] Grant to Kimberley (10 Mar. 1872) (No. 47) with Minutes of Taylor (15 Apr.)
and Herbert (17 Apr.), CO137/462.
[4] Grant to Kimberley (9 May 1873) (No. 79) with Minute of Herbert (20 June)
and Kimberley (22 June), CO137/470.
[5] Grant to Kimberley (4 Aug. 1871) (No. 103), P.P., 1872, xlii [C. 523], 30–1.
On the origins of the fruit trade, see P. Abrahams, *Jamaica*, pp. 149–50.

after his time the price of sugar, which was still important to Jamaica, again began to fall. But the new sense of direction he had given to the colony was not lost. What is more, he had rehabilitated Crown Colony government and shown it to be the best method of doing what needed to be done in the West Indies. The constitutional reforms of the fifties had increased the powers of the Crown in island administration and finance. But the legislative machinery still creaked badly. It was difficult to pass laws which offended vested interests or to carry reforms which cost money. Even the policy of the Colonial Office, except perhaps in Lord Grey's time, seemed to lack a sense of direction after emancipation, no doubt in part because of the prevailing philosophy of government but also because of the continual frustrations of dealing with the jealous island Assemblies. But the Morant Bay rebellion had convinced wide circles in England that narrowly based oligarchies, whether pure white or with some admixture of coloured blood, were a mockery of self-government.[1] The real trouble was not the lack of liaison between the Executive and the Assembly but the lack of contact between the Assembly and the people. In what sense (to revert to Darling's dispatch of 1860) could an electorate of fewer than 1,500 voters be 'assumed to be the people' of Jamaica?[2] With the backing of English opinion, the Colonial Office now at last had the opportunity to do what Henry Taylor had urged in 1839 and use the authority of the Crown to reform Jamaican society. And some at least may have had the vision to discern in the distance the lineaments of a new, broadly based self-government.

[1] See, for instance, the *Spectator*, 11 and 18 Nov. 1865. Cf. also a letter from Cardwell to Grant (15 Oct. 1867), 'It seems like awakening from an evil dream to read of affairs in Jamaica conducted on sound principles for the public good', Cardwell Papers, P.R.O. 30/48, 7/43.

[2] 'The whole 47 members of the House of Assembly were returned by 1457 voters', Eyre to Cardwell (19 Apr. 1865), P.P., 1866, li [3595] 31.

# XIV

## CROWN COLONY GOVERNMENT AND FEDERATION IN THE LESSER ANTILLES

THE Lesser Antilles underwent no such traumatic experience in this period as the Morant Bay rebellion. Riots in St. John's, Antigua, on 25 and 26 March 1858 were suppressed by the police with the loss of ten lives. Governor Hamilton, being without any troops, had applied to the nearest available source, Guadeloupe; they were immediately sent, but, as order had been restored, they were not landed. A company arrived from Barbados a few days later.[1] In St. Vincent more serious and widespread rioting occurred after a reduction of wages and stoppage of sugar and rum allowances on certain estates in September 1862. The riots were quelled by volunteers, special constables, and the ordinary police, of whom a large proportion were Negroes; and some 250 arrests were made.[2] In neither case did the disturbances shake the fabric of society. On the whole these were peaceful years in the smaller islands, though only St. Kitts could be called prosperous. Antigua, for instance, between 1862 and 1865 suffered a smallpox epidemic and then three years of intense drought, which reduced the sugar export from 250,000 to 50,000 hundredweight.

It became clear, however, that here too the device of an Executive Committee, though it made for smoother working of the machine of government, was no adequate remedy for the weaknesses of the superannuated representative system of the islands. The colonial Assemblies, moreover, would not leave well alone.

[1] The 'tumult' was reported in Hamilton to Stanley (27 Mar. 1858) (No. 21), CO 7/109. In a Minute (5 May) on a later dispatch (No. 22 of 7 Apr.) Taylor complained that the Governor had not reported in sufficient detail on the riots and their suppression. The Colonial Office, uneasy at the precedent created by the appeal to the French, urged on the War Office the importance of keeping a detachment at Antigua, CO7/111.

[2] The documents are in P.P., 1863, xxxviii (H.C. 509)—a parliamentary Paper of 170 pages, which the Duke of Newcastle had printed to vindicate the character of Lieutenant-Governor Musgrave against unfair attacks.

In Tobago, which had been the first colony to follow Jamaica's lead, the Assembly, after neglecting to pass an Appropriation Act, passed in 1863 a motion expunging the rule of the House reserving the initiative in money votes to the Crown, an essential part of the Executive Committee system.[1] The St. Vincent Assembly in 1862 passed an 'Act to repeal so much of the Council and Committee Act 1859 as gives salaries to the members of the Administrative Committee';[2] and in 1864, when the original Act expired, the Administrative Committee was virtually swallowed up in a reconstituted Executive Council with the Colonial Secretary as clerk, though one or two members of this Council were to act as organs of communication between the Governor and the House of Assembly.[3] Sir Benjamin Pine, an unusually experienced Lieutenant-Governor for a small West Indian island, reported the Administrative Committee to be working well in St. Kitts. He had given one member charge of public works, another of finance, and the third of other business.[4] But in Antigua the salaries of the Committee were abolished in 1863. This saved £750, but made it 'more difficult to get competent men to devote themselves to the public work'.[5]

In the long run the trend towards a single chamber, already discernible in the fifties, proved more significant. Montserrat's first attempt in this direction, in 1853, had broken down over the Assembly's refusal to make the amendments required by the Colonial Office. President Rushworth in 1859 reported it to be determinedly opposed to any constitutional change. Yet, in the words of the Colonial Secretary, E. D. Baynes,

the privilege of selecting members of the Assembly for nearly all the electoral districts was almost exclusively exercised by the inhabitants of the town of Plymouth, the majority of whom, under the system which conferred the right of voting on the freehold possession of any

[1] Drysdale to Walker (11 Mar. 1863) with Enclosure, CO285/81. Minutes of Legislative Assembly (27 Mar. 1863), CO288/26. H. I. Woodcock, *History of Tobago* (Ayr, 1867), p. 132.
[2] Musgrave to Walker (22 May) in Walker to Newcastle (10 June 1862) (No. 46), CO260/97.
[3] Walker to Newcastle (19 Apr. 1864) (No. 219), CO260/101.
[4] Pine to Hill (17 Oct.) in Hill to Cardwell (24 Oct. 1865) (No. 148), P.P., 1866, xlix [3719], 123-4.
[5] Address of Pine to Legislative Council and House of Assembly (10 Oct. 1866) in Hill to Buckingham (27 Aug. 1867) (No. 98), P.P., 1867-8, xlviii [3995], 91-2. Pine had been in temporary charge of the Leeward Islands in 1866.

portion of land, however small, have acquired the nominal possession of small lots in the different parishes, or had been made trustees (who were also held entitled to vote) under some deed of settlement.

At one election 'fifty-seven persons appeared at the hustings and exercised a right to vote on the joint possession of a single acre'.[1] Rushworth's successor Cockburn, on his arrival in 1860, was 'struck . . . with the desolate appearance of the Country—its uncultivated fields and neglected agriculture—its crippled commerce and diminished resources—its dilapidated buildings—its indigence and its poverty'.[2] He determined to rouse Montserrat from its lethargy. He first persuaded the Assembly to pass a Franchise Act, restricting the vote to freeholders of one acre with residence or 20 without or of the value of £14 per annum, or leaseholders of land valued at £50 per annum. Later, when the House persistently refused to meet (an old failing) he dissolved it June 1861 and persuaded Baynes, another Councillor, and other people of standing to offer themselves for election. With a working majority in the new Assembly he passed an Act reconstituting it as a Legislative Assembly of four nominated and eight elected members.[3]

Dominica, whose Assembly was once unkindly described as a body of 'ignorant coloured hucksters' was another island in which the executive found it difficult to get a quorum together. Lieutenant-Governor Price nevertheless managed in 1863 to overthrow the ruling party, dominated by the editor and proprietor of the *Dominican*, Falconer, and secure the consolidation of the Assembly into a single chamber of nineteen elective and nine non-elective members. W. C. F. Robinson, transferred from Montserrat early in 1865, found Dominica still unresponsive to executive leadership and 'disorganized by violent party feeling'.[4] He gained the consent of the Secretary of State to an attempt to transform it

[1] Baynes to Robinson (16 June) in Hamilton to Newcastle (23 July 1862) (No. 176), P.P., 1863, xxxix [3165], 82. This was a retrospect.

[2] Cockburn to Hamilton (31 Oct.) in Hamilton to Newcastle (23 Nov. 1861) (No. 87), CO175/10. Cockburn's successor, W. C. F. Robinson, brother of Sir Hercules, 'was carried ashore on the coxswain's back, there being no jetty', P. J. Boyce, 'The Governors of Western Australia under Representative Government' in *University Studies in History*, iv. 1 (Nedlands, W. A., 1962), 108.

[3] Baynes to Robinson (16 June) in Hamilton to Newcastle (23 July 1862) (No. 176), P.P., 1863, xxxix [3165], 81–3.

[4] Robinson to Hill (9 Jan. and 19 Jan., Confidential) in Hill to Cardwell (18 Jan. 1865, No. 3, and 31 Jan. 1865, No. 6), CO71/130.

into a Crown Colony before Falconer had recovered from his defeat. He did not quite bring this off, but Falconer agreed to a compromise, and a Bill constituting a chamber of seven nominees and seven elected members, presided over by the Lieutenant-Governor in person, was introduced. Falconer went back on his agreement and his party invaded the House, shouting down speakers of the opposite party. But the opportune arrival of H.M.S. *Aurora* enabled Robinson to clear the House with a marine guard and the restraining influence of the Roman Catholic Bishop enabled him to get the Bill through on 20 April.[1] Cardwell confirmed the Act. It had not been carried by the votes of the nominees and the weight of property and influence appeared to be for it.[2]

By the end of the year Jamaica had created another precedent in favour of such a change. Benjamin Pine, with his active mind and restless temperament, was just the man to improve the occasion. His second marriage in 1859 had presumably brought to an end the philandering which had offered a target for ridicule in Natal, and after seven years he had the government of St. Kitts well under control. By his own account the Executive had 'of late years acquired so much power that it has become a common remark, that the Island is really a Crown Colony . . . under the guise of popular Institutions'. After a general election favourable to the Government, the Assembly passed two Bills reconstituting itself as a single chamber of ten elected and ten nominated members, with a paid President, and substituting for the Administrative Committee an Executive Council of paid officials.[3] The departure of Colonel Hill, Governor of the Leeward Islands, on leave enabled Pine, as Acting Governor, to repeat the performance in Nevis. These two neighbouring islands presented a contrast socially and economically. The St. Kitts proprietors were mostly new, progressive men. In Nevis there were many old-established resident proprietary families, deeply divided by a feud between the Maynards and the Hugginses, one of whom had once been killed by a Maynard in a duel; but in agriculture it was 'a century

[1] Robinson to Hill (21 Apr.) in Hill to Cardwell (26 Apr. 1865) (No. 21), CO 71/130.

[2] Cardwell to Hill (16 June 1865) (No. 51) (Draft), ibid.

[3] Pine to Cardwell (25 Apr. 1866) (No. 68), CO239/115. Pine recommended that Challenger, the member of the Administrative Committee in charge of Finance, be appointed Auditor-General. The other two Executive Councillors were the Secretary to Government and Attorney-General.

behind . . . St. Kitts' and little had been done for the ignorant, superstitious Negro population. The Assembly was 'a hot bed of jobbers', mostly coloured men. The Collector of Customs audited his own accounts. The Excise Officer, who was also Speaker of the Assembly, was himself a manufacturer of rum. Capitalists threatened to withdraw altogether if the existing system of government continued.[1] In July Pine carried two Acts to 'amend and simplify the Legislature' by transforming it into a mixed chamber of two *ex officio* members, three other nominees, and five elective members, and to replace the Administrative Committee by an official Executive Council.[2]

Antigua's turn came next. There was local support for a simplified constitution; but a pure Crown Colony regime, in Pine's opinion, would have caused 'heartburnings which it would have taken years to allay' among the mainly coloured 'popular party'. During a two months' prorogation, their leaders were finally persuaded to support a mixed chamber on the St. Kitts model, provided Pine saw to it that the island did not lose every vestige of representation.[3] When the Assembly was reconvened in October it carried by comfortable majorities a Bill constituting a single Legislative Chamber of twelve officers and nominees of the Crown and twelve elected members, with a casting vote for the Crown. Pine rounded off his year's work by proceeding in December to Montserrat, dissolving the Assembly and, despite much misrepresentation in a fierce election campaign, passing through the new House an Act making this sadly mismanaged island a Crown Colony.[4] Next year President Rumbold, backed by Pine, made a similar change in the Virgin Islands. Elections under the constitution of 1853 had become a farce; there were only six registered voters, but one of the Crown nominees in the Legislative Council, who had systematically opposed every

[1] Pine to Cardwell (26 June 1866) (No. 115), CO184/14. The Excise Officer, an adventurer from Jamaica named Scott, and the Collector of Customs were both on the Administrative Committee until Pine replaced them by two members of the Huggins family, for once sitting with a Maynard.
[2] The Acts, No. 4 and 5 of 1866, were specially confirmed by Order in Council forwarded on 28 Nov. 1866, No. 5 being thought *ultra vires* in parts.
[3] Pine to Carnarvon (23 Oct. 1866) (No. 94), CO7/128. As a sequel Pine in 1869 proposed to supersede a number of irresponsible Boards and Commissions handling public revenue.
[4] Pine to Carnarvon (29 Dec. 1866, No. 118 and 11 Jan. 1867, No. 4), CO175/15 and 16.

measure of the Executive, was buying up lands for labourers with a view to controlling all elections.[1] The new Legislative Council, under a Constitution Ordinance based on a Colonial Office draft, would consist simply of the President, two other officials, and three non-official nominees.[2]

Constitutional reform had thus been carried through in the Leeward Islands virtually at one stroke and mainly by one man. The Windwards lagged behind. Only St. Vincent, where the Assembly had been more co-operative since the riots of 1862, showed much inclination to follow Jamaica's example. In an address to Lieutenant-Governor Berkeley, the Assembly requested a dissolution and expressed an opinion in favour of Crown Colony government; but popular opinion 'ran so strongly against the entire abandonment of the representative element' that members were obliged to give pledges against any such measure. The Bill passed in December 1866 provided for a single chamber of three officials, three other nominees, and seven elective members, with a Speaker elected by the House.[3] Lord Carnarvon, however, on Taylor's advice, insisted that this Bill be amended so as to give a casting vote to the Crown.[4] The Assembly complied readily enough, reducing the elective members to six and providing for a President, appointed by the Governor, with a deliberative and a casting vote.[5] The executive government was also remodelled in 1868 and made mainly official; but one non-official member was retained on the Executive Council and next year non-official representation was increased to four.[6]

The Colonial Office had been careful to leave the initiative in these constitutional changes to the Governors, warning them, however, not to press such measures on the legislatures if they seemed likely to create discontent. But both the Secretaries of

[1] Rumbold to Pine (7 Jan. 1867), CO414/17. Rumbold had already suggested a purely nominee Council on 14 June 1866, CO314/16.

[2] Rumbold to Buckingham (27 Apr. 1867), ibid. Rumbold was mildly reproved for not forwarding the Ordinance through Governor Hill.

[3] Walker to Carnarvon (26 Dec. 1866) (No. 433), CO260/105. Berkeley to Walker (27 July) in Walker to Buckingham (29 Aug. 1867) (No. 479), P.P., 1867-8, xlviii [3995], 53-5.

[4] Carnarvon to Walker (30 Jan. 1867) (No. 30) (draft), CO260/105.

[5] Berkeley to Walker (27 July 1867), loc. cit. The new Act also abandoned the provision for all the elective members to be chosen by one constituency, which obviously favoured the capital, Kingstown.

[6] Berkeley to Rawson (24 June 1869) (No. 621), P.P., 1870, xlix [C. 85], 54-8. See also P.P., 1871, xlviii [C. 334], 73.

State and their senior officials warmly approved of the changes. 'These Colonies', wrote Taylor, 'have thrown themselves upon the Crown for good government, renouncing their own power and authority for the sake of it.'[1] In 1868 constitutional reform had advanced far enough for the Duke of Buckingham to send a circular dispatch, for communication to the legislatures, reviewing its course and giving it his blessing.

The object of all parties was to establish a system of Government and Legislation by which the financial condition of the colonies should be improved and their agricultural and commercial interests be promoted, by which industry might be encouraged, crime repressed and the welfare of all classes be better provided for. . . . Her Majesty's Government . . . considered that where there is no wide basis for constituent and representative power and responsibility substantially to rest upon, there is no eligible alternative but to vest power and responsibility substantially in the Crown.

The Duke went on to discuss the duties of Crown nominees in the remodelled legislatures. The same implicit obedience would not necessarily be expected from *ex officio* members in their legislative as in their executive capacities. They might reasonably expect to be excused from taking part in measures to which they had conscientious scruples; but they could not be expected to be continued in their offices if their consciences precluded them from giving the Governor the support required to carry on Government business in the legislature. The same considerations applied to nominee but not *ex officio* members who were salaried servants of the Crown; and non-official nominees should 'not oppose the Crown on any important question without strong and substantial reasons'. If elective members thought official interests were being allowed to prevail over public interests they had the right to protest, through the Governor, to the Secretary of State; and in such cases, or where there were serious differences of opinion, Governors were advised to refer questions to the Secretary of State unless the public interests would suffer materially by delay. All parties were advised to co-operate and not press their powers to the limit.[2]

[1] Minute of Taylor on Colonel S. J. Hill's application for the Government of British Guiana (9 May 1867), CO111/365. About this time Taylor dubbed these colonies with equal numbers of nominated and elected members with a casting vote for the Crown 'quasi-Crown colonies'.

[2] Buckingham to Governors of Antigua, Dominica, St. Kitts, Nevis, Montserrat, the Virgin Islands, and St. Vincent (17 Aug. 1868), CO7/158.

Already, however, the Colonial Office was considering wider schemes of consolidation and simplification. The Governor of the Leeward Islands at Antigua had five subordinate governments under him, each with its own legislature, officials, and judges; the Governor of Barbados had the four island governments of St. Lucia, St. Vincent, Grenada, and Tobago. The first move, in 1866, came from the Treasury. Official salaries in Dominica had fallen nine months into arrear until a loan of £4,000 was raised to pay them. The Treasury, though approving the loan, asked whether some reduction might not be made in a judicial establishment 'out of all proportion' with its population. Rogers in his turn suggested that Pine be asked to report whether it might not be more efficient and economical to consolidate the judicial staff of all the Leeward and perhaps the Windward Islands into one circuit court: 'it is in his line.'[1] Pine indeed carried the question a stage further, to the subsidiary questions of a uniform code of procedure for all the islands, a uniform law of property and criminal law, and finally to the question whether an indirectly elected General Legislature or Federal Council might not be desirable for the Leeward Islands. It would, 'instead of over-shadowing the local Legislatures . . . rather tend to increase their importance and dignity' and he had reason to believe that 'the leading and most intelligent men at least in this Island [Antigua], St. Kitts and Nevis' would support such a measure.[2]

Henry Taylor was sceptical. 'It would be best', he wrote, 'to try what can be done by the reconstituted local Legislatures to improve and assimilate the several Colonial Codes and feel the want of a General Legislature before we attempt to supply it.'[3] Rogers, on the other hand, after tabulating the advantages and disadvantages of centralization, came to the conclusion that it would be worth working for a combination of the Windward and Leeward Islands into one government under a Governor-in-Chief

[1] Childers to Rogers (30 Apr. 1866) with Minute of Rogers (4 May), CO71/133. The operative dispatch was Cardwell to Pine (17 May 1866) (No. 112), CO72/6. There were already Courts of Appeal, set up under an Act of 1850 for the Leeward Islands in 1853 and for the Windward Islands in 1859. Dominica, geographically, is one of the Windward Islands, but it formed part of the Leeward Islands government.
[2] Pine to Carnarvon (20 Oct. and 17 Dec. 1866, General Nos. 2 and 3), CO7/128. A former General Legislature met for the last time in 1798.
[3] Minute of Taylor (28 Feb. 1867) on Pine to Carnarvon (17 Dec. 1866) (General No. 3), CO7/128.

at Barbados. On the legislative side Pine's list of subjects (procedure, law of property, criminal law, post office, bankruptcy and insolvency, quarantine, militia and police) was a good basis for discussion. One Attorney-General and Surveyor-General at Barbados would require only 'subordinate officers of a wholly inferior class' in the separate islands. One Auditor-General would suffice. Imperial expenditure on West Indian government would be diminished and should, Rogers thought, be confined to payment of the central staff. All this, he admitted, could not be achieved at once. The first step was to press on with the transformation of representative into Crown Colony or quasi-Crown Colony governments. The next to appoint 'a person of an active, organizing mind and familiar with colonial public business and the West Indies', such as Pine or Rushworth, as Governor of both the Leeward and the Windward Islands. An Act of Parliament authorizing the constitution of a Central Legislature would be the final stage.[1] Adderley had 'no doubt of the desirability of concentration' and thought the Leeward Islands offered 'a present opportunity for a first experiment'.[2] The Duke of Buckingham, new to office, did not at this stage record an opinion.

Some months later, presumably at Buckingham's request, Taylor prepared an elaborate minute on the subject. There were still traces of his original scepticism on the degree to which concentration and reduction of Imperial expenditure would be possible. To enforce payments in relief of the Imperial Treasury would be a most ungracious use of the new authority of the Crown. The colonies would be displeased if Lieutenant-Governors were reduced in status; and there was also the question 'how far this cluster of Lieutenant-Governments and Presidencies can be conveniently dispensed with in its capacity of a nursery and training school for the Governmental service in its higher walks'. He agreed with Pine that 'it would not be expedient to do anything by which the local Legislatures might feel themselves to be degraded and set aside'. But he had clearly come round to a support, if rather a lukewarm support, of the plan.[3] Rogers, 'with more of an inclination to centralization in the abstract', agreed

[1] Minute of Rogers (30 Mar. 1867), ibid.
[2] Minute of Adderley (13 Apr. 1867), ibid.
[3] Minute of Taylor on Consolidation of West Indian Governments and Legislatures (10 Feb. 1868), CO71/135, 11393.

442 CROWN COLONY GOVERNMENT AND

that all that could be done at the moment was to prepare the way: he also noted that 'the possession of a Government yacht to enable the chief officers and Governor to visit the out islands would prove a necessity'.[1] Adderley thought the general object, to secure Governors and judges of higher standard, 'most desirable and even urgent'. It would mean higher salaries, but they would 'soon cover that by preventing constant little causes of expense and trouble'. 'Island administrators', he declared, 'should be only Mayors and the idea of Lieutenant-Governors got rid of.' Arthur Gordon, Governor of Trinidad, suggested about this time that Tobago should be brought under his government: Adderley suggested this might be done with Grenada also.[2] Buckingham had now been won over to Rogers's scheme of 'consolidation of all the Windward and Leeward island governments under one Governor-General resident at Barbados'. He should be provided with a steamer and required to visit each island once a year. There should be at least one resident European officer in each island, a circuit court, and an appellate court at Barbados. There should be a Council composed of one member or representative from each colony to legislate on matters of general interest.[3]

The scheme then disappears from view for some months but comes to the surface again with a minute of Rogers on 2 November. He pointed out that these questions would remain theoretical rather than practical 'till we have got the consent of the Islands to abandon their independence . . . or an Act of Parliament to compel them to do so, either of which is a question of years I should think'. 'To my mind the question is not one of amalgamation or confederation—' he added, 'but of good government.'[4] But after some further consideration in the Office, the plan was submitted to the Treasury on 21 November. Two days later Disraeli had the audience with the Queen which foreshadowed his resignation after his defeat at the polls. Buckingham, however, had already made the two crucial appointments of Sir Benjamin Pine as

---

[1] Minute of Rogers (14 Feb. 1868), CO71/135.
[2] Minute of Adderley (15 Feb. 1868), ibid. For Gordon's part see Gordon to Gladstone (24 Apr. 1869) (Private), 'Gladstone-Gordon Correspondence' (ed. P. Knaplund), *American Philosophical Society Transactions*, n.s. li, Part 4 (1961), 50. But Gordon did not go on leave until June 1868, J. K. Chapman, *The Career of Arthur Hamilton Gordon* (Toronto, 1964), p. 76. The original suggestion to annex Tobago to Trinidad must surely have preceded the suggestion about Grenada.
[3] Minute of Buckingham (18 Feb. 1868), CO 71/135.
[4] Minute of Rogers (2 Nov. 1868), ibid.

Governor of the Leeward Islands and R. W. Rawson, Governor of the Bahamas since 1864, as Governor of Barbados and the Windward Islands. Pine was an obvious choice. The choice of the cautious, conservative Rawson was not so obvious. The isolated community of the Bahamas with its old-style legislature was no special preparation for the complexities of the Windward Islands and neither in the Bahamas nor, as Colonial Secretary, at the Cape had Rawson shown any particular aptitude for political management.[1] It is clear that there were long discussions between the two new Governors and the new Secretary of State, Lord Granville, in the Colonial Office in February and March 1869. In the course of these discussions the plan of attaching Tobago and Grenada to Trinidad was dropped, much to Gordon's annoyance;[2] and Pine's advocacy of immediate action in the Leeward Islands gained the day over Rogers's preference for the inevitability of gradualness.

Pine was sent out with the instruction that 'the end you will keep steadily in view is to form these islands into one colony, with one Governor, one Council, one Superior Court, one Corps of Police'.[3] It was for him to produce a detailed scheme. One proposal, a common Treasury for the Leeward Islands, he soon found to be impracticable, especially in St. Kitts.

'What!' they say, 'shall the rich and prosperous island of St. Kitts share its overflowing treasury with the bankrupt island of Antigua?' . . . They say the scheme emanated from some Birmingham and Manchester men, who have bought property in islands involved in difficulty, and now want to save themselves at the expense of St. Kitts.

He urged Lord Granville 'not to make shipwreck of a scheme which comprises so much that is practicable and eminently advantageous to the islands for the sake of this one point'.[4] Granville pointed out that in any kind of union it was impossible

---

[1] In fact he exchanged offices with his predecessor Walker, possibly for health reasons, as Walker retired after two years in the Bahamas. On the Bahamas, which are not discussed in this book, see M. Craton, *History of the Bahamas* (London, 1962).

[2] Gordon to Gladstone (24 Apr. 1869) (Private), loc. cit. The inhabitants of Tobago, according to Rawson, had no desire to be united to Trinidad: Rawson to Granville (16 Dec. 1869) (Confidential), CO28/209.

[3] Granville to Pine (10 Apr. 1869) (No. 75), P.P., 1871, xlviii [C. 353], 1.

[4] Pine to Granville (10 Sept. 1869, No. 30, and 27 Sept. 1869, No. 31), ibid., pp. 2–3.

'to dispense with a general revenue raised for general purposes, by taxation imposed by the General Legislature'; but he was quite ready to drop the idea of uniting the island Treasuries and let each island have a revenue of its own.[1] Pine favoured choice of the General Legislature by the island legislatures, in the quasi-Crown colonies partly from the nominated, partly from the elected, portion of the House. The General Legislature should have fifteen members, four each from Antigua and St. Kitts, two each from Dominica, Nevis, and Montserrat and one from the Virgin Islands. In view of the strength of local jealousies, 'its legislation should be confined to eleven heads (1) the law of real and personal property (2) mercantile law (3) family law (4) criminal law (5) constitution of courts, administration of justice and procedure (6) the post office (7) quarantine (8) weights and measures (9) audit of public accounts in all the islands (10) common penal establishment and prison discipline (11) general police and other protective forces'.[2] Granville approved this scheme, with reservations on a few points. On Rogers's advice, he preferred that the General Legislature should have supreme legislative power in all cases: 'if this is done', he added, 'you may be very liberal in granting concurrent powers of legislation to the insular authorities.' He also approved Pine's suggested procedure—resolutions to be passed by the various legislatures and then form the basis of a parliamentary Bill.[3]

Taylor and Rogers had their private doubts about Pine's methods. 'Sir B. Pine', wrote Rogers, 'was originally intended, I think, to approach federation by degrees. He preferred to be instructed to carry it at once. . . . I would rather that he should fail, than that the Imperial Government should be inconsistent or oppressive.'[4] But he did not fail. He modified his scheme in some details. The General Legislative Council was to be enlarged to twenty, with a President, three *ex officio* members, one other nominee from each island legislature, and ten elected by those having an elective element, four by Antigua, three by St. Kitts,

---

[1] Granville to Pine (5 Nov. 1869, No. 160, and 17 Nov. 1869, No. 170), P.P., 1871, xlviii [C353], 3–4.

[2] Pine to Granville (25 Oct. 1869, No. 35), ibid., pp. 5–9.

[3] Granville to Pine (15 Jan. 1870) (No. 190), ibid., pp. 10–11. This was based on a Minute of Rogers (11 Nov. 1869), CO7/137.

[4] Minute of Rogers (16 Dec.) on Pine to Granville (27 Oct.) (Confidential), CO7/138.

two by Dominica, and one by Nevis; and four more heads of legislation were allocated to it—currency, education, immigration, lunatics and lunatic asylum. Expenses were to be divided into as many parts as there were representative members, each island paying as many parts as it had representatives.[1] The Imperial Treasury, after some argument, had agreed to place a steamer at the disposal of the new Government, at Imperial cost, for five years.[2] On 11 July Pine was able to announce that the Antigua Legislative Council had passed his resolutions unanimously. St. Kitts, the most prosperous of the islands, was much more difficult to handle. The planters prepared a memorial against federation and the loss of their Lieutenant-Governor and a deputation saw Lord Granville. But Granville stood by Pine, telling them 'that I was strongly in favour of Confederation, that I had neither from them nor from the memorial of the planters any strong argument against, that there was obviously misrepresentation of the plan'.[3] He also removed any impression of Imperial lukewarmness by a dispatch commending the scheme and soothing the island's fears.[4] Pine rejected the idea of dissolving the Assembly, preferring to 'win over the nominees by argument, courtesy and just concessions' and carried his resolutions on 18 August by 10 to 8.[5] Five of the eight opponents lost their seats in an election at the end of the year. On urgent representations from Lieutenant-Governor Freeling, Pine then went to Dominica. On 7 September he addressed the Assembly and it passed the resolutions next day. Though notice had been given on 18 August, five of the seven elected members protested against this hasty consideration of 'a measure so vitally affecting the population'.[6] The Virgin Islands and Montserrat, being Crown Colonies, presented no difficulty. Nevis was more troublesome. Walter Maynard, senior nominated member and a supporter of the

[1] Resolutions of Antigua Legislative Council in Pine to Granville (11 July 1870) (No. 116), P.P., 1871, xlviii [C. 353], 27–8.
[2] Treasury to Colonial Office (31 Mar. and 18 May 1870), ibid., pp. 33, 35. Pine announced this to the Antigua Legislative Council on 23 June.
[3] Minute of Granville (1 May) on Pine to Granville (22 Mar. 1870) (Confidential), CO239/123. For the Memorial see [C. 353], 37.
[4] Granville to Pine (16 May 1870) (No. 248), P.P., 1871, xlviii [C. 353], 38–9.
[5] Pine to Kimberley (23 Aug. 1870) (No. 114), ibid., pp. 40–1. Pine thought an adjournment over the week-end might have produced a 12 to 6 majority.
[6] Pine to Kimberley (10 Sept. 1870) (No. 59), ibid., p. 60. For the protest see ibid., p. 63.

plan, resigned on the ground of the hostility of his family and the excitement among the people. 'A party, supported by brute force,' Pine explains, 'was attempting to coerce and intimidate the men representing the greater part of the wealth and nearly all the intelligence of the island.' Pine was not deterred. He landed a party of marines from H.M.S. *Danae*, ostensibly as a guard of honour, and passed his federation resolution on 1 December.[1] He had won his campaign within the year and the Colonial Office may not have been right in thinking that with more gradual methods 'the result would have been the same and the victory . . . won in better style'.[2] Pine knew his West Indies and it was harder to believe in the ultimate victory of pure reason in a West Indian island than in Downing Street. Early in the New Year he came home on leave, and a Bill, based on the island resolutions and forming the Leeward Islands into one colony of six presidencies, passed through Parliament with only a brief debate in the House of Lords.[3] The Act followed the scheme of distribution of members and expenses among the islands which their legislatures had already approved. It added three more heads of general legislation, copyrights and patents, constitution and procedure of the General Legislative Council, and 'such other subjects in respect of each presidency as the Island Legislature thereof may declare to be within the competency of the General Legislature'. Presidency laws were to be void so far as repugnant to any general law. The Legislative Council might alter the Act by reserved Bill. Power was taken to admit other islands to the federation by Order in Council, on address from the legislative body.[4]

Two speakers in the House of Lords, notably Carnarvon, looked to this measure as 'the germ of a still larger federation'; but there was the difficulty that three of the Windward group, Grenada, Tobago, and Barbados, still jealously retained the old representative system, which left little or no initiative to the Crown. Rawson found Grenada 'over-officered . . . the legislation . . . slow and inefficient; the Assembly incompetent and the island retro-

---

[1] Pine to Kimberley (12 Dec. 1870) (No. 153), CO184/19. Extracts only were printed in Command Papers 353.

[2] Minute of Herbert (4 Nov. 1870) on the Protest of the Dominica Elected Members, CO71/141.

[3] *Hansard*, 3rd Ser. ccvi. 1022–7.

[4] The 'Act for the Federation and General Government of the Leeward Islands' was 34 & 35 Vict., c. 107.

grading', and was not long in coming to the conclusion that 'the smaller Islands of this Government might well be governed without a local legislature';[1] but Granville cautioned him 'not to rely, as you appear to do, upon Imperial legislation for the constitution of a central Windward Islands Legislature at Barbados, except in conformity with the wishes of the people'.[2] Rawson later confirmed his first impression that the island legislatures for various reasons —local pride, fear that their local affairs would not receive enough attention, inability of the best qualified men to spare time for a General Legislature—were not prepared to assent to a federation. It was known that the Duke of Buckingham favoured it; but this would cause any move towards a single chamber to be regarded as the thin end of the wedge. Rawson therefore advised that the Government should introduce and promote administrative reforms, consolidation of officers, and reduction of expenditure: if these were resisted by the legislatures, it might be possible to 'enlist the public opinion in support of the Government'.[3] Granville accepted this argument (as did Rogers) and approved the policy.[4]

There was a special difficulty in the Windward Islands which did not exist in the Leewards. Barbados would be entitled to nearly half as many councillors again as all the others on the score of population, and on the score of production, trade, and wealth to even more.[5] Its planter aristocracy was still in firm control of the Government, in spite of an increasing and intelligent middle class of small landowners, businessmen, clerks, tradesmen, and mechanics, mainly coloured; and a network of Joint or House of Assembly Committees had usurped most of the executive power. Rawson thought the Assembly 'composed, with few exceptions, of incompetent, narrow-minded men'; but in Rogers's opinion the Barbadians had on the whole managed their affairs well, and according to Governor Hincks their success in sugar production was due to skilful and economical management and not to

---

[1] Rawson to Granville (9 Aug. 1869) (Confidential), CO28/208.

[2] Granville to Rawson (12 Sept. 1869) (Confidential), CO29/41. The dispatch was based on a Minute of Taylor of 7 Sept.

[3] Rawson to Granville (25 Jan. 1870) (Confidential), CO28/211. Further comments in Rawson to Kimberley (8 Sept. 1871), P.P., 1876, xiii [C. 1539].

[4] Minute of Rogers (26 Feb.) on Rawson to Granville (25 Jan. 1870), CO28/211. Granville to Rawson (26 Mar. 1870) (No. 143), CO29/41.

[5] The census of 1871 gave the population of Barbados as 161,594; St. Lucia 31,610; St. Vincent 35,688; Grenada 37,684; Tobago 17,054.

specially low wages, which were in any case supplemented by
encouragement to the Negroes to grow cane on their allotments.[1]
It was natural that these men should not wish to surrender their
autonomy and Rawson's predecessor, Sir James Walker (who
had tried in vain in 1863 to introduce Crown initiative in
money votes) had not made matters easier by falling out with
the Assembly.

Lord Kimberley, however, was less patient than Lord Granville
with Rawson's methods, and in the summer of 1872 Gore, the
Colonial Secretary of Barbados, and Sir Graham Briggs, a leading
planter, told Wodehouse, Kimberley's Private Secretary, that 'in
their opinion an attempt might now be made, with a very good
prospect of success, to substitute a single Legislative Council for
the present Legislative Council and the House of Assembly of
Barbadoes, but the initiative of Governor Rawson is wanting'.[2]
Kimberley thereupon sent Rawson a dispatch impressing upon
him the importance he attached to this change, which might be
practicable in Grenada and Tobago also.[3] After some kite-flying
in the Barbados press Rawson admitted the change might be
possible in these two islands, pointing out, however, that the
stumbling block was 'the creation of a numerical preponderance
in favour of the Government' and the power this would give it
to force federation on them.[4] 'Mr. Rawson is great at finding
reasons how not to do it', Kimberley noted resignedly, 'and it is
only fair to add that the difficulties he would have to encounter
are serious. . . . We shall have to wait until there is a new Governor.'[5] But in a memorandum sent to H. T. Holland early in 1873
Rawson returned to the subject, asking whether Barbadian preponderance might not be countered by throwing the Windward
and Leeward Islands into a single group. Even this must be the
work of time: 'the current of events in the Leeward Islands has

[1] Rawson to Granville (9 Aug. 1869) (Confidential) with Minute of Rogers
(11 Sept.), CO28/208. Hincks to Lytton (1 Sept. 1858) (No. 48), P.P., 1859, Sess.,
2, xxi [2567], 74–6. W. G. Sewell, *The Ordeal of Free Labour in the British West
Indies* (New York, 1861) has interesting comments.
[2] Minute of Wodehouse (18 Aug. 1872), CO28/215. E. R. Wodehouse was the
son of Sir Philip and a third cousin, once removed, of Lord Kimberley. He was
afterwards Liberal (Unionist) M.P. for Bath.
[3] Kimberley to Rawson (30 Aug. 1872) (No. 159), P.P., 1876, liii [C. 1539], 3.
[4] Rawson to Kimberley (26 Sept. 1872) (Confidential), ibid., p. 4.
[5] Minute of Kimberley (24 Oct.) on Rawson to Kimberley (26 Sept. 1872)
(Confidential), CO28/217.

not tended to weaken the objections felt here to the change.'[1] At last, Kimberley felt, Rawson was 'ready to work heartily in the direction of Federation'. He sent a dispatch arguing that the Leeward Islands federation had already justified itself by its legislation and declaring that 'Her Majesty's Government have not contemplated, unless possibly as a temporary measure, that Barbados and the other Windward Islands should form a federation separate from that of the Leeward Islands.'[2] But Rawson still asked for, and was given, 'a reasonable latitude in determining when and how to commence action'.[3] Only one step forward was taken in his time. A general election in Tobago in 1873 on an extended franchise produced a majority in favour of a single chamber, which was known to be desired by the Imperial authorities. The Act 'to amend and simplify the Legislature of the Island of Tobago', passed in 1874, created a mixed chamber of six nominees (three of whom might be officials) and eight elected members. An Executive Committee of two was retained. The new chamber was soon giving general satisfaction.[4]

The sequel takes us beyond the period covered in this book, but must be briefly treated. When Rawson retired in 1875 the Disraeli Government chose as his successor a brilliant and charming but impulsive, eccentric, disputatious Irishman, John Pope-Hennessy, who like him had previously been Governor of the Bahamas.[5] He had no instructions to force on federation. 'It would not be convenient at the present time to *initiate here* any steps for another Confederation', wrote Herbert, 'as our hands are full enough with the South African matter.'[6] But if he could persuade the Barbadian leaders to discuss it, that was another question. Hennessy began quietly by formulating six points of practical reform, extending the degree of co-operation already existing with the

[1] Memo. of Rawson on Federation in the Windward Islands (28 Feb. 1873), CO28/218.

[2] Minute of Kimberley (23 Mar.) on Rawson Memo. ibid. Kimberley to Rawson (1 May 1873) (No. 19), P.P., 1876, liii [C. 1539], 7–8.

[3] Rawson to Kimberley (7 June 1873) (Confidential) and Kimberley to Rawson (7 July 1873) (draft), CO28/218.

[4] Usher to Freeling (n.d.) in Freeling to Carnarvon (16 Aug. 1875), P.P., 1875, li [C. 1336], 87.

[5] On Pope-Hennessy see his grandson James Pope-Hennessy's entertaining book *Verandah* (London, 1964). On the whole episode the fullest and best treatment is B. Hamilton's *Barbados and the Confederation Question, 1871–1885* (London, 1956).

[6] Herbert to Carnarvon (n.d.–1875?); quoted by James Pope-Hennessy, op. cit., p. 165.

Windward Islands in matters of justice, police, prisons, and the auditing of accounts. He believed he had won over a small but influential group of Barbadians when he set out on a visit to the other islands of his government, partly at least as 'a canvassing tour for the cause of Federation'.[1] But the Barbadians, egged on by the press, were now beginning to be suspicious, though the House at first seemed disposed to consider some at least of the Six Points. They were confirmed in their suspicions when Hennessy drew attention to a 'grave scandal' in one of the prisons and ordered the release on ticket of leave of a number of good-conduct prisoners. Then the ill-timed arrival of letters patent (suggested by Rawson) constituting a separate Executive Council antagonized Councillors, some of them hitherto supporters of the Governor, who had thus been deprived of their executive functions.[2] Feeling that events were slipping out of his control, Hennessy decided to make a bid for popular support. In a long speech to the Assembly on 3 March he not only outlined his policy on the Six Points and admitted Confederation to be his ultimate aim but made some disparaging remarks on the social condition of the island and in conclusion expressed his confidence that 'no intelligent person who loves Barbados will take the serious responsibility of standing between his poor countrymen and the wise policy of the British Government'.[3] It was magnificent in its way; but it was not good politics. The Negroes in the public gallery cheered; and Hennessy reported to Carnarvon that 'Confederation is opposed by one class in Barbados and those immediately surrounding that class, but the masses of the population are decidedly in favour of it.'[4] The masses had responded to Hennessy's sympathy and the hopes he held out of emigration to the other islands; but the planters were enraged and they held the power. The more extreme of them formed a Barbados Defence Association, circulated damaging rumours in the island, and stirred up their friends at home. The rising excitement among the Negroes culminated at Easter in a week of rioting. Hennessy coolly and promptly suppressed the riots and declined to proclaim martial law; but Confederation was dead. Rawson's hesitations had been justified after all.

[1] Pope-Hennessy to Carnarvon (28 December 1875) (No. 65), CO321/6. The quotation is from James Pope-Hennessy, op. cit., p. 167.
[2] On this see Hamilton, op. cit., pp. 52–4.
[3] P.P., 1876, liii [C. 1539], 131.
[4] Pope-Hennessy to Carnarvon (11 Mar. 1876), ibid., p. 116.

The Colonial Office was not unduly alarmed by the pressure of the Barbados Defence Association for Hennessy's immediate recall, and a deputation from the West India Committee to Lord Carnarvon proved to be ill-informed about the facts. But some account had to be taken of the point made by the former Governor Sir James Walker, even though he was connected by marriage with the Barbadian planting interest: 'The system of Colonial Government in the West Indies has changed very much when intead of discussions, sometimes warm, sometimes not very constitutional, but never disloyal, there has come a necessity for intimidation to carry out the behests of the Crown.'[1] This was before news of the riots had reached England. Though the Barbados Defence Association's telegrams were much too highly coloured, Carnarvon had reason to be worried. He instructed Hennessy to issue a proclamation declaring 'that it would be a great mistake to suppose that Confederation could either injure or benefit in any considerable degree the social condition of any class'.[2] He also approved of Hennessy's idea of a Special Commission to try the rioters and appointed Mr. Justice Lushington Phillips of Natal. In a speech in the House of Lords on 1 August he continued to resist the demand for Hennessy's recall. But towards the end of the year he was moved to Hong Kong.

The Office had to be content with the success of its policy of reversion to Crown Colony government in the remaining Windward Islands. In 1875 St. Vincent, Tobago, and Grenada agreed to empower Her Majesty 'to create and constitute a legislature . . . in such form and with such powers as Her Majesty in Council may determine'. Parliament in 1876 passed an empowering statute accordingly and in 1876–7 all three became, like St. Lucia, Crown Colonies.[3] Even Barbados, on the motion of an able coloured barrister, Conrad Reeves, adopted an Executive Committee system which, like Barkly's in Jamaica, formed 'a bridge between Executive and Legislature' and endured until 1946.[4] But, though Barbados was separated from the Windward Islands in

---

[1] Walker to Carnarvon (22 April 1876), P.P., 1876, liii [C. 1539], 178. Walker had recently visited Barbados, see Hamilton, op. cit., pp. 69, 128.
[2] Carnarvon to Hennessy (1 May 1876), P.P., 1876, liii [C. 1539], 226–8. The Proclamation was issued on 25 May.
[3] 39 & 40 Vict., c. 47. The St. Vincent and Tobago Acts are in the schedule to the Act, an Address from the Grenada Assembly (9 Feb. 1876) in the preamble.
[4] On this see Hamilton, op. cit., pp. 105–11, 144–5.

1884, an attempt to federate the four Crown Colonies was as unsuccessful in winning popular support as the wider scheme. The fact is that these small islands cherish their individuality. To do the Colonial Office justice, it had not favoured federation in these West Indian islands because of any theoretical preference for federal institutions but to simplify the working of government and to improve the laws and their administration—and incidentally to reduce Imperial expenditure. But even in the Leewards hopes of economy were disappointed and the federation worked rather uneasily. The policy of constitutional reform, on the other hand, now appears as a necessary stage of the transition from a narrowly based to a democratic form of government.

# XV

## ASIAN IMMIGRATION WITH SPECIAL REFERENCE TO BRITISH GUIANA

THE destiny of the West Indies was not to be worked out by white, coloured, and Negro alone. The disinclination of the Negroes to field labour after emancipation had led the sugar colonies, Mauritius first and then some of the West India colonies, to seek to replace them with immigrants from India. The first planter to introduce them into the West Indies was John Gladstone, father of the statesman, who landed two ship-loads of 'hill coolies' in British Guiana in 1838. An outcry from Exeter Hall led to the prohibition of emigration from India, pending full investigation, in 1839; but, after a report favouring immigration from a Parliamentary Committee on the West Indies, the Government of India in 1844 re-opened emigration to British Guiana, Trinidad, and Jamaica (as it had already done to Mauritius) under stricter regulation. Immigrants began to arrive in those colonies in 1845 and some thousands had arrived when the immigration was again brought to a stop by the commercial crisis of 1847-8. A guaranteed loan of £500,000 for immigration was, however, one of the relief measures proposed by the Russell Ministry in 1848; and after a period of sulking, British Guiana and Trinidad, though not Jamaica, agreed to avail themselves of it. In the course of 1851 Indian immigration got under way again.

Thomas Caird, a covenanted servant of the East India Company, as Resident Agent at Calcutta, was responsible for the dispatch of the numbers of immigrants ordered by the colonies; and J. T. White, a British Guiana planter, was appointed by the Court of Policy in 1850 to act in co-operation with Caird, and, by arrangement with Lord Harris and the Trinidad Legislative Council, acted for Trinidad as well. Caird also visited the West Indies in 1853. Conditions on the ships were regulated by the

United Kingdom Passenger Acts. Agents-General for Immigration in the colonies were responsible for the distribution of the immigrants among employers and (with the magistrates) for supervision on the estates. The whole system of legislation and administration was supervised by the Colonial Land and Emigration Board, which was in effect a sub-department of the Colonial Office.[1] Three-year contracts were now permitted and immigrants were entitled to free return passages after five years' 'industrial residence'. T. W. C. Murdoch, Chairman of the Colonial Land and Emigration Commissioners, justified the system a few years later, in sentences worth quoting, in an office memorandum printed for Parliament.

The advantage to the coolie . . . admits of no doubt. In his own country his wages do not exceed 2d or 3d a day. He is not always able to obtain that. . . . In the West Indies he receives wages averaging 1s. to 2s. a day, in addition to which he is allowed a house and garden, and is provided with medical attendance. Before the indenture system was established the coolies abandoned their work and wandered about the country and in many instances . . . perished miserably from disease and want. . . . If the planters cannot obtain labour which will enable them to continue sugar cultivation, they will . . . abandon their estates. The land will fall out of cultivation or be appropriated by the creole population. The whites will disappear, and with them civilization, morality and religion; the creole would be the greatest sufferer by such a result.[2]

The time was now come when British Guiana and Trinidad would themselves have to finance this immigration, the costs of which had so far been defrayed from the guaranteed loan of 1848. The British Guiana Court of Policy proposed to introduce 4,000 immigrants a year—2,500 from India and 1,500 from China. Employers were to pay one-third of the cost of introducing them or commuting their return passages. An export tax on produce was also to be allocated to immigration. But the ordinance passed by the Court (No. 3 of 1853) proposed to legalize five-year contracts and impose a further indenture for the full period on all immigrants who had accepted a bonus in commutation of their

[1] On all this see my *British Colonial Policy in the Age of Peel and Russell*, chs. vii and xi; I. M. Cumpston, *Indians Overseas in British Territories, 1834–1854* (London, 1953); and F. H. Hitchins, *The Colonial Land and Emigration Commission* (Philadelphia, 1931).

[2] Memo. on Immigration into the West Indies (18 Feb. 1859), P.P., 1859, Sess. 2, xx (H.C. 31), 500–2.

return passages and engaged to remain in the colony for a further term. It also required annual payments as a condition of a return passage. The Duke of Newcastle disallowed the ordinance and the arguments of four elective members of the Court against the disallowance received short shrift from the Land and Emigration Commissioners.[1] But the Government of India agreed that immigrants should not be entitled to a return passage until after ten years and Newcastle offered some further concessions, which were embodied in Ordinance 7 of 1854. Indians were to be indentured for three years in the first instance, after which they might renew the indenture for a further two years or commute for a payment of £5. After ten years they might have a back passage free if under contract for the whole period or for $35 (£7) if they had been released from indenture.[2] The Colonial Office still objected to certain provisions of the new ordinance, especially one permitting private individuals to import immigrants for their own estates; but an amended ordinance was speedily passed and received the royal assent.[3] Trinidad asked for a further immigration loan, but neither Pakington nor Newcastle would agree. Newcastle softened the blow by offering the colony £25,000 of the £47,000 still remaining from the original £500,000.[4] Trinidad also wanted a different system of indentures, which were to be for a year, renewable but with the option of commutation at the rate of 5s. a month, payable in advance. Indians were to be entitled to a return passage after ten years' industrial residence on payment of $35.[5] Ordinance No. 24 of 1854 provided for an initial three years' indenture but with renewals for one year only.

It looked for a time as if concessions to the planters had gone too far. Caird could not secure the 3,500 labourers ordered for the

[1] Barkly to Newcastle (11 Feb. 1853) (No. 21), P.P., 1852-3, lxviii (H.C. 986), 27 ff. Wood and Rogers to Merivale (30 Sept. 1853), CO318/203.
[2] Newcastle to Walker (16 Jan. 1854) (No. 175), P.P., 1859, xvi [2452], 1-4. Taylor's comment on the concessions is interesting: 'It will be generally found that the steady pressure of one invariable pecuniary interest through a series of years will overcome the resistance of Governmental Bodies in cases where they have nothing else to support them but a feeling in favour of dumb interests', Minute (30 Oct. 1853), CO318/203.
[3] Sir G. Grey to Wodehouse (13 Sept. 1854) (No. 33), P.P., 1859, xvi [2452], 54-6. Assent to the amended Ordinance was conveyed on 15 Nov.
[4] Newcastle to Harris (1 Apr. 1853) (Private), Newcastle Papers, NeC9553.
[5] Wood and Rogers to Merivale (2 June 1854), P.P., 1859, xvi [2452], 273-4. For the Trinidad Ordinance see ibid., pp. 458-65.

West Indies in the season 1853-4: 'a large number', he explained, 'most positively refused to go to the West Indies for ten years, but they gave me to understand that they were willing to engage for five.'[1] Yet in March 1855 the British Guiana Combined Court expressed the opinion that 'the cost of the passage hither of Indian Immigrants or its equivalent $50 should subject to certain conditions be borne by the planters to whom they may be indentured for the first five years of their industrial residences'.[2] This implied five-year indentures. The Chinese were already coming on five-year contracts. In the circumstances Lord John Russell felt he must accept the principle, though he pointed out that it cost more than $50 to introduce immigrants and that, West Indian emigration being 'anything but popular', the Agents in India were likely to find it difficult to fulfil the requirements of British Guiana and Trinidad.[3] A further difficulty was the Duke of Newcastle's insistence, confirmed by his successor Sir George Grey, that 'Coolie immigration should be stopped unless means could be found of rectifying the disproportion which exists between the numbers of male and female immigrants.'[4] Governor Wodehouse argued temperately against undue rigour. A bonus on female immigrants would be cheerfully paid; but 'little good will be derived from too strict inquiries as to their being married or single or as to their morals'. Russell instructed West Indian Governors nevertheless to observe the proportion of one female to three males suggested by the Emigration Commissioners.[5]

White had been instructed by the British Guiana Government to go to China in the off-season for Calcutta emigration and in October 1852 he was notified of his appointment as Emigration Agent at the port of Victoria (Hong Kong) and such other ports on or near the coast of China as might be named by the Governor of Hong Kong. Her Majesty's Government had sanctioned the dispatch of three shiploads of Chinese immigrants on the bounty system to Trinidad and private shipowners had sent ships to

[1] Caird to Walcott (18 Apr.) in Sir G. Grey to Wodehouse (26 June 1854) (No. 8), P.P., 1849, xvi [2452]; pp. 49 ff.

[2] Combined Court (19 Mar.) in Wodehouse to Herbert (24 Mar. 1855) (No. 36), ibid., p. 175. The money was to be used to repay a loan of £150,000.

[3] Russell to Wodehouse (29 June 1855) (No. 29), ibid., pp. 74-5. The phrase 'anything but popular' was Caird's.

[4] Newcastle to Wodehouse (12 June 1854), ibid., p. 44.

[5] Wodehouse to Herbert (24 Mar. 1855), loc. cit. Russell to West Indian Governors (23 June 1855) (Circular), ibid., pp. 67-9.

transport 1,700 to British Guiana under a recent ordinance.[1] As a matter of fact nine ships had reached Amoy by the beginning of August and John Bowring, Consul at Canton, complained with some justice of this 'sudden irruption of a fleet of ships' before he had received any instructions from the Foreign Office.[2] There was serious trouble at Amoy later in the year. Bowring pointed out that 'while the premium paid on coolies continues at anything like the present rate, no Consular authority, no interference of any emigration agent, will make the trade anything but one of great irregularity and abuses'.[3] It happened that 164 of the 811 sent on the first three British Guiana ships died, but Barkly reported that the planters were pleased with the Chinese and believed the weaknesses in the system were remediable. More suitable ships should be chosen; indiscriminate immigration on bounty should cease, and selection be left to White.[4] Trinidad's experience with its ships was more fortunate and Lord Harris reported in similar terms of the quality of the immigrants and the defects of the bounty system.[5] The presence in England of Barkly, Bowring, White, and Dr. Winchester, Assistant Consul at Amoy, enabled conferences to be held in 1853 with the Emigration Commissioners and the decision was reached that all emigration to the British West Indies should be conducted by a responsible agent and should as far as possible start from Hong Kong.[6] But White found shipping very hard to get in competition with sailings for California, for which upwards of 40,000 Chinese had left, Cuba, Peru, and now Australia also, and, to the Commissioners' regret and the annoyance of the Foreign Office, authorized one or two ships to be dispatched from Namoa (Nan-ao) which was not a treaty port.[7] He admitted that West

[1] Walcott to White (23 Oct.) in Murdoch and Rogers to Merivale (28 Oct. 1852), P.P., 1852–3, lxvii (H.C. 936), 222–3.

[2] Bowring to Malmesbury (3 Aug. 1852), P.P., 1852–3, lxviii [1686], 4. The shipper, Tait, was Spanish, Dutch, and Portuguese Consul at Amoy.

[3] Bowring to Malmesbury (5 Jan. 1853), ibid., pp. 83–6.

[4] Barkly to Pakington (24 Jan. 1853) (No. 8, (P.P., 1852–3, lxviii (H.C. 986), 9–10.

[5] Harris to Newcastle (10 Mar. 1853, No. 26, and 22 Mar. 1853, No. 30), ibid., pp. 137–40.

[6] Merivale to Addington (15 Sept. 1853), P.P., 1854–5, xxxix (O. 7), 1. In 1855, the Chinese Passengers Act (17 & 18 Vict., c. 104) was passed, applying to all Chinese ships clearing from Hong Kong and all British ships from any Chinese port carrying more than 20 passengers.

[7] Murdoch and Rogers to Merivale (25 Feb. 1854) with Enclosures from White of 10 and 26 Dec. 1853, ibid., pp. 10 ff.

Indian emigration was 'viewed with distrust by respectable Chinese' and permitted only because the local authorities derived pecuniary benefit from it. The wages, even with clothes and food, were 'not . . . sufficient inducement for any man of respectable character'. The absence of women was a deterrent to permanent settlement and in any case 'families never emigrate from China'. The only means of obtaining women would be a bounty to married emigrants equal to the price paid by a Chinese labourer for his wife.[1] This suggestion, though defended by the Emigration Commissioners against Bowring's criticisms, did not meet with the approval of the Foreign Office; and Labouchere told Bowring, now Governor of Hong Kong, in 1856 that no emigration to the British colonies at the public expense was contemplated 'unless such means as would meet the approval of Her Majesty's Government can be devised for securing a due proportion of females'.[2] There had in fact been no such emigration from China since 1854.

Some of the smaller West Indian islands wished to share in the benefits of Indian immigration and the Imperial Government was willing to allow them small portions of its guaranteed loan. St. Lucia in 1854 and Grenada in 1855 passed laws on the subject, both taking the British Guiana ordinance as their model. In 1855 the Government of India opened its doors to both colonies. But the Indian authorities did not think St. Lucia's appointment of an Agent at £50 per annum would afford sufficient protection to Indian immigrants. They would be the first to come to St. Lucia: 'some provision ought to be made for the appointment of a protector acquainted with their languages and habits and who could devote the whole of his time in superintending over their interests.'[3] There would, as the Emigration Commissioners pointed out, be only a few hundred immigrants, and such an appointment would absorb a large part of the available funds.[4] Governor Hincks

---

[1] J. T. White, 'Remarks on Emigration from China and on the General Management of Chinese Emigrants in the British West Indies' (8 Feb.) in New-castle to Wodehouse (12 June 1854) (No. 38), P.P., 1859, xvi [2452], 35–40. White left China in 1854.

[2] Labouchere to Bowring (25 Sept. 1856) (No. 111), P.P., 1857–8, xliii (H.C. 481), 41.

[3] Minute of Peacock (2 Jan. 1856) in Labouchere to Hincks (31 May 1856) (No. 18), P.P., 1859, xvi [2452], 377.

[4] Murdoch and Rogers to Merivale (14 May 1856), ibid., pp. 378–9.

of Barbados also criticized the Grenada and St. Lucia proposals, alleging that their object was to reduce wages.[1] Both colonies, however, persevered; the Government of India withdrew its objections and the qualification for a return passage was reduced to eight years' industrial residence to compensate for the lower wages as compared with the larger colonies. Grenada took nearly 1,000 Indian immigrants in 1857-9 and St. Lucia 555 in 1859 and 660 in 1860.[2] St. Vincent, which in 1857 also passed Acts making provision for immigration, received 700 Indians in 1860 and 1861.[3]

Creole and Indian, said Governor Wodehouse of British Guiana, 'do not associate, but they do not quarrel'.[4] But in February 1856 serious riots broke out in British Guiana against the Portuguese, thousands of whom had arrived over the years from Madeira. A religious fanatic, J. S. Orr, returning to the colony of his birth, had whipped up the passions of the Negro and coloured population; but, in the words of Governor Wodehouse, once the riots had begun, 'the pope, the bishops, the nuns were clean forgotten. Nothing remained in the minds of the actors but the long subsisting hatred and jealousy of the Portuguese immigrants.' There was no loss of life, but many Portuguese shops, both in Georgetown and in the country, were broken into and gutted before the disturbances were suppressed by police, special constables, and troops.[5] Over a hundred of the rioters were sentenced to terms of imprisonment, a few being flogged into the bargain, but a number of others were given conditional pardons—an unusual measure but one, the Secretary of State thought, 'well adapted to the occasion'.[6] Wodehouse turned down Taylor's suggestion of a levy on disturbed districts for compension for property owners, but he did pass an ordinance for the registration of all property,

[1] Hincks to Labouchere (9 Nov. 1857) (No. 57), P.P., 1859, Sess. 2 (H.C. 31-I), 4. Answered by Murdoch and Rogers to Merivale (15 Mar. 1858), ibid., pp. 63-4.
[2] The figures are taken from Annual Returns of Immigrants and Liberated Africans in the Parliamentary Papers.
[3] Ibid. For the Acts see Hincks to Labouchere (9 Nov. 1857) (No. 86), P.P., 1859, Sess. 2 (H.C. 31-I), 116-17, 305-18.
[4] Wodehouse to Merivale (28 Jan.) in Stanley to Hincks (16 Apr. 1858), ibid., p. 58.
[5] Wodehouse to Labouchere (24 Feb. 1856, No. 16, and 10 Mar. 1856, No. 25), P.P., 1856, xliv (H.C. 432), 3-9, 34-8.
[6] Labouchere to Wodehouse (1 and 16 Apr. 1856, Nos. 56 and 65), ibid., pp. 87-9.

which would make such a levy possible in future.[1] The Registration Ordinance and a fee for registration levied by the Tax
Ordinance earned Wodehouse some unpopularity among the
Negroes and a protest from the Anti-Slavery Society, but the
storm soon blew over.

The protests of Governor Hincks against the whole system of
subsidized immigration also had little effect. His assertion that 'it
is . . . looked upon as a system of mitigated slavery in foreign
countries, but especially in the United States' was accepted by
Merivale, but not by other Colonial Office officials, and even
Merivale agreed with Cox and Taylor that he mistook such exceptions as Barbados and Antigua for the rule. No doubt immigration
into the other colonies diminished the competitive advantage of
Barbados, but that was not a reason for stopping it.[2] Immigration
appeared to be proceeding smoothly; a dispatch of Lord Stanley
conceding to the several colonies the right to employ their
own Emigration Agents in India gave satisfaction;[3] and Charles
Buxton, in moving in 1859 for a Committee to inquire into the
state of the West Indies and the best means of promoting immigration into them, expressly dissociated himself from the Anti-
Slavery Society's criticisms. 'So far from the competition of the
immigrants being any bane to the negroes,' he declared, 'it would
be a healthy spur to them.'[4] Underhill also, visiting Trinidad in
1859, found the system 'approved by every class of persons in
the island'. He spoke, often on the roadside, with people from
Eastern Bengal, Bihar, the North-West Provinces, and Oude,
and found the people better housed than in India, well fed, happy,
and contented.[5]

By this time West Indian hopes of China as a source were reviving. Emigration was condoned by the provincial authorities, but
the unsophisticated, underfed population of south-western China
were an easy prey for the crimps and coolie-brokers and there was

---

[1] Wodehouse to Labouchere (23 June 1856) (No. 83), P.P., 1857, Sess. 2, xxviii
(H.C. 305). For the protest of the Anti-Slavery Society, see ibid., pp. 17–18.
[2] See especially Hincks to Labouchere (22 Aug. 1857) (No. 42), P.P., 1859
Sess. 2, xxi (H.C. 31–I), 31–6. Also Minutes on this dispatch in CO28/187.
[3] Wodehouse to Lytton (24 July 1858) (No. 94), P.P., 1859, Sess. 2, xx (H.C.
31), 62–3. Stanley's dispatch was of 4 June 1858.
[4] House of Commons, 3 Mar. 1859: Hansard, 3rd Ser. clii. 1219–24. Buxton,
after a short debate, withdrew his motion, saying he would study the papers about
to be presented, which were in fact very voluminous. On Buxton's motion see also
Letters of Lord Blachford, pp. 213–14.          [5] Underhill, The West Indies, p. 82.

still an Imperial law against it. When Lord Elgin was sent out in 1857 as High Commissioner to put an end to the pinpricks of the Governor of Kwangtung by a direct appeal to the Emperor at Peking, he was instructed if possible to secure formal sanction for the emigration of Chinese men and women. The Treaty of Tientsin (26 June 1858) did not cover the question, but the capture of Canton by British and French troops at the end of the previous year gave them command of the principal source of supply. J. G. Austin, the British Guiana Agent-General for Immigration, had been nominated by the Court of Policy to prepare a scheme of legalized emigration; and in the meantime Lord Stanley was persuaded to agree to a year's experiment in immigration by private parties under an ordinance drafted by the Emigration Commissioners themselves.[1] Two ships were dispatched, but their methods of recruitment gave rise to severe criticism and in fact proved the necessity for Government control. Anger was rising in Canton against the prevailing abuses in the coolie trade and the Governor of Kwangtung was persuaded to issue on 9 April 1859 a proclamation forbidding kidnapping on pain of death, but allowing voluntary emigration. Meanwhile Austin, as Emigration Agent in China, had secured Colonial Office sanction for his scheme. With the assent of the Chinese authorities, he opened in November an Emigration House in Canton for the reception of emigrants for the British West Indian colonies. They were to be encouraged to take their wives and families with them. By 7 March 1860, in spite of the intrigues of crimps recruiting for Cuba, some 1,850 emigrants (1,489 men and 259 women) had been dispatched to British Guiana;[2] and by the end of 1862, over 8,500 had arrived, though Trinidad only received 647. But, according to Governor Hincks, the immigration of the 1861-2 season was 'most disastrous'. He admitted that the new season's Chinese were 'very superior to the last', but the demand was falling off.[3] Austin was not reappointed and in his speech opening the Combined Court in April 1863 Hincks hinted that he would

---

[1] Stanley to Wodehouse (1 Apr. 1858) (No. 15), P.P., 1857-8, xli (H.C. 525), 147-8. The Ordinance was No. 17 of 1858; Trinidad passed a similar Ordinance (No. 11), though Governor Keate would have preferred Government emigration.

[2] Parkes (Commissioner at Canton) to Bruce (10, 15, 26 Nov. 1959), P.P., 1860, lxix [2714], 11-12, 40, 44. The figures are on p. 136.

[3] Hincks to Newcastle (3 Feb. 1862, No. 8, and 8 Mar. 1862, No. 31), CO111/334. Hincks became Governor of British Guiana early in 1862.

prefer to abandon Chinese immigration as too expensive.[1] There was an upward swing in 1865—1,691 immigrants from China arrived in British Guiana and 593 in Trinidad—and on 5 March 1866 British and French representatives at last negotiated an Emigration Convention with the Government of China. But the Chinese insisted on a free return passage after five years or its equivalent in money. This, the West India Committee, the Emigration Commissioners, and the Governors agreed, would make Chinese far too expensive in comparison with Indians and was unfair to Chinese who had come without it.[2] As the Chinese Government refused to budge, the emigration came to a standstill. It had never realized the high hopes of its initiators.

The British West Indies were now competing not only with Mauritius but with the French colonies for immigrants from India. *Engagés* were being shipped from West Africa to the French West Indies and others were recruited, under treaties with Zanzibar and later with Portugal, in East Africa for Reunion, Mayotta in the Comoros, and Nossi Bé off Madagascar. This seemed to the Colonial Office very like a slave trade. To wean the French from it, Palmerston and Clarendon offered to let them recruit in India on equal terms with the British. Sir Frederic Rogers went to Paris and, after many interruptions, the negotiations ended in a draft Convention in June 1860. The Government of India passed the necessary legislation and on 1 July 1861 the Convention was duly signed.[3] One result was to extend the term of the first indenture in British colonies to five years, another to lower the proportion of women required to 25 per cent of the men, though it was to increase after three years. In 1864 the Government of India tightened up its regulations. The Presidency Governments were to appoint Protectors and Medical Inspectors. Depots were to be established, licensed, and visited weekly. Recruiters were to have

[1] Speech of H.E. the Governor (14 Apr.) in Hincks to Newcastle (29 June 1863) (No. 115), P.P., 1864, x [3304], 41.

[2] Murdoch to Rogers (7 Nov. 1866), CO318/247. On the Convention see Persia C. Campbell, *Chinese Coolie Emigration to Countries Within the British Empire* (London, 1923), pp. 140–50; on the general diplomatic background W. C. Costin, *Great Britain and China, 1833–1860* (Oxford, 1937) and J. L. Morison, *The Eighth Earl of Elgin* (London, 1928).

[3] *Letters of Lord Blachford*, ch. vi, *passim*, and p. 231; W. L. Mathieson, *Great Britain and the Slave Trade* (London, 1929), pp. 166–9; Sir R. Coupland, *East Africa and its Invaders* (Oxford, 1938), pp. 429–35. The Convention is in *British and Foreign State Papers, 1860–61*, pp. 35 ff.

a license, countersigned by their local magistrate, and to bring intending emigrants before a magistrate or Protector. The Medical Inspector, Agent, and Protector were to examine them at the depot, and ships were to sail within 24 hours of the embarkation of the first emigrants.[1]

Trinidad introduced Indian labourers in the sixties at an average rate of 2,200–2,300 a year. Grenada, St. Lucia, St. Vincent, St. Kitts, and Antigua took some hundreds at irregular intervals, though some doubted whether the stimulus to the sugar industry would be permanent.[2] Heavy mortality on a sugar estate in Grenada in 1866 led to an inquiry which revealed culpable neglect on the part of the manager. A Bill providing for central hospitals on the estates, which the Assembly had shelved, was now pushed through; but when the Indians were removed from the estate in question, the planters refused to employ them. Others refused to re-indenture the immigrants—a necessary condition of a free return passage. Thereupon Lord Carnarvon stopped all immigration into Grenada. It was five years before it was resumed.[3]

Throughout the period British Guiana retained its primacy in Indian immigration. Hincks, 'an able, astute, scheming, uncompromising, terribly energetic Scotch-Irishman', who had raised himself to the first place in Canadian politics before he deserted them for colonial government, had already shown himself to be genuinely interested in the Negroes.[4] He passed a Village Ordinance for regulating, taxing, and improving the Negro villages which had sprung up on abandoned estates after emancipation.[5] He pointed out the importance to the estates of the heavy work done by Negroes, often 'task gangs' who travelled considerable distances to work for some weeks or even

[1] Report of J. Geoghegan (Under-Secretary to the Government of India, Department of Agriculture, Revenue, and Commerce) (n.d.), P.P., 1874, xlvii (H.C. 314), 30–41.
[2] Cf. (on St. Lucia) Grant to Walker (2 May 1868), P.P., 1868–9, xliii [4090], 72.
[3] Baynes to Walker (24 June and 8 Nov.) in Walker to Cardwell (1 Aug. 1866) (No. 335) and to Carnarvon (21 Nov. 1866) (No. 359), CO101/123 and 124. Minute of Carnarvon (3 Oct.) on Walcott to Rogers (26 Sept. 1866), CO318/247. Report of Geoghegan, loc. cit., pp. 52–3.
[4] The characterization is from [J. E. Jenkins], *The Coolie: his Rights and Wrongs* (London, 1871), p. 79.
[5] Taylor thought this the most noteworthy feature of his government: Minute (14 Feb.) on Hincks to Granville (23 Jan. 1869) (No. 29), CO111/371.

months on a particular estate.[1] But at first he seemed intent on
reducing Indian immigration, telling Newcastle he was 'very
doubtful as to the expediency of ordering even the small number
of Indians that have been applied for. No new capital is likely to
be employed in producing Sugar, and my own conviction is, that
there is an ample supply of labour in the Colony for the next two
or three years'. He also mentioned the inadequacy of some estates'
hospitals and dwellings.[2] The number of Indians arriving during
his government, varying from two to four thousand, remained
well below the 1862 figures of 5,625 (with 2,590 Chinese as well)
for which he was not, of course, responsible. In transmitting the
British Guiana Blue Book for 1867 he remarked: 'The superintendence of these immigrant labourers is a constant source of anxiety,
but I have great satisfaction in expressing my conviction that no
just ground of complaint as to their treatment will be found to
exist.'[3] He had in fact come to terms with the planters—a fact
which gains added significance from his quarrel with Chief Justice
Beaumont.

Beaumont, who took up his post in 1863, was clearly a lawyer
who insisted on his rights and on the observance of the tech-
nicalities of the law. He declined to sit on the Court of Policy
unless he was regarded as 'an independent supporter of Government' and, when Hincks would not concede this point, he secured
permission to retire from the Court of Policy.[4] He gave an opening for attack by accusing the Government of tampering with the
clerk of his Court in order to falsify its records by entering certain
commutations of sentences by the Governor, which he held to be
invalid, and was suspended.[5] But the suspension was revoked by
Cardwell, who accepted Taylor's view that the grounds were insufficient.[6] Hincks acquiesced in the decision, saying he had 'never
entertained feelings of personal animosity towards Mr. Beaumont';

[1] Hincks to Newcastle (3 Mar. 1865) (No. 50), CO111/345.
[2] Hincks to Newcastle (7 Feb. 1862, No. 14, and 22 Feb. 1862, No. 19), CO111/334.
[3] Hincks to Buckingham (31 Aug. 1868) (No. 135), P.P., 1868-9, xliii [4090], 37-8.
[4] Hincks to Cardwell (23 June 1864) (No. 109) with Enclosures, CO111/346. Cardwell to Hincks (31 Oct. 1864) (No. 101), CO112/37.
[5] Hincks to Cardwell (5 Aug. 1865, No. 128, and 21 Aug. 1865, No. 129), CO111/353.
[6] Cardwell to Hincks (17 Nov. 1865) (No. 297), CO112/38. Based on Minute of Taylor (6 Oct.) on Hincks to Cardwell (21 Aug. 1865), CO111/353.

but next year the Court of Policy adopted an Address and
Memorial to the Queen praying for the Chief Justice's removal.[1]
It seems unlikely that the Court of Policy would have gone so far
merely because the Chief Justice was pedantically picking holes
in colonial legislation: Des Voeux's statement that he continually
overruled magistrates' decisions favourable to the planters seems
to lie closer to the heart of the matter.[2] When the Court of Policy's
Memorial seemed to be hanging fire, the Combined Court early
in 1868 refused to include the Chief Justice's salary in the civil list,
then due for renewal. Rogers believed that 'a judicious and conciliatory Governor' could have come to terms with the Chief
Justice, and a civil list without his salary was of course unacceptable; but a point had been reached where the Imperial authorities
were 'bound if possible . . . to stop the existing evils by recalling
Mr. Hincks or dismissing Mr. Beaumont'. Hincks's term was nearing its end; but, as Adderley pointed out, the Chief Justice's
relations with the Court of Policy made it impossible for him to
remain 'with any chance of peace or good government in the
Colony'.[3] At last, on 10 July, the Judicial Committee of the Privy
Council gave its decision on the Court of Policy's Memorial: it
was adverse to Beaumont. The charge of judicial misconduct had
not been made out; but their Lordships had found evidence that
the Chief Justice had 'allowed himself to be influenced in the
exercise of his judicial office by a desire to embarrass the Executive
Government'.[4] 'No doubt,' said Taylor in a minute four years
later, 'Sir F. Hincks, with his cold, self-possessed temper, had a
great gift of provocation.'[5] He had sacrificed the Chief Justice to
keep the goodwill of the planters. The 9,000 small freeholders
who presented an address against his removal doubtless saw the
issue in those terms.[6]

[1] Memorial in Hincks to Cardwell (23 May 1866) (No. 123), CO111/358.
[2] Sir G. W. Des Voeux, *My Colonial Service* (London, 1903), i. 122–3.
[3] Hincks to Buckingham (18 Mar. 1868) (No 26) with Minute of Rogers (n.d.)
Hincks to Buckingham (7 Apr. 1868) (No. 46) with Minutes of Taylor (10 May),
Rogers (15 May), and Adderley (20 May), CO111/366. Taylor attributed the
delay in action on the Memorial partly to the 'preoccupations with Parliament
and subsequent promotion to the Bench' of Cairns (the Court of Policy's counsel).
[4] Reeve to Rogers (16 July 1868) enclosing Report of Judicial Committee and
Order in Council for Beaumont's removal, CO111/370.
[5] Minute of Taylor (17 May 1872), in CO111/390.
[6] Address (9,170 signatures) in Hincks to Buckingham (7 July 1868) (No. 98),
CO111/367.

Early in 1869 Hincks was succeeded by John Scott. Gordon had been offered the government, but declined. The storm burst after Hincks's departure. Des Voeux, whose sympathies with Beaumont were known, was transfered to a less congenial magistracy and applied to Lord Granville for an appointment elsewhere. He had friends in high places and was offered, and accepted, the Administratorship of St. Lucia.[1] Towards the end of the year he heard news of trouble in British Guiana and an application for more troops. On Christmas Day he wrote to Granville alleging that there was 'very widespread discontent and disaffection existing throughout the immigrant population, both Indian and Chinese (and especially the latter)'. This he attributed to bad hospital conditions, poor housing, planter influence over medical men and magistrates, and a badly understaffed Immigration Department, whose head, Crosby, he nevertheless declared to be 'thoroughly upright, conscientious and indefatigable'. The number of re-indentures, he held, was no argument in favour of the system: 'for those who have no capital freedom is really of little value as against indentures made more attractive by the bounty and . . . privacy of living.'[2] Such charges could not be ignored. After discussion in the Colonial Office, Granville instructed Scott to ask the Combined Court to make provision for two Commissioners to be named by the Secretary of State in consultation with the Secretary of State for India.[3] Gordon was willing to lend Charles Mitchell, who had acted as Agent-General for Immigration in Trinidad in place of his father, but urged the 'absolute necessity of a sharp lawyer on the . . . Commission'.[4] Finally Sir George Young, Bart., of Lincoln's Inn, agreed to act with Mitchell and the India Office nominee, W. E. Frere, an elder brother of Sir Bartle Frere. The planting interests in London sent out as their counsel a former Advocate-General of Bengal and the Aborigines Protection Society a rising barrister, Edward Jenkins.

The Commission presented an exhaustive report in February 1871. After visiting 55 of the 124 estates employing immigrant

[1] Des Voeux, op. cit., i. 127.
[2] Dex Voeux to Granville (25 Dec. 1869) in Report of Commissioners appointed to inquire into the Treatment of Immigrants in British Guiana (23 Feb. 1871), P.P., 1871, xx [C. 393], 1-13.
[3] Granville to Scott (10 Mar. 1870) (No. 187), CO112/40.
[4] Gordon to Taylor (8 Apr. 1870) (Private), CO111/375. Sir George Young (1837-1930) was afterwards for many years a Charity Commissioner.

labour, it found Des Voeux's charges too sweeping, but by no means baseless. Des Voeux, who had suffered head injuries in a fall from a horse while visiting Gordon in Trinidad, was in poor health and confessedly made a poor showing. But the Commissioners admitted that his complaint of the undue rigour of magistrates in labour cases was 'to a great extent well-founded'.¹ Moreover they were clearly impressed by Crosby and strongly criticized Hincks for reducing him to the level of 'a sort of chief clerk in an office directed in its minutest details by the Governor in person' and, more specifically, for accepting 'a promise of redress more or less indefinite' when charges could have been brought against employers and managers. The planters had not given the Chinese the scale of provisions promised them in their indentures: failing to allow for the expense of the immigration or for 'the natural shrewdness of the Chinese', they found themselves 'involved in a series of dear bargains, from which they extricated themselves in a manner not creditable to the colony'. The Indians were often entered as agricultural labourers when they were not and medical inspection at the port of embarkation was perfunctory; clearly many of them were poor types. But they were often miserably paid, and their pay was liable to be stopped quite illegally. As Des Voeux had hinted, the practice of re-indenture for five years certain, made legal by Ordinance 3 of 1863, virtually abolished free labour so far as immigrants were concerned. The estates' hospitals had many defects. Dr. Shier, their Inspector, had carried his policy of forbearance too far. Moreover this new country, needing population, was making little effort to retain it: 'for the present this great experiment in colonization is merely in embryo'.² This was also the theme of Jenkins's able book: the policy of colonial legislation had hitherto been one of coercion 'where only a policy of broad and liberal kindness can succeed'.³

Hincks, who, being Finance Minister in Canada, had not been heard by the Commission, defended himself and Dr. Shier; and Sir Clinton Murdoch, with his great experience of immigration, considered that the defects the Commission had pointed out were

¹ In addition to Des Voeux's own book, see Jenkins, op. cit., pp. 139–40.
² Report of Commission, P.P., 1871, xx [C. 393], 192. On the five years' pre-indenture, see above, p. 455–6.
³ Jenkins, op. cit., p. 367.

'caused by errors of judgement, by insufficiency of the law, or by want of foresight, not by intentional neglect or indifference to the wellbeing of the people, still less by oppression or cruelty'.[1] But the elective members went much too far when they claimed that the inquiry had exposed misrepresentations and practically vindicated the planters.[2] Governor Scott accepted the Commission's recommendation that the medical supervision of immigrant labourers should be taken over by a salaried medical service and agreed that the Immigration Ordinance needed revision in many of its details. In particular he suggested that an immigrant should be given the option of re-indenturing for one or more, up to five, years as he might himself select, with a right to commute, by proportionate repayment of bounty, at any time after the first year. He did not, on the other hand, agree with the Commission's proposal that the state should pay the cost of supervision, the planter the cost of introduction. He held, with Murdoch, that there were no grounds at present for disturbing the Duke of Newcastle's arrangement that the planters should bear two-thirds of the cost: this might revive embarrassing questions.[3]

Sir George Young undertook the drafting of the new Immigration Ordinance. Its chief departure from Scott's suggestions was the adoption of a fixed limit of one year for re-indenture, which worked well in Trinidad, rather than the optional system with a right of commutation, which was 'much disliked by the planters, as drawing from them at uncertain intervals their best hands as soon as they begin to accumulate money'.[4] Lord Kimberley accepted this and also the Commission's proposal, which Scott disliked, that the Agent-General for Immigration should be a member of the Court of Policy.[5] After all, he was responsible for the welfare of 48,363 Indians and 6,880 Chinese in a total population in 1871 of some 193,000; and he enjoyed their confidence. He died in 1880 when just about to retire after twenty-two years' service; and 'more than half a century after his demise, all his

[1] Murdoch to Rogers (15 May 1871), P.P., 1872, xliii [C. 641], 8–18.
[2] Address in Reply (15 May) in Scott to Kimberley (18 May 1871) (No. 74), CO111/385.
[3] Scott to Kimberley (25 July 1871, No. 115, and 21 Dec. 1871, No. 180), P.P., 1872, xliii [C. 641], 20–2, 27–45.
[4] Young to Herbert (8 Mar. 1872), ibid., pp. 51–3.
[5] Scott to Kimberley (10 Jan. 1872) (No. 5); Kimberley to Scott (16 May 1872) (No. 295), ibid., pp 47–50, 86–9.

successors in office . . . continued to be known by that name' (*Krasbi*).[1]

The new Immigration Ordinance met with opposition from the elected members of the Court of Policy despite the warning, passed on by Kimberley, that if the existing state of affairs were not remedied the Government of India would 'take into serious consideration the question of suspending emigration from this country to British Guiana'.[2] But Kimberley insisted on most of the clauses, though he was willing to agree that one year re-indentures might be optional and that six days of seven hours might be substituted for five of nine. The ordinance was then passed, though not without a protest from the elective members against Kimberley's 'dictation'.[3] It marked the beginning of a series of reforms which, according to the historian of Guyana Indians, made British Guiana the model colony for indentured labour.[4] The number of unindentured Indians also increased, though in 1874 (according to Crosby) about half of these continued to work on the estates.[5]

Disturbances on some Essequibo estates in 1872, in which five Indians were killed in a clash between 24 police and 200 estate labourers, led Kimberley to address some sharp questions to Governor Scott. Inquiries suggested that there were faults on both sides: one of the Indian ringleaders had been provocative and the magistrate concerned was a new arrival. The wages were among the highest in the colony, though the hours worked in the factory were excessive.[6] The unwillingness of Portuguese jurors to convict the persons arrested of unlawful, riotous, and tumultuous assembly may have been due to the fact that the British Guiana Portuguese had grievances of their own, with which Scott had not been sympathetic.[7] British Guiana in fact remained, as Taylor remarked in a minute about this time, 'a merchants' and planters' oligarchy,

[1] Dwarka Nath, *A History of Indians in British Guiana* (Edinburgh, 1950), p. 60.
[2] Government of India to Argyll (Secretary of State) (22 Mar. 1872), P.P., 1872, xliii [C. 641], 118.
[3] Scott to Kimberley (25 Sept. 1872) (No. 123), CO111/391. Kimberley to Scott (14 Nov. 1872) (draft), CO111/392. Protest in Scott to Kimberley (2 Dec. 1872) (No. 170), CO111/393.        [4] Dwarka Nath, op. cit., p. 78.
[5] Longden to Carnarvon (17 Dec. 1875) transmitting Blue Book for 1874, P.P., 1875, li [C. 1336], 69–70.
[6] The correspondence is all in P.P., 1873, xlix [C. 879] with the exception of Scott to Kimberley (24 Mar. 1873) (Confidential), CO111/396.
[7] These also were the subject of a Special Blue Book, P.P., 1871, xlvii [C. 458]. The grievances were largely concerned with liquor and timber licenses.

not much tempered perhaps by any apprehension that the Crown will really exert the latent power it claims of supreme and absolute legislation'. Nevertheless the planters' continuing need of immigrant labour gave the Crown leverage which it could on occasions use.[1]

Trinidad was free from these constitutional complications. Unlike British Guiana it drew large numbers of immigrants from smaller West Indian islands, such as St. Vincent. It also assimilated its Indian immigrants more easily, especially after Governor Gordon in 1869 had made its extensive waste lands available on reasonable terms.[2] Trinidad controversies, which were not infrequent, centred rather in Catholic–Protestant rivalry, which powerfully affected education policy and the question of religious disestablishment, which the Gladstone Government was pressing forward. In both these colonies, as in Barbados, whose special circumstances have already been touched on, sugar production was now much higher than in the early days of emancipation. Trinidad and British Guiana had bought their relative prosperity at the cost (which they were hardly yet beginning to count) of becoming more than ever a plural society. To say this is by no means to condemn the immigration policy. Their economies might well have stagnated without it; and it brought to thousands of immigrants standards of living and opportunities of advancement few of them would have had in the overcrowded lands from which they came. Moreover the Colonial Office, as it learned from experience, was able to deal more purposefully with the problems to which immigration gave rise than in the early years of the experiment. Its guidance was still needed. Time was required for these new societies to mature gradually until, after many vicissitudes, they could justifiably claim freedom to determine their own destiny.

[1] Minute of Taylor (5 Dec. 1871) on Scott to Kimberley (7 Nov. 1871) (No. 160) transmitting an east coast petition for constitutional reform, CO111/387.

[2] Ordinance 8 of 1869. On Gordon's important governorship see J. K. Chapman, *The Career of Arthur Hamilton Gordon, First Lord Stanmore, 1829–1912* (Toronto, 1964), ch. iii.

# XVI

## CONCLUSION

SINCE Lord Durham's Report the main theme of British colonial policy has been the extension and deepening of his conception of responsible government. Lord Grey and Lord John Russell made the concession to the British North American colonies (Newfoundland excepted) and Lord Elgin's wise guidance ensured its success in the first critical stage in Canada. Sir William Molesworth's elaborations of Durham's reservations into a scheme of statutory delimitation of Imperial and colonial subjects was rejected in the course of the debates on the Australian Colonies Government Bill (and again when the newly framed Australian constitutions came before the Cabinet in 1855).[1] It was, therefore, left to the Imperial and Colonial Governments to settle, in the course of time and in the light of accumulating experience, what limitations upon colonial self-government, if any, were expedient and mutually acceptable.

The control of the public lands, one of Durham's proposed reservations, was conceded to Canada and, before this study begins, to the Australian colonies and New Zealand also. His others—'the constitution of the form of government—the regulation of foreign relations, and of trade with the mother country, the other British Colonies, and foreign nations'[2]—were as yet hardly questioned. But the question what colonies were entitled to self-government was a fundamental one and could not be settled all at once. Lord Grey indeed held that representative governments could not safely be created until colonies had attained a certain maturity and that 'the principal bar' to their establishment was 'their being inhabited by a population of which a large proportion is not of European race'.[3] This had not deterred him

---

[1] *British Colonial Policy in the Age of Peel and Russell*, pp. 492–6; Knaplund, *Gladstone and Britain's Imperial Policy*, pp. 73–8.

[2] *Lord Durham's Report on the Affairs of British North America* (ed. C. P. Lucas) (Oxford, 1912), ii. 282.

[3] Earl Grey, *The Colonial Policy of Lord John Russell's Administration* (London, 1853), i. 27.

from initiating policies which led to the introduction of representative institutions in New Zealand and at the Cape. He intended the Cape Coloured people, if they acquired the property qualification, to receive the franchise and probably thought the Maoris would in due course receive it also, for it was not only in South Africa that he believed 'the ultimate amalgamation of the two races . . . not impracticable, if the superior power of this Country is wisely and generously used to enforce on both sides a respect for each other's rights'.[1]

But representative institutions were one thing; responsible government was another. It never entered Lord Grey's mind that New Zealand or the Cape should be given responsible government yet. He later protested that the grant to New Zealand had been premature. The missionary bodies, the Anti-Slavery Society, and the Aborigines Protection Society were still forces to be reckoned with: though less potent than they had been a generation earlier, they made their voices heard in criticism of colonial policies if occasion arose. But their principles were yielding ground to the desire to be rid of colonial responsibilities and to the belief that self-government entailed self-defence and that self-defence could make colonial wars less likely, for prudential reasons. Self-defence was not, or at least not until Gladstone became Prime Minister and Cardwell went to the War Office, a policy to which the Cabinet gave high priority. Among the leading officials at the Colonial Office Merivale and Elliot were sceptical of it, though Rogers supported it more and more strongly. The steady pressure for such a policy came from the House of Commons. It appealed to the Manchester economists, the businessmen, and the remaining 'Colonial Reformers'. The Select Committee of 1861, set up on a private member's motion, which formulated the policy in express terms, was engineered by one of these Reformers, Godley, now Assistant Under-Secretary for War.

This policy had gained an early success when disgust at the continual 'Kaffir Wars' in South Africa led to British withdrawal from the Orange River Sovereignty in 1854 in defiance of the Cape colonists and a large section at least of the European inhabitants of the Sovereignty itself, not to mention the Griquas and the Basuto on its borders. Yet the Imperial Government, determined though it was to limit its responsibilities in South Africa, was not

[1] Earl Grey, op. cit., ii. 253.

prepared at that stage to abandon them and leave the Cape Colony, which it had just endowed with a representative constitution, to manage its own frontier policy and defend itself. The Cape, and the Eastern Province in particular, did not want responsible government on those terms and Natal, though already asking for representative institutions, did not and could not contemplate self-defence. In short, the Imperial Government admitted it still had responsibilities in South Africa, and by sending out Sir George Grey as Governor of the Cape and High Commissioner in the very year of the withdrawal by implication accepted his idea that the peace of the frontier was best secured by exercising a bene-volent civilizing influence over the frontier tribes. On the eastern frontier Grey's policy won a measure of success in the face of many difficulties; but his bid to reverse the policy of 1854 and secure the peace of South Africa by joining the Cape, the Orange Free State and Natal in a federation with responsible government was too ambitious and bound to fail. His last attempt to extend the frontier by annexing the Transkei, a policy which Sir Philip Wodehouse inherited, was reversed when it seemed on the point of accomplishment. The Cape Colony was now forced to in-corporate British Kaffraria and thus relieve the Imperial Govern-ment of another inconvenient responsibility. But in 1868, when Wodehouse intervened to save the Basuto from conquest by the Orange Free State, the Duke of Buckingham accepted his action. The discovery of diamonds placed a further strain on the policy of limited responsibility. Thousands of diamond diggers swarmed northwards over the colonial frontier; the land rights of a Griqua chief at least appeared to be involved; and even Gladstone was constrained to agree to an annexation which, being challenged by the Orange Free State, amounted to an assertion of British paramountcy in South Africa. He solaced himself with the thought that the new High Commissioner, Sir Henry Barkly, was to give Imperial backing to the responsible government party at the Cape and see to it that the Cape Colony assumed responsibility for both Basutoland and Griqualand West. It was too much to expect of a newly fledged responsible Ministry. The Cape took over Basutoland—for a time—but refused to annex Griqualand West until 1880. The responsible government principle had won the day; but Imperial responsibilities diminished but little, even in defence. There was no question of responsible government for

Natal as yet; the Imperial Government revived the idea of federation as the best course for South Africa and soon found itself more deeply involved than ever. The enthusiasts for self-government and self-defence could hardly feel satisfied with the outcome.

The problem in New Zealand had seemed simpler. Sir George Grey's policy of pacification and 'amalgamation' in his first governorship appeared to have been crowned with success.[1] After his departure the new constitution came into force and the Aberdeen Ministry made no difficulty about conceding responsible government when the first General Assembly asked for it in 1854. But Grey's successor, Gore Browne, regarded Native affairs and Native land purchase as 'Imperial subjects' and thus still under his control as representative of the Crown. Neither his Ministers nor the Colonial Office demurred, though both had doubts whether the arrangement would work. The presence of Imperial troops was the most potent argument in its favour and the Imperial Government, though anxious to reduce their number, willingly reinforced them when war broke out in Taranaki. But the war brought out into the open the differences between the Imperial and the colonial point of view. The New Zealand Ministry had used its control over legislation and finance to whittle away the Governor's independent power in Native affairs and an attempt by Gore Browne and the Duke of Newcastle to secure through Imperial legislation an independent Native Council was obnoxious to colonial opinion and came to nothing. Yet the responsible Ministers insisted that the war was an Imperial war. When New Zealand missionaries and philo-Maoris began to impugn the justice of the war British public opinion began to turn against New Zealand. In its perplexity the Imperial Government was glad to accept the offer of Sir George Grey to return as Governor and peace-maker to New Zealand.

The early stages of responsible government imposed a heavy burden on the representative of the Crown. Elgin had been given a practically free hand in Canada. He had kept out of politics, though this was not fully appreciated until in his last year he admitted the Conservatives to office, and had triumphantly overcome his difficulties. Sir George Grey had a practically free hand so long as Newcastle was in office but events were too strong for

---

[1] My view of Sir G. Grey's policy is no longer so favourable as it was in 1930. Yet in pacification at any rate he had achieved much.

him. Moreover, he could not keep out of politics. The legacy of distrust which his first government had left caused the Fox Ministry at once to face him with a demand for responsible government in Native affairs. He conceded the point, confident that with his knowledge of the Maoris he could keep the reins in his own hands. He nevertheless wanted Imperial assistance in his plans of pacification. Then the General Assembly, alarmed at the military and financial implications of responsible government in Native affairs, tried to shuffle out of the demand which Ministers had made on its behalf. The Duke of Newcastle, disgusted at this shuffling, stood firm, refused to resume a responsibility which had become merely nominal and roundly declared the war to be a colonial and not an Imperial war, though he pointed out that New Zealand was still defended by Imperial troops. This censorious dispatch achieved the desired end: New Zealand Ministers made no further difficulty about assuming responsibility. But it left a feeling of soreness. When war broke again, the Imperial Government once more unhesitatingly reinforced the troops. But it did not like the way in which Grey and his New Zealand Ministers proposed to face their new responsibilities—an Imperially guaranteed loan, confiscation of the lands of the Maori tribes involved, and military settlement upon the confiscated lands as a security against war in future. The Duke of Newcastle rather hesitantly approved the confiscation policy. His successor Cardwell did not conceal his dislike of it. Unable to resume responsibility, he relied on the restraining power of Sir George Grey. Grey for the time was prepared to play the Imperial game, but the result was merely to embroil him with his Ministers and bring the machinery of responsible government to a standstill.

With the formation of Weld's 'self-reliant' Ministry, a new way out of the difficulty appeared. Weld abandoned all idea of making the war a profitable enterprise. He could not leave the military settlers in the lurch and drop the confiscation policy but he proposed to dispense with the Imperial troops and raise a sufficient colonial force. Grey had no choice but to co-operate with his new Ministry, but he did not really believe in self-reliance and knew that the Imperial troops were the main prop of his personal power. When Weld fell ill and lost his grip and the Assembly rejected the new taxation needed to finance his policy, Grey saw his chance. He had already moved over from the Imperial to the

colonial side, quarrelling with General Cameron and further dis-
illusioning the Imperial authorities. Now he formed an alliance
with Stafford and the pair fought a long rearguard action against
the withdrawal of the troops, haggling over terms for retaining
them but never explicitly disavowing self-reliance and indeed
employing colonial rather than Imperial troops to do the actual
fighting. The Imperial Government, tiring of Grey's evasions,
deprived him of all control over the movements of the troops
and did not conceal its relief in announcing that his term of office
had come to an end. But when the war flared up again in 1868,
it became clear that the difficulty did not merely arise out of the
personality of Sir George Grey. The New Zealand Government
wished to retain an Imperial military presence, though disclaiming
any desire to use the one remaining regiment in active operations.
The Gladstone Ministry insisted on withdrawing it and gave
fresh offence by a hint that New Zealand would be well advised
to come to terms with the Maori King. It maintained this stand
when Stafford was replaced by Fox, who frankly asked for
Imperial assistance in men and in finance. But Fox, instead of
bandying words with the Imperial Government across the ocean,
sent Featherston and Bell to negotiate face to face. Their firm and
yet conciliatory diplomacy secured the assistance asked for, not
indeed in men, for which the need was passing, but in an Imperial
guarantee for a loan of £1,000,000.

The relaxation of tension showed that both sides had learned
some lessons. New Zealand had been slow to shoulder the burdens that the much desired 'responsible government' entailed.
The colonists wished to be free of the leading strings of the mother
country but at the same time to have Imperial troops fight their
wars without any but incidental expense to the colony. The
Imperial connection could not be expected to endure on such a
basis as that. On the other hand, the rigid British military mind, the
narrow, doctrinaire Treasury view of politics and the didacticism
of the Colonial Office all found it difficult to adjust themselves to
the implications of colonial self-government. The reservation of
control of Native affairs, though it had some advantages as a
transitional arrangement, was essentially artificial and when it was
seriously questioned by responsible Ministers was bound to break
down. Even when the Colonial Office relinquished this responsibility it still sought to have the last word through the presence of

the Imperial troops and the constitutional authority of the Governor as an Imperial officer. Lord John Russell had foreseen this dilemma in his famous dispatch of 14 October 1839.[1] But if Sir George Grey could not persuade his ministers to adopt the Imperial view, he had in the long run to accept the colonial view. He held out against Whitaker and Fox but he had to give in to Weld. When in alliance with Stafford he tried to pull the wool over the eyes of the Imperial Government the Colonial Office was not deceived and broke him. But that did not mean that Colonial Office policy had succeeded. If the Imperial connection was to endure under responsible government the terms must not be laid down in acrimonious dispatches but worked out in personal negotiation. This was already beginning to be appreciated. If the missions of Crosbie Ward and Reader Wood had failed, the success of Sewell in 1857 and Fitzherbert in 1867–8 prepared the way for Featherston and Dillon Bell. Before long Featherston returned as the first New Zealand Agent-General. Soon the Colonial Agents-General, of whom he was only one, were recognized as an essential link between the self-governing colonies and the Imperial Government. Under its new permanent head, Sir Robert Herbert, the role of the Colonial Office began to change.

In the twenty years we have been considering, neither South Africa nor New Zealand shows the Colonial Office at its best; but it had some achievements to its credit in the West India colonies. Self-government had had a different meaning in these islands, most of which inherited the representative system of the old Empire, but in a narrowly oligarchical form. Their political institutions had survived the transition from slavery to freedom, the only change being the gradual admission of the coloured classes, through the election of their leaders to the Assemblies, to some share in political power. Governments were generally weak, Assemblies irresponsible and forward-looking policies out of the question. In Jamaica, the most important, the Duke of Newcastle and Sir Henry Barkly had some success at first in their attempt to approximate to responsible government by the formation of an Executive Committee as the organ of government in the Assembly; and some of the smaller colonies followed

[1] W. P. M. Kennedy, *Statutes, Treaties and Documents of the Canadian Constitution* (Oxford, 1930), pp. 421–3.

Jamaica's lead. But under less skilled management the new machinery began to creak and the Morant Bay rebellion, which revealed the fundamental weakness of these narrowly based oligarchies, frightened the Assemblies (except in Barbados) into a surrender of power. A remedy for West Indian ills was sought in Crown Colony government. Inspired by men of reforming temper whom the Colonial Office sent out, the island governments, with Jamaica again in the lead, at last broke out of the stagnation which had followed abolition. Much-needed reforms were introduced, even though in the smaller islands Governors were inclined to underrate the difficulties which still beset reform. In British Guiana, whose peculiar institutions still gave the oligarchy considerable power, the Colonial Office at last began to look upon the Indian immigrants as a permanent element in the colony's population and to take a more active interest in their integration in colonial society. For the present at least, however, enlightened Crown Colony rule was the most promising approach to a more broadly based franchise and can be justified as a necessary stage in the gradual evolution of self-government.

These mid Victorian years are not an exciting period in the history of British colonial policy. The all-important concession of the principle of responsible government belonged to the past; the lush growth of late Victorian imperialism was not yet discernible. But the Imperial Government was acquiring experience in the application of responsible government to the varied conditions of the British Colonial Empire. Precedents had been created in New Zealand and at the Cape. The presence of a large non-European population had not after all been a bar to the concession of responsible government to European settlers. The Colonial Office doubtless shared the liberal hope that the franchise would remain open to non-Europeans with the requisite qualification and that in due course they would have representation in the legislature. On the other hand, the idea of introducing responsible government in the West Indian oligarchies had been abandoned.

At the same time a readjustment of relations between the Colonial Office, as the responsible organ of the Imperial Government, and the self-governing colonies was quietly proceeding. The principle that they had 'the main responsibility of providing for their internal order and security' had been established and

accepted in New Zealand (and in the North American and Australian colonies). It hardly had been in Cape Colony—but then the
Cape was the base from which Great Britain exercised the paramountcy it claimed in Southern Africa and paramountcy entailed
some, even if an ill-defined, responsibility. The establishment
of Agents-General (whose functions of course were by no means
exclusively political) had forged a new link in the chain which
bound Great Britain and the colonies together. They were a
useful supplement to the official connection through the Governors and gave a permanent personal contact which accorded well
with the spirit of responsible government. The Empire clearly
possessed more cohesion than critics like Goldwin Smith had
supposed. Non-official opinion had begun to assert itself in favour
of maintaining the imperial connection and had perhaps been
decisive in the critical years 1869–70. The ties of commerce,
finance, and investment were increasing in importance. Unofficial
societies, notably the Royal Colonial Institute (now, under its
new name of the Royal Commonwealth Society, celebrating its
centenary) were beginning to play their part as store-houses of
information and meeting-places of people from all corners of the
Empire. The Empire was changing, but growing, not disintegrat-
ing. A 'policy of Imperial consolidation', on less spectacular lines
than those of which Disraeli spoke, had unostentatiously begun.
That was the mid Victorian achievement.

# BIBLIOGRAPHY

## 1. GENERAL

### Manuscript Sources

Colonial Office Papers at the Public Record Office, London.
The series used are specified under later heads in the bibliography.
Russell Papers: Public Record Office 30/22.
Granville Papers: Public Record Office 30/29.
Cardwell Papers: Public Record Office 30/48.
Gladstone Papers: British Museum Additional MS. 44118/9 (Cardwell), 44262-3 (Newcastle), 44224 (Kimberley), 44534-41 (Letter Books).
Newcastle Papers: University of Nottingham Library: NeC9553-5, 10885-914, 10930-6 (in microfilm).

### Printed Sources

Parliamentary Papers, 1852-3 to 1875.
Detailed lists seem unnecessary in view of the lists in volumes ii, iii, vii, part ii, and viii of the *Cambridge history of the British Empire* (Cambridge, 1929-59).
Public General Statutes of the United Kingdom.
*Hansard's Parliamentary Debates*, Third Series.
Here again the lists in the *Cambridge history of the British Empire* are generally satisfactory. The debates on the military defence of the colonies on 25 July 1859 (clv. 391-411) and on Mills's motion on the subject on 4 March 1862 (clxv. 1032-61) are, however, omitted. Certain other omissions are noted under later heads of this bibliography.

### Newspapers and Reviews

*The Times*, 1853-72.
*Spectator*, 1853-72.
*Saturday Review*, 1855-72.
Occasional references have been made to the *Edinburgh Review, Quarterly Review, Fortnightly Review, Contemporary Review*, and *Daily News*.

### Contemporary Books, Pamphlets, etc.

GLADSTONE, W. E. *Our colonies.* London, 1855. A speech, reprinted in P. Knaplund, *Gladstone and Britain's imperial policy* (see below).
MILLS, ARTHUR. *Colonial constitutions.* London, 1856.
ADDERLEY, C. B. *Letter to the Right Hon. B. Disraeli on the present relations of England with the colonies.* London, 1861. Reprinted with a new preface in 1862.
MERIVALE, H. *Lectures on colonization and colonies.* New edition. London, 1861. Reprinted Oxford, 1928.
MILL, J. S. *Considerations on representative government.* London, 1861. Many times reprinted.

GODLEY, J. R. *Extracts from letters to C. B. Adderley*. Privately printed, London, 1863.

GREY, H. G. (3rd Earl). *Parliamentary government considered with reference to reform*. London, 1863.

MILLS, A. *Colonial military expenditure*. London, 1863.

SMITH, GOLDWIN. *The Empire: a series of letters*. London, 1863.

VOGEL, J. *Great Britain and her colonies*. London, 1865.

BAGEHOT, W. *The English constitution*. London, 1867.

DILKE, SIR C. W. *Greater Britain*. London, 1868.

ADDERLEY, SIR C. B. *Review of 'The colonial policy of Lord John Russell's administration', by Earl Grey . . . and of subsequent colonial history*. London, 1869. See also the critical review of this book in the *Edinburgh Review*, xccci (Jan. 1870).

CLODE, C. M. *The military Forces of the Crown*. 2 vols. London, 1869.

MERIVALE, H. 'The colonial question in 1870' in the *Fortnightly Review*, N.S. vii (Feb. 1870).

FROUDE, J. A. 'England and her colonies', *Fraser's Magazine*, N.S. i (Jan. 1870).

—— 'The colonies once more', *Fraser's Magazine* (Aug. 1870).

MACFIE, R. A. *Papers on colonial questions*. London, 1871.

JENKINS, E. (ed.) *Discussions on colonial questions: report of the proceedings of a conference*. London, 1872.

*Proceedings of the Royal Colonial Institute*, 1869–73.

*The letters of John Stuart Mill*. Ed. with Introduction by H. S. R. Elliot. London, 1910. [A few letters in vol. ii bear on the Jamaica crisis.]

*The political correspondence of Mr. Gladstone and Lord Granville, 1868–1876*. Ed. A. Ramm. Camden 3rd Ser. lxxxi–lxxxii. London, 1952.

KIMBERLEY, 1ST EARL OF. *A journal of events during the Gladstone ministry, 1868–1874*. Ed. E. Drus. Camden Miscellany, xxi. London, 1958.

### Secondary Works

BIDDULPH, SIR R. *Lord Cardwell at the War Office*. London, 1904.

BLACHFORD, LORD (SIR F. ROGERS). *Letters* (ed. G. E. Marindin). London, 1896. [An important first-hand source.]

BLAKE, R. N. W. *Disraeli*. London, 1966.

BODELSEN, C. A. *Studies in mid-Victorian imperialism*. Copenhagen, 1924.

BOWEN, SIR G. F. *Thirty years of colonial government* (ed. S. Lane Poole). London, 1889.

BUXTON, S. *Finance and politics: an historical study, 1783–1885*. London, 1888.

CAMPBELL, PERSIA C. *Chinese coolie emigration to countries within the British Empire*. London, 1923.

CARRINGTON, C. E. *John Robert Godley of Canterbury*. Christchurch, 1950.

CELL, J. W. 'The Colonial Office in the 1850's', *Historical studies: Australia and New Zealand*, xii (1965).

CHILDE-PEMBERTON, W. S. *Life of Sir C. Adderley, Lord Norton*. London, 1909.

CHILDERS, E. S. C. *Life and correspondence of Hugh C. E. Childers*. 2 vols. London, 1901.

CREIGHTON, D. G. *The road to confederation: the emergence of Canada, 1863–1867*. Toronto, 1964.

D'EGVILLE, SIR H. *Imperial defence: Sir John Colomb*. London, 1913.

ERICKSON, A. B. 'Edward Cardwell, Peelite', *Transactions of the American Philosophical Society*, xlix, part 2. Philadelphia, 1959.

ESCOTT, T. H. SWEET. *Edward Bulwer, first Baron Lytton*. London, 1910.

FARR, D. M. L. *The Colonial Office and Canada, 1867–1887*. Toronto, 1955.

FAWCETT, M. G. *Life of Sir William Molesworth*. London, 1901.

FIDDES, SIR G. V. *The Dominions and Colonial Offices*. London, 1926.

FITZMAURICE, LORD E. *Life of the second Earl Granville*. 2 vols. London, 1905.

FOLSOM, A. *The Royal Empire Society: the formative years*. London, 1933.

FORTESCUE, SIR J. W. *History of the British Army*, vol. xiii. London, 1930.

GREVILLE, C. C. F. *Memoirs*. [The older edition, edited by H. Reeve (London, 1887), being more accessible, has been used.]

GUEDALLA, P. (ed.) *Gladstone and Palmerston*. London, 1928. [This is, of course, an original source.]

HALL, H. DUNCAN. *The British Commonwealth of nations*. London, 1920.

HALL, H. L. *The Colonial Office: a history*. Royal Empire Society Imperial Studies, No. 13. London, 1927.

HARDINGE, SIR A. H. *The Fourth Earl of Carnarvon*. 3 vols. London, 1925.

HIRST, F. W. *Gladstone as Financier and Economist*. London, 1931.

KNAPLUND, P. *Gladstone and Britain's Imperial Policy*. London, 1927.

KNOX, B. A. 'Colonial Influence on Imperial Policy, 1858–1866: Victoria and the Colonial Naval Defence Act 1865', *Historical studies: Australia and New Zealand*, xi (1963).

—— 'The provision of legal advice and Colonial Office reorganization, 1866–7', *Bulletin of the Institute of Historical Research*, xxxv (1962).

LUCAS, SIR C. P. *The Empire at war*, vol. i. Oxford, 1921.

LUVAAS, J. *The Education of an army: British military thought, 1815–1940*. London, 1965.

MARTIN, B. KINGSLEY. *The triumph of Lord Palmerston*. London, 1924.

MARTINEAU, J. *Life of Henry Pelham, fifth Duke of Newcastle*. London, 1908.

MERIVALE, C. *Herman Merivale, C.B.* Reprinted from *Transactions of the Devonshire Association for the Advancement of Science*, 1884.

MERIVALE, H. C. *Bar, stage and platform: autobiographic memories, etc.* London, 1902.

MONYPENNY, W. F., and BUCKLE, G. E. *Life of Benjamin Disraeli Earl of Beaconsfield*. New ed. in 2 vols. London, 1929.

MORLEY, J. (VISCOUNT). *Life of Richard Cobden*. London, 1881.

—— *Life of Gladstone*. 3 vols. London, 1903.

—— *Recollections*. 2 vols. London, 1917.

ST. AUBYN, GILES. *The Royal George . . . life of H.R.H. Prince George Duke of Cambridge*. London, 1963.

SCHURMAN, D. M. *The education of a navy: the development of British naval strategic thought, 1867–1914*. London, 1965.

SCHUYLER, R. L. *The fall of the old colonial system: a study in British free trade, 1770–1870*. New York, 1945.

SMITH, GOLDWIN. *Reminiscences*. Ed. A. Haultain. New York, 1910.

STACEY, C. P. *Canada and the British Army, 1846–1871: a study in the practice of responsible government*. Revised ed. Toronto, 1963.

STANMORE, BARON (SIR A. H. GORDON). *Sidney Herbert: a memoir*. 2 vols. London, 1906.

TAYLOR, SIR H. *Autobiography*. 2 vols. London, 1885.
—— *Correspondence*. Ed. E. Dowden. London, 1888.
*The Times. History of The Times*, vol. ii, *The tradition established, 1841–1884*. London, 1939.
TYLER, J. E. *The struggle for imperial unity, 1868–1895*. Royal Empire Society Imperial Studies, No. 16. London, 1938.
VICTORIA, H.M. QUEEN. *Letters*. 1st Ser. Ed. A. C. Benson and Viscount Esher. 2nd Ser. Ed. G. E. Buckle. London, 1907 and 1927.
VINCENT, J. *The formation of the Liberal Party, 1857–1868*. London, 1966.
WAITE, P. B. *The life and times of confederation, 1864–1867*. Toronto, 1962.
WIGHT, M. *The development of the Legislative Council, 1606–1945*. London, 1946.
YOUNG, D. M. *The Colonial Office in the early nineteenth century*. Royal Commonwealth Society Imperial Studies, No. 22. London, 1961.

*Unpublished Theses*

SELLERS, G. J. 'Edward Cardwell at the Colonial Office.' Univ. of Oxford, B.Litt. thesis, 1958.
TYLER, W. P. N. 'Sir Frederic Rogers, Permanent Under-Secretary at the Colonial Office, 1860–1871.' Duke Univ., Ph.D. dissertation, 1962.

## 2. SOUTH AFRICA

*Manuscript Sources*

Cape Archives, Cape Town.
Government House Records: Dispatches from Secretary of State, 1853–72: G.H. 1/47–68; G.H. 4/1.
—— Dispatches to Secretary of State, 1852–72: G.H. 23/22–31; G.H. 27/1, 3.
—— Enclosures to Dispatches, 1854–72: G.H. 28/66–91.
   These volumes cover the same field as the Public Record Office series Colonial Office 48/337–463 and Colonial Office 49/48–62, but do not of course include the minutes of Colonial Office officials, which I consulted in England in 1958. It seemed more convenient in most cases to give the Public Record Office reference.
Natal Archives, Pietermaritzburg:
Government House Records: Secretary of State Dispatches Received, 1853–72: G.H. 1–19, 66.
—— Dispatches Outward, 1853–72: G.H. 270–8, 298.
   These volumes cover the field of Colonial Office 179/28–110, and Colonial Office 405/1–7, Public Records Office, with the exception noted under the Cape head. The Colonial Office minutes were consulted in 1958 and references are normally given to the CO series.
Grey Collection, Auckland Public Library. Contains some South African letters of interest.
Private Correspondence of Sir P. E. Wodehouse; Colonial Office Library, London.
The Southey Papers in the Cape Archives were consulted in part in 1952.
After some correspondence with the South African Government Archives

I had reluctantly to abandon my intention to obtain a microfilm of at least a selection of the remaining papers.

### Printed Sources

Cape Colony: *Minutes of the Legislative Council with Annexures, 1854–1872.*
—— *Votes and Proceedings of the House of Assembly with Annexures, 1854–1872.*
—— *The Advertiser and Mail's Parliamentary Debates, 1854–55.*
*Statutes of the Cape of Good Hope, 1854–1872.* Cape Town, 1906–9.
For United Kingdom Parliamentary Papers and Debates, readers are referred to the *Cambridge history of the British Empire*, vol. viii: *South Africa.*

### Collected Historical Records and Selected Documents

THEAL, G. M. (ed.) *Basutoland Records*, vols. i–iii. Cape Town, 1883. Volumes iv–vi exist in manuscript in the Cape Archives and were also consulted.
BELL, K. N., and MORRELL, W. P. (eds.) *Select documents on British colonial policy, 1830–1860.* Oxford, 1928.
EYBERS, G. W. (ed.) *Select constitutional documents illustrating South African history, 1795–1910.* London, 1918.
HATTERSLEY, A. F. (ed.) *More annals of Natal.* London, 1936. *Later annals of Natal.* London, 1938. *The Natalians.* Pietermaritzburg, 1940.

### Newspapers

*Grahamstown Journal, 1856–72.*
The issues for 1853–6 and for the first half of 1869 were missing from the file in the Grahamstown Public Library. In 1861 this journal claimed to have the largest circulation of any newspaper in South Africa.
Occasional references were made to the *Cape Frontier Times* (Grahamstown).

### Contemporary Books, Pamphlets, etc.

GREEN, J. *The Kat River settlement in 1851.* Grahamstown, 1853.
KING, W. R. *Campaigning in Kaffirland.* London, 1853.
MERRIMAN, N. J. *The Kaffir, the Hottentot and the frontier farmer.* London, 1853. The journals from which this book was compiled were published without the author's consent. In 1957 as No. 37 of its publications the Van Riebeeck Society published them in full as *The Cape journals of Archdeacon N. J. Merriman.* Ed. D. H. Varley and H. M. Matthew.
MOLESWORTH, SIR W. *Materials for a speech in defence of the policy of abandoning the Orange River Territory.* London, 1854.
STOCKENSTROM, SIR A. *Light and shade. . . . The Hottentots of the Kat River Settlement.* Cape Town, 1854.
COLENSO, THE RIGHT REVD. J. W. *Ten weeks in Natal.* Cambridge, 1855.
HOLDEN, THE REVD. W. C. *History of the Colony of Natal.* London, 1855.
CATHCART, SIR G. *Correspondence . . . relating to his military operations in Kaffraria.* London, 1856. [Posthumously published; an important source.]
ORPEN, J. M. *History of the Basutus of South Africa.* Cape Town, 1857.
CARTER, T. T. *A memoir of John Armstrong, D.D., late Lord Bishop of Grahamstown.* Oxford, 1857.
CALDERWOOD, REVD. H. *Caffres and Caffre missions.* London, 1858.

MACLEAN, COL. J. (ed.) *A compendium of Kafir laws and customs*. Mount Coke, 1858.

CASALIS, E. *Les Bassoutos*. Paris, 1859.

HODGES, SIR W. *Federation in South Africa*. Cape Town, 1859.

SHAW, THE REVD. W. *The story of my mission in South Eastern Africa*. Lodnon, 1860.

GROUT, THE REVD. L. *Zululand or life among the Zulu Kafirs*. London, 1862.

HOLDEN, THE REVD. W. C. *The past and future of the Kaffir races*. London, 1866.

WILSON, E. *Reminiscences of a Frontier Armed and Mounted Police officer in South Africa*. Grahamstown, 1866.

TAYLOR, THE REVD. W. *Christian adventures in South Africa*. London, 1867.

WILMOT, A. *Diamonds and the South African diamond fields*. Cape Town, 1869.

MCKAY, J. *Reminiscences of the last Kafir war*. Grahamstown, 1871.

ROBINSON, J. *Notes on Natal: an old colonist's book for new settlers*. Durban and London, 1872.

PHILIP, THE REVD. W. B. 'The Griquas and their Exodus', *Cape Monthly Magazine* (December 1872). [Valuable.]

BOYCE, W. B. *Memoir of the Rev. William Shaw*. London, 1874.

BISSET, J. J. *Sport and war or recollections . . . 1834–1867*. London, 1875.

GOVAN, W. *Memorials of the Rev. James Laing*. Glasgow, 1875.

LESLIE, D. *Among the Zulus and Amatongas*. Glasgow, 1875.

CHALMERS, J. A. *Tiyo Soga: a page of South African mission work*. Edinburgh, 1878.

ROGERS, SIR F. 'South Africa', *Edinburgh Review*, cxlix (1879).

FEILDEN, E. W. *My African home*. London, 1887.

DUFF, GORDON, L. *Letters from the Cape* [1861–2]. Ed. D. Fairbridge, London, 1927.

DOBIE, J. S. *South African journal, 1862–6*. Ed. A. F. Hattersley. Van Riebeeck Society Publications, No. 26. Cape Town, 1945.

*The chronicle of Jeremiah Goldswain, Albany settler of 1820*. Ed. U. Long. Van Riebeeck Society Publications, Nos. 27–9. Cape Town, 1946–9.

STANFORD, SIR W. *Reminiscences*, vol. i, 1850–85. Ed. J. W. Macquarrie. Van Riebeeck Society Publications, No. 39. Cape Town, 1958.

### Secondary Works

AGAR-HAMILTON, J. A. I. *The native policy of the Voortrekkers*. Cape Town, 1928.

—— *The road to the north: South Africa, 1852–1886*. London, 1937.

ATTREE, E. M. 'The Closer union movement between the Orange Free State, South African Republic and Cape Colony', *Archives year book for South African history*, No. 12, vol. i. Cape Town, 1949.

AYLIFF, THE REVD. J. and WHITESIDE, THE REV. J. *History of the Abambo, generally known as Fingos*. Butterworth, 1912.

BROOKES, E. H. *History of Native policy in South Africa from 1830*. Cape Town, 1934.

BROWNLEE, C. *Reminiscences of Kaffir life and history*. Lovedale, 1896.

BUCHANAN, BARBARA. *Pioneer days in Natal*. Pietermaritzburg, 1934.

BUTLER, GENERAL SIR W. F. *Life of Sir George Pomeroy Colley*. London, 1899.

CAMPBELL, W. B. 'The South African frontier, 1865–85', *Archives year book for South African history*, No. 22, vol. i. Cape Town, 1959.

COLLINS, W. W. *Free Statia . . . reminiscences, 1852–1875*. Bloemfontein, 1907.
CORY, SIR G. E. *The rise of South Africa*, vol. v. London, 1930. Vol. vi. *Archives year book for South African history*, No. 2, vol. i. Cape Town, 1939.
DE KIEWIET, C. W. *British Colonial policy and the South African republics, 1848–1872*. Royal Empire Society Imperial Studies, No. 3. London, 1929.
DU TOIT, A. E. 'The Cape frontier: a study of native policy, 1847–1866.' *Archives year book for South African history*, No. 17, vol. i. Cape Town, 1954.
ELLENBERGER, D. F. *History of the Basuto, ancient and modern*. Trans. Macgregor. London, 1912.
GALBRAITH, J. S. *Reluctant empire: British policy on the South African frontier, 1834–1854*. Berkeley and Los Angeles, 1963.
GALLIENNE, G. *Un pionnier de 1833 au Lessouto: Thomas Arbousset (1810–1877)*. Paris, [1933].
GRAY, C. *Life of Robert Gray, Bishop of Cape Town*. London, 1876.
GROBBELAAR, J. J. G. 'Die Vrystaatse Republiek en Die Bassoetoe Vraagstuk'. *Archives year book for South African history*, No. 2, vol. ii. Cape Town, 1939.
HATTERSLEY, A. F. *Portrait of a colony: the story of Natal*. Cambridge, 1940.
—— *The British settlement of Natal: a study in imperial migration*. Cambridge, 1950.
HOOK, D. B. *With sword and statute on the Cape of Good Hope frontier*. Cape Town, 1905.
KISTNER, W. 'The anti-slavery agitation against the Transvaal Republic, 1852–1868', *Archives year book for South African history*, No. 15, vol. ii. Cape Town, 1952.
LAGDEN, SIR G. *The Basutos*. London, 1909.
LOMBARD, P. J. 'Die Stigting en Vroeë Geskiednis van Queenstown, 1853–1859', *Archives year book for South African history*, No. 15, vol. ii. Cape Town, 1952.
LUGG, H. C. *Historic Natal and Zululand*. Pietermaritzburg, 1949.
MACMILLAN, W. M. *Bantu, Boer, and Briton*. London, 1929.
MARAIS, J. S. *The Cape coloured people, 1652–1937*. London, 1939.
MIDGLEY, J. F. 'The Orange River Sovereignty, 1848–1854', *Archives year book for South African history*, No. 12, vol. ii. Cape Town, 1949.
MOLTENO, P. A. *Life and times of Sir J. C. Molteno*. London, 1900.
MURRAY, R. W. *South African reminiscences*. Cape Town, 1894.
ORPEN, J. M. *Reminiscences of life in South Africa*. Durban, 1915.
ROBERTSON, H. M. *150 years of economic contact between black and white*. Reprinted from *South African journal of economics*. Cape Town, 1935.
ROBINSON, SIR J. *A lifetime in South Africa*. London, 1900.
RUSSELL, R. *Natal: the land and its story*. Pietermaritzburg, 1891.
RUTHERFORD, J. *Sir George Grey, K.C.B., 1812–1898: a study in colonial government*. London, 1961.
SCHNELL, E. L. G. *For men must work: a study in German immigration to the Cape*. Cape Town, 1954.
SHEPHERD, THE REVD. R. H. W. *Lovedale, South Africa: the story of a century, 1841–1941*. Lovedale, 1941.
SMITH, THE REVD. E. W. *The Mabilles of Basutoland*. London, 1939.
—— *Life and times of Daniel Lindley*. London, 1949.
SOGA, J. H. *The south-eastern Bantu*. Johannesburg, 1930.

—— *The Ama-Xosa: life and customs.* Lovedale, [1932].

SOLOMON, W. E. G. *Saul Solomon.* Cape Town, 1948.

THEAL, G. M. *History of South Africa.* New ed. in 11 vols. Vols. vii and viii. Cape Town, 1964.

THOMPSON, L. M. 'Indian immigration into Natal, 1860–1872', *Archives year book for South African history*, No. 15, vol. ii. Cape Town, 1952.

TYLDEN, G. *The rise of the Basuto.* Cape Town, 1950.

UYS, C. J. *In the era of Shepstone.* Lovedale, 1933.

VAN DER HORST, S. *Native labour in South Africa.* London, 1942.

VAN DER POEL, J. 'Basutoland as a factor in South African politics, 1852–1870', *Archives year book for South African history*, No. 4, vol. i. Cape Town, 1941.

WALKER, E. A. *Lord de Villiers and his Times: South Africa, 1842–1914.* London, 1925.

—— *Historical atlas of South Africa.* Cape Town, 1922.

—— *History of Southern Africa.* 3rd ed. London, 1957.

WILMOT, A. *Life and times of Sir Richard Southey,* London, 1904.

YOUNG, L. M. 'The Native Policy of Benjamin Pine in Natal, 1850–1855', *Archives year book for South African history*, No. 14, vol. ii. Cape Town, 1951.

*Unpublished theses*

BROKENSHA, D. W. 'Political institutions of some southern Nguni tribes.' Univ. of Oxford, B.Litt. thesis, 1950.

DOWSLEY, E. D'A. 'An investigation into . . . the cattle-killing delusion in Kaffraria.' Univ. of South Africa, M.A. thesis, 1932.

McGILL, D. C. 'History of the Transvaal, 1853–1864.' Univ. of Cape Town, Ph.D. thesis, 1943.

SOLE, D. B. 'The Separation Movement and the Demand for Resident Government in the Eastern Province.' Rhodes Univ. Coll., M.A. thesis, 1939.

GILLESPIE, G. G. 'The pensioner settlements' [in New Zealand]. Univ. of New Zealand (Otago), M.A. thesis, 1954.

3. NEW ZEALAND

*Manuscript Sources*

The Public Records Office series Colonial Office 209 has been consulted in part at the Office in London and in part in microfilm in New Zealand. Certain series in the National Archives (G16, G36, EC1, PM1) have also been consulted. They contain a few important documents not available elsewhere. Several New Zealand libraries now contain useful collections of private papers. The Gore Browne Papers (important) and the Weld Papers (slight) are in the National Archives; the voluminous Richmond–Atkinson Papers are in the General Assembly Library (but I have relied on the published *Richmond–Atkinson Papers*, ed. G. H. Scholefield, 2 vols., Wellington, 1960). The Turnbull Library, Wellington, has the papers of Sir Donald McLean (important) and of Sir E. W. Stafford. The Canterbury Museum has papers of J. R. Godley and some of J. E. FitzGerald's papers. The Grey Collection in the Auckland Public Library contains some interesting papers on public but none on private affairs. The University of Canterbury has the custody of the valuable Journal of Henry Sewell. The papers of H. S. Selfe, legal adviser to the Canterbury Association, now in the Hocken Library, Dunedin, contain some interesting letters, especially from FitzGerald.

### Printed Sources

*Journals and appendices to journals of the House of Representatives*, 1854–72.
*Journals of the Legislative Council.*
*Statutes of New Zealand.*
*New Zealand Government Gazette.*
*New Zealand Parliamentary Debates.* (The published debates down to 1866 are a recension of contemporary newspaper reports.)

For United Kingdom Parliamentary Papers (which include an unusually high proportion of the dispatches of the Governors and Secretaries of State) refer to the bibliography in *Cambridge history of the British Empire*, vol. vii, part ii. Its list of Parliamentary Debates, however, unaccountably omits the important debates in 1864 in *Hansard*, 3rd Ser., vol. clxxvi, and others in 1861 (vol. clxii) and 1865 (vol. clxxxviii).

### Newspapers

My aim here was to secure a good coverage at critical periods of the localities most affected. The following were consulted:
*Taranaki Herald* (New Plymouth), 1854–5, 1858–61.
*Press* (Christchurch), 1861–5.
*Daily Southern Cross* (Auckland), 1863.
*New Zealander* (Auckland), 1863.
*Nelson Examiner* (Nelson), 1864–5.
*Wellington Independent*, 1864–5.

I also made use of notes taken many years ago of the *Otago Witness* and *Otago Daily Times* (Dunedin).

### Contemporary Books, Pamphlets, etc.

GREY, SIR G. *Memorandum upon a letter addressed by Lord Lyttelton to Sir George Grey.* London, 1854.
SELWYN, G. A. (BISHOP). *Pastoral letter . . . to the members of the Church of England in the Settlement of New Plymouth.* New Plymouth, 1855.
TAYLOR, THE REVD. R. *Te Ika A Maui or New Zealand and its inhabitants.* London, 1855. 2nd edition, 1870.
ABRAHAM, C. J. (ARCHDEACON). *Journal of a walk . . . from Auckland to Taranaki.* London, 1856.
SWAINSON, W. *New Zealand.* London, 1856.
—— *New Zealand and its colonization.* London, 1859.
THOMSON, A. S. *The story of New Zealand.* London, 1859.
HADFIELD, THE REVD. O. *One of England's little wars.* London, 1860. [A brilliant polemical pamphlet.]
BROWNE, THE REVD. E. H. *The case of the war in New Zealand.* London, 1860. [Answer to Hadfield by the Governor's brother.]

[JOHNSTON, A. J.] *Notes on Maori matters.* Auckland, 1860. [By one of the judges of the Supreme Court.]

MARTIN, SIR W. *The Taranaki question.* Auckland, 1860. [Very able criticism of Government policy.]

CARRINGTON, F. A. *The land question of Taranaki.* New Plymouth, 1860.

FOX, W. *The war in New Zealand.* Auckland, London, and Edinburgh, 1860.

[TORLESSE, C. O.] *The New Zealander war.* Christchurch, 1860.

BUDDLE, THE REVD. T. *The Maori king movement in New Zealand.* Auckland, 1860.

HADFIELD, O. *A sequel to 'One of England's little wars'.* London, 1861.

—— *The New Zealand war: the second year.* London, 1861.

JOHNSTONE, J. C. *The Maoris and the cause of the present anarchy in New Zealand.* Auckland, 1861.

[BELL, F. D., and WHITAKER, F.] *Notes on Sir William Martin's pamphlet . . . 'The Taranaki question'.* Auckland, 1861.

MARTIN, SIR W. *Remarks on 'Notes Published for the New Zealand Government'.* Auckland, 1861.

*Memorial* [of the Church Missionary Society] *to His Grace the Secretary of State for the Colonies together with a memorandum on New Zealand affairs.* London, 1861.

*A vindication of the character of the Church missionaries and native Christians.* London, 1861.

*Letters from New Zealand on the war question.* Privately printed, London, 1861.

[ABORIGINES PROTECTION SOCIETY.] *The New Zealand war of 1860.* London, 1861.

*Further remarks on New Zealand affairs.* London, 1861.

PASLEY, E. B. 'The war in New Zealand', *Journal of the United Service Institution* (1862).

SWAINSON, W. *New Zealand and the war.* London, 1862.

WHITE, W. *Memorials of Sergeant W. Marjouram, R.A.* London, 1862.

ALEXANDER, SIR J. E. *Incidents of the Maori war.* London, 1863.

CAREY, LT.-COL. R. *Narrative of the late war in New Zealand.* London, 1863.

WAKEFIELD, E. J. *What will they do in the General Assembly?* Auckland, 1863.

WARD, CROSBIE. *Letter to the Right Hon. Lord Lyttelton on the relations of Great Britain with the colonists and aborigines of New Zealand.* London, 1863.

GORST, J. E. *The Maori king.* London and Cambridge, 1864. Ed. K. Sinclair, Hamilton and London, 1959.

[ABORIGINES PROTECTION SOCIETY.] *The New Zealand Government and the Maori war of 1863-4 with especial reference to the confiscation of native lands and the Colonial Ministry's defence of their war policy.* London, 1864.

SEWELL, H. *The New Zealand native rebellion: letter to Lord Lyttelton.* London, 1864.

FITZGERALD, J. E. *Letters on the present state of Maori affairs.* Christchurch, 1865.

FOX, W. *The revolt in New Zealand.* London, 1865.

HURSTHOUSE, C. F. *Letters on New Zealand subjects.* London, 1865.

FOX, W. *The war in New Zealand.* London, 1866.

RICHARDSON, MAJOR J. L. C. *Address to the electors of Dunedin and suburbs north.* Dunedin, 1866.

WILLIAMS, [BISHOP] W. *Christianity among the New Zealanders.* London, 1867.

Barsanti, O. *I protestanti tra I selvaggi della Nuova Zelanda*. Turin, 1868.

Taylor, The Revd. R. *The past and future of New Zealand*. London, 1868.

Firth, J. C. *Conference with Tamati Ngapora and the king natives*. Auckland, 1869.

[McDonnell, T.] *Explanation of the principal causes which led to the present war on the west coast of New Zealand*. Wanganui, 1869.

Wakefield, E. J. *True self-reliance: a brief review of the causes of the present condition and suggestions for the relief of New Zealand*. Wellington, 1869.

Weld, F. A. *Notes on New Zealand affairs*. London, 1869. [An able and informative pamphlet.]

FitzGerald, J. E. *The self-reliant policy in New Zealand*. London, 1870.

Meade, H. *A ride through the disturbed districts of New Zealand*. London, 1870.

Colenso, W. *Fiat Justitia: being a few thoughts respecting the Maori prisoner Kereopa*. Napier, 1871.

Alexander, Sir J. E. *Bush fighting*. London, 1873.

Gore Browne, Harriet L. *Narrative of the Waitara purchase and the Taranaki war*. Ed. W. P. Morrell. Dunedin, 1965. [An incomplete account, written in 1861 by the Governor's wife.]

### Secondary Works

Airey, W. T. G. (ed.) *Studies in a small democracy*. Auckland, 1963.

*Cambridge history of the British Empire*, vol. vii, part ii, *New Zealand*. Cambridge, 1933.

Condliffe, J. B. *New Zealand in the making*. London, 1930.

Cowan, J. *The New Zealand wars: a history of the Maori campaigns and the pioneering period*. 2 vols. Wellington, 1922–23.

Dalton, B. J. *War and politics in New Zealand, 1855–1870*. Sydney, 1967.

Gisborne, W. *New Zealand rulers and statesmen, 1840–1885*. London, 1886. [Well-drawn portraits by an Under-Secretary.]

—— *The colony of New Zealand*. London, 1888.

Gorton, E. *Some home truths re the Maori war*. London, 1901.

Grace, J. TeH. *Tuwharetoa*. Wellington, 1959.

Grace, M. S. *A sketch of the New Zealand war*. London, 1899.

Grace, T. S. *A pioneer missionary among the Maoris*. Ed. S. J. Brittain and G. S., C. W., and A. V. Grace. Palmerston North, 1928.

Gudgeon, T. W. *Reminiscences of the war in New Zealand*. London, 1879.

Harrop, A. J. *England and the Maori wars*. London, 1937.

Herron, D. G. 'Sir G. Grey and the summoning of the first General Assembly', *Historical studies: Australia and New Zealand*, viii.

Holt, E. *The strangest war*. London, 1962.

Lovat, Alice (Lady). *Life of Sir F. Weld*. London, 1914.

Miller, H. G. *Race conflict in New Zealand 1814–1865*. Auckland, 1966. [Documentary extracts with a well-informed commentary.]

Morrell, W. P. *The provincial system in New Zealand, 1852–76*. London, 1932. Reprinted with corrections, Christchurch, 1964.

Norris, H. C. M. *Armed settlers*. Hamilton, 1956. [The best account of military settlement in the Waikato.]

Oliver, W. H. *The story of New Zealand*. London, 1960.

Reeves, W. P. *The long white cloud*. London, 1898.

RICHMOND, J. C. *Reminiscences of a minister of native affairs in New Zealand.* Wellington, 1888. [Reprint of a speech.]

RUSDEN, G. W. *History of New Zealand.* 3 vols. London, 1883.

RUTHERFORD, J. *Sir George Grey.* London, 1961.

SAUNDERS, A. *History of New Zealand.* 2 vols. Christchurch, 1896–9.

SINCLAIR, K. *The Maori land league.* Auckland, 1950.

—— *Origins of the Maori wars.* Wellington, 1957.

—— *History of New Zealand.* Harmondsworth, 1959.

TUCKER, H. W. *Memoir of the life and episcopate of G. A. Selwyn.* 2 vols. London, 1879.

WELLS, B. *History of Taranaki.* New Plymouth, 1878.

WHITMORE, MAJ.-GEN. SIR G. S. *The last Maori war in New Zealand.* London, 1902.

WILLIAMS, F. W. *Through ninety years: notes of the lives of William and William Leonard Williams.* Christchurch, [1940].

WILSON, G. H. ORMOND. *War in the Tussock.* Wellington, 1961. [This booklet is the best account of Te Kooti's career.]

*Unpublished Theses*

BEAGLEHOLE, T. H. 'Maori schools, 1815–1886.' Univ. of New Zealand (Wellington), M.A. thesis, 1955.

FARGHER, R. W. S. 'Donald McLean, Chief Land Purchase Agent and Native Secretary.' Univ. of New Zealand (Auckland), M.A. thesis, 1948.

HENSLEY, G. C. 'The Withdrawal of the British Troops from New Zealand.' Univ. of New Zealand (Canterbury), M.A. thesis, 1957.

HENSLEY, G. C. 'The Withdrawal of the British Troops from New Zealand.' Univ. of New Zealand (Canterbury), M.A. thesis, 1957.

HERRON, D. G. 'The course and structure of New Zealand politics, 1853–1858.' Univ. of New Zealand (Otago), Ph.D. thesis, 1959.

HUNT, R. T. 'Independence agitation in New Zealand, 1869–1871.' Univ. of New Zealand (Otago), M.A. thesis, 1950.

McNAB, R. G. C. 'Life of Bishop Hadfield.' Univ. of New Zealand (Auckland), M.A. thesis, 1924.

SORRENSON, M. P. K. 'The Purchase of Maori Lands, 1865–1892.' Univ. of New Zealand (Auckland), M.A. thesis, 1955.

SINCLAIR, K. 'The Aborigines Protection Society and New Zealand.' Univ. of New Zealand (Auckland), M.A. thesis, 1946.

## 4. THE WEST INDIES

*Manuscript Sources*

Colonial Office Papers, Public Record Office. The following series were examined by me:

CO111/293–401; CO112/32–42 (British Guiana).

CO137/316–475; CO138/69–83 (Jamaica).

CO7/109, 111 (1858), 128 (1866), 136–43 (1869–71); CO393/13 (1866), 15 (1868–72) (Antigua).

CO28/178–80 (1853–4), 211–12 (1870); CO29/39 (1854–64) (Barbados).

CO71/130, 132–3 (1865–6) (Dominica).
CO101/113–5 (1857–9), 118 (1862), 123–5 (1866–7); CO102/23 (Grenada).
CO175/4–5 (1855–6), 10 (1861), 15–16 (1866–7) (Montserrat).
CO184/14–15 (1866), 19–20 (1870–2) (Nevis).
CO239/100–02 (1857–9), 115–6 (1866), 123 (1870) (St. Kitts).
CO260/79–85 (1854–6), 92 (1859), 97–8 (1862), 101–2 (1864), 104–6 (1866–7); CO261/16 (St. Vincent).
CO285/68–70 (1854–5), 81 (1863), 89 (1871) (Tobago).
CO314/16–17 (1866–7) (Virgin Islands).
CO318/203 (1853), 207 (1854), 247 (1866) (West Indies General).
CO321/6 (1875), 9 (1876) (Windward Islands).
Certain dispatches from other series have been obtained on microfilm.
Correspondence of Sir H. Barkly with the Duke of Newcastle and H. Roberts, 1853–4. Newcastle Papers, University of Nottingham.

*Printed Sources*

The United Kingdom Parliamentary Papers and Parliamentary Debates relating to the West Indies for this period are listed in the appropriate sections of the Bibliographies in the *Cambridge history of the British Empire*, vols. ii and iii; but some important papers on Chinese immigration are omitted, especially P.P., 1852–3, lxviii [1686] and H.C. 986; 1854–5, xxxix [O. 7]; 1860, lxix [2714].

*Contemporary Books, Pamphlets, etc.*

DAVY, J. *The West Indies before and since slave emancipation.* London, 1854.
DALTON, H. G. *History of British Guiana.* 2 vols. London, 1855.
BARRETT, W. G. *Immigration to the British West Indies: is it the slave trade revived or not?* London, 1859.
SWINTON, E. and J. *Journal of a voyage with coolie emigrants from Calcutta to Trinidad.* London, [1859].
BUXTON, C. *Slavery and freedom in the British West Indies.* London, 1860.
TROLLOPE, ANTHONY. *The West Indies and the Spanish Main.* London, 1860.
SEWELL, W. G. *The Ordeal of free labour in the British West Indies.* New York, 1861.
UNDERHILL, E. B. *The West Indies: their social and religious condition.* London, 1862.
—— *Letter addressed to the Right Hon. E. Cardwell.* London, 1865.
JAMAICA COMMITTEE, LONDON. *Jamaica papers no. 3.* London [1866].
LUDLOW, J. M. *A quarter century of Jamaica legislation.* Jamaica Papers No. 4. London, 1866.
NOEL, B. W. *The case of G. W. Gordon.* London, 1866.
PIM, B. C. T. *The Negro and Jamaica.* London, 1866.
PRICE, G. E. *Jamaica and the Colonial Office: who caused the crisis?* London, 1866.
ROUNDELL, C. S. *England and her subject races with special reference to Jamaica.* London, 1866.
WILLIAMS, B. T. *The case of G. W. Gordon.* London, 1866.
GORRIE, J. *Illustrations of martial law in Jamaica.* Jamaica Papers No. 6. London, 1867.

HARRISON, F. *Martial law: six letters to the 'Daily News'*. Jamaica Papers No. 5. London, 1867.

HARVEY, T., and BREWIN, W. *Jamaica in 1866*. London, 1867.

WOODCOCK, H. I. *History of Tobago*. Ayr, 1867.

BLEBY, H. *The reign of terror*. London, 1868.

FINLASON, W. F. *History of the Jamaica case*. 2nd ed., enlarged and corrected. London, 1869.

[PRINGLE, H.] *Fall of the sugar planters in Jamaica*. London, 1869.

HINCKS, SIR F. *Observations on a letter addressed by G. W. Des Voeux to the Right Hon. Earl Granville*. Ottawa, 1870.

[JENKINS, J. E.] *The coolie: his rights and wrongs*. London, 1871. [Valuable.]

'A WEST INDIAN'. *A few words upon 'The coolie, his rights and wrongs'*. London, 1871.

WHITFIELD, R. H. *Present position and future prospects of British Guiana considered*. London and Liverpool, 1872.

—— *Present position and future prospects of British Guiana: a second letter*. London, 1872.

*Secondary Works*

BEACHEY, R. W. *The British West Indies sugar industry in the late nineteenth century*. Oxford, 1957.

BURN, W. L. *Emancipation and apprenticeship in the British West Indies*. London, 1937. [Valuable as a background study.]

CHAPMAN, J. K. *The career of Arthur Hamilton Gordon, first Lord Stanmore*. Toronto, 1964.

CLEMENTI, SIR C. *Constitutional history of British Guiana*. London, 1937.

COSTIN, W. C. *Great Britain and China, 1833–1860*. Oxford, 1937.

CRATON, M. *A History of the Bahamas*. London, 1962.

CUMPSTON, I. M. *Indians overseas in British Territories, 1834–1854*. London, 1953.

CURTIN, P. D. *Two Jamaicas: the role of Ideas in a tropical colony, 1830–1865*. Cambridge, Mas., 1955. [A book of first-rate importance.]

—— 'The sugar duties and West Indian prosperity', *Journal of economic history*, xiv (1954).

*Daily Gleaner. Morant Bay: A centenary special supplement*. Kingston, Jamaica, 1965.

DES VOEUX, SIR G. W. *My colonial service*. 2 vols. London, 1903.

EISNER, G. *Jamaica, 1830–1930: a study in economic growth*. Manchester, 1961.

FARLEY, R. 'The rise of the peasantry in British Guiana', *Social and economic studies*, ii, no. 4 (1954).

GARDNER, W. J. *History of Jamaica*. Revised ed., London, 1909.

HALL, D. *Free Jamaica, 1838–1865: an economic history*. New Haven, 1959.

HAMILTON, B. *Barbados and the confederation question, 1871–1885*. London, 1956. [A scholarly study.]

HIGHAM, C. S. S. 'Sir Henry Taylor and the establishment of Crown Colony government in the West Indies, 1871', *Scottish Historical Review*, xxiii (1926).

HITCHINS, F. H. *The colonial land and emigration commission*. Philadelphia, 1931.

HUME, A. H. *Life of Edward John Eyre*. London, 1867.

JAMAICA INFORMATION SERVICE. *The Morant Bay rebellion*. Kingston, [1965.] [Booklet with contemporary illustrations.]

KNOX, G. 'British colonial policy and the problems of establishing a free society in Jamaica', *Caribbean Studies*, ii, no. 4 (1963).

MATHIESON, W. L. *The Sugar colonies and Governor Eyre*. London, 1936.

MURRAY, D. J. *The West Indies and the development of colonial government, 1801–1834*. Oxford, 1965.

OLIVIER, S. (BARON). *The myth of Governor Eyre*. London, 1933. [Highly critical of Eyre.]

POPE-HENNESSY, J. *Verandah*. London, 1964. [Lively biography of his grandfather, Sir J. Pope-Hennessy.]

SEMMEL, B. *The Governor Eyre controversy*. London, 1962. [Comprehensive and valuable, but lacks references.]

—— 'The issue of race in the British attitude to the Morant Bay uprising of 1865', *Caribbean Studies*, ii, no. 3, 1962.

SIRES, R. V. 'Constitutional change in Jamaica, 1834–1860', *Journal of Comparative Legislation and International Law*, 3rd Ser. xxii.

—— 'Government crisis in Jamaica, 1860–1866', *Jamaican Historical Review*, ii, no. 3 (1953).

—— 'Sir Henry Barkly and the labour problem in Jamaica', *Journal of Negro History*, xxv (1940).

SPURDLE, F. G. *Early West Indian government*. Palmerston North [1962]. [Useful for constitutional background.]

UNDERHILL, E. B. *The tragedy of Morant Bay*. London, 1895.

WADDELL, D. A. G. *British Honduras: a historical and contemporary survey*. London, 1961.

WILLIAMS, E. E. *British historians and the West Indies*. London, 1966. [Polemical in tone.]

WISE, K. S. (ed.) *Historical sketches of Trinidad and Tobago*. 4 vols. Port of Spain, 1934–8.

WRONG, H. H. *The Government of the West Indies*. Oxford, 1923. [A pioneering survey, still useful.]

# INDEX

Military expenditure, imperial, in the colonies, 3, 4–9, 10, 138, 274, 276, 287–8, 300.
Mill, J. S., 15, 33, 424, 425.
Mills, Arthur, 6, 8, 14, 141 n., 147 n., 252, 302, 303, 304, 305, 321.
Molapo (Basuto chief), 158, 161, 164, 170.
Molesworth, Sir W., 2, 3, 33.
— as Colonial Secretary, 21–2, 68–9, 70–1, 77, 88, 212, 471.
Molteno, J. C., 63, 131, 150, 173, 182, 188.
Monck, Viscount, 11.
Monro, (Sir) David, 205, 206, 248, 279, 353.
Monsell, W., 170, 174, 195, 363–4, 365.
Montserrat, 2.
— and the federation of the Leeward Islands, 444–5.
— Assembly of, 379, 434, 435, 437.
— constitutional reform in, 395–6, 434, 435, 437.
Mopeli (Basuto chief), 46, 161, 163, 164, 167.
Morant Bay (Jamaica), 409, 410.
— rebellion in, 410–14, 418, 432, 433, 478.
Morija Mission Station, 109.
Moroko (Barolong chief), 45.
Moshesh (Basuto chief), 45–8, 56, 72, 103–10, 113, 152–67, 171.
Murdoch, (Sir) T. W. C., 454, 467–8.
— on Indian immigration into West Indies, 454.
Murray, Revd. Andrew, 53, 54, 59.
Murray, Lieutenant-Colonel, 239–40, 244.
Musgrave, (Sir) Anthony, 197, 200.

Napier, 230, 238, 349, 353.
Natal, 60, 114–15, 133, 134.
— and Basutoland, 158, 162, 163–7, 171, 181, 192.
— electoral franchise in, 98, 190–1.
— European settlement in, 94, 100–1.
— Indian immigration into, 101–3, 125, 188, 191, 193, 198–200.
— Legislative Council of, 122–5, 167, 188–91.
— 'location' policy in, 94, 190–1.
— Native Management Commission, 95.

— Native policy in, 95–8, 122, 190, 197–8.
— representative institutions in, 31, 96, 98–100.
— sugar-growing in, 101.
Native Circuit Courts Act (New Zealand), 225.
Native Districts Regulation Act, 225, 250, 273.
Native Land Court (New Zealand), 286, 332–3, 375.
Native Reserves Act, 223.
Native Territorial Rights Bill, 225–9, 286.
Naval Defence, 8, 23, 152, 373–4.
Ndhlambi tribe, 72, 88–9.
Negroes, health of, in the West Indies, 378, 430.
Nehemiah Moshesh (Basuto chief), 46, 47, 108–9, 135, 136, 161.
Nelson, Colonel A. A., 412, 418, 425, 426.
Nelson, Major, 245–6.
Nelson, Province of, 205, 215.
*Nelson Examiner*, 308.
Nevis, 377, 440.
— and federation of the Leeward Islands, 446.
— Assembly of, 437.
— Constitutional reform in, 437.
— Executive Government of, 394.
Newcastle, 5th Duke of, 2, 5, 6, 11, 23, 28, 29, 30, 47–8, 56, 58, 233, 270, 273, 297–8, 381, 389–90, 383, 396, 455, 468.
— character and policies of, 16–19.
— policy of, in New Zealand, 203, 207, 250, 252, 255, 268–9, 274, 287–9, 291–2, 299–300, 354.
— policy of, in South Africa, 48–56, 62, 98, 99, 119–21, 126–9, 132–3, 136–8, 149–50, 155, 189–90.
— policy of, in Jamaica, 382, 388, 401.
New Plymouth, 204, 209, 229, 230, 239, 261, 318, 322, 340, 353.
New South Wales, responsible government in, 17, 207.
New Zealand, armed constabulary in, 329, 348–9, 355, 360.
— Colonial Defence Force in, 329, 344–5.
— confiscation policy in, 18, 20, 31,

—— *The Ama-Xosa: life and customs.* Lovedale, [1932].

SOLOMON, W. E. G. *Saul Solomon.* Cape Town, 1948.

THEAL, G. M. *History of South Africa.* New ed. in 11 vols. Vols. vii and viii. Cape Town, 1964.

THOMPSON, L. M. 'Indian immigration into Natal, 1860–1872', *Archives year book for South African history*, No. 15, vol. ii. Cape Town, 1952.

TYLDEN, G. *The rise of the Basuto.* Cape Town, 1950.

UYS, C. J. *In the era of Shepstone.* Lovedale, 1933.

VAN DER HORST, S. *Native labour in South Africa.* London, 1942.

VAN DER POEL, J. 'Basutoland as a factor in South African politics, 1852–1870', *Archives year book for South African history*, No. 4, vol. i. Cape Town, 1941.

WALKER, E. A. *Lord de Villiers and his Times: South Africa, 1842–1914.* London, 1925.

—— *Historical atlas of South Africa.* Cape Town, 1922.

—— *History of Southern Africa.* 3rd ed. London, 1957.

WILMOT, A. *Life and times of Sir Richard Southey*, London, 1904.

YOUNG, L. M. 'The Native Policy of Benjamin Pine in Natal, 1850–1855', *Archives year book for South African history*, No. 14, vol. ii. Cape Town, 1951.

### Unpublished theses

BROKENSHA, D. W. 'Political institutions of some southern Nguni tribes.' Univ. of Oxford, B.Litt. thesis, 1950.

DOWSLEY, E. D'A. 'An investigation into . . . the cattle-killing delusion in Kaffraria.' Univ. of South Africa, M.A. thesis, 1932.

McGILL, D. C. 'History of the Transvaal, 1853–1864.' Univ. of Cape Town, Ph.D. thesis, 1943.

SOLE, D. B. 'The Separation Movement and the Demand for Resident Government in the Eastern Province.' Rhodes Univ. Coll., M.A. thesis, 1939.

GILLESPIE, G. G. 'The pensioner settlements' [in New Zealand]. Univ. of New Zealand (Otago), M.A. thesis, 1954.

### 3. NEW ZEALAND

#### Manuscript Sources

The Public Records Office series Colonial Office 209 has been consulted in part at the Office in London and in part in microfilm in New Zealand. Certain series in the National Archives (G16, G36, EC1, PM1) have also been consulted. They contain a few important documents not available elsewhere. Several New Zealand libraries now contain useful collections of private papers. The Gore Browne Papers (important) and the Weld Papers (slight) are in the National Archives; the voluminous Richmond–Atkinson Papers are in the General Assembly Library (but I have relied on the published *Richmond–Atkinson Papers*, ed. G. H. Scholefield, 2 vols., Wellington, 1960). The Turnbull Library, Wellington, has the papers of Sir Donald McLean (important) and of Sir E. W. Stafford. The Canterbury Museum has papers of J. R. Godley and some of J. E. FitzGerald's papers. The Grey Collection in the Auckland Public Library contains some interesting papers on public but none on private affairs. The University of Canterbury has the custody of the valuable Journal of Henry Sewell. The papers of H. S. Selfe, legal adviser to the Canterbury Association, now in the Hocken Library, Dunedin, contain some interesting letters, especially from FitzGerald.

### Printed Sources

*Journals and appendices to journals of the House of Representatives,* 1854–72.
*Journals of the Legislative Council.*
*Statutes of New Zealand.*
*New Zealand Government Gazette.*
*New Zealand Parliamentary Debates.* (The published debates down to 1866 are a recension of contemporary newspaper reports.)

For United Kingdom Parliamentary Papers (which include an unusually high proportion of the dispatches of the Governors and Secretaries of State) refer to the bibliography in *Cambridge history of the British Empire,* vol. vii, part ii. Its list of Parliamentary Debates, however, unaccountably omits the important debates in 1864 in *Hansard,* 3rd Ser., vol. clxxvi, and others in 1861 (vol. clxii) and 1865 (vol. clxxxviii).

### Newspapers

My aim here was to secure a good coverage at critical periods of the localities most affected. The following were consulted:
*Taranaki Herald* (New Plymouth), 1854–5, 1858–61.
*Press* (Christchurch), 1861–5.
*Daily Southern Cross* (Auckland), 1863.
*New Zealander* (Auckland), 1863.
*Nelson Examiner* (Nelson), 1864–5.
*Wellington Independent,* 1864–5.

I also made use of notes taken many years ago of the *Otago Witness* and *Otago Daily Times* (Dunedin).

### Contemporary Books, Pamphlets, etc.

GREY, SIR G. *Memorandum upon a letter addressed by Lord Lyttelton to Sir George Grey.* London, 1854.
SELWYN, G. A. (BISHOP). *Pastoral letter . . . to the members of the Church of England in the Settlement of New Plymouth.* New Plymouth, 1855.
TAYLOR, THE REVD. R. *Te Ika A Maui or New Zealand and its inhabitants.* London, 1855. 2nd edition, 1870.
ABRAHAM, C. J. (ARCHDEACON). *Journal of a walk . . . from Auckland to Taranaki.* London, 1856.
SWAINSON, W. *New Zealand.* London, 1856.
—— *New Zealand and its colonization.* London, 1859.
THOMSON, A. S. *The story of New Zealand.* London, 1859.
HADFIELD, THE REVD. O. *One of England's little wars.* London, 1860. [A brilliant polemical pamphlet.]
BROWNE, THE REVD. E. H. *The case of the war in New Zealand.* London. 1860. [Answer to Hadfield by the Governor's brother.]

[JOHNSTON, A. J.] *Notes on Maori matters*. Auckland, 1860. [By one of the judges of the Supreme Court.]

MARTIN, SIR W. *The Taranaki question*. Auckland, 1860. [Very able criticism of Government policy.]

CARRINGTON, F. A. *The land question of Taranaki*. New Plymouth, 1860.

FOX, W. *The war in New Zealand*. Auckland, London, and Edinburgh, 1860.

[TORLESSE, C. O.] *The New Zealander war*. Christchurch, 1860.

BUDDLE, THE REVD. T. *The Maori king movement in New Zealand*. Auckland, 1860.

HADFIELD, O. *A sequel to 'One of England's little wars'*. London, 1861.

—— *The New Zealand war: the second year*. London, 1861.

JOHNSTONE, J. C. *The Maoris and the cause of the present anarchy in New Zealand*. Auckland, 1861.

[BELL, F. D., and WHITAKER, F.] *Notes on Sir William Martin's pamphlet . . . 'The Taranaki question'*. Auckland, 1861.

MARTIN, SIR W. *Remarks on 'Notes Published for the New Zealand Government'*. Auckland, 1861.

*Memorial* [of the Church Missionary Society] *to His Grace the Secretary of State for the Colonies together with a memorandum on New Zealand affairs*. London, 1861.

*A vindication of the character of the Church missionaries and native Christians.* London, 1861.

*Letters from New Zealand on the war question*. Privately printed, London, 1861.

[ABORIGINES PROTECTION SOCIETY.] *The New Zealand war of 1860*. London, 1861.

*Further remarks on New Zealand affairs*. London, 1861.

PASLEY, E. B. 'The war in New Zealand', *Journal of the United Service Institution* (1862).

SWAINSON, W. *New Zealand and the war*. London, 1862.

WHITE, W. *Memorials of Sergeant W. Marjouram, R.A.* London, 1862.

ALEXANDER, SIR J. E. *Incidents of the Maori war*. London, 1863.

CAREY, LT.-COL. R. *Narrative of the late war in New Zealand*. London, 1863.

WAKEFIELD, E. J. *What will they do in the General Assembly?* Auckland, 1863.

WARD, CROSBIE. *Letter to the Right Hon. Lord Lyttelton on the relations of Great Britain with the colonists and aborigines of New Zealand*. London, 1863.

GORST, J. E. *The Maori king*. London and Cambridge, 1864. Ed. K. Sinclair, Hamilton and London, 1959.

[ABORIGINES PROTECTION SOCIETY.] *The New Zealand Government and the Maori war of 1863–4 with especial reference to the confiscation of native lands and the Colonial Ministry's defence of their war policy*. London, 1864.

SEWELL, H. *The New Zealand native rebellion: letter to Lord Lyttelton*. London, 1864.

FITZGERALD, J. E. *Letters on the present state of Maori affairs*. Christchurch, 1865.

FOX, W. *The revolt in New Zealand*. London, 1865.

HURSTHOUSE, C. F. *Letters on New Zealand subjects*. London, 1865.

FOX, W. *The war in New Zealand*. London, 1866.

RICHARDSON, MAJOR J. L. C. *Address to the electors of Dunedin and suburbs north*. Dunedin, 1866.

WILLIAMS, [BISHOP] W. *Christianity among the New Zealanders*. London, 1867.

BARSANTI, O. *I protestanti tra I selvaggi della Nuova Zelanda.* Turin, 1868.
TAYLOR, THE REVD. R. *The past and future of New Zealand.* London, 1868.
FIRTH, J. C. *Conference with Tamati Ngapora and the king natives.* Auckland, 1869.
[McDONNELL, T.] *Explanation of the principal causes which led to the present war on the west coast of New Zealand.* Wanganui, 1869.
WAKEFIELD, E. J. *True self-reliance: a brief review of the causes of the present condition and suggestions for the relief of New Zealand.* Wellington, 1869.
WELD, F. A. *Notes on New Zealand affairs.* London, 1869. [An able and informative pamphlet.]
FITZGERALD, J. E. *The self-reliant policy in New Zealand.* London, 1870.
MEADE, H. *A ride through the disturbed districts of New Zealand.* London, 1870.
COLENSO, W. *Fiat Justitia: being a few thoughts respecting the Maori prisoner Kereopa.* Napier, 1871.
ALEXANDER, SIR J. E. *Bush fighting.* London, 1873.
GORE BROWNE, HARRIET L. *Narrative of the Waitara purchase and the Taranaki war.* Ed. W. P. Morrell. Dunedin, 1965. [An incomplete account, written in 1861 by the Governor's wife.]

### Secondary Works

AIREY, W. T. G. (ed.) *Studies in a small democracy.* Auckland, 1963.
*Cambridge history of the British Empire,* vol. vii, part ii, *New Zealand.* Cambridge, 1933.
CONDLIFFE, J. B. *New Zealand in the making.* London, 1930.
COWAN, J. *The New Zealand wars: a history of the Maori campaigns and the pioneering period.* 2 vols. Wellington, 1922–23.
DALTON, B. J. *War and politics in New Zealand, 1855–1870.* Sydney, 1967.
GISBORNE, W. *New Zealand rulers and statesmen, 1840–1885.* London, 1886. [Well-drawn portraits by an Under-Secretary.]
—— *The colony of New Zealand.* London, 1888.
GORTON, E. *Some home truths re the Maori war.* London, 1901.
GRACE, J. TeH. *Tuwharetoa.* Wellington, 1959.
GRACE, M. S. *A sketch of the New Zealand war.* London, 1899.
GRACE, T. S. *A pioneer missionary among the Maoris.* Ed. S. J. Brittain and G. S., C. W., and A. V. Grace. Palmerston North, 1928.
GUDGEON, T. W. *Reminiscences of the war in New Zealand.* London, 1879.
HARROP, A. J. *England and the Maori wars.* London, 1937.
HERRON, D. G. 'Sir G. Grey and the summoning of the first General Assembly', *Historical studies: Australia and New Zealand,* viii.
HOLT, E. *The strangest war.* London, 1962.
LOVAT, ALICE (LADY). *Life of Sir F. Weld.* London, 1914.
MILLER, H. G. *Race conflict in New Zealand 1814–1865.* Auckland, 1966. [Documentary extracts with a well-informed commentary.]
MORRELL, W. P. *The provincial system in New Zealand, 1852–76.* London, 1932. Reprinted with corrections, Christchurch, 1964.
NORRIS, H. C. M. *Armed settlers.* Hamilton, 1956. [The best account of military settlement in the Waikato.]
OLIVER, W. H. *The story of New Zealand.* London, 1960.
REEVES, W. P. *The long white cloud.* London, 1898.

RICHMOND, J. C. *Reminiscences of a minister of native affairs in New Zealand.* Wellington, 1888. [Reprint of a speech.]
RUSDEN, G. W. *History of New Zealand.* 3 vols. London, 1883.
RUTHERFORD, J. *Sir George Grey.* London, 1961.
SAUNDERS, A. *History of New Zealand.* 2 vols. Christchurch, 1896–9.
SINCLAIR, K. *The Maori land league.* Auckland, 1950.
—— *Origins of the Maori wars.* Wellington, 1957.
—— *History of New Zealand.* Harmondsworth, 1959.
TUCKER, H. W. *Memoir of the life and episcopate of G. A. Selwyn.* 2 vols. London, 1879.
WELLS, B. *History of Taranaki.* New Plymouth, 1878.
WHITMORE, MAJ.-GEN. SIR G. S. *The last Maori war in New Zealand.* London, 1902.
WILLIAMS, F. W. *Through ninety years: notes of the lives of William and William Leonard Williams.* Christchurch, [1940].
WILSON, G. H. ORMOND. *War in the Tussock.* Wellington, 1961. [This booklet is the best account of Te Kooti's career.]

*Unpublished Theses*

BEAGLEHOLE, T. H. 'Maori schools, 1815–1886.' Univ. of New Zealand (Wellington), M.A. thesis, 1955.
FARGHER, R. W. S. 'Donald McLean, Chief Land Purchase Agent and Native Secretary.' Univ. of New Zealand (Auckland), M.A. thesis, 1948.
HENSLEY, G. C. 'The Withdrawal of the British Troops from New Zealand.' Univ. of New Zealand (Canterbury), M.A. thesis, 1957.
HENSLEY, G. C. 'The Withdrawal of the British Troops from New Zealand.' Univ. of New Zealand (Canterbury), M.A. thesis, 1957.
HERRON, D. G. 'The course and structure of New Zealand politics, 1853–1858.' Univ. of New Zealand (Otago), Ph.D. thesis, 1959.
HUNT, R. T. 'Independence agitation in New Zealand, 1869–1871.' Univ. of New Zealand (Otago), M.A. thesis, 1950.
McNAB, R. G. C. 'Life of Bishop Hadfield.' Univ. of New Zealand (Auckland), M.A. thesis, 1924.
SORRENSON, M. P. K. 'The Purchase of Maori Lands, 1865–1892.' Univ. of New Zealand (Auckland), M.A. thesis, 1955.
SINCLAIR, K. 'The Aborigines Protection Society and New Zealand.' Univ. of New Zealand (Auckland), M.A. thesis, 1946.

## 4. THE WEST INDIES

*Manuscript Sources*

Colonial Office Papers, Public Record Office. The following series were examined by me:
CO111/293–401; CO112/32–42 (British Guiana).
CO137/316–475; CO138/69–83 (Jamaica).
CO7/109, 111 (1858), 128 (1866), 136–43 (1869–71); CO393/13 (1866), 15 (1868–72) (Antigua).
CO28/178–80 (1853–4), 211–12 (1870); CO29/39 (1854–64) (Barbados).

CO71/130, 132–3 (1865–6) (Dominica).
CO101/113–5 (1857–9), 118 (1862), 123–5 (1866–7); CO102/23 (Grenada).
CO175/4–5 (1855–6), 10 (1861), 15–16 (1866–7) (Montserrat).
CO184/14–15 (1866), 19–20 (1870–2) (Nevis).
CO239/100–02 (1857–9), 115–6 (1866), 123 (1870) (St. Kitts).
CO260/79–85 (1854–6), 92 (1859), 97–8 (1862), 101–2 (1864), 104–6 (1866–7);
    CO261/16 (St. Vincent).
CO285/68–70 (1854–5), 81 (1863), 89 (1871) (Tobago).
CO314/16–17 (1866–7) (Virgin Islands).
CO318/203 (1853), 207 (1854), 247 (1866) (West Indies General).
CO321/6 (1875), 9 (1876) (Windward Islands).
Certain dispatches from other series have been obtained on microfilm.
Correspondence of Sir H. Barkly with the Duke of Newcastle and H. Roberts,
    1853–4. Newcastle Papers, University of Nottingham.

*Printed Sources*

The United Kingdom Parliamentary Papers and Parliamentary Debates relating
    to the West Indies for this period are listed in the appropriate sections of the
    Bibliographies in the *Cambridge history of the British Empire*, vols. ii and iii;
    but some important papers on Chinese immigration are omitted, especially
    P.P., 1852–3, lxviii [1686] and H.C. 986; 1854–5, xxxix [O. 7]; 1860,
    lxix [2714].

*Contemporary Books, Pamphlets, etc.*

DAVY, J. *The West Indies before and since slave emancipation.* London, 1854.
DALTON, H. G. *History of British Guiana.* 2 vols. London, 1855.
BARRETT, W. G. *Immigration to the British West Indies: is it the slave trade revived
    or not?* London, 1859.
SWINTON, E. and J. *Journal of a voyage with coolie emigrants from Calcutta to
    Trinidad.* London, [1859].
BUXTON, C. *Slavery and freedom in the British West Indies.* London, 1860.
TROLLOPE, ANTHONY. *The West Indies and the Spanish Main.* London, 1860.
SEWELL, W. G. *The Ordeal of free labour in the British West Indies.* New York,
    1861.
UNDERHILL, E. B. *The West Indies: their social and religious condition.* London,
    1862.
—— *Letter addressed to the Right Hon. E. Cardwell.* London, 1865.
JAMAICA COMMITTEE, LONDON. *Jamaica papers no. 3.* London [1866].
LUDLOW, J. M. *A quarter century of Jamaica legislation.* Jamaica Papers No. 4.
    London, 1866.
NOEL, B. W. *The case of G. W. Gordon.* London, 1866.
PIM, B. C. T. *The Negro and Jamaica.* London, 1866.
PRICE, G. E. *Jamaica and the Colonial Office: who caused the crisis?* London, 1866.
ROUNDELL, C. S. *England and her subject races with special reference to Jamaica.*
    London, 1866.
WILLIAMS, B. T. *The case of G. W. Gordon.* London, 1866.
GORRIE, J. *Illustrations of martial law in Jamaica.* Jamaica Papers No. 6. London,
    1867.

BIBLIOGRAPHY 493

HARRISON, F. *Martial law: six letters to the 'Daily News'*. Jamaica Papers No. 5. London, 1867.

HARVEY, T., and BREWIN, W. *Jamaica in 1866*. London, 1867.

WOODCOCK, H. I. *History of Tobago*. Ayr, 1867.

BLEBY, H. *The reign of terror*. London, 1868.

FINLASON, W. F. *History of the Jamaica case*. 2nd ed., enlarged and corrected. London, 1869.

[PRINGLE, H.] *Fall of the sugar planters in Jamaica*. London, 1869.

HINCKS, SIR F. *Observations on a letter addressed by G. W. Des Voeux to the Right Hon. Earl Granville*. Ottawa, 1870.

[JENKINS, J. E.] *The coolie: his rights and wrongs*. London, 1871. [Valuable.]

'A WEST INDIAN'. *A few words upon 'The coolie, his rights and wrongs'*. London, 1871.

WHITFIELD, R. H. *Present position and future prospects of British Guiana considered*. London and Liverpool, 1872.

—— *Present position and future prospects of British Guiana: a second letter*. London, 1872.

*Secondary Works*

BEACHEY, R. W. *The British West Indies sugar industry in the late nineteenth century*. Oxford, 1957.

BURN, W. L. *Emancipation and apprenticeship in the British West Indies*. London, 1937. [Valuable as a background study.]

CHAPMAN, J. K. *The career of Arthur Hamilton Gordon, first Lord Stanmore*. Toronto, 1964.

CLEMENTI, SIR C. *Constitutional history of British Guiana*. London, 1937.

COSTIN, W. C. *Great Britain and China, 1833–1860*. Oxford, 1937.

CRATON, M. *A History of the Bahamas*. London, 1962.

CUMPSTON, I. M. *Indians overseas in British Territories, 1834–1854*. London, 1953.

CURTIN, P. D. *Two Jamaicas: the role of Ideas in a tropical colony, 1830–1865*. Cambridge, Mas., 1955. [A book of first-rate importance.]

—— 'The sugar duties and West Indian prosperity', *Journal of economic history*, xiv (1954).

*Daily Gleaner. Morant Bay: A centenary special supplement*. Kingston, Jamaica, 1965.

DES VOEUX, SIR G. W. *My colonial service*. 2 vols. London, 1903.

EISNER, G. *Jamaica, 1830–1930: a study in economic growth*. Manchester, 1961.

FARLEY, R. 'The rise of the peasantry in British Guiana', *Social and economic studies*, ii, no. 4 (1954).

GARDNER, W. J. *History of Jamaica*. Revised ed., London, 1909.

HALL, D. *Free Jamaica, 1838–1865: an economic history*. New Haven, 1959.

HAMILTON, B. *Barbados and the confederation question, 1871–1885*. London, 1956. [A scholarly study.]

HIGHAM, C. S. S. 'Sir Henry Taylor and the establishment of Crown Colony government in the West Indies, 1871', *Scottish Historical Review*, xxiii (1926).

HITCHINS, F. H. *The colonial land and emigration commission*. Philadelphia, 1931.

HUME, A. H. *Life of Edward John Eyre*. London, 1867.

JAMAICA INFORMATION SERVICE. *The Morant Bay rebellion.* Kingston, [1965.] [Booklet with contemporary illustrations.]

KNOX, G. 'British colonial policy and the problems of establishing a free society in Jamaica', *Caribbean Studies*, ii, no. 4 (1963).

MATHIESON, W. L. *The Sugar colonies and Governor Eyre.* London, 1936.

MURRAY, D. J. *The West Indies and the development of colonial government, 1801–1834.* Oxford, 1965.

OLIVIER, S. (BARON). *The myth of Governor Eyre.* London, 1933. [Highly critical of Eyre.]

POPE-HENNESSY, J. *Verandah.* London, 1964. [Lively biography of his grandfather, Sir J. Pope-Hennessy.]

SEMMEL, B. *The Governor Eyre controversy.* London, 1962. [Comprehensive and valuable, but lacks references.]

—— 'The issue of race in the British attitude to the Morant Bay uprising of 1865', *Caribbean Studies*, ii, no. 3, 1962.

SIRES, R. V. 'Constitutional change in Jamaica, 1834–1860', *Journal of Comparative Legislation and International Law*, 3rd Ser. xxii.

—— 'Government crisis in Jamaica, 1860–1866', *Jamaican Historical Review*, ii, no. 3 (1953).

—— 'Sir Henry Barkly and the labour problem in Jamaica', *Journal of Negro History*, xxv (1940).

SPURDLE, F. G. *Early West Indian government.* Palmerston North [1962]. [Useful for constitutional background.]

UNDERHILL, E. B. *The tragedy of Morant Bay.* London, 1895.

WADDELL, D. A. G. *British Honduras: a historical and contemporary survey.* London, 1961.

WILLIAMS, E. E. *British historians and the West Indies.* London, 1966. [Polemical in tone.]

WISE, K. S. (ed.) *Historical sketches of Trinidad and Tobago.* 4 vols. Port of Spain, 1934–8.

WRONG, H. H. *The Government of the West Indies.* Oxford, 1923. [A pioneering survey, still useful.]

# INDEX

PRINTED IN GREAT BRITAIN
AT THE UNIVERSITY PRESS, OXFORD
BY VIVIAN RIDLER
PRINTER TO THE UNIVERSITY